Historical Introductions to the Book of Concord

# Historical Introductions
## to the
# Book of Concord

## F. Bente

## Concordia Publishing House
## St. Louis, Missouri

Concordia Publishing House, Saint Louis, Missouri 63118

Concordia Publishing House Ltd., London, E. C. 1

First published in *Concordia Triglotta*, 1921

Reprint of Historical Introductions, 1965

# Contents

# Foreword

July 4, 1965, marked the 44th anniversary of the completion of the Preface to the *Concordia Triglotta* by Dr. F. Bente. In his Preface the author calls attention to the format and the purpose of this synodically authorized edition of the Book of Concord. This jubilee edition was intended — in the words of the author — "to strengthen this loyalty [to the confessional symbols] and to further and facilitate the study of our 'Golden Concordia.'" During the three decades following its publication the *Concordia Triglotta* became the source book for several generations of theological students in their study and use of the confessional symbols of the Lutheran Church.

One of the notable contributions of this edition of the Book of Concord is the material entitled Historical Introductions to the Symbolical Books of the Evangelical Lutheran Church. Historical circumstances and doctrinal tensions are among the decisive originators and framers of confessional formulations and pronouncements. Acquaintance with and evaluation of these circumstances are therefore not only indispensable for the correct understanding of confessional symbols but also invaluable for their application in the thought and life of the church.

The extent to which this applies to the Lutheran Symbols is evident to casual reader and serious student alike. The extent to which the coeditor of the *Triglot* was of similar persuasion is attested by the fact that more than one fifth of the volume — 264 of 1285 pages — is devoted to the Historical Introductions.

At present many students of the Lutheran Symbols have access to the scholarly edition which was first published in 1930 in Göttingen under the title *Die Bekenntnisschriften der evangelisch-lutherischen Kirche*. It is no reflection on the *Concordia Triglotta* when it is asserted that the Göttingen publication has found no peers or even any equals in scholarliness and detail of critical apparatus. Also its various *Einleitungen* are superb.

But the hurdle which frequently confronts the American theological student is the language barrier. Here the *Triglot* offers invaluable assistance. There is scarcely another English edition of the Book of Concord which contains such a wealth of historical background as does the *Triglotta*.

This reprint of the *Historical Introductions* is offered with the hope that they may assist the theological student in gaining a deeper insight into the origin of the Lutheran Symbols, a better understanding of their final form, and a more enduring appreciation of their ultimate purpose.

5th Sunday after Trinity
1965

Lorenz Wunderlich
Concordia Seminary
St. Louis, Missouri

# HISTORICAL INTRODUCTIONS TO THE SYMBOLICAL BOOKS OF THE EVANGELICAL LUTHERAN CHURCH.

## I. The Book of Concord, or The Concordia.

### 1. General and Particular Symbols.

Book of Concord, or Concordia, is the title of the Lutheran *corpus doctrinae*, *i. e.*, of the symbols recognized and published under that name by the Lutheran Church. The word symbol, σύμβολον, is derived from the verb συμβάλλειν, to compare two things for the purpose of perceiving their relation and association. Σύμβολον thus developed the meaning of *tessara*, or sign, token, badge, banner, watchword, parole, countersign, confession, creed. A Christian symbol, therefore, is a mark by which Christians are known. And since Christianity is essentially the belief in the truths of the Gospel, its symbol is of necessity a confession of Christian doctrine. The Church, accordingly, has from the beginning defined and regarded its symbols as a rule of faith or a rule of truth. Says Augustine: "Symbolum est regula fidei brevis et grandis: brevis numero verborum, grandis pondere sententiarum. A symbol is a rule of faith, both brief and grand: brief, as to the number of words; grand, as to the weight of its thoughts."

Cyprian was the first who applied the term symbol to the baptismal confession, because, he said, it distinguished the Christians from non-Christians. Already at the beginning of the fourth century the Apostles' Creed was universally called symbol; and in the Middle Ages this name was applied also to the Nicene and the Athanasian Creeds. In the Introduction to the Book of Concord the Lutheran confessors designate the Augsburg Confession as the "symbol of our faith," and in the Epitome of the Formula of Concord, as "our symbol of this time."

Symbols may be divided into the following classes: 1. Ecumenical symbols, which, at least in the past, have been accepted by all Christendom, and are still formally acknowledged by most of the evangelical Churches; 2. particular symbols, adopted by the various denominations of divided Christendom; 3. private symbols, such as have been formulated and published by individuals, for example, Luther's Confession of the Lord's Supper of 1528. The publication of private confessions does not necessarily involve an impropriety; for according to Matt. 10, 32 33 and 1 Pet. 3, 15 not only the Church as a whole, but individual Christians as well are privileged and in duty bound to confess the Christian truth over against its public assailants. Self-evidently, only such are symbols of particular churches as have been approved and adopted by them. The symbols of the Church, says the Formula of Concord, "should not be based on private writings, but on such books as have been composed, approved, and received in the name of the churches which pledge themselves to one doctrine and religion." (CONC. TRIGL., 851, 2.)

Not being formally and explicitly adopted by all Christians, the specifically Lutheran confessions also are generally regarded as particular symbols. Inasmuch, however, as they are in complete agreement with Holy Scripture, and in this respect differ from all other particular symbols, the Lutheran confessions are truly ecumenical and catholic in character. They contain the truths believed universally by true Christians everywhere, explicitly by all consistent Christians, implicitly even by inconsistent and erring Christians. Christian truth, being one and the same the world over, is none other than that which is found in the Lutheran confessions.

### 2. The German Book of Concord.

The printing of the official German edition of the Book of Concord was begun in 1578, under the editorship of Jacob Andreae. The 25th of June, 1580, however, the fiftieth anniversary of the presentation of the Augsburg Confession to Emperor Charles V, was chosen as the date for its official publication at Dresden and its promulgation to the general public. Following are the contents of one of the five Dresden folio copies which we have compared: 1. The title-page, concluding with the words, "Mit Churf. G. zu Sachsen Befreiung. Dresden MDLXXX." 2. The preface, as adopted and signed by the estates at Jueterbock in 1579, which supplanted the explanation, originally planned, of the theologians against the various attacks made upon the Formula of Concord. 3. The three Ecumenical Symbols. 4. The Augsburg Confession of 1530. 5. The Apology of 1530. 6. The Smalcald Articles of 1537, with the appendix, "Concerning the Power and Supremacy of the Pope." 7. Luther's Small Catechism, omitting the "Booklets of Marriage and Baptism," found in some copies. 8. Luther's Large Catechism. 9. The Formula of Concord, with separate title-pages for the Epitome and the Solida Declaratio, both dated 1580. 10. The signatures of the theologians, etc., amounting to about 8,000.

11. The Catalogus Testimoniorum, with the superscription "Appendix" (found in some copies only). The Preface is followed by a *Privilegium* signed by Elector August and guaranteeing to Matthes Stoeckel and Gimel Bergen the sole right of publication, a document not found in the other copies we compared. The Formula of Concord is followed by a twelve-page index of the doctrines treated in the Book of Concord; and the list of signatures, by a page containing the trade-mark of the printer. The center of this page features a cut inscribed, "Matthes Stoeckel Gimel Bergen 1579." The cut is headed by Ps. 9, 1. 2: "Ich danke dem Herrn von ganzem Herzen und erzaehle all deine Wunder. Ich freue mich und bin froehlich in dir und lobe deinen Namen, du Allerhoechster. I thank the Lord with all my heart and proclaim all Thy wonders. I am glad and rejoice in Thee, and praise Thy name, Thou Most High." Under the cut are the words: "Gedruckt zu Dresden durch Matthes Stoeckel. Anno 1580. Printed by Matthes Stoeckel, Dresden, 1580."

In a letter dated November 7, 1580, Martin Chemnitz speaks of two Dresden folio editions of the German Book of Concord, while Feuerlinus, in 1752, counts seven Dresden editions. As a matter of fact, the Dresden folio copies differ from one another, both as to typography and contents. Following are the chief differences of the latter kind: 1. Only some copies have the liturgical Forms of Baptism and of Marriage appended to the Small Catechism. 2. The Catalogus is not entitled "Appendix" in all copies, because it was not regarded as a part of the confession proper. 3. In some copies the passage from the Augsburg Confession, quoted in Art. 2, 29 of the Solida Declaratio, is taken, not from the Mainz Manuscript, but from the quarto edition of 1531, which already contained some alterations. 4. Some copies are dated 1580, while others bear the date 1579 or 1581. Dr. Kolde gives it as his opinion that in spite of all these and other (chiefly typographical) differences they are nevertheless all copies of one and the same edition, with changes only in individual sheets. (*Historische Einleitung in die Symbolischen Buecher der ev.-luth. Kirche*, p. 70.) Dr. Tschackert inclines to the same view, saying: "Such copies of this edition as have been preserved exhibit, in places, typographical differences. This, according to Polycarp Leyser's *Kurzer und gegruendeter Bericht*, Dresden, 1597 (Kolde, 70), is due to the fact that the manuscript was rushed through the press and sent in separate sheets to the interested estates, and that, while the forms were in press, changes were made on the basis of the criticisms sent in from time to time, yet not equally, so that some copies differ in certain sheets and insertions." (*Die Entstehung der luth. und der ref. Kirchenlehre*, 1910, p. 621.)

However, while this hypothesis explains a number of the variations in the Dresden folio copies, it does not account for all of them, especially not for those of a typographical nature. In one of the five copies which we compared, the title-page, radically differing

from the others, reads as follows: "Formula Concordiae. Das ist: Christliche, Heilsame, Reine Vergleichunge, in welcher die Goettliche Leer von den vornembsten Artikeln vnserer wahrhafftigen Religion, aus heiliger Schrifft in kurtze bekanntnues oder Symbola vnd Leerhafte Schrifften, : welche allbereit vor dieser zeit von den Kirchen Gottes Augspurgischer Confession, angenommen vnd approbiert:, verfasset. Sampt bestendiger, in Gottes wort wolgegruendeter, richtiger, endlicher widerholung, erklerung und entscheidung deren Streit, welche vnter etlichen Theologen, so sich zu ermelter Confession bekant, fuergefallen. Alles nach inhalt der heiligen Schrifft, als der einigen Richtschnur der Goettlichen wahrheit, vnd nach anleitung obgemeldter in der Kirchen Gottes, approbierten Schrifften. Auff gnedigsten, gnedigen, auch guetigsten beuehl, verordnung und einwilligung nach beschriebener Christlichen Churfuersten, Fuersten vnd Stende des heiligen Roemischen Reichs Deutscher Nation, Augspurgischer Confession, derselben Landen, Kirchen, Schulen vnd Nachkommen zum trost vnd besten in Druck vorfertiget. M. D. LXXIX." ("Formula of Concord, that is, Christian, wholesome, pure agreement, in which the divine doctrine of the chief articles of our true religion have been drawn up from the Holy Scripture in short confessions or symbols and doctrinal writings, which have already before this time been accepted and approved by the Churches of God of the Augsburg Confession, together with a firm, Scripturally well-founded, correct, final repetition, explanation and decision of those controversies which have arisen among some theologians who have subscribed to said Confession, all of which has been drawn up according to the contents of Holy Scripture, the sole norm of divine Truth, and according to the analogy of the above-named writings which have the approval of the Churches of God. Published by the most gracious, kind, and benevolent command, order, and assent of the subscribed Christian Electors, princes, and estates of the Holy Roman Empire, of the German nation, of the Augsburg Confession, for the comfort and benefit of said lands, churches, schools, and posterity. 1579.")

Apart from the above title this copy differs from the others we examined in various ways. Everywhere (at four different places) it bears the date 1579, which, on the chief title-page, however, seems to have been entered in ink at a later date. Also the place of publication, evidently Dresden, is not indicated. Two variations are found in the Preface to the Book of Concord, one an omission, the other an addition. The signatures of the princes and estates to the Preface are omitted. Material and formal differences are found also on the pages containing the subscriptions of the theologians to the Formula of Concord; and the Catalogus is lacking entirely. The typography everywhere, especially in the portions printed in Roman type, exhibits many variations and divergences from our other four copies, which, in turn, are also characterized by numerous typographical and other variations. The copy of which, above, we have given the contents is dated throughout 1580. Our third copy bears the same date, 1580, excepting on the title-page of the Solida Declaratio, which has 1579. In both of these copies the typography of the signatures to the Book of Concord is practically alike. In our fourth copy the date 1580 is found on the title-page of the Concordia, the Catalogus, and the appended Saxon Church Order, which covers 433 pages, while the title-pages of the Epitome and the Declaratio and the page carrying the printer's imprint are all dated 1579. In this copy the typography of the signatures closely resembles that of the copy dated everywhere 1579. In our fifth Dresden folio copy, the title-page of the Book of Concord and the Catalogus are dated 1580, while the title-pages of the Epitome and Solida Declaratio are dated 1579. This is also the only copy in which the Catalogus is printed under the special heading "Appendix."

In view of these facts, especially the variation of the Roman type in all copies, Kolde's hypothesis will hardly be regarded as firmly established. Even if we eliminate the copy which is everywhere dated 1579, the variations in our four remaining Dresden folio copies cannot be explained satisfactorily without assuming either several editions or at least several different compositions for the same edition, or perhaps for the two editions mentioned by Chemnitz. Feuerlinus distinguishes seven Dresden editions of the Book of Concord — one, printed for the greater part in 1578, the second, third, and fourth in 1580, the fifth in 1581, the sixth also in 1581, but in quarto, and the seventh in 1598, in folio. (*Bibliotheca Symbolica*, 1752, p. 9.) A copy like the one referred to above, which is everywhere dated 1579, does not seem to have come to the notice of Feuerlinus.

In the copy of the Tuebingen folio edition which is before us, the Index follows the Preface. The appendices of the Small Catechism are omitted, likewise the superscription Appendix of the Catalogus. Our copy of the Heidelberg folio edition of 1582 omits the Catalogus and adds the Apology of the Book of Concord of 1583, as also the Refutation of the Bremen Pastors of the same year. A copy of the Magdeburg quarto edition lying before us has the year 1580 on the title-pages of the Book of Concord, the Epitome, the Declaratio, and the Catalogus. The Preface is followed by three pages, on which Joachim Frederick guarantees to "Thomas Frantzen Buchvorlegern" (Thomas Frantzen, publishers) the sole right of publication for a period of five years, and prohibits the introduction of other copies, excepting only those of the Dresden folio edition of 1580. Luther's Booklets of Marriage and of Baptism are appended to the Small Catechism, and to the Large Catechism is added "Eine kurze Vermahnung zu der Beicht, A Brief Exhortation to Confession." (None of the Dresden folio copies we compared contain these appendices, nor are they found in the Latin editions of 1580 and 1584.)

The index is followed by a page of corrected misprints. The last page has the following imprint: "Gedruckt zu Magdeburg durch Johann Meiszner und Joachim Walden Erben, Anno 1580, Printed at Magdeburg by John Meissner's and Joachim Walden's heirs. In the year 1580."

### 3. The Latin Concordia.

Even before the close of 1580, Selneccer published a Latin Concordia containing a translation of the Formula of Concord begun by Lucas Osiander in 1578 and completed by Jacob Heerbrand. It was a private undertaking and, owing to its numerous and partly offensive mistakes, found no recognition. Thus, for instance, the passage of the Tractatus, "De Potestate et Primatu Papae," in § 24: "Christ gives the highest and final judgment to the church," was rendered as follows: "Et.Christus summum et ultimum ferculum apponit ecclesiae." (p. 317.) Besides, Selneccer had embodied in his Concordia the objectionable text of the Augsburg Confession found in the octavo edition of 1531, which Melanchthon had altered extensively.

The necessary revision of the Latin text was made at the convention in Quedlinburg during December, 1582, and January, 1583, Chemnitz giving material assistance. The revised edition, which constitutes the Latin *textus receptus* of the Formula of Concord, was published at Leipzig in 1584. Aside from many corrections, this edition contains the translation of the Formula of Concord as already corrected by Selneccer in 1582 for his special Latin-German edition, and afterwards thoroughly revised by Chemnitz. The texts of the Augsburg Confession and the Apology follow the *editio princeps* of 1531. The 8,000 signatures, embodied also in the Latin edition of 1580, were omitted, lest any one might complain that his name was appended to a book which he had neither seen nor approved. In keeping herewith, the words in the title of the Book of Concord: *"et nomina sua huic libro subscripserunt* — and have subscribed their names to this book," which Mueller retained in his edition, were eliminated. The title-page concludes as in the edition of 1580, the word "denuo" only being added and the date correspondingly changed. On the last two pages of this edition of 1584 Selneccer refers to the edition of 1580 as follows: "Antea publicatus est liber Christianae Concordiae, Latine, sed privato et festinato instituto, Before this the Book of Concord has been published in Latin, but as a private and hasty undertaking." In the edition of 1584, the text of the Small Catechism is adorned with 23 Biblical illustrations.

Among the later noteworthy editions of the Book of Concord are the following: Tuebingen, 1599; Leipzig, 1603, 1622; Stuttgart, 1660, 1681. Editions furnished with introductions or annotations or both: H. Pipping, 1703; S. J. Baumgarten, 1747; J. W. Schoepff, Part I, 1826, Part II, 1827; F. A. Koethe, 1830; J. A. Detzer, 1830; F. W. Bodemann, 1843. In America the entire Book of Concord was printed in German by H. Ludwig, of New York, in 1848, and by the Concordia Publishing House of St. Louis, Mo., in 1880. In Leipzig, Latin editions appeared in the years 1602, 1606, 1612, 1618, 1626, 1654, 1669, 1677. Adam Rechenberg's edition "with an appendix in three parts and new indices" (*cum appendice tripartita et novis indicibus*) saw five editions — 1678, 1698, 1712, 1725, 1742. We mention also the edition of Pfaffius, 1730; Tittmann, 1817; H. A. G. Meyer, 1830, containing a good preface; Karl Hase, in his editions of 1827, 1837, and 1845, was the first to number the paragraphs. Reineccius prepared a German-Latin edition in 1708. This was followed in 1750 by the German-Latin edition of Johann Georg Walch. Mueller's well-known German-Latin Concordia saw eleven editions between 1847 and 1912. Since 1907 it appears with historical introductions by Th. Kolde.

### 4. English Translations.

All of the Lutheran symbols have been translated into the English language repeatedly. In 1536 Richard Tavener prepared the first translation of the Augsburg Confession. Cranmer published, in 1548, "A Short Instruction into the Christian Religion," essentially a translation of the Ansbach-Nuernberg Sermons on the Catechism. In 1834 a translation of the German text of the Augsburg Confession with "Preliminary Observations" was published at Newmarket, Va., by Charles Henkel, Prof. Schmidt of the Seminary at Columbus, O., assisting in this work. The Introduction to the Newmarket Book of Concord assigns Henkel's translation of the Augsburg Confession to the year 1831. Our copy, however, which does not claim to be a second edition, is dated 1834. In his *Popular Theology* of 1834, S. S. Schmucker offered a translation of the Latin text, mutilated in the interest of his *American Lutheranism*. Hazelius followed him with a translation in 1841. In 1848, Ludwig, of New York, issued a translation of the German text of the Unaltered Augsburg Confession, as well as of the Introduction, prepared by C. H. Schott, together with the Ecumenical Symbols, also with introductions. The title-page of our copy lists the price of the book at 12½ cents. C. P. Krauth's translation of the Augsburg Confession appeared in 1868. The first complete translation of the German text of the entire Book of Concord was published in 1851 by the publishing house of Solomon D. Henkel & Bros., at Newmarket, Va. In this translation, however, greater stress was laid on literary style than upon an exact reproduction of the original. Ambrose and Socrates Henkel prepared the translation of the Augsburg Confession, the Apology, the Smalcald Articles, the Appendix, and the Articles of Visitation. The Small Catechism was offered in the translation prepared by David Henkel in 1827. The Large Catechism was translated by J. Stirewalt; the Epitome, by H. Wetzel; the Declaratio, by J. R. Moser. The second, improved edition of 1854 contained a translation of the Augsburg Confession by C. Philip Krauth, the Apology was translated by W. F. Lehmann, the Smalcald Articles by W. M. Reynolds, the two Catechisms by J. G. Morris, and the Formula of Concord together with the Catalogus by C. F. Schaeffer. In both editions the historical introductions present a reproduction of the material in J. T. Mueller's *Book of Concord*. In 1882 a new English translation of the entire Book of Concord, together with introductions and other confessional material, appeared in two volumes, edited by Dr. H. E. Jacobs. The first volume of this edition embraces the confessional writings of the Lutheran Church. It contains C. P. Krauth's translation of the Augsburg Confession as revised for Schaff's *Creeds of Christendom*. Jacobs translated the Apology (from the Latin, with insertions, in brackets, of translations from the German text), the Smalcald Articles (from the German), the Tractatus (from the Latin), and the Formula of Concord. The translation of the Small Catechism was prepared by a committee of the Ministerium of Pennsylvania. The Large Catechism was done into English by A. Martin. A reprint of this edition appeared in 1911, entitled "People's Edition," in which the Augsburg Confession is presented in a translation prepared by a committee of the General Council, the General Synod, the United Synod in the South, and the Ohio Synod. The second volume of Jacobs's edition of the Book of Concord embodies historical introductions to the Lutheran symbols, translations of the Marburg Articles, the Schwabach Articles, the Torgau Articles, the Altered Augsburg Confession of 1540 and 1542, Zwingli's Ratio Fidei, the Tetrapolitana, the Romish Confutatio, Melanchthon's Opinion of 1530, Luther's Sermon on the Descent into Hell of 1533, the Wittenberg Concordia, the Leipzig Interim, the Catalogus Testimoniorum, the Articles of Visitation, and the Decretum Upsaliense of 1593. The Principles of Faith and Church Polity of the General Council and an index complete this volume. A Norwegian and a Swedish translation of the Book of Concord have also been published in America.

### 5. Corpora Doctrinae Supplanted by Book of Concord.

More than twenty different Lutheran collections of symbols or *corpora doctrinae* (a term first employed by Melanchthon), most of them bulky, had appeared after the death of Luther and before the adoption of the Formula of Concord, by which quite a number of them were supplanted. From the signatures to its Preface it appears that the entire Book of Concord was adopted by 3 electors, 20 princes, 24 counts, 4 barons, and 35 imperial cities. And the list of signatures appended to the Formula of Concord contains about 8,000 names of theologians, preachers, and schoolteachers. About two-thirds of the German territories which professed adherence to the Augsburg Confession adopted and introduced the Book of Concord as their *corpus doctrinae.* (Compare Historical Introduction to the Formula of Concord.)

Among the *corpora doctrinae* which were gradually superseded by the Book of Concord are the following: 1. Corpus Doctrinae Philippicum, or Misnicum, or Wittenbergense of 1560, containing, besides the three Ecumenical Symbols, the following works of Melanchthon: Variata, Apologia, Repetitio Augustanae Confessionis, Loci, Examen Ordinandorum of 1552, Responsio ad Articulos Bavaricae Inquisitionis, Refutatio Serveti. Melanchthon, shortly before his death, wrote the preface for the Latin as well as the German edition of this Corpus. 2. Corpus Doctrinae Pomeranicum of 1564, which adds Luther's Catechisms, the Smalcald Articles, and three other works of Luther to the Corpus Doctrinae Philippicum, which had been adopted 1561. 3. Corpus Doctrinae Prutenicum, or Borussicum, of Prussia, 1567, containing the Augsburg Confession, the Apology, the Smalcald Articles, and Repetition of the Sum and Content of the True, Universal Christian Doctrine of the Church, written by Moerlin and Chemnitz. 4. Corpus Doctrinae Thuringicum in Ducal Saxony, of 1570, containing the three Ecumenical Symbols, Luther's Catechisms, the Smalcald Articles, the Confession of the Landed Estates in Thuringia (drawn up by Justus Menius in 1549), and the Prince of Saxony's Book of Confutation (*Konfutationsbuch*) of 1558. 5. Corpus Doctrinae Brandenburgicum of 1572, containing the Augsburg Confession according to the Mainz Manuscript, Luther's Small Catechism, Explanation of the Augsburg Confession drawn from the postils and doctrinal writings "of the faithful man of God Dr. Luther" by Andreas Musculus, and a Church Agenda. 6. Corpus Doctrinae Wilhelminum of Lueneburg, 1576, containing the three Ecumenical Symbols, the Augsburg Confession, the Apology, the Smalcald Articles, Luther's Catechisms, Formulae Caute Loquendi (Forms of Speaking Cautiously) by Dr. Urbanus Regius, and Formulae Recte Sentiendi de Praecipuis Horum Temporum Controversiis (Forms of Thinking Correctly concerning the Chief Controversies of These Times) by Martin Chemnitz. 7. Corpus Doctrinae Iulium of Duke Julius of Braunschweig-Wolfenbuettel, 1576, containing the documents of the Wilhelminum, with the sole addition of the Short Report of Some Prominent Articles of Doctrine, from the Church Order of Duke Julius, of 1569. 8. The Hamburg Book of Confession of 1560, which was also adopted by Luebeck and Lueneburg, and contained a confession against the Interim, drawn up by Aepinus in 1548, and also four declarations concerning Adiaphorism, Osiandrism, Majorism, and the doctrine of the Lord's Supper, drawn up since 1549. 9. The Confessional Book of Braunschweig, adopted in 1563 and reaffirmed in 1570, containing, The Braunschweig Church Order of 1528, the Unaltered Augsburg Confession, the Apology thereof, the Smalcald Articles, Explanation, etc., drawn up at Lueneburg in 1561 against the Crypto-Calvinists. 10. The Church Order

of the city of Goettingen, 1568, containing the Church Order of Goettingen of 1531, Luther's Small Catechism, the Smalcald Articles, the Augsburg Confession, and the Apology. (Tschackert, *l. c.*, 613 f.; Feuerlinus, *l. c.*, 1 f.)

## 6. Subscription to Confessions.

The position accorded the symbols in the Lutheran Church is clearly defined by the Book of Concord itself. According to it Holy Scripture alone is to be regarded as the sole rule and norm by which absolutely all doctrines and teachers are to be judged. The object of the Augustana, as stated in its Preface, was to show "what manner of doctrine has been set forth, in our lands and churches, from the Holy Scripture and the pure Word of God." And in its Conclusion the Lutheran confessors declare: "Nothing has been received on our part against Scripture or the Church Catholic," and "we are ready, God willing, to present ampler information according to the Scriptures." "Iuxta Scripturam" — such are the closing words of the Augsburg Confession. The Lutheran Church knows of no other principle.

In the Formula of Concord we read: "Other writings, however, of ancient or modern teachers, whatever name they bear, must not be regarded as equal to the Holy Scriptures, but all of them together be subjected to them, and should not be received otherwise or further than as witnesses, [which are to show] in what manner after the time of the apostles, and at what places, this doctrine of the prophets and apostles was preserved." (777, 2.) In the Conclusion of the Catalog of Testimonies we read: "The true saving faith is to be founded upon no church-teachers, old or new, but only and alone upon God's Word, which is comprised in the Scriptures of the holy prophets and apostles, as unquestionable witnesses of divine truth." (1149.)

The Lutheran symbols, therefore, are not intended to supplant the Scriptures, nor do they do so. They do, however, set forth what has been at all times the unanimous understanding of the pure Christian doctrine adhered to by sincere and loyal Lutherans everywhere; and, at the same time, they show convincingly from the Scriptures that our forefathers did indeed manfully confess nothing but God's eternal truth, which every Christian is in duty bound to, and consistently always will, believe, teach, and confess.

The manner also in which Lutherans pledge themselves confessionally appears from these symbols. The Augsburg Confession was endorsed by the princes and estates as follows: "The above articles we desire to present in accordance with the edict of Your Imperial Majesty, in order to exhibit our Confession and let men see a summary of the doctrine of our teachers." (95, 6.) In the preamble to the signatures of 1537 the Lutheran preachers unanimously confess: "We have reread the articles of the Confession presented to the Emperor in the Assembly at Augsburg, and by the favor of God all the preachers who have been present in this Assembly at Smalcald harmoniously declare that they believe and teach in their churches according to the articles of the Confession and Apology." (529.) John Brenz declares that he had read and reread, time and again, the Confession, the Apology, etc., and judged "that all these agree with Holy Scripture, and with the belief of the true and genuine catholic Church (*haec omnia convenire cum Sacra Scriptura et cum sententia verae καὶ γνησίης catholicae ecclesiae*)." (529.) Another subscription — to the Smalcald Articles — reads: "I, Conrad Figenbotz, for the glory of God subscribe that I have thus believed and am still preaching and firmly believing as above." (503, 13.) Brixius writes in a similar vein: "I . . . subscribe to the Articles of the reverend Father Martin Luther, and confess that hitherto I have thus believed and taught, and by the Spirit of Christ I shall continue thus to believe and teach." (503, 27.)

In the Preface to the Thorough Declaration of the Formula of Concord the Lutheran confessors declare: "To this Christian Augsburg Confession, so thoroughly grounded in God's Word, we herewith pledge ourselves again from our inmost hearts. We abide by its simple, clear, and unadulterated meaning as the words convey it, and regard the said Confession as a pure Christian symbol, with which at the present time true Christians ought to be found next to God's Word. . . . We intend also, by the grace of the Almighty, faithfully to abide until our end by this Christian Confession, mentioned several times, as it was delivered in the year 1530 to the Emperor Charles V; and it is our purpose, neither in this nor in any other writing, to recede in the least from that oft-cited Confession, nor to propose another or new confession." (847, 4. 5.) Again: "We confess also the First, Unaltered Augsburg Confession as our symbol for this time (not because it was composed by our theologians, but because it has been taken from God's Word and is founded firmly and well therein), precisely in the form in which it was committed to writing in the year 1530, and presented to the Emperor Charles V at Augsburg." (851, 5.)

In like manner the remaining Lutheran symbols were adopted. (852. 777.) Other books, the Formula of Concord declares, are accounted useful, "as far as (*wofern, quatenus*) they are consistent with" the Scriptures and the symbols. (855, 10.) The symbols, however, are accepted "that we may have a unanimously received, definite, common form of doctrine, which all our Evangelical churches together and in common confess, from and according to which, because (*cum, weil*) it has been derived from God's Word, all other writings should be judged and adjusted, as to how far (*wiefern, quatenus*) they are to be approved and accepted." (855, 10.)

After its adoption by the Lutheran electors, princes, and estates, the Formula of Concord, and with it the entire Book of Concord, was, as stated, solemnly subscribed by about 8,000 theologians, pastors, and teachers, the pledge reading as follows: "Since now, in the sight of God and of all Christendom, we wish to testify to those now living and those who shall come after us that this declaration herewith presented concerning all the controverted articles aforementioned and explained, and no other, is our faith, doctrine, and confession, in which we are also willing, by God's grace, to appear with intrepid hearts before the judgment-seat of Jesus Christ, and give an account of it; and that we will neither privately nor publicly speak or write anything contrary to it, but, by the help of God's grace, intend to abide thereby: therefore, after mature deliberation, we have, in God's fear and with the invocation of His name, attached our signatures with our own hands." (1103, 40.)

Furthermore, in the Preface to the Book of Concord the princes and estates declare that many churches and schools had received the Augsburg Confession "as a symbol of the present time in regard to the chief articles of faith, especially those involved in controversy with the Romanists and various corruptions of the heavenly doctrine." (7.) They solemnly protest that it never entered their minds "either to introduce, furnish a cover for, and establish any false doctrine, or in the least even to recede from the Confession presented in the year 1530 at Augsburg." (15.) They declare: "This Confession also, by the help of God, we will retain to our last breath, when we shall go forth from this life to the heavenly fatherland, to appear with joyful and undaunted mind and with a pure conscience before the tribunal of our Lord Jesus Christ." (15.) "Therefore we also have determined not to depart even a finger's breadth either from the subjects themselves or from the phrases which are found in them (*vel a rebus ipsis vel a phrasibus, quae in illa habentur, discedere*), but, the Spirit of the Lord aiding us, to persevere constantly, with the greatest harmony, in this godly agreement, and we intend to examine all controversies according to this true norm and declaration of the pure doctrine." (23.)

## 7. Pledging of Ministers to the Confessions.

Such being the attitude of the Lutherans towards their symbols, and such their evaluation of pure doctrine, it was self-evident that the public teachers of their churches should be pledged to the confessions. In December, 1529, H. Winckel, of Goettingen, drew up a form in which the candidate for ordination declares: "I believe and hold also of the most sacred Sacrament . . . as one ought to believe concerning it according to the contents of the Bible, and as Doctor Martin Luther writes and confesses concerning it especially in his Confession" (of the Lord's Supper, 1528). The Goettingen Church Order of 1530, however, did not as yet embody a vow of ordination. The first pledges to the symbols were demanded by the University of Wittenberg in 1533 from candidates for the degree of Doctor of Divinity. In 1535 this pledge was required also of the candidates for ordination. The oath provided that the candidate must faithfully teach the Gospel without corruption, steadfastly defend the Ecumenical Symbols, remain in agreement with the Augsburg Confession, and before deciding difficult controversies consult older teachers of the Church of the Augsburg Confession. Even before 1549 the candidates for philosophical degrees were also pledged by oath to the Augsburg Confession.

In 1535, at the Diet of Smalcald, it was agreed that new members entering the Smalcald League should promise "to provide for such teaching and preaching as was in harmony with the Word of God and the pure teaching of our [Augsburg] Confession." According to the Pomeranian Church Order, which Bugenhagen drew up in 1535, pastors were pledged to the Augsburg Confession and the Apology thereof. Capito, Bucer, and all others who took part in the Wittenberg Concord of 1536, promised, over their signatures, "to believe and to teach in all articles according to the Confession and the Apology." (*Corpus Reformatorum*, opp. Melanthonis, 3, 76.) In 1540, at Goettingen, John Wigand promised to accept the Augsburg Confession and its Apology, and to abide by them all his life. "And," he continued, "if I should be found to do otherwise or be convicted of teaching and confessing contrary to such Confession and Apology, then let me, by this signature, be condemned and deposed from this divine ministry. This do I swear; so help me God." Also at Goettingen, Veit Pflugmacher vowed, in 1541, that he would preach the Gospel in its truth and purity according to the Augsburg Confession and the contents of the postils of Anton Corvinus. He added: "Should I be found to do otherwise and not

living up to what has been set forth above, then shall I by such act have deposed myself from office. This do I swear; so help me God."

In 1550 and 1552, Andrew Osiander attacked the oath of confession which was in vogue at Wittenberg, claiming it to be "an entanglement in oath-bound duties after the manner of the Papists." "What else," said he, "does this oath accomplish than to sever those who swear it from the Holy Scriptures and bind them to Philip's doctrine? Parents may therefore well consider what they do by sending their sons to Wittenberg to become Masters and Doctors. Money is there taken from them, and they are made Masters and Doctors. But while the parents think that their son is an excellent man, well versed in the Scriptures and able to silence enthusiasts and heretics, he is, in reality, a poor captive, entangled and embarrassed by oath-bound duties. For he has abjured the Word of God and has taken an oath on Philip's doctrine." Replying to this fanatical charge in 1553, Melanchthon emphasized the fact that the doctrinal pledges demanded at Wittenberg had been introduced, chiefly by Luther, for the purpose of "maintaining the true doctrine." "For," said Melanchthon, "many enthusiasts were roaming about at that time, each, in turn, spreading new silly nonsense, *e. g.*, the Anabaptists, Servetus, Campanus, Schwenckfeld, and others. And such tormenting spirits are not lacking at any time (*Et non desunt tales furiae ullo tempore*)." A doctrinal pledge, Melanchthon furthermore explained, was necessary "in order correctly to acknowledge God and call upon Him to preserve harmony in the Church, and to bridle the audacity of such as invent new doctrines." (*C. R.* 12, 5.)

# II. The Three Ecumenical or Universal Symbols.

## 8. Ecumenical Symbols.

The Ecumenical (general, universal) Symbols were embodied in the Book of Concord primarily for apologetic reasons. Carpzov writes: "The sole reason why our Church appealed to these symbols was to declare her agreement with the ancient Church in so far as the faith of the latter was laid down in these symbols, to refute also the calumniations and the accusations of the opponents, and to evince the fact that she preaches no new doctrine and in no wise deviates from the Church Catholic." (*Isagoge*, 37.) For like reasons Article I of the Augsburg Confession declares its adherence to the Nicene Creed, and the first part of the Smalcald Articles, to the Apostles' and Athanasian Creeds. The oath introduced by Luther in 1535, and required of the candidates for the degree of Doctor of Divinity, also contained a pledge on the Ecumenical Symbols. In 1538 Luther published a tract entitled "The Three Symbols or Confessions of the Faith of Christ Unanimously Used in the Church," containing the Apostles' Creed, the Athanasian Creed, and

the Te Deum of Ambrose and Augustine. To these was appended the Nicene Creed.

In the opening sentences of this tract, Luther remarks: "Whereas I have previously taught and written quite a bit concerning faith, showing both what faith is and what faith does, and have also published my Confession [1528], setting forth both what I believe and what position I intend to maintain; and whereas the devil continues to seek new intrigues against me, I have decided, by way of supererogation, to publish conjointly, in the German tongue, the three so-called Symbols, or Confessions, which have hitherto been received, read, and chanted throughout the Church. I would thereby reaffirm the fact that I side with the true Christian Church, which has adhered to these Symbols, or Confessions, to the present day, and not with the false, vainglorious church, which in reality is the worst enemy of the true Church, having introduced much idolatry beside these beautiful confessions." (St. L. 10, 993; Erl. 23, 252.) Luther's translation of the Ecumenical Symbols, together with the captions which appeared in his tract, were embodied in the Book of Concord. The superscription, "Tria Symbola Catholica seu Oecumenica," occurs for the first time in Selneccer's edition of the Book of Concord of 1580. Before this, 1575, he had written: "Quot sunt Symbola fidei Christianae in Ecclesia? Tria sunt praecipua, quae nominantur oecumenica, sive universalia et authentica, id est, habentia auctoritatem et non indigentia demonstratione aut probatione, videlicet Symbolum Apostolicum, Nicaenum et Athanasianum." (Schmauk, *Confessional Principle*, 834.)

## 9. The Apostles' Creed.

The foundation of the Apostles' Creed was, in a way, laid by Christ Himself when He commissioned His disciples, saying, Matt. 28, 19. 20: "Go ye therefore and teach all nations, baptizing them in the name of the Father, and of the Son, and of the Holy Ghost: teaching them to observe all things whatsoever I have commanded you." The formula of Baptism here prescribed, "In the name of the Father, and of the Son, and of the Holy Ghost," briefly indicates what Christ wants Christians to be taught, to believe, and to confess. And the Apostles' Creed, both as to its form and contents, is evidently but an amplification of the trinitarian formula of Baptism. Theo. Zahn remarks: "It has been said, and not without a good basis either, that Christ Himself has ordained the baptismal confession. For the profession of the Triune God made by the candidates for Baptism is indeed the echo of His missionary and baptismal command reechoing through all lands and times in many thousand voices." (*Skizzen aus dem Leben der Kirche*, 252.)

But when and by whom was the formula of Baptism thus amplified? — During the Medieval Ages the Apostles' Creed was commonly known as "The Twelve Articles," because it was generally believed that the twelve apostles, assembled in joint session before they were separated, soon after Pentecost, drafted this Creed, each contributing a clause. But, though retained in the Catechismus Romanus, this is a legend which originated in Italy or Gaul in the sixth or seventh (according to Zahn, toward the end of the fourth) century and was unknown before this date. Yet, though it may seem more probable that the Apostles' Creed was the result of a silent growth and very gradual formation corresponding to the ever-changing environments and needs of the Christian congregations, especially over against the heretics, there is no sufficient reason why the apostles themselves should not have been instrumental in its formulation, nor why, with the exception of a number of minor later additions, its original form should not have been essentially what it is to-day.

Nathanael confessed: "Rabbi, Thou art the Son of God; Thou art the King of Israel," John 1, 49; the apostles confessed: "Thou art the Christ, the Son of the living God," Matt. 16, 16; Peter confessed: "We believe and are sure that Thou art that Christ, the Son of the

living God," John 6, 69; Thomas confessed: "My Lord and my God," John 20, 28. These and similar confessions of the truth concerning Himself were not merely approved of, but solicited and demanded by, Christ. For He declares most solemnly: "Whosoever therefore shall confess Me before men, him will I confess also before My Father which is in heaven. But whosoever shall deny Me before men, him will I also deny before My Father which is in heaven," Matt. 10, 32. 33. The same duty of confessing their faith, *i. e.*, the truths concerning Christ, is enjoined upon all Christians by the Apostle Paul when he writes: "If thou shalt confess with thy mouth the Lord Jesus and shalt believe in thine heart that God hath raised Him from the dead, thou shalt be saved," Rom. 10, 9.

In the light of these and similar passages, the trinitarian baptismal formula prescribed by Christ evidently required from the candidate for Baptism a definite statement of what he believed concerning the Father, Son, and Holy Ghost, especially concerning Jesus Christ the Savior. And that such a confession of faith was in vogue even in the days of the apostles appears from the Bible itself. Of Timothy it is said that he had "professed a good profession before many witnesses," 1 Tim. 6, 12. Heb. 4, 14 we read: "Let us hold fast our profession." Heb. 10, 23: "Let us hold fast the profession of our faith without wavering." Jude urges the Christians that they "should earnestly contend for the faith which was once delivered unto the saints," and build up themselves on their "most holy faith," vv. 3. 20. Compare also 1 Cor. 15, 3. 4; 1 Tim. 3, 16; Titus 1, 13; 3, 4—7.

## 10. Apostles' Creed and Early Christian Writers.

The Christian writers of the first three centuries, furthermore, furnish ample proof for the following facts: that from the very beginning of the Christian Church the candidates for Baptism everywhere were required to make a confession of their faith; that from the beginning there was existing in all the Christian congregations a formulated confession, which they called the rule of faith, the rule of truth, etc.; that this rule was identical with the confession required of the candidates for Baptism; that it was declared to be of apostolic origin; that the summaries and explanations of this rule of truth, given by these writers, tally with the contents and, in part, also with the phraseology of the Apostles' Creed; that the scattered Christian congregations, then still autonomous, regarded the adoption of this rule of faith as the only necessary condition of Christian unity and fellowship.

The manner in which Clement, Ignatius, Polycarp, Justin, Aristides, and other early Christian writers present the Christian truth frequently reminds us of the Apostles' Creed and suggests its existence. Thus Justin Martyr, who died 165, says in his first Apology, which was written about 140: "Our teacher of these things is Jesus Christ, who also was born for this purpose and was crucified under Pontius Pilate, procurator of Judea, that we reasonably worship Him, having learned that He is the Son of the true God Himself, and holding Him in the second place, and the prophetic Spirit in the third." "Eternal praise to the Father of all, through the name of the Son and of the Holy Spirit." Similar strains, sounding like echoes of the Second Article, may be found in the Epistles to the Trallians and to the Christians at Smyrna, written by Ignatius, the famous martyr and bishop of Antioch, who died 107.

Irenaeus, who died 189, remarks: Every Christian "who retains immovable in himself the rule of the truth which he received through Baptism (ὁ τὸν κανόνα τῆς ἀληθείας ἀκλινῆ ἐν ἑαυτῷ κατέχων, ὃν διὰ τοῦ βαπτίσματος εἴληφε)" is able to see through the deceit of all heresies. Irenaeus here identifies the baptismal confession with what he calls the "rule of truth, κανὼν τῆς ἀληθείας," i. e., the truth which is the rule for everything claiming to be Christian. Apparently, this "rule of truth" was the sum of doctrines which every Christian received and confessed at his baptism. The very phrase "rule of truth" implies that it was a concise and definite formulation of the chief Christian truths. For "canon, rule," was the term employed by the ancient Church to designate such brief sentences as were adopted by synods for the practise of the Church. And this "rule of truth" is declared by Irenaeus to be "the old tradition," "the old tradition of the apostles": ἥ τε ἀπὸ τῶν ἀποστόλων ἐν τῇ ἐκκλησίᾳ παράδοσις. (Zahn, l. c., 379 f.) Irenaeus was the pupil of Polycarp the Martyr; and what he had learned from him, Polycarp had received from the Apostle John. Polycarp, says Irenaeus, "taught the things which he had learned from the apostles, and which the Church has handed down, and which alone are true." According to Irenaeus, then, the "rule of truth" received and confessed by every Christian at his baptism was transmitted by the apostles.

The contents of this rule of truth received from the apostles are repeatedly set forth by Irenaeus. In his *Contra Haereses* (I, 10, 1) one of these summaries reads as follows: "The Church dispersed through the whole world, to the ends of the earth, has received from the apostles and their disciples the faith in one God, the Father Almighty, who has made heaven and earth and the sea and all things that are in them; and in one Jesus Christ, the Son of God, who became incarnate for our salvation; and in the Holy Spirit, who has proclaimed through the prophets the dispensations, and the advents, and the birth from a virgin, and the passion, and the resurrection from the dead, and the bodily assumption into heaven of the beloved Christ Jesus, our Lord, and His manifestation from heaven in the glory of the Father." It thus appears that the "rule of truth" as Irenaeus knew it,

the formulated sum of doctrines mediated by Baptism, which he, in accordance with the testimony of his teacher Polycarp, believed to have been received from the apostles, at least approaches our present Apostolic Creed.

## 11. Tertullian and Cyprian on Apostles' Creed.

A similar result is obtained from the writings of Tertullian, Cyprian, Novatian, Origen, and others. "When we step into the water of Baptism," says Tertullian, who died about 220, "we confess the Christian faith according to the words of its law," i. e., according to the law of faith or the rule of faith. Tertullian, therefore, identifies the confession to which the candidates for Baptism were pledged with the brief formulation of the chief Christian doctrines which he variously designates as "the law of faith," "the rule of faith," frequently also as *tessara*, watchword, and *sacramentum*, a term then signifying the military oath of allegiance. This Law or Rule of Faith was, according to Tertullian, the confession adopted by Christians everywhere, which distinguished them from unbelievers and heretics. The unity of the congregations, the granting of the greeting of peace, of the name brother, and of mutual hospitality, — these and similar Christian rights and privileges, says Tertullian, "depend on no other condition than the similar tradition of the same oath of allegiance," i. e., the adoption of the same baptismal rule of faith. (Zahn, 250.)

At the same time Tertullian most emphatically claims, "that this rule of faith was established by the apostles, aye, by Christ Himself," inasmuch as He had commanded to baptize "in the name of the Father, and of the Son, and of the Holy Ghost." (Zahn, 252.) In his book *Adversus Praxeam*, Tertullian concludes an epitome which he gives of "the rule of faith" as follows: "That this rule has come down from the beginning of the Gospel, even before the earlier heretics, and so, of course, before the Praxeas of yesterday, is proved both by the lateness of all heretics and by the novelty of this Praxeas of yesterday." (Schaff, *Creeds of Christendom*, 2, 18.) The following form is taken from Tertullian's *De Virginibus Velandis:* "For the rule of faith is altogether one, alone (*sola*), immovable, and irreformable, namely, believing in one God omnipotent, the Maker of the world, and in His Son Jesus Christ, born of the Virgin Mary, crucified under Pontius Pilate, raised from the dead the third day, received into the heavens, sitting now at the right hand of the Father, who shall come to judge the living and the dead, also through the resurrection of the flesh." Cyprian the Martyr, bishop of Carthage, who died 257, and who was the first one to apply the term *symbolum* to the baptismal creed, in his Epistle to Magnus and to Januarius, as well as to other Numidian bishops, gives the following as the answer of the candidate for Baptism to the question,

"Do you believe?": "I believe in God the Father, in His Son Christ, in the Holy Spirit. I believe the remission of sins, and the life eternal through the holy Church."

## 12. Variations of the Apostles' Creed.

While there can be no reasonable doubt either that the Christian churches from the very beginning were in possession of a definite and formulated symbol, or that this symbol was an amplification of the trinitarian formula of Baptism, yet we are unable to ascertain with any degree of certainty what its exact original wording was. There has not been found in the early Christian writers a single passage recording the precise form of the baptismal confession or the rule of truth and faith as used in the earliest churches. This lack of contemporal written records is accounted for by the fact that the early Christians and Christian churches refused on principle to impart and transmit their confession in any other manner than by word of mouth. Such was their attitude, not because they believed in keeping their creed secret, but because they viewed the exclusively oral method of impartation as the most appropriate in a matter which they regarded as an affair of deepest concern of their hearts. It is universally admitted, even by those who believe that the apostles were instrumental in formulating the early Christian Creed, that the wording of it was not absolutely identical in all Christian congregations, and that in the course of time various changes and additions were made. "Tradition," says Tertullian with respect to the baptismal confession, received from the apostles, "has enlarged it, custom has confirmed it, faith observes and preserves it." (Zahn, 252. 381.) When, therefore, Tertullian and other ancient writers declare that the rule of faith received from the apostles is "altogether one, immovable, and irreformable," they do not at all mean to say that the phraseology of this symbol was alike everywhere, and that in this respect no changes whatever had been made, nor that any clauses had been added. Such variations, additions, and alterations, however, involved a doctrinal change of the confession no more than the Apology of the Augsburg Confession implies a doctrinal departure from this symbol. It remained the same Apostolic Creed, the changes and additions merely bringing out more fully and clearly its true, original meaning. And this is the sense in which Tertullian and others emphasize that the rule of faith is "one, immovable, and irreformable." The oldest known form of the Apostles' Creed, according to A. Harnack, is the one used in the church at Rome, even prior to 150 A. D. It was, however, as late as 337 or 338, when this Creed, which, as the church at Rome claimed, was brought thither by Peter himself, was for the first time quoted as a whole by Bishop Marcellus of Ancyra in a letter to Bishop Julius of Rome, for the purpose of vindicating his orthodoxy. During the long period intervening, some changes, however, may have been, and probably were,

made also in this Old Roman Symbol, which reads as follows: —

Πιστεύω εἰς θεὸν πατέρα παντοκράτορα· καὶ εἰς Χριστὸν Ἰησοῦν [τὸν] υἱὸν αὐτοῦ τὸν μονογενῆ, τὸν κύριον ἡμῶν, τὸν γεννηθέντα ἐκ πνεύματος ἁγίου καὶ Μαρίας τῆς παρθένου, τὸν ἐπὶ Ποντίου Πιλάτου σταυρωθέντα καὶ ταφέντα, τῇ τρίτῃ ἡμέρᾳ ἀναστάντα ἐκ [τῶν] νεκρῶν, ἀναβάντα εἰς τοὺς οὐρανούς, καθήμενον ἐν δεξιᾷ τοῦ πατρός, ὅθεν ἔρχεται κρῖναι ζῶντας καὶ νεκρούς· καὶ εἰς πνεῦμα ἅγιον, ἁγίαν ἐκκλησίαν, ἄφεσιν ἁμαρτιῶν, σαρκὸς ἀνάστασιν. (Herzog, R. E. 1, 744.)

## 13. Present Form of Creed and Its Contents.

The complete form of the present *textus receptus* of the Apostles' Creed, evidently the result of a comparison and combination of the various preexisting forms of this symbol, may be traced to the end of the fifth century and is first found in a sermon by Caesarius of Arles in France, about 500. — In his translation, Luther substituted "Christian" for "catholic" in the Third Article. He regarded the two expressions as equivalent in substance, as appears from the Smalcald Articles, where he identifies these terms, saying: "Sic enim orant pueri: Credo sanctam ecclesiam catholicam sive Christianam." (472, 5; 498, 3.) The form, "I believe a holy Christian Church," however, is met with even before Luther's time. (Carpzov, *Isagoge*, 46.) — In the Greek version the received form of the Apostles' Creed reads as follows: —

Πιστεύω εἰς θεὸν πατέρα, παντοκράτορα, ποιητὴν οὐρανοῦ καὶ γῆς. Καὶ εἰς Ἰησοῦν Χριστόν, υἱὸν αὐτοῦ τὸν μονογενῆ, τὸν κύριον ἡμῶν, τὸν συλληφθέντα ἐκ πνεύματος ἁγίου, γεννηθέντα ἐκ Μαρίας τῆς παρθένου, παθόντα ἐπὶ Ποντίου Πιλάτου, σταυρωθέντα, θανόντα, καὶ ταφέντα, κατελθόντα εἰς τὰ κατώτατα, τῇ τρίτῃ ἡμέρᾳ ἀναστάντα ἀπὸ τῶν νεκρῶν, ἀνελθόντα εἰς τοὺς οὐρανούς, καθεζόμενον ἐν δεξιᾷ θεοῦ πατρὸς παντοδυνάμου, ἐκεῖθεν ἐρχόμενον κρῖναι ζῶντας καὶ νεκρούς. Πιστεύω εἰς τὸ πνεῦμα τὸ ἅγιον, ἁγίαν καθολικὴν ἐκκλησίαν, ἁγίων κοινωνίαν, ἄφεσιν ἁμαρτιῶν, σαρκὸς ἀνάστασιν, ζωὴν αἰώνιον. Ἀμήν.

As to its contents, the Apostles' Creed is a positive statement of the essential facts of Christianity. The Second Article, says Zahn, is "a compend of the Evangelical history, including even external details." (264.) Yet some of the clauses of this Creed were probably inserted in opposition to prevailing, notably Gnostic, heresies of the first centuries. It was the first Christian symbol and, as Tertullian and others declare, the bond of unity and fellowship of the early Christian congregations everywhere. It must not, however, be regarded as inspired, much less as superior even to the Holy Scriptures; for, as stated above, it cannot even, in any of its existing forms, be traced to the apostles. Hence it must be subjected to, and tested and judged by, the Holy Scriptures, the inspired Word of God and the only infallible rule and norm of all doctrines, teachers, and symbols. In accordance herewith the Lutheran Church receives the Apostles' Creed, as also the two other ecumenical confessions, not as *per se* divine and authoritative, but because its doctrine is taken from, and well grounded in, the prophetic and apostolic writings of the Old and New Testaments. (CONC. TRIGL., 851, 4.)

## 14. The Nicene Creed.

In the year 325 Emperor Constantine the Great convened the First Ecumenical Council at Nicaea, in Bithynia, for the purpose of settling the controversy precipitated by the teaching of Arius, who denied the true divinity of Christ. The council was attended by 318 bishops and their assistants, among whom the young deacon Athanasius of Alexandria gained special prominence as a theologian of great eloquence, acumen, and learning. "The most valiant champion against the Arians," as he was called, Athanasius turned the tide of victory in favor of the Homoousians, who believed that the essence of the Father and of the Son is identical. The discussions were based upon the symbol of Eusebius of Caesarea, which by changes and the insertion of Homoousian phrases (such as ἐκ τῆς οὐσίας τοῦ πατρός; γεννηθείς, οὐ ποιηθείς; ὁμοούσιος τῷ πατρί) was amended into an unequivocal, clean-cut, anti-Arian confession. Two Egyptian bishops who refused to sign the symbol were banished, together with Arius, to Illyria. The text of the original Nicene Creed reads as follows: —

Πιστεύομεν εἰς ἕνα θεόν, πατέρα παντοκράτορα, πάντων ὁρατῶν τὲ καὶ ἀοράτων ποιητήν. Καὶ εἰς ἕνα κύριον Ἰησοῦν Χριστόν, τὸν υἱὸν τοῦ θεοῦ, γεννηθέντα ἐκ τοῦ πατρὸς μονογενῆ, τουτέστιν ἐκ τῆς οὐσίας τοῦ πατρός, θεὸν ἐκ θεοῦ, φῶς ἐκ φωτός, θεὸν ἀληθινὸν ἐκ θεοῦ ἀληθινοῦ, γεννηθέντα, οὐ ποιηθέντα, ὁμοούσιον τῷ πατρί, δι' οὗ τὰ πάντα ἐγένετο, τά τε ἐν τῷ οὐρανῷ καὶ τὰ ἐπὶ τῆς γῆς· τὸν δι' ἡμᾶς τοὺς ἀνθρώπους καὶ διὰ τὴν ἡμετέραν σωτηρίαν κατελθόντα καὶ σαρκωθέντα καὶ ἐνανθρωπήσαντα, παθόντα, καὶ ἀναστάντα τῇ τρίτῃ ἡμέρᾳ, καὶ ἀνελθόντα εἰς τοὺς οὐρανούς, καὶ ἐρχόμενον πάλιν κρῖναι ζῶντας καὶ νεκρούς. Καὶ εἰς τὸ πνεῦμα τὸ ἅγιον. Τοὺς δὲ λέγοντας, ὅτι ἦν ποτὲ ὅτε οὐκ ἦν, καὶ πρὶν γεννηθῆναι οὐκ ἦν, καὶ ὅτι ἐξ οὐκ ὄντων ἐγένετο, ἢ ἐξ ἑτέρας ὑποστάσεως ἢ οὐσίας φάσκοντας εἶναι, ἢ κτιστόν, ἢ ἀλλοιωτὸν ἢ τρεπτὸν τὸν υἱὸν τοῦ θεοῦ, τούτους ἀναθεματίζει ἡ καθολικὴ καὶ ἀποστολικὴ ἐκκλησία. (Mansi, *Amplissima Collectio*, 2, 665 sq.)

## 15. Niceno-Constantinopolitan Creed.

In order to suppress Arianism, which still continued to flourish, Emperor Theodosius convened the Second Ecumenical Council, in 381, at Constantinople. The bishops here assembled, 150 in number, resolved that the faith of the Nicene Fathers must ever remain firm and unchanged, and that its opponents, the Eunomians, Anomoeans, Arians, Eudoxians, Semi-Arians, Sabellians, Marcellians, Photinians, and Apollinarians, musᵗ be rejected. At this council also Macedonius was condemned, who taught that the Holy Spirit is not God: ἔλεγε γὰρ αὐτὸ μὴ εἶναι θεόν, ἀλλὰ τῆς θεότητος τοῦ πατρὸς ἀλλότριον. (Mansi, 3, 558. 566. 573.

577. 600.) By omissions, alterations, and additions (in particular concerning the Holy Spirit) this council gave to the Nicene Creed its present form. Hence it is also known as the Niceno-Constantinopolitan Creed. The Third Ecumenical Council, which assembled at Toledo, Spain, in 589, inserted the word "Filioque," an addition which the Greek Church has never sanctioned, and which later contributed towards bringing about the great Eastern Schism. A. Harnack considers the Constantinopolitanum (CPanum), the creed adopted at Constantinople, to be the baptismal confession of the Church of Jerusalem, which, he says, was revised between 362 and 373 and amplified by the Nicene formulas and a rule of faith concerning the Holy Ghost. (Herzog, *R. E.*, 11, 19 f.) Following is the text of the CPanum according to Mansi: —

Πιστεύομεν εἰς ἕνα θεὸν πατέρα, παντοκράτορα, ποιητὴν οὐρανοῦ καὶ γῆς, ὁρατῶν τε πάντων καὶ ἀοράτων. Καὶ εἰς ἕνα κύριον Ἰησοῦν Χριστὸν τὸν υἱὸν τοῦ θεοῦ τὸν μονογενῆ, τὸν ἐκ τοῦ πατρὸς γεννηθέντα πρὸ πάντων τῶν αἰώνων, φῶς ἐκ φωτός, θεὸν ἀληθινὸν ἐκ θεοῦ ἀληθινοῦ, γεννηθέντα, οὐ ποιηθέντα, ὁμοούσιον τῷ πατρί, δι' οὗ τὰ πάντα ἐγένετο, τὸν δι' ἡμᾶς τοὺς ἀνθρώπους καὶ διὰ τὴν ἡμετέραν σωτηρίαν κατελθόντα ἐκ τῶν οὐρανῶν, καὶ σαρκωθέντα ἐκ πνεύματος ἁγίου καὶ Μαρίας τῆς παρθένου, καὶ ἐνανθρωπήσαντα, σταυρωθέντα τε ὑπὲρ ἡμῶν ἐπὶ Ποντίου Πιλάτου, καὶ παθόντα, καὶ ταφέντα, καὶ ἀναστάντα τῇ τρίτῃ ἡμέρᾳ κατὰ τὰς γραφάς, καὶ ἀνελθόντα εἰς τοὺς οὐρανούς, καὶ καθεζόμενον ἐκ δεξιῶν τοῦ πατρός, καὶ πάλιν ἐρχόμενον μετὰ δόξης κρῖναι ζῶντας καὶ νεκρούς· οὗ τῆς βασιλείας οὐκ ἔσται τέλος. Καὶ εἰς τὸ πνεῦμα τὸ ἅγιον, τὸ κύριον, τὸ ζωοποιόν, τὸ ἐκ τοῦ πατρὸς ἐκπορευόμενον, τὸ σὺν πατρὶ καὶ υἱῷ συμπροσκυνούμενον καὶ συνδοξαζόμενον, τὸ λαλῆσαν διὰ τῶν προφητῶν, εἰς μίαν ἁγίαν καθολικὴν καὶ ἀποστολικὴν ἐκκλησίαν. Ὁμολογοῦμεν ἓν βάπτισμα εἰς ἄφεσιν ἁμαρτιῶν· προσδοκῶμεν ἀνάστασιν νεκρῶν, καὶ ζωὴν τοῦ μέλλοντος αἰῶνος. Ἀμήν. (3, 565.)

## 16. The Athanasian Creed.

From its opening word this Creed is also called Symbolum Quicunque. Roman tradition has it that Athanasius, who died 373, made this confession before Pope Julius when the latter summoned him "to submit himself to him [the Pope], as to the ecumenical bishop and supreme arbiter of matters ecclesiastical (*ut ei, seu episcopo oecumenico et supremo rerum ecclesiasticarum arbitro, sese submitteret*)." However, Athanasius is not even the author of this confession, as appears from the following facts: 1. The Creed was originally written in Latin. 2. It is mentioned neither by Athanasius himself nor by his Greek eulogists. 3. It was unknown to the Greek Church till about 1200, and has never been accorded official recognition by this Church nor its "orthodox" sister churches. 4. It presupposes the post-Athanasian Trinitarian and Christological controversies. — Up to the present day it has been impossible to reach a final verdict concerning the author of the Quicunque and the time and place of its origin. Koellner's *Symbolik* allocates it to Gaul. Loofs inclines to the same opinion and ventures the conjecture that the source of this symbol must be sought in Southern Gaul between 450 and 600. (Herzog, *R. E.*, 2, 177.) Gieseler and others look to Spain for its origin.

Paragraphs 1, 2, and 40 of the Athanasian Creed have given offense not only to theologians who advocate an undogmatic Christianity, but to many thoughtless Christians as well. Loofs declares: The Quicunque is unevangelical and cannot be received, because its very first sentence confounds *fides* with *expositio fidei.* (H., *R. E.*, 2, 194.) However, the charge is gratuitous, since the Athanasian Creed deals with the most fundamental Christian truths: concerning the Trinity, the divinity of Christ, and His work of redemption, without the knowledge of which saving faith is impossible. The paragraphs in question merely express the clear doctrine of such passages of the Scriptures as Acts 4, 12: "Neither is there salvation in any other; for there is none other name under heaven given among men whereby we must be saved"; John 8, 21: "If ye believe not that I am He, ye shall die in your sins"; John 14, 6: "Jesus saith unto him, I am the Way, the Truth, and the Life; no man cometh unto the Father but by Me." In complete agreement with the impugned statements of the Athanasian Creed, the Apology of the Augsburg Confession closes its article "Of God" as follows: "Therefore we do freely conclude that they are all idolatrous, blasphemers, and outside of the Church of Christ who hold or teach otherwise." (102.)

In the early part of the Middle Ages the Quicunque had already received a place in the order of public worship. The Council of Vavre resolved, 1368: "Proinde Symbolum Apostolorum silenter et secrete dicitur quotidie in Completorio et in Prima, quia fuit editum tempore, quo nondum erat fides catholica propalata. Alia autem duo publice in diebus Dominicis et festivis, quando maior ad ecclesiam congregatur populus, decantantur, quia fuere edita tempore fidei propalatae. Symbolum quidem Nicaenum post evangelium cantatur in Missa quasi evangelicae fidei expositio. Symbolum Athanasii de mane solum cantatur in Prima, quia fuit editum tempore, quo maxime fuerunt depulsa et detecta nox atra et tenebrae haeresium et errorum." (Mansi, 26, 487.) Luther says: "The first symbol, that of the apostles, is indeed the best of all, because it contains a concise, correct, and splendid presentation of the articles of faith and is easily learned by children and the common people. The second, the Athanasian Creed, is longer . . . and practically amounts to an apology of the first symbol." "I do not know of any more important document of the New Testament Church since the days of the apostles" [than the Athanasian Creed]. (St. L. 10, 994; 6, 1576; E. 23, 253.)

### 17. Luther on Ecumenical Creeds.

The central theme of the three Ecumenical Symbols is Christ's person and work, the paramount importance of which Luther extols as follows in his tract of 1538: "In all the histories of the entire Christendom I have found and experienced that all who had and held the chief article concerning Jesus Christ correctly remained safe and sound in the true Christian faith. And even though they erred and sinned in other points, they nevertheless were finally preserved." "For it has been decreed, says Paul, Col. 2, 9, that in Christ should dwell all the fulness of the Godhead bodily, or personally, so that he who does not find or receive God in Christ shall never have nor find Him anywhere outside of Christ, even though he ascend above heaven, descend below hell, or go beyond the world." "On the other hand, I have also observed that all errors, heresies, idolatries, offenses, abuses, and ungodliness within the Church originally resulted from the fact that this article of faith concerning Jesus Christ was despised or lost. And viewed clearly and rightly, all heresies militate against the precious article of Jesus Christ, as Simeon says concerning Him, Luke 2, 34, that He is set for the falling and the rising of many in Israel and for a sign which is spoken against; and long before this, Isaiah, chapter 8, 14, spoke of Him as 'a stone of stumbling and a rock of offense.'" "And we, in the Papacy, the last and greatest of saints, what have we done? We have confessed that He [Christ] is God and man; but that He is our Savior, who died and rose *for us*, etc., this we have denied and persecuted with might and main" (those who taught this). "And even now those who claim to be the best Christians and boast that they are the Holy Church, who burn the others and wade in innocent blood, regard as the best doctrine [that which teaches] that we obtain grace and salvation through our own works. Christ is to be accorded no other honor with regard to our salvation than that He made the beginning, while we are the heroes who complete it with our merit."

Luther continues: "This is the way the devil goes to work. He attacks Christ with three storm-columns. One will not suffer Him to be God; the other will not suffer Him to be man; the third denies that He has merited salvation for us. Each of the three endeavors to destroy Christ. For what does it avail that you confess Him to be God if you do not also believe that He is man? For then you have not the entire and the true Christ, but a phantom of the devil. What does it avail you to confess that He is true man if you do not also believe that He is true God? What does it avail you to confess that He is God and man if you do not also believe that whatever He became and whatever He did was done for you?" "Surely, all three parts must be believed, namely, that He is God, also, that He is man, and that He became such a man for us, that is, as the first symbol says: conceived by the Holy Ghost, born of the Virgin Mary, suffered, was crucified, died, and rose again, etc. If one small part is lacking, then all parts are lacking. For faith shall and must be complete in every particular. While it may indeed be weak and subject to afflictions, yet it must be entire and not false.

Weakness [of faith] does not work the harm, but false faith — that is eternal death." (St. L. 10, 998; E. 23, 258.)

Concerning the mystery involved in the doctrine of the Holy Trinity, the chief topic of the Ecumenical Creeds, Luther remarks in the same tract: "Now, to be sure, we Christians are not so utterly devoid of all reason and sense as the Jews consider us, who take us to be nothing but crazy geese and ducks, unable to perceive or notice what folly it is to believe that God is man, and that in one Godhead there are three distinct persons. No, praise God, we perceive indeed that this doctrine cannot and will not be received by reason. Nor are we in need of any sublime Jewish reasoning to demonstrate this to us. We believe it knowingly and willingly. We confess and also experience that, where the Holy Spirit does not, surpassing reason, shine into the heart, it is impossible to grasp, or to believe, and abide by, such article; moreover, there must remain in it [the heart] a Jewish, proud, and supercilious reason deriding and ridiculing such article, and thus setting up itself as judge and master of the Divine Being, whom it has never seen nor is able to see, and hence does not know what it is passing judgment on, nor whereof it thinks or speaks. For God dwells in a 'light which no man can approach unto,' 1 Tim. 6, 16. He must come to us, yet hidden in the lantern, and as it is written, John 1, 18: 'No man hath seen God at any time; the only-begotten Son, which is in the bosom of the Father, He hath declared Him,' and as Moses said before this, Ex. 33: 'There shall no man see Me [God] and live.' " (St. L. 10, 1007; E. 23, 568.)

# III. The Augsburg Confession.

## 18. Diet Proclaimed by Emperor.

January 21, 1530, Emperor Charles V proclaimed a diet to convene at Augsburg on the 8th of April. The manifesto proceeded from Bologna, where, three days later, the Emperor was crowned by Pope Clement VII. The proclamation, after referring to the Turkish invasion and the action to be taken with reference to this great peril, continues as follows: "The diet is to consider furthermore what might and ought to be done and resolved upon regarding the division and separation in the holy faith and the Christian religion; and that this may proceed the better and more salubriously, [the Emperor urged] to allay divisions, to cease hostility, to surrender past errors to our Savior, and to display diligence in hearing, understanding, and considering with love and kindness the opinions and views of everybody, in order to reduce them to one single Christian truth and agreement, to put aside whatever has not been properly explained or done by either party, so that we all may adopt and hold one single and true religion; and may all live in one communion, church, and unity, even as we all live and do battle under one Christ."

In his invitation to attend the diet, the Emperor at the same time urged the Elector of Saxony by all means to appear early enough (the Elector reached Augsburg on May 2, while the Emperor did not arrive before June 16), "lest the others who arrived in time be compelled to wait with disgust, heavy expenses, and detrimental delay such as had frequently occurred in the past." The Emperor added the warning: In case the Elector should not appear, the diet would proceed as if he had been present and assented to its resolutions. (Foerstemann, *Urkundenbuch,* 1, 7 f.)

March 11 the proclamation reached Elector John at Torgau. On the 14th Chancellor Brueck advised the Elector to have "the opinion on which our party has hitherto stood and to which they have adhered," in the controverted points, "properly drawn up in writing, with a thorough confirmation thereof from the divine Scriptures." On the same day the Elector commissioned Luther, Jonas, Bugenhagen, and Melanchthon to prepare a document treating especially of "those articles on account of which said division, both in faith and in other outward church customs and ceremonies, continues." (43.) At Wittenberg the theologians at once set to work, and the result was presented at Torgau March 27 by Melanchthon. On April 4 the Elector and his theologians set out from Torgau, arriving at Coburg on the 15th, where they rested for eight days. On the 23d of April the Elector left for Augsburg, while Luther, who was still under the ban of both the Pope and the Emperor, remained at the fortress Ebernburg. Nevertheless he continued in close touch with the confessors, as appears from his numerous letters written to Augsburg, seventy all told, about twenty of which were addressed to Melanchthon.

## 19. Apology Original Plan of Lutherans.

The documents which the Wittenberg theologians delivered at Torgau treated the following subjects: Human Doctrines and Ordinances, Marriage of Priests, Both Kinds, Mass, Confession, Power of Bishops, Ordination, Monastic Vows, Invocation of the Saints, German Singing, Faith and Works, Office of the Keys (Papacy), Ban, Marriage, and Private Mass. Accordingly, the original intention of the Lutherans was not to enter upon, and present for discussion at Augsburg, such doctrines as were not in controversy (Of God, etc.), but merely to treat of the abuses and immediately related doctrines, especially of Faith and Good Works. (66 ff.) They evidently regarded it as their chief object and duty to justify before the Emperor and the estates both Luther and his protectors, the electors of Saxony. This is borne out also by the original Introduction to the contemplated Apology, concerning which we read in the prefatory remarks to the so-called Torgau Articles mentioned above: "To this end [of justifying the Elector's peaceable frame of mind] it will be advantageous to begin [the projected Apology] with a lengthy rhetorical introduction." (68; *C. R.*, 26, 171.) This introduction, later on replaced by another, was composed by Melanchthon at Coburg and polished by him during the first days at Augsburg. May 4 he remarks in a letter to Luther: "I have shaped the Exordium of our Apology somewhat more rhetorical (*ῥητορικώτερον*) than I had written it at Coburg." (*C. R.*, 2, 40; Luther, St. L. 16, 652.) In this introduction Melanchthon explains: Next to God the Elector builds his hope on the Emperor, who had always striven for peace, and was even now prepared to adjust the religious controversy in mildness. As to the Elector and his brother Frederick, they had ever been attached to the Christian religion, had proved faithful to the Emperor, and had constantly cultivated peace. Their present position was due to the fact that commandments of men had been preached instead of faith in Christ. Not Luther, but Luther's opponents, had begun the strife. It was for conscience' sake that the Elector had not proceeded against Luther. Besides, such action would only have made matters worse, since Luther had resisted the Sacramentarians and the Anabaptists. Equally unfounded were also the accusations that the Evangelicals had abolished all order as well as all ceremonies, and had undermined the authority of the bishops. If only the bishops would tolerate the Gospel and do away with the gross abuses, they would suffer no loss of power, honor, and prestige. In concluding Melanchthon emphatically protests: "Never has a reformation been undertaken so utterly without any violence as this [in Saxony]; for it is a public fact that our men have prevailed with such as were already in arms to make peace." (Kolde, *l. c.*, 13.) The document, accordingly, as originally planned for presentation at Augsburg, was to be a defense of Luther and his Elector. In keeping herewith it was in the beginning consistently designated "Apology."

## 20. Transformation of Apology into Confession Due to Eck's Slanders.

This plan, however, was modified when the Lutherans, after reaching Augsburg, heard of and read the 404 Propositions published by Dr. John Eck, in which Luther was classified with Zwingli, Oecolampadius, Carlstadt, Pirkheimer, Hubmaier, and Denk, and was charged with every conceivable heresy. In a letter of March 14, accompanying the copy of his Propositions which Eck sent to the Emperor, he refers to Luther as the domestic enemy of the Church (*hostis ecclesiae domesticus*), who has fallen into every Scylla and Charybdis of iniquity; who speaks of the Pope as the Antichrist and of the Church as the harlot; who has praise for none but heretics and schismatics; whom the Church has to thank for the Iconoclasts, Sacramentarians, New Hus-

sites, Anabaptists, New Epicureans, who teach that the soul is mortal, and the Cerinthians; who rehashes all the old heresies condemned more than a thousand years ago, etc. (Plitt, *Einleitung in die Augustana*, 1, 527 ff.) Such and similar slanders had been disseminated by the Papists before this, and they continued to do so even after the Lutherans, at Augsburg, had made a public confession of their faith and had most emphatically disavowed all ancient and modern heresies. Thus Cochlaeus asserted in his attack on the Apology, published 1534, that Lutheranism was a concoction of all the old condemned heresies, that Luther taught fifteen errors against the article of God, and Melanchthon nine against the Nicene Creed, etc. Luther, he declared, had attacked the doctrine of the Trinity in a coarser fashion than Arius. (Salig, *Historie d. Augsb. Konf.*, 1, 377.)

These calumniations caused the Lutherans to remodel and expand the defense originally planned into a document which should not merely justify the changes made by them with regard to customs and ceremonies, but also present as fully as possible the doctrinal articles which they held over against ancient and modern heresies, falsely imputed to them. Thus to some extent it is due to the scurrility of Eck that the contemplated Apology was transformed into an all-embracing Confession, a term employed by Melanchthon himself. In a letter to Luther, dated May 11, 1530, he wrote: "Our Apology is being sent to you, — though it is rather a Confession. *Mittitur tibi apologia nostra, quamquam verius confessio est.* I included [in the Confession] almost all articles of faith, because Eck published most diabolical lies against us, *quia Eckius edidit διαβολικώτατας διαβολάς contra nos.* Against these it was my purpose to provide an antidote." (*C. R.* 2, 45; Luther, St. L. 16, 654.)

This is in accord also with Melanchthon's account in his Preface of September 29, 1559, to the German *Corpus Doctrinae* (Philippicum), stating: "Some papal scribblers had disseminated pasquinades at the diet [at Augsburg, 1530], which reviled our churches with horrible lies, charging that they taught many condemned errors, and were like the Anabaptists, erring and rebellious. Answer had to be made to His Imperial Majesty, and in order to refute the pasquinades, it was decided to include all articles of Christian doctrine in proper succession, that every one might see how unjustly our churches were slandered in the lying papal writings. . . . Finally, this Confession was, as God directed and guided, drawn up by me in the manner indicated, and the venerable Doctor Martin Luther was pleased with it." (*C. R.* 9, 929.)

The original plan, however, was not entirely abandoned, but merely extended by adding a defense also against the various heresies with which the Lutherans were publicly charged. This was done in an objective presentation of the principal doctrines held by the Lutherans, for which the Marburg and Schwabach Articles served as models and guides.

## 21. Marburg, Schwabach, and Torgau Articles.

The material from which Melanchthon constructed the Augsburg Confession is, in the last analysis, none other than the Reformation truths which Luther had proclaimed since 1517 with ever-increasing clarity and force. In particular, he was guided by, and based his labor on, the Marburg Articles, the Schwabach Articles, and the so-called Torgau Articles. The Marburg Articles, fifteen in number, had been drawn up by Luther, in 1529, at the Colloquy of Marburg, whence he departed October 5, about six months before the Diet at Augsburg. (Luther, St. L., 17, 1138 f.) The seventeen Schwabach Articles were composed by Luther, Melanchthon, Jonas, Brenz, and Agricola, and presented to the Convention at Smalcald about the middle of October, 1529. According to recent researches the Schwabach Articles antedated the Marburg Articles and formed the basis for them. (Luther, Weimar Ed., 30, 3, 97. 107.) In 1530 Luther published these Articles, remarking: "It is true that I helped to draw up such articles; for they were not composed by me alone." This public statement discredits the opinion of v. Schubert published in 1908, according to which Melanchthon is the sole author of the Schwabach Articles, Luther's contribution and participation being negligible. The Schwabach Articles constitute the seventeen basic articles of the first part of the Augsburg Confession. (St. L. 16, 638. 648. 564; C. R. 26, 146 f.)

The so-called Torgau Articles are the documents referred to above, touching chiefly upon the abuses. Pursuant to the order of the Elector, they were prepared by Luther and his assistants, Melanchthon, Bugenhagen, and possibly also Jonas. They are called Torgau Articles because the order for drafting them came from Torgau (March 14), and because they were presented to the Elector at Torgau. (Foerstemann, 1, 66; C. R. 26, 171; St. L. 16, 638.) With reference to these articles Luther wrote (March 14) to Jonas, who was then still conducting the visitation: "The Prince has written to us, that is, to you, Pomeranus, Philip, and myself, in a letter addressed to us in common, that we should come together, set aside all other business, and finish before next Sunday whatever is necessary for the next diet on April 8. For Emperor Charles himself will be present at Augsburg to settle all things in a friendly way, as he writes in his bull. Therefore, although you are absent, we three shall do what we can to-day and to-morrow; still, in order to comply with the will of the Prince, it will be incumbent upon you to turn your work over to your companions and be present with us here on the morrow. For things are in a hurry. *Festinata enim sunt omnia.*" (St. L. 16, 638.) Melanchthon also wrote to Jonas on the 15th of March: "Luther is summoning you by order of the Prince; you will therefore come as soon as it is at all possible. The Diet, according to the proclamation, will convene at Augsburg. And the Emperor graciously promises that he will investigate the

matter, and correct the errors on both sides. May Christ stand by us!" (*C. R.* 2, 28; Foerstemann, 1, 45.) It was to these articles (Torgau Articles) that the Elector referred when he wrote to Luther from Augsburg on the 11th of May: "After you and others of our learned men at Wittenberg, at our gracious desire and demand, have drafted the articles which are in religious controversy, we do not wish to conceal from you that Master Philip Melanchthon has now at this place perused them further and drawn them up in one form." (*C. R.* 2, 47.)

## 22. Luther's Spokesman at Augsburg.

The material, therefore, out of which Melanchthon, who in 1530 was still in full accord with Luther doctrinally, framed the fundamental symbol of the Lutheran Church were the thoughts and, in a large measure, the very words of Luther. Melanchthon gave to the Augsburg Confession its form and its irenic note; its entire doctrinal content, however, must be conceded to be "*iuxta sententiam Lutheri*, according to the teaching of Luther," as Melanchthon himself declared particularly with respect to the article of the Lord's Supper. (*C. R.* 2, 142.) On the 27th of June, two days after the presentation of the Confession, Melanchthon wrote to Luther: "We have hitherto followed your authority, *tuam secuti hactenus auctoritatem*," and now, says Melanchthon, Luther should also let him know how much could be yielded to the opponents. (2, 146.) Accordingly, in the opinion of Melanchthon, Luther, though absent, was the head of the Evangelicals also at Augsburg.

In his answer Luther does not deny this, but only demands of Melanchthon to consider the cause of the Gospel as his own. "For," says he, "it is indeed my affair, and, to tell the truth, my affair more so than that of all of you." Yet they should not speak of "authority." "In this matter," he continues, "I will not be or be called your author [authority]; and though this might be correctly explained, I do not want this word. If it is not your affair at the same time and in the same measure, I do not desire that it be called mine and be imposed upon you. If it is mine alone, I shall direct it myself." (St. L. 16, 906. 903. Enders, *Luthers Briefwechsel*, 8, 43.)

Luther, then, was the prime mover also at Augsburg. Without him there would have been no Evangelical cause, no Diet of Augsburg, no Evangelical confessors, no Augsburg Confession. And this is what Luther really meant when he said: "*Confessio Augustana mea;* the Augsburg Confession is mine." (Walch 22, 1532.) He did not in the least thereby intend to deprive Melanchthon of any credit properly due him with reference to the Confession. Moreover, in a letter written to Nicolaus Hausmann on July 6, 1530, Luther refers to the Augustana as "our confession, which our Philip prepared; *quam Philippus noster paravit.*" (St. L. 16, 882; Enders 8, 80.) As a matter of fact, however, the day of Augsburg, even as the day of Worms, was the day of Luther and of the Evangelical truth once more restored to light by Luther. At Augsburg, too, Melanchthon was not the real author and moving spirit, but the instrument and mouthpiece of Luther, out of whose spirit the doctrine there confessed had proceeded. (See Formula of Concord 983, 32—34.)

Only blindness born of false religious interests (indifferentism, unionism, etc.) can speak of Melanchthon's theological independence at Augsburg or of any doctrinal disagreement between the Augsburg Confession and the teaching of Luther. That, at the Diet, he was led, and wished to be led, by Luther is admitted by Melanchthon himself. In the letter of June 27, referred to above, he said: "The matters, as you [Luther] know, have been considered before, though in the combat it always turns out otherwise than expected." (St. L. 16, 899; C. R. 2, 146.) On the 31st of August he wrote to his friend Camerarius: "Hitherto we have yielded nothing to our opponents, except what Luther judged should be done, since the matter was considered well and carefully before the Diet; re bene ac diligenter deliberata ante conventum." (2, 334.)

Very pertinently E. T. Nitzsch said of Melanchthon (1855): "With the son of the miner, who was destined to bring good ore out of the deep shaft, there was associated the son of an armorer, who was well qualified to follow his leader and to forge shields, helmets, armor, and swords for this great work." This applies also to the Augsburg Confession, in which Melanchthon merely shaped the material long before produced by Luther from the divine shafts of God's Word. Replying to Koeller, Rueckert, and Heppe, who contend that the authorship of the Augsburg Confession must in every way be ascribed to Melanchthon, Philip Schaff writes as follows: "This is true as far as the spirit [which Luther called 'pussyfooting,' Leisetreten] and the literary composition are concerned; but as to the doctrines Luther had a right to say, 'The Catechism, the Exposition of the Ten Commandments, and the Augsburg Confession are mine.'" (Creeds 1, 229.)

### 23. Drafting the Confession.

May 11 the Confession was so far completed that the Elector was able to submit it to Luther for the purpose of getting his opinion on it. According to Melanchthon's letter of the same date, the document contained "almost all articles of faith, omnes fere articulos fidei." (C. R. 2, 45.) This agrees with the account written by Melanchthon shortly before his death, in which he states that in the Augsburg Confession he had presented "the sum of our Church's doctrine," and that in so doing he had arrogated nothing to himself; for in the presence of the princes, etc., each individual sentence had been discussed. "Thereupon," says Melanchthon, "the entire Confession was sent also to Luther, who informed the princes that he had read it and approved it. The princes and other honest and learned men still living will remember that such was the case. Missa est denique et

Luthero tota forma Confessionis, qui Principibus scripsit, se hanc Confessionem et legisse et probare. Haec ita acta esse, Principes et alii honesti et docti viri adhuc superstites meminerint." (9, 1052.) As early as May 15 Luther returned the Confession with the remark: "I have read Master Philip's Apology. I am well pleased with it, and know nothing to improve or to change in it; neither would this be proper, since I cannot step so gently and softly. Christ, our Lord, grant that it may produce much and great fruit, which, indeed, we hope and pray for. Amen." (St. L. 16, 657.) Luther is said to have added these words to the Tenth Article: "And they condemn those who teach otherwise; et improbant secus docentes." (Enders, 7, 336.)

Up to the time of its presentation the Augsburg Confession was diligently improved, polished, perfected, and partly recast. Additions were inserted and several articles added. Nor was this done secretly and without Luther's knowledge. May 22 Melanchthon wrote to Luther: "Daily we change much in the Apology. I have eliminated the article On Vows, since it was too brief, and substituted a fuller explanation. Now I am also treating of the Power of the Keys. I would like to have you read the articles of faith. If you find no shortcoming in them, we shall manage to treat the remainder. For one must always make some changes in them and adapt oneself to conditions. Subinde enim mutandi sunt, atque ad occasiones accommodandi." (C. R. 2, 60; Luther, 16, 689.) Improvements suggested by Regius and Brenz were also adopted. (Zoeckler, Die A. K., 18.)

Even Brueck is said to have made some improvements. May 24 the Nuernberg delegates wrote to their Council: "The Saxon Plan [Apology] has been returned by Doctor Luther. But Doctor Brueck, the old chancellor, still has some changes to make at the beginning and the end." (C. R. 2, 62.) The expression "beginning and end (hinten und vorne)," according to Tschackert, is tantamount to "all over (ueberall)." However, even before 1867 Plitt wrote it had long ago been recognized that this expression refers to the Introduction and the Conclusion of the Confession, which were written by Brueck. (Aug. 2, 11.) Bretschneider is of the same opinion. (C. R. 2, 62.) June 3 the Nuernberg delegates wrote: "Herewith we transmit to Your Excellencies a copy of the Saxon Plan [Confession] in Latin, together with the Introduction or Preamble. At the end, however, there are lacking one or two articles [20 and 21] and the Conclusion, in which the Saxon theologians are still engaged. When that is completed, it shall be sent to Your Excellencies. Meanwhile Your Excellencies may cause your learned men and preachers to study it and deliberate upon it. When this Plan [Confession] is drawn up in German, it shall not be withheld from Your Excellencies. The Saxons, however, distinctly desire that, for the present, Your Excellencies keep this Plan or document secret, and that you permit no copy to be given to any one until it has been delivered to His Imperial

Majesty. They have reasons of their own for making this request. . . . And if Your Excellencies' pastors and learned men should decide to make changes or improvements in this Plan or in the one previously submitted, these, too, Your Excellencies are asked to transmit to us." (2, 83.) June 26 Melanchthon wrote to Camerarius: "Daily I changed and recast much; and I would have changed still more if our advisers (συμφράδμονες) had permitted us to do so." (2, 140.)

### 24. Public Reading of the Confession.

June 15, after long negotiations, a number of other estates were permitted to join the adherents of the Saxon Confession (C. R. 2, 105.) As a result, Melanchthon's Introduction, containing a defense of the Saxon Electors, without mentioning the other Lutheran estates, no longer fitted in with the changed conditions. Accordingly, it was supplanted by the Preface composed by Brueck, and translated into Latin by Justus Jonas, whose acknowledged elegant Latin and German style qualified him for such services. At the last deliberation, on June 23, the Confession was signed. And on June 25, at 3 P. M., the ever-memorable meeting of the Diet took place at which the Augustana was read by Chancellor Beyer in German, and both manuscripts were handed over. The Emperor kept the Latin copy for himself, and gave the German copy to the Imperial Chancellor, the Elector and Archbishop Albrecht, to be preserved in the Imperial Archives at Mainz. Both texts, therefore, the Latin as well as the German, have equal authority, although the German text has the additional distinction and prestige of having been publicly read at the Diet.

As to where and how the Lutheran heroes confessed their faith, Kolde writes as follows: "The place where they assembled on Saturday, June 25, at 3 P. M., was not the courtroom, where the meetings of the Diet were ordinarily conducted, but, as the Imperial Herald, Caspar Sturm, reports, the 'Pfalz,' the large front room, i. e., the Chapter-room of the bishop's palace, where the Emperor lived. The two Saxon chancellors, Dr. Greg. Brueck and Dr. Chr. Beyer, the one with the Latin and the other with the German copy of the Confession, stepped into the middle of the hall, while as many of the Evangelically minded estates as had the courage publicly to espouse the Evangelical cause arose from their seats. Caspar Sturm reports: 'Als aber die gemeldeten Commissarii und Botschaften der oesterreichischen Lande ihre Werbung und Botschaft vollendet und abgetreten, sind darauf von Stund' an Kurfuerst von Sachsen, naemlich Herzog Johannes, Markgraf Joerg von Brandenburg, Herzog Ernst samt seinem Bruder Franzisko, beide Herzoege zu Braunschweig und Lueneburg, Landgraf Philipp von Hessen, Graf Wolf von Anhalt usw. von ihrer Session auf- und gegen Kaiserliche Majestaet gestanden.' The Emperor desired to hear the Latin text. But when Elector John had called attention to the fact that the meeting was held on German soil, and expressed the hope that the Emperor would permit the reading

to proceed in German, it was granted. Hereupon Dr. Beyer read the Confession. The reading lasted about two hours; but he read with a voice so clear and plain that the multitude, which could not gain access to the hall, understood every word in the courtyard." (19 f.)

The public reading of the Confession exercised a tremendous influence in every direction. Even before the Diet adjourned, Heilbronn, Kempten, Windsheim, Weissenburg, and Frankfurt on the Main professed their adherence to it. Others had received the first impulse which subsequently induced them to side with the Evangelicals. Brenz has it that the Emperor fell asleep during the reading. However, this can have been only temporarily or apparently, since Spalatin and Jonas assure us that the Emperor, like the other princes and King Ferdinand, listened attentively. Their report reads: "*Satis attentus erat Caesar*, The Emperor was attentive enough." Duke William of Bavaria declared: "Never before has this matter and doctrine been presented to me in this manner." And when Eck assured him that he would undertake to refute the Lutheran doctrine with the Fathers, but not with the Scriptures, the Duke responded, "Then the Lutherans, I understand, sit in the Scriptures and we of the Pope's Church beside the Scriptures! *So hoer' ich wohl, die Lutherischen sitzen in der Schrift und wir Pontificii daneben!*" The Archbishop of Salzburg declared that he, too, desired a reformation, but the unbearable thing about it was that one lone monk wanted to reform them all. In private conversation, Bishop Stadion of Augsburg exclaimed, "What has been read to us is the truth, the pure truth, and we cannot deny it." (St. L. 16, 882; Plitt, *Apologie*, 18.) Father Aegidius, the Emperor's confessor, said to Melanchthon, "You have a theology which a person can understand only if he prays much." Campegius is reported to have said that for his part he might well permit such teaching; but it would be a precedent of no little consequence, as the same permission would then have to be given other nations and kingdoms, which could not be tolerated. (Zoeckler, *A. K.*, 24.)

### 25. Luther's Mild Criticism.

June 26 Melanchthon sent a copy of the Confession, as publicly read, to Luther, who, adhering to his opinion of May 15, praised it, yet not without adding a grain of gentle criticism. June 29 he wrote to Melanchthon: "I have received your Apology and cannot understand what you may mean when you ask what and how much should be yielded to the Papists. . . . As far as I am concerned, too much has already been yielded (*plus satis cessum est*) in this Apology; and if they reject it, I see nothing that might be yielded beyond what has been done, unless I see the proofs they proffer, and clearer Bible-passages than I have hitherto seen. . . . As I have always written — I am prepared to yield everything to them if we are but given the liberty to teach the Gospel. I cannot yield anything that militates against the Gospel."

(St. L. 16, 902; Enders, 8, 42. 45.) The clearest expression of Luther's criticism is found in a letter to Jonas, dated July 21, 1530. Here we read: "Now I see the purpose of those questions [on the part of the Papists] whether you had any further articles to present. The devil still lives, and he has noticed very well that your Apology steps softly, and that it has veiled the articles of Purgatory, the Adoration of the Saints, and especially that of the Antichrist, the Pope." Another reading of this passage of Luther: "*Apologiam vestram, die Leisetreterin, dissimulasse,*" is severer even than the one quoted: "*Apologiam vestram leise treten et dissimulasse.*" (St. L. 16, 2323; Enders, 8, 133.)

Brenz regarded the Confession as written "very courteously and modestly, *valde civiliter et modeste.*" (*C. R.* 2, 125.) The Nuernberg delegates had also received the impression that the Confession, while saying what was necessary, was very reserved and discreet. They reported to their Council: "Said instruction. [Confession], as far as the articles of faith are concerned, is substantially like that which we have previously sent to Your Excellencies, only that it has been improved in some parts, and throughout made as mild as possible (*allenthalben aufs glimpflichste gemacht*), yet, according to our view, without omitting anything necessary." (2, 129.) At Smalcald, in 1537, the theologians were ordered by the Princes and Estates "to look over the Confession, to make no changes pertaining to its contents or substance, nor those of the Concord [of 1536], but merely to enlarge upon matters regarding the Papacy, which, for certain reasons, was previously omitted at the Diet of Augsburg in submissive deference to His Imperial Majesty." (Kolde, *Analecta*, 297.)

Indirectly Melanchthon himself admits the correctness of Luther's criticism. True, when after the presentation of the Confession he thought of the angry Papists, he trembled, fearing that he had written too severely. June 26 he wrote to his most intimate friend, Camerarius: "Far from thinking that I have written milder than was proper, I rather strongly fear (*mirum in modum*) that some have taken offense at our freedom. For Valdes, the Emperor's secretary, saw it before its presentation and gave it as his opinion that from beginning to end it was sharper than the opponents would be able to endure." (*C. R.* 2, 140.) On the same day he wrote to Luther: "According to my judgment, the Confession is severe enough. For you will see that I have depicted the monks sufficiently." (141.)

In two letters to Camerarius, however, written on May 21 and June 19, respectively, hence before the efforts at toning down the Confession were completed, Melanchthon expressed the opinion that the Confession could not have been written "in terms more gentle and mild, *mitior et lenior.*" (2, 57.) No doubt, Melanchthon also had in mind his far-reaching irenics at Augsburg, when he wrote in the Preface to the Apology of the Augsburg Confession: "It has always been my custom in these controversies to retain, so far as I was at all able, the form of the customarily received doctrine, in order that at some time concord might the more readily be effected. Nor, indeed, am I now departing far from this custom, although I could justly lead away the men of this age still farther from the opinions of the adversaries." (101, 11.) Evidently, Melanchthon means to emphasize that in the Augustana he had been conservative, criticizing only when compelled to do so for conscience' sake.

### 26. Luther Praising Confession and Confessors.

Luther's criticism did not in the least dampen his joy over the glorious victory at Augsburg nor lessen his praise of the splendid confession there made. In the above-mentioned letter of June 27 he identifies himself fully and entirely with the Augustana, and demands that Melanchthon, too, consider it an expression of his own faith, and not merely of Luther's faith. July 3 he wrote to Melanchthon: "Yesterday I reread carefully your entire Apology, and it pleases me extremely (*vehementer*)." (St. L. 16, 913; Enders, 8, 79.) July 6 he wrote a letter to Cordatus in which he speaks of the Augustana as "altogether a most beautiful confession, *plane pulcherrima confessio.*" At the same time he expresses his great delight over the victory won at Augsburg, applying to the Confession Ps. 119, 46: "I will speak of Thy testimonies also before kings, and will not be ashamed," — a text which ever since has remained the motto, appearing on all of its subsequent manuscripts and printed copies.

Luther said: "I rejoice beyond measure that I lived to see the hour in which Christ was publicly glorified by such great confessors of His, in so great an assembly, through this in every respect most beautiful Confession. And the word has been fulfilled [Ps. 119, 46]: 'I will speak of Thy testimonies also before kings'; and the other word will also be fulfilled: 'I was not confounded.' For, 'Whosoever confesses Me before men' (so speaks He who lies not), 'him will I also confess before My Father which is in heaven.'" (16, 915; E. 8, 83.) July 9 Luther wrote to Jonas: "Christ was loudly proclaimed by means of the public and glorious Confession (*publica et gloriosa confessione*) and confessed in the open (*am Lichte*) and in their [the Papists'] faces, so that they cannot boast that we fled, had been afraid, or had concealed our faith. I only regret that I was not able to be present when this splendid Confession was made (*in hac pulchra confessione*)." (St. L. 16, 928; E. 8, 94.)

On the same day, July 9, Luther wrote to the Elector: "I know and consider well that our Lord Christ Himself comforts the heart of Your Electoral Grace better than I or any one else is able to do. This is shown, too, and proved before our eyes by the facts; for the opponents think that they made a shrewd move by having His Imperial Majesty prohibit preaching. But the poor deluded people do not see that, through the written Confession presented to them, more has been preached than otherwise perhaps ten preachers could have done. Is it not keen wisdom and great wit that Magister Eisleben and others must keep silence? But in lieu thereof the Elector of Saxony, together with other princes and lords, arises with the written Confession and preaches freely before His Imperial Majesty and the entire realm, under their noses, so that they must hear and cannot gainsay. I think that thus the order prohibiting preaching was a success indeed. They will not permit their servants to hear the ministers, but must themselves hear something far worse (as they regard it) from such great lords, and keep their peace. Indeed, Christ is not silent at the Diet; and though they be furious, still they must hear more by listening to the Confession than they would have heard in a year from the preachers. Thus is fulfilled what Paul says: God's Word will nevertheless have free course. If it is prohibited in the pulpit, it must be heard in the palaces. If poor preachers dare not speak it, then mighty princes and lords proclaim it. In brief, if everything keeps silence, the very stones will cry out, says Christ Himself." (16, 815.) September 15, at the close of the Diet, Luther wrote to Melanchthon: "You have confessed Christ, offered peace, obeyed the Emperor, endured reproach, been sated with slander, and have not recompensed evil for evil; in sum, you have performed the holy work of God, as becomes saints, in a worthy manner. . . . I shall canonize you (*canonizabo vos*) as faithful members of Christ." (16, 2319; E. 8, 259.)

### 27. Manuscripts and Editions of Augustana.

As far as the text of the Augsburg Confession is concerned, both of the original manuscripts are lost to us. Evidently they have become a prey to Romish rage and enmity. Eck was given permission to examine the German copy in 1540, and possibly at that time already it was not returned to Mainz. It may have been taken to Trent for the discussions at the Council, and thence carried to Rome. The Latin original was deposited in the Imperial Archives at Brussels, where it was seen and perused by Lindanus in 1562. February 18, 1569, however, Philip II instructed Duke Alva to bring the manuscript to Spain, lest the Protestants "regard it as a Koran," and in order that "such a damned work might forever be destroyed; *porque se hunda para siempre tan malvada obra.*" The keeper of the Brussels archives himself testifies that the manuscript was delivered to Alva. There is, however, no lack of other manuscripts of the Augsburg Confession. Up to the present time no less than 39 have been found. Of these, five German and four Latin copies contain also the signatures. The five German copies are in verbal agreement almost throughout, and therefore probably offer the text as read and presented at Augsburg.

The printing of the Confession had been expressly prohibited by the Emperor. June 26 Melanchthon wrote to Veit Dietrich: "Our Confession has been presented to the Emperor. He ordered that it be not printed. You will therefore see that it is not made public." (*C. R.* 2, 142.) However, even during the sessions of the Diet a number of printed editions, six in German and one in Latin, were issued by irresponsible parties. But since these were full of errors, and since, furthermore, the Romanists asserted with increasing boldness and challenge that the Confession of the Lutherans had been refuted, by the Roman Confutation, from the Scriptures and the Fathers, Melanchthon, in 1530, had a correct edition printed, which was issued, together with the Apology, in May, 1531. This quarto edition ("Beide, Deutsch Und Lateinisch Ps. 119") is regarded as the *editio princeps*.

For years this edition was also considered the authentic edition of the Augsburg Confession. Its Latin text was embodied 1584 in the Book of Concord as the *textus receptus*. But when attention was drawn to the changes in the German text of this edition (also the Latin text had been subjected to minor alterations), the Mainz Manuscript was substituted in the German Book of Concord, as its Preface explains. (14.) This manuscript, however, contains no original signatures and was erroneously considered the identical document presented to the Emperor, of which it was probably but a copy. In his Introduction to the Symbolical Books, J. T. Mueller expresses the following opinion concerning the Mainz Manuscript: "To say the least, one cannot deny that its text, as a rule, agrees with that of the best manuscripts, and that its mistakes can easily be corrected according to them and the *editio princeps*, so that we have no reason to surrender the text received by the Church and to accept another in place thereof, of which we cannot prove either that it is any closer to the original." (78.) Tschackert, who devoted much study to the manuscripts of the Augsburg Confession, writes: "The Saxon theologians acted in good faith, and the Mainz copy is still certainly better than Melanchthon's original imprint [the *editio princeps*]; yet, when compared with the complete and — because synchronous with the originally presented copy — reliable manuscripts of the signers of the Confession, the Mainz Manuscript proves to be defective in quite a number of places." (*L. c.* 621 f.)

However, even Tschackert's minute comparison shows that the Mainz Manuscript deviates from the original presented to the Emperor only in unimportant and purely formal points. For example, in § 20 of the Preface the words: "Papst das Generalkonzilium zu halten nicht geweigert, so waere E. K. M. gnaediges Erbieten, zu fordern und zu handeln, dass der" are omitted. Art. 27, § 48 we are to read: "dass die erdichteten geistlichen Orden Staende sind christlicher Vollkommenheit" instead of: "dass die erdichteten geistlichen Ordensstaende sind christliche Vollkommenheit." Art. 27, § 61 reads, "die Uebermass der Werke," instead of, "die Uebermasswerke," by the way, an excellent expression, which should again be given currency in the German. The conclusion of § 2 has "Leichpredigten" instead of "Beipredigten." According to the manuscripts, also the Mainz Manuscript, the correct reading of § 12 of the Preface is as follows: "Wo aber bei unsern Herrn, Freunden und besonders den Kurfuersten, Fuersten und Staenden des andern Teils die Handlung dermassen, wie E. K. M. Ausschreiben vermag ('bequeme Handlung unter uns selbst in Lieb' und Guetigkeit') nicht verfangen noch erspriesslich sein wollte" etc. The words, "bequeme Handlung unter uns selbst in Lieb' und Guetigkeit," are quoted from the imperial proclamation. (Foerstemann, 7, 378; Plitt, 2, 12.)

Originally only the last seven articles concerning the abuses had separate titles, the doctrinal articles being merely numbered, as in the Marburg and Schwabach Articles, which Melanchthon had before him at Augsburg. (Luther, Weimar 30, 3, 86. 160.) Nor are the present captions of the doctrinal articles found in the original German and Latin editions of the Book of Concord, Article XX forming a solitary exception; for in the German (in the Latin Concordia, too, it bears no title) it is superscribed: "Vom Glauben und guten Werken, Of Faith and Good Works." This is probably due to the fact that Article XX was taken from the so-called Torgau Articles and, with its superscription there, placed among the doctrinal articles. In the German edition of 1580 the word "Schluss" is omitted where the Latin has "Epilogus."

As to the translations, even before the Confession was presented to the Emperor, it had been rendered into French. (This translation was published by Foerstemann, 1, 357.) The Emperor had it translated for his own use into both Italian and French. (C. R. 2, 155; Luther, St. L., 16, 884.) Since then the Augustana has been done into Hebrew, Greek, Spanish, Portuguese, Belgian, Slavic, Danish, Swedish, English, and many other languages. As to the English translations, see page 6.

## 28. Signatures of Augsburg Confession.

Concerning the signatures of the Augustana, Tschackert writes as follows: "The names of the signers are most reliably determined from the best manuscript copies of the original of the Confession, which have been preserved to us. There we find the signatures of eight princes and two free cities, to wit, Elector John of Saxony, Margrave George of Brandenburg-Ansbach, Duke Ernest of Braunschweig-Lueneburg, Landgrave Philip of Hesse, then John Frederick, the Electoral Prince of Saxony, Ernest's brother Francis of Braunschweig-Lueneburg, Prince Wolfgang of Anhalt, Count Albrecht of Mansfeld, and the cities Nuernberg and Reutlingen." (L. c. 285; see also Luther's letter of July 6, 1530, St. L. 16, 882.) Camerarius, in his Life of Melanchthon, relates that Melanchthon desired to have the Confession drawn up in the name of the theologians only, but that his plan did not prevail because it was believed that the signatures of the princes would lend prestige and splendor to the act of presenting this confes-

sion of faith. Besides, this plan of Melanchthon's was excluded by the Emperor's proclamation.

Although Philip of Hesse, in the interest of a union with the Swiss, had zealously, but in vain, endeavored to secure for the article concerning the Lord's Supper a milder form, still, in the end, he did not refuse to sign. Regius wrote to Luther, May 21, that he had discussed the entire cause of the Gospel with the Landgrave, who had invited him to dinner, and talked with him for two hours on the Lord's Supper. The Prince had presented all the arguments of the Sacramentarians and desired to hear Regius refute them. But while the Landgrave did not side with Zwingli (non sentit cum Zwinglio), yet he desired with all his heart an agreement of the theologians, as far as piety would permit (exoptat doctorum hominum concordiam, quantum sinit pietas). He was far less inclined to dissension than rumor had it before his arrival. He would hardly despise the wise counsel of Melanchthon and others. (Kolde, Analecta, 125; see also C. R. 2, 59, where the text reads, "nam sentit cum Zwinglio" instead of, "non sentit cum Zwinglio.") Accordingly, the mind of the Landgrave was not outright Zwinglian, but unionistic. He regarded the followers of Zwingli as weak brethren, who must be borne with, and to whom Christian fellowship should not be refused. This also explains how the Landgrave could sign the Augustana, and yet continue his endeavors to bring about a union. May 22 Melanchthon wrote to Luther: "The Macedonian [Philip of Hesse] now contemplates signing our formula of speech, and it appears as if he can be drawn back to our side; still, a letter from you will be necessary. Therefore I beg you most urgently that you write him, admonishing him not to burden his conscience with a godless doctrine." Still the Landgrave did not change his position in the next few weeks. June 25, however, Melanchthon reported to Luther: "The Landgrave approves our Confession and has signed it. You will, I hope, accomplish much if you seek to strengthen him by writing him a letter." (C. R. 2, 60. 92. 96. 101. 103. 126; Luther, St. L., 16, 689; 21a, 1499.)

At Augsburg, whither also Zwingli had sent his Fidei Ratio, the South-German imperial cities (Strassburg, Constance, Memmingen, Lindau) presented the so-called Confessio Tetrapolitana, prepared by Bucer and Capito, which declares that the Sacraments are "holy types," and that in the Lord's Supper the "true body" and the "true blood" of Christ "are truly eaten and drunk as meat and drink for the souls, which are thereby nourished unto eternal life." However, in 1532 these cities, too, signed the Augsburg Confession.

Thus the seed which Luther sowed had grown wonderfully. June 25, 1530, is properly regarded as the real birthday of the Lutheran Church. From this day on she stands before all the world as a body united by a public confession and separate from the Roman Church. The lone, but courageous confessor of Worms saw himself surrounded with a stately host of true Christian heroes, who were not afraid to place their names under his Confession, although they knew that it might cost them goods and blood, life and limb. When the Emperor, after entering Augsburg, stubbornly demanded that the Lutherans cease preaching, Margrave George of Brandenburg finally declared: "Rather than deny my God and suffer the Word of God to be taken from me, I will kneel down and have my head struck off." (*C. R.* 2, 115.) That characterizes the pious and heroic frame of mind of all who signed the Augustana in 1530. In a letter, of June 18, to Luther, Jonas relates how the Catholic princes and estates knelt down to receive the blessing of Campegius when the latter entered the city, but that the Elector remained standing and declared: "To God alone shall knees be bowed; *In Deo flectenda sunt genua.*" (Kolde, *Analecta*, 135.) When Melanchthon called the Elector's attention to the possible consequences of his signing the Augsburg Confession, the latter answered that he would do what was right, without concerning himself about his electoral dignity; he would confess his Lord, whose cross he prized higher than all the power of the world.

Brenz wrote: "Our princes are most steadfast in confessing the Gospel, and surely, when I consider their great steadfastness, there comes over me no small feeling of shame because we poor beggars [theologians] are filled with fear of the Imperial Majesty." (*C. R.* 2, 125.) Luther praises Elector John for having suffered a bitter death at the Diet of Augsburg. There, says Luther, he had to swallow all kinds of nasty soups and poison with which the devil served him; at Augsburg he publicly, before all the world, confessed Christ's death and resurrection, and hazarded property and people, yea, his own body and life; and because of the confession which he made, we shall honor him as a Christian. (St. L. 12, 2078 f.) And not only the Lutheran Church, but all Protestant Christendom, aye, the entire world has every reason to revere and hold sacred the memory of the heroes who boldly affixed their names to the Confession of 1530.

### 29. Tributes to Confession of Augsburg.

From the moment of its presentation to the present day, men have not tired of praising the Augsburg Confession, which has been called *Confessio augusta, Confessio augustissima,* the *"Evangelischer Augapfel,"* etc. They have admired its systematic plan, its completeness, comprehensiveness, and arrangement; its balance of mildness and firmness; its racy vigor, freshness, and directness; its beauty of composition, "the like of which can-

not be found in the entire literature of the Reformation period." Spalatin exclaims: "A Confession, the like of which was never made, not only in a thousand years, but as long as the world has been standing!" Sartorius: "A confession of the eternal truth, of true ecumenical Christianity, and of all fundamental articles of the Christian faith!" "From the Diet of Augsburg, which is the birthday of the Evangelical Church Federation, down to the great Peace Congress of Muenster and Osnabrueck, this Confession stands as the towering standard in the entire history of those profoundly troublous times, gathering the Protestants about itself in ever closer ranks, and, when assaulted by the enemies of Evangelical truth with increasing fury, is defended by its friends in severe fighting, with loss of goods and blood, and always finally victoriously holds the field. Under the protection of this banner the Evangelical Lutheran Church in Germany has been built up on firm and unassailable foundations; under the same protection the Reformed Church in Germany has found shelter. But the banner was carried still farther; for all Swedes, Danes, Norwegians, and Prussians have sworn allegiance to it, and the Esthonians, Letts, Finns, as well as all Lutherans of Russia, France, and other lands recognize therein the palladium of their faith and rights. No other Protestant confession has ever been so honored." (Guericke, *Kg.*, 3, 116 f.)

Vilmar says in praise of the Confession: "Whoever has once felt a gentle breath of the bracing mountain air which is wafted from this mighty mountain of faith [the Augsburg Confession] no longer seeks to pit against its firm and quiet dignity his own uncertain, immature, and wavering thoughts, nor to direct the vain and childish puff of his mouth against that breath of God in order to give it a different direction." (*Theol. d. Tatsachen,* 76.) In his Introduction to the Symbolical Books, J. T. Mueller says: "Luther called the Diet of Augsburg 'the last trumpet before Judgment Day'; hence we may well call the confession there made the *blast* of that trumpet, which, indeed, has gone forth into all lands, even as the Gospel of God, which it proclaims in its purity." (78.) The highest praise, however, is given the Augsburg Confession by the Church which was born with it, when, *e. g.*, in the Formula of Concord, the Lutherans designate it as "the symbol of our time," and glory in it as the Confession, which, though frowned upon and assailed by its opponents, "down to this day has remained unrefuted and unoverthrown (bis auf diesen Tag unwiderlegt und unumgestossen geblieben)." (777, 4; 847, 3.)

# IV. Melanchthon's Alterations of the Augsburg Confession.

### 30. Changes Unwarranted.

Melanchthon continued uninterruptedly to polish and correct the Augsburg Confession till immediately before its presentation on June 25, 1530. While, indeed, he cannot be censured for doing this, it was, though originally not so intended by Melanchthon, an act of presumption to continue to alter the document after it had been adopted, signed, and publicly presented. Even the *editio princeps* of 1531 is no longer in literal agreement with the original manuscripts. For this reason the

German text embodied in the Book of Concord is not the one contained in the *editio princeps*, but that of the Mainz Manuscript, which, as stated, was erroneously believed to be the identical German copy presented to the Emperor. The Latin text of the *editio princeps*, embodied in the Book of Concord, had likewise undergone some, though unessential, changes. These alterations became much more extensive in the Latin octavo edition of 1531 and in the German revision of 1533. The Variata of 1540 and 1542, however, capped the climax as far as changes are concerned, some of them being very questionable also doctrinally. In their "Approbation" of the Concordia Germanico-Latina, edited by Reineccius, 1708, the Leipzig theologians remark pertinently: Melanchthon found it "impossible to leave a book as it once was." Witness his *Loci* of 1521, which he remodeled three times — 1535, 1542, and 1548. However, the *Loci* were his own private work, while the Augustana was the property and confession of the Church.

Tschackert is right when he comments as follows: "To-day it is regarded as an almost incomprehensible trait of Melanchthon's character, that immediately after the Diet and all his lifetime he regarded the Confession as a private production of his pen, and made changes in it as often as he had it printed, while he, more so than others, could but evaluate it as a state-paper of the Evangelical estates, which, having been read and delivered in solemn session, represented an important document of German history, both secular and ecclesiastical. In extenuation it is said that Melanchthon made these changes in pedagogical interests, namely, in order to clarify terms or to explain them more definitely; furthermore, that for decades the Evangelical estates and theologians did not take offense at Melanchthon's changes. Both may be true. But this does not change the fact that the chief editor of the Confession did not appreciate the world-historical significance of this state-paper of the Evangelical estates." (*L. c.* 288.) Nor can it be denied that Melanchthon made these changes, not merely in pedagogical interests, but, at least a number of them, also in the interest of his deviating dogmatic views and in deference to Philip of Hesse, who favored a union with the Swiss. Nor can Melanchthon be fully cleared of dissimulation in this matter. The revised Apology of 1540, for example, he openly designated on the title-page as "diligently revised, *diligenter recognita*"; but in the case of the Augsburg Confession of 1540 and 1542 he in no way indicated that it was a changed and augmented edition.

As yet it has not been definitely ascertained when and where the terms "Variata" and "Invariata" originated. At the princes' diet of Naumburg, in 1561, the Variata was designated as the "amended" edition. The Reuss Confession of 1567 contains the term "unaltered Augsburg Confession." In its Epitome as well as in its Thorough Declaration the Formula of Concord speaks of "the First Unaltered Augsburg Confession — *Augustana illa prima et non mutata Confessio*." (777, 4; 851, 5.) The Preface to the Formula of Concord repeatedly speaks of the Variata of 1540 as "the other edition of the Augsburg Confession — *altera Augustanae Confessionis editio*." (13 f.)

## 31. Detrimental Consequences of Alterations.

The changes made in the Augsburg Confession brought great distress, heavy cares, and bitter struggles upon the Lutheran Church, both from within and without. Church history records the manifold and sinister ways in which they were exploited by the Reformed as well as the Papists; especially by the latter (the Jesuits) at the religious colloquies, beginning 1540, until far into the time of the Thirty Years' War, in order to deprive the Lutherans of the blessings guaranteed by the religious Peace of Augsburg, 1555. (Salig, *Gesch. d. A. K.*, 1, 770 ff.; *Lehre und Wehre* 1919, 218 ff.)

On Melanchthon's alterations of the Augsburg Confession the Romanists, as the Preface to the Book of Concord explains, based the reproach and slander that the Lutherans themselves did not know "which is the true and genuine Augsburg Confession." (15.) Decrying the Lutherans, they boldly declared "that not two preachers are found who agree in each and every article of the Augsburg Confession, but that they are rent asunder and separated from one another to such an extent that they themselves no longer know what is the Augsburg Confession and its proper sense." (1095.) In spite of the express declaration of the Lutherans at Naumburg, 1561, that they were minded to abide by the original Augsburg Confession as presented to Emperor Charles V at Augsburg, 1530, the Papists and the Reformed did not cease their calumniations, but continued to interpret their declarations to mean, "as though we [the Lutherans] were so uncertain concerning our religion, and so often had transfused it from one formula to another, that it was no longer clear to us or our theologians what is the Confession once offered to the Emperor at Augsburg." (11.)

As a result of the numerous and, in part, radical changes made by Melanchthon in the Augsburg Confession, the Reformed also, in the course of time more and more, laid claim to the Variata and appealed to it over against the loyal Lutherans. In particular, they regarded and interpreted the alteration which Melanchthon had made in Article X, Of the Lord's Supper, as a correction of the original Augustana in deference to the views of Calvinism. Calvin declared that he (1539 at Strassburg) had signed the Augustana "in the sense in which its author [Melanchthon] explains it (*sicut eam auctor ipse interpretatur*)." And whenever the Reformed, who were regarded as confessionally related to the Augsburg Confession (*Confessioni Augustanae addicti*), and as such shared in the blessings of the Peace of Augsburg (1555) and the

Peace of Westphalia (1648), adopted, and appealed to, the Augustana, they interpreted it according to the Variata.

Referring to this abuse on the part of the Reformed and Crypto-Calvinists, the Preface to the Book of Concord remarks: "To these disadvantages [the slanders of the Romanists] there is also added that, under the pretext of the Augsburg Confession [Variata of 1540], the teaching conflicting with the institution of the Holy Supper of the body and blood of Christ and also other corruptions were introduced here and there into the churches and schools." (11. 17.) — Thus the changes made in the Augsburg Confession did much harm to the Lutheran cause. Melanchthon belongs to the class of men that have greatly benefited our Church, but have also seriously harmed it. "These fictions" of the adversaries, says the Preface to the Book of Concord concerning the slanders based on Melanchthon's changes, "have deterred and alienated many good men from our churches, schools, doctrine, faith, and confession." (11.)

## 32. Attitude toward Variata.

John Eck was the first who, in 1541, at the religious colloquy of Worms, publicly protested against the Variata. But since it was apparent that most of the changes were intended merely as reenforcements of the Lutheran position against the Papists, and Melanchthon also declared that he had made no changes in "the matter and substance or in the sense," i. e., in the doctrine itself, the Lutherans at that time, as the Preface to the Book of Concord shows, attached no further importance to the matter. The freedom with which in those days formal alterations were made even in public documents, and the guilelessness with which such changes were received, appears, for example, from the translation of the Apology by Justus Jonas. However, not all Lutherans even at that time were able to view Melanchthon's changes without apprehension and indifference. Among these was Elector John Frederick, who declared that he considered the Augustana to be the confession of those who had signed it, and not the private property of Melanchthon.

In his admonition to Brueck of May 5, 1537, he says: "Thus Master Philip also is said to have arrogated to himself the privilege of changing in some points the Confession of Your Electoral Grace and the other princes and estates, made before His Imperial Majesty at Augsburg, to soften it and to print it elsewhere [a reprint of the changed Latin octavo edition of 1531 had been published 1535 at Augsburg and another at Hagenau] without the previous knowledge and approval of Your Electoral Grace and of the other estates, which, in the opinion of Your Electoral Grace, he should justly have refrained from, since the Confession belongs primarily to Your Electoral Grace and the other estates; and from it [the alterations made] Your Electoral Grace and the other related estates might be charged that they are not certain of their doctrine and are also unstable. Besides, it is giving an offense to the people." (C. R. 3, 365.) Luther, too, is said to have remonstrated with Melanchthon for having altered the Confession. In his Introduction to the Augsburg Confession (Koenigsberg, 1577) Wigand reports: "I heard from Mr. George Rorarius that Dr. Luther said to Philip, 'Philip, Philip, you are not doing right in changing Augustanam Confessionem so often; for it is not your, but the Church's book.'" Yet it is improbable that this should have occurred between 1537 and 1542, for in 1540 the Variata followed, which was changed still more in 1542, without arousing any public protest whatever.

After Luther's death, however, when Melanchthon's doctrinal deviations became apparent, and the Melanchthonians and the loyal Lutherans became more and more opposed to one another, the Variata was rejected with increasing determination by the latter as the party-symbol of the Philippists. In 1560 Flacius asserted at Weimar that the Variata differed essentially from the Augustana. In the Reuss-Schoenburg Confession of 1567 the Variata was unqualifiedly condemned; for here we read: We confess "the old, true, unaltered Augsburg Confession, which later was changed, mutilated, misinterpreted, and falsified . . . by the Adiaphorists in many places both as regards the words and the substance (nach den Worten und sonst in den Haendeln), which thus became a buskin, Bundschuh, pantoffle, and a Polish boot, fitting both legs equally well [suiting Lutherans as well as Reformed], or a cloak and a changeling (Wechselbalg), by means of which Adiaphorists, Sacramentarians, Antinomians, new teachers of works, and the like hide, adorn, defend, and establish their errors and falsifications under the cover and name of the Augsburg Confession, pretending to be likewise confessors of the Augsburg Confession, for the sole purpose of enjoying with us under its shadow, against rain and hail, the common peace of the Empire, and selling, furthering, and spreading their errors under the semblance of friends so much the more easily and safely." (Kolde, Einleitung, 30.) In a sermon delivered at Wittenberg, Jacob Andreae also opposed the Variata very zealously.

Thus the conditions without as well as within the Lutheran Church were such that a public declaration on the part of the genuine Lutherans as to their attitude toward the alterations of Melanchthon, notably in the Variata of 1540, became increasingly imperative. Especially the continued slanders, intrigues, and threats of the Papists necessitated such a declaration. As early as 1555, when the Peace of Augsburg was concluded, the Romanists attempted to limit its provisions to the adherents of the Augustana of 1530. At the religious colloquy of Worms, in 1557, the Jesuit Canisius, distinguishing between a pure and a falsified Augustana, demanded that the adherents of the latter be condemned, and excluded from the discussions.

## 33. Alterations in Editions of 1531, 1533, 1540.

As to the alterations themselves, the Latin text of the *editio princeps* of the Augsburg Confession of 1531 received the following additions: § 3 in Article 13, § 8 in Article 18, and § 26 in Article 26. Accordingly, these passages do not occur in the German text of the Book of Concord. Originally § 2 in the conclusion of Article 21 read: "*Tota* dissensio est de paucis quibusdam abusibus," and § 3 in Article 24: "Nam ad hoc *praecipue* opus est ceremoniis, ut doceant imperitos." The additions made to Articles 13 and 18 are also found in the German text of the *editio princeps*. (*C. R.* 26, 279. 564.)

In the "Approbation" of the Leipzig theologians mentioned above we read: The octavo edition of the Augustana and the Apology, printed 1531 by George Rauh, according to the unanimous testimony of our theologians, cannot be tolerated, "owing to the many additions and other changes originating from Philip Melanchthon. For if one compares the 20th Article of the Augsburg Confession as well as the last articles on the Abuses: 'Of Monastic Vows' and 'Of Ecclesiastical Authority,' it will readily be seen what great additions (*laciniae*) have been patched onto this Wittenberg octavo edition of 1531. The same thing has also been done with the Apology, especially in the article 'Of Justification and Good Works,' where often entire successive pages may be found which do not occur in the genuine copies. Furthermore, in the declaration regarding the article 'Of the Lord's Supper,' where Paul's words, that the bread is a communion of the body of Christ, etc., as well as the testimony of Theophylact concerning the presence of the body of Christ in the Supper have been omitted. Likewise in the defense of the articles 'Of Repentance,' 'Of Confession and Satisfaction,' 'Of Human Traditions,' 'Of the Marriage of Priests,' and 'Of Ecclesiastical Power,' where, again, entire pages have been added." (*L. c.* 8, 13; *C. R.* 27, 437.) In the German edition of the Augsburg Confession of 1533 it was especially Articles 4, 5, 6, 12, 13, 15, and 20 that were remodeled. These alterations, however, involve no doctrinal changes, with the possible exception of Article 5, where the words "where and when He will" are expunged. (*C. R.* 26, 728.)

As to the Variata of 1540, however, the extent of the 21 doctrinal articles was here almost doubled, and quite a number of material alterations were made. Chief among the latter are the following: In Article 5 the words, "ubi et quando visum est Deo," are omitted. In the 10th Article the rejection of the Reformed doctrine is deleted, and the following is substituted for the article proper: "De coena Domini docent, quod cum pane et vino vere exhibeantur corpus et sanguis Christi vescentibus in Coena Domini." (*C. R.* 26, 357.) The following sentences have also given offense: "Et cum hoc modo consolamur nos promissione seu Evangelio et erigimus nos fide, certo consequimur remissionem peccato-

rum, et *simul* datur nobis Spiritus Sanctus." "Cum Evangelium audimus aut cogitamus aut sacramenta tractamus et fide nos consolamur, *simul* est efficax Spiritus Sanctus." (354.) For the words of the 18th Article: "sed haec fit in cordibus, cum per Verbum Spiritus Sanctus concipitur," the Variata substitutes: "Et Christus dicit: Sine me nihil potestis facere. Efficitur autem spiritualis iustitia in nobis, cum *adiuvamur* a Spiritu Sancto. Porro Spiritum Sanctum concipimus, cum Verbo Dei assentimur, ut nos fide in terroribus consolemur." (362.) Toward the end of the same article we read: "Quamquam énim externa opera aliquo modo potest efficere humana natura per sese, . . . verum timorem, veram fiduciam, patientiam, castitatem non potest efficere, nisi Spiritus Sanctus gubernet et *adiuvet* corda nostra." (363.) In the 19th Article the phrase "non adiuvante Deo" is erased, which, by the way, indicates that Melanchthon regarded these words as equivalent to those of the German text: "so Gott die Hand abgetan," for else he would have weakened the text against his own interests. (363.) To the 20th Article Melanchthon added the sentence: "Debet autem ad haec dona [Dei] accedere exercitatio nostra, quae et *conservat* ea et meretur incrementum, iuxta illud: Habenti dabitur. Et Augustinus praeclare dixit: Dilectio meretur incrementum dilectionis, cum videlicet exercetur." (371.)

## 34. Alterations Render Confession Ambiguous.

True, in making all these changes, Melanchthon did not introduce any direct heresy into the Variata. He did, however, in the interest of his irenic and unionistic policy and dogmatic vacillations, render ambiguous and weaken the clear sense of the Augustana. By his changes he opened the door and cleared the way, as it were, for his deviations in the direction of Synergism, Calvinism (Lord's Supper), and Romanism (good works are necessary to salvation). Nor was Melanchthon a man who did not know what he was doing when he made alterations. Whenever he weakened and trimmed the doctrines he had once confessed, whether in his *Loci* or in the Augustana, he did so in order to satisfy definite interests of his own, interests self-evidently not subservient to, but conflicting with, the clear expression and bold confession of the old Lutheran truth.

Kolde, referring in particular to the changes made in the 10th Article, says: "It should never have been denied that these alterations involved real changes. The motives which actuated Melanchthon cannot be definitely ascertained, neither from his own expressions nor from contemporary remarks of his circle of acquaintances" [As late as 1575 Selneccer reports that Philip of Hesse had asked Melanchthon to erase the *improbatio* of the 10th Article, because then also the Swiss would accept the Augustana as their confession]. "A comparison with the Wittenberg Concord of May, 1536 (*cum pane et vino vere et substantialiter adesse* — that the body and blood [of Christ] are really and substantially present with the bread and wine, *C. R.* 3, 75) justifies the assumption that by using the form: *cum pane et vino vere exhibeantur*, he endeavored to take into account the existing agreement with the South Germans (*Oberlaender*). However, when, at the same time, he omits the words: *vere et substantialiter adesse*, and the *improbatio*, it cannot, in view of his gradually changed conception of the Lord's Supper, be doubted that he sought to leave open for himself and others the possibility of associating also with the Swiss." (25.)

An adequate answer to the question what prompted Melanchthon to make his alterations will embrace also the following points: (1.) Melanchthon's mania for changing and remodeling in general. (2.) His desire, especially after the breach between the Lutherans and the Papists seemed incurable, to meet and satisfy the criticism that the Augustana was too mild, and to reenforce the Lutheran position over against the Papists. (3.) Melanchthon's doctrinal deviations, especially in Reformed and synergistic directions.

## 35. Variata Disowned by Lutheran Church.

It cannot be denied that during Luther's life and for quite a time after his death the Variata was used by Lutherans without any public opposition and recognized as the Augsburg Confession. Martin Chemnitz, in his "Iudicium de Controversiis quibusdam circa quosdam Augustanae Confessionis Articulos — Decision concerning Certain Controversies about Some Articles of the Augsburg Confession," printed 1597, says that the edition of 1540 was employed at the religious colloquies with the previous knowledge and approval of Luther; in fact, that it was drawn up especially for the Colloquy at Hagenau, which the opponents (Cochlaeus at Worms, Pighius at Regensburg) had taken amiss. "Graviter tulerant," says Chemnitz, "multis articulis pleniori declaratione plusculum lucis accessisse, unde videbant veras sententias magis illustrari et Thaidis Babyloniae turpitudinem manifestius denudare — They took it amiss that more light had been shed on many articles by a fuller explanation, whence they perceived the true statements to be more fully illustrated and the shame of the Babylonian Thais to be more fully disclosed." (Mueller, *Einleitung*, 72.)

Furthermore, it is equally certain that, on the part of the Lutheran princes, the Variata was employed without any sinister intentions whatever, and without the slightest thought of deviating even in the least from the doctrine of the original Augustana, as has been falsely asserted by Heppe, Weber, and others. Wherever the Variata was adopted by Lutheran princes and theologians, it was never for the purpose of weakening the doctrine of the Augsburg Confession in any point. Moreover, the sole reason always was to accentuate and present more clearly the contrast between themselves and the Papists; and, generally

speaking, the Variata did serve this purpose. True, Melanchthon at the same time, no doubt, planned to prepare the way for his doctrinal innovations; but wherever such was the case, he kept it strictly to himself.

The complete guilelessness and good faith in which the Lutheran princes and theologians employed the Variata, and permitted its use, appears from the Preface to the Book of Concord. For here they state: "Therefore we have decided in this writing to testify publicly, and to inform all, that we wished neither then nor now in any way to defend, or excuse, or to approve, as agreeing with the Gospeldoctrine, false and godless doctrines and opinions which may lie concealed under certain coverings of words [in the Variata]. We, indeed, never received the latter edition [of 1540] in a sense differing in any part from the former which was presented [at Augsburg]. Neither do we judge that other useful writings of Dr. Philip Melanchthon, or of Brenz, Urban Regius, Pomeranus, etc., should be rejected and condemned, as far as, in all things, they agree with the norm which has been set forth in the Book of Concord." (17.)

Accordingly, when the Variata was boldly exploited by the Romanists to circulate all manner of slanders about the Lutherans; when it also became increasingly evident that the Reformed and Crypto-Calvinists employed the Variata as a cover for their false doctrine of the Lord's Supper; when, furthermore, within the Lutheran Church the suspicion gradually grew into conviction that Melanchthon, by his alterations, had indeed intended to foist doctrinal deviations upon the Lutheran Church; and when, finally, a close scrutiny of the Variata had unmistakably revealed the fact that it actually did deviate from the original document not only in extent, but also with regard to intent, not merely formally, but materially as well, — all loyal Lutheran princes and theologians regarded it as self-evident that they unanimously and solemnly declare their exclusive adherence to the Augsburg Confession as presented to Emperor Charles at Augsburg, and abandon the Variata without delay. At Naumburg, in 1561, the Lutheran princes, therefore, after some vacillation, declared that they would adhere to the original Augsburg Confession and its "genuine Christian declaration and norm," the Smalcald Articles. Frederick III of the Palatinate alone withdrew, and before long joined the Calvinists by introducing the Heidelberg Catechism, thus revealing the spuriousness of his own Lutheranism.

It was due especially to the Crypto-Calvinists in Electoral Saxony and to the *Corpus Doctrinae Philippicum* that the Variata retained a temporary and local authority, until it was finally and generally disowned by the Lutheran Church and excluded from its symbols by the adoption of the Formula of Concord. For here our Church pledges adherence to "the First, Unaltered Augsburg Confession, delivered to the Emperor Charles V at Augs-

burg in the year 1530, in the great Diet."
(777, 4; 847, 5; 851, 5.) And in the Preface
to the Book of Concord the princes and estates
declare: "Accordingly, in order that no persons may permit themselves to be disturbed
by the charges of our adversaries spun out of
their own minds, by which they boast that not
even we are certain which is the true and
genuine Augsburg Confession, but that both
those who are now among the living and posterity may be clearly and firmly taught and
informed what that godly Confession is which
we and the churches and schools of our realms
at all times professed and embraced, we emphatically testify that next to the pure and
immutable truth of God's Word we wish to
embrace the first Augsburg Confession alone
which was presented to the Emperor Charles V,
in the year 1530, at the famous Diet of Augsburg, this alone (we say), and no other." (15.)
At the same time the princes furthermore protest that also the adoption of the Formula of
Concord did not make any change in this respect. For doctrinally the Formula of Concord was not, nor was it intended to be,
a "new or different confession," i. e., different
from the one presented to Emperor Charles V.
(20.)

# V. The Pontifical Confutation of the Augsburg Confession.

### 36. Papal Party Refusing Conciliation.

At the Diet of Augsburg, convened in order
to restore the disturbed religious peace, the
Lutherans were the first to take a step
towards reconciliation by delivering their Confession, June 25, 1530. In accordance with
the manifesto of Emperor Charles, they now
expected that the papal party would also
present its "view and opinion," in order that
the discussions might thereupon proceed "in
love and kindness," as the Emperor put it.
In the Preface to their Confession the Lutherans declared: "In obedience to Your Imperial Majesty's wishes, we offer, in this matter of religion, the Confession of our preachers
and of ourselves, showing what manner of
doctrine from the Holy Scriptures and the
pure Word of God has been up to this time
set forth in our lands, dukedoms, dominions,
and cities, and taught in our churches. And
if the other Electors, Princes, and Estates of
the Empire will, according to the said imperial proposition, present similar writings,
to wit, in Latin and German, giving their
opinions in this matter of religion, we, with
the Princes and friends aforesaid, here before
Your Imperial Majesty, our most clement
Lord, are prepared to confer amicably concerning all possible ways and means, in order
that we may come together, as far as this
may be honorably done, and, the matter between us on both sides being peacefully discussed without offensive strife, the dissension,
by God's help, may be done away and brought
back to one true accordant religion; for as
we all are under one Christ and do battle
under Him, we ought to confess the one
Christ, after the tenor of Your Imperial
Majesty's edict, and everything ought to be
conducted according to the truth of God; and
this is what, with most fervent prayers, we
entreat of God." (39, 8.)

The Lutherans did not believe that the
manifesto of the Emperor could be construed
in any other way than that both parties
would be treated as equals at the Diet. Not
merely as a matter of good policy, but bona
fide, as honest Germans and true Christians,
they clung tenaciously to the words of the
Emperor, according to which the Romanists,
too, were to be regarded as a party summoned
for the trial, the Emperor being the judge.
The Lutherans simply refused to take the
word of the Emperor at anything less than
par, or to doubt his good will and the sincerity
of his promise. The fact that from the very
beginning his actions were in apparent contravention of the manifesto was attributed by
the Lutherans to the sinister influence of such
bitter, baiting, and unscrupulous theologians
as Eck, Cochlaeus, and Faber, who, they
claimed, endeavored to poison and incite the
guileless heart of the Emperor. Thus the
Lutherans would not and could not believe
that Charles had deceived them, — a simple
trust, which, however, stubborn facts finally
compelled them to abandon.

The Romanists, on the other hand, boasting
before the Emperor that they had remained
with the true Christian faith, the holy Gospel,
the Catholic Church, the bull of the Pope, and
the Edict of Worms, refused with equal
tenacity to be treated as a party summoned
for trial. June 25, 1530, Elector John wrote
to Luther: "Thus we and the other princes
and estates who are related to us in this
matter had to consent to submit our opinion
and confession of faith. Our opponents, however, as we are told, declined to present theirs
and decided to show to the Emperor that
they adhered to the Edict [of Worms] and to
the faith which their fathers had bequeathed
to and bestowed upon them, and which they
intended to adhere to even now; if, however,
the Pope or, in his place, the Legate, together
with His Imperial Majesty, would point out,
and expect them to adopt, a different and new
faith, they would humbly hear the Emperor's
opinion." (Luther, St. L. 16, 758.)

Thus presupposing what they were summoned to prove at Augsburg, namely, that the
doctrine of the Pope was identical with the
old Christian faith, the Romanists declared
a presentation of their views unnecessary.
The Lutherans, they maintained, were convicted apostates and rebels against Pope and
Church, against Emperor and realm; sentence
was not first to be pronounced upon them, but
had been pronounced long ago, the Diet's duty
merely being to confirm and execute it; hence,
there was nothing else to be done by the Emperor than to attend to his office as warden
and protector of the Church, and, together
with the princes and estates, to proceed

against the heretics with drastic measures. Also in the later discussions, conducted with a view of effecting a reconciliation, the Romanists refused to relinquish this position. From beginning to end they acted as the accusers, judges, and henchmen of the Lutherans. Nor was anything else to be expected, since, unlike the Lutherans, they considered not God's Word, but the Pope the supreme arbiter in religious matters. Thus, from the very outset, the gulf between the two parties was such that it could not be bridged. Common ground was lacking. On the one side conscience, bound by the Word of God! On the other, blind subjection to human, papal authority! Also Romanists realized that this fundamental and irreconcilable difference was bound to render futile all discussions. It was not merely his own disgust which the papal historian expressed when he concluded his report on the prolonged discussions at Augsburg: "Thus the time was wasted with vain discussions." (Plitt, *Apologie*, 43.)

### 37. Further Success Not Hoped for by Luther.

Luther regarded the public reading of the Confession as an unparalleled triumph of his cause. Further results, such as a union with the Romanists, he did not expect. On July 9, 1530, he wrote to Jonas: "*Quid sperem de Caesare, quantumvis optimo, sed obsesso?* What can I hope of the Emperor, even the best, when he is obsessed" [by the papal theologians]? The most Luther hoped for was mutual political toleration. In the letter quoted he continues: "But they [the Papists] must expect a sad, and we a happy issue. Not, indeed, that there ever will be unity of doctrine; for who can hope that Belial will be united with Christ? Excepting that perhaps marriage [of priests] and the two kinds [of the Sacrament] be permitted (here too, however, this adverb 'perhaps' is required, and perhaps too much 'perhaps'). But this I wish and earnestly hope for, that, the difference in doctrine being set aside, a political union may be made. If by the blessing of Christ this takes place, enough and more than enough has been done and accomplished at this Diet. . . . Now, if we obtain also the third thing, that we adjourn with worldly peace secured, then we shall have clearly defeated Satan in this year." (Enders, 8, 95; St. L. 16, 927. 1666.)

July 21, 1530, Luther wrote in a similar vein to Jonas: "The fact that these frogs [the papal theologians who wrote the Confutation] with their croakings [*coaxitatibus* = pasquinades against Luther, instead of answers to the Augustana] have free access [to the Emperor] chagrins me very much in this great work in the most important matters. . . . But this happens to prove that I am a true prophet; for I have always said that we work and hope in vain for a union in doctrine; it would be enough if we could obtain worldly peace." (16, 927. 2324.) August 25, when the prolonged discussions of reconciliation were nearing their end, he wrote

to Melanchthon: "In sum, it does not please me at all that unity of doctrine is to be discussed, since this is utterly impossible, unless the Pope would abolish his entire popery. It would have sufficed if we had presented to them the reasons for our faith and desired peace. But how can we hope that we shall win them over to accept the truth? We have come to hear whether they approve our doctrine or not, permitting them to remain what they are, only inquiring whether they acknowledge our doctrine to be correct or condemn it. If they condemn it, what does it avail to discuss the question of unity any longer with avowed enemies? If they acknowledge it to be right, what necessity is there of retaining the old abuses?" (16, 1404.)

Though willing to yield to the Catholic party in all other matters, Luther refused to compromise the divine truth in any point or in any way. For this reason he also insisted that the Emperor should not be recognized as judge and arbiter without qualification, but only with the proviso that his decision would not conflict with the clear Word of God. According to Luther, everybody, Pope and Emperor included, must submit to the authority of the Scriptures. In a letter of July 9, 1530, he wrote to the Elector: "In the first place: Should His Imperial Majesty desire that the Imperial Majesty be permitted to decide these matters, since it was not His Majesty's purpose to enter into lengthy discussions, I think Your Electoral Grace might answer that His Imperial Majesty's manifesto promises that he would graciously listen to these matters. If such was not intended, the manifesto would have been needless, for His Imperial Majesty might have rendered his decision just as well in Spain without summoning Your Electoral Grace to Augsburg at such great labor and expense. . . . In the second place: Should His Imperial Majesty insist that the Imperial Majesty be permitted to decide these matters, Your Electoral Grace may cheerfully answer: Yes, the Imperial Majesty shall decide these matters, and Your Electoral Grace would accept and suffer everything, provided only that His Imperial Majesty make no decision against the clear Scriptures, or God's Word. For Your Electoral Grace cannot put the Emperor above God, nor accept his verdict in opposition to God's Word." (16, 815.)

### 38. Papal Peace Sought by Emperor.

By their obstinate refusal to regard themselves as a party summoned, the Romanists, from the outset, made it impossible for the Emperor to maintain the role of an impartial judge, which, probably, he had never really intended to be. At any rate, though earnestly desirous of religious peace, his actions throughout the Diet do not reveal a single serious effort at redeeming his promise and putting his beautiful words into practise. Being bound to the Pope and the papal party both religiously and politically, Charles did not require of the Romanists a fulfilment of the obligations imposed upon them by his manifesto. All the concessions were to be made by the Lutherans. *Revoca!* — that was the first and only word which Rome had hitherto spoken to Luther. "Revoke and submit yourselves!" — that, in the last analysis, was also the demand of the Emperor at Augsburg with respect to the Lutheran princes, both when he spoke in tones friendly and gentle and when he uttered severe and threatening words. Charles, it is true, desired peace, but a Roman peace, a peace effected by universal blind submission to the Pope; not a peace by mutual understanding and concessions; least of all a peace by political religious tolerance, such as Luther desired, and which in our days is generally regarded as the outstanding feature of modern civilization, notably of Americanism. To force the Lutherans into submission and obedience to the Pope, that was the real object of the Emperor. And the political situation demanded that this be accomplished by peaceable and gentle means — if possible.

Self-evidently, in his endeavors to establish a Papal Peace, the Emperor, who was haunted and tormented by the fear that all efforts might prove futile, was zealously seconded, encouraged, and prodded on by the papal theologians. To bring about a religious peace, such as the Emperor contemplated, this, they flattered Charles, would be an ever-memorable achievement, truly worthy of the Emperor; for the eyes of all Christendom were upon him, and he had staked his honor upon the success of this glorious undertaking. June 3 the Father Confessor of the Emperor, Garsia, then at Rome, wrote to Charles: "At present there is nothing so important in this life as that Your Majesty emerge victorious in the German affair. In Italy you will be accounted the best prince on earth if God should vouchsafe this grace unto us that the heresies which have arisen in that nation be cured by your hand." (Plitt, 4.) June 6 Garsia wrote: "Gracious Lord! After the letters from the legate [Campegius, concerning the return of Christian II to the Roman Church, the disagreement between Philip of Hesse and the Elector, etc.] had been read at to-day's Consistorial Meeting, almost all the cardinals said that Your Majesty was the angel sent from heaven to restore Christendom. God knows how much I rejoiced, and although the sun burned fiercely when I returned to my home, how patiently I bore it! I was not sensitive to it from sheer joy at hearing such sweet words about my master from those who a year ago had maligned him. My chief comfort, however, was to behold that they were right; for it seems as if God were performing miracles by Your Majesty, and to judge by the beginning you have made in curing this ailment, it is evident that we may expect the issue to prove far more favorable than our sins merit." (11. 67.)

### 39. Compulsion Advocated by Theologians.

All Romanists, the Emperor included, were of the opinion that the Protestants must be brought back to the papal fold. But they differed somewhat as to the means of accomplishing this purpose. Some demanded that force be resorted to forthwith, while others counseled that leniency be tried first. Campegius advised kindness at the beginning, and greater severity only in dealing with certain individuals, but that sharper measures and, finally, force of arms ought to follow. At Rome force was viewed as the "true rhubarb" for healing the breach, especially among the common people. July 18 Garsia wrote to the Emperor: "If you are determined to bring Germany back to the fold, I know of no other or better means than by presents and flattery to persuade those who are most eminent in science or in the empire to return to our faith. Once that is done, you must, in dealing with the remaining common people, first of all publish your imperial edicts and Christian admonitions. If they will not obey these, then the true rhubarb to cure them is force. This alone cured Spain's rebellion against its king. And force is what will also cure Germany's unfaithfulness to God, unless, indeed, divine grace should not attend Your Majesty in the usual measure. God would learn in this matter whether you are a faithful son of His, and should He so find, then I promise you that among all creatures you will find no power sufficiently strong to resist you. All will but serve the purpose of enabling you to obtain the crown of this world." (42.)

Among the open advocates of force were Cochlaeus, Eck, Faber, and the theologians and monks who flocked to Augsburg in large numbers about the time the Augsburg Confession was read. They all considered it their prime duty to rouse the passions of the Emperor, as well as of the Catholic princes and estates, and to incite them against the Lutherans. Their enmity was primarily directed against the Augustana, whose objective and moderate tone had gained many friends even among the Catholics, and which had indirectly branded Eck and his compeers as detractors and calumniators. For had not Duke William of Bavaria, after the reading of the Confession, rebuked Eck, in the presence of the Elector of Saxony, for having misrepresented the Lutheran doctrine to him? The moderation of the Augustana, said these Romanists, was nothing but the cunning of serpents, deception and misrepresentation, especially on the part of the wily Melanchthon; for the true Luther was portrayed in the 404 theses of Eck. Cochlaeus wrote that the Lutherans were slyly hiding their ungodly doctrines in order to deceive the Emperor: "astute occultari in illorum Confessione prava eorum dogmata, de quibus ibi tacendo dissimulabant, ut in hypocrisi loquentes Maiestati Tuae aliisque principibus imponerent." (Laemmer, *Vortridentinische Theologie*, 39.) Thus while the malice and fanaticism of the papal theologians and the monks rose in proportion as friendliness was shown the Lutherans by Catholic princes and the Emperor. They feared that every approach toward the Lutherans would jeopardize the *pax Pontificia*.

The fanaticism of the papal theologians is

frequently referred to by the Lutherans. June 26 Melanchthon wrote to Luther: "Sophists and monks are daily streaming into the city, in order to inflame the hatred of the Emperor against us." (C. R. 2, 141.) June 27: "Our Confession was presented last Saturday. The opponents are now deliberating upon how to answer; they flock together, take great pains, and incite the princes, who already have been sufficiently aroused. Eck vehemently demands of the Archbishop of Mainz that the matter be not debated, since it has already been condemned." (144.) June 29 Jonas wrote to Luther: "Faber is goaded on by furies, and Eck is not a whit more sensible. Both insist in every manner imaginable that the affair ought to be managed by force and must not be heard." (154.) Melanchthon, July 8: "By chance Eck and Cochlaeus came to the legate [Campegius, with whom Melanchthon was deliberating]. I heard them say, distinctly enough, I believe, that the opponents are merely deliberating upon how to suppress us by force." (175.) July 15: "Repeatedly have I been with certain enemies who belong to that herd of Eck. Words fail me to describe the bitter, Pharisaical hatred I noticed there. They do nothing, they plan nothing else than how they may incite the princes against us, and supply the Emperor with impious weapons." (197.) The implacable theologians also succeeded in fanaticizing some of the princes and bishops, who gradually became more and more opposed to any kind of settlement by mutual understanding. (175.)

The chief exponent of force was Cochlaeus. In his *Expostulatio*, which appeared at Augsburg in May, 1530, he argued that not only according to papal, but according to imperial law as well, which the Evangelicals also acknowledged, and according to the Scriptures, heretics might, aye, must be punished with death. The treatise concludes as follows: "Thus it is established that obdurate heretics may be executed by every form of law. We, however, much prefer to have them return to the Church, be converted, healed, and live, and we beseech them to do so. *Constat igitur, haereticos pertinaces omni iure interimi posse. Nos tamen longe magis optamus et precamur, ut redeuntes ad ecclesiam convertantur, sanentur et vivant.*" (Plitt, 1, 5.)

Naturally Eck, too, was prominent among those who counseled the employment of compulsory measures; indeed, he could not await the hour when the order would be given to proceed against the heretics with fire and sword. He lamented, in bitter terms, the fact that the Emperor had not made use of stern measures as soon as he arrived in Germany. For now, said he, procrastination and the conciliatory demeanor of the Evangelicals, especially of Melanchthon and Brueck, had made it impossible to rouse the Emperor to such a degree as the exigency of the case demanded. (Plitt, 63.) Luther wrote: "For that shameless gab and bloodthirsty sophist, Doctor Eck, one of their chief advisers, publicly declared in the presence of our people that if the Emperor had followed the resolution made at Bononia, and, immediately on entering Germany, had courageously attacked the Lutherans with the sword, and beheaded one after another, the matter would have been easily settled. But all this was prevented when he permitted the Elector of Saxony to speak and be heard through his chancellor." (St. L. 16, 1636.)

## 40. Emperor Employs Mildness.

While a number of the Catholic estates, incited by the theologians, were also in favor of immediately resorting to brutal force, the Emperor, for political reasons, considered it more advisable to employ kindness. Lauding the extreme affability and leniency of Charles, Melanchthon wrote to Luther, January 25: "The Emperor greets our Prince very kindly; and I would that our people, in turn, were more complaisant towards him. I would ask you to admonish our Junior Prince by letter in this matter. The Emperor's court has no one milder than himself. All others harbor a most cruel hatred against us. *Caesar satis benigne salutat nostrum principem; ac velim vicissim nostros erga ipsum officiosiores esse. Ea de re utinam iuniorem principem nostrum litteris admonueris. Nihil ipso Caesare mitius habet ipsius aula. Reliqui omnes crudelissime nos oderunt.*" (C. R. 2, 125.)

The reading of the Augustana strengthened this friendly attitude of Charles. Both its content and its conciliatory tone, which was not at all in harmony with the picture of the Lutherans as sketched by Eck, caused him to be more kindly disposed toward Protestantism, and nourished his hope that religious peace might be attained by peaceable means. Other Catholic dignitaries and princes had been impressed in the same manner. July 6 Luther wrote to Hausmann: "Many bishops are inclined to peace and despise the sophists, Eck and Faber. One bishop [Stadion of Augsburg] is said to have declared in a private conversation, 'This [the Confession of the Lutherans] is the pure truth, we cannot deny it.' The Bishop of Mainz is being praised very much for his endeavors in the interest of peace. Likewise Duke Henry of Brunswick, who extended a friendly invitation to Philip to dine with him, and admitted that he was not able to disprove the articles treating of both kinds, the marriage of priests, and the distinction of meats. Our men boast that, of the entire Diet, no one is milder than the Emperor himself. Such is the beginning. The Emperor treats our Elector not only graciously, but most respectfully. So Philip writes. It is remarkable how all are aglow with love and good will toward the Emperor. It may happen, if God so wills, that, as the first Emperor [Charles at Worms] was very hostile, so this last Emperor [Charles at Augsburg] will be very friendly. Only let us pray; for the power of prayer is clearly perceived." (St. L. 16, 882.) The Emperor's optimism was, no doubt, due to the fact that, unlike his theologians, he did not perceive and realize the impassable gulf fixed between Lutheranism and the Papacy, as appeared also from the Augustana, in which, however, the Emperor mistook moderation of tone for surrender of substance.

### 41. Augustana Submitted to Catholic Party.

Full of hope the Emperor, on June 26, immediately after its public presentation, submitted the Lutheran Confession to the Catholic estates for deliberation. These, too, though not in the least inclined to abandon their arrogant attitude, seem to have given themselves over to the delusion that the Lutherans could now be brought to recede from their position. Accordingly, their answer (Responsum) of June 27, couched in conciliatory language, recommended as "the humble opinion of the electors and estates that the Imperial Roman Majesty would submit this great and important matter to a number of highly learned, sensible, honest, conciliating, and not spiteful persons, to deliberate on, and to consider, the writing [the Augustana], as far as necessary, enumerating, on the one hand, whatsoever therein was found to be in conformity and harmony with the Gospel, God's Word, and the holy Christian Church, but, on the other hand, refuting with the true foundation of the Gospel and the Holy Scripture and its doctrine, and bringing into true Christian understanding, such matters as were found to be against, and out of harmony with, the Gospel, the Word of God, and the Christian Church." (Laemmer, 32.) They recommended, however, that in this entire matter Campegius be consulted, and for that purpose be furnished with a copy of the Lutheran Confession.

The Romanists furthermore resolved that the Lutherans be asked whether they had any additional points to present, and, if so, to do this immediately. The Lutherans, considering this a snare, declared, on July 10, that in their Confession they had made it a special point to present the chief articles which it is necessary to believe in order to be saved, but had not enumerated all abuses, desiring to emphasize such only as burdened the consciences, lest the paramount questions be obscured; that they would let this [all that was enumerated in their Confession] suffice, and have included other points of doctrine and abuses which were not mentioned; that they would not fail to give an answer from the Word of God in case their opponents should attack the Confession or present anything new. (Foerstemann, 2, 16. C. R. 2, 181.) No doubt, the Papists felt that the Lutherans really should have testified directly also against the Papacy, etc. This, too, was the interpretation which Luther put on the inquiry of the Romanists. July 21, 1530, he wrote to Jonas: "But now I see what the questions aimed at whether you had other articles to present. For Satan still lives and has noticed very well that your Apology [Augustana] steps softly and has passed by the articles concerning purgatory, the adora-

tion of the saints, and especially Antichrist, the Pope." (St. L. 16, 2323; Enders, 8, 133.)

July 5 the Emperor accepted the opinion of the estates and appointed the confutators. At the same time he declared with reference to the Lutherans that he "was the judge of the content of their writing" (Augustana); that, in case they should not be satisfied with his verdict, the final decision must remain with the Council; but that meanwhile the Edict of Worms would be enforced everywhere. (Laemmer, 34; C. R. 2, 175.) Thus the Emperor, in unmistakable terms, indicated that the Roman Confutation would bring his own final verdict, which no further discussions could modify, and that he would compel the Lutherans by force to observe the Edict of Worms if they refused to submit willingly. The Catholic estates endorsed the Emperor's declaration, but added the petition that, after the Confutation had been read, the Lutherans be asked in all kindness to return, and that, in case this remained fruitless, an attempt be made to bring about an agreement to be reached by a committee appointed by both parties. Evidently, the estates as well as the Emperor expected the Lutherans to yield and surrender. Still, for the present, they were willing and preferred to attain this end by mild and gentle means.

### 42. Rabid Theologians Appointed as Confutators.

Campegius, to whom the entire matter was entrusted, manipulated things in such a manner that the result was the very opposite of what the Emperor and estates had resolved upon. To be sure, he made it appear as though he were entirely neutral, leaving everything to the discretion of the German princes. He knew also how to hide his real sentiments from the Lutherans. Jonas, for example, reports that in his address of June 24 Campegius had said "nothing harsh, or hateful (nihil acerbe, nihil odiose) against the Lutherans." Spalatin reports: "Some one besought the Legate and Cardinal Campegius to assist in obtaining peace for the cause of the Gospel. To this he responded: Since the papal power was suspicious to us, the matter rested with the Emperor and the German princes. Whatever they did would stand." (Koellner, Symbolik, 403.) Thus Campegius created the impression of absolute neutrality, while in reality he was at the same time busy with secret intrigues against the Lutherans.

Among the Confutators (Brueck mentions 19, Spalatin 20, others 22, still others 24), selected by Campegius and appointed by the Emperor, were such rabid, abusive, and inveterate enemies of Luther as Eck, Faber, Cochlaeus, Wimpina, Colli (author of a slanderous tract against Luther's marriage), Dietenberger, etc. The first three are repeatedly designated as the true authors of the Confutation. In his Replica ad Bucerum, Eck boasts: "Of all the theologians at Augsburg I was chosen unanimously to prepare the answer to the Saxon Confession, and I obeyed."

*Augustae ab omnibus theologis fui delectus unanimiter, qui responsum pararem contra confessionem Saxonicam, et parui.*" (Koellner, 407.) July 10 Brenz wrote to Myconius: "Their leader (*antesignanus*) is that good man Eck. The rest are 23 in number. One might call them an Iliad [Homer's Iliad consists of 24 books] of sophists." (*C. R.* 2, 180.) Melanchthon, too, repeatedly designates Eck and Faber as the authors of the Confutation. July 14 he wrote to Luther: "With his leger-demain (*commanipulatione*) Eck presented to the Emperor the Confutation of our Confession." (193.) August 6: "This Confutation is the most nonsensical of all the nonsensical books of Faber." (253.) August 8, to Myconius: "Eck and Faber have worked for six entire weeks in producing the Confutation of our Confession." (260.) Hence also such allusions in Melanchthon's letters as "confutatio Fabrilis," "Fabriliter scripta," and in the Apology: "Nullus Faber Fabrilius cogitare quidquam posset, quam hae ineptiae excogitatae sunt ad eludendum ius naturae." (366, 10.) Brueck was right when he said that some of the Confutators were "purely partial, and altogether suspicious characters." (Koellner, 411.)

### 43. Confutation Prepared.

The resolution which the Catholic estates passed June 27 was to the effect that the imperial answer to the Lutheran Confession be made "by sober and not spiteful men of learning." The Emperor's Prolog to the Confutation, accordingly, designated the confutators as "certain learned, valiant, sensible, sober, and honorable men of many nations." (*C. R.* 27, 189.) At the same time they were told to couch their answer in winning, convincing, moderate, and earnest terms. The imperial instruction read: "To this end it is indeed good and needful that said document [the Augustana] be carefully considered and diligently studied by learned, wise, and sober persons, in order that they [the Lutherans] be shown in all kindness (*durch gute Wege*) where they err, and be admonished to return to the good way; likewise, to grant them whatsoever may be serviceable and adapted to our holy Christian faith; and to set forth the errors, moderately and politely, with such good and holy arguments as the matter calls for; to defend and prove everything with suitable evangelical declarations and admonitions, proceeding from Christian and neighborly love; and at the same time to mingle therewith earnestness and severity with such moderation as may be likely to win the five electors and princes, and not to destroy their hope or to harden them still more." (Koellner, 403.)

However, inspired by Campegius and goaded on by blind hatred, the Confutators employed their commission for the purpose of casting suspicion on the Lutherans and inciting the Emperor against them. They disregarded the imperial admonition for moderation, and instead of an objective answer to the Augustana, they produced a long-winded pasquinade

against Luther and the Evangelical preachers, a fit companion piece to the 404 theses of Eck, — a general accusation against the Protestants, a slanderous anthology of garbled quotations from Luther, Melanchthon, and other Evangelical preachers. The insinuation lurking in the document everywhere was that the Confession of the Lutheran princes was in glaring contradiction to the real doctrine of their pastors. The sinister scheme of the Romanists, as the Elector in 1536 reminded the Lutheran theologians, was to bring the princes in opposition to their preachers. (*C. R.* 3, 148.) The mildness and moderation of the Augustana, they openly declared, was nothing but subtle cunning of the smooth and wily Melanchthon, who sought to hide the true state of affairs. In a book which Cochlaeus published against the Apology in 1534, he said that the open attacks of Luther were far more tolerable than the serpentine cunning and hypocrisy of Melanchthon (*instar draconis insidiantis fraudes intendens*), as manifested in particular by his demeanor toward Campegius at Augsburg in 1530. (Laemmer, 56; Salig, 1, 376.) Thus the Roman Confutators disregarded their commission to refute the Augustana, and substituted a caricature of Luther and his doctrines, designed to irritate the Emperor.

### 44. A Bulky, Scurrilous Document.

The Confutation, compiled by Eck and Faber from various contributions of the Confutators, was ready by the 8th of July, and was presented to the Emperor on the 12th or 13th. The German translation was prepared by the Bavarian Chancellor, Leonhard von Eck. July 10 Brenz had written: "It is reported that they are preparing wagonloads of commentaries against our Confession." (*C. R.* 2, 180.) Spalatin reports that the Confutators delivered to the Emperor "a pile of books against Doctor Martin with most scurrilous titles." The chief document was entitled: "Catholic and, as it were, Extemporaneous Response concerning Certain Articles Presented in These Days at the Diet to the Imperial Majesty by the Illustrious Elector of Saxony and Certain Other Princes as well as Two Cities. *Catholica et quasi extemporanea Responsio super nonnullis articulis Caesareae Maiestati hisce diebus in dieta imperiali Augustensi per Illustrem Electorem Saxoniae et alios quosdam Principes et duas Civitates oblatis.*" It was supplemented by nine other treatises on all manner of alleged contradictions and heresies of Luther and Anabaptistic as well as other fruits of his teaching. (Laemmer, 37; *C. R.* 2, 197.) The pasquinade with its supplements comprised no less than 351 folios, 280 of which were devoted to the answer proper. Cochlaeus also designates it as "very severe and extended, *acrior extensiorque.*" July 14 Melanchthon reported he had heard from friends that the Confutation was "long and filled with scurrilities." (193. 218.) July 15: "I am sending you [Luther] a list of the treatises which our opponents have presented to the Emperor, from which you will see that the Confutation is supplemented by antilogs and other treatises in order to stir up against us the most gentle heart of the Emperor. Such are the stratagems these slanderers (*sycophantae*) devise." (197.)

The effect of the Confutation on the Emperor, however, was not at all what its authors desired and anticipated. Disgusted with the miserable bulky botch, the Emperor convened the estates on July 15, and they resolved to return the bungling document to the theologians for revision. Tone, method, plan, everything displeased the Emperor and estates to such an extent that they expunged almost one-third of it. Intentionally they ignored the nine supplements, and demanded that reflections on Luther be eliminated from the document entirely; moreover, that the theologians confine themselves to a refutation of the Augustana. (Laemmer, 39.) Cochlaeus writes: "Since the Catholic princes all desired peace and concord, they deemed it necessary to answer in a milder tone, and to omit all reference to what the [Lutheran] preachers had formerly taught and written otherwise than their Confession stated." (Koellner, 405.) In a letter to Brueck he declared that such coarse extracts and articles [with which the first draft of the Confutation charged Luther] should not be mentioned in the reply to the Confession, lest any one be put to shame or defamed publicly. (Laemmer, 39.)

In his Annals, Spalatin reports: "At first there were perhaps 280 folios. But His Imperial Majesty is said to have weeded out many folios and condensed the Confutation to such an extent that not more than twelve folios remained. This is said to have hurt and angered Eck severely." (St. L. 21a, 1539.) In a letter to Veit Dietrich, dated July 30, Melanchthon remarks sarcastically: "Recently Eck complained to one of his friends that the Emperor had deleted almost the third part of his treatise: and I suspect that the chief ornaments of the book were rooted out, that is, the glaring lies and the most stupid tricks, *insignia mendacia et sycophantiae stolidissimae.*" (C. R. 2, 241.) Brenz regarded this as an evidence of the extent to which the Augustana had perturbed the opponents, leaving them utterly helpless. July 15 he wrote to Isemann: "Meanwhile nothing new has taken place in our midst, except that I heard that the confession of the sophists was to-day returned by the Emperor to its authors, the sophists, and this for the reason that it was so confused, jumbled, vehement, bloodthirsty, and cruel (*confusa, incondita, violenta, sanguinolenta et crudelis*) that he was ashamed to have it read before the Imperial Senate. . . . We experience daily that we have so bewildered, stunned, and confused them that they know not where to begin or to end." (198.) "Pussyfooting (*Leisetreten*)!" — such was the slogan at Augsburg; and in this Melanchthon was nowhere equaled. Privately also Cochlaeus elaborated a milder answer to the Lutheran Confession. But even the friends who had induced him to undertake this task considered his effort too harsh to be presented to the Emperor.

The first, rejected draft of the Confutation has been lost, with the sole exception of the second article, preserved by Cochlaeus. On the difference between this draft and the one finally adopted, Plitt comments as follows: "The Confutation as read simply adopted the first article of the Confession [Augustana] as in complete agreement with the Roman Church. The original draft also approved this article's appeal to the Council of Nicaea, but added that now the Emperor should admonish the confessing estates to accept everything else taught by the Catholic Church, even though it was not verbally contained in the Scriptures, as, for example, the Mass, Quadragesimal fasting, the invocation of the saints, etc.; for the wording of the doctrine of the Trinity could be found in the Scriptures just as little as that of the points mentioned; furthermore, that he also call upon them to acknowledge said Synod of Nicaea in all its parts, hence also to retain the hierarchical degrees with their powers; that he admonish them to compel their preachers and teachers to retract everything which they had said and written against that Synod, especially Luther and Melanchthon, its public defamers. Refusal of such retraction would invalidate their appeal to that Synod and prove it to be nothing but a means of deception. Finally, they were to be admonished, not to believe their teachers in anything which was against the declarations of the Church catholic. Such was the form in which the first draft of the Confutation was couched. Everywhere the tendency was apparent to magnify the differences, make invidious inferences, cast suspicion on their opponents, and place them in a bad light with the Emperor and the majority. This was not the case in the answer which was finally read." (37.)

### 45. Confutation Adopted and Read.

Only after repeated revisions, in which Campegius and the imperial counselors Valdés and Granvella took part, was an agreement reached regarding the form of the Confutation. July 30 the Emperor received the fourth revision, and on August 1 he presented it to the bishops, princes, and estates for their opinion. There still remained offensive passages which had to be eliminated. A fifth revision was necessary before the approval of the Emperor and the estates was forthcoming. A Prolog and an Epilog were added, according to which the Confutation is drawn up in the name of the Emperor. Thus the original volume was boiled down to a comparatively small document. But, to speak with Kolde, even in its final form the Confutation is "still rather an accusation against the Evangelicals, and an effort to retain all the medieval church customs, than a refutation of the Augustana." (34.) August 6 Jonas wrote to Luther: "The chaplain [John Henkel] of Queen Maria informed us that they had five times changed their Confutation, casting and recasting, minting and reminting it, and still there finally was produced nothing but an uncouth and confused conglomeration and a hodgepodge, as when a cook pours different soups into one pot. At first they patched together an enormous volume, as Faber is known to be a verbose compiler; the book grew by reason of the multitude of its lies and scurrilities. However, at the first revision the Emperor eliminated the third part of the book, so that barely twelve or sixteen folios remained, which were read." (St. L. 21 a, 1539.)

On August 3, 1530, in the same hall in which the Augsburg Confession had been submitted thirty-eight days before, in the presence of all the estates of the empire, the Augustanae Confessionis Responsio, immediately called Confutatio Pontificia by the Protestants, was read in the German language by Alexander Schweiss, the Imperial Secretary. However, the reading, too, proved to be a discreditable affair. Owing to the great haste in which the German copy had been prepared, an entire portion had been omitted; the result was that the conclusion of Article 24 as well as Articles 25 and 26 were not presented. Furthermore, Schweiss, overlooking the lines of erasure, read a part which had been stricken, containing a very bold deliverance on the sacrifice of the Mass, in which they labored to prove from the Hebrew, Greek, and Latin that the word *facite* in the institution of the Sacrament was synonymous with "sacrifice." (Kolde, 34.) August 6, 1530, Jonas wrote to Luther: The opponents presented their Confutation to the Emperor on July 30, and on the 3d of August it was read in the presence of the Emperor and the estates, together with a Prolog and an Epilog of the Emperor. "The reading also consumed two entire hours, but with an incredible aversion, weariness, and disgust on the part of some of the more sensible hearers, who complained that they were almost driven out by this utterly cold, threadbare songlet (*cantilena*), being extremely chagrined that the ears of the Emperor should be molested with such a lengthy array of worthless things masquerading under the name of Catholic doctrines." (St. L. 21a, 1539.) August 4 Brenz wrote to Isemann: "The Emperor maintains neutrality; for he slept both when the Augustana and when the Confutation was read. *Imperator neutralem sese gerit; nam cum nostra confessio legeretur obdormivit; rursus cum adversariorum responsio legeretur, iterum obdormivit in media negotii actione.*" (*C. R.* 2, 245.)

The Confutation was neither published, nor was a copy of it delivered to the Lutherans. Apparently the Romanists, notably the Emperor and the estates, were ashamed of the document. True, Cochlaeus reports that toward the close of the Diet Charles authorized him and Eck to publish it, but that this was not done, because Duke George and the Emperor left Augsburg shortly after, and the printer also moved away. (Koellner, 414.) All subsequent pleading and imploring, however, on the part of Eck and others, to induce the Emperor to publish the Confutation fell on deaf ears. Evidently Charles no longer took any interest in a document that had so shamefully shattered his fond ambition

of reconciling the religious parties. What appeared in print, early in 1531, was merely an extract prepared by Cochlaeus, entitled, *Summary of the Imperial Answer*, etc. The first Latin edition of the Confutation appeared as late as 1573; the first German edition, in 1808. All previous German impressions (also the edition of 1584) are translations of the Latin edition of 1573. (*C. R.* 27, 25. 82.) Concerning the German text of the Confutation Kolde remarks: "Since changes were made even after it had been read, we have even less definite knowledge, respecting details, as to what was read than in the case of the Augustana." (35.) One may therefore also speak of a Confutatio Variata. The doctrine of the Confutation does not differ essentially from that which was later on affirmed by the Council of Trent (1545—1563). However, says Kolde, "being written by the German leaders of the Catholic party under the eye of the Papal Legate, and approved by the Emperor, the German bishops, and the Roman-minded princes, it [the Confutation] must be reckoned among the historically most important documents of the Roman Catholic faith of that day."

## 46. Confutation Denounced by Lutherans.

In the opinion of the Lutherans, the final draft of the Confutation, too, was a miserable makeshift. True, its tone was moderate, and, with few exceptions, personal defamations were omitted. The arrangement of subjects was essentially the same as in the Augustana. Still it was not what it pretended to be. It was no serious attempt at refuting the Lutheran Confession, but rather an accumulation of Bible-texts, arbitrarily expounded, in support of false doctrines and scholastic theories. These efforts led to exegetical feats that made the Confutators butts of scorn and derision. At any rate, the Lutherans were charged with having failed, at the public reading, to control their risibilities sufficiently. Cochlaeus complains: "During the reading many of the Lutherans indulged in unseemly laughter. *Quando recitata fuit, multi e Lutheranis inepte cachinnabantur.*" (Koellner, 411.) If this did not actually occur, it was not because the Confutators had given them no cause for hilarity.

"Altogether childish and silly" — such is Melanchthon's verdict on many of their exegetical pranks. August 6 he wrote letter after letter to Luther, expressing his contempt for the document. "After hearing that Confutation," says Melanchthon, "all good people seem to have been more firmly established on our part, and the opponents, if there be among them some who are more reasonable, are said to be disgusted (*stomachari*) that such absurdities were forced upon the Emperor, the best of princes." (*C. R.* 2, 252.) Again: Although the Emperor's verdict was very stern and terrible, "still, the Confutation being a composition so very puerile, a most remarkable congratulation followed its reading. No book of Faber's is so childish but that this Confutation is still more childish." (253.) In another letter he remarked that, according to the Confutation, in which the doctrine of justification by faith was rejected, "the opponents had no knowledge of religion whatever." (253.)

August 4 Brenz wrote to Isemann: "All things were written in the fashion of Cochlaeus, Faber, and Eck. Truly a most stupid comment, so that I am ashamed of the Roman name, because in their whole Church they can find no men able to answer us heretics at least in a manner wise and accomplished. *Sed omnia conscripta erant Cochleice et Fabriliter et Eccianice. Commentum sane stupidissimum, ut pudeat me Romani nominis, quod in sua religione non conquirant viros, qui saltem prudenter et ornate nobis haereticis responderent.*" (245.) August 15 Luther answered: "We received all of your letters, and I praise God that he made the Confutation of the adversaries so awkward and foolish a thing. However, courage to the end! *Verum frisch hindurch!*" (Enders, 8, 190.)

### 47. Luther on the Confutation.

Derision increased when the Papists declined to publish the Confutation, or even to deliver a copy of it to the Lutherans for further inspection. This refusal was universally interpreted as an admission, on the part of the Romanists, of a guilty conscience, and of being ashamed themselves of the document. In his *Warning to My Beloved Germans*, which appeared early in 1531, Luther wrote as follows: "But I am quite ready to believe that extraordinary wisdom prompted them [the Papists at Augsburg] to keep this rebuttal of theirs and that splendid booklet [Confutation] to themselves, because their own conscience tells them very plainly that it is a corrupt, wicked, and frigid thing, of which they would have to be ashamed if it were published and suffered itself to be seen in the light or to endure an answer. For I very well know these highly learned doctors who have cooked and brewed over it for six weeks, though with the ignorant they may be able to give the matter a good semblance. But when it is put on paper, it has neither hands nor feet, but lies there in a disorderly mass, as if a drunkard had spewed it up, as may be seen, in particular, in the writings of Doctor Schmid and Doctor Eck. For there is neither rhyme nor rhythm in whatsoever they are compelled to put into writing. Hence they are more sedulous to shout and prattle. Thus I have also learned that when our Confession was read, many of our opponents were astonished, and confessed that it was the pure truth, which they could not refute from the Scriptures. On the other hand, when their rebuttal was read, they hung their heads, and showed by their gestures that they considered it a mean and useless makeshift as compared with our Confession. Our people, however, and many other pious hearts were greatly delighted and mightily strengthened when they heard that with all the strength and art which our opponents were then called upon to display, they were capable of producing nothing

but this flimsy rebuttal, which now, praise God! a woman, a child, a layman, a peasant, are fully able to refute with good arguments taken from the Scriptures, the Word of Truth. And that is also the true and ultimate reason why they refused to deliver [to the Lutherans a copy of] their refutation. Those fugitive evil consciences were filled with horror at themselves, and dared not await the answer of Truth. And it is quite evident that they were confident, and that they had the Diet called together in the conviction that our people would never have the boldness to appear, but if the Emperor should only be brought to Germany in person, every one would be frightened and say to them: Mercy, dear lords, what would you have us do? When they were disappointed in this, and the Elector of Saxony was the very first to appear on the scene, good Lord, how their breeches began to ——! How all their confidence was confounded! What gathering together, secret consultations, and whisperings resulted! . . . The final sum and substance of it all was to devise ways and means (since our men were the first joyously and cheerfully to appear) how to keep them from being heard [block the reading of the Augustana]. When also this scheme of theirs was defeated, they finally succeeded in gaining the glory that they did not dare to hand over their futile rebuttal nor to give us an opportunity to reply to it! . . . But some one might say: The Emperor was willing to deliver the answer to our party, provided they would promise not to have it published nor its contents divulged. That is true, for such a pledge was expected of our men. Here, however, every one may grasp and feel (even though he is able neither to see nor hear) what manner of people they are who will not and dare not permit their matter to come to the light. If it is so precious a thing and so well founded in the Scriptures as they bellow and boast, why, then, does it shun the light? What benefit can there be in hiding from us and every one else such public matters as must nevertheless be taught and held among them? But if it is unfounded and futile, why, then, did they, in the first resolution [of the Diet], have the Elector of Brandenburg proclaim and publish in writing that our Confession had been refuted [by the Confutation] with the Scriptures and stanch arguments? If that were true, and if their own consciences did not give them the lie, they would not merely have allowed such precious and well-founded Refutation to be read, but would have furnished us with a written copy, saying: There you have it; we defy any one to answer it! as we did and still do with our Confession. . . . What the Elector of Brandenburg said in the resolution [read at the Diet], that our Confession was refuted with the Scriptures and with sound arguments, is not the truth, but a lie. . . . For this well-founded refutation [Confutation] has as yet not come to light, but is perhaps sleeping with the old Tannhaeuser on Mount Venus (*Venusberg*)." (St. L. 16, 1635.)

# VI. The Apology of the Augsburg Confession.

## 48. Emperor Demands Adoption of Confutation.

The Confutation was written in the name of the Emperor. This is indicated by the title: "Roman Imperial Confutation, *Roemisch-Kaiserliche Konfutation.*" (*C. R.* 27, 189.) And according to his declaration of July 5, demanding that the Lutherans acknowledge him as judge, the Emperor, immediately before the reading, announced: The Confutation contained his faith and his verdict on the Confession of the Lutherans; he demanded that they accept it; should they refuse to do so, he would prove himself the warden and protector of the Church. In the Epilog the Emperor gave expression to the following thoughts: From this Confutation he saw that the Evangelicals "in many articles agree with the Universal and also the Roman Church, and reject and condemn many wicked teachings current among the common people of the German nation." He therefore did not doubt that, having heard his answer to their Confession, they would square themselves also in the remaining points, and return to what, by common consent, had hitherto been held by all true believers. Should they fail to heed his admonition, they must consider that he would be compelled to reveal and demean himself in this matter in such manner as "by reason of his office, according to his conscience, behooved the supreme warden and protector of the Holy Christian Church." (27, 228.) Immediately after the reading, Frederick, Duke of the Palatinate, declared in the name of the Emperor that the Confutation was the Emperor's answer to the Lutherans, the verdict he rendered against their Confession; and they were now called upon to relinquish the articles of their Confession that were refuted in the Confutation, and to return to the Roman Church in unity of faith. (See the reports of Brenz, Melanchthon, and the delegates from Nuernberg, *C. R.* 2, 245. 250. 253.) Thus the Emperor, who had promised to have the deliberations carried on in love and kindness, demanded blind submission, and closed his demand with a threat. His manifesto was Protestant; his actions remained Papistical. In the estimation of the Romanists, the Emperor, by condescending to an extended reply to the Lutheran Confession, had done more than his duty, and much more than they had considered expedient. Now they rejoiced, believing that everything they wished for had been accomplished, and that there was no other way open for the Lutherans than to submit, voluntarily or by compulsion.

Naturally the attitude of the Emperor was a great disappointment to the Lutherans, and it caused much alarm and fear among them. From the very beginning they had declared themselves ready, in the interest of peace, to do whatever they could "with God and conscience." And this remained their position to the very last. They dreaded war, and were determined to leave no stone unturned towards avoiding this calamity. In this interest even Philip of Hesse was prepared to go to the very limits of possibility. Melanchthon wrote: "The Landgrave deports himself with much restraint. He has openly declared to me that in order to preserve peace, he would accept even sterner conditions, as long as he did not thereby disgrace the Gospel." (*C. R.* 2, 254.) But a denial of God, conscience, and the Gospel was precisely what the Emperor expected. Hence the Lutherans refer to his demands as cruel, impossible of fulfilment, and as a breach of promise. Outraged by the Emperor's procedure, and fearing for his own safety, the Landgrave secretly left the Diet on August 6. War seemed inevitable to many. The reading of the Confutation had shattered the last hopes of the Lutherans for a peaceful settlement. They said so to each other, and wrote it to those at home, though not all of them in the lachrymose tone of the vacillating Melanchthon, who, filled with a thousand fears, was temporarily more qualified for depriving others of their courage than for inspiring courage. (Plitt, 24.)

## 49. Sustained by Luther.

In these days of severe trials and sore distress the Lutherans were sustained by the comforting letters of Luther and the bracing consciousness that it was the divine truth itself which they advocated. And the reading of the Confutation had marvelously strengthened this conviction. Brueck reports an eyewitness of the reading of the Augustana as saying: "The greater portion among them [the Papists] is not so ignorant as not to have seen long ago that they are in error." (Plitt, 18.) Because of this conviction there was, as Melanchthon reported, a "marvelous congratulation" among the Lutherans after the reading of the Confutation. "We stand for the divine truth, which God cannot but lead to victory, while our opponents are condemned by their own consciences," — such was the buoying conviction of the Lutherans. And in this the powerful letters of Luther strengthened the confessors at Augsburg. He wrote: "This is the nature of our Christian doctrine, that it must be held and grasped as certain, and that every one must think and be convinced: The doctrine is true and sure indeed and cannot fail. But whoever falls to reasoning and begins to waver within himself, saying: My dear friend, do you believe that it is true, etc.? such a heart will never be a true Christian." (Plitt, 12.)

Concerning the spiritual support which the confessors at Augsburg, notably Melanchthon, received from Luther, Plitt remarks: "What Luther did during his solitary stay in the Castle at Coburg cannot be rated high enough. His ideal deportment during these days, so trying for the Church, is an example which at all times Evangelical Christians may look up to, in order to learn from him and to emulate him. What he wrote to his followers in order to comfort and encourage them, can and must at all times refresh and buoy up those who are concerned about the course of the Church." (24.) June 30 Veit Dietrich, who shared Luther's solitude at Coburg, wrote to Melanchthon: "My dear Philip, you do not know how concerned I am for your welfare, and I beseech you for Christ's sake not to regard as vain the Doctor's [Luther's] letters to you. I cannot sufficiently admire that man's unique constancy, joy, confidence, and hope in these days of most sore distress. And daily he nourishes them by diligent contemplation of the Word of God. Not a day passes in which he does not spend in prayer at least three hours, such as are most precious for study. On one occasion I chanced to hear him pray. Good Lord, what a spirit, what faith spoke out of his words! He prayed with such reverence that one could see he was speaking with God, and withal with such faith and such confidence as is shown by one who is speaking with his father and friend. I know, said he, that Thou art our Father and our God. Therefore I am certain that Thou wilt confound those who persecute Thy children. If Thou dost not do it, the danger is Thine as well as ours. For the entire matter is Thine own. We were compelled to take hold of it; mayest Thou therefore also protect it, etc. Standing at a distance, I heard him praying in this manner with a loud voice. Then my heart, too, burned mightily within me, when he spoke so familiarly, so earnestly, and reverently with God, and in his prayer insisted on the promises in the Psalms, as one who was certain that everything he prayed for would be done. Hence I do not doubt that his prayer will prove a great help in the desperately bad affair of this Diet. And you, my teacher, would do far better to imitate our father, the Doctor, also in this point. For with your miserable cares and your weakling tears you will accomplish nothing, but prepare a sad destruction for yourself and us all, who take pleasure in, and are benefited by, nothing more than your welfare." (*C. R.* 2, 158 f.; St. L. 16, 929 f.)

### 50. Copy of Confutation Refused to Lutherans.

Since the Confutation, in the manner indicated, had been presented as the Emperor's final verdict upon the Augsburg Confession, the Lutherans were compelled to declare themselves. Accordingly, Chancellor Brueck at once responded to the demand for submission made through the Palatinate after the reading of the Confutation, saying: The importance of this matter, which concerned their salvation, required that the Confutation be delivered to the Lutherans for careful inspection and examination to enable them to arrive at a decision in the matter. The delegates from Nuernberg reported, in substance: After the Confutation was read, Doctor Brueck answered: Whereas, according to their Confession, the Lutherans were willing to do and yield everything that could be so done with a good conscience; whereas, furthermore, according to the Confutation, some of their [the

Lutherans'] articles were approved, others entirely rejected, still others partly admitted to be right and partly repudiated; and whereas the Confutation was a somewhat lengthy document: therefore the Electors, princes, and cities deemed it necessary to scan these articles more closely, the more so, because many writings were adduced in them that made it necessary to show to what intent, and if at all, they were rightly quoted, and accordingly requested the Emperor, since he had promised to hear both parties, to submit the Confutation for their inspection. The Emperor answered: "As it was now late and grown dark, and since the matter was important, he would consider their request and reply to it later." Hereupon, according to the Nuernberg delegates, "the chancellor pleaded again and most earnestly that His Imperial Majesty would consider this important and great affair as a gracious and Christian emperor ought to do, and not deny their prayer and petition, but deliver to them the document which had been read." (*C. R.* 2, 251.)

Now, although the Romanists were in no way minded and disposed to submit the Confutation to the Lutherans, they nevertheless did not consider it wise to refuse their petition outright and bluntly; for they realized that this would redound to the glory neither of themselves nor of their document. The fanatical theologians, putting little faith in that sorry fabrication of their own, and shunning the light, at first succeeded in having a resolution passed declaring the entire matter settled with the mere reading. However, in order to save their faces and to avoid the appearance of having refused the Confutation as well as "the scorn and ridicule on that account" (as the Emperor naively put it), and "lest any one say that His Imperial Majesty had not, in accordance with his manifesto, first dealt kindly with" the Lutherans, the estates resolved on August 4 to grant their request. At the same time, however, they added conditions which the Lutherans regarded as dangerous, insinuating, and impossible, hence rendering the Catholic offer illusory and unacceptable.

August 5 the Emperor communicated the resolutions adopted by the Catholic estates to the Lutherans. According to a report of the Nuernberg delegates the negotiations proceeded as follows: The Emperor declared that the Confutation would be forwarded to the Lutherans, but with the understanding that they must come to an agreement with the Catholic princes and estates; furthermore, that they spare His Imperial Majesty with their refutations and make no further reply; and, above all, that they keep this and other writings to themselves, nor let them pass out of their hands, for instance, by printing them, or in any other way. Hereupon Brueck, in the name of the Lutherans, thanked the Emperor, at the same time voicing the request "that, considering their dire necessity, His Imperial Majesty would permit his Elector and princes to make answer to the Confutation." Duke Frederick responded: The Emperor was inclined to grant them permission to reply, but desired the answer to be "as profitable and brief as possible," also expected them to come to an agreement with the Catholics, and finally required a solemn promise that they would not permit the document to pass out of their hands. Brueck answered guardedly: The Lutherans would gladly come to an agreement "as far as it was possible for them to do so with God and their conscience"; and as to their answer and the preservation of the document, they would be found "irreprehensible." The Emperor now declared: "The document should be delivered to the Lutherans in case they would promise to keep it to themselves and not allow it to fall into other hands; otherwise His Imperial Majesty was not minded to confer with them any longer." Brueck asked for time to consider the matter, and was given till evening. In his response he declined the Emperor's offer, at the same time indicating that an answer to the Confutation would be forthcoming nevertheless. The Lutherans, he said, felt constrained to relinquish their petition, because the condition that the document be kept in their hands had been stressed in such a manner that they could not but fear the worst interpretation if it would nevertheless leak out without their knowledge and consent; still, they offered to answer the Confutation, since they had noted the most important points while it was read; in this case, however, they asked that it be not charged to them if anything should be overlooked; at the same time they besought the Emperor to consider this action of theirs as compelled by dire necessity, and in no other light. (C. R. 2, 255 ff.) In the Preface to the Apology, Melanchthon says: "This [a copy of the Confutation] our princes could not obtain, except on the most perilous conditions, which it was impossible for them to accept." (99.)

## 51. Lutherans on Roman Duplicity and Perfidy.

The duplicity and perfidy of the Emperor and the Romanists in their dealings with the Lutherans was characterized by Chancellor Brueck as follows: "The tactics of the opponents in offering a copy [of the Confutation] were those of the fox when he invited the stork to be his guest and served him food in a broad, shallow pan, so that he could not take the food with his long bill. In like manner they treated the five electors and princes, as well as the related cities, when they offered to accede to their request and submit a copy to them, but upon conditions which they could not accept without greatly violating their honor." (Koellner, 419.) Over against the Emperor's demand of blind submission and his threat of violence, the Lutherans appealed to their pure Confession, based on the Holy Scriptures, to their good conscience, bound in the Word of God, and to the plain wording of the imperial manifesto, which had promised discussions in love and kindness. In an Answer of August 9, e. g., they declared: The articles of the Augustana which we have pre-

sented are drawn from the Scriptures, and "it is impossible for us to relinquish them with a good conscience and peace of heart, unless we find a refutation founded on God's Word and truth, on which we may rest our conscience in peace and certainty." (Foerstemann, 2, 185.) In the Preface to the Apology, Melanchthon comments as follows on the demand of the Romanists: "Afterwards, negotiations for peace were begun, in which it was apparent that our princes declined no burden, however grievous, which could be assumed without offense to conscience. But the adversaries obstinately demanded that we should approve certain manifest abuses and errors; and as we could not do this, His Imperial Majesty again demanded that our princes should assent to the Confutation. This our princes refused to do. For how could they, in a matter pertaining to religion, assent to a writing which they had not been able to examine, especially as they had heard that some articles were condemned in which it was impossible for them, without grievous sin, to approve the opinions of the adversaries?" (99.)

Self-evidently the Lutherans also protested publicly that the procedure of the Romanists was in contravention of the proclamation of the Emperor as well as of his declaration on June 20, according to which both parties were to deliver their opinions in writing for the purpose of mutual friendly discussion. In the Answer of August 9, referred to above, they said: "We understand His Imperial Majesty's answer to mean nothing else than that, after each party had presented its meaning and opinion, such should here be discussed among us in love and kindness." Hence, they said, it was in violation of this agreement to withhold the Confutation, lest it be answered. (Foerstemann, 2, 184 f.) Luther expressed the same conviction, saying: "All the world was awaiting a gracious diet, as the manifesto proclaimed and pretended, and yet, sad to say, it was not so conducted." (St. L. 16, 1636.) That the Romanists themselves fully realized that the charges of the Lutherans were well founded, appears from the subterfuges to which they resorted in order to justify their violence and duplicity, notably their refusal to let them examine the Confutation. In a declaration of August 11 they stated "that the imperial laws expressly forbid, on pain of loss of life and limb, to dispute or argue (gruppeln) about the articles of faith in any manner whatever," and that in the past the edicts of the Emperor in this matter of faith had been despised, scorned, ridiculed, and derided by the Lutherans. (Foerstemann, 2, 190.) Such were the miserable arguments with which the Romanists defended their treachery. Luther certainly hit the nail on the head when he wrote that the Romanists refused to deliver the Confutation "because their consciences felt very well that it was a corrupt, futile, and frigid affair, of which they would have to be ashamed in case it should become public and show itself in the light, or endure an answer." (St. L. 16, 1635.)

## 52. Original Draft of Apology.

August 5 the Lutherans had declared to the Emperor that they would not remain indebted for an answer to the Confutation, even though a copy of it was refused them. They knew the cunning Romanists, and had prepared for every. emergency. Melanchthon, who, according to a letter addressed to Luther (*C. R.* 2, 254), was not present at the reading of the Confutation, writes in the Preface to the Apology: "During the reading some of us had taken down the chief points of the topics and arguments." (101.) Among these was Camerarius. August 4 the Nuernberg delegates reported to their senate that the Confutation, comprising more than fifty pages, had been publicly read on August 3, at 2 P. M., and that the Lutherans had John Kammermeister "record the substance of all the articles; this he has diligently done in shorthand on his tablet, as far as he was able, and more than all of us were able to understand and remember, as Your Excellency may perceive from the enclosed copy." (*C. R.* 2, 250.)

On the basis of these notes the council of Nuernberg had a theological and a legal opinion drawn up, and a copy of the former (Osiander's refutation of the Confutation) was delivered to Melanchthon on August 18 by the Nuernberg delegates. Osiander specially stressed the point that the demand of the Romanists to submit to the decision of the Church in matters of faith must be rejected, that, on the contrary, everything must be subordinated to the Holy Scriptures. (Plitt, 87.) In drawing up the Apology, however, Melanchthon made little, if any, use of Osiander's work. Such, at least, is the inference Kolde draws from Melanchthon's words to Camerarius, September 20: "Your citizens [of Nuernberg] have sent us a book on the same subject [answer to the Confutation], which I hope before long to discuss with you orally." (383.) There can be little doubt that Melanchthon privately entertained the idea of writing the Apology immediately after the reading of the Confutation. The commission, however, to do this was not given until later; and most of the work was probably done in September. For August 19 the Nuernberg delegates reported that their "opinion" had been given to Melanchthon, who as yet, however, had not received orders to write anything in reply to the Confutation, "unless he is privately engaged in such undertaking." (*C. R.* 2, 289.)

At Augsburg the execution of the resolution to frame an answer to the Confutation had been sidetracked for the time being, by the peace parleys between the Lutherans and the Catholics, which began soon after the Confutation was read and continued through August. But when these miscarried, the Evangelical estates, on the 29th of August, took official action regarding the preparation of an Apology. Of the meeting in which the matter was discussed the Nuernberg delegates report: "It was furthermore resolved: 'Since we have recently declared before His Majesty that, in case His Majesty refused to deliver to us the Confutation of our Confession without restrictions [the aforementioned conditions], we nevertheless could not refrain from writing a reply to it, as far as the articles had been noted down during the reading, and from delivering it to His Imperial Majesty: we therefore ought to prepare ourselves in this matter, in order to make use of it in case of necessity.' In this we, the delegates of the cities, also acquiesced. . . . I, Baumgaertner, also said: In case such a work as was under discussion should be drawn up, we had some opinions [the theological and the legal opinions of the city of Nuernberg], which might be of service in this matter, and which we would gladly submit. Hereupon it was ordered that Dr. Brueck and other Saxons be commissioned to draft the writing." (321.) The assumption, therefore, that Melanchthon was the sole author of the first draft of the Apology is erroneous. In the Preface to the Apology he writes: "They had, however, commanded me *and some others* to prepare an Apology of the Confession, in which the reasons why we could not accept the Confutation should be set forth to His Imperial Majesty, and the objections made by the adversaries be refuted." (101.) In the same Preface he says that he had originally drawn up the Apology at Augsburg, "*taking counsel with others.*" (101.) However, we do not know who, besides Brueck, these "others" were.

## 53. Apology Presented, But Acceptance Refused.

By September 20 Melanchthon had finished his work. For on the same day he wrote to Camerarius: "The verdict [decision of the Diet] on our affair has not yet been rendered. . . . Our Prince thought of leaving yesterday, and again to-day. The Emperor, however, kept him here by the promise that he would render his decision within three days. . . . Owing to the statements of evil-minded people, I am now remaining at home and have in these days written the Apology of our Confession, which, if necessary, shall also be delivered; for it will be opposed to the Confutation of the other party, which you heard when it was read. I have written it sharply and more vehemently" (than the Confession). (*C. R.* 2, 383.)

Before long, a good opportunity also for delivering this Apology presented itself. It was at the meeting of the Diet on September 22, when the draft of a final resolution (*Abschied*) was read to the estates. According to this decision, the Emperor offered to give the Evangelicals time till April 15, 1531, to consider whether or not they would unite with the Christian Church, the Holy Father, and His Majesty "in the other articles," provided, however, that in the mean time nothing be printed and absolutely no further innovations be made. The imperial decision also declared emphatically that the Lutheran Confession had been refuted by the Confutation. The verdict claimed the Emperor "had, in the presence of the other electors, princes, and estates of the holy empire, graciously heard the opinion and confession [of the Evangelical princes], had given it due and thorough consideration, and had refuted and disproved it with sound arguments from the holy gospels and the Scriptures." (Foerstemann, 2, 475.)

Self-evidently, the Lutherans could not let this Roman boast pass by in silence. Accordingly, in the name of the Elector, Brueck arose to voice their objections, and, while apologizing for its deficiencies, presented the Apology. In his protest, Brueck dwelt especially on the offensive words of the Imperial decision which claimed that the Augustana was refuted by the Confutation. He called attention to the fact that the Lutherans had been offered a copy only under impossible conditions; that they had nevertheless, on the basis of what was heard during the reading, drawn up a "counter-plea, or reply"; this he was now holding in his hands, and he requested that it be read publicly; from it every one might learn "with what strong, irrefutable reasons of Holy Scripture" the Augustana was fortified. (Foerstemann, 2, 479.) Duke Frederick took the Apology, but returned it on signal from the Emperor, into whose ear King Ferdinand had been whispering. Sleidan relates: "Cumque hucusce perventum esset, Pontanus apologiam Caesari defert; eam ubi Fridericus Palatinus accepit, subnuente Caesare, cui Ferdinandus aliquid ad aures insusurraverat, reddit." A similar report is found in the annals of Spalatin. (Koellner, 422.)

By refusing to accept the Apology, the Emperor and the Romanists de facto broke off negotiations with the Lutherans; and the breach remained, and became permanent. September 23 the Elector left Augsburg. By the time the second imperial decision was rendered, November 19, all the Evangelical princes had left the Diet. The second verdict, dictated by the intolerant spirit of the papal theologians, was more vehement than the first. Confusing Lutherans, Zwinglians, and Anabaptists, Charles emphasized the execution of the Edict of Worms; sanctioned all dogmas and abuses which the Evangelicals had attacked; confirmed the spiritual jurisdiction of the bishops; demanded the restoration of all abolished rites; identified himself with the Confutation, and repeated the assertion that the Lutheran Confession had been refuted from the Scriptures. (Foerstemann, 2, 839 f.; Laemmer, 49.)

In his *Gloss on the Alleged Imperial Edict* of 1531, Luther dilates as follows on the Roman assertion of having refuted the Augustana from the Scriptures: "In the first place, concerning their boasting that our Confession was refuted from the holy gospels, this is so manifest a lie that they themselves well know it to be an abominable falsehood. With this rouge they wanted to tint their faces and to defame us, since they noticed very well that their affair was leaky, leprous, and filthy, and despite such deficiency nevertheless was to be honored. Their heart thought: Ours is an evil cause, this we know very well; but we shall say the Lutherans were refuted; that's enough. Who will compel us to prove such

a false statement? For if they had not felt that their boasting was lying, pure and simple, they would not only gladly, and without offering any objections, have surrendered their refutation as was so earnestly desired, but would also have made use of all printing-presses to publish it, and heralded it with all trumpets and drums, so that such defiance would have arisen that the very sun would not have been able to shine on account of it. But now, since they so shamefully withheld their answer and still more shamefully hide and secrete it, by this action their evil conscience bears witness to the fact that they lie like reprobates when they boast that our Confession has been refuted, and that by such lies they seek not the truth, but our dishonor and a cover for their shame." (St. L. 16, 1668.)

## 54. Apology Recast by Melanchthon.

Owing to the fact that Melanchthon, immediately after the presentation of the Apology, resolved to revise and recast it, the original draft was forced into the background. It remained unknown for a long time and was published for the first time forty-seven years after the Diet. Chytraeus embodied it in his *Historia Augustanae Confessionis*, 1578, with the caption, "*Prima Delineatio Caesari Carolo Die 22. Septembris Oblata, sed Non Recepta* — The First Draft which was Offered to Emperor Charles on September 22, but Not Accepted." The German and Latin texts are found in *Corp. Ref.* 27, 275 ff. and 322. Following is the Latin title: "Apologia Confessionis, 1530. Ps. 119: Principes persecuti sunt me gratis." The German title runs: "Antwort der Widerlegung auf unser Bekenntnis uebergeben." (245. 378.) Plitt says of the original Apology: "It was well qualified to be presented to the Emperor, and, in form also, far surpassed the Confutation of the Papists. Still the Evangelical Church suffered no harm when the Emperor declined to accept it. The opportunity for revision which was thus offered and fully exploited by Melanchthon, who was never able to satisfy himself, resulted in a great improvement. The Apology as it appeared the following year is much riper, sharper in its rebuttal, and stronger in its argumentation." (88.)

The draft of the Apology presented at Augsburg concluded as follows: "If the Confutation had been forwarded to us for inspection, we would perhaps have been able to give a more adequate answer on these and additional points." (*C. R.* 27, 378.) When, therefore, the Emperor had refused to accept it, Melanchthon determined to revise, reenforce, and augment the document. September 23 he left Augsburg in the company of the Elector; and already while *en route* he began the work. In his *History of the Augsburg Confession*, 1730, Salig remarks: "Still the loss of the first copy [of the Apology] does not seem to be so great, since we now possess the Apology in a more carefully elaborated form. For while the Diet was still in session, and also after the theologians had returned home, Melanchthon was constantly engaged upon it, casting it into an entirely different mold, and making it much more extensive than it was before. When the theologians had returned to Saxony from the Diet, Melanchthon, in Spalatin's house at Altenburg, even worked at it on Sunday, so that Luther plucked the pen from his hand, saying that on this day he must rest from such work." (1, 377.) However, since the first draft was presented to the Emperor on September 22, and Melanchthon, together with the Elector, left Augsburg on the following day, it is evident that he could not have busied himself very much with the revision of the Apology at Augsburg. And that Luther, in the Altenburg incident, should have put especial stress on the Sunday, for this neither Salig nor those who follow him (e. g., Schaff, Creeds, 1, 243) offer any evidence. In his Seventeen Sermons on the Life of Luther, Mathesius gives the following version of the incident: "When Luther, returning home with his companions from Coburg, was visiting Spalatin, and Philip, constantly engrossed in thoughts concerning the Apology, was writing during the meal, he arose and took the pen away from him [saying]: 'God can be honored not alone by work, but also by rest and recreation; for that reason He has given the Third Commandment and commanded the Sabbath.'" (243.) This report of Mathesius certainly offers no ground for a Puritanic explanation of the incident in Spalatin's home.

Originally Melanchthon does not seem to have contemplated a revision on a very large scale. In the Preface, which was printed first, he merely remarks that he made "some additions" (quaedam adieci) to the Apology drawn up at Augsburg. (101.) Evidently, at the time when he wrote this, he had no estimate of the proportions the work, which grew under his hands, would finally assume. Before long also he obtained a complete copy of the Confutation. It was probably sent to him from Nuernberg, whose delegate had been able to send a copy home on August 28, 1530. (Kolde, 37.) Says Melanchthon in the Preface to the Apology: "I have recently seen the Confutation, and have noticed how cunningly and slanderously it was written, so that on some points it could deceive even the cautious." (101.) Eck clamored that the Confutation "had gotten into Melanchthon's hands in a furtive and fraudulent manner, furtim et fraudulenter ad manus Melanchthonis eandem pervenisse." (Koellner, 426.) The possession of the document enabled Melanchthon to deal in a reliable manner with all questions involved, and spurred him on to do most careful and thorough work.

### 55. Completion of Apology Delayed.

Owing to the fact that Melanchthon spent much more time and labor on the work than he had anticipated and originally planned, the publication of the Apology was unexpectedly delayed. October 1, 1530, Melanchthon wrote to Camerarius: "Concerning the word 'liturgy' [in the Apology] I ask you

again and again carefully to search out for me its etymology as well as examples of its meaning." November 12, to Dietrich: "I shall describe them [the forms of the Greek mass] to Osiander as soon as I have completed the Apology, which I am now having printed and am endeavoring to polish. In it I shall fully explain the most important controversies, which, I hope, will prove profitable." (C. R. 2, 438.) In a similar strain he wrote to Camerarius, November 18. (440.) January 1, 1531, again to Camerarius: "In the Apology I experience much trouble with the article of Justification, which I seek to explain profitably." (470.) February, 1531, to Brenz: "I am at work on the Apology. It will appear considerably augmented and better founded. For this article, in which we teach that men are justified by faith and not by love, is treated exhaustively." (484.) March 7, to Camerarius: "My Apology is not yet completed. It grows in the writing." (486.) Likewise in March, to Baumgaertner: "I have not yet completed the Apology, as I was hindered, not only by illness, but also by many other matters, which interrupted me, concerning the syncretism Bucer is stirring up." (485.) March 17, to Camerarius: "My Apology is making slower progress than the matter calls for." (488.) Toward the end of March, to Baumgaertner: "The Apology is still in press; for I am revising it entirely and extending it." (492.) April 7, to Jonas: "In the Apology I have completed the article on Marriage, in which the opponents are charged with many real crimes." (493.) April 8, to Brenz: "We have almost finished the Apology. I hope it will please you and other good people." (494.) April 11, to Camerarius: "My Apology will appear one of these days. I shall also see that you receive it. At times I have spoken somewhat vehemently, as I see that the opponents despise every mention of peace." (495.) Finally, in the middle of April, to Bucer: "My Apology has appeared, in which, in my opinion, I have treated the articles of Justification, Repentance, and several others in such a manner that our opponents will find themselves heavily burdened. I have said little of the Eucharist." (498.)

These letters show that Melanchthon took particular pains with the article of Justification, which was expanded more than tenfold. January 31, he was still hard at work on this article. Kolde says: "This was due to the fact that he suppressed five and one-half sheets [preserved by Veit Dietrich] treating this subject because they were not satisfactory to him, and while he at first treated Articles 4 to 6 together, he now included also Article 20, recasting anew the entire question of the nature of justification and the relation of faith and good works. Illness and important business, such as the negotiations with Bucer on the Lord's Supper, brought new delays. He also found it necessary to be more explicit than he had contemplated. Thus it came about that the work could first appear, together with the Augustana, end of April, or, at the latest, beginning of May." (37.) Ac-

quatenus - in as far as it is in accord with God's word.
quia - accept because they are in accord with God's word.

VI. The Apology of the Augsburg Confession. 43

cording to the resolution of the Diet, the Lutherans were to have decided by April 15, 1531, whether they would accept the Confutation or not. The answer of the Lutherans was the appearance, on the bookstalls, of the Augustana and the Apology, and a few days prior, of Luther's "Remarks on the Alleged Imperial Edict, *Glossen auf das vermeinte kaiserliche Edikt.*"

## 56. German Translation by Jonas.

The Apology was written in Latin. The *editio princeps* in quarto of 1531 contained the German and the Latin texts of the Augsburg Confession, and the Latin text of the Apology. From the very beginning, however, a German translation was, if not begun, at least planned. But, though announced on the title-page of the quarto edition just referred to, it appeared six months later, in the fall of 1531. It was the work of Justus Jonas. The title of the edition of 1531 reads: "*Apologie der Konfession, aus dem Latein verdeutscht durch Justus Jonas, Wittenberg.* Apology of the Confession done into German from the Latin by Justus Jonas, Wittenberg." For a time Luther also thought of writing a "German Apology." April 8, 1531, Melanchthon wrote to Brenz: "*Lutherus nunc instituit apologiam Germanicam.* Luther is now preparing a German Apology." (*C. R.* 2, 494. 501.) It is, however, hardly possible that Luther was contemplating a translation. Koellner comments on Melanchthon's words: "One can understand them to mean that Luther is working on the German Apology." *Instituit,* however, seems to indicate an independent work rather than a translation. Koestlin is of the opinion that Luther thought of writing an Apology of his own, because he was not entirely satisfied with Melanchthon's. (*Martin Luther* 2, 382.) However, if this view is correct, it certainly cannot apply to Melanchthon's revised Apology, to which Luther in 1533 expressly confessed himself, but to the first draft at Augsburg, in which, *e. g.,* the 10th Article seems to endorse the concomitance doctrine. (*Lehre und Wehre* 1918, 385.) At all events, Luther changed his plan when Jonas began the translation of the new Apology.

The translation of Jonas is not a literal reproduction of the Latin original, but a version with numerous independent amplifications. Also Melanchthon had a share in this work. In a letter of September 26, 1531, he says: "They are still printing the German Apology, the improvements of which cost me no little labor." (*C. R.* 2, 542.) The deviations from the Latin original therefore must perhaps be traced to Melanchthon rather than to Jonas. Some of them are due to the fact that the translation was based in part not on the text of the *editio princeps,* but on the altered Latin octavo edition, copies of which Melanchthon was able to send to his friends as early as September 14. See, for example, the 10th Article, where the German text follows the octavo edition in omitting the quotation from Theophylact. The German text

appeared also in a separate edition, as we learn from the letter of the printer Rhau to Stephen Roth of November 30, 1531: "I shall send you a German Apology, most beautifully bound." (Kolde, 39.) German translations adhering strictly to the text of the *editio princeps* are of a much later date.

## 57. Alterations of Apology.

Melanchthon, who was forever changing and improving, naturally could not leave the Apology as it read in the first edition. This applies to both the German and the Latin text. He was thinking of the Latin octavo edition when he wrote to Brenz, June 7, 1531: "The Apology is now being printed, and I am at pains to make some points in the article of Justification clearer. It is an extremely great matter, in which we must proceed carefully, that Christ's honor may be magnified." (2, 504.) The same edition he had in mind when he wrote to Myconius, June 14, 1531: "My Apology is now in press, and I am endeavoring to present the article of Justification even more clearly; for there are some things in the solution of the arguments which are not satisfactory to me." (506.) Accordingly, this octavo edition, of which Melanchthon was able to send a copy to Margrave George on September 14, revealed important alterations: partly improvements, partly expansions, partly deletions. The changes in the 10th Article, already referred to, especially the omission of the quotation from Theophylact, attracted most attention. The succeeding Latin editions likewise revealed minor changes. The Apology accompanying the Altered Augsburg Confession of 1540, was designated by Melanchthon himself as "*diligenter recognita,* diligently revised." (*C. R.* 26, 357. 419.)

Concerning the German Apology, Melanchthon wrote to Camerarius on January 1, 1533: "I have more carefully treated the German Apology and the article of Justification, and would ask you to examine it. If you have seen my Romans [Commentary on the Epistle to the Romans], you will be able to notice how exactly and methodically I am endeavoring to explain this matter. I also hope that intelligent men will approve it. For I have done this in order to explain necessary matters and to cut off all manner of questions, partly false, partly useless." (*C. R.* 2, 624.) About the same time he wrote to Spalatin: "Two articles I have recast entirely: Of Original Sin and Of Righteousness. I ask you to examine them, and hope that they will profit pious consciences. For in my humble opinion I have most clearly presented the doctrine of Righteousness and ask you to write me your opinion." (625.) Kolde says of this second revision of the German text of 1533: "This edition, which Melanchthon described as 'diligently amended,' is much sharper in its tone against the Romanists than the first and reveals quite extensive changes. Indeed, entire articles have been remodeled, such as those Of Justification and Good Works, Of Repentance, Of the Mass, and also the statements on Christian perfection." (41.) These altera-tions in the Latin and German texts of the Apology, however, do not involve changes in doctrine, at least not in the same degree as in the case of the Augustana Variata of 1540. Self-evidently, it was the text of the first edition of the German as well as the Latin Apology that was embodied in the Book of Concord.

## 58. Purpose, Arrangement, and Character of Apology.

The aim of the Apology was to show why the Lutherans "do not accept the Confuta-tion," and to puncture the papal boast that the Augustana had been refuted with the Holy Scriptures. In its Preface we read: "After-wards a certain decree was published [by the Emperor], in which the adversaries boast that they have refuted our Confession from the Scriptures. You have now, therefore, reader, our Apology, from which you will understand not only what the adversaries have judged (for we have reported in good faith), but also that they have condemned several articles con-trary to the manifest Scripture of the Holy Ghost; so far are they from overthrowing our propositions by means of the Scriptures." (101.) The Apology is, on the one hand, a refutation of the Confutation and, on the other hand, a defense and elaboration of the Augus-tana, presenting theological proofs for the cor-rectness of its teachings. Hence constant ref-erence is made to the Augsburg Confession as well as the Confutation; and scholastic the-ology is discussed as well. On this account also the sequence of the articles, on the whole, agrees with that of the Augustana and the Confutation. However, articles treating of related doctrines are collected into one, e. g., Articles 4, 5, 6, and 20. Articles to which the Romanists assented are but briefly touched upon. Only a few of them have been elabo-rated somewhat, e. g., Of the Adoration of the Saints, Of Baptism, Of the Lord's Supper, Of Repentance, Of Civil Government. The four-teen articles, however, which the Confutation rejected are discussed extensively, and fur-nished also with titles, in the editio princeps as well as in the Book of Concord of 1580 and 1584. In Mueller's edition of the Sym-bolical Books all articles of the Apology are for the first time supplied with numbers and captions corresponding with the Augsburg Confession.

In the Apology, just as in the Augsburg Confession, everything springs from, and is regulated by, the fundamental Lutheran prin-ciple of Law and Gospel, sin and grace, faith and justification. Not only is the doctrine of justification set forth thoroughly and com-fortingly in a particular article, but through-out the discussions it remains the dominant note, its heavenly strain returning again and again as the motif in the grand symphony of divine truths — a strain with which the Apol-ogy also breathes, as it were, its last, depart-ing breath. For in its Conclusion we read: "If all the scandals [which, according to the Papists, resulted from Luther's teaching] be

brought together, still the one article concern-ing the remission of sins (that for Christ's sake, through faith, we freely obtain the re-mission of sins) brings so much good as to hide all evils. And this, in the beginning [of the Reformation], gained for Luther not only our favor, but also that of many who are now contending against us." (451.)

In Kolde's opinion, the Apology is a com-panion volume, as it were, to Melanchthon's Loci Communes, and a theological dissertation rather than a confession. However, theolog-ical thoroughness and erudition do not con-flict with the nature of a confession as long as it is not mere cold intellectual reflection and abstraction, but the warm, living, and immediate language of the believing heart. With all its thoroughness and erudition the Apology is truly edifying, especially the Ger-man version. One cannot read without being touched in his inmost heart, without sensing and feeling something of the heart-beat of the Lutheran confessors. Jacobs, who translated the Apology into English, remarks: "To one charged with the cure of souls the frequent reading of the Apology is invaluable; in many (we may say, in most) parts it is a book of practical religion." (The Book of Concord 2, 41.) The Apology does not offer all man-ner of theories of idle minds, but living testi-monies of what faith, while struggling hotly with the devil and languishing in the fear of death and the terrors of sin and the Law, found and experienced in the sweet Gospel as restored by Luther. In reading the Apology, one can tell from the words employed how Melanchthon lived, moved, and fairly reveled in this blessed truth which in opposition to all heathen work-righteousness teaches terri-fied hearts to rely solely and alone on grace. In his History of Lutheranism (2, 206) Secken-dorf declares that no one can be truly called a theologian of our Church who has not dili-gently and repeatedly read the Apology or familiarized himself with it. (Salig, 1, 375.)

## 59. Moderate Tone of Apology.

The tone of the Apology is much sharper than that of the Augsburg Confession. The situation had changed; hence the manner of dealing with the opposition also changed. The Romanists had fully revealed themselves as implacable enemies, who absolutely refused a peace on the basis of truth and justice. In the Conclusion of the Apology we read: "But as to the want of unity and dissension in the Church, it is well known how these matters first happened, and who caused the division, namely, the sellers of indulgences, who shame-fully preached intolerable lies, and afterwards condemned Luther for not approving of those lies, and besides, they again and again excited more controversies, so that Luther was in-duced to attack many other errors. But since our opponents would not tolerate the truth, and dared to promote manifest errors by force, it is easy to judge who is guilty of the schism. Surely, all the world, all wisdom, all power ought to yield to Christ and His holy Word. But the devil is the enemy of God, and therefore rouses all his might against Christ to extinguish and suppress the Word of God. Therefore the devil with his members, setting himself against the Word of God, is the cause of the schism and want of unity. For we have most zealously sought peace, and still most eagerly desire it, provided only we are not forced to blaspheme and deny Christ. For God, the discerner of all men's hearts, is our witness that we do not delight and have no joy in this awful disunion. On the other hand, our adversaries have so far not been willing to conclude peace without stipulating that we must abandon the saving doctrine of the forgiveness of sin by Christ without our merit, though Christ would be most foully blasphemed thereby." (451.)

Such being the attitude of the Romanists, there was no longer any reason for Melanchthon to have any special consideration for these implacable opponents of the Lutherans and hardened enemies of the Gospel, of the truth, and of religious liberty and peace. Reconciliation with Rome was out of the question. Hence he could yield more freely to his impulse here than in the Augustana; for when this Confession was written, an agreement was not considered impossible. In a letter of July 15, 1530, informing Luther of the pasquinades delivered to the Emperor, Melanchthon declared: "If an answer will become necessary, I shall certainly remunerate these wretched, bloody men. *Si continget, ut respondendum sit, ego profecto remunerabor istos nefarios viros sanguinum.*" (*C. R.* 2, 197.) And when about to conclude the Apology, he wrote to Brenz, April 8, 1531: "I have entirely laid aside the mildness which I formerly exercised toward the opponents. Since they will not employ me as a peacemaker, but would rather have me as their enemy, I shall do what the matter requires, and faithfully defend our cause." (494.) But while Melanchthon castigates the papal theologians, he spares and even defends the Emperor.

In Luther's *Remarks on the Alleged Imperial Edict*, of 1531, we read: "I, Martin Luther, Doctor of the Sacred Scriptures and pastor of the Christians at Wittenberg, in publishing these *Remarks*, wish it to be distinctly understood that anything I am writing in this booklet against the alleged imperial edict or command is not to be viewed as written against His Imperial Majesty or any higher power, either of spiritual or civil estate. . . . I do not mean the pious Emperor nor the pious lords, but the traitors and reprobates (be they princes or bishops), and especially that fellow whom St. Paul calls God's opponent (I should say God's vicar), the arch-knave, Pope Clement, and his servant Campegius, and the like, who plan to carry out their desperate, nefarious roguery under the imperial name, or, as Solomon says, at court." (16, 1666.) Luther then continues to condemn the Diet in unqualified terms. "What a disgraceful Diet," says he, "the like of which was never held and never heard of, and nevermore shall be held or heard of, on account of such disgraceful action! It cannot but re-

main an eternal blot on all princes and the entire empire, and makes all Germans blush before God and all the world." But he continues exonerating and excusing the Emperor: "Let no one tremble on account of this edict which they so shamefully invent and publish in the name of the pious Emperor. And should they not publish their lies in the name of a pious Emperor, when their entire blasphemous, abominable affair "was begun and maintained for over six hundred years in the name of God and the Holy Church?" (16, 1634.)

In a similar manner Melanchthon, too, treats the Emperor. He calls him "*optimum imperatorem,*" and speaks of "the Emperor's most gentle disposition, *mansuetissimum Caesaris pectus,*" which Eck and his party were seeking to incite to bloodshed. (*C. R.* 2, 197.) In the Preface he says: "And now I have written with the greatest moderation possible; and if any expression appears too severe, I must say here beforehand that I am contending with the theologians and monks who wrote the Confutation, and not with the Emperor or the princes, whom I hold in due esteem." (101.) In Article 23 Melanchthon even rises to the apostrophe: "And these their lusts they ask you to defend with your chaste right hand, Emperor Charles (whom even certain ancient predictions name as the king of modest face; for the saying appears concerning you: 'One modest in face shall reign everywhere')." (363.)

The Confutators, however, the avowed enemies of truth and peace, were spared no longer. Upon them Melanchthon now pours out the lye of bitter scorn. He excoriates them as "desperate sophists, who maliciously interpret the holy Gospel according to their dreams," and as "coarse, sluggish, inexperienced theologians." He denounces them as men "who for the greater part do not know whereof they speak," and "who dare to destroy this doctrine of faith with fire and sword," etc. Occasionally Melanchthon even loses his dignified composure. Article 6 we read: "*Quis docuit illos asinos hanc dialecticam?*" Article 9: "*Videant isti asini.*" In his book of 1534 against the Apology, Cochlaeus complains that the youthful Melanchthon called old priests asses, sycophants, windbags, godless sophists, worthless hyocrites, etc. In the margin he had written: "Fierce and vicious he is, a barking dog toward those who are absent, but to those who were present at Augsburg, Philip was more gentle than a pup. *Ferox et mordax est, latrator in absentes, in praesentes erat Augustae omni catello blandior Philippus.*" (Salig, 1, 377.)

On this score, however, Cochlaeus and his papal compeers had no reason to complain, for they had proved to be past masters in vilifying and slandering the Lutherans, as well as implacable enemies, satisfied with nothing short of their blood and utter destruction. As a sample of their scurrility W. Walther quotes the following from a book written by Duke George of Saxony: "Er [Luther] ist gewiss mit dem Teufel besessen, mit der ganzen Legion, welche Christus von den Besessenen austrieb und erlaubte ihnen, in die Schweine zu fahren. Diese Legion hat dem Luther seinen Moenchschaedel hirnwuetig und wirbelsuechtig gemacht. Du unruhiger, treuloser und meineidiger Kuttenbube! Du bist allein der groesste, groebste Esel und Narr, du verfluchter Apostat! Hieraus kann maenniglich abnehmen die Verraeterei und Falschheit deines blutduerstigen Herzens, rachgierigen Gemuets und teuflischen Willens, so du, Luther, gegen deinen Naechsten tobend, als ein toerichter Hund mit offenem Maul ohne Unterlass wagest. Du treuloser Bube und teuflischer Moench! Du deklarierter Mameluck und verdammter Zwiedarm, deren neun einen Pickharden gelten. Ich sage vornehmlich, dass du selbst der allerunverstaendigste Bacchant und zehneckichte Cornut und Bestia . bist. Du meineidiger, treuloser und ehrenbloser Fleischboesewicht! Pfui dich nun, du sakrilegischer, der ausgelaufenen Moenche und Nonnen, der abfaelligen Pfaffen und aller Abtruennigen Hurenwirt! Ei, Doktor Schandluther! Mein Doktor Erzesel, ich will dir's prophezeit haben, der allmaechtige Gott wird dir kuerzlich die Schanze brechen und deiner boshaftigsten, groebsten Eselheit Feierabend geben. Du Sauboze, Doktor Sautrog! Doktor Eselsohr! Doktor Filzhut! Zweiundsiebzig Teufel sollen dich lebendig in den Abgrund der Hoelle fuehren. Ich will machen, dass du als ein Hoellenhund sollst Feuer ausspruehen und dich endlich selbst verbrennen. Ich will dich dem wuetenigen Teufel und seiner Hurenmutter mit einem blutigen Kopf in den Abgrund der Hoelle schicken." (*Luthers Charakter,* 148.)

Despite the occasional asperity referred to, the Apology, as a whole, is written with modesty and moderation. Melanchthon sought to keep the track as clear as possible for a future understanding. In the interest of unity, which he never lost sight of entirely, he was conservative and not disposed needlessly to widen the existing gulf. In the Preface to the Apology he declares: "It has always been my custom in these controversies to retain, so far as I was at all able, the form of the customarily received doctrine, in order that at some time concord could be reached the more readily. Nor, indeed, am I now departing far from this custom, although I could justly lead away the men of this age still farther from the opinions of the adversaries." (101.) This irenic feature is perhaps most prominent in the 10th Article, Of the Lord's Supper, where Melanchthon, in order to satisfy the opponents as to the orthodoxy of the Lutherans in the doctrine of the Real Presence, emphasizes the agreement in such a manner that he has been misunderstood as endorsing also the Romish doctrine of Transubstantiation.

## 60. Symbolical Authority of Apology.

The great importance ascribed to the Apology appears both from its numerous reprints and the strenuous endeavors of the opponents to oppose it with books, which, however, no one was willing to print. The reception accorded it by the Lutherans is described in a letter which Lazarus Spengler sent to Veit Dietrich May 17: "We have received the Apology with the greatest joy and in good hope that it will be productive of much profit among our posterity." Brenz declares it worthy of the canon [worthy of symbolical authority]: "Apologiam, me iudice, canone dignam" (*C. R.* 2, 510), a phrase which Luther had previously applied to Melanchthon's *Loci.* The joy of the Lutherans was equaled only by the consternation of their enemies. The appearance of the Apology surprised and perturbed them. They keenly felt that they were again discredited in the public opinion and had been outwitted by the Lutherans. On November 19 Albert of Mayence sent a copy of the Apology to the Emperor in order to show him how the Catholic religion was being destroyed while the Confutation remained unpublished. Cochlaeus complained that, to judge from letters received, the Apology found approval even in Rome, whereas no printer could be found for Catholic replies to the Apology. He wrote: "Meantime, while we keep silence, they flaunt the Apology and other writings, and not only insult us, but cause our people and cities to doubt and to grow unstable in the faith." (Kolde, 40.)

The Apology, as revised and published by Melanchthon, was a private work. His name, therefore, appeared on the title-page of the edition of 1531, which was not the case with respect to the Confession and Apology presented at Augsburg. The latter were official documents, drawn up by order of the Lutheran princes and estates, while the revised Apology was an undertaking for which Melanchthon had received no commission. Accordingly, as he was not justified in publishing a work of his own under the name of the princes, there was nothing else for him to do than to affix his own signature. In the Preface to the Apology he says: "As it passed through the press, I made some additions. Therefore I give my name, so that no one can complain that the book has been published anonymously." (100.) Melanchthon did not wish to make any one beside himself responsible for the contents of the revised Apology.

Before long, however, the Apology received official recognition. At Schweinfurt, 1532, in opposition to the Papists, the Lutherans appealed to the Augustana and Apology as the confession of their faith, designating the latter as "the defense and explanation of the Confession." And when the Papists advanced the claim that the Lutherans had gone farther in the Apology than in the Augustana, and, April 11, 1532, demanded that they abide by the Augustana, refrain from making the Apology their confession, and accordingly substitute "Assertion" for the title "Apology," the Lutherans, considering the Apology to be the adequate expression of their faith, insisted on the original title. April 17 they declared: "This book was called Apology because it was presented to Caesar after the Confession; nor could they suffer its doctrine and the Word of God to be bound and limited, or their preachers restricted to teach nothing else than the letter of the Augsburg Confession, thus making it impossible for them to rebuke freely and most fully all doctrinal errors, abuses, sins, and crimes. *Nominatum fuisse Apologiam scriptum illud, quod Caesari post Confessionem exhibitum sit, neque se pati posse, ut doctrina sua et Verbum Dei coangustetur, imminuatur et concionatores astringantur, ut nihil aliud praedicent quam ad litteram Augustanae Confessionis, neque libere et plenissime adversus omnes errores doctrinae, abusus, peccata et crimina dicere possint."* Hereupon the Romanists, on April 22, demanded that at least a qualifying explanation be added to the title Apology. Brueck answered on the 23d: "It is not possible to omit this word. The Apology is the correlate of the Confession. Still the princes and their associates do not wish any articles taught other than those which have so far begun to be discussed. *Omitti istud verbum non posse; Apologiam esse correlatum Confessionis; nolle tamen Principes et socios, ut alii articuli docerentur, quam hucusque tractari coepti sint."* (Koellner, 430.)

In his Letter of Comfort, 1533, to the Leipzig Lutherans banished by Duke George, Luther says: "There is our Confession and Apology.... Adhere to our Confession and Apology." (10, 1956.) Membership in the Smalcald League was conditioned on accepting the Apology as well as the Augustana. Both were also subscribed to in the Wittenberg Concord of 1536. (*C. R.* 3, 76.) In 1537, at Smalcald, the Apology (together with the Augustana and the Appendix Concerning the Primacy of the Pope) was, by order of the Evangelical estates, subscribed by all of the theologians present, and thereby solemnly declared a confession of the Lutheran Church. In 1539 Denmark reckoned the Apology among the books which pastors were required to adopt. In 1540 it was presented together with the Augustana at Worms. It was also received into the various *corpora doctrinae.* The Formula of Concord adopts the Apology, saying: "We unanimously confess this [Apology] also, because not only is the said Augsburg Confession explained in it as much as is necessary and guarded [against the slanders of the adversaries], but also proved by clear, irrefutable testimonies of Holy Scripture." (853, 6.)

# VII. Smalcald Articles and Tract concerning Power and Primacy of Pope.

## 61. General Council Demanded by Lutherans.

In order to settle the religious controversy between themselves and the Papists, the Lutherans, from the very beginning, asked for a general council. In the course of years this demand became increasingly frequent and insistent. It was solemnly renewed in the Preface of the Augsburg Confession. The Emperor had repeatedly promised to summon a council. At Augsburg he renewed the promise of convening it within a year. The Roman Curia, however, dissatisfied with the arrangements made at the Diet, found ways and means of delaying it. In 1532, the Emperor proceeded to Bologna, where he negotiated with Clement VII concerning the matter, as appears from the imperial and papal proclamations of January 8 and 10, 1533, respectively. As a result, the Pope, in 1533, sent Hugo Rangon, bishop of Resz, to Germany, to propose that the council be held at Placentia, Bologna, or Mantua. Clement, however, was not sincere in making this offer. In reality he was opposed to holding a council. Such were probably also the real sentiments of his successor, Paul III. But when the Emperor, who, in the interest of his sweeping world policy, was anxious to dispose of the religious controversy, renewed his pressure, Paul finally found himself compelled to yield. June 4, 1536, he issued a bull convoking a general council to meet at Mantua, May 8, 1537. Nothing, however, was said about the principles according to which it was to be formed and by which it should be governed in transacting its business. Self-evidently, then, the

rules of the former councils were to be applied. Its declared purpose was the peace of the Church through the extinction of heresy. In the Bull *Concerning the Reforms of the Roman Court,* which the Pope issued September 23, he expressly declared that the purpose of the council would be "the utter extirpation of the poisonous, pestilential Lutheran heresy." (St. L. 16, 1914.) Thus the question confronting the Protestants was, whether they could risk to appear at such a council, and ought to do so, or whether (and how) they should decline to attend.

Luther, indeed, still desired a council. But after 1530 he no longer put any confidence in a council convened by the Pope, although, for his person, he did not refuse to attend even such a council. This appears also from his conversation, November 7, 1535, with the papal legate Peter Paul Vergerius (born 1497; accused of Lutheranism 1546; deprived of his bishopric 1549; defending Protestantism after 1550; employed by Duke Christoph of Wuerttemberg 1553; died 1564.) Koestlin writes: "Luther relates how he had told the legate: 'Even if you do call a council, you will not treat of salutary doctrine, saving faith, etc., but of useless matters, such as laws concerning meats, the length of priest's garments, exercises of monks, etc.' While he was thus dilating, says Luther, the legate, holding his head in his hand, turned to a near-by companion and said: 'He strikes the nail on the head.' The further utterances of Luther: 'We do not need a council for ourselves and our adherents, for we already have the firm Evangelical doctrine and order; Christendom, how-

*reason why Luther wanted the council*

ever, needs it, in order that those whom error still holds captive may be able to distinguish between error and truth,' appeared utterly intolerable to Vergerius, as he himself relates. He regarded them as unheard-of arrogance. By way of answer, he asked, whether, indeed, the Christian men assembled from all parts of the world, upon whom, without doubt, the Holy Spirit descends, must only decide what Luther approved of. Boldly and angrily interrupting him, Luther said: 'Yes, I will come to the council and lose my head if I shall not defend my doctrine against all the world'; furthermore he exclaimed: 'This wrath of my mouth is not my wrath, but the wrath of God.' Vergerius rejoiced to hear that Luther was perfectly willing to come to the council; for, so he wrote to Rome, he thought that nothing more was needed to break the courage of the heretics than the certain prospect of a council, and at the same time he believed that in Luther's assent he heard the decision of his master, the Elector, also. Luther declared that it was immaterial to him where the council would meet, at Mantua, Verona, or at any other place. Vergerius continued: 'Are you willing to come to Bologna?' Luther: 'To whom does Bologna belong?' Vergerius: 'To the Pope.' Luther: 'Good Lord, has this town, too, been grabbed by the Pope? Very well, I shall come to you there.' Vergerius: 'The Pope will probably not refuse to come to you at Wittenberg either.' Luther: 'Very well, let him come; we shall look for him with pleasure.' Vergerius: 'Do you expect him to come with an army or without weapons?' Luther: 'As he pleases; in whatsoever manner he may come, we shall expect him and shall receive him.' — Luther and Bugenhagen remained with Vergerius until he departed with his train of attendants. After mounting, he said once more to Luther: 'See that you be prepared for the council.' Luther answered: 'Yes, sir, with this my neck and head.'" (*Martin Luther* 2, 382 sq.)

### 62. Luther's Views Regarding the Council.

What Luther's attitude toward a general council was in 1537 is expressed in the Preface to the Smalcald Articles as follows: "But to return to the subject. I verily desire to see a truly Christian council, in order that many matters and persons might be helped. Not that we need it; for our churches are now, through God's grace, so enlightened and equipped with the pure Word and right use of the Sacraments, with knowledge of the various callings and of right works, that we on our part ask for no council, and on such points have nothing better to hope or expect from a council. But we see in the bishoprics everywhere so many parishes vacant and desolate that one's heart would break, and yet neither the bishops nor canons care how the poor people live or die, for whom nevertheless Christ has died, and who are not permitted to hear Him speak with them as the true Shepherd with His sheep. This causes me to shudder and fear that at some time He may

send a council of angels upon Germany utterly destroying us, like Sodom and Gomorrah, because we so wantonly mock Him, with the council." (457.)

From a popish council Luther expected nothing but condemnation of the truth and its confessors. At the same time he was convinced that the Pope would never permit a truly free, Christian council to assemble. He had found him out and knew "that the Pope would see all Christendom perish and all souls damned rather than suffer either himself or his adherents to be reformed even a little, and his tyranny to be limited." (455.) "For with them conscience is nothing, but money, honors, power, are everything." (455. 477.) The Second Part of his Articles Luther concludes as follows: "In these four articles they will have enough to condemn in the council. For they cannot and will not concede to us even the least point in one of these articles. Of this we should be certain, and animate ourselves with the hope that Christ, our Lord, has attacked His adversary, and He will press the attack home both by His Spirit and coming. Amen. For in the council we will stand not before the Emperor or the political magistrate, as at Augsburg (where the Emperor published a most gracious edict, and caused matters to be heard kindly), but before the Pope and devil himself, who intends to listen to nothing, but merely to condemn, to murder, and to force us to idolatry. Therefore we ought not here to kiss his feet or to say, 'Thou art my gracious lord,' but as the angel in Zechariah 3, 2 said to Satan, The Lord rebuke thee, O Satan." (475.) Hence his Preface also concludes with the plaint and prayer: "O Lord Jesus Christ, do Thou Thyself convoke a council, and deliver Thy servants by Thy glorious advent! The Pope and his adherents are done for; they will have none of Thee. Do Thou, then, help us, who are poor and needy, who sigh to Thee, and beseech Thee earnestly, according to the grace which Thou hast given us, through Thy Holy Ghost, who liveth and reigneth with Thee and the Father, blessed forever. Amen." (459.)

### 63. Elector Opposed to Hearing Papal Legate.

From the very beginning, Elector John Frederick was opposed to a council. And the question which particularly engaged his attention was, whether the Lutherans should receive and hear the papal legate who would deliver the invitation. Accordingly, on July 24, the Elector came to Wittenberg and through Brueck delivered four (five) articles to the local theologians and jurists for consideration, with instructions to submit their answer in writing. (*C. R.* 3, 119.) August 1, Melanchthon wrote to Jonas: "Recently the Prince was here and demanded an opinion from all theologians and jurists. . . . It is rumored that a cardinal-legate will come to Germany to announce the council. The Prince is therefore inquiring what to answer, and under what condition the synod might be permitted."

(106.) The articles which Brueck presented dealt mainly with the questions: whether, in view of the fact that the Pope is a party to the issue and his authority to convene a council is questioned, the legate should be heard, especially if the Emperor did not send a messenger along with him; whether one would not already submit himself to the Pope by hearing the legate; whether one ought not to protest, because the Pope alone had summoned the council; and what should be done in case the legate would summon the Elector as a party, and not for consultation, like the other estates. (119 f.)

In the preparation of their answer, the Elector desired the Wittenberg scholars to take into careful consideration also his own view of the matter, which he persistently defended as the only correct one. For this purpose he transmitted to them an opinion of his own on Brueck's articles referred to in the preceding paragraph. In it he maintained that the papal invitation must be declined, because acceptance involved the recognition of the Pope "as the head of the Church and of the council." According to the Elector the proper course for the Lutheran confederates would be to inform the legate, immediately on his arrival in Germany, that they would never submit to the authority which the Pope had arrogated to himself in his proclamation, since the power he assumed was neither more nor less than abominable tyranny; that they could not consider the Pope as differing from, or give him greater honor than, any other ordinary bishop; that, besides, they must regard the Pope as their greatest enemy and opponent; that he had arranged for the council with the sinister object of maintaining his antichristian power and suppressing the holy Gospel; that there was no need of hearing the legate any further, since the Pope, who was sufficiently informed as to their teaching, cared neither for Scripture nor for law and justice, and merely wished to be their judge and lord; that, in public print, they would unmask the roguery of the Pope, and show that he had no authority whatever to convoke a council, but, at the same time, declare their willingness to take part in, and submit their doctrine to, a free, common, Christian, and impartial council, which would judge according to the Scriptures. Nor did the Elector fail to stress the point that, by attending at Mantua, the Lutherans would *de facto* waive their former demand that the council must be held on German soil. (99 ff.)

## 64. Elector Imbued with Luther's Spirit.

Evidently, the Elector had no desire of engaging once more in diplomatic jugglery, such as had been indulged in at Augsburg. And at Smalcald, despite the opposing advice of the theologians, his views prevailed, to the sorrow of Melanchthon, as appears from the latter's complaint to Camerarius, March 1, 1537. (*C. R.* 3, 293.) The Elector was thoroughly imbued with the spirit of Luther, who never felt more antagonistic toward Rome than at Smalcald, although, as shown above,

he was personally willing to appear at the council, even if held at Mantua. This spirit of bold defiance appears from the articles which Luther wrote for the convention, notably from the article on the Papacy and on the Mass. In the latter he declares: "As Campegius said at Augsburg that he would be torn to pieces before he would relinquish the Mass, so, by the help of God, I, too, would suffer myself to be reduced to ashes before I would allow a hireling of the Mass, be he good or bad, to be made equal to Christ Jesus, my Lord and Savior, or to be exalted above Him. Thus we are and remain eternally separated and opposed to one another. They feel well enough that when the Mass falls, the Papacy lies in ruins. Before they will permit this to occur, they will put us all to death if they can." (465.) In the Pope, Luther had recognized the Antichrist; and the idea of treating, seeking an agreement, and making a compromise with the enemy of his Savior, was intolerable to him. At Smalcald, while suffering excruciating pain, he declared, "I shall die as the enemy of all enemies of my Lord Christ." When seated in the wagon, and ready to leave Smalcald, he made the sign of the cross over those who stood about him and said: "May the Lord fill you with His blessing and with hatred against the Pope!" Believing that his end was not far removed, he had chosen as his epitaph: "Living, I was thy pest; dying, I shall be thy death, O Pope! *Pestis eram vivus, moriens ero mors tua, Papa!*"

The same spirit of bold defiance and determination not to compromise the divine truth in any way animated the Elector and practically all of the princes and theologians at Smalcald, with, perhaps, the sole exception of Melanchthon. Koestlin writes: "Meanwhile the allies at Smalcald displayed no lack of 'hatred against the Pope.' His letters, delivered by the legate, were returned unopened. They decidedly refused to take part in the council, and that in spite of the opinion of their theologians, whose reasons Melanchthon again ardently defended. For, as they declared in an explanation to all Christian rulers, they could not submit to a council which, according to the papal proclamation, was convoked to eradicate the Lutheran heresy, would consist only of bishops, who were bound to the Pope by an oath, have as its presiding officer the Pope, who himself was a party to the matter, and would not decide freely according to the Word of God, but according to human and papal decrees. And from the legal standpoint they could hardly act differently. Theologians like Luther could have appeared even before such a council in order to give bold testimony before it. Princes, however, the representatives of the law and protectors of the Church, dared not even create the appearance of acknowledging its legality." (2, 402.)

## 65. Opinion of Theologians.

August 6 the Wittenberg professors assembled to deliberate on Brueck's articles and the views of the Elector. The opinion resolved upon was drawn up by Melanchthon. Its contents may be summarized as follows: The Lutherans must not reject the papal invitation before hearing whether the legate comes with a citation or an invitation. In case they were invited like the rest of the princes to take part in the deliberations, and not cited as a party, this would mean a concession on the part of the Pope, inasmuch as he thereby consented "that the opinion of our gracious Lord [the Elector] should be heard and have weight, like that of the other estates." Furthermore, by such invitation the Pope would indicate that he did not consider these princes to be heretics. If the legate were rebuffed, the Romanists would proceed against the Lutherans as obstinate sinners (contumaces) and condemn them unheard, which, as is well known, would please the enemies best. The Lutherans would then also be slandered before the Emperor as despisers of His Majesty and of the council. Nor did the mere hearing of the legate involve an acknowledgment of the papal authority. "For with such invitation [to attend the council] the Pope does not issue a command, nor summon any one to appear before his tribunal, but before another judge, namely, the Council, the Pope being in this matter merely the commander of the other estates. By hearing the legate, therefore, one has not submitted to the Pope or to his judgments.... For although the Pope has not the authority to summon others by divine law, nevertheless the ancient councils, as, for example, that of Nicaea, have given him this charge, which external church regulation we do not attack. And although in former years, when the empire was under one head, some emperors convoked councils, it would be in vain at present for the Emperor to proclaim a council, as foreign nations would not heed such proclamation. But while the Pope, at present, according to the form of the law, has the charge to proclaim councils, he is thereby not made the judge in matters of faith, for even popes themselves have frequently been deposed by councils. Pope John proclaimed the Council of Constance, but was nevertheless deposed by it." Accordingly the opinion continues: "It is not for us to advise that the council be summarily declined, neither do we consider this profitable, for we have always appealed to a council. What manner of suspicion, therefore, would be aroused with His Imperial Majesty and all nations if at the outset we would summarily decline a council, before discussing the method of procedure!" And even if the Lutherans should be cited [instead of invited], one must await the wording of the citation, "whether we are cited to show the reason for our teaching, or to hear ourselves declared and condemned as public heretics." In the latter case it might be declined. In the former, however, the citation should be accepted, but under the protest "that they had appealed to a free Christian council," and did not acknowledge the Pope as judge. "And if (caeteris paribus, that is, provided the procedure is correct otherwise) the council is considered the highest tribunal,

as it ought to be considered, one cannot despise the command of the person to whom the charge is given to proclaim councils, whoever he may be. But if afterwards the proceedings are not conducted properly, one can then justly lodge complaint on that account." "To proclaim a council is within the province of the Pope; but the judgment and decision belongs to the council. ... For all canonists hold that in matters of faith the council is superior to the Pope, and that in case of difference the council's verdict must be preferred to that of the Pope. For there must be a supreme court of the Church, i. e., the council." On account of the place, however, they should not refuse to appear. (C. R. 3, 119.)

In their subsequent judgments the theologians adhered to the view that the Protestants ought not to incur the reproach of having prevented the council by turning down the legate. Luther says, in an opinion written at Smalcald, February, 1537: "I have no doubt that the Pope and his adherents are afraid and would like to see the council prevented, but in such a manner as would enable them to boast with a semblance of truth that it was not their fault, since they had proclaimed it, sent messengers, called the estates, etc., as they, indeed, would brag and trump it up. Hence, in order that we might be frightened and back out, they have set before us a horrible devil's head by proclaiming a council, in which they mention nothing about church matters, nothing about a hearing, nothing about other matters, but solely speak of the extirpation and eradication of the poisonous Lutheran heresy, as they themselves indicate in the bull De Reformatione Curiae [of September 23, 1536; St. L. 16, 1913 ff.]. Here we have not only our sentence, which is to be passed upon us in the council, but the appeal also with hearing, answer, and discussion of all matters is denied us, and all pious, honorable men who might possibly have been chosen as mediators are also excluded. Moreover, these knaves of the devil are bent on doing their pleasure, not only in condemning (for according to the said bull launched against us they want to be certain of that), but also in speedily beginning and ordering execution and eradication, although we have not yet been heard (as all laws require), nor have they, the cardinals, ever read our writing or learned its doctrine, since our books are proscribed everywhere, but have heard only the false writers and the lying mouths, having not heard us make a reply, although in Germany both princes and bishops know, also those of their party, that they are lying books and rascals, whom the Pope, Italy, and other nations believe. ... Hence they would like to frighten us into refusing it [the Council]; for then they could safely say that we had prevented it. Thus the shame would not only cleave to us, but we would have to bear that, by our refusal, we had helped to strengthen such abominations of the Pope, which otherwise might have been righted." Such and similar reasons prompted Luther to declare that, even though he knew "it would finally end in a scuffle," he was not afraid of "the lousy, contemptible council," and would neither give the legate a negative answer, nor "entangle himself," and therefore not be hasty in the matter. (St. L. 16, 1997.) Even after the princes at Smalcald had resolved not to attend the council, Luther expressed the opinion that it had been false wisdom to decline it; the Pope should have been left without excuse; in case it should convene, the council would now be conducted without the Protestants.

## 66. Elector's Strictures on Opinion of Theologians.

Elector John Frederick was not at all satisfied with the Wittenberg opinion of August 6. Accordingly, he informed the theologians assembled August 30 at Luther's house, through Brueck, that they had permitted themselves to be unduly influenced by the jurists, had not framed their opinion with the diligence required by the importance of the matter, and had not weighed all the dangers lurking in an acceptance of the invitation to the council. If the Lutherans would be invited like the other estates, and attend, they must needs dread a repetition of the craftiness attempted at Augsburg, namely, of bringing their princes in opposition to their preachers. Furthermore, in that case it would also be considered self-evident that the Lutherans submit to the decision of the majority in all matters. And if they refused, what then? "On this wise we, for our part, would be lured into the net so far that we could not, with honor, give a respectable account of our action before the world. For thereupon to appeal from such decision of the council to another would by all the world be construed against our part as capriciousness pure and simple. At all events, therefore, the Lutherans could accept the papal invitation only with a public protest, from which the Pope and every one else could perceive in advance, before the council convened, that the Lutherans would not allow themselves to be lured into the net of a papal council, and what must be the character of the council to which they would assent." (C. R. 3, 147.) In this Protest, which the Elector presented, and which Melanchthon translated into Latin, we read: "By the [possible] acceptance [of the invitation to the council], they [the Lutherans] assent to no council other than a general, free, pious, Christian, and impartial one; not to one either which would be subject to, and bound by, papal prejudices (as the one promised by Clement VII), but to such a synod as will endeavor to bring godly and Christian unity within the Church by choosing pious, learned, impartial, and unsuspected men for the purpose of investigating the religious controversies and adjudicating them from the Word of God, and not in accordance with usage and human traditions, nor on the basis of decisions rendered by former synods that militate against the Word of God." (152. 157.)

## 67. Counter-Council Disadvised.

The other matters which engaged the Elector's attention dealt primarily with measures of defense, the convening of a counter-council *(Gegenkonzil)* and the preparation of articles which all would unanimously accept, and by which they proposed to stand to the uttermost. August 20 Brueck brought these points up for discussion. And in a "memorandum" which the Elector personally presented to the theologians at Wittenberg on December 1, 1536, he expressed his opinion as follows: The Lutherans were not obligated to attend the council, neither would it be advisable. One could not believe or trust the opponents. Nothing but trickery, deception, harm, and destruction might be expected. At the council the Lutheran doctrine would be condemned, and its confessors excommunicated and outlawed. To be sure, the Lutheran cause was in God's hands. And as in the past, so also in the future God would protect it. Still they must not on this account neglect anything. Luther should therefore draw up articles from which he was determined not to recede. After they had been subscribed by the Wittenbergers and by all Evangelical pastors at the prospective meeting [at Smalcald], the question might also be discussed whether the Lutherans should not arrange for a counter-council, "a universal, free, Christian council," possibly at Augsburg. The proclamation for this council might be issued "by Doctor Luther together with his fellow-bishops and ecclesiastics, as the pastors." However, one might also consider whether this should not preferably be done by the princes and estates. In such an event, however, one had to see to it that the Emperor be properly informed, and that the entire blame be saddled upon the Pope and his adherents, the enemies and opponents of our side. (141.)

The seriousness with which the Elector considered the idea of a counter-council appears from the details on which he entered in the "memorandum" referred to, where he puts especial emphasis on the following points: At this free, universal council the Lutherans were minded "to set forth their doctrine and faith according to the divine, holy Scriptures." Every one, whether priest or layman, should be heard in case he wanted to present anything concerning this doctrine from the Holy Scriptures. A free, safe, Christian passport was to be given to all, even to the worst enemy, leaving it to his discretion when to come and go. Only matters founded in the Scriptures were to be presented and discussed at such council. Human laws, ordinances, and writings should under no circumstances be listened to in matters pertaining to faith and conscience, nor be admitted as evidence against the Word of God. "Whoever would submit such matters, should not be heard, but silence enjoined upon him." To the verdict of such a holy and Christian council the Lutherans would be willing to submit their doctrine. (141.)

The theologians answered in an opinion of December 6, 1536, endorsing the Protest referred to above, but disapproving the counter-council. Concerning the first point they advised that a writing be published and sent to the Emperor and all rulers in which the Lutherans were to "request that ways and means be considered of adopting a lawful procedure [at the council] promoting the true Christian unity of Christendom." Concerning the counter-council, however, they advised "at all events not to hasten with it. For to convoke it would produce a great and terrible appearance of creating a schism, and of setting oneself against all the world and contemplating taking the field soon. Therefore such great, apparent resistance should not be undertaken till one intends to do something in the matter openly and in deed." Concerning the defense, the Wittenberg theologians were of the opinion that it was the right and duty of the princes to protect and defend their subjects against notorious injuries (if, for example, an attempt should be made to force upon them the Romish idolatry, or to rend asunder the marriages of their pastors), and also against the Emperor, even after the council had condemned them as heretics. Luther signed this opinion with the following words: "I, too, Martin Luther, will help with my prayers and, if necessary, also with my fist." (126.)

### 68. Articles Drafted by Luther.

In the "memorandum" of December 1 the Elector spoke of the articles Luther was to frame as follows: "Although, in the first place, it may easily be perceived that whatsoever our party may propose in such a [popish] council as has been announced will have no weight with the opposition, miserable, blinded, and mad men that they are, no matter how well it is founded on Holy Scripture, moreover, everything will have to be Lutheran heresy, and their verdict, which probably has already been decided and agreed upon, must be adopted and immediately followed by their proposed ban and interdict [decree excommunicating and outlawing our party], it will, nevertheless, be very necessary for Doctor Martin to prepare his foundation and opinion from the Holy Scriptures, namely, the articles as hitherto taught, preached, and written by him, and which he is determined to adhere to and abide by at the council, as well as upon his departure from this world and before the judgment of Almighty God, and in which we cannot yield without becom'ng guilty of treason against God, even though property and life, peace or war, are at stake. Such articles, however, as are not necessary, and in which, for the sake of Christian love, yet without offense against God and His Word, something might be yielded (though, doubtless, they will be few in number), should in this connection also be indicated separately by said Doctor Martin. And when Doctor Martin has completed such work (which, if at all possible for the Doctor, must be done between the present date and that of the Conversion of St. Paul [January 25], at the latest), he shall thereupon present it to the other Wittenberg

theologians, and likewise to some prominent preachers whose presence he should require, to hear from them, at the same time admonishing them most earnestly, and asking them whether they agreed with him in these articles which he had drawn up, or not, and thereupon, as they hoped for their souls' salvation, their sentiment and opinion be learned in its entirety, but not in appearance, for the sake of peace, or because they did not like to oppose the Doctor, and for this reason would not fully open their hearts, and still, at a later time, would teach, preach, write, and make public something else or advise the people against said articles, as some have in several instances done before this." An agreement having been reached, the articles were to be subscribed by all and prepared in German and Latin. At the prospective meeting [at Smalcald] they should be submitted to the religious confederates for discussion and subscription. Hence, in the invitation, every prince should be asked "to bring with him two or three theologians, in order that a unanimous agreement might be reached there, and no delay could be sought or pretended." (139.) Accordingly, the Elector planned to have Luther draw up articles which were to be accepted by all, first at Wittenberg and then at Smalcald, without compulsion and for no other reason than that they expressed their own inmost convictions. The situation had changed since 1530, and the Elector desired a clearer expression, especially on the Papacy. Hence he did not appoint Melanchthon, but Luther, to compose the articles. The truth was to be confessed without regard to anything else.

Luther had received the order to draw up these articles as early as August 20, 1536. September 3 Brueck wrote to the Elector on this matter: "I also delivered to Doctor Martin the credentials which Your Electoral Grace gave to me, and thereupon also spoke with him in accordance with the command of Your Electoral Grace. He promised to be obedient in every way. It also appears to me that he already has the work well in hand, to open his heart to Your Electoral Grace on religion, which is to be, as it were, his testament." (147.) Luther, who at the time thought that his end would come in the near future, had, no doubt, used such an expression himself. His articles were to be his testament. In the preface to the articles he touched upon it once more, saying: "I have determined to publish these articles in plain print, so that, should I die before there will be a council (as I fully expect and hope, because the knaves who flee the light and shun the day take such wretched pains to delay and hinder the council), those who live and remain after my demise may be able to produce my testimony and confession in addition to the Confession which I previously issued, whereby up to this time I have abided, and by God's grace will abide." (455.)

The Elector seems also to have enjoined silence on Luther with respect to the articles until they had been approved at Wittenberg.

For in his letter to Spalatin, of December 15, 1536, Luther wrote: "But you will keep these matters [his journey to Wittenberg to discuss the articles] as secret as possible, and pretend other reasons for your departure. *Sed haec secreta teneas quantum potes, et finge alias causas abeundi.*" (St. L. 21 b, 2135.) December 11 the Elector again called attention to the articles, desiring that Amsdorf, Agricola, and other outside theologians be called to Wittenberg at his expense to take part in the discussion. Shortly after, Luther must have finished the articles. The numerous changes and improvements appearing in the original manuscript, which is still preserved in the Heidelberg library, show how much time and labor he spent on this work. Concluding his articles, Luther says: "These are the articles on which I must stand, and, God willing, shall stand even to my death; and I do not know how to change or to yield anything in them. If any one wishes to yield anything, let him do it at the peril of his conscience." (501, 3.)

Toward the close of the year Luther submitted the draft to his colleagues, Jonas, Bugenhagen, Cruciger, Melanchthon, and those who had come from abroad, Spalatin, Amsdorf, and Agricola. After thorough discussion it was adopted by all with but few changes, *e. g.*, regarding the adoration of the saints, concerning which Luther had originally said nothing. (Kolde, 44.) Spalatin reports that all the articles were read, and successively considered and discussed. The Elector had spoken also of points in which a concession might be possible. In the discussion at Wittenberg, Spalatin mentioned as such the question whether the Evangelicals, in case the Pope would concede the cup to them, should cease preaching against the continuance of the one kind among the Papists; furthermore, what was to be done with respect to ordination and the adiaphora. Luther had not entered upon a discussion of these questions, chiefly, perhaps, because he was convinced that the council would condemn even the essential articles. (Compare Melanchthon's letter of August 4, 1530, to Campegius, *C. R.* 2, 246.) After the articles had been read and approved, Spalatin prepared a copy (now preserved in the archives at Weimar), which was signed by the eight theologians present, by Melanchthon, however, with the limitation that the Pope might be permitted to retain his authority "iure humano," "in case he would admit the Gospel." Perhaps Melanchthon, who probably would otherwise have dissimulated, felt constrained to add this stricture on account of the solemn demand of the Elector that no one should hide any dissent of his, with the intention of publishing it later. (*C. R.* 3, 140.)

## 69. Articles Endorsed by Elector.

With these first subscriptions, Luther sent his articles to the Elector on January 3, 1537, by the hand of Spalatin. In the accompanying letter of the same date he informed the Elector that he had asked Amsdorf, Eisleben [Agricola], and Spalatin to come to Wittenberg on December 28 or the following days. "I presented the articles which I had myself drawn up according to the command of Your Electoral Grace, and talked them over with them for several days, owing to my weakness, which intervened (as I think, by the agency of Satan); for otherwise I had expected to deliberate upon them no longer than one day. And herewith I am sending them, as affirmed with their signatures, by our dear brother and good friend, Magister George Spalatin, to deliver them to Your Electoral Grace, as they all charged and asked me so to do. At the same time, since there are some who, by suspicion and words, insinuate that we parsons (*Pfaffen*), as they call us, by our stubbornness desire to jeopardize you princes and lords, together with your lands and people, etc., I very humbly ask, also in the name of all of us, that by all means Your Electoral Grace would reprimand us for this. For if it would prove dangerous for other humble people, to say nothing of Your Electoral Grace, together with other lords, lands, and people, we would much rather take it upon ourselves alone. Accordingly, Your Electoral Grace will know well how far and to what extent you will accept these articles, for we would have no one but ourselves burdened with them, leaving it to every one whether he will, or will not, burden also himself with them." (St. L. 21 b, 2142.)

In his answer of January 7, 1537, the Elector expressed his thanks to Luther for having drawn up the articles "in such Christian, true, and pure fashion," and rejoiced over the unanimity of his theologians. At the same time he ordered Chancellor Brueck to take steps toward having the most prominent pastors of the country subscribe the articles, "so that these pastors and preachers, having affixed their names, must abide by these articles and not devise teachings of their own, according to their own opinion and liking, in case Almighty God would summon Doctor Martin from this world, which rests with His good will." (Kolde, 45.) In the letter which the Elector sent to Luther, we read: "We give thanks to Almighty God and to our Lord Christ for having granted you health and strength to prepare these articles in such Christian, true, and pure fashion; also that He has given you grace, so that you have agreed on them with the others in Christian, also brotherly and friendly unity. . . . From them we also perceive that you have changed your mind in no point, but that you are steadfastly adhering to the Christian articles, as you have always taught, preached, and written, which are also built on the foundation, namely, our Lord Jesus Christ, against whom the gates of hell cannot prevail, and who shall also remain in spite of the Pope, the council, and its adherents. May Almighty God, through our Lord Christ, bestow His grace on us all, that with steadfast and true faith we abide by them, and suffer no human fear or opinion to turn us therefrom! . . . After reading them over for the second time, we can entertain no other opinion of them, but accept them as divine, Christian, and true, and accordingly shall also confess them and have them confessed freely and publicly before the council, before the whole world, and whatsoever may come, and we shall ask God that He would vouchsafe grace to our brother and to us, and also to our posterity, that steadfastly and without wavering we may abide and remain in them." (21 b, 2143.)

### 70. Melanchthon's Qualified Subscription.

In his letter to Luther the Elector made special reference also to the qualified subscription of Melanchthon. "Concerning the Pope," he said, "we have no hesitation about resisting him most vehemently. For if, from good opinion, or for the sake of peace, as Magister Philip suggests, we should suffer him to remain a lord having the right to command us, our bishops, pastors, and preachers, we would expose ourselves to danger and burden (because he and his successors will not cease in their endeavors to destroy us entirely and to root out all our posterity), for which there is no necessity, since God's Word has delivered and redeemed us therefrom. And if we, now that God has delivered us from the Babylonian captivity, should again run into such danger and thus tempt God, this [subjection to the Pope] would, by a just decree of God, come upon us through our wisdom, which otherwise, no doubt, will not come to pass." (2145.) Evidently, the Elector, though not regarding Melanchthon's deviation as a false doctrine, did not consider it to be without danger.

At the beginning of the Reformation, Luther had entertained similar thoughts, but he had long ago seen through the Papacy, and abandoned such opinions. In the Smalcald Articles he is done with the Pope and his superiority, also by human right. And this for two reasons: first, because it would be impossible for the Pope to agree to a mere superiority *iure humano*, for in that case "he must suffer his rule and estate to be overturned and destroyed together with all his laws and books; in brief, he cannot do it"; in the second place, because even such a purely human superiority would only harm the Church. (473, 7. 8.) Melanchthon, on the other hand, still adhered to the position which he had occupied in the compromise discussions at Augsburg, whence, *e. g.*, he wrote to Camerarius, August 31, 1530: "Oh, would that I could, not indeed fortify the domination, but restore the administration of the bishops. For I see what manner of church we shall have when the ecclesiastical body has been disorganized. I see that afterwards there will arise a much more intolerable tyranny [of the princes] than there ever was before." (*C. R.* 2, 334.) At Smalcald, however, his views met with so little response among the princes and theologians that in his "Tract on the Primacy of the Pope" he omitted them entirely and followed Luther's trend of thought. March 1, 1537, Melanchthon himself wrote concerning his defeat at the deliberations of the theologians on the question in which articles concessions might be made in the interest of

peace, saying that the unlearned and the more vehement would not hear of concessions, since the Lutherans would then be charged with inconsistency, and the Emperor would only increase his demands. (*C. R.* 3, 292.) Evidently, then, even at that time Melanchthon was not entirely cured of his utopian dream.

"If the Pontiff would admit the Gospel, *si pontifex evangelium admitteret*." A. Osiander remarked: "That is, if the devil would become an apostle." In the Jena edition of Luther's works Melanchthon's phrase is commented upon as follows: "And yet the Pope with his wolves, the bishops, even now curses, blasphemes, and outlaws the holy Gospel more horribly than ever before, raging and fuming against the Church of Christ and us poor Christians in most horrible fashion, both with fire and sword, and in whatever way he can, like a real werwolf, aye, like the very devil himself." (6, 557 b.) The same comment is found in the edition of the Smalcald Articles prepared 1553 by Stolz and Aurifaber, where the passage begins: "O quantum mutatus ab illo [the former Melanchthon]!" (Koellner, 448. 457.) Carpzov remarks pertinently: "This subscription [of Melanchthon] is not a part of the Book of Concord [it does not contain the doctrine advocated by the Book of Concord], nor was it approved by Luther; moreover, it was later on repudiated by Philip himself." (*Isagoge* 823. 894.)

### 71. Luther's Articles Sidetracked at Smalcald.

It was a large and brilliant assembly, especially of theologians, which convened at Smalcald in February, 1537. Luther, too, was present. On January 7 the Elector had written: "We hope that our God will grant you grace, strength, and health that you may be able to make the journey to Smalcald with us, and help us to right, and bring to a good issue, this [matter concerning the Pope] and other matters."

As stated above, the Elector's plan was to elevate Luther's articles to a confession officially recognized and subscribed to by all Lutheran princes, estates, and theologians. Accordingly, on February 10, at the first meeting held at Smalcald, Chancellor Brueck moved that the theologians deliberate concerning the doctrine, so that, in case the Lutherans would attend the council, they would know by what they intended to stand, and whether any concessions were to be made, or, as Brueck put it, "whether anything good [perhaps a deliverance on the Papacy] should be adopted, or something should be conceded."

Self-evidently, Brueck had Luther's articles in mind, although it cannot be proved that he directly and expressly mentioned them or submitted them for discussion and adoption. Perhaps, he felt from the very beginning that the Elector would hardly succeed with his plans as smoothly and completely as anticipated. For Luther, desiring to clear the track for the whole truth in every direction, the Reformed as well as the Papistic, both against the "false brethren who would be of our party"

(Preface to Sm. Art. 455, 4), as well as against the open enemies, had in his articles so sharpened the expressions employed in the Wittenberg Concord of 1536 concerning the Lord's Supper that the assent of Philip of Hesse and the attending South German delegates and theologians (Bucer, Blaurer, Wolfart, etc.) was more than doubtful. Luther's letter to the adherents of Zwingli, December 1, 1537, shows that he did not at all desire unnecessarily to disturb the work of union begun by the Wittenberg Concord. (St. L. 17, 2143.) Still, he at the same time endeavored to prevent a false union resting on misunderstanding and self-deception. And, no doubt, his reformulation of the article on the Lord's Supper was intended to serve this purpose. Besides, owing to a very painful attack of gravel, Luther was not able to attend the sessions, hence could not make his influence felt in a decisive manner as desired by the Elector.

This situation was exploited by Melanchthon in the interest of his attitude toward the Zwinglians, which now was much more favorable than it had been at Augsburg, 1530. From the very outset he opposed the official adoption of Luther's articles. He desired more freedom with regard to both the Romanists and the Reformed than was offered by Luther's articles. The first appears from his subscription. Concerning the article of the Lord's Supper, however, which the Strassburgers and others refused to accept, Melanchthon does not seem to have voiced any scruples during the deliberations at Wittenberg. Personally he may even have been able to accept Luther's form, and this, too, more honestly than Bucer did at Smalcald. For as late as September 6, 1557, he wrote to Joachim of Anhalt: "I have answered briefly that in doctrine all are agreed, and that we all embrace and retain the Confession with the Apology and Luther's confession written before the Synod of Mantua. *Respondi breviter, consensum esse omnium de doctrina: amplecti nos omnes et retinere Confessionem cum Apologia et confessione Lutheri scripta ante Mantuanam Synodum.*" (*C. R.* 9, 260.) But, although Melanchthon, for his person, accepted Luther's article on the Lord's Supper, he nevertheless considered it to be dangerous to the Concord with the Southern Germans and to the Smalcald League. Privately he also made known his dissatisfaction in no uncertain manner. And in so doing, he took shelter behind Philip of Hesse, who, as at Augsburg, 1530, still desired to have the Zwinglians regarded and treated as weak brethren.

Kolde relates: "On the same day (February 10) Melanchthon reported to the Landgrave: 'One article, that concerning the Sacrament of the Holy Supper, has been drawn up somewhat vehemently, in that it states that the bread *is* the body of the Lord, which Luther at first did not draw up in this form, but, as contained in the [Wittenberg] Concord, namely, that the body of the Lord is given with the bread; and this was due to Pomeranus, for he is a vehement man and

a coarse Pomeranian. Otherwise he [Melanchthon] knew of no shortcoming or complaint in all the articles.' . . . 'He also said' (this the Landgrave reports to Jacob Sturm of Strassburg as an expression of Melanchthon) 'that Luther would hear of no yielding or receding, but declared: This have I drawn up; if the princes and estates desired to yield anything, it would rest with them,' etc. The estates, Melanchthon advised, might therefore in every way declare that they had adopted the Confession and the Concord, and were minded to abide by them. At the same time he promised to demand at the prospective deliberation of the theologians, 'that the article of the Sacrament be drawn up as contained in the Concord.' Melanchthon's assertion that Bugenhagen influenced Luther's formulation of the article on the Lord's Supper is probably correct. At any rate, it can be proved that Luther really changed the article. For a glance at the original manuscript shows that he had at first written, in conformity with the Concord, 'that the true body and blood of Christ is under the bread and wine,' but later on changed it to read: 'that the bread and wine of the Lord's Supper are the true body and blood of Christ.'" (48.) Melanchthon was diplomatic enough to hide from the Landgrave his strictures on Luther's articles about the Pope, knowing well that in this point he could expect neither approval nor support.

## 72. Articles Not Discussed in Meeting of League.

As the Southern Germans regarded Luther's formulation of the article on the Lord's Supper with disfavor, the Landgrave found little difficulty in winning over (through Jacob Sturm) the delegates of Augsburg and Ulm to Melanchthon's view of declaring adherence only to the Confession and the Wittenberg Concord. Already on February 11 the cities decided to "decline on the best grounds" the Saxon proposition. Following were the reasons advanced: It was not necessary at present to enter upon the proposition, since the council would make slow progress, as the Emperor and the King of France were not yet at peace. They had not understood this (the adoption of the Saxon proposition) to be the purpose of the invitation to bring scholars with them. They had a confession, the Augustana, presented to the Emperor. It was also to be feared that deliberations on the question whether any concessions should be made, might lead to a division; nor would this remain concealed from the Papists. If the Elector desired to present some articles, he might transmit them, and they, in turn, would send them to their superiors for inspection. (Kolde, *Analecta*, 296.)

In the afternoon of February 11 the princes, according to the report of the Strassburgers, expressed their satisfaction with the resolution of the cities. At the same time they declared that they were not minded to make any concessions to the Papists, nor to dispute about, or question, anything in the Confession or the

Wittenberg Concord, "but merely to review the Confession, not to change anything against its contents and substance, nor that of the Concord, but solely to enlarge on the Papacy, which before this, at the Diet, had been omitted, in order to please His Imperial Majesty and for other reasons"; that such was the purpose of the deliberation for which the scholars had been summoned; and that this was not superfluous, since "they were all mortal, and it was necessary that their posterity be thoroughly informed as to what their doctrine had been, lest others who would succeed to their places accept something else." The report continues: "The cities did not object to this." (296.) According to this report, then, Luther's articles were neither discussed nor adopted at the official meeting of the princes and estates belonging to the Smalcald League. Without mentioning them, they declared in their final resolution: Our scholars have "unanimously agreed among themselves in all points and articles contained in our Confession and Apology, presented at the Diet of Augsburg, excepting only that they have expanded and drawn up more clearly than there contained one article, concerning the Primacy of the Pope of Rome." (Koellner, 468.) Koestlin remarks: "Since the princes decided to decline the council absolutely, they had no occasion to discuss Luther's articles." (2, 403.)

### 73. Meeting of Theologians.

At Smalcald the first duty imposed upon the scholars and theologians was once more to discuss the Augustana and the Apology carefully, and to acknowledge both as their own confessions by their signatures. Thereupon they were, in a special treatise, to enlarge on the Papacy. The Strassburg delegates report: "It has also come to pass that the scholars received orders once more to read the articles of the Confession and to enlarge somewhat on the Papacy, which they did." (Kolde, *Analecta*, 298.) However, since neither the Augustana nor its Apology contained an article against the Papacy, the demand of the princes could only be satisfied by a special treatise, the "Tractatus de Potestate et Primatu Papae," which Melanchthon wrote and completed by February 17, whereupon it was immediately delivered to the princes.

The princes had furthermore ordered the theologians, while reviewing and discussing the Augustana (and its Apology), to reenforce its doctrine with additional proofs. Owing to lack of time and books, this was not carried out. February 17 Osiander reports to the Nuernberg preachers: "We are enjoying good health here, although we traveled in stormy weather and over roads that offered many difficulties, and are living under a constantly beclouded sky, which unpleasantries are increased by troublesome and difficult questions in complicated matters. . . . The first business imposed on us by the princes embraces two things: first, to fortify the Confession and the Apology with every kind

of argument from the Holy Scriptures, the fathers, councils, and the decrees of the Popes; thereupon, diligently to discuss in detail everything concerning the Primacy, which was omitted in the Confession because it was odious. The latter we completed so far to-day that we shall immediately deliver a copy to the princes. The former, however, will be postponed to another time and place, since it requires a longer time, as well as libraries, which are lacking here." (*C. R.* 3, 267.)

The discussion of the Confession was also to serve the purpose of obtaining mutual assurance whether they were all really agreed in doctrine. This led to deliberations on the doctrine of the Lord's Supper as well as on the question what concessions might be made to the Romanists. According to a report of Melanchthon, March 1, the theologians were to discuss the doctrines, not superficially, but very thoroughly, in order that all disagreement might be removed, and a harmonious and complete system of doctrines exist in our churches. They were to review the Confession in order to learn whether any one deviated in any article or disapproved of anything. But Melanchthon remarks that this object was not reached, since the special request had been voiced not to increase the disagreement by any quarrel and thus to endanger the Smalcald League. (*C. R.* 3, 292.) In a second letter of the same date he says that a real doctrinal discussion had never come to pass, partly because Luther's illness prevented him from taking part in the meetings, partly because the timidity of certain men [the Landgrave and others] had prevented an exact disputation, lest any discord might arise. (295.) March 3 he wrote to Jonas in a similar vein, saying that the reports of violent controversies among the theologians at Smalcald were false. For although they had been in consultation with one another for the purpose of discovering whether all the theologians in attendance there agreed in doctrine, the matter had been treated briefly and incidentally. (298.)

As far as the Lord's Supper is concerned, Melanchthon's report concerning the superficial character of the doctrinal discussions is little, if at all, exaggerated. He himself was one of those timid souls of whom he spoke, having from the beginning done all he could not only to bar Luther's articles from the deliberations, but also to prevent any penetrating discussion of the Lord's Supper. Assent to the Wittenberg Concord was considered satisfactory, although all felt, and believed to know, that some of the Southern Germans did not agree with the loyal Lutherans in this matter. Of the attending theologians who were under suspicion, Bucer, Blaurer, Fagius, Wolfart, Fontanus, and Melander, only the first two took part in the deliberations. (292.) March 1 Melanchthon wrote to Camerarius: "Bucer spoke openly and clearly of the Mystery [the Lord's Supper], affirming the presence of Christ. He satisfied all of our party, also those who are more severe. Blaurer, however, employed such general expressions as, that Christ was present. Afterward he added several more ambiguous expressions. Osiander pressed him somewhat hotly; but since we did not desire to arouse any very vehement quarrel, I terminated the discussion. Thus we separated, so that agreement was restored among all others, while he [Blaurer] did not seem to contradict. I know that this is weak, but nothing else could be done at this time, especially since Luther was absent, being tortured by very severe gravel pains." (292.)

This agrees with the report Veit Dietrich made to Foerster, May 16, stating: At the first meeting of the committee of the theologians they completed the first nine articles of the Augustana. Blaurer, Wolfart, and some others of those who were doctrinally under suspicion (*nobis suspecti de doctrina*) were present. "However, when the article of the Lord's Supper was to be discussed on the following day, the meeting was prevented, I do not know by whom. It is certain that the princes, too, desired another meeting, because they feared a rupture of the [Smalcald] Alliance, if any doctrinal difference should become evident, which, however, would occur if the matter were thoroughly discussed. Since the disputation was prevented, we were commissioned to write on the Power of the Pope, in order to have something to do. Report had it that Blaurer did not approve the Concord of Wittenberg; certainly, he asked Philip for expressions of the Fathers (which are now in my possession), in order to be better furnished with arguments. This prompted Pomeranus and Amsdorf again to convene the theologians against Melanchthon's will. Then the Lord's Supper was discussed. Bucer indeed satisfied all. Blaurer, however, while speaking vaguely of the other matters, nevertheless publicly attacked the statement that the ungodly do not receive the body of Christ." Wolfart declared that he was present at the Concord made at Wittenberg, and had approved it. It was unpleasant for him [Dietrich] when hereupon Stephanus Agricola and then Wolfart rehashed some old statements, *vetera quaedam dicta*. (370.)

## 74. Luther's Articles Subscribed.

As to the articles of Luther, Veit Dietrich reports that they were privately circulated at Smalcald and read by all. They were also to be read at the meeting of the theologians on February 18. (*C. R.* 3, 371.) As a matter of fact, however, neither a public reading nor a real discussion, nor an official adoption resulted. The Strassburg delegates report: "Doctor Martin Luther has also drawn up some special articles, which he purposed to send to the council on his own accord, copies of which we have designated with W." The Strassburgers, then, were in position to send home a copy of these articles. Furthermore, Osiander relates in a letter dated February 17: "Besides this, Luther has also written articles at Wittenberg, short indeed, but splendid and keen (*illustres et argutos*), in which everything is summed up in German wherefrom we

cannot recede in the council without committing sacrilege. To-morrow we shall read them publicly in our meeting, in order that any one who wishes to add anything to them may present this in the presence of all. They will also, as I hope, deliberate on the [Wittenberg] Concord in the matter concerning the Lord's Supper. I regard Bucer as being sincerely one of us; Blaurer, however, by no means. For Philip tells of his having remarked that he was not able to agree with us." (268.) On February 18, however, Luther was taken ill, and an official, public reading and discussion of his articles did not take place on this day, nor, as already stated, at a later date.

Luther's articles, however, were nevertheless adopted at Smalcald, though not by the South Germans. When all other business had been transacted, they were presented for voluntary subscription. Bugenhagen had called the theologians together for this purpose. He proposed that now all those who wished (*qui velint*) should sign the articles Luther had brought with him. Hereupon Bucer declared that he had no commission to do this. However, in order to obliterate the impression that he declined to subscribe because of doctrinal differences, he added that he knew nothing in Luther's articles which might be criticized. Blaurer of Constance, Melander of Hesse, and Wolfart of Augsburg followed his example in declaring that they had no commission to sign the articles. In order not to endanger the Smalcald League, Bugenhagen, as appears from his proposition, refrained from urging any one to sign. This was also the position of the other theologians.

Veit Dietrich reports: "Bucer was the first to say that he had no orders to sign. He added, however, that he knew of nothing in these articles that could be criticized, but that his magistrates had reasons for instructing him not to sign them. Afterwards Blaurer, Dionysius Melander, and your Boniface [Wolfart of Augsburg] said the same [that they had not been authorized by their superiors to sign]. The thought came to me immediately why Bucer, who taught correctly, should have been the first to refuse his signature, since it was certain that the others, Blaurer and, if you will, also your man, would not subscribe because they did not approve of the dogma of the Lord's Supper. This would have led to an open doctrinal schism, which the Elector, Ernst of Lueneburg, and the Counts of Anhalt would, under no circumstances, have tolerated among the confederates. But, since Bucer did not subscribe, it was not necessary to dispute about the doctrine. When we saw this, I was also pleased that Luther's articles received no attention [in the official subscription], and that all subscribed merely to the Augustana and the Concord. And there was no one who refused to do this." (371.)

While thus Bucer, Fagius, Wolfart, Blaurer, and Fontanus refused to affix their signatures, the attending loyal Lutheran theologians endorsed Luther's articles all the more enthusiastically. And while the signatures affixed to the Augustana and the Apology total 32, including the suspected theologians, 44 names appear under Luther's articles. Among these is found also the abnormal subscription of Melander of Hesse: "I subscribe to the Confession, the Apology, and the Concord in the matter of the Eucharist," which is probably to be interpreted as a limitation of Luther's Article of the Lord's Supper.

Although, therefore, the subscription of the Smalcald Articles lacked the official character and was not by order of the Smalcald League as such, it nevertheless is in keeping with the actual facts when the Formula of Concord refers to Luther's Articles as "subscribed at that time [1537] by the chief theologians." (777, 4; 853, 7.) All true Lutheran pastors assembled at Smalcald recognized in Luther's articles their own, spontaneous confession against the Papists as well as against the Zwinglians and other enthusiasts.

### 75. Endorsed by Princes and Estates.

The Thorough Declaration of the Formula of Concord makes the further statement that the Smalcald Articles were to be delivered in the Council at Mantua "in the name of the Estates, Electors, and Princes." (853, 7.) Evidently this is based on Luther's Preface to the Smalcald Articles, written 1538, in which he says concerning his Articles: "They have also been accepted and unanimously confessed by our side, and it has been resolved that, in case the Pope with his adherents should ever be so bold as seriously and in good faith, without lying and cheating, to hold a truly free Christian Council (as, indeed, he would be in duty bound to do), they be publicly delivered in order to set forth the Confession of our Faith." (455.)

Kolde and others surmise that Luther wrote as he did because, owing to his illness, he was not acquainted with the true situation at Smalcald. Tschackert, too, takes it for granted that Luther, not being sufficiently informed, was under the erroneous impression that the princes and estates as well as the theologians had adopted, and subscribed to, his articles. (300. 302.) Nor has a better theory of solving the difficulty hitherto been advanced. Yet it appears very improbable. If adopted, one must assume that Luther's attention was never drawn to this error of his. For Luther does not merely permit his assertion to stand in the following editions of the Smalcald Articles, but repeats it elsewhere as well. In an opinion written 1541 he writes: "In the second place, I leave the matter as it is found in the articles adopted at Smalcald; I shall not be able to improve on them; nor do I know how to yield anything further." (St. L. 17, 666.)

The Elector, too, shared Luther's opinion. In a letter of October 27, 1543, he urged him to publish in Latin and German (octavo), under the title, *Booklet of the Smalcald Agreement — Buechlein der geschehenen Schmalkaldischen Vergleichung,* the "Articles of Agreement, Vergleichungsartikel," on which he and Melanchthon had come to an agreement in 1537, at Smalcald, with the other allied

estates, scholars, and theologians. (St. L. 21, 2913.) October 17, 1552, immediately afte. he had obtained his liberty, the Elector made a similar statement. (*C. R.* 7, 1109.) Nor did Spalatin possess a knowledge in this matter differing from that of Luther and the Elector. He, too, believed that not only the theologians, but the princes and estates as well, with the exception of Hesse, Wuerttemberg, Strassburg, etc., had subscribed to Luther's articles. (Kolde, 51.)

Evidently, then, Luther's statement was generally regarded as being substantially and approximately correct and for all practical purposes in keeping, if not with the exact letter and form, at least with the real spirit of what transpired at Smalcald and before as well as after this convention. It was not a mere delusion of Luther's, but was generally regarded as agreeing with the facts, that at Smalcald his articles were not only subscribed by the theologians, but adopted also by the Lutheran princes and estates, though, in deference to the Landgrave and the South German cities, not officially and by the Smalcald League as such.

### 76. Symbolical Authority of Smalcald Articles.

The importance attached to the Smalcald Articles over against the Reformed and Crypto-Calvinists appears from a statement made by the Elector of Saxony, October 17, 1552 (shortly after his deliverance from captivity), in which he maintained that the Lutheran Church could have been spared her internal dissensions if every one had faithfully abided by the articles of Luther. He told the Wittenberg theologians that during his captivity he had heard of the dissensions and continued controversies, "which caused us no little grief. And we have therefore often desired with all our heart that in the churches of our former lands and those of others no change, prompted by human wisdom, had been undertaken nor permitted in the matters [doctrines] as they were held during the life of the blessed Doctor Martin Luther and during our rule, and confirmed at Smalcald, in the year 1537, by all pastors and preachers of the estates of the Augsburg Confession then assembled at that place. For if this had been done, no doubt, the divisions and errors prevailing among the teachers of said Confession, together with the grievous and harmful offenses which resulted therefrom, would, with the help of God, have been avoided." (*C. R.* 7, 1109.)

In the Prolegomena to his edition of the Lutheran Confessions, Hase remarks concerning the symbolical authority of Luther's articles: "The formula of faith, drawn up by such a man, and adorned with such names, immediately enjoyed the greatest authority. *Fidei formula a tali viro profecta talibusque nominibus ornata maxima statim auctoritate floruit.*" To rank among the symbolical books, Luther's articles required a special resolution on the part of the princes and estates as little as did his two catechisms; contents and the

Reformer's name were quite sufficient. Voluntarily the articles were subscribed at Smalcald. On their own merits they won their place of honor in our Church. In the situation then obtaining, they voiced the Lutheran position in a manner so correct and consistent that every loyal Lutheran spontaneously gave and declared his assent. In keeping with the changed historical context of the times, they offered a correct explanation of the Augsburg Confession, adding thereto a declaration concerning the Papacy, the absence of which had become increasingly painful. They struck the timely, logical, Lutheran note also over against the Zwinglian and Bucerian [Reformed and Unionistic] tendencies. Luther's articles offered quarters neither for disguised Papists nor for masked Calvinists. In brief, they gave such a clear expression to genuine Lutheranism that false spirits could not remain in their company. It was the recognition of these facts which immediately elicited the joyful acclaim of all true Lutherans. To them it was a recommendation of Luther's articles when Bucer, Blaurer, and others, though having subscribed the Augsburg Confession, refused to sign them. Loyal Lutherans everywhere felt that the Smalcald Articles presented an up-to-date touchstone of the pure Lutheran truth, and that, in taking their stand on them, their feet were planted, over against the aberrations of the Romanists as well as the Zwinglians, on ground immovable.

In the course of time, the esteem in which Luther's articles were held, rose higher and higher. Especially during and after the controversies on the Interim, as well as in the subsequent controversies with the Crypto-Calvinists, the Lutherans became more and more convinced that the Smalcald Articles, and not the Variata, contained the correct exposition of the Augsburg Confession. At the Diet of Regensburg, in 1541, the Elector, by his delegates, sent word to Melanchthon "to stand by the Confession and the Smalcald Agreement [Smalcald Articles] in word and in sense." The delegates answered that Philip would not yield anything "which was opposed to the Confession and the Smalcald Agreement," as he had declared that "he would die rather than yield anything against his conscience." (*C. R.* 4, 292.) In an opinion of 1544 also the theologians of Hesse, who at Smalcald had helped to sidetrack Luther's articles, put them on a par with the Augustana. At Naumburg, in 1561, where Elector Frederick of the Palatinate and the Crypto-Calvinists endeavored to undermine the authority of Luther, Duke John Frederick of Saxony declared that he would abide by the original Augustana and its "true declaration and norm," the Smalcald Articles.

Faithful Lutherans everywhere received the Smalcald Articles into their *corpora doctrinae.* In 1557 the Convention of Coswig declared them to be "the norm by which controversies are to be decided, *norma decidendi controversias.*" Similarly, the Synod of Moelln, 1559. In 1560 the ministerium of Luebeck and the

Senate of Hamburg confessionally accepted the Articles. Likewise, the Convention of Lueneburg in 1561, and the theologians of Schleswig-Holstein in 1570. The Thorough Declaration could truthfully say that the Smalcald Articles had been embodied in the confessional writings of the Lutheran Church, "for the reason that these have always and everywhere been regarded as the common, unanimously accepted meaning of our churches, and, moreover, have been subscribed at that time by the chief and most enlightened theologians, and have held sway in all evangelical churches and schools." (855, 11.)

## 77. Editions of Smalcald Articles.

In 1538 Luther published his Articles, which *editio princeps* was followed by numerous other editions, two of them in the same year. In the copy of the Articles which Spalatin took at Wittenberg the title reads: "Opinion concerning the Faith, and What We Must Adhere to Ultimately at the Future Council. *Bedenken des Glaubens halben, und worauf im kuenftigen Konzil endlich zu beharren sei.*" The *editio princeps* bears the title: "Articles which were to be Delivered on Behalf of Our Party at the Council of Mantua, or Where Else It Would Meet. *Artikel, so da haetten aufs Konzilium zu Mantua, oder wo es wuerde sein, ueberantwortet werden von unsers Teils wegen.*" These titles designate the purpose for which the articles were framed by order of the Elector. In the edition of 1553, published by John Stolz and John Aurifaber, Luther's Articles are designated as "prepared for the Diet of Smalcald in the year 1537, *gestellt auf den Tag zu Schmalkalden Anno 1537.*" Says Carpzov: "They are commonly called Smalcald Articles after the place where they were composed [an error already found in Brenz's letter of February 23, 1537, appended to the subscriptions of the "Tract on the Power and Primacy of the Pope" (529). See also Formula of Concord 777, 4; 853, 7], as well as solemnly approved and subscribed, since the articles were composed by Luther and approved by the Protestants at Smalcald, a town in the borders of Saxony and Ducal Hesse, and selected for the convention of the Protestants for the reason that the individuals who had been called thither might have an easy and safe approach." (*Isagoge,* 769.)

The text of the Smalcald Articles, as published by Luther, omits the following motto found in the original: "This is sufficient doctrine for eternal life. As to the political and economic affairs, there are enough laws to trouble us, so that there is no need of inventing further troubles much more burdensome. Sufficient unto the day is the evil thereof. *His satis est doctrinae pro vita aeterna. Caeterum in politia et oeconomia satis est legum, quibus vexamur, ut non sit opus praeter has molestias fingere alias quam miserrimas [necessarias]. Sufficit diei malitia sua.*" (Luther, Weimar 50, 192. St. L. 16, 1918.) Apart from all kinds of minor corrections, Luther added to the text a Preface (written 1538) and several additions, some of them quite long, which, however, did not change the sense. Among these are § 5, §§ 13 to 15, and §§ 25—28 of the article concerning the Mass; §§ 42—45 concerning the False Repentance of the Papists; §§ 3—13 about Enthusiasm in the article concerning Confession. The editions of 1543 and 1545 contained further emendations. The German text of Luther's first edition of 1538 was received into the Book of Concord, "as they were first framed and printed." (853, 7.) The first Latin translation by Peter Generanus appeared in 1541, with a Preface by Veit Amerbach (later on Catholic Professor of Philosophy at Ingolstadt). In 1542 it was succeeded by an emended edition. In the following year the Elector desired a Latin-German edition in octavo. The Latin translation found in the Book of Concord of 1580 was furnished by Selneccer; this was revised for the official Latin Concordia of 1584.

### 78. Tract on the Power and Primacy of the Pope.

Melanchthon's "Tract Concerning the Power and Primacy of the Pope, *Tractatus de Potestate et Primatu Papae*," presents essentially the same thoughts Luther had already discussed in his article "Of the Papacy." Melanchthon here abandons the idea of a papal supremacy *iure humano*, which he had advocated at Augsburg 1530 and expressed in his subscription to Luther's articles, and moves entirely in the wake of Luther and in the trend of the Reformer's thoughts. The Tract was written not so much from his own conviction as from that of Luther and in accommodation to the antipapal sentiment which, to his grief, became increasingly dominant at Smalcald. (*C. R.* 3, 270. 292 f. 297.) In a letter to Jonas, February 23, he remarks, indicating his accommodation to the public opinion prevailing at Smalcald: "I have written this [Tract] somewhat sharper than I am wont to do." (271. 292.) Melanchthon always trimmed his sails according to the wind; and at Smalcald a decidedly antipapal gale was blowing. He complains that he found no one there who assented to his opinion that the papal invitation to a council ought not be declined. (293.) It is also possible that he heard of the Elector's criticism of his qualified subscription to Luther's articles. At all events, the Tract amounts to a retraction of his stricture on Luther's view of the Papacy. In every respect, Smalcald spelled a defeat for Melanchthon. His policy toward the South Germans was actually repudiated by the numerous and enthusiastic subscriptions to Luther's articles, foreshadowing, as it were, the final historical outcome, when Philippism was definitely defeated in the Formula of Concord. And his own Tract gave the *coup de grace* to his mediating policy with regard to the Romanists. For here Melanchthon, in the manner of Luther, opposes and denounces the Pope as the Antichrist, the protector of ungodly doctrine and customs, and the persecutor of the true confessors of Christ, from whom one must separate. The second part

of the Tract, "Concerning the Power and the Jurisdiction of the Bishops, *De Potestate et Iurisdictione Episcoporum*," strikes an equally decided note.

The Tract, which was already completed by February 17, received the approval of the estates, and, together with the Augustana and the Apology, was signed by the theologians upon order of the princes. (*C. R.* 3, 286.) Koellner writes: "Immediately at the convention Veit Dietrich translated this writing [the Tract] into German, and (as appears from the fact that the Weimar theologians in 1553 published the document from the archives with the subscriptions) this German translation was, at the convention, presented to, and approved by, the estates as the official text, and subscribed by the theologians." (464.) Brenz's letter appended to the subscriptions shows that the signing did not take place till after February 23, perhaps the 25th of February. For on the 26th Melanchthon and Spalatin refer to it as finished.

With reference to the Concord of 1536, let it be stated here that, although mentioned with approval by the theologians and also included in Brenz's and Melander's subscriptions to the Smalcald Articles, the princes and estates nevertheless passed no resolution requiring its subscription. Melanchthon writes that the princes had expressly declared that they would abide by the Wittenberg Concord. (*C. R.* 3, 292.) Veit Dietrich's remark to Foerster, May 16, 1537, that only the Augustana and the Concord were signed at Smalcald, is probably due to a mistake in writing. (372.)

### 79. Authorship of Tract.

The Tract first appeared in print in 1540. A German translation, published 1541, designates it as "drawn up by Mr. Philip Melanchthon and done into German by Veit Dietrich." (*C. R.* 23, 722.) In the edition of the Smalcald Articles by Stolz and Aurifaber, 1553, the Tract is appended with the caption: "Concerning the Power and Supremacy of the Pope, Composed by the Scholars. Smalcald, 1537." In the Jena edition of Luther's Works the Smalcald Articles are likewise followed by the Tract with the title: "Concerning the Power and Supremacy of the Pope, Composed by the Scholars in the Year 37 at Smalcald and Printed in the Year 38." (6, 523.) This superscription gave rise to the opinion that the German was the original text. At any rate, such seems to have been the belief of Selneccer, since he incorporated a Latin translation, based on the German text, into the Latin edition of his Book of Concord, privately published 1580. Apart from other errors, this Latin version contained also the offensive misprint referred to in our article on the Book of Concord (p. 5). In the official edition of 1584 it was supplanted by the original text of Melanchthon. The subtitle, however, remained: "Tractatus per Theologos Smalcaldicos Congregatos Conscriptus."

To-day it is generally assumed that by 1553 it was universally forgotten both that Melanchthon was the author of the Tract, and that it was originally composed in Latin. However, it remains a mystery how this should have been possible — only twelve years after Dietrich had published the Tract under a title which clearly designates Melanchthon as its author, and states that the German text is a translation. The evidence for Melanchthon's authorship which thus became necessary was furnished by J. C. Bertram in 1770. However, before him Chytraeus and Seckendorf, in 1564, had expressly vindicated Melanchthon's authorship. Be it mentioned as a curiosity that the Papist Lud. Jac. a St. Carolo mentioned a certain "Articulus Alsmalcaldicus, Germanus, Lutheranus" as the author of the Tract. In the Formula of Concord and in the Preface to the Book of Concord the Tract is not enumerated as a separate confessional writing, but is treated as an appendix to the Smalcald Articles.

## 80. A Threefold Criticism.

On the basis of the facts stated in the preceding paragraphs, Kolde, followed by others, believes himself justified in offering a threefold criticism. In the first place, he opines that Luther's Articles are "very improperly called 'Smalcald Articles.'" However, even if Luther's Articles were not officially adopted by the Smalcald League as such, they were, nevertheless, written for the Convention of Smalcald, and were there signed by the assembled Lutheran theologians and preachers, and privately adopted also by most of the princes and estates. For Luther's Articles, then, there is and can be no title more appropriate than "Smalcald Articles." Tschackert remarks: "Almost all [all, with the exception of the suspected theologians] subscribed, and thereby they became weighty and important for the Evangelical churches of Germany; and hence it certainly is not inappropriate to call them 'Smalcald Articles,' even though they were written at Wittenberg and were not publicly deliberated upon at Smalcald." (302.)

"It is entirely unhistorical," Kolde continues in his strictures, "to designate Melanchthon's Tract, which has no connection with Luther's Articles, as an 'Appendix' to them, when in fact it was accepted as an appendix of the Augustana and Apology." (50.) It is a mistake, therefore, says Kolde, that the Tract is not separately mentioned in the Book of Concord, nor counted as a separate confessional writing. (53.) Likewise Tschackert: "On the other hand, it is a mistake to treat Melanchthon's Tract as an appendix to the Smalcald Articles, as is done in the Book of Concord. The signatures of the estates have rather given it an independent authority in the Church." (302.) However, there is much more of a connection between Luther's Articles and the Tract than Kolde and Tschackert seem to be aware of. Luther's Articles as well as the Tract were prepared for the Convention at Smalcald. Both were there signed by practically the same Lutheran theologians. The fact that in the case of the Smalcald Articles this was done voluntarily rather enhances,

and does not in the least diminish, their importance. Both also, from the very beginning, were equally regarded as Lutheran confessional writings. The Tract, furthermore, follows Luther's Articles also in substance, as it is but an acknowledgment and additional exposition of his article "Of the Papacy." To be sure, the Tract must not be viewed as an appendix to Luther's Articles, which, indeed, were in no need of such an appendix. Moreover, both the Articles and the Tract may be regarded as appendices to the Augsburg Confession and the Apology. Accordingly, there is no reason whatever why, in the Book of Concord, the Tract should not follow Luther's Articles or be regarded as closely connected with it, and naturally belonging to it. Koellner is right when he declares it to be "very appropriate" that the Tract is connected and grouped with the Smalcald Articles. (469.)

Finally, Kolde designates the words in the title "composed, conscriptus, by the scholars" as false in every respect. Likewise Tschackert. (303.) The criticism is justified inasmuch as the expression "composed, zusammengezogen, conscriptus, by the scholars" cannot very well be harmonized with the fact that Melanchthon wrote the Tract. But even this superscription is inappropriate, at least not in the degree assumed by Kolde and Tschackert. For the fact is that the princes and estates did not order Melanchthon, but the theologians, to write the treatise concerning the Papacy, and that the Tract was presented in their name. Koellner writes: "It is certainly a splendid testimony for the noble sentiments of those heroes of the faith that the Elector should know of, and partly disapprove, Melanchthon's milder views, and still entrust him with the composition of this very important document [the Tract], and, on the other hand, equally so, that Melanchthon so splendidly fulfilled the consideration which he owed to the views and the interests of the party without infringing upon his own conviction." "Seckendorf also," Koellner adds, "justly admires this unusual phenomenon." (471.) However, Koellner offers no evidence for the supposition that the Elector charged Melanchthon in particular with the composition of the Tract. According to the report of the Strassburg delegates, the princes declared that "the scholars" should peruse the Confession and enlarge on the Papacy. The report continues: "The scholars received orders . . . to enlarge somewhat on the Papacy, which *they* did, and thereupon transmitted *their* criticism to the Elector and the princes." (Kolde, *Anal.*, 297.) This is corroborated by Melanchthon himself, who wrote to Camerarius, March 1, 1537: "We received orders (*iussi sumus*) to write something on the Primacy of Peter or the Roman Pontiff." (*C. R.* 3, 292.) February 17 Osiander reported: "The first business imposed on *us* by the princes was . . . diligently to explain the Primacy, which was omitted from the Confession because it was regarded as odious. The latter of these duties *we* have to-day completed, so that *we* shall immediately deliver a copy to the princes." (3, 267.) These statements might even warrant the conclusion that the theologians also participated, more or less, in the drawing up of the Tract, for which, however, further evidence is wanting. Nor does it appear how this view could be harmonized with Veit Dietrich's assertion in his letter to Foerster, May 16: "Orders given to write about the power of the Pope, the primacy of Peter, and the ecclesiastical jurisdiction. Philip alone performed this very well." (3, 370.)

However, entirely apart from the statement of Osiander, the mere fact that the *theologians* were ordered to prepare the document, and that it was delivered by, and in the name of, these theologians, sufficiently warrants us to speak of the document as "The Tract of the Scholars at Smalcald" with the same propriety that, for example, the opinion which Melanchthon drew up on August 6, 1536, is entitled: "The First Proposal of the Wittenberg Scholars concerning the Future Council." (*C. R.* 3, 119.)

# VIII. Luther's Efforts at Restoring Catechetical Instruction.

## 81. Modern Researches Respecting Luther's Catechisms.

Besides G. v. Zezschwitz (*System der christlich-kirchlichen Katechetik*, 3 volumes, 1862 to 1874) and numerous other contemporary and later students, G. Buchwald, F. Cohrs, and O. Albrecht have, since the middle of the past century, rendered no mean service by their researches pertaining to Luther's Catechisms. Buchwald edited the three series of sermons on the Five Chief Parts which Luther delivered in 1528, pointed out their important bearing on his Catechisms, and shed new light on their origin by discovering and exploiting the Stephan Roth correspondence. He published the results of his labors in 1894 under the title, "The Origin of the Two Catechisms of Luther and the Foundation of the Large Catechism. *Die Entstehung der beiden Katechismen Luthers und die Grundlage des Grossen Katechismus.*" F. Cohrs enriched this department of knowledge by his articles in the third edition of Herzog's *Realenzyklopaedie*, and especially by his five-volume work on *The Evangelical Catechism-Attempts Prior to Luther's Enchiridion*, in *Monumenta Germaniae Paedagogica*, 1900 to 1907. In 1905 O. Albrecht was entrusted with the preparation of Luther's Catechisms for the Weimar Critical Edition of Luther's Complete Works. He also contributed the extensive historical sections of the first of the three parts of Vol. 30, where the Catechisms are treated.

This first part of 826 pages, which appeared in 1910, represents the latest important research work on the origin of Luther's Catechisms. In its preface R. Drescher says: "The writings of 1529 to 1530, in their totality, were a difficult mountain, and it gives us particular joy finally to have surmounted it. And the most difficult and laborious part of the way, at least in view of the comprehensive treatment it was to receive, was the publication of the Large and the Small Catechism, including the three series of Catechism Sermons. . . . The harvest which was garnered fills a large volume of our edition."

## 82. Meaning of the Word Catechism.

The term *catechismus* (catechism), like its related terms, *catechesis, catechizari, catechumeni*, was common in the ancient Church. In his *Glossarium*, Du Cange defines it as "*institutio puerorum etiam recens natorum, ante-*

*quam baptizentur* — the instruction of children, also those recently born, before their baptism." The synonymous expression, *catechesis*, he describes as "*institutio primorum fidei Christianae rudimentorum, de quibus χατηχήσεις suas scripsit S. Cyrillus Jerusolymitanus* — instruction in the first rudiments of the Christian faith, about which St. Cyril of Jerusalem wrote his catechizations." (2, 222 f.). Also Luther was acquainted with this usage in the ancient Church. He began his Catechism sermon of November 30, 1528, with the words: "These parts which you heard me recite the old Fathers called catechism, *i. e.*, a sermon for children, which children should know and all who desire to be Christians." (Weimar 30, 1, 57.) At first Luther seems to have employed the term but seldom; later on, however, especially after 1526, more frequently. Evidently he was bent on popularizing it. Between the Preface and the Decalog of the first Wittenberg book edition of the Small Catechism we find the title, "A Small Catechism or Christian Training — *Ein kleiner Katechismus oder christliche Zucht.*" No doubt, Luther added the explanation "christliche Zucht" because the word catechism had not yet become current among the people. May 18, 1528, he began his sermon with the explanation: "*Catechismus dicitur instructio* — Catechism is instruction"; likewise the sermon of September 14: "Catechism, *i. e.*, an instruction or Christian teaching"; the sermon of November 30: "Catechism, *i. e.*, a sermon for children." In the Preface to his Small Catechism he again explains the term as "Christian doctrine." Thus Luther endeavored to familiarize the people with the word catechism.

The meaning of this term, however, is not always the same. It may designate the act of instructing, the subject-matter or the doctrine imparted, a summary thereof, the text of the traditional chief parts, or a book containing the catechismal doctrine, text, or text with explanation. Luther used the word most frequently and preferably in the sense of instruction. This appears from the definitions quoted in the preceding paragraph, where catechism is defined as "sermon," "instruction," "Christian training," etc. "You have the catechism" (the doctrine), says Luther, "in small and large books." Bugenhagen defines thus: "Katechismus, dat is, christlike

underrichtinge ut den teyn gebaden Gades."
In the Apology, Melanchthon employs the
word catechism as identical with *κατήχησις
puerorum*, instruction of the young in the
Christian fundamentals. (324, 41.) "Accordingly," says O. Albrecht, "catechism means
elementary instruction in Christianity, conceived, first, as the act; then, as the material
for instruction; then, as the contents of a
book; and finally, as the book itself. This
usage must be borne in mind also where Luther speaks of his own Catechisms. "German
Catechism" means instruction in, or preaching on, the traditional chief parts in the German language. And while "Enchiridion" signifies a book of small compass, the title "Small
Catechism" (as appears from the old subtitle:
"Ein kleiner Katechismus oder christliche
Zucht") means instruction in the chief parts,
proceeding with compact brevity, and, at the
same time, these parts themselves together
with the explanations added. (W. 30, 1, 454.
539.) As the title of a book the word catechism was first employed by Althamer in 1528,
and by Brenz as the subtitle of his "Questions" (*Fragestuecke*). A school-book written
by John Colet in the beginning of the sixteenth
century bears the title "*Catechyzon*, The Instructor." (456.)

Not every kind of Christian instruction,
however, is called catechism by Luther. Whenever he uses the word, he has in mind begin-
ners, children, and unlearned people. In his
"German Order of Worship, *Deutsche Messe*,"
of 1526, he writes: "Catechism is an instruction whereby heathen who desire to become
Christians are taught and shown what they
must believe, do, not do, and know in Christianity; hence the name catechumens was
given to pupils who were accepted for such
instruction and who learned the Creed previous to their baptism." (19, 76.) In his sermon of November 30, 1528: "The Catechism
is a sermon for children, which the children
and all who desire to be Christians must
know. Whoever does not know it cannot be
numbered among the Christians. For if he
does not know these things, it is evident that
God and Christ mean nothing to him."
(30, 1, 57.) In his sermon of September 14:
"This [catechism] is preaching for children,
or, the Bible of the laity, which serves the
plain people. Whoever, then, does not know
these things, and is unable to recite them and
understand them, cannot be considered a Christian. It is for this reason, too, that it bears
the name catechism, *i. e.*, instruction and
Christian teaching, since all Christians at the
very least should know this much. Afterward
they ought to learn more of the Scriptures.
Hence, let all children govern themselves accordingly, and see that they learn it." (27.)
May 18 Luther began his sermon thus: "The
preaching of the Catechism was begun that
it might serve as an instruction for children
and the unlearned. . . . For every Christian
must necessarily know the Catechism. Whoever does not know it cannot be numbered
among the Christians." (2.) In the short
Preface to the Large Catechism: "This ser-

mon is designed and undertaken that it might
be an instruction for children and the simple-
minded. Hence, of old it was called in Greek
catechism, *i. e.*, instruction for children, what
every Christian must needs know, so that he
who does not know this could not be numbered
with the Christians nor be admitted to any
Sacrament." (CONC. TRIGL., 575, 1; 535, 11.)

## 83. Chief Parts of Catechism.

In Luther's opinion the elementary doctrines
which form the subject-matter of the Catechism are comprised in the three traditional
parts: Decalog, Creed, and Lord's Prayer.
These he considered to be the gist of the doctrine every one must learn if he would be regarded and treated as a Christian. "Those
who are unwilling to learn it," says Luther,
"should be told that they deny Christ and are
no Christians; neither should they be admitted to the Sacraments, accepted as sponsors
at Baptism, nor exercise any part of Christian
liberty." (CONC. TRIGL. 535, 11.) Of course,
Luther considered these three parts only a
minimum, which, however, Christians who
partake of the Lord's Supper should strive
to exceed, but still sufficient for children and
plain people. (575, 5.) Even in his later years,
Luther speaks of the first three parts as the
Catechism proper.

However, probably in consequence of the
controversy with the Enthusiasts, which began in 1524, Luther soon added as supplements the parts treating of Baptism, the
Lord's Supper, and Confession. In the Large
Catechism, where Baptism and the Lord's
Supper appear as appendices, Luther emphasizes the fact that the first three parts form
the kernel of the Catechism, but that instruction in Baptism and the Lord's Supper must
also be imparted. "These" (first three), says
he, "are the most necessary parts, which one
should first learn to repeat word for word. . . .
Now, when these three parts are apprehended,
it behooves a person also to know what to say
concerning our Sacraments, which Christ Himself instituted, Baptism and the holy body
and blood of Christ, namely, the text which
Matthew and Mark record at the close of their
gospels, when Christ said farewell to His disciples and sent them forth." (579, 20.) Luther regarded a correct knowledge of Baptism
and the Lord's Supper not only as useful, but
as necessary. Beginning his explanation of
the Fourth Chief Part, he remarks: "We have
now finished the three chief parts of the common Christian doctrine. Besides these we
have yet to speak of our two Sacraments instituted by Christ, of which also every Christian ought to have at least an ordinary, brief
instruction, because without them there can
be no Christian; although, alas! hitherto no
instruction concerning them has been given."
(733, 1.) Thus Luther materially enlarged
the Catechism. True, several prayer- and con-
fession-books, which appeared in the late
Middle Ages, also treat of the Sacraments.
As for the people, however, it was considered
sufficient for laymen to be able to recite the
names of the seven Roman sacraments. Hence

Luther, in the passage cited from the Large Catechism, declares that in Popery practically nothing of Baptism and the Lord's Supper was taught, certainly nothing worth while or wholesome.

### 84. Parts Inherited from Ancient Church.

The text of the first three chief parts, Luther considered a sacred heirloom from the ancient Church. "For," says he in his Large Catechism, "the holy Fathers or apostles have thus embraced in a summary the doctrine, life, wisdom, and art of Christians, of which they speak and treat, and with which they are occupied." (579, 19.) Thus Luther, always conservative, did not reject the traditional catechism, both bag and baggage, but carefully distinguished between the good, which he retained, and the worthless, which he discarded. In fact, he no more dreamt of foisting a new doctrine or catechism on the Christian Church than he ever thought of founding a new church. On the contrary, his sole object was to restore the ancient Apostolic Church; and his catechetical endeavors were bent on bringing to light once more, purifying, explaining, and restoring, the old catechism of the fathers.

In his book *Wider Hans Worst*, 1541, Luther says: "We have remained faithful to the true and ancient Church; aye, we are the true and ancient Church. You Papists, however, have apostatized from us, *i. e.*, from the ancient Church, and have set up a new church in opposition to the ancient Church." In harmony with this view, Luther repeatedly and emphatically asserted that in his Catechism he was merely protecting and guarding an inheritance of the fathers, which he had preserved to the Church by his correct explanation. In his *German Order of Worship* we read: "I know of no simpler nor better arrangement of this instruction or doctrine than the arrangement which has existed since the beginning of Christendom, *viz.*, the three parts, Ten Commandments, Creed, and the Lord's Prayer." (W. 19, 76.) In the ancient Church the original parts for catechumens and sponsors were the *Symbolum* and the *Paternoster*, the Apostles' Creed and the Lord's Prayer. To these the Ten Commandments were added as a formal part of doctrine only since the thirteenth century. (30, 1, 434.) The usual sequence of these parts was: Lord's Prayer, Apostles' Creed, and, wherever it was not supplanted by other matter, the Decalog. It was with deliberation, then, that Luther substituted his own objective, logical order.

In his *Short Form of the Ten Commandments, the Creed, and the Lord's Prayer*, 1520, Luther speaks as follows of the three traditional parts, which God preserved to the Church in spite of the Papacy: "It did not come to pass without the special providence of God, that, with reference to the common Christian, who cannot read the Scriptures, it was commanded to teach and to know the Ten Commandments, Creed, and Lord's Prayer, which three parts indeed thoroughly and completely embrace all that is contained in the Scripture and may ever be preached, all also

that a Christian needs to know, and this, too, in a form so brief and simple that no one can complain or offer the excuse that it is too much, and that it is too hard for him to remember what is essential to his salvation. For in order to be saved, a man must know three things: First, he must know what he is to do and leave undone. Secondly, when he realizes that by his own strength he is unable to do it and leave it undone, he must know where he may take, seek, and find that which will enable him to do and to refrain. Thirdly, he must know *how* he may seek and obtain it. Even as a sick man needs first of all to know what disease he has, what he may or may not do, or leave undone. Thereupon he needs to know where the medicine is which will help him, that he may do and leave undone like a healthy person. Fourthly, he must desire it, seek and get it, or have it brought to him. In like manner the commandments teach a man to know his disease, that he may see and perceive what he can do and not do, leave and not leave, and thus perceive that he is a sinner and a wicked man. Thereupon the Creed holds before his eyes and teaches him where to find the medicine, the grace, which will help him become pious, that he may keep the commandments, and shows him God and His mercy as revealed and offered in Christ. Fifthly, the Lord's Prayer teaches him how to ask for, get and obtain it, namely, by proper, humble, and comforting prayer. These three things comprise the entire Scriptures." (W. 7, 204.) It was things such as the chief parts of the Catechism that Luther had in mind when he wrote against the fanatics, 1528: "We confess that even under the Papacy there are many Christian blessings, aye, all Christian blessings, and thence they have come to us: the true Holy Scriptures, true Baptism, the true Sacrament of the Altar, true keys for the forgiveness of sins, the true office of the ministry, the true catechism, such as the Lord's Prayer, the Ten Commandments, the Articles of Faith, etc." (26, 147.) Luther's meaning is, that in the midst of antichristendom and despite the Pope, the text of the three chief parts was, among other things, preserved to the Church.

### 85. Service Rendered Catechism by Luther.

The fact that the text of the three chief parts existed long before Luther does not detract from the service which he rendered the Catechism. Luther's work, moreover, consisted in this, (1) that he brought about a general revival of the instruction in the Catechism of the ancient Church; (2) that he completed it by adding the parts treating of Baptism, Confession, and the Lord's Supper; (3) that he purged its material from all manner of papal ballast; (4) that he eliminated the Romish interpretation and adulteration in the interest of work-righteousness; (5) that he refilled the ancient forms with their genuine Evangelical and Scriptural meaning. Before Luther's time the study of the Catechism had everywhere fallen into decay.

There were but few who knew its text, and when able to recite it, they did not understand it. The soul of all Christian truths, the Gospel of God's free pardon for Christ's sake, had departed. Concerning "the three parts which have remained in Christendom from of old" Luther said that "little of it had been taught and treated correctly." (CONC. TRIGL. 575, 6.)

In his *Warning to My Dear Germans*, of 1531, he enlarges on the same thought as follows: "Thanks to God, our Gospel has produced much and great good. Formerly no one knew what was Gospel, what Christ, what Baptism, what Confession, what Sacrament, what faith, what spirit, what flesh, what good works, what the Ten Commandments, what the Lord's Prayer, what praying, what suffering, what comfort, what civil government, what matrimony, what parents, what children, what lords, what servant, what mistress, what maid, what devil, what angel, what world, what life, what death, what sin, what right, what forgiveness of sin, what God, what bishop, what pastor, what Church, what a Christian, what the cross. Sum, we knew nothing of what a Christian should know. Everything was obscured and suppressed by the papal asses. For in Christian matters they are asses indeed, aye, great, coarse, unlearned asses. For I also was one of them and know that in this I am speaking the truth. And all pious hearts who were captive under the Pope, even as I, will bear me out that they would fain have known one of these things, yet were not able nor permitted to know it. We knew no better than that the priests and monks alone were everything; on their works we based our hope of salvation and not on Christ. Thanks to God, however, it has now come to pass that man and woman, young and old, know the Catechism, and how to believe, live, pray, suffer, and die; and that is indeed a splendid instruction for consciences, teaching them how to be a Christian and to know Christ." (W. 30, 3, 317.)

Thus Luther extols it as the great achievement of his day that now every one knew the Catechism, whereas formerly Christian doctrine was unknown or at least not understood aright. And this achievement is preeminently a service which Luther rendered. He revived once more the ancient catechetical parts of doctrine, placed them in the proper Biblical light, permeated them with the Evangelical spirit, and explained them in conformity with the understanding of the Gospel which he had gained anew, stressing especially the *finis historiae* (the divine purpose of the historical facts of Christianity, as recorded in the Second Article), the forgiveness of sins not by works of our own, but by grace, for Christ's sake.

## 86. Catechetical Instruction before Luther.

In the Middle Ages the Lord's Prayer and the Creed were called the chief parts for sponsors (*Patenhauptstuecke*), since the canons required sponsors to know them, and at Baptism they were obligated to teach these parts to their godchildren. The children, then, were to learn the Creed and the Lord's Prayer from their parents and sponsors. Since the Carolingian Epoch these regulations of the Church were often repeated, as, for example, in the *Exhortation to the Christian Laity* of the ninth century. From the same century dates the regulation that an explanation of the Creed and the Lord's Prayer should be found in every parish, self-evidently to facilitate preaching and the examination in confession. In confession, which, according to the Lateran Council, 1215, everybody was required to make at least once a year, the priests were to inquire also regarding this instruction and have the chief parts recited. Since the middle of the thirteenth century the Creed, the Lord's Prayer, together with the Benedicite, Gratias, Ave Maria, Psalms, and other matter, were taught also in the Latin schools, where probably Luther, too, learned them. In the *Instruction for Visitors*, Melanchthon still mentions "der Kinder Handbuechlein, darin das Alphabet, Vaterunser, Glaub' und andere Gebet' innen stehen — Manual for Children, containing the alphabet, the Lord's Prayer, the Creed, and other prayers," as the first school-book. (W. 26, 237.) After the invention of printing, chart-impressions with pictures illustrating the Creed, the Lord's Prayer, and the Ten Commandments came into the possession also of some laymen. The poorer classes, however, had to content themselves with the charts in the churches, which especially Nicolaus of Cusa endeavored to introduce everywhere. (Herzog's *Realenzyklopaedie* 10, 138.) They were followed by confessional booklets, prayer-booklets, and also by voluminous books of devotion. Apart from other trash, these contained confessional and communion prayers, instructions on Repentance, Confession, and the Sacrament of the Altar; above all, however, a mirror of sins, intended as a guide for self-examination, on the basis of various lists of sins and catalogs of virtues, which, supplanting the Decalog, were to be memorized. Self-evidently, all this was not intended as a schoolmaster to bring them to Christ and to faith in the free grace of God, but merely to serve the interest of the Romish penances, satisfactions, and work-righteousness. Says Luther in the Smalcald Articles: "Here, too, there was no faith nor Christ, and the virtue of the absolution was not declared to him, but upon his enumeration of sins and his self-abasement depended his consolation. What torture, rascality, and idolatry such confession has produced is more than can be related." (485, 20.) The chief parts of Christian doctrine but little taught and nowhere correctly taught, — such was the chief hurt of the Church under the Papacy.

In the course of time, however, even this deficient and false instruction gradually fell into decay. The influence of the Latin schools was not very far-reaching, their number being very small in proportion to the young. Public schools for the people did not exist in the

Middle Ages. As a matter of fact, not a single synod concerned itself specifically with the instruction of the young. (*H. R.* 10, 137.) At home, parents and sponsors became increasingly indifferent and incompetent for teaching. True, the reformers of the fourteenth and fifteenth centuries did attempt to elevate the instruction also in the Catechism. Geiler's sermons on the Lord's Prayer were published. Gerson admonished: "The reformation of the Church must begin with the young," and published sermons on the Decalog as models for the use of the clergy. John Wolf also urged that the young be instructed, and endeavored to substitute the Decalog for the prevalent catalogs of sins. The Humanists John Wimpheling, Erasmus, and John Colet (who wrote the *Catechyzon*, which Erasmus rendered into Latin hexameters) urged the same thing. Peter Tritonius Athesinus wrote a similar book of instruction for the Latin schools. However, all of these attempts proved ineffectual, and even if successful, they would have accomplished little for truly Christian instruction, such as Luther advocated, since the real essence of Christianity, the doctrine of justification, was unknown to these reformers.

Thus in the course of time the people, and especially the young, grew more and more deficient in the knowledge of even the simplest Christian truths and facts. And bishops and priests, unconcerned about the ancient canons, stolidly looked on while Christendom was sinking deeper and deeper into the quagmire of total religious ignorance and indifference. Without fearing contradiction, Melanchthon declared in his Apology: "Among the adversaries there is no catechization of the children whatever, concerning which even the canons give commands. . . . Among the adversaries, in many regions [as in Italy and Spain], during the entire year no sermons are delivered, except in Lent." (325, 41.)

## 87. Medieval Books of Prayer and Instruction.

Concerning the aforementioned Catholic books of prayer and edification which, during the Middle Ages, served the people as catechisms, Luther, in his Prayer-Booklet of 1522 (which was intended to supplant the Romish prayer-books), writes as follows: "Among many other harmful doctrines and booklets which have seduced and deceived Christians and given rise to countless superstitions, I do not consider as the least the prayer-booklets, by which so much distress of confessing and enumerating sins, such unchristian folly in the prayers to God and His saints was inculcated upon the unlearned, and which, nevertheless, were highly puffed with indulgences and red titles, and, in addition, bore precious names, one being called *Hortulus Animae*, the other *Paradisus Animae*, and so forth. They are in sore need of a thorough and sound reformation, or to be eradicated entirely, a sentence which I also pass on the Passional or Legend books, to which also a great deal has been added by the devil." (W. 10, 1, 375.)

The *Hortulus Animae*, which is mentioned even before 1500, was widely circulated at the beginning of the sixteenth century. It embraced all forms of edifying literature. Sebastian Brandt and Jacob Wimpheling helped to compile it. The *Paradisus Animae* had the same contents, but was probably spread in Latin only. The *Hortulus Animae* contains very complete rosters of sins and catalogs of virtues for "confessing and enumerating sins." Among the virtues are listed the bodily works of mercy (Matt. 25, 35) and the seven spiritual works of mercy: to instruct the ignorant, give counsel to the doubtful, comfort the afflicted, admonish sinners, pardon adversaries, suffer wrong, and forgive the enemies. Among the virtues were counted the seven gifts of the Holy Ghost: wisdom, understanding, ability, kindness, counsel, strength, and fear. Furthermore the three divine virtues: faith, hope, and charity. The four cardinal virtues: prudence, justice, fortitude, and temperance. The eight beatitudes according to Matt. 5, 3 ff. The twelve counsels: poverty, obedience, chastity, love of enemies, meekness, abundant mercy, simplicity of words, not too much care for temporal things, correct purpose and simplicity of deeds, harmony of doctrine and works, fleeing the cause of sin, brotherly admonition. Finally also the seven sacraments. The list of sins contains the nine foreign sins, the six sins against the Holy Ghost, the four sins that cry to God for vengeance, the five senses, the Ten Commandments, and the seven mortal sins: pride, covetousness, unchastity, anger, gluttony, envy, and sloth. Each of these mortal sins is again analyzed extensively. The Weimar edition of Luther's Works remarks: "If these catalogs were employed for self-examination, confusion, endless torment, or complete externalization of the consciousness of sin was bound to result. We can therefore understand why the Reformer inveighs against this 'enumerating of sins.'" (10, 2, 336.)

The *Hortulus Animae* also shows how Luther was obliged to purge the Catechism from all manner of "unchristian follies," as he calls them. For the entire book is pervaded by idolatrous adoration of the saints. An acrostic prayer to Mary addresses her as *mediatrix, auxiliatrix, reparatrix, illuminatrix, advocatrix.* In English the prayer would read as follows: "O Mary, thou mediator between God and men, make of thyself the medium between the righteous God and me, a poor sinner! O Mary, thou helper in all anguish and need, come to my assistance in all sufferings, and help me resist and strive against the evil spirits and overcome all my temptations and afflictions. O Mary, thou restorer of lost grace to all men, restore unto me my lost time, my sinful and wasted life! O Mary, thou illuminator, who didst give birth to the eternal Light of the whole world, illumine my blindness and ignorance, lest I, poor sinner that I am, enter the darkness of eternal death! O Mary, thou advocate of all miserable men, be thou my advocate at my last end before the stern judgment of God, and obtain for me the grace and the fruit of thy womb, Jesus Christ! Amen." Another prayer calls Mary the "mighty queen of heaven, the holy empress of the angels, the one who stays divine wrath." A prayer to the eleven thousand virgins reads as follows: "O ye, adorned with chastity, crowned with humility, clad with patience, covered with the blossoms of virtue, well polished with moderation — O ye precious pearls and chosen virgin maids, help us in the hour of death!'"

With this idolatry and saint-worship silly superstition was combined. In order to be efficacious, a certain prayer prescribed in the *Hortulus* must be spoken not only with "true contrition and pure confession," but also "before a figure which had appeared to St. Gregory." Whoever offers a certain prayer "before the image of Our Lady in the Sun" "will not depart this life unshriven, and thirty days before his death will see the very adorable Virgin Mary prepared to help him." Another prayer is good "for pestilence" when spoken "before the image of St. Ann"; another prayer to St. Margaret profits "every woman in travail"; still another preserves him who says it from "a sudden death." All of these promises, however, are far surpassed by the indulgences assured. The prayer before the apparition of St. Gregory obtains 24,600 years and 24 days of indulgence; another promises "indulgence for as many days as our Lord Jesus Christ received wounds during His passion, *viz.*, 5,475." Whoever prays the Bridget-prayers not only obtains indulgence for himself, but 15 souls of his kin are thereby delivered from purgatory, 15 sinners converted, and 15 righteous "confirmed and established in their good standing." (W. 10, 2, 334.)

Also in the chart booklets for the Latin schools of the Middle Ages the Ave Maria and Salve Regina played an important part. — Such were the books which, before Luther, were to serve the people as catechisms, or books of instruction and prayer. In them, everything, even what was right and good in itself, such as the Creed, the Lord's Prayer, and the Decalog, was made to serve Romish superstition and work-righteousness. Hence one can easily understand why Luther demanded that they be either thoroughly reformed or eradicated.

Indeed, the dire need of the Church in this respect was felt and lamented by none sooner and more deeply than Luther. Already in his tract *To the Christian Nobility of the German Nation*, 1520, he complained that Christian instruction of the young was being neglected. He writes: "Above all, the chief and most common lesson in the higher and lower schools ought to be the Holy Scriptures and for the young boys, the Gospel. Would to God every city had also a school for girls, where the little maids might daily hear the Gospel for an hour, either in German or in Latin! Truly, in the past the schools and convents for men and women were founded for this purpose, with very laudable Christian intention, as we read of St. Agnes and other saints. There grew up holy virgins and martyrs, and Christendom fared very well. But now it amounts to nothing more than praying and singing. Ought not, indeed, every Christian at the age of nine or ten years know the entire holy Gospel, in which his name and life is written? Does not the spinner and the seamstress teach the same handicraft to her daughter when she is still young? But now even the great men, the learned prelates and bishops, do not know the Gospel. How unjustly do we deal with the poor youth entrusted to us, failing, as we do, to govern and instruct them! What a severe reckoning will be required of us because we do not set before them the Word of God! For unto them is done as Jeremiah says, Lam. 2, 11. 12: 'Mine eyes do fail with tears, my bowels are troubled, my liver is poured upon the earth, for the destruction of the daughter of my people; because the children and the sucklings swoon in the streets of the city. They say to their mothers, Where is corn and wine? when they swooned as the wounded in the streets of the city, when their soul was poured out into their mothers' bosom.' But we do not see the wretched misery, how the young people, in the midst of Christendom, now also languish and perish miserably for lack of the Gospel, in which they should always be instructed and drilled." (W. 6, 461; E. 21, 349.)

## 88. Church Visitation Reveals Deplorable Ignorance.

The Saxon Visitation brought to light such a total decay of all Christian knowledge and of Christian instruction as even Luther had not anticipated. Aside from other evils (clergymen cohabiting with their cooks, addicted to drink, or even conducting taverns, etc.), the people, especially in the villages, were found to be grossly ignorant of even the simplest rudiments of Christian doctrine and most unwilling to learn anything, while many pastors were utterly incompetent to teach. According to the official records, one priest, who enjoyed a great reputation as an exorcist, could not even recite the Lord's Prayer and the Creed fluently. (Koestlin, *Martin Luther*, 2, 41.) Luther took part in the visitation of the Electoral circuit from the end of October till after the middle of November, 1528, and again from the end of December, 1528, till January, 1529, and on April 26, 1529, at Torgau, he, too, signed the report on visitation. When Luther therefore describes the decay of instruction in Popery, he speaks from personal experience. About the middle of January, 1529, he wrote to Spalatin: "Moreover, conditions in the congregations everywhere are pitiable, inasmuch as the peasants learn nothing, know nothing, never pray, do nothing but abuse their liberty, make no confession, receive no communion, as if they had been altogether emancipated from religion. They have neglected their papistical affairs (ours they despise) to such extent that it is terrible to contemplate the administration of the papal bishops." (Enders 7, 45.) The intense heartache and mingled feelings which came over Luther when he thought of the ignorance which he found during the visitation, are described in the Preface to the Small Catechism as follows: "The deplorable, miserable condition which I discovered lately when I, too, was a visitor, has forced and urged me to prepare this Catechism, or Christian doctrine, in this small, plain, simple form. Mercy! Good God! what manifold misery I beheld! The common people, especially in the villages, have no knowledge whatever of Christian doctrine, and, alas! many pastors are altogether incapable, and incompetent to teach. Nevertheless, all maintain that they are Christians, all have been baptized and receive the holy Sacrament. Yet they cannot recite either the Lord's Prayer, or the Creed, or the Ten Commandments; they live like dumb brutes and irrational swine; and yet, now that the Gospel has come, they have nicely learned to abuse all liberty like experts. O ye bishops! what will ye ever answer to Christ for having so shamefully neglected the people and never for a moment discharged your office? May all misfortune flee you! You command the Sacrament in one form and insist on your human laws, and yet at the same time you do not care in the least whether the people know the Lord's Prayer, the Creed, the Ten Commandments, or any part of the Word of God. Woe, woe, unto you forever!" (533, 1 ff.)

To these experiences made during the visitation, Luther also refers when he says in the Short Preface to the Large Catechism: "For I well remember the time, indeed, even now it is a daily occurrence that one finds rude, old persons who knew nothing and still know nothing of these things, and who, nevertheless, go to Baptism and the Lord's Supper, and use everything belonging to Christians, notwithstanding that those who come to the Lord's Supper ought to know more and have a fuller understanding of all Christian doctrine than children and new scholars." (575, 5.) In his "Admonition to the Clergy" of 1530, Luther describes the conditions before the Reformation as follows: "In brief, preaching and teaching were in a wretched and heart-rending state. Still all the bishops kept silence and saw nothing new, although they are now able to see a gnat in the sun. Hence all things were so confused and wild, owing to the discordant teaching and the strange new opinions, that no one was any longer able to know what was certain or uncertain, what was a Christian or an unchristian. The old doctrine of faith in Christ, of love, of prayer, of cross, of comfort in tribulation was entirely trodden down. Aye, there was in all the world no doctor who knew the entire Catechism, that is, the Lord's Prayer, the Ten Commandments, and the Creed, to say nothing of understanding and teaching it, as now, God be praised, it is being taught and learned, even by young children. In support of this statement I appeal to all their books, both of theologians and jurists. If a single part of the Catechism can be correctly learned therefrom, I am ready to be broken upon the wheel and to have my veins opened." (W. 30, 1, 301.)

Melanchthon, Jonas, Brenz, George of Anhalt, Mathesius, and many others draw a similar picture of the religious conditions prevailing in Germany, England, and other lands immediately prior to the Reformation. To be sure, Papists, particularly Jesuits, have disputed the accuracy and truth of these descriptions from the pen of Luther and his contemporaries. But arrayed against these Romish apologetes is also the testimony of Papists themselves. In his *Catholicus Catechismus*, published at Cologne, 1543, Nausea writes: "I endeavored to renew the instruction, once well known among all churches, which, however, not only recently, but long ago (I do not khow to whose stupidity, negligence, or ignorance this was due) was altogether forgotten, not without lamentable loss to the catholic religion. *Veterem illam catechesin, per omnes quondam ecclesias percelebrem non modo tum, sed et ante pridem, nescio quorum vel socordia vel negligentia vel ignorantia, non sine poenitenda catholicae religionis iactura prorsus in oblivionem coeptam repetere coepi.*" (W. 30, 1, 467.) Moreover, when Romanists dispute Luther's assertions, they refer to the one point only, that religious instruction (as conceived by Catholics) had not declined in the measure claimed by Luther. As to the chief point in Luther's assertion, however, *viz.*, the correct Evangelical explanation of the Catechism, which, in Luther's opinion, is essential to all truly Christian instruction, the Catholic Church has always been utterly devoid of it, not only prior to the Reformation, but also after it, and down to the present day.

True, even during the Reformation some Papists were incited to greater zeal in preaching and teaching. It was a reaction against the Reformation of Luther, who must be regarded as the indirect cause also of the formal improvement in the instruction of the young among the Romanists. To maintain their power, bishops and priests were compelled to resume and cultivate it. This revival, however, meant only an intensified instruction in the old work-righteousness, and therefore was the very opposite of the instruction which Luther desired and advocated. In the Apology, Melanchthon, after charging the Papists with totally neglecting the instruction of the young, continues: "A few among them now also begin to preach of good works. But of the knowledge of Christ, of faith, of the consolation of consciences they are unable to preach anything, moreover, this blessed doctrine, the precious holy Gospel, they call Lutheran." (326, 44.)

## 89. Luther Devising Measures to Restore Catechism.

Fully realizing the general decay of Christian training, Luther at once directed all his efforts toward bringing about a change for the better. And well aware of the fact that the future belongs to the rising generation, the instruction of the common people, and particularly of the young, became increasingly an object of his especial concern. If the Church, said he, is to be helped, if the Gospel is to be victorious, if the Reformation is to succeed, if Satan and Antichrist are to be dealt a mortal blow, a blow from which they will not recover, it must be done through the young. For every cause which is not, or cannot be made, the cause of the rising generation, is doomed from the very outset. "This is the total ruin of the Church," said Luther as early as 1516; "for if ever it is to flourish again, one must begin by instructing the young. *Haec est enim ecclesiae ruina tota; si enim unquam debet reflorere, necesse est, ut a puerorum institutione exordium fiat.*" (W. 1, 494.) For, apart from being incapable of much improvement, the old people would soon disappear from the scene. Hence, if Christianity and its saving truths were to be preserved to the Church, the children must learn them from earliest youth.

In his Large Catechism Luther gave utterance to these thoughts as follows: "Let this, then, be said for exhortation, not only for those of us who are old and grown, but also for the young people, who ought to be brought up in the Christian doctrine and understanding. For thereby the Ten Commandments, the Creed, and the Lord's Prayer might be the more easily inculcated upon our youth, so that they would receive them with pleasure and earnestness, and thus would practise them from their youth and accustom themselves to them. For the old are now well-nigh done for, so that these and other things cannot be attained, unless we train the people who are to come after us and succeed us in our office and work, in order that they also may bring up their children successfully, that the Word of God and the Christian Church may be preserved. Therefore let every father of a family know that it is his duty, by the injunction and command of God, to teach these things to his children, or have them learn what they ought to know." (773, 85.)

A thorough and lasting revival of the Catechism can be hoped for only through the young — such were Luther's convictions. Accordingly he implored and adjured pastors and parents not to refuse their help in this matter. In the Preface to his Small Catechism we read: "Therefore I entreat you all for God's sake, my dear sirs and brethren, who are pastors or preachers, to devote yourselves heartily to your office, to have pity on the people who are entrusted to you, and to help us inculcate the Catechism upon the people, especially upon the young." (533, 6.) And as he earnestly admonished the pastors, so he also tenderly invited them to be faithful in this work. He was firmly convinced that nothing except the Gospel, as rediscovered and preached by himself, was able to save men. How, then, could he remain silent or abandon this work because of the hatred and ungratefulness of men! It was this new frame of mind, produced by the Gospel, to which Luther appealed in the interest of the Catechism. "Therefore look to it, ye pastors and preachers," says he, concluding the Preface to his Small Catechism. "Our office is now become a different thing from what it was under the Pope; it is now become serious and salutary. Accordingly it

now involves much more trouble and labor, danger and trials, and in addition thereto, secures but little reward and gratitude in the world. But Christ Himself will be our reward if we labor faithfully." (539, 26.)

At the same time Luther also took proper steps toward giving the preachers frequent opportunity for Catechism-work. Since 1525 Wittenberg had a regulation prescribing quarterly instruction in the Catechism by means of special sermons. The *Instruction for Visitors*, of 1527, demanded "that the Ten Commandments, the Articles of Faith, and the Lord's Prayer be steadily preached and expounded on Sunday afternoons.... And when the Ten Commandments, the Lord's Prayer, and the Creed have been preached on Sundays in succession, matrimony, and the sacraments of Baptism and the Lord's Supper shall also be preached diligently. In this interest the Ten Commandments, the Lord's Prayer, and the Articles of Faith shall be recited word for word, for the sake of the children and other simple and ignorant folk." (W. 26, 230.) November 29, 1528, in an admonition to attend these Catechism-sermons, Luther proclaimed from the pulpit: "We have ordered, as hitherto has been customary with us, that the first principles and the fundamentals of Christian knowledge and life be preached four times each year, two weeks in each quarter, four days per week, at 10 A. M." (W. 27, 444; 29, 146.) In Luther's sermon of November 27, 1530, we read: "It is our custom to preach the Catechism four times a year. Therefore attend these services, and let the children and the rest of the household come." (32, 209.) September 10, 1531, Luther concluded his sermon with the following admonition: "It is the custom, and the time of the Catechism-sermons is at hand. I admonish you to give these eight days to your Lord and permit your household and children to attend, and you yourself may also come and profit by this instruction. No one knows as much as he ought to know. For I myself am constrained to drill it every day. You know that we did not have it under the Papacy. Buy while the market is at the door; some day you will behold the fruit. We would, indeed, rather escape the burden, but we do it for your sakes." (34, 2, 195.)

## 90. Cooperation of Parents Urged by Luther.

In order to bring the instruction of the young into vogue, Luther saw that church, school, and home must needs cooperate. The home especially must not fail in this. Accordingly, in his admonitions, he endeavored to interest the fathers and mothers in this work. He was convinced that without their vigorous cooperation he could achieve but little. In his *German Order of Worship*, 1526, we read: "For if the parents and guardians of the young are unwilling to take such pains with the young, either personally or through others, Catechism [catechetical instruction] will never be established." (W. 19, 76.) In this he was confirmed by the experiences he had while on his tour of visitation. If the children were to memorize the Catechism and learn to understand it, they must be instructed and questioned individually, a task to which the Church was unequal, and for the accomplishment of which also the small number of schools was altogether inadequate. Parents, however, were able to reach the children individually. They had the time and opportunity, too, morning, noon, and evening, at the table, etc. Furthermore, they had the greatest interest in this matter, the children being their own flesh and blood. And they, in the first place, were commanded by God to provide for the proper training of their children. The fathers and mothers, therefore, these natural and divinely appointed teachers of the children, Luther was at great pains to enlist for the urgent work of instructing the young. They should see that the children and servants did not only attend the Catechism-sermons in church, but also memorized the text and learned to understand it. The Christian homes should again become home-churches, home-schools, where the housefathers were both house-priests and house-teachers, performing the office of the ministry there just as the pastors did in the churches.

With ever-increasing energy Luther, therefore, urged the parents to study the Catechism in order to be able to teach it to their children. In his sermons on the Ten Commandments, 1516, he admonishes them to bring up their children in the fear and admonition of the Lord. "But alas," he exclaims, "how has not all this been corrupted! Nor is it to be wondered at, since the parents themselves have not been trained and educated." In a sermon of 1526: "Here are two doctrines, Law and Gospel. Of them we preach frequently; but very few there are who take it to heart. I hear that many are still so ignorant that they do not know the Ten Commandments nor are able to pray. It plainly shows that they are altogether careless. Parents ought to see what their children and family are doing. In the school at home they should learn these three. I hear that in the city, too, there are wicked people. We cannot enter the homes; parents, masters, and mistresses ought to be sufficiently skilled to require their children and servants to say the prayers before retiring. But they do not know any themselves. What, then, avails it that we do a great deal of preaching concerning the kingdom of Christ? I thought conditions had improved. I admonish you master — for it is your duty — to instruct the servants, the mistress, the maids, and the children; and it is publicly preached in church for the purpose that it may be preached at home." (W. 20, 485.)

In his sermon of September 14, 1528, Luther declares that the Catechism is the laymen's Bible, which every one must know who wishes to be considered a Christian and to be admitted to the Lord's Supper. He then proceeds: "Hence all children should behave accordingly, and learn. And you parents are bound to have your children learn these things.

Likewise you lords, take pains that your family, etc. Whoever does not know these things does not deserve any food. These five points are a brief summary of the Christian doctrine. When the question is put, 'What is the First Commandment?' every one should be able to recite: 'Namely this,'" etc. (W. 30, 1, 27.) Exhorting the people to attend the Catechism-services, Luther declared November 29, 1528: "Think not, ye housefathers, that you are freed from the care of your household when you say: 'Oh, if they are unwilling to go [to Catechism instruction], why should I force them? I am not in need of it.' You have been appointed their bishop and housepastor; beware lest you neglect your duty toward them!" (27, 444.) On the following day, beginning the sermons he had announced, Luther said: "Therefore I have admonished you adults to have your children and your servants, attend it [the Catechism-sermon], and also be present yourselves; otherwise we shall not admit you to Holy Communion. For if you parents and masters will not help us, we shall accomplish little by our preaching. If I preach an entire year, the household comes, gapes at the walls and windows of the church, etc. Whoever is a good citizen is in duty bound to urge his people to learn these things; he should refuse them food unless, etc. If the servants complain, slam the door on them. If you have children, accustom them to learn the Ten Commandments, the Symbol, the Paternoster, etc. If you will diligently urge them, they will learn much in one year. When they have learned these things, there are everywhere in the Scriptures fine passages which they may learn next; if not all, at least some. For this reason God has appointed you a master, a mistress, that you may urge your household to do this. And this you are well able to accomplish: that they pray in the morning and evening, before and after meals. In this way they would be brought up in the fear of God. I am no idle prattler; I ask you not to cast my words to the winds. I would not think you so rude if I did not daily hear it. Every housefather is a priest in his own house, every housemother is a priestess; therefore see that you help us to perform the office of the ministry in your homes as we do in church. If you do, we shall have a propitious God, who will defend us from all evil. In the Psalm [78, 5] it is written: 'He appointed a law in Israel, which He commanded our fathers, that they should make them known to their children.'" (30, 1, 57.) In the same sermon: "Able teachers are necessary because of the great need, since parents do not concern themselves about this. But each master and mistress must remember that they are priests and priestesses over Hans and Gretchen," their sons and daughters.

In the same way Luther urges this matter in his Catechisms. For here we read: "Therefore it is the duty of every father of a family to question and examine his children and servants at least once a week and to ascertain what they know of it [the Catechism], or are learning, and, if they do not know it, to keep them faithfully at it." (575, 4.) "Likewise every head of a household is obliged to do the same with respect to his domestics, man-servants and maid-servants, and not to keep them in his house if they do not know these things and are unwilling to learn them. For a person who is so rude and unruly as to be unwilling to learn these things is not to be tolerated; for in these three parts everything that we have in the Scriptures is compre-hended in short, plain, and simple terms." (577, 17.) "Therefore let every father of a family know that it is his duty, by the in-junction and command of God, to teach these things to his children, or have them learn what they ought to know. For since they are baptized and received into the Christian Church, they should also enjoy this com-munion of the Sacrament, in order that they may serve us and be useful to us; for they must all indeed help us to believe, love, pray, and fight against the devil." (773, 87.)

In confession and before visitors, house-fathers were also to render account of the manner in which they discharged these duties. In his sermon of July 11, 1529, Luther said: "You will therefore instruct your children and servants according to this Catechism. . . . For you have the Catechism in small and large books; therefore study it. You had the vis-itors, and you have furthermore those who will examine you housefathers and your house-hold, that they may see how you have im-proved. . . . You should have given money and property for it; yet you neglect it when it is offered freely; therefore you house-fathers ought to be diligent students of this preaching, that as you learn you may instruct, *discendo doceatis.*" (W. 29, 472; 30, 1, 121.)

## 91. German Services with German Catechism.

With great emphasis Luther advocated dili-gent Catechism instruction in his *Deutsche Messe* (German Mass, *i. e.,* German Service or German Order of Worship), which he com-pleted toward the end of 1525 and published in 1526. Luther issued this Service "because German masses and services are everywhere insisted upon." The demand was made es-pecially in the interest of the unlearned and the children, for whose benefit, according to Luther, all such measures were adopted. "For," says he, "we do not at all establish such orders for those who are already [ad-vanced] Christians. . . . But we are in need of such orders for the sake of those who are still to become Christians or to grow stronger. Just as a Christian does not need Baptism, the Word, and Sacrament as a Christian, since he already has everything, but as a sinner. Chiefly, however, this is done for the sake of the unlearned and the young people, who should and must be exercised daily and brought up in the Scriptures, the Word of God, that they may become accustomed to the Scripture, skilled, fluent, and at home in it, in order that they may be able to defend their faith, and in time teach others and help to increase the kingdom of Christ. For their

sake one must read, sing, preach, write, and compose. And if it would help and promote this aim, I would have all bells rung, all organs played, and everything that is capable of giving sound to sound forth. For the Cath-olic services are so damnable because they [the Papists] made laws, works, and merits of them, thereby smothering faith, and did not adapt them to the young and unlearned, to exercise them in the Scriptures, in the Word of God, but themselves clung to them [as works], regarding them as beneficial and necessary for salvation to themselves; that is the devil."

While Luther, in his *German Worship,* as well as in other places, favors also Latin masses, yet he demands that "for the sake of the unlearned laity" German services be in-troduced. And since the unlearned could be truly served only by instruction in the funda-mental truths of Christianity, the Catechism, according to Luther, was to constitute a chief part in these services. "Very well," says he, "in God's name! First of all a clear, simple, plain, good Catechism is needed in the Ger-man service. Catechism, however, is an in-struction whereby heathen who desire to be-come Christians are taught and instructed in what they must believe, do, not do, and know concerning Christianity. Pupils who were ac-cepted for such instruction and learned the faith before being baptized were therefore called catechumens. Nor do I know how to present this instruction, or teaching, in a form more simple than it already has been presented since the beginning of Christianity, and hitherto retained, to wit, the three parts: the Ten Commandments, the Creed, and the Lord's Prayer. These three parts contain in simple and brief form everything that a Chris-tian must know. And since as yet we have no special congregation (*weil man noch keine sonderliche Gemeinde hat*), this instruction must proceed in the following manner, by preaching from the pulpit at various times or daily, as necessity demands, and by repeating and reading it to the children and servants at home in the houses morning and evening (if one would make Christians of them). Yet not only so that they memorize the words or recite them, as was done hitherto, but by ques-tioning them part for part, and having them state in their answer what each part means, and how they understand it. If all parts can-not be asked at one time, take one, the next day another. For if the parents or guardians are unwilling to take such pains with the young, either personally or through others, the Catechism will never be established." (19, 76.) German Catechism in German ser-vices — such, then, was the slogan which Lu-ther now sounded forth with ever-increasing emphasis.

## 92. Luther Illustrating Method of Procedure.

According to Luther's *German Worship,* pas-tors were to preach the Catechism on Mondays and Tuesdays. To insure the desired results (memorizing and understanding the text), the children should be questioned, especially at home by the parents. Exemplifying such catechization, Luther writes: "For so shall they be asked: 'What do you pray?' Answer: 'The Lord's Prayer.' What do you mean by saying: 'Our Father who art in heaven?' Answer: 'That God is not an earthly, but a heavenly Father, who would make us rich and blessed in heaven.' 'What does "Hallowed be Thy name" mean?' Answer: 'That we should honor God's name and not use it in vain, lest it be profaned.' 'How, then, is it profaned and desecrated?' Answer: 'When we who are regarded as His children lead wicked lives, teach and believe what is wrong.' And so forth, what God's kingdom means; how it comes; what God's will is; what daily bread, etc. Likewise also of the Creed: 'What do you believe?' Answer: 'I believe in God the Father,' etc. Thereupon part for part, as leisure permits, one or two at a time. Thus: 'What does it mean to believe in God the Father Almighty?' Answer: 'It means that the heart trusts Him entirely, and confidently looks to Him for all grace, favor, help, and comfort, here and hereafter.' 'What does it mean to believe in Jesus Christ, His Son?' Answer: 'It means that the heart believes we should all be lost eternally if Christ had not died for us,' etc. In like manner one must also question on the Ten Commandments, what the first, the second, the third and other commandments mean. Such questions you may take from our Prayer-Booklet, where the three parts are briefly explained, or you may formulate others yourself, until they comprehend with their hearts the entire sum of Christian knowledge in two parts, as in two sacks, which are faith and love. Let faith's sack have two pockets; into the one pocket put the part according to which we believe that we are altogether corrupted by Adam's sin, are sinners and condemned, Rom. 5, 12 and Ps. 51, 7. Into the other pocket put the part telling us that by Jesus Christ we have all been redeemed from such corrupt, sinful, condemned condition, Rom. 5, 18 and John 3, 16. Let love's sack also have two pockets. Into the one put this part, that we should serve, and do good to, every one, even as Christ did unto us, Rom. 13. Into the other put the part that we should gladly suffer and endure all manner of evil." (19, 76.)

In like manner passages of Scripture were also to be made the child's property, as it were; for it was not Luther's idea that instruction should cease at the lowest indispensably necessary goal (the understanding of the text of the chief parts). In his *German Order of Worship* he goes on to say: "When the child begins to comprehend this [the text of the Catechism], accustom it to carry home passages of Scripture from the sermons and to recite them to the parents at the table, at meal-time, as it was formerly customary to recite Latin, and thereupon to store the passages into the sacks and pockets, as one puts *pfennige*, and *groschen*, or *gulden* into his pocket. Let the sack of faith be, as it were, the gulden sack. Into the first pocket let this

passage be put, Rom. 5: 'By one man's disobedience many were made sinners'; and Ps. 51: 'Behold, I was shapen in iniquity, and in sin did my mother conceive me.' Those are two Rheinish gulden in the pocket. The other pocket is for the Hungarian gulden, such as this passage, Rom. 5: 'Christ was delivered for our offenses, and was raised again for our justification'; again, John 1: 'Behold the Lamb of God, which taketh away the sin of the world.' That would be two good Hungarian gulden in the pocket. Let love's sack be the silver sack. Into the first pocket belong the passages of well-doing, such as Gal. 5: 'By love serve one another'; Matt. 25: 'Inasmuch as ye have done it unto one of the least of these My brethren, ye have done it unto Me.' That would be two silver groschen in the pocket. Into the other pocket this passage belongs, Matt. 5: 'Blessed are ye when men shall persecute you for My sake'; Heb. 12: 'For whom the Lord loveth He chasteneth; He scourgeth every son whom He receiveth.' Those are two Schreckenbergers [a coin made of silver mined from Schreckenberg] in the pocket." (19, 77 f.)

Believing that understanding, not mere mechanical memorizing, of the Catechism is of paramount import, Luther insisted that the instruction must be popular throughout. Preachers and fathers are urged to come down to the level of the children and to prattle with them, in order to bring the Christian fundamentals home even to the weakest and simplest. In his *German Mass* Luther concludes the chapter on instruction as follows: "And let no one consider himself too wise and despise such child's play. When Christ desired to train men, He had to become a man. If we are to train children, we also must become children with them. Would to God that such child's play were carried on well; then we should in a short time see a great wealth of Christian people, and souls growing rich in the Scriptures and the knowledge of God, until they themselves would give more heed to these pockets as *locos communes* and comprehend in them the entire Scriptures; otherwise they come daily to hear the preaching and leave again as they came. For they believe that the object is merely to spend the time in hearing, no one intending to learn or retain anything. Thus many a man will hear preaching for three, four years and still not learn enough to be able to give account of his faith in one particular, as I indeed experience every day. Enough has been written in books. True, but not all of it has been impressed on the hearts." (19, 78.)

### 93. Value Placed on Memorizing.

Modern pedagogs have contended that Luther's method of teaching the Catechism unduly multiplies the material to be memorized, and does not sufficiently stress the understanding. Both charges, however, are without any foundation. As to the first, it is true that Luther did not put a low estimate on the memorizing of the Catechism. In the Large Catechism he says: "Therefore we must have the young learn the parts which belong to the Catechism or instruction for children well, and fluently and diligently exercise themselves in them and keep them occupied with them. Hence it is the duty of every father of a family to question and examine his children and servants at least once a week, and to ascertain what they know of it, or are learning, and, if they do not know it, to keep them faithfully at it." (575, 3 f.) Again: "These are the most necessary parts which one should first learn to repeat word for word, and which our children should be accustomed to recite daily when they arise in the morning, when they sit down to their meals, and when they retire at night; and until they repeat them, they should be given neither food nor drink." (577, 15.)

According to the Preface to the Small Catechism, the teacher is to abide with rigid exactness by the text which he has once chosen, and have the children learn it verbatim. "In the first place," says Luther, "let the preacher above all be careful to avoid many kinds of or various texts and forms of the Ten Commandments, the Lord's Prayer, the Creed, the Sacraments, etc., but choose one form to which he adheres, and which he inculcates all the time, year after year. For young and simple people must be taught by uniform, settled texts and forms, otherwise they easily become confused when the teacher to-day teaches them thus, and in a year some other way, as if he wished to make improvements, and thus all effort and labor will be lost. Also our blessed fathers understood this well; for they all used the same form of the Lord's Prayer, the Creed, and the Ten Commandments. Therefore we, too, should teach the young and simple people these parts in such a way as not to change a syllable, or set them forth and repeat them one year differently than in another. Hence, choose whatever form you please, and adhere to it forever. But when you preach in the presence of learned and intelligent men, you may exhibit your skill, and may present these parts in as varied and intricate ways and give them as masterly turns as you are able. But with the young people stick to one fixed, permanent form and manner, and teach them, first of all, these parts, namely, the Ten Commandments, the Creed, the Lord's Prayer, etc., according to the text, word for word, so that they, too, can repeat it in the same manner after you and commit it to memory." (533, 7 ff.) Thus Luther indeed placed a high value on exact memorizing of the Catechism.

As to the quantity of memorizing, however, Luther did not demand more than even the least gifted were well able to render. He was satisfied if they knew, as a minimum, the text of the first three chief parts and the words of institution of Baptism and the Lord's Supper. (579, 22. 25.) That was certainly not overburdening even a weak memory. Luther was right when he declared in his *Short Form of the Ten Commandments*, of 1520: In the three chief parts everything "is summed up with such brevity and simplicity that no one can complain or offer the excuse that it is too much or too hard for him to remember what he must know for his salvation." (W. 7, 204.)

Self-evidently, it was not Luther's opinion that instruction or memorizing should end here. In the Preface to the Small Catechism he says: "In the third place, after you have thus taught them this Short Catechism, then take up the Large Catechism, and give them also a richer and fuller knowledge. Here explain at length every commandment, petition, and part with its various works, uses, benefits, dangers, and injuries as you find these abundantly stated in many books written about these matters." (535, 17.) Then, as Luther often repeats, Bible-verses, hymns, and Psalms were also to be memorized and explained. Nor did he exclude the explanation of the Small Catechism from the material for memorizing. For this very reason he had written the Small Catechism in questions and answers, because he wished to have it learned, questioned, and recited from memory. "However," says Luther in the Large Catechism, "for the common people we are satisfied with the three parts, which have remained in Christendom from of old." (575, 5.) As far, then, as the material for memorizing is concerned, Luther certainly did not demand more than even the least gifted were well able to render.

## 94. Memorizing to Serve Understanding.

The second charge, that Luther attached no special importance to the understanding of what was memorized, is still more unfounded. The fact is that everywhere he was satisfied with nothing less than correct understanding. Luther was a man of thought, not of mere sacred formulas and words. To him instruction did not mean mere mechanical memorizing, but conscious, personal, enduring, and applicable spiritual appropriation. Says he: "However, it is not enough for them to comprehend and recite these parts according to the words only, but the young people should also be made to attend the preaching, especially during the time which is devoted to the Catechism, that they may hear it explained, and may learn to understand what every part contains, so as to be able to recite it as they have heard it, and, when asked, may give a correct answer, so that the preaching may not be without profit and fruit." (579, 26.) In the Preface to the Small Catechism, Luther instructs the preachers: "After they [the children] have well learned the text, then teach them the sense also, so that they know what it means." (535, 14.) Correct understanding was everything to Luther. Sermons in the churches and catechizations at home were all to serve this purpose.

In the same interest, viz., to enrich the brief text of the Catechism and, as it were, quicken it with concrete perceptions, Luther urged the use of Bible-stories as illustrations. For the same reason he added pictures to both of his Catechisms. His *Prayer-Booklet* contained as its most important part the text and explanation of the Catechism and, in addition, the passional booklet, a sort of Bible History. To this Luther remarks: "I considered it wise to add the ancient passional booklet [augmented by Luther] to the *Prayer-Booklet*, chiefly for the sake of the children and the unlearned, who are more apt to remember the divine histories if pictures and parables are added, than by mere words and teaching, as St. Mark testifies, that for the sake of the simple Christ, too, preached to them only in parables." (W. 10, 2, 458.) Indeed, Luther left no stone unturned to have his instruction understood. On words and formulas, merely memorized, but not appropriated intellectually, he placed but little value.

Memorizing, too, was regarded by Luther not as an end in itself, but as a means to an end. It was to serve the explanation and understanding. And its importance in this respect was realized by Luther much more clearly than by his modern critics. For when the text is safely embedded, as it were, in the memory, its explanation is facilitated, and the process of mental assimilation may proceed all the more readily. In this point, too, the strictures of modern pedagogs on Luther's Catechism are therefore unwarranted. Where Luther's instructions are followed, the memory is not overtaxed, and the understanding not neglected.

The instruction advocated by Luther differed fundamentally from the mechanical methods of the Middle Ages. He insisted on a thorough mental elaboration, by means of sermons, explanations, questions and answers, of the material memorized, in order to elevate it to the plane of knowledge. With Luther we meet the questions: "What does this mean? What does this signify? Where is this written? What does it profit?" He engages the intellect. The *Table of Christian Life* of the Middle Ages, which "all good Christians are in duty bound to have in their houses, for themselves, their children, and household," is regarded by Cohrs as a sort of forerunner of Luther's Small Catechism. "At the same time, however," Cohrs adds, "it clearly shows the difference between the demands made by the Church of the Middle Ages and the requirements of the Evangelical Church; yonder, numerous parts without any word of explanation, sacred formulas, which many prayed without an inkling of the meaning; here, the five chief parts, in which the emphasis is put on 'What does this mean?'" (Herzog, *R.* 10, 138.)

It was due to the neglect of Christian teaching that Christendom had fallen into decay. Force on the part of the popes and priests and blind submission on the part of the people had supplanted instruction and conviction from the Word of God. Hence the cure of the Church, first of all, called for an instructor in Christian fundamentals. And just such a catechist Luther was, who made it his business to teach and convince the people from the Bible. Indeed, in his entire work as a Reformer, Luther consistently appealed to the intellect, as was strikingly demonstrated in

the turmoil which Carlstadt brought about at Wittenberg. Instruction was the secret, was the method, of Luther's Reformation. In the Preface to the Small Catechism he says that one cannot and must not force any one to believe nor drive any one to partake of the Sacrament by laws, lest it be turned into poison, that is to say, lest the very object of the Gospel, which is spontaneous action flowing from conviction, be defeated. (539, 24; 535, 13.)

### 95. Manuals Preceding Luther's Catechism.

When Luther, in his *German Order of Worship*, sounded the slogan: German services with German instruction in Christian fundamentals! he did not lose sight of the fact that this required certain helps for both parents and preachers. A book was needed that would contain not only the text to be memorized, but also necessary explanations. Accordingly, in his *German Order of Worship*, Luther referred to his *Prayer-Booklet* as a help for instruction. However, the *Brief Form of the Ten Commandments*, etc., incorporated in the *Prayer-Booklet*, was not adapted for children and parents, as it was not drawn up in questions and answers. To the experienced teacher it furnished material in abundance, but children and parents had need of a simpler book. Hardeland says: "It is certain that Luther in 1526 already conceived the ideal catechism to be a brief summary of the most important knowledge [in questions and answers], adapted for memorizing and still sufficiently extensive to make a thorough explanation possible, at once confessional in its tone, and fitted for use in divine service." (*Katechismusgedanken* 2.) But if Luther in 1526 had conceived this idea, it was not carried out until three years later.

However, what Luther said on teaching the Catechism by questions and answers, in the *German Order of Worship*, was reprinted repeatedly (probably for the first time at Nuernberg) under the title: "Doctor Martin Luther's instruction how to bring the children to God's Word and service, which parents and guardians are in duty bound to do, 1527." This appeal of Luther also called forth quite a number of other explanations of the Catechism. Among the attempts which appeared before Luther's Catechisms were writings of Melanchthon, Bugenhagen, Eustasius Kannel, John Agricola, Val. Ickelsamer, Hans Gerhart, John Toltz, John Bader, Petrus Schultz, Caspar Graeter, Andr. Althamer, Wenz. Link, Conr. Sam, John Brenz, O. Braunfels, Chr. Hegendorfer, Caspar Loener, W. Capito, John Oecolampad, John Zwick, and others. The work of Althamer, the Humanist and so-called Reformer of Brandenburg-Ansbach, was the first to bear the title "Catechism." As yet it has not been ascertained whether, or not, Luther was acquainted with these writings. Cohrs says: "Probably Luther followed this literature with interest, and possibly consulted some of it; the relationship is nowhere close enough to exclude chance; still the frequent allusions must not be overlooked; as yet it cannot be simply denied that Luther was influenced by these writings." On the other hand, it has been shown what an enormous influence Luther exercised on that literature, especially by his *Brief Form* and his *Prayer-Booklet.* "In fact," says Cohrs, "Luther's writings can be adduced as the source of almost every sentence in most of these books of instruction." (W. 30, 1, 474.) Evidently, Luther's appeal of 1526 had not fallen on deaf ears.

### 96. Luther's Catechetical Publications.

Luther not only stirred up others to bring the Catechism back into use, but himself put his powerful shoulder to the wheel. From the very beginning he was, time and again, occupied with reading the text of the Catechism to the people, and then explaining it in sermons. From the end of June, 1516, to Easter, 1517, he preached on the Ten Commandments and the Lord's Prayer. (W. 1, 394; 2, 74; 9, 122.) In 1518 the explanation of the Ten Commandments appeared in print: "*Decem Praecepta Wittenbergensi Praedicata Populo.* The Ten Commandments Preached to the People of Wittenberg." (1, 398. 521.) Oecolampadius praised the work, saying that Luther had here "taken the veil from the face of Moses." Sebastian Muenster said: Luther explains the Ten Commandments "in such a spiritual, Christian, and Evangelical way, that its like cannot be found, though many teachers have written on the subject." (1, 394.) Agricola published Luther's sermons on the Lord's Prayer at the beginning of 1518 with some additions of his own, which fact induced Luther to publish them himself. April 5, 1519, his *Explanation of the Lord's Prayer in German* appeared in print. It was intended for the plain people, "not for the learned." (2, 81 to 130.) July 2, 1519, the Humanist Beatus Rhenanus wrote to Zwingli that he would like to see this explanation of the Lord's Prayer offered for sale throughout all Switzerland, in all cities, markets, villages, and houses. Mathesius reports: "At Venice Doctor Martin's Lord's Prayer was translated into Italian, his name being omitted. And when the man saw it from whom the permission to print it was obtained, he exclaimed: Blessed are the hands that wrote this, blessed the eyes that see it, and blessed will be the hearts that believe this book and cry to God in such a manner." (W. 2, 75.) This work passed through many editions. In 1520 it appeared in Latin and Bohemian, and as late as 1844 in English. March 13, 1519, Luther wrote to Spalatin: "I am not able to turn the Lord's Prayer [Explanation of the Lord's Prayer in German of 1518] into Latin, being busy with so many works. Every day at evening I pronounce the commandments and the Lord's Prayer for the children and the unlearned, then I preach." (Enders 1, 449.) Thus Luther preached the Catechism, and at the same time was engaged in publishing it.

The *Brief Instruction How to Confess,* printed 1519, was also essentially an explana-

tion of the Ten Commandments. It is an extract from Luther's Latin work, *Instructio pro Confessione Peccatorum,* published by Spalatin. Luther recast this work and published it in March, 1520, entitled: *Confitendi Ratio.* (W. 2, 59. 65.) As a late fruit of his *Explanation of the Lord's Prayer in German* there appeared, in 1519, the *Brief Form for Understanding and Praying the Lord's Prayer,* which explains it in prayers. (6, 11—19.) In 1519 there appeared also his *Short and Good Explanation Before Oneself and Behind Oneself* ("vor sich und hinter sich"), a concise explanation how the seven petitions must be understood before oneself ("vor sich"), *i. e.,* being ever referred to God, while many, thinking only of themselves, put and understand them behind themselves ("hinter sich"). (6, 21. 22.) June, 1520, it was followed by the *Brief Form of the Ten Commandments, the Creed, the Lord's Prayer,* a combination of the revised *Brief Explanation of the Ten Commandments,* of 1518, and the *Brief Form for Understanding the Lord's Prayer,* of 1519, with a newly written explanation of the Creed. With few changes Luther embodied it in his *Prayer-Booklet,* which appeared for the first time in 1522. Here he calls it a "simple Christian form and mirror to know one's sins, and to pray." The best evidence of the enthusiastic reception of the *Prayer-Booklet* are the early editions which followed hard upon each other, and the numerous reprints during the first years. (10, 2, 350—409.) In 1525 Luther's sermons on Baptism, Confession, and the Lord's Supper were also received into the *Prayer-Booklet,* and in 1529 the entire Small Catechism.

After his return from the Wartburg, Luther resumed his Catechism-labors with increased energy. March 27 Albert Burer wrote to Beatus Rhenanus: "Luther intends to nourish the weak, whom Carlstadt and Gabriel aroused by their vehement preaching, with milk alone until they grow strong. He daily preaches the Ten Commandments." At Wittenberg special attention was given to the instruction of the young, and regular Catechism-sermons were instituted. In the spring of 1521 Agricola was appointed catechist of the City Church, to instruct the young in religion. Lent 1522 and 1523, Luther also delivered Catechism-sermons, Latin copies of which have been preserved. In the same year Bugenhagen was appointed City Pastor, part of his duties being to deliver sermons on the Catechism, some of which have also been preserved.

Maundy Thursday, 1523, Luther announced that instead of the Romish confession, abolished during the Wittenberg disturbances, communicants were to announce for communion to the pastor and submit to an examination in the Catechism. As appears from Luther's *Formula Missae* of this year, the pastor was to convince himself whether they were able to recite and explain the words of institution by questioning them on what the Lord's Supper is, what it profits, and for what purpose they desired to partake of it. (12, 215.

479.) To enable the people to prepare for such examination, Luther (or Bugenhagen, at the instance of Luther) published a few short questions on the Lord's Supper, culled from one of Luther's sermons. This examination became a permanent institution at Wittenberg. In a sermon on the Sacrament of 1526, Luther says: "Confession, though it serve no other purpose, is a suitable means of instructing the people and of ascertaining what they believe, how they learn to pray, etc.; for else they live like brutes. Therefore I have said that the Sacrament shall be given to no one except he be able to give an account of what he receives [in the Sacrament] and why he is going. This can best be done in confession." (19, 520.)

Furthermore, on Sundays, after the sermon, the Catechism was read to the people, a custom which likewise became a fixture in Wittenberg. According to a small pamphlet of 1526, entitled, "What Shall be Read to the Common People after the Sermon?" it was the text of the five chief parts that was read. (Herz., R. 10, 132.) These parts came into the hands of the people by means of the Booklet for Laymen and Children, of 1525, written probably by Bugenhagen. He also reorganized the Wittenberg school which the fanatics had dissolved; and, self-evidently, there, too, Catechism instruction was not lacking. In a similar way religious instruction of the young was begun at other places, as appears, for example, from the Opinions on Reformation by Nicolaus Hausmann (Zwickau), of 1523 and 1525. Melanchthon's Instructions for Visitors (Articuli, de quibus egerunt per visitatores), drawn up in 1527, and used in the visitation of 1528 and 1529 as the guide by which pastors were examined, and pointing out what they should be charged to do, provide, above all, for Catechism-preaching on every Sunday, and give instructions for such sermons. (C. R. 26, 9. 48.)

Thus Luther's strenuous efforts at establishing the Catechism were crowned with success. In the Apology of 1530 Melanchthon declares triumphantly: "Among the opponents there is no Catechism, although the canons require it. Among us the canons are observed, for pastors and ministers instruct the children and the young in God's Word, publicly and privately." (526, 41.)

## 97. Immediate Forerunners of Luther's Catechisms.

Luther's entire pastoral activity was essentially of a catechetical nature and naturally issued in his two Catechisms, which, more than any other of his books, are the result of his labor in the congregation. Three writings, however, must be regarded as their direct precursors, viz., the Short Form of the Ten Commandments, the Creed, and the Lord's Prayer, of 1520, the Booklet for Laymen and Children, of 1525, and the three series of Catechism-sermons of 1528, delivered in Bugenhagen's absence. True, they are not yet real catechisms, but they paved the way for them. The Short Form is a summary and explanation of the three traditional chief parts. In the preface to this work, Luther expresses him-

self for the first time on the value and the coherence of these parts, which he considered to be the real kernel of the Catechism. In the Short Form he also abandoned the traditional division of the Creed into twelve parts, choosing, instead, the threefold division of the later Small Catechism. In 1522 he embodied the Short Form into his Prayer-Booklet, in consequence of which it was given extended circulation. It has been called Luther's first catechism, and Luther himself regarded it so; for in his German Order of Worship he recommends its use for catechetical instruction. In it are summed up Luther's catechetical efforts since 1516.

The Booklet for Laymen and Children appeared at Wittenberg in 1525, at first in Low German (Ein Boekeschen vor de leyen unde Kinder), but done into High German in the same year. Though Bugenhagen is probably its author, no doubt, the book was written at the suggestion and under the influence of Luther, parts of whose earlier explanations it contains, and who also, since 1526, made use of it in his public services. Besides the three traditional parts, it offered for the first time also those on Baptism (without the baptismal command) and on the Lord's Supper. The wording of the text was practically the same as that of Luther's Enchiridion. Several prayers, later found in Luther's Enchiridion, were also added. Hence the Booklet for Laymen and Children is properly considered a forerunner of Luther's Catechisms.

The three series of Catechism-sermons of 1528 must be considered the last preparatory work and immediate source of the explanation of the Catechisms. Luther delivered the first series May 18 to 30; the second, from September 14 to 25; the third, from November 30 to December 19. Each series treats the same five chief parts. We have these sermons in a transcript which Roerer made from a copy (Nachschrift); the third series also in a copy by a South German. In his Origin of the Catechism, Buchwald has shown how Luther's Large Catechism grew out of these sermons of 1528. In his opinion, Luther, while engaged on the Large Catechism, "had those three series of sermons before him either in his own manuscript or in the form of a copy (Nachschrift)." This explains the extensive agreement of both, apparent everywhere.

Luther himself hints at this relation; for said sermons must have been before him when he began the Large Catechism with the words: "This sermon is designed and undertaken that it might be an instruction for children and the simple-minded." (575, 1.) This was also Roerer's view; for he calls the Large Catechism "Catechism preached by D. M.," a title found also in the second copy (Nachschrift) of the third series: Catechism Preached by Doctor Martin Luther. In the conclusion of the first edition of the Large Catechism, Luther seems to have made use also of his sermon on Palm Sunday, 1529, and others; and in the Short Exhortation to Confession, which was appended to the second edition, of the sermon of Maundy Thursday, 1529, and others.

Some historians, however, have expressed the opinion that the relationship might here be reversed. The substance of the sermon-series is essentially that also of the Large Catechism. In form the Catechism differs from the sermons by summing up in each case what is contained in the corresponding three sermons, and by giving in German what the copies of the sermons offer in a mixture of Latin and German (principally Latin, especially in the first series).

Following is a sample of the German-Latin form in which Roerer preserved these sermons: "Zaehlet mir her illos, qui reliquerunt multas divitias, wie reiche Kinder sie gehabt haben; du wirst finden, dass ihr Gut zerstoben und zerflogen ist; antequam 3. et 4. generatio venit, so ist's dahin. Die Exempel gelten in allen Historien. Saul 1. fuit bonus etc. Er musste ausgerottet werden, ne quidem uno puello superstite, quia es musste wahr bleiben, quod Deus hic dicit. Sed das betreugt uns, dass er ein Jahr oder 20 regiert hat, et fuit potens rex; das verdreusst uns, ut credamus non esse verum. Sed verba Dei non mentiuntur, et exempla ostendunt etc. Econtra qui Verbo Dei fidunt, die muessen genug haben etc., ut David, qui erat vergeucht [verjagt] und verscheucht ut avicula; tamen mansit rex. Econtra Saul. Sic fit cum omnibus piis. Ideo nota bene 1. praeceptum, i. e., debes ex tota corde fidere Deo et praeterea nulli aliae rei, sive sit potestas etc., ut illis omnibus utaris, ut sutor subula etc., qui tantum laborat cum istis suis instrumentis. Sic utere bonis et donis; sie sollen dein Abgott nicht sein, sed Deus." (30, 1, 29.) The three series of sermons of 1528, therefore, were to the explanation of Luther's Catechisms what the *Booklet for Laymen* was to the text.

## 98. Catechism of Bohemian Brethren.

The assertion has been made that Luther, in his Small Catechism, followed the Children's Questions of the Bohemian Brethren, which at that time had been in use for about sixty years. This catechism, which was not clear in its teaching on the Lord's Supper, came to the notice of Luther 1520 in Bohemian or Latin, and 1523 in German and Bohemian. In his treatise, *Concerning the Adoration of the Sacrament of the Holy Body of Christ,* 1523, Luther remarks: "A book has been circulated by your people [the Bohemian Brethren] in German and Bohemian which aims to give Christian instruction to the young."

Among other things the statement is made that [the presence of] Christ in the Sacrament is not a personal and natural one, and that He must not be adored there, which disquiets us Germans very much. For without doubt it is known to you how, through the delegates you sent to me, I requested you to make this particular article clear in a separate booklet. For by word of mouth I heard them confess that you hold unanimously that Christ is truly in the Sacrament with His flesh and blood as it was born of Mary and hung on the cross, as we Germans believe. That booklet has now been sent to me by Mr. Luca in Latin. Still, in this article it has not yet been made as pure and clear as I should like to have seen it. Hence I did not have it translated into German nor printed as I promised, fearing I might not render the obscure words correctly, and thus fail to give your meaning correctly. For it may be regarded as a piece of good luck if one has hit upon an exact translation, even if the passage is very clear and certain, as I daily experience in the translations I am making. Now, that this matter may come to an end, and that the offense of the German booklet which you have published may be removed, I shall present to you and everybody, as plainly and as clearly as I am able to do, this article as we Germans believe it, and as one ought to believe according to the Gospel. There you may see whether I have stated correctly what you believe or how much we differ from one another. Perhaps my German language will be clearer to you than your German and Latin is to me." (11, 431.) Luther, then, was familiar with the catechism of the Bohemians, which contained, besides the chief parts of the ancient Church, also the doctrine of the Sacraments. This, therefore, may have suggested to him the idea of publishing a small book for children with questions and answers, which would also contain the parts of Baptism and the Lord's Supper. Such at least is the opinion of Cohrs, Kolde, Koestlin, Kawerau, and Albrecht. (W. 30, 1, 466.) But we have no sure knowledge of this. At any rate, it is not likely that it was the book of the Bohemian Brethren which prompted Luther to embody the Sacraments in his Catechism. The further assertion of Ehrenfeuchter, Moenckeberg, *et al.,* that Luther in his Table of Duties followed the Bohemian Brethren, is incorrect, since the Table of Duties appeared much later in their catechism.

# IX. The Small and the Large Catechism of Luther.

## 99. Luther Beginning Work on Catechisms.

Luther first mentioned the plan of publishing a catechism in a letter of February 2, 1525, to Nicolaus Hausmann. He informs him: "Jonas and Eisleben [Agricola] have been instructed to prepare a catechism for children. I am devoting myself to the Postil [last part of the Winter Postil] and to

Deuteronomy, where I have sufficient work for the present." (Enders, 5, 115.) In a letter of March 26, 1525, also to Hausmann, Luther repeats: "The Catechism, as I have written before, has been given to its authors, *ist seinen Verfassern aufgetragen worden.*" (144.) However, when Jonas and Agricola (who soon moved from Wittenberg to Eisleben) failed, Luther resolved to undertake the work himself, which, according to his letter of February 2, he had declined merely for the reason that he was already sufficiently burdened. The execution of his plan, however, was deferred. September 27, 1525, he wrote to Hausmann: "I am postponing the Catechism, as I would like to finish everything at one time in *one* work." (246.) The same letter shows what Luther meant. For here he speaks of the reformation of the parishes and of the introduction of uniform ceremonies. Evidently, then, he at that time desired to publish the Catechism together with a visitation tract, such as Melanchthon wrote in 1527. Besides, his *Prayer-Booklet*, containing the "Brief Form," as well as the *Booklet for Laymen and Children*, offered a temporary substitute for the contemplated Catechism. The deplorable conditions, however, which the Saxon visitation brought to light would not permit him to tarry any longer. "The deplorable, miserable condition," says Luther in the Preface to his Small Catechism, "which I discovered lately when I, too, was a visitor, has forced and urged me to prepare this Catechism, or Christian doctrine, in this small, plain, simple form." (553, 1.) Thus the Small Catechism sprang, as it were, directly from the compassion Luther felt for the churches on account of the sad state of destitution to which they had been brought, and which he felt so keenly during the visitation. However, Luther's statements in the *German Order of Worship* concerning the catechetical procedure in question and answer quoted above show that the thought of such a Catechism did not first occur to him at this time. Still it was the visitation that added the decisive impulse to put the idea into immediate execution. Besides, it was a time in which Luther was entirely engrossed in the Catechism, having preached in 1528 on the five chief parts no less than three times. Thus the harvest was at hand. In January, 1529, according to his own letters, Luther was engaged in this work, having probably begun about the close of 1528. He was able to make rapid progress, since ample material was at his command.

The old moot question which of the two Catechisms appeared first was decided when Buchwald discovered the Stephan Roth letters, which show that the Small Catechism appeared in chart form in January and March, 1529, while the first Wittenberg book edition appeared in May, after the Large Catechism had meanwhile come off the press in April. From the fact that Luther simply called his Large Catechism "German Catechism" one may infer that he began work on this first, and that, when writing the title, he had not yet begun the Small Catechism nor planned it definitely; but not, that Luther completed the Large Catechism first. On the other hand, from the title "Small Catechism" one can only infer that Luther, when he wrote thus, had already begun to write, and was working on, the Large Catechism, but not, that the Small Catechism appeared later than the Large. Albrecht: "One may certainly speak of a small book before the appearance of a large

book of similar kind, if the latter has been definitely planned, worked out at the same time, and is almost completed." (W. 30, 1, 569.)

## 100. Tables Published First.

January 15, 1529, Luther wrote to Martin Goerlitz: "*Modo in parando catechismo pro rudibus paganis versor.* I am now busy preparing the Catechism for the ignorant heathen" (not "peasants," for in his *German Order of Worship*, Luther says: "Catechism is an instruction by means of which heathen who desire to become Christians are taught"). It was formerly asserted that the expression "*pro rudibus paganis*" showed that Luther here meant the Small Catechism. Appealing to the statement in the Preface to the Large Catechism: "This sermon is designed and undertaken that it might be an instruction for children and the simple-minded," Koellner was the first one to assert that Luther's phrase of January 15 referred to the Large Catechism. In this he was followed by Cohrs, Enders, and others. (Enders, 7, 44.) However, according to the usage of the word catechism described above, the statement quoted does not preclude that Luther, when writing thus, was engaged on *both* Catechisms. And such indeed was the case. For on January 20, 1529, Roerer, the Wittenberg proofreader, wrote to Roth: "Nothing new has appeared. I believe that the Catechism as preached by D. M. for the unlettered and simple will be published for the coming Frankfurt mass. Yet, while writing this, I glance at the wall of my dwelling, and fixed to the wall I behold tables embracing in shortest and simplest form Luther's Catechism for children and the household, and forthwith I send them to you as a sample, so that by the same messenger they may be brought to you immediately. *Iam novi nihil in lucem prodiit; ad nundinas credo Francofurdenses futuras Catechismus per D. M. praedicatus pro rudibus et simplicibus edetur. Hoc vero scribens inspicio parietem aestuarioli mei, affixas parieti video tabulas complectentes brevissime simul et crasse catechismum Lutheri pro pueris et familia, statim mitto pro exemplari, ut eodem tabellario iam ad te perferantur.*" (W. 30, 1, 428; Enders, 7, 44.)

This letter of January 20 is the first time that both of Luther's Catechisms are mentioned together and distinguished from each other. By catechism Roerer means the text of the five chief parts which Luther put at the head of his Large Catechism. "*Catechismus per D. M. praedicatus*" designates the explanation of this text as comprised in Luther's three series of sermons of 1528 and summed up in the Large Catechism. From this preached and later on so-called Large Catechism, which appeared in April, entitled "German Catechism," Roerer distinguishes "tables, summing up Luther's Catechism in shortest and simplest form for children and the household." He means the series of charts containing the first three chief parts, which Luther considered the Catechism *par excellence*. And at the time when Roerer spoke of the prospective publication of the Large Catechism for the Frankfurt mass, these tables were already hanging on his wall.

Albrecht comments: "For the moment Roerer had not remembered the very interesting novelty, which had already appeared in the first tables of the later so-called Small Catechism. However, a glance at the wall of his room reminded him of it. And from a letter of his dated March 16 we must infer that they were the three charts containing the Ten Commandments, the Creed, and the Lord's Prayer with Luther's explanation. These he calls 'tables which in shortest and simplest form embrace Luther's Catechism for the children and the household.' Thus he wrote in view of the superscription: 'As the head of the family should teach them in a simple way to his household,' without implying a difference between the expression *pro pueris et familia* and the preceding *pro rudibus et simplicibus*, since the former are included in the latter. The difference between the two works is rather indicated by the words *brevissime simul et crasse*. But at the same time their inner connection is asserted, for by sending the tables *pro exemplari*, he characterizes them as a model or sample of Luther's manner of treating the Catechism. They are the *catechismus Lutheri*, that is, the aforementioned *catechismus per D. M. praedicatus* in its shortest form and draft (conceived as an extract of the sermons or of the Large Catechism). He thought that this sample would indicate what was to be expected from the forthcoming larger work." (W. 30, 1, 429.)

When, therefore, Luther wrote on January 15: "Modo in parando catechismo pro rudibus paganis versor," he was engaged on both Catechisms, and had proceeded far enough to enable him to send the first tables of the Small Catechism to the printer. Buchwald remarks regarding the letter of January 20 that Roerer probably had just received the tables from the press. However, Roerer's letter to Roth of February 12, 1529, shows that already about a month ago he had sent the "tables of the Catechism" (evidently the same to which he referred January 20) to Spalatin. Accordingly, these tables were forwarded about January 12. The following remark in the Church Order for Schoenewald in the district of Schweinitz: "First to pronounce for the people the Ten Commandments, the Creed, and the Lord's Prayer, thereupon to explain them in the most simple way, *as published* [*each*] *on a printed table*," takes us back still a few days more. For the visitation in the district of Schweinitz, in which Luther took part, was held January 7 to 9, the time from which also the Schoenewald Church Order dates. At this visitation, therefore, even prior to January 7, Luther himself distributed the first series of tables, comprising the first three chief parts, of his Small Catechism. Cohrs opines that Luther sent this series to the printer about Christmas 1528 at the latest. However, it does not appear why the printing should have consumed three to four weeks. Seb. Froeschel, however, is mistaken when he declares in his book on the *Priesthood of*

*Christ*, 1565, that, at a table conversation of 1528, Luther had advised Hans Metsch constantly to have with him a good small catechism, such as the one he had written. Knaake surmises that 1528 is a misprint; it should be 1538. (W. 30, 1, 430 f.)

## 101. Completion of Catechisms Delayed.

It was almost two months after the first table-series had appeared before the second was published. This delay is accounted for by Luther's illness and his being burdened with other work, especially with his book against the Turk. March 3 he wrote to Hausmann: "By reason of Satan's afflictions I am almost constantly compelled to be a sick well man (*als Gesunder krank zu sein*); hence I am much hindered in writing and other work." (Enders, 7, 61.) However, in the same letter Luther informed his impatiently waiting friend: "The Catechism is not completed, my dear Hausmann, but it will be completed shortly." Enders remarks that this refers to the Large Catechism. However, it harmonizes best with Luther's usage and with the facts if the words are understood as referring to both Catechisms. "Shortly," Luther had written; and on March 16 Roerer, according to his letter of this date, forwarded "the tables of Confession, the German Litany, the tables of the Sacrament of Baptism and of the blood of Christ." Roerer calls them a novelty, *recens excussa*, recently printed, from which it appears that the *tabulae catechismum Lutheri brevissime simul et crasse complectentes*, to which he referred on January 20, did not contain the Sacraments. Thus, then, the five chief parts, Decalog, Creed, Lord's Prayer, Baptism, and Lord's Supper, were completed by March 16, 1529. Buchwald and Cohrs surmise, but without further ground for their assumption, that the table with the Benedicite and the Gratias was issued together with the first series in January. At the latest, however, the prayers appeared with the second series. For March 7, 1529, Levin Metzsch wrote to Roth, evidently referring to Luther's tables: "I am herewith also sending to you the Benedicite and the Gratias, also the Morning and Evening Prayers, together with the Vice of Drunkenness." (W. 30, 1, 432.) The exact time when Luther composed the Table of Duties is not known. And the first evidence we have of the Small Catechism's appearing in book form is Roerer's letter of May 16, 1529, saying that he is sending two copies of the Small Catechism, the price of which, together with other books, is two groschen. (432.) The necessary data are lacking to determine how long Luther's manuscript was ready before it was printed, and before the printed copies were distributed.

As to the Large Catechism, it was not completed when the second table series appeared in March. In a letter, the date of which must probably be fixed about the end of March, Roerer says: "The Turk is not yet entirely struck off, neither the Catechism." April 23, however, the Large Catechism was on the market, for on this day Roerer wrote: "I am sending three copies of the Catechism." It was the Large Catechism; for the price of each copy was two groschen, whereas on May 16, 1529, Roerer had sent two copies of the Small Catechism and other books for two groschen. (432.) The Large Catechism probably had appeared several weeks before April 23. Albrecht: "Even if all [of Luther's] sermons from Palm Sunday to Maundy Thursday, 1529, are considered preliminary works, according to which the last paragraphs of the Large Catechism were elaborated, we can assume that its appearance in the beginning or the first half of April, 1529, was possible. To be sure, the printing must then have been advanced so far before Holy Week that the rest could be finished speedily on the basis of the manuscript delivered immediately after the sermons of Monday and Maundy Thursday had been preached.

This theory fits in with the facts that John Lonicer of Marburg had already completed his Latin translation on May 15, 1529 (although, according to the title-page, it first appeared in September), and that Roerer in a letter of April 23 merely mentions the Large Catechism in passing, without designating it as an important novelty. Stephen Roth, the recipient of the letter, spent some time at Wittenberg during April, and probably purchased his first copy there; so Roerer refers to copies which were ordered subsequently. (482.)

While thus the Small Catechism in chart form was completed and published before the Large Catechism, the former succeeded the latter in book form. However, though completed after the Small Catechism, it can be shown that the beginning and perhaps even part of the printing of the Large Catechism dates back to 1528, thus preceding in this respect even the Charts of January 9. If the short Preface to the Large Catechism, as well as the exhortation at the beginning: "Let the young people also come to the preaching, that they hear it explained and learn to understand it," etc., had been written after the 9th of January, Luther would probably have mentioned the Tables, just as he refers to the Large Catechism in the Preface to the Small Catechism, which was written about the end of April or the beginning of May. (535, 17.) Since, however, Luther makes no such indication, these paragraphs of the Large Catechism were, no doubt, composed before January, 1529. (574, 1; 578, 26.) The same inference may be drawn from the fact that, in the explanation of the First Commandment, the wording of the conclusion of the Ten Commandments shows a number of variations from its wording in the Small Catechism, whereas its wording at the close of the explanation of the commandments is in conformity with it. (588, 30; 672, 320.)

## 102. Similarity and Purpose of Catechisms.

As great as is the dissimilarity between Luther's two Catechisms, on the one hand, so great, on the other, is the similarity. If one did not know that the Large Catechism was begun before the Small, and that both originated in the sermons of 1528, he might either view the Large Catechism as a subsequent expansion of the Small, or the latter as a summary of the former. Yet neither the one nor the other is the case. If the Large Catechism influenced the Small, so also the latter the former. Albrecht says: "It is more probable that the Small Catechism influenced the Large Catechism than *vice versa.*" (W. 30, 1, 558.) At all events, the second table-series could not have been extracted from the Large Catechism as such, since the latter was only completed after March 25, whereas these tables were published already on March 16. The Small Catechism has been characterized as "a small basketful of ripe fruit gathered from that tree" [the Large Catechism]. In substance that is true, since both originate from the same source, the sermons of 1528. Already Roerer calls attention to this similarity, when, in the aforementioned letter, he designates the Large Catechism as "*Catechismus per D. M. praedicatus,*" and then describes the Small Catechism as "*tabulae complectentes brevissime simul et crasse catechismum Lutheri pro pueris et familia.*" Both treat of the same five chief parts; the explanation of both presupposes the knowledge of the text of these parts; both owe their origin to the doctrinal ignorance, uncovered particularly in the Saxon visitation; and the purpose of both is the instruction of the plain people and the young. Indeed, it was not for scholars, but for the people that Luther lived, labored, and contended. "For," says he in his *German Mass,* "the paramount thing is to teach and lead the people." (W. 19, 97.)

Above all, Luther endeavored to acquaint the "dear youth" with the saving truths, not merely for their own sakes, but in the interest of future generations as well. He desired to make them mature Christians, able to confess their faith and to impart instruction to their children later on. In particular, the two Catechisms were to serve the purpose of properly preparing the children and the unlearned for the Holy Eucharist, as appears from the Preface to the Small Catechism and from the last paragraphs of the Large (536, 21 ff.; 760, 39 ff.); for both end in admonitions diligently to partake of the Lord's Supper. The Sacrament of the Altar, in Luther's estimation, is the goal of all catechetical instruction. For this reason he added to the ancient chief parts those of Baptism, Confession, and the Lord's Supper.

Accordingly, both Catechisms, though in various respects, are intended for all: people, youth, parents, preachers, and teachers. It is not correct to say that Luther wrote his Large Catechism only for scholars, and the other only for the unlearned. He desired to instruct all, and, at the same time, enable parents and pastors to teach. According to Luther, it is the duty of every Christian to learn constantly, in order also to be able to teach others in turn. If any one, said he, really no longer needed the Catechism for himself, he should study it nevertheless for the sake of the ignorant. Nor did Luther exempt himself from such study. In the Long Preface to the Large

Catechism we read: "But for myself I say this: I am also a doctor and preacher, yea, as learned and experienced as all those may be who have such presumption and security; yet I do as a child who is being taught the Catechism, and every morning, and whenever I have time, I read and say, word for word, the Ten Commandments, the Creed, the Lord's Prayer, the Psalms, etc. And I must still read and study daily, and yet I cannot master it as I wish, but must remain a child and pupil of the Catechism, and am glad so to remain." (569, 7.)

April 18, 1530, Luther repeated this in a sermon as follows: "Whoever is able to read, let him, in the morning, take a psalm or some other chapter in the Bible and study it for a while. For that is what I do. When I rise in the morning, I pray the Ten Commandments, the Creed, the Lord's Prayer, and also a psalm with the children. I do so because I wish to remain familiar with it, and not have it overgrown with mildew, so that I know it." (W. 32, 65.) In a sermon of November 27, of the same year, Luther warns: "Beware lest you become presumptuous, as though, because you have heard it often, you knew enough of the Catechism. For this knowledge ever desires us to be its students. We shall never finish learning it, since it does not consist in speech, but in life. . . . For I also, D. M., doctor and preacher, am compelled day by day to pray and to recite the words of the Decalog, the Symbol, and the Lord's Prayer as children are wont to do. Hence you need not be ashamed; for much fruit will result." (209.)

### 103. Particular Purpose of Large Catechism.

In his sermons of 1529 Luther declared repeatedly that his purpose was to instruct the plain people and the children in those things which he regarded as the minimum every Christian ought to know. (30, 1, 2. 27. 57.) And he did not abandon this purpose when he condensed his sermons into the Large Catechism. Accordingly, he begins it with the words: "This sermon is designed and undertaken that it might be an instruction for children and the simple-minded." (575, 1.) Again: "For the reason why we exercise such diligence in preaching the Catechism so often is that it may be inculcated on our youth, not in a high and subtile manner, but briefly and with the greatest simplicity, so as to enter the mind readily and be fixed in the memory." (581, 27.) Hence Roerer also characterized the Large Catechism as "Catechismus per D. M. praedicatus pro rudibus et simplicibus." Many expressions of the Large Catechism also point to the fact that everything was here intended for the young and the common people. For example: "All this I say that it may be well impressed upon the young." (621, 140.) "But now for young scholars let it suffice to indicate the most necessary points." (681, 12.) "But to explain all these single points separately belongs not to brief sermons for children, but rather to the ampler ser-

mons that extend throughout the entire year." (687, 32.) Thus Luther aimed to serve the people and the children also by his Large Catechism. Not, indeed, that it was to be given into the hands of the children (the Small Catechism served that purpose), but that preachers, teachers, and parents were to use it with a view to teaching them by example how to expound the articles of the Christian doctrine for the simple-minded.

In particular, the Large Catechism was to enable the less educated pastors in the villages and in the country to do justice to their sacred duty. The instructions of the visitors called for regular Catechism-sermons. For this purpose Luther sought to furnish the preachers with material. From the Large Catechism they were to learn how to deliver simple, plain sermons on the five chief parts. In the longer Preface Luther therefore directs his admonition "to all Christians, but especially to all pastors and preachers, that they should daily exercise themselves in the Catechism, which is a short summary and epitome of the entire Holy Scriptures, and that they may always teach the same." And why? Luther explains: "We have no slight reasons for treating the Catechism so constantly, and for both desiring and beseeching others to teach it, since we see to our sorrow that many pastors and preachers are very negligent in this, and slight both their office and this teaching; some from great and high art, but others from sheer laziness and care for their paunches," etc. (567.)

Ministers, according to Luther, were to study the Catechism for their own instruction and edification as well as in the interest of their office. Hence he concludes his Preface, saying: "Therefore I again implore all Christians, especially pastors and preachers, not to be doctors too soon, and imagine that they know everything (for imagination and cloth unshrunk fall far short of the measure), but that they daily exercise themselves well in these studies and constantly treat them; moreover, that they guard with all care and diligence against the poisonous infection of such security and vain imagination, but steadily keep on reading, teaching, learning, pondering, and meditating, and do not cease until they have made a test and are sure that they have taught the devil to death, and have become more learned than God Himself and all His saints." (573, 19; 534, 17.)

From the Large Catechism, therefore, pastors were to learn how to preach the fundamental Christian truths. "To be sure," says Albrecht, "Luther did not make it as easy for the pastors as was later done by Osiander and Sleupner in the Nuernberg Children's Sermons, where the individual sermons are exactly marked off, the form of address to the children is retained, and, in each instance, a short explanation, to be memorized, is added to the longer explanation." (W. 30, 1, 478.) — That it was Luther's purpose to have his Large Catechism serve also parents appears from the instructions at the beginning and the end of it. (574, 17; 772, 87.)

## 104. Special Purpose of Small Catechism.

The Large Catechism was to serve all; the same applies to the Small Catechism. But above all it was to be placed into the hands of the children, who were to use and to memorize it at home, and to bring it with them for instruction in the church. Buchwald and Cohrs surmise that Luther published the second table series during Lent with special reference to "grown people." However, Luther was accustomed to direct his admonition to partake of the Lord's Supper diligently also to children and that, too, to children of comparatively tender years. In his sermon of March 25, 1529, he says: "This exhortation ought not only to move us older ones, but also the young and the children. Therefore you parents ought to instruct and educate them in the doctrine of the Lord: the Decalog, the Creed, the Prayer, and the Sacraments. Such children ought also to be admitted to the Table that they may be partakers" [of the Lord's Supper]. (W. 30, 1, 233.) In his sermon of December 19, 1528, we read: "Hence, you parents and heads of families, invite your subordinates to this Sacrament; and we shall demand an account of you if you neglect it. If you will not go yourselves, let the young go; we are much concerned about them. When they come, we shall learn, by examining them, how you instruct them in the Word as prescribed. Hence, do come more frequently to the Sacrament, and also admonish your children to do so when they have reached the age of discretion. For in this way we want to learn who are Christians, and who not. If you will not do so, we shall speak to you on the subject. For even though you older people insist on going to the devil, we shall still inquire about your children. Necessity: because sin, the devil, and death are ever present. Benefit: because the remission of sins and the Holy Spirit are received." (121 f.) The tender age at which the young were held to partake of the Lord's Supper appears from Bugenhagen's preface to the Danish edition of the Enchiridion of 1538, where he says "that, after this confession is made, also the little children of about eight years or less should be admitted to the table of Him who says: 'Suffer the little children to come unto Me.'" (433.) The conjecture, therefore, that the tables of Confession and the Sacraments were not intended for children, but specifically for adults, is without foundation. In all its parts the Small Catechism was intended to serve the children.

When the first table appeared, it bore the superscription: "The Ten Commandments, as *the head of the family* should teach them in a simple way to his household." Similar to this were the titles of the remaining charts. And these superscriptions were permitted to stand when Luther published the Enchiridion in book form. The book edition, therefore, as well as the chart edition, was to render services also to parents, who were to take upon themselves a large part of the work in teaching the young. But how were they to do it,

in view of the fact that many of them did not know the Catechism themselves? This had occurred also to Luther. He realized that, besides the Large Catechism, parents were in need of a text-book containing questions and answers, adapted for catechizing the children on the meaning of each part of the Catechism. This, too, was the reason why the Small Catechism was rapidly completed before the Large, which had been begun first. Luther intended parents to use it, first of all for their own instruction and edification, but also for the purpose of enabling them to discharge their duty by their children and household.

## 105. Small Catechism Intended Also for Pastors.

That Luther intended his Small Catechism as a help also for pastors was, in so many words, stated on the title-page of the first book edition. For, surprising as it may seem, here he mentions neither the parents nor the children, but solely the "ordinary pastors and preachers." The Preface also is addressed to "all faithful, pious pastors and preachers," and it shows in detail how they were to make use of the book. Evidently, then, the book edition was intended to render special services also to preachers. The reason, however, was not, as has been surmised, because it embodied the booklet on Marriage (the booklet on Baptism was added in the second edition); for the Preface, which is addressed to the preachers, does not even mention it. The pastors, moreover, were especially designated on the title-page as the recipients of the Enchiridion, inasmuch as they were to employ it in their religious instruction and catechetical sermons, in order to imbue the young with its contents. The expression "ordinary pastors and preachers" referred primarily to the plain preachers in the villages, where no properly regulated school system existed, and where, at best, the sexton might assist the pastor in seeing to it that the Catechism was memorized. Albrecht: "When Luther prepared both Catechisms at the same time and with reference to each other, he evidently desired their simultaneous use, especially on the part of the plain pastors, who in the Small Catechism possessed the leading thoughts which were to be memorized, and in the Large Catechism their clear and popular explanation." (W. 30, 1, 548.)

Luther's intention was to make the Small Catechism the basis of instruction in the church as well as in the homes; for uniform instruction was required to insure results. Having, therefore, placed the Catechism into the hands of the parents, Luther could but urge that it be introduced in the churches, too. He also showed them how to use it. On June 11, 1529, for instance, he expounded the First Article after he had read the text and the explanation of the Small Catechism. (549.) This the pastors were to imitate, a plan which was also carried out. The charts were suspended in the churches; the people and children were wont to bring the book edition with them to church; the preachers read the text, expounded it, and had it recited. The Schoene-wald Church Order prescribed that the pastor "first pronounce for the people" the text of the chief parts, and then expound it as on Luther's charts. (549.)

### 106. A Book Also for Schools and Teachers.

When planning and writing his Small Catechism, Luther self-evidently did not overlook the schools and the schoolteachers. The first booklet of the charts for the Latin schools of the Middle Ages contained the abc; the second, the first reading-material, viz., the Paternoster, Ave Maria, and the Credo; the third, the Benedicite, Gratias, and similar prayers. Albrecht writes: "We may surmise that Luther, when composing the German tables and combining them in a book, had in mind the old chart-booklets. This view is supported by the fact that in it he embodied the prayers, the Benedicite and Gratias, and probably also by the title Enchiridion, which, besides the titles 'Handbooklet' or 'The Children's Handbooklet' was applied to such elementary books." (W. 30, 1, 546.) In the Instruction for the Visitors we read: "A certain day, either Saturday or Wednesday, shall be set aside for imparting to the children Christian instruction. . . . Hereupon the schoolteacher shall simply and correctly expound at one time the Lord's Prayer, at another the Creed, at another the Ten Commandments, etc." (W. 26, 238.) In these schools Luther's Small Catechism served as text-book. From 1529 until the beginning of the eighteenth century Sauermann's Latin translation (Parvus Catechismus pro Pueris in Schola) was employed in the Latin schools of Saxony. In the German schools the German Enchiridion was used as the First Reader. Hence, the Marburg reprint of the first Wittenberg edition of the Catechism begins with the alphabet, and makes it a point to mention this fact on its title-page.

Down to the present day no other book has become and remained a schoolbook for religious instruction to such an extent as Luther's Small Catechism. And rightly so; for even Bible History must be regarded as subordinate to it. The assertion of modern educators that instruction in Bible History must precede instruction in Luther's Catechism rests on the false assumption that Luther's Catechism teaches doctrines only. But the truth is that it contains all the essential facts of salvation as well, though in briefest form, as appears particularly from the Second Article, which enumerates historical facts only. The Small Catechism is "the Laymen's Bible, der Laien Biblia," as Luther called it in a sermon of September 14, 1528, an expression adopted also by the Formula of Concord. (777, 5.) Luther's Enchiridion presents both the facts of salvation and their divine interpretation. The picture for which the Small Catechism furnishes the frame is Christ, the historical Christ, as glorified by the Holy Spirit, particularly in the writings of the Apostle Paul. In the Lutheran Church the Small Catechism, therefore, deserves to be and always to remain what it became from the first moment of its publication: the book of religious instruction for home, school, and church; for parents, children, teachers, and preachers, just as Luther had planned and desired.

### 107. Titles of Large Catechism.

"Deutsch Katechismus, German Catechism," was the title under which the Large Catechism first appeared, and which Luther never changed. In the Preface to the Small Catechism he used the expression "Large Catechism," having in mind his own Catechism, though not exclusively, as the context shows. (534, 17.) Yet this was the natural title, since the shorter Catechism was from the beginning known as the "Small Catechism." And before long it was universally in vogue. The Church Order for Brueck, of 1530, designates the Large Catechism as "the Long Catechism." In the catalog of his writings of 1533, which Luther prefaced, but did not compile, it is called "Large Catechism, Catechismus Gross." Likewise in the Corpus Doctrinae Pomeranicum. The Articles of the Visitors in Meiszen, 1533, first employed the designation "The Large and Small Catechisms." The Church Order for Gera of the same year also distinguishes: "The Large Catechism and the Small Catechism." The Eisfeld Order of 1554 distinguishes: "The Small Catechism of Luther" and "The Large Catechism of Luther." In his treatise on the Large Catechism of 1541, Spangenberg first employed the new form as a title: "The Large Catechism and Children's Instruction of Dr. M. Luther."

The title of the Low German edition of 1541 runs: "De Grote Katechismus Duedesch." The Latin translation by Obsopoeus of 1544 is entitled "Catechismus Maior." The Index of the Wittenberg complete edition of Luther's Works of 1553 has "Der grosse Katechismus," while the Catechism itself still bears the original title, "Deutscher Katechismus." The Jena edition of 1556 also has the original title, but paraphrases in the Index: "Zweierlei Vorrede, gross und klein, D. M. L. auf den Katechismum, von ihm gepredigt Anno 1529. Two Prefaces, large and small, of Dr. M. L. to the Catechism, preached by him in the year 1529." Since 1570, the Corpora Doctrinae give the title, "The Large Catechism, German. Der Grosse Katechismus, deutsch." So also the Book of Concord of 1580. In the Leipzig edition and in Walch's the word "deutsch" is omitted. (W. 30, 1, 474 f.)

"German Catechism," corresponding to the title "German Mass," means German preaching for children, German instruction in the fundamental doctrines of Christianity. Luther wrote "German Mass" in order to distinguish it from the Latin, which was retained for many years at Wittenberg beside the German service (this is also what Wolfgang Musculus meant when he reported in 1536 that in Wittenberg services were conducted predominantly in papistic fashion, ad morem papisticum).

So also "German Catechism" is in contrast to the Latin instruction in the churches and especially in the schools. Concerning the latter we read, *e. g.*, in the instruction of the visitors: "The boys shall also be induced to speak Latin, and the schoolteachers shall, as far as possible, speak nothing but Latin with them." (26, 240.) Ever since the early part of the Middle Ages the Latin Credo, Paternoster, etc., had been regarded and memorized as sacred formulas, the vernacular being permitted only rarely, and reluctantly at that. Also in the Lutheran Church the Latin language was not immediately abolished. A number of Evangelical catechisms, antedating Luther's, were written in, and presuppose the use of, the Latin language, for example, Melanchthon's *Enchiridion*, Urerius's *Paedagogia*, Agricola's *Elementa Pietatis*, etc. The Brunswick Liturgy of 1528, drafted by Bugenhagen, prescribed that on Saturday evening and early on Sunday morning the chief parts of the Catechism be read in Latin in the churches "on both galleries, slowly, without chanting (*sine tono*), alternately (*ummeschicht*)." The Wittenberg Liturgy provided: "Before the early sermon on Sundays or on festival-days the boys in the choir, on both sides, shall read the entire Catechism in Latin, verse by verse, without ornamental tone (*sine tono distincto*)." (477.) Accordingly, when Luther began to preach on the chief parts in German, he was said to conduct "German Catechism." And since German services with German instruction were instituted by Luther in the interest of the unlearned and such as were unable to attend the Latin schools, the term "German Catechism" was equivalent to popular instruction in religion. That Luther's Catechism, also in point of racy language, was German to the core, appears from the frequent use of German words and expressions which, in part, have since become obsolete. (Mueller, *Symb. Buecher*, 857—860.)

## 108. Editions of Large Catechism.

The first edition (quarto) of the Large Catechism, of which Roerer forwarded copies on April 23, 1529, contains, as text, the Commandments, the Creed, the Lord's Prayer, and the words of institution of the Sacraments. The text is preceded by a Brief Preface, which, however, Luther, considering it a part of the Catechism, did not designate and superscribe as such. Some instructions and admonitions are inserted between the Catechism-text, which is followed by the detailed explanation. Such is the form in which the Large Catechism first appeared, and which, in the main, it also retained. The second edition (also in quarto and from the year 1529) reveals numerous textual corrections and adds a longer section to the Lord's Prayer, *viz.*, paragraphs 9 to 11: "at the risk of God's wrath . . . seek His grace." (699.) This addition, though not found in the German Book of Concord of 1580, was received into the official Latin Concordia of 1584. Furthermore, the second edition of 1529 adds the "Short Admonition to Confession"; hence the subtitle: "Increased

by a New Instruction and Admonition to Confession." This addition, however, was embodied in neither the German nor the Latin Concordia. In the Seventh Commandment the second edition of 1529 omits the words "with whom [arch-thieves] lords and princes keep company" (644, 230), which, according to Albrecht, was due to a timid proof-reader. Numerous marginal notes, briefly summarizing the contents, were also added to this edition and retained in the Latin Concordia of 1584. Furthermore, it contained 24 woodcuts, the first three of which were already used in Melanchthon's fragmentary Catechism sermons of 1528, for which book probably also the remaining cuts were originally intended. Albrecht remarks: "Let it remain undecided whether the cuts, which Melanchthon probably was first to select for his catechism sermons of 1528, were received into the edition of 1529 (which Luther corrected) upon a suggestion of the printer Rhau, or Bugenhagen, or Luther himself." (W. 30, 1, 493.)

Two Latin as well as a Low German translation (by Bugenhagen) also appeared in 1529. The Low German edition, printed by Rhau, seems to have paved the way in using the aforementioned pictures. Of the Latin translations, one was prepared by Lonicer and printed at Marburg, while the other, by Vicentius Obsopoeus, rector of the school at Ansbach, was printed at Hagenau. After making some changes, which were not always improvements, Selnecter embodied the latter in the Latin Concordia, adding the longer Preface from the Frankfurt edition of 1544. In the Large Catechism this new Preface is found for the first time in Rhau's quarto edition of 1530. Literal allusions to Luther's letter of June 30, 1530, to J. Jonas have given rise to the assumption that it was written at Castle Coburg. (Enders, 8, 47. 37.) In the Jena edition of Luther's Works, the Dresden edition of the Book of Concord of 1580, the Magdeburg edition of 1580, the Heidelberg folio edition of 1582, and the Latin edition of 1580, this longer Preface follows the shorter. However, since the shorter Preface forms part of the Catechism itself, the longer Preface ought to precede it, as is the case in the official Latin Concordia of 1584. In the Low German edition of 1531 Bugenhagen defends the expressions, criticized by some: I believe "an Gott, an Christum" in the Low German edition of 1529, instead of "in Gott, in Christum." (W. 30, 1, 493.) In Rhau's edition of 1532 and 1535 the morning and evening prayers are added, probably only as fillers. The changes in Rhau's edition of 1538, styling itself, "newly corrected and improved," consist in linguistic improvements and some additions and omissions. Albrecht believes that most, but not all, of these changes were made by Luther himself, and that the omissions are mostly due to inadvertence.

## 109. Title of Small Catechism.

Luther seems to have published the chart catechism of January, 1529, without any special title, though Roerer, from the very first, calls it a catechism. In the first Wittenberg book edition, however, one finds inserted, between the Preface and the Decalog, the superscription: *"Ein kleiner Katechismus oder christliche Zucht.* A Small Catechism or Christian Discipline." This may have been the title of the charts, since it would hardly have been introduced for the book edition, where it was entirely superfluous, the title-page designating it as "The Small Catechism for the Ordinary Pastors and Preachers." Likewise, it cannot be proved that the opening word on the title-page of this first book edition was "Enchiridion," since this edition has disappeared without a trace, and the only remaining direct reprint does not contain the word "Enchiridion." All subsequent editions, however, have it.

The word "Enchiridion" is already found in the writings of Augustine, and later became common. In his Glossary, Du Cange remarks: "This name [Enchiridion] St. Augustine gave to a most excellent little work on faith, hope, and charity, which could easily be carried in the hand, or, rather, ought continually to be so carried, since it contained the things most necessary for salvation." (3, 265.) The Erfurt *Hymn-Booklet* of 1524 was called "Enchiridion or Handbooklet, very profitable for every Christian to have with him for constant use and meditation." In 1531 Luther praised the Psalter, saying: "It may be called a little Bible, wherein all that is found in the entire Bible is most beautifully and briefly summed up and has been made and prepared to be a splendid Enchiridion, or Handbook." (E. 63, 28.) The *Instruction for Visitors* calls the primer "the handbooklet of the children, containing the alphabet, the Lord's Prayer, the Creed, and other prayers." In 1523 Melanchthon had published such a book, entitled "Enchiridion." Thus Enchiridion denotes a book of pithy brevity, an elementary book. The various Church Orders employ the word in a similar sense. (W. 30, 1, 540.)

## 110. Editions of Small Catechism.

At Wittenberg, George Rhau printed the Large Catechism and Michel Schirlentz the Small Catechism (the chart impressions of which must be considered the first edition). In the Preface to the Small Catechism, Luther speaks of "these tables" and "the form of these tables," thus referring to the chief parts, which were already printed on placards. However, since "table" also denotes a list, the term could be applied also to the chief parts in book form. It was nothing new to employ tables (*"Zeddeln,"* i. e., placards printed on one side) in order to spread the parts of the Catechism in churches, homes, and schools. In 1518 Luther published his "Ten Commandments with a brief exposition of their fulfilment and transgression," on placards. Of the charts of the Small Catechism only a Low German copy has as yet been discovered. It contains Luther's Morning and Evening Prayers, a reduced reproduction of which is found in the Weimar Edition of Lu-

ther's Works. (30, 1, 241.) The book editions soon took their place beside the charts. It seems (but here the traces are rather indefinable) that the first three tables were summed up into a booklet as early as January or February, 1529. At Hamburg, Bugenhagen published the charts, which he had received till then, as a booklet, in Low German. It contained the five chief parts and the Benedicite and Gratias. Shortly after the first Wittenberg book edition had reached him, Bugenhagen translated the Preface and had it printed as a supplement.

Shortly after the completion of the Large Catechism Luther made arrangements to have the Small Catechism appear in book form. May 16 Roerer sent two copies of the *Catechismus Minor.* But, as stated above, all copies of this edition were completely used up. The edition has been preserved in three reprints, two of which appeared at Erfurt and one at Marburg. Th. Harnack published the one Erfurt and the Marburg reprint, and H. Hartung the other Erfurt reprint in separate facsimile editions. Evidently these reprints appeared before the second Wittenberg edition of June, 1529, was known at Erfurt and Marburg. In estimating their value, however, modern scholars are not agreed as to whether they represent three direct or one direct and two indirect reprints. Albrecht is of the opinion that only one of the three may be looked upon as a direct reprint. Judging from these reprints, the original edition was entitled: *"Der kleine Katechismus fuer die gemeinen Pfarrherrn und Prediger.* The Small Catechism for Ordinary Pastors and Preachers." Aside from the five chief parts, it contained the Preface, the Morning and Evening Prayers, the Table of Duties, and the Marriage Booklet. On the other hand, these reprints omit not only the word Enchiridion, but also the question, "How can bodily eating and drinking do such great things?" together with its answer. Now, in case all three should be direct reprints, the omitted question and answer evidently were not contained in the first Wittenberg edition either. On the other hand, if only one of them is a direct reprint, the mistake must be charged to the original Wittenberg impression or to the reprint. That the omission is an error, probably due to the printer, appears from the fact that the omitted question and answer were already found on the charts; for the Hamburg book edition of the charts in Low German has them, as also Stifel's written copies of the charts. (W. 30, 1, 573.)

Of the Wittenberg editions which followed the *editio princeps,* those of 1529, 1531, and 1542 deserve special mention. The first appeared under the title: "Enchiridion. The Small Catechism for the Ordinary Pastors and Preachers, enlarged and improved." On the 13th of June this edition was completed, for Roerer reports on this date: "Parvus Catechismus sub incudem iam tertio revocatus est et in ista postrema editione adauctus." (Kolde, *l. c.,* 60.) Roerer designates this edition as the third, probably because two imprints had been made of the *editio princeps*. According to a defective copy, the only one preserved, this edition adds to the contents of the *editio princeps* the word Enchiridion in the title, the Booklet of Baptism, A Brief Form of Confessing to the Priest, for the Simple, and the Litany. The fifth chief part has the question: "How can bodily eating and drinking do such great things?" In the Lord's Prayer, however, the explanation of the introduction is still lacking. This emended edition of 1529 furthermore had the pictures, for the first time as it seems. The booklets on Marriage and Baptism were retained, as additions, in all editions of the Small Catechism published during the life of Luther, and in many later editions as well. As yet, however, it has not been proved directly that such was intended and arranged for by Luther himself.

Also in the succeeding editions Luther made various material and linguistic changes. In the edition of 1531 he omitted the Litany, and for the "Short Form of Confession" he substituted an instruction in confession, which he inserted between the fourth and fifth chief parts, under the caption, "How the Unlearned Shall be Taught to Confess." The Lord's Prayer was complemented by the addition of the Introduction and its explanation, and the number of cuts was increased to 23. This edition of 1531, of which but one copy (found in the Bodleiana of Oxford) is in existence, shows essentially the form in which the Enchiridion was henceforth regularly printed during and after Luther's life. (W. 30, 1, 608.) The editions of 1537 reveal several changes in language, especially in the Bible-verses, which are made to conform to Luther's translation. In the edition of 1542 the promise of the Fourth Commandment appears for the first time, and the Table of Duties is expanded. The Bible-verses referring to the relation of congregations to their pastors were added, and the verses setting forth the relation of subjects to their government were considerably augmented. Hence the title: "Newly revised and prepared, *aufs neue uebersehen und zugerichtet*." Probably the last edition to appear during Luther's life was the one of 1543, which, however, was essentially a reprint of the edition of 1542.

Knaake declared that all the editions which we possess "must be attributed to the enterprise of the book dealers," and that one cannot speak of a direct influence of Luther on any of these editions. In opposition to this extreme skepticism, Albrecht points out that, for instance, the insertion of the explanation of the Introduction to the Lord's Prayer and the new form of confession, as well as its insertion between Baptism and the Lord's Supper, could not have taken place "without the direct cooperation of Luther."

## 111. Translations and Elaborations of Small Catechism.

Two of the Latin translations of the Small Catechism date back to 1529. The first was inserted in the *Enchiridion Piarum Precationum*, the Latin translation of Luther's *Prayer-*

*Booklet*, which appeared toward the end of August, 1529. Roerer met with great difficulties in editing the book. August, 1529, he wrote: "You may not believe me if I tell you how much trouble I am having with the Latin *Prayer-Booklet* which is now being printed. Somebody else, it is true, translated it from German into Latin, but I spent much more labor in this work than he did." (W. 30, 1, 588.) We do not know who the translator was to whom Roerer refers. It certainly was not Lonicer, the versatile Humanist of Marburg, who at that time had completed the Large Catechism with a Preface dated May 15, 1529. Kawerau surmises that it was probably *G. Major*. Evidently Luther himself had nothing to do with this translation. This Catechism is entitled: *Simplicissima et Brevissima Catechismi Expositio*. Almost throughout the question form was abandoned. In 1532 a revised form of this translation appeared, entitled: *Nova Catechismi Brevioris Translatio*. From these facts the theory (advocated also by v. Zezschwitz and Knaake) has been spun that the Small Catechism sprang from a still shorter one, which was not throughout cast in questions and answers, and offered texts as well as explanations in a briefer form. This would necessitate the further inference that the Preface to the Small Catechism was originally written in Latin. All of these suppositions, however, founder on the fact that the charts as we have them in the handwriting of Stifel are in the form of questions and answers. The *Prayer-Booklet* discarded the form of questions and answers, because its object was merely to reproduce the contents of Luther's Catechism for such as were unacquainted with German.

The second Latin translation of 1529 was furnished by John Sauermann, not (as v. Zezschwitz and Cohrs, 1901, in Herzog's *R. E.*, 10, 135, assume) the Canon of Breslau, who died 1510, but probably Johannes Sauermann of Bambergen, who matriculated at Wittenberg in the winter semester of 1518. (W. 30, 1, 601.) Sauermann's translation was intended as a school edition of the Small Catechism. First came the alphabet, then followed the texts: Decalog, Creed, the Lord's Prayer, Baptism, the Lord's Supper. Luther's Preface, the Litany, and the Booklets of Marriage and Baptism were omitted as not adapted for school use. The chapter on Confession, from the second Wittenberg book edition, was inserted between the fourth and fifth chief parts. The note to the Benedicite was put into the text with the superscription "Scholion" (instead of the incorrect "Scholia" of the German edition, found also in the Book of Concord). "Paedagogus" was substituted for "head of the family (*Hausvater*)." The word "Haustafel" remained untranslated. The words of the Third Petition, "so uns den Namen Gottes nicht heiligen und sein Reich nicht kommen lassen wollen," are rendered: "quae nobis nomen Dei non *sanctificent* regnumque eius ad nos pervenire non sinant."

In the Preface, dated September 19, 1529, "Johannes Sauromannus" writes: "Every one is of the opinion that it is clearly the best thing from early youth carefully and diligently to instruct the boys in the principles of Christian piety. And since I believe that of all the elementary books of the theologians of this age none are better adapted for this purpose than those of Dr. Martin Luther, I have rendered into Latin the booklet of this man which is called the Small Catechism, hoping that it might be given to the boys to be learned as soon as they enter the Latin school." At the same time Sauermann declares that his translation was published "by the advice and order (*consilio ac iussu*) of the author [Luther] himself." (30, 1, 673.) One cannot doubt, therefore, that Sauermann's translation received Luther's approval. And being in entire conformity with the *Instruction for Visitors*, of 1528, for the Latin city schools, the book was soon in general use. In 1556 Michael Neander speaks of it as "the common Latin version, hitherto used in all schools." (603.) The Latin Concordia of 1584 contains Sauermann's version, essentially, though not literally. The Preface, which Sauermann had not translated, is taken over from the *Prayer-Booklet*. The part On Confession was newly translated from the German edition of the Catechism of 1531. The textual changes which were made in Sauermann's translation for the Concordia of 1584 "show that he was careful and usually felicitous, and are partly to be explained as combinations of the first and second Latin translations." (604.)

When, in 1539, Justus Jonas translated the Nuernberg *Sermons for Children*, he made a third Latin translation of the Small Catechism. He calls it "this my Latin translation, not carefully finished indeed, but nevertheless rendered in good faith." (627.) This Latin text obtained special importance since it was immediately done into English, Polish, and Icelandic. In 1560 Job Magdeburg furnished a fourth Latin version. Concerning the translations into Greek, Hebrew, and other languages see Weimar Edition of Luther's Complete Works (10, 1, 718 f.).

Among the earliest elaborations of the Small Catechism was the Catechism of Justus Menius, 1532, and the Nuernberg *Children's Sermons* of 1533. Both exploit Luther's explanations without mentioning his name. At the same time some changing, abbreviating, polishing, etc., was done, as Luther's text was considered difficult to memorize. Albrecht says of Menius's emendations: "Some of his formal changes are not bad; most of them, however, are unnecessary. The entire book finally serves the purpose of bringing to light the surpassing merit of the real Luther-Catechism." (617.) The same verdict will probably be passed on all the substitute catechisms which have hitherto appeared. John Spangenberg's Small Catechism of 1541, which was widely used, is, as he himself says, composed "from the Catechism of our beloved father, Dr. Martin, and those of others." It contains Luther's Catechism mainly as changed by Menius. The Nuernberg *Children's Sermons*,

which embodied also the pictures of Luther's Catechism and received a wide circulation, were written by Osiander and Sleupner in 1532, and printed at Nuernberg, 1533. They contain almost complete the five chief parts of Luther's Small Catechism as concluding sentences of the individual sermons, but in original minting, with abbreviations, additions, and other changes, which, however, are not nearly as marked as those of Menius. These changes were also made to facilitate memorizing. Between Baptism and the Lord's Supper was found the doctrinal part on the Office of the Keys, which in this or a similar form was, after Luther's death, appended to, or inserted in, the Small Catechism as the sixth or fifth chief part, respectively.

## 112. The Part "Of Confession."

The Small Catechism did not spring from Luther's mind finished and complete at one sitting. Originally he considered the first three chief parts as constituting the Catechism. Before long, however, he added the parts of Baptism and the Lord's Supper. These five parts are for the first time mentioned in the *German Order of Worship*, and printed together in the Booklet for Laymen and Children. The Introduction to the Large Catechism also offers no more. The chart and book editions added as real parts of the Catechism (the Booklets of Marriage and of Baptism cannot be viewed as such) the Benedicite and Gratias, the Morning and Evening Prayers, the Table of Duties, and Confession. It is the last of these parts which played a peculiar rôle in the history of the Small Catechism. Albrecht writes: "In the textual history of the Small Catechism, Confession (besides the Table of Duties) is the most restless and movable part. In the Low German editions since 1531 and 1534 it is found after the Lord's Supper as a sort of sixth chief part. In individual instances it is entirely omitted. On the other hand, in elaborations of the Catechism, notably in the Nuernberg Catechism-sermons, it is supplanted by the Office of the Keys, and in later prints also combined with it or otherwise recast." (W. 30, 1, 607.)

As for Luther, evidently, as soon as he began to work on the Catechism, he planned to include also a part on Confession. Among the charts there were already those which dealt with Confession. In fact, Luther must have here treated this part at comparative length. For Roerer reports that the price of the Confession charts was three pfennige, whereas the price of the Sacrament charts was two pfennige. Yet nothing of Confession was embodied in the first book edition of the Small Catechism. The first edition also of the Large Catechism had no part treating of Confession. But the second Wittenberg edition, of 1529, appeared "augmented with a new instruction and admonition concerning Confession." Likewise the "augmented and improved" Small Catechism of 1529, superscribed, "Enchiridion," contained a "Short Form how the Unlearned shall Confess to the Priest. *Eine kurze Weise zu beichten fuer die Einfaeltigen, dem Priester."* This Form was not to serve the pastor in admonishing, etc., but Christians when going to confession. Possibly it was one of the charts which Roerer, March 16, mentioned as novelties. The addition of this part was, no doubt, caused by Luther himself. This is supported by the fact that Sauermann's translation, which appeared by Luther's "advice and order," also contained it. And while in the German book edition it was found in the Appendix, following the Booklet on Baptism, Sauermann inserted it between Baptism and the Lord's Supper with the superscription: "How schoolmasters ought in simplest manner to teach their boys a brief form of confession. *Quo pacto paedagogi suos pueros brevem confitendi rationem simplicissime docere debeant."* Evidently this, too, was done with Luther's approval (*auctoris consilio et iussu*). "Thus Luther at that time already," says Albrecht, "selected this place for Confession and retained it later on, when [1531] he furnished another form of confession for the Catechism which to him seemed more appropriate." The gradual insertion of a new chief part (of Confession and Absolution) between Baptism and the Lord's Supper was therefore entirely according to Luther's mind; indeed, it had virtually been carried out by him as early as 1529.

The original part Of Confession, however, was no catechetical and doctrinal part in the proper sense of the word, but purely a liturgical formula of Confession, even the Absolution being omitted. It merely contained two confessions similar to the forms found in the Book of Concord, page 552, sections 21 to 23. Hence Luther, in the edition of 1531, replaced it with a catechetico-liturgical form entitled, "How the Unlearned Should be Taught to Confess." It is identical with the one found in the Book of Concord of 1580, save only that the original contained the words, "What is Confession? Answer," which are omitted in the German Concordia. Luther placed the part Of Confession between Baptism and the Lord's Supper, thereby actually making this the fifth and the Lord's Supper the sixth chief part. And when later on (for in Luther's editions the chief parts are not numbered) the figures were added, Confession could but receive the number 5, and the Lord's Supper, 6. Thus, then, the sequence of the six parts, as found in the Book of Concord, was, in a way, chosen by Luther himself.

## 113. Office of the Keys and Christian Questions.

The three questions on the Office of the Keys in the fifth chief part form the most important and independent addition to Luther's Small Catechism. However, they are not only in complete agreement with Luther's doctrine of Absolution, but, in substance, also contained in what he himself offered in the part Of Confession. For what Luther says in paragraphs 26 to 28 in a liturgical form is expressed and explained in the three questions on the Office of the Keys in a doctrinal and catechetical

form. Not being formulated by Luther, however, they were not received into the Book of Concord. In the Nuernberg *Text-Booklet* of 1531 they are placed before Baptism. Thence they were taken over into the Nuernberg *Children's Sermons* of 1533 as a substitute for Luther's form of Confession. Andrew Osiander, in the draft of his Church Order of 1531, in the article on "Catechism and the Instruction of Children," added as sixth to the five chief parts: "Of the Keys of the Church, or the Power to Bind and to Unbind from Sins," quoting as Bible-verse the passage: "The Lord Jesus breathed on His disciples," etc. Brenz, though not, as frequently assumed, the author of the Nuernberg Catechism, also contributed toward introducing and popularizing this part of the Catechism. In his Questions of 1535 and 1536, which appeared in the Appendix to the Latin translation of Luther's Large Catechism, he offered an original treatment to the Keys of Heaven, as the sixth chief part, on the basis of Matt. 16, 19; Luke 19, 16; John 20, 22 f. Thirty-six years after the first publication of Luther's Catechisms, Mathesius, in his *Sermons on the Life of Luther,* also speaks of six chief parts of catechetical instruction; but he enumerates Absolution as the part between Baptism and the Lord's Supper, hence as the fifth chief part of the Catechism.

As to the Christian Questions for Those Who Intend to Go to the Sacrament, it was claimed very early that Luther was the author. They were first published in 1549, and a number of separate impressions followed. After 1558 they are usually found in the appendix to the Small Catechism. The Note, "These questions and answers," etc., designating Luther as the author, first appeared in an edition of 1551. Together with this Note, the Questions are found in an undated Wittenberg edition of the Small Catechism, which appeared about 1560, containing pictures dated 1551. Referring to this edition, the Wittenberg proof-reader, Christopher Walther, in a polemical writing (1566) against Aurifaber, asserted that the Questions were not written by Luther, but by John Lang of Erfurt († 1548). The question at issue has not yet been decided. For while the contents of the Questions reproduce, from beginning to end, Luther's thoughts, and the last answers are almost literally taken from the Large Catechism, we have no evidence that Luther compiled them; but, on the other hand, also no convincing proof against this. Claus Harms and Koellner asserted that Luther is the author of the Questions, while Kliefoth and Loehe declared it as probable. — The Introduction to the Ten Commandments, "I the Lord, thy God," and the Doxology, at the close of the Lord's Prayer, were added after Luther's death.

## 114. The Table of Duties — Haustafel.

The eighth and last chart of the Catechism differed from the preceding ones in that it was superscribed: "Table of Duties (Haustafel), Consisting of Certain Passages of Scripture for Various Holy Orders and Stations, Whereby These are to be Admonished, as by a Special Lesson, Regarding Their Office and Service." The exact time when Luther drew up this Table is not known. The latest date to which its composition can be assigned is the end of April or the beginning of May, 1529. It may, however, be questioned whether it was published at all as a placard. The two groups of passages: "What the Hearers Owe to Their Pastors," and: "What Subjects Owe to Their Government," are probably not from Luther. Following are the grounds supporting this view: 1. They are not contained in the German editions, but appeared for the first time in the Latin translation. 2. Their superscriptions differ in form from those of the other groups. 3. They adduce quite a number of Bible-verses, and repeat some already quoted, e. g., 1 Tim. 2, 1; Rom. 13, 1. The German Book of Concord omitted these passages, while the Latin Concordia of 1580 and 1584 embodied them. Albrecht writes: "The Table of Duties is an original part of the Catechism, bearing a true Lutheran stamp. But it was old material worked over, as is the case almost throughout the Small Catechism." The oft-repeated assertion, however, that the Table of Duties was borrowed from the catechism of the Waldensians or Bohemian Brethren, is not correct. For this Table is not found in the Catechism of the Brethren of 1522, with which Luther was acquainted, but first in Gyrick's Catechism of 1554, in which Lutheran material is embodied also in other places." (W. 30, 1, 645.)

The confession books of the Middle Ages, however, which classified sins according to the social estates, and especially John Gerson's tract (*De Modo Vivendi Omnium Fidelium*, reprinted at Wittenberg 1513), which treated of the offices of all sorts of lay-people in every station of life, may have prompted Luther to draw up this Table. But, says Albrecht, "it certainly grew under his hand into something new and characteristic. The old material is thoroughly shortened, sifted, supplemented, newly arranged, recast. While Gerson's tract throughout bears the stamp of the Middle Ages, Luther's Table of Duties, with its appeal to the Scriptures alone, its knowledge of what is a 'holy estate,' its teaching that, as divine ordinances, civil government and the household (when embraced by the common order of Christian love) are equally as holy as the priesthood, reveals the characteristic marks of the Reformer's new ideal of life, which, rooting in his faith, and opposed to the hierarchy and monkery of the Middle Ages, as well as to the fanaticism of the Anabaptists, became of far-reaching importance for the entire moral thought of the succeeding centuries." (647.)

Grimm's Lexicon defines "Haustafel" as "*der Abschnitt des Katechismus, der ueber die Pflichten des Hausstandes handelt*, that section of the Catechism which treats of the duties of the household." This verbal definition, suggested by the term, is too narrow, since Luther's "Haustafel" is designed "for various holy orders and estates," magistrates and pastors included. Still, the term is not on this account inappropriate. Table (*Tafel, tabula*) signifies in general a roster, a list, or index of leading points, with or without reference to the chart form. And such a table, suspended in the home and employed in the instruction of the home congregation, is properly termed "Haustafel." Agreeably to this, Andreas Fabricius, in 1569, called the "Haustafel" a domestic table of works, *tabula operum domestica*. Daniel Kauzmann, in his *Handbook* (16 sermons on the Catechism) of 1569, says: "It is called 'Haustafel' of the Christians because every Christian should daily view it and call to mind therefrom his calling, as from a table which portrays and presents to every one what pertains to him. It teaches all the people who may be in a house what each one ought to do or to leave undone in his calling." (642.)

In his *Catechismus Lutheri* of 1600 Polycarp Leyser offers the following explanation: "Why are these passages called a table? Beyond doubt this is due to the fact that, from of old, good ordinances have been written and graven on tables. So did God, who prescribed His Law to the Jews in ten commandments on two tables. Similarly Solon wrote the laws of Athens on tables. The Romans also had their law of twelve tables brought from Athens. And so, when the government to-day issues certain commands, it is customary to suspend them on tables, as also princes and lords suspend on tables their court rules. But why is it called 'Haustafel' when it also treats of preachers and the government? The reason for this is given by St. Paul, 1 Tim. 3, where he calls the Church a house of the living God. For as the housefather in a large house summons his servants and prescribes to each one what he is to do, so God is also wont to call into certain stations those who have been received into His house by Holy Baptism, and to prescribe to them in this table how each one in his calling shall conduct himself." (641.)

Concerning the purpose of the Table of Duties, Albrecht remarks: "If I am correct, Luther, by these additions, would especially inculcate that Christianity, the essence of which is set forth in the preceding chief parts, must daily be practised." That is certainly correct, for the Catechism must not only be learned, but lived. And the Table of Duties emphasizes the great truth, brought to light again by Luther, that Christianity does not consist in any peculiar form of life, as Romish priests, monks, and nuns held, who separated themselves from the world outwardly, but that it is essentially faith of the heart, which, however, is not to flee into cloisters and solitudes, but courageously and cheerfully to plunge into practical life with its natural forms and relations as ordained by Creation, there to be tried as well as glorified. In his *Admonition to the Clergy*, 1530, Luther says: "Furthermore, by such abominable doctrine all truly good works which God appointed and ordained were despised and utterly set at naught [by the Papists]. For instance, lord, subject, father, mother, son, daughter, servant, maid were not regarded as good works, but were called worldliness, dangerous estates, and lost works." (W. 30, 2, 291.) The Table of Duties is a protest against such perverted views. For here Luther considers not only the calling of preachers and teachers, but also all those of government and subjects, of fathers, mothers, and children, of masters and servants, of mistresses and maids, of employees and employers, as "holy orders and estates," in which a Christian may live with a good conscience, and all of which the Catechism is to permeate with its truths. "Out into the stream of life with the Catechism you have learned!" Such, then, is the admonition which, in particular, the Table of Duties adds to the preceding parts of the Catechism.

## 115. Symbolical Authority of Catechisms.

The symbolical authority of Luther's Catechisms must be distinguished from the practical use to which they were put in church, school, and home. As to his doctrine, Luther knew it to be the pure truth of the divine Word. Hence he could not but demand that every one acknowledge it. Self-evidently this applies also to the doctrinal contents of the Catechisms. Luther, however, did not insist that his Catechisms be made the books of instruction in church, school, and home; he only desired and counseled it. If for the purpose of instruction the form of his Small Catechism did not suit any one, let him, said Luther, choose another. In the Preface to the Small Catechism he declared: "Hence, choose whatever form you think best, and adhere to it forever." Again, "Take the form of these tables or some other short, fixed form of your choice, and adhere to it without the change of a single syllable." Self-evidently Luther is here not speaking of the doctrine of the Catechism, but of the form to be used for instruction. And with respect to the latter he makes no demands whatever. However, the contents of these books and the name of the author sufficed to procure for them the widest circulation and the most extensive use. Everywhere the doors of churches, schools, and homes were opened to the writings of Luther.

The tables had hardly been published when catechism instruction already generally was given according to Luther's Explanation. The church regulations, first in Saxony, then also in other lands, provided that Luther's Small Catechism be memorized word for word, and that preaching be according to the Large Catechism. The Church Order of Henry the Pious, 1539, declares: "There shall not be taught a different catechism in every locality, but one and the same form, as presented by Dr. Martin Luther at Wittenberg, shall be observed everywhere." In 1533 the ministers of Allstaedt were ordered "to preach according to Luther's Large Catechism." (Kolde, 63.) The authority of the Catechisms grew during the controversies after Luther's death, when the faithful Lutherans appealed to the Smalcald Articles and especially to Luther's Catechisms.

The Lueneburg Articles of 1561 designate them, together with the Smalcald Articles, as the correct "explication and explanation" of the true sense of the Augustana. The *Corpus Doctrinae Pomeranicum* of 1564 declares that "the sum of Christian and evangelical doctrine is purely and correctly contained in Luther's Catechisms." Their authority as a genuinely Lutheran norm of doctrine increased when the Reformed of Germany, in 1563, made the Heidelberg Catechism their particular confession.

Like the Smalcald Articles, Luther's Catechisms achieved their symbolical authority by themselves, without resolutions of princes, estates, and theologians. The Thorough Declaration of the Formula of Concord is merely chronicling actual facts when it adopts the Catechisms for this reason: "because they have been unanimously approved and received by all churches adhering to the Augsburg Confession, and have been publicly used in churches, schools, and homes, and, moreover, because the Christian doctrine from God's Word is comprised in them in the most correct and simple way, and, in like manner, is explained, as far as necessary for simple laymen." (852, 8.) The Epitome adds: "And because such matters concern also the laity and the salvation of their souls, we also confess the Small and Large Catechisms of Dr. Luther, as they are included in Luther's works, as the Bible of the laity, wherein everything is comprised which is treated at greater length in Holy Scripture, and is necessary for a Christian man to know for his salvation." (777, 5.)

## 116. Enemies and Friends of Small Catechism.

In recent times liberal German theologians, pastors, and teachers have endeavored to dislodge Luther's Small Catechism from its position in church, school, and home. As a rule, these attacks were made in the name of pedagogy; the real cause, however, were their liberal dogmatical views. The form was mentioned and assailed, but the contents were meant. As a sample of this hostility we quote the pedagog, philologian, and historian Dr. Ludwig Gurlitt (*Die Zukunft*, Vol. 17, No. 6, p. 222): "At the beginning of the sixteenth century," he says, "a monk eloped from a cloister and wrote a religious book of instruction for the German children. At the time it was a bold innovation, the delight of all freethinkers and men of progress, of all who desired to serve the future. This book, which will soon celebrate its five-[four-]hundredth anniversary, is still the chief book of instruction for German children. True, its contents already are so antiquated that parents reject almost every sentence of it for themselves; true, the man of to-day understands its language only with difficulty — what of it, the children must gulp down the moldy, musty food. How we would scoff and jeer if a similar report were made about the school system of China! To this Lutheran Catechism, which I would best like to see in state libraries only, are added many antiquated hymns of mystical turgidity, which a simple youth, even with the best will, does not know how to use. All outlived! Faith in the Bible owes its existence only to the tough power and law of inertia. It is purely mechanical thinking and speaking which the schoolmaster preaches to them and pounds into them. We continue thus because we are too indolent to fight, or because we fear an enlightened people."

The best refutation of such and similar aspersions is a reference to the enormous circulation which Luther's Small Catechism has enjoyed, to its countless editions, translations, elaborations, and its universal use in church, school, and home for four centuries. Thirty-seven years after the publication of Luther's Catechisms, Mathesius wrote: "Praise God, it is said that in our times over one hundred thousand copies have been printed and used in great numbers in all kinds of languages in foreign lands and in all Latin and German schools." And since then, down to the present day, millions and millions of hands have been stretched forth to receive Luther's catechetical classic. While during the last four centuries hundreds of catechisms have gone under, Luther's Enchiridion is afloat to-day and is just as seaworthy as when it was first launched. A person, however, endowed with an average measure of common sense will hardly be able to believe that the entire Lutheran Church has, for four centuries, been so stupid as would have been the case if men of Dr. Gurlitt's stripe had spoken only half the truth in their criticisms.

Moreover, the number of detractors disappears in the great host of friends who down to the present day have not tired of praising the Catechisms, especially the Enchiridion. They admire its artistic and perfect form; its harmonious grouping, as of the petals of a flower; the melody and rhythm of its language, notably in the explanation of the Second Article; its clarity, perspicuity, and popularity; its simplicity, coupled with depth and richness of thought; the absence of polemics and of theological terminology, etc. However, with all this and many other things which have been and might be said in praise of the Catechism, the feature which made it what it truly was, a Great Deed of the Reformation, has not as yet been pointed out. Luther Paulinized, Evangelicalized, the Catechism by properly setting forth in his explanations the *finis historiae*, the blessed meaning of the great deeds of God, the doctrine of justification. Indeed, also Luther's Catechism is, in more than one way, conditioned by its times, but in its kernel, in its doctrine, it contains, as Albrecht puts it, "timeless, never-aging material. For in it pulsates the heart-beat of the primitive Christian faith, as witnessed by the apostles, and experienced anew by the Reformer." (648.) This, too, is the reason why Luther's Enchiridion is, indeed, as G. v. Zezschwitz remarks, "a booklet which a theologian never finishes learning, and a Christian never finishes living."

## 117. Evaluation of Small Catechism.

Luther himself reckoned his Catechisms among his most important books. In his letter to Wolfgang Capito, July 9, 1537, he writes: "I am quite cold and indifferent about arranging my books, for, incited by a Saturnine hunger, I would much rather have them all devoured, *eo quod Saturnina fame percitus magis cuperem eos omnes devoratos.* For none do I acknowledge as really my books, except perhaps *De Servo Arbitrio* and the Catechism." (Enders, 11, 247.) Justus Jonas declares: "The Catechism is but a small booklet, which can be purchased for six pfennige, but six thousand worlds could not pay for it." He believed that the Holy Ghost inspired the blessed Luther to write it. Mathesius says: "If in his career Luther had produced and done no other good thing than to give his two Catechisms to homes, schools, and pulpits, the entire world could never sufficiently thank or repay him for it." J. Fr. Mayer: "*Tot res, quot verba. Tot utilitates, quot apices complectens. Pagellis brevis, sed rerum theologicarum amplitudine incomparabilis.* As many thoughts as words; as many uses as there are characters in the book. Brief in pages, but incomparable in amplitude of theological thoughts."

In his dedicatory epistle of 1591, to Chemnitz's *Loci,* Polycarp Leyser says: "That sainted man, Martin Luther, never took greater pains than when he drew up into a brief sum those prolix expositions which he taught most energetically in his various books. . . . Therefore he composed the Short Catechism, which is more precious than gold or gems, in which the pure doctrine of the prophets and apostles (*prophetica et apostolica doctrinae puritas*) is summed up into one integral doctrinal body, and set forth in such clear words that it may justly be considered worthy of the Canon (for everything has been drawn from the canonical Scriptures). I can truthfully affirm that this very small book contains such a wealth of so many and so great things that, if all faithful preachers of the Gospel during their entire lives would do nothing else in their sermons than explain aright to the common people the secret wisdom of God comprised in those few words, and set forth from the divine Scriptures the solid ground upon which each word is built, they could never exhaust this immense abyss."

Leopold von Ranke, in his *German History of the Time of the Reformation,* 1839, declares: "The Catechism which Luther published in 1529, and of which he said that he, old Doctor though he was, prayed it, is as childlike as it is deep, as comprehensible as it is unfathomable, simple, and sublime. Blessed is the man who nourishes his soul with it, who adheres to it! He has imperishable comfort in every moment: under a thin shell the kernel of truth, which satisfies the wisest of the wise."

Loehe, another enthusiastic panegyrist of Luther, declares: "The Small Lutheran Catechism can be read and spoken throughout with a praying heart; in short, it can be prayed. This can be said of no other catechism. It contains the most definitive doctrine, resisting every perversion, and still it is not polemical — it exhales the purest air of peace. In it is expressed the manliest and most developed knowledge, and yet it admits of the most blissful contemplation the soul may wish for. It is a confession of the Church, and of all, the best known, the most universal, in which God's children most frequently meet in conscious faith; and still this universal confession speaks in a most pleasing personal tone. Warm, hearty, childlike, yet it is so manly, so courageous, so free the individual confessor speaks here. Of all the confessions comprised in the Concordia of 1580, this is the most youthful, the clearest, and the most penetrating note in the harmonious chime, and, withal, as rounded and finished as any. One may say that in it the firmest objectiveness appears in the garb of the most pleasing subjectiveness."

Schmauk writes: "The Small Catechism is the real epitome of Lutheranism in the simplest, the most practical, the most modern and living, and, at the same time, the most radical form. It steers clear of all obscure historical allusions; it contains no condemnatory articles; it is based on the shortest and the oldest of the ecumenical symbols. It is not a work for theologians, but for every Lutheran; and it is not nearly as large as the Augsburg Confession." (Conf. Prin., 696.)

McGiffert says: "In 1529 appeared his [Luther's] Large and Small Catechisms, the latter containing a most beautiful summary of Christian faith and duty, wholly devoid of polemics of every kind, and so simple and concise as to be easily understood and memorized by every child. It has formed the basis of the religious education of German youth ever since. Though preceded by other catechisms from the pen of this and that colleague or disciple, it speedily displaced them all, not simply because of its authorship, but because of its superlative merit, and has alone maintained itself in general use. The versatility of the Reformer in adapting himself with such success to the needs of the young and immature is no less than extraordinary. Such a little book as this it is that reveals most clearly the genius of the man." (Life of Luther, 316.)

O. Albrecht writes: "Reverently adhering to the churchly tradition and permeating it with the new understanding of the Gospel, such are the characteristics of Luther's Catechisms, especially the Small Catechism." "On every page new and original features appear beside the traditional elements." "The essential doctrinal content of the booklet is thoroughly original; in it Luther offered a carefully digested presentation of the essence of Christianity, according to his own understanding as the Reformer, in a manner adapted to the comprehension of children — a simple, pithy description of his own personal Christian piety, without polemics and systematization, but with the convincing power of experienced truth." (W. 30, 1, 647.) — Similar testimonies might easily be multiplied and have been collected and published repeatedly.

The best praise, however, comes from the enemy in the form of imitation or even verbal appropriation. Albrecht says: "Old Catholic catechetes, and not the worst, have not hesitated to draw on Luther's Large Catechism. If one peruses the widely spread catechism of the Dominican monk John Dietenberger, of 1537 (reprinted by Maufang in his work on the Catholic Catechisms of the sixteenth century, 1881), one is frequently edified and delighted by the diligence with which, besides older material, Luther's Large and Small Catechisms, as well as the Nuernberg Catechismsermons of 1533, have been exploited." (W. 30, 1, 497.)

## 118. Literary Merit of Small Catechism.

Moenckeberg remarks: The Small Catechism betrays "the imperfection of the haste in which it had to be finished." As a matter of fact, however, Luther, the master of German, paid much attention also to its language, in order, by pithy brevity and simple, attractive form, to make its glorious truths the permanent property of the children and unlearned who memorized it. In his publication "Zur Sprache und Geschichte des Kleinen Katechismus Luthers, Concerning the Language and History of Luther's Small Catechism," 1909, J. Gillhoff writes: "Here, if ever, arose a master of language, who expressed the deepest mysteries in sounds most simple. Here, if ever, there was created in the German language and spirit, and in brief compass, a work of art of German prose. If ever the gods blessed a man to create, consciously or unconsciously, on the soil of the people and their needs, a perfect work of popular art in the spirit of the people and in the terms of their speech, to the weal of the people and their youth throughout the centuries, it was here. The explanation of the Second Article is one of the chief creations of the home art of German poetry. And such it is, not for the reason that it rises from desert surroundings, drawing attention to itself alone, but because it sums up and crowns the character of the book throughout." (16.)

Speaking in particular of the Second Article, Bang, in 1909, said in his lecture "Luthers Kleiner Katechismus, ein Kleinod der Volksschule — Luther's Small Catechism, a Jewel of the Public Schools": "The Catechism is precious also for the reason that Luther in the explanations strikes a personal, subjective, confessional note. When at home I read the text of the Second Article in silence, and then read Luther's explanation aloud, it seems to me as if a hymn rushing heavenward arises from the lapidary record of facts. It is no longer the language of the word, but of the sound as well. The text reports objectively, like the language of a Roman, writing tables of law. The explanation witnesses and confesses subjectively. It is Christianity transformed into flesh and blood. It sounds like an oath of allegiance to the flag. In its ravishing tone we perceive the marching tread of the myriads of believers of nineteen centuries; we see them moving onward under the fluttering banner of the cross in war, victory, and peace. And we, too, by a power which cannot be expressed in words, are drawn into the great, blessed experience of our ancestors and champions. Who would dare to lay his impious hands on this consecrated, inherited jewel, and rob the coming generations of it?!" (20.)

# X. The Smalcald War and the Augsburg and Leipzig Interims.

## 119. Bulwark of Peace Removed.

Luther died on the day of Concordia, February 18, 1546. With him peace and concord departed from the Lutheran Church. His death was everywhere the signal for action against true Lutheranism on the part of both its avowed enemies and false brethren. As long as that hero of faith and prayer was still living, the weight of his personal influence and authority proved to be a veritable bulwark of peace and doctrinal purity against the enemies within as well as without the Church. Though enemies seeking to devour had been lurking long ago, the powerful and commanding personality of Luther had checked all forces making for war from without and for dissension from within. The Emperor could not be induced to attack the Lutherans. He knew that they would stand united and strong as long as the Hero of the Reformation was in their midst. Nor were the false brethren able to muster up sufficient courage to come out into the open and publish their errors while the voice of the lion was heard. But no sooner had Luther departed than strife began its distracting work. War, political as well as theological, followed in the wake of his death. From the grave of the fallen hero a double specter began to loom up. Pope and Emperor now joined hands to crush Protestantism by brute force as they had planned long ago. The result was the Smalcald War. The secret enemies which Lutheranism harbored within its own bosom began boldly to raise their heads. Revealing their true colors and coming out in the open with their pernicious errors, they caused numerous controversies which spread over all Germany (Saxony, the cradle of the Reformation, becoming the chief battlefield), and threatened to undo completely the blessed work of Luther, to disrupt and disintegrate the Church, or to pervert it into a unionistic or Reformed sect. Especially these discreditable internal dissensions were a cause of deep humiliation and of anxious concern to all loyal Lutherans. To the Romanists and Reformed, however, who united in predicting the impending collapse of Lutheranism, they were a source of malicious and triumphant scoffing and jeering. A prominent theologian reported that by 1566 matters had come to such a pass in Germany that the old Lutheran doctrine was publicly proclaimed only in relatively few places. In the Calvinized Palatinate public thanks were rendered to God in the churches that also Electoral Saxony was now about to join them. The Jesuits insisted that, having abandoned the doctrine of the real presence in the Lord's Supper, the Lutherans were no longer genuine Lutherans and hence no more entitled to the privileges guaranteed by the Peace of Augsburg (1555). That the final result of this turmoil, political as well as theological, proved a blessing to the Lutheran Church must be regarded and ever gratefully remembered as a special grace and a remarkable favor of Almighty God.

## 120. Luther Foretold Coming Distress.

Though fully conscious of the gravity of the political and theological situation, and convinced that war and dissensions were bound to come, Luther was at the same time confident that it would not occur during his life. With respect to the coming war he said: "With great earnestness I have asked God, and still pray daily, that He would thwart their [the Papists'] plan and suffer no war to come upon Germany during my life. And I am confident that God surely hears such prayer of mine, and I know that there will be no war in Germany as long as I shall live." (St. L. 9, 1856.) In his Commentary on the Book of Genesis he wrote: "It is a great consolation when he says (Is. 57, 1) that the righteous are taken away from the evil to come. Thus we, too, shall die in peace before misfortune and misery overtake Germany." (St. L. 1, 1758.)

Luther spoke frequently also of the impending doctrinal dissensions. As early as 1531 he declared that the Gospel would abide only a short time. "When the present pious, true preachers will be dead," said he, "others will come who will preach and act as it pleases the devil." (8, 72.) In 1546 he said in a sermon preached at Wittenberg: "Up to this time you have heard the real, true Word; now beware of your own thoughts and wisdom. The devil will kindle the light of reason and lead you away from the faith, as he did the Anabaptists and Sacramentarians. . . . I see clearly that, if God does not give us faithful preachers and ministers, the devil will tear our church to pieces by the fanatics (Rottengeister), and will not cease until he has finished. Such is plainly his object. If he cannot accomplish it through the Pope and the Emperor, he will do it through those who are [now] in doctrinal agreement with us. . . . Therefore pray earnestly that God may preserve the Word to you, for things will come to a dreadful pass." (12, 1174. 437.)

Reading the signs of the times, Melanchthon also realized that Luther's prophecies would be fulfilled. His address to the students of Wittenberg University, on February 19, 1546, in which he announced the death of Luther, concludes: "Obiit auriga et currus Israel. He is dead, the chariot of Israel and the horsemen thereof, who guided the Church in this last old age of the world. For the doctrine of the forgiveness of sins and of faith in the Son of God was not discovered by human sagacity, but revealed by God through this man. Let us therefore love his memory and his teaching; and may we be all the more humble and ponder the terrible calamity and the great changes which will follow this misfortune." (*C. R.* 6, 59.)

Nor were these prophecies of Luther mere intuitions or deductions based on general reflections only. They were inductions from facts which he had not failed to observe at Wittenberg, even in his immediate surroundings. Seckendorf relates that Luther, when sick at Smalcald in 1537, told the Elector of Saxony that after his death, discord would break out in the University of Wittenberg, and that his doctrine would be changed. (*Comm. de Lutheranismo* 3, 165.) In his Preface to Luther's Table Talk, John Aurifaber reports that Luther had frequently predicted that after his death his doctrine would wane and decline because of false brethren, fanatics, and sectarians, and that the truth, which in 1530 had been placed on a pinnacle at Augsburg, would descend into the valley, since the Word of God had seldom flourished more than forty years in one place. (Richard, *Conf. Hist.*, 311.) Stephanus Tucher, a faithful Lutheran preacher of Magdeburg, wrote in 1549: "Doctor Martin Luther, of sainted memory, has frequently repeated before many trustworthy witnesses, and also before Doctor Augustine Schurf, these words: 'After my death not one of these [Wittenberg] theologians will remain steadfast.'" Tucher adds: "This I have heard of Doctor Augustine Schurf not once, but frequently. Therefore I also testify to it before Christ, my Lord, the righteous Judge," etc. (St. L. 12, 1177; Walther, *Kern und Stern,* 7.)

It was, above all, the spirit of indifferentism toward false doctrine, particularly concerning the Lord's Supper, which Luther observed and deplored in his Wittenberg colleagues: Melanchthon, Bugenhagen, Cruciger, Eber, and Major. Shortly before his last journey to Eisleben he invited them to his house, where he addressed to them the following solemn words of warning: They should "remain steadfast in the Gospel; for I see that soon after my death the most prominent brethren will fall away. I am not afraid of the Papists," he added; "for most of them are coarse, unlearned asses and Epicureans; but *our brethren* will inflict the damage on the Gospel; for 'they went out from us, but they were not of us' (1 John 2, 19); they will give the Gospel a harder blow than did the Papists." About the same time Luther had written above the entrance to his study: "Our professors are to be examined on the Lord's Supper." When Major, who was about to leave for the colloquy at Regensburg, entered and inquired what these words signified, Luther answered: "The meaning of these words is precisely what you read and what they say; and when you and I shall have returned, an examination will have to be held, to which

you as well as others will be cited." Major protested that he was not addicted to any false doctrine. Luther answered: "It is by your silence and cloaking that you cast suspicion upon yourself. If you believe as you declare in my presence, then speak so also in the church, in public lectures, in sermons, and in private conversations, and strengthen your brethren, and lead the erring back to the right path, and contradict the contumacious spirits; otherwise your confession is sham pure and simple, and worth nothing. Whoever really regards his doctrine, faith, and confession as true, right, and certain cannot remain in the same stall with such as teach, or adhere to, false doctrine; nor can he keep on giving friendly words to Satan and his minions. A teacher who remains silent when errors are taught, and nevertheless pretends to be a true teacher, is worse than an open fanatic and by his hypocrisy does greater damage than a heretic. Nor can he be trusted. He is a wolf and a fox, a hireling and a servant of his belly, and ready to despise and to sacrifice doctrine, Word, faith, Sacrament, churches, and schools. He is either a secret bedfellow of the enemies, or a skeptic and a weathervane, waiting to see whether Christ or the devil will prove victorious; or he has no convictions of his own whatever, and is not worthy to be called a pupil, let alone a teacher; nor does he want to offend anybody, or say a word in favor of Christ, or hurt the devil and the world." (Walther, 39 f.)

## 121. Unfortunate Issue of Smalcald War.

All too soon the predictions of Luther, and the fears expressed by Melanchthon and others, were realized. June 26, 1546, four months after Luther's death, Pope and Emperor entered into a secret agreement to compel the Protestants by force of arms to acknowledge the decrees of the Council of Trent, and to return to the bosom of the Roman Church. The covenant provided that, "in the name of God and with the help and assistance of His Papal Holiness, His Imperial Majesty should prepare himself for war, and equip himself with soldiers and everything pertaining to warfare against those who objected to the Council, against the Smalcald League, and against all who were addicted to the false belief and error in Germany, and that he do so with all his power and might, in order to bring them back to the old [papal] faith and to the obedience of the Holy See." The Pope promised to assist the Emperor with 200,000 Krontaler, more than 12,000 Italian soldiers, and quite a number of horsemen. He furthermore permitted the Emperor to appropriate, for the purpose of this war, one half of the total income of the church property in Spain and 500,000 Krontaler from the revenue of the Spanish cloisters.

While the Emperor endeavored to veil the real purpose of his preparations, the Pope openly declared in a bull of July 4, 1546: "From the beginning of our Papacy it has always been our concern how to root out the weeds of godless doctrines which the heretics have sowed throughout Germany. . . . Now it has come to pass that, by the inspiration of the Holy Ghost, our dearest son in Christ, Charles, the Roman Emperor, has decided to employ the sword against these enemies of God. And for the protection of religion we intend to promote this pious enterprise with all our own and the Roman Church's possessions. Accordingly, we admonish all Christians to assist in this war with their prayers to God and their alms, in order that the godless heresy may be rooted out and the dissension removed. . . . To each and all who do these things we grant the most complete indulgence and remission of all their sins." (St. L. 17, 1453 ff. Walther, 10.)

The Smalcald War, so called because it was directed against the Smalcald League, was easily won by the Emperor. Among the causes of this unfortunate issue were the neutral attitude of Joachim II of Brandenburg and of other Lutheran princes, and especially the treachery of the ambitious and unscrupulous Maurice, Duke of Saxony and nephew of Elector John Frederick of Saxony, who, in order to gain the Electorate of Saxony, had made a secret agreement with the Emperor according to which he was to join his forces with those of the Emperor against the Lutherans. The decisive battle was fought at Muehlberg on the Elbe, April 24, 1547. It proved to be a crushing defeat for the Protestants. The Elector himself was taken captive, treated as a rebel, and sentenced to death. The sentence was read to him while he was playing chess with his fellow-captive, Duke Ernest of Lueneburg. John Frederick answered, he did not believe that the Emperor would deal so severely with him; if, however, he were in earnest, they should let him know that he might order his affairs with his wife and children. He then calmly turned to the Duke, saying: "Let us continue the game; it's your move." (Jackel, G. d. Ref. 1, 114.) The day after the battle at Muehlberg, Torgau fell into the hands of the Emperor; and when he threatened to execute the Elector, having already erected a scaffold for this purpose, Wittenberg, too, though well protected by 5,000 soldiers, signed a capitulation on May 19, in order to save the Elector's life. On the 23d of May, Wittenberg was occupied by the Emperor. Here Charles, when standing at the grave of Luther, and urged to have the body of "the heretic" exhumed, spoke the memorable words that he was warring not with the dead, but with the living. The death-sentence was rescinded, but, apart from other cruel conditions forced upon the Elector, he was compelled to resign in favor of Maurice and promise to remain in captivity as long as the Emperor should desire. His sons were granted the districts of Weimar, Jena, Eisenach, and Gotha. Philip of Hesse surrendered without striking a blow, and was likewise treacherously held in captivity and humiliated in every possible way by the Emperor. The imperial plenipotentiaries had assured

the Landgrave that he would not be imprisoned. Afterwards, however, the words in the document, "not any bodily captivity — nit eenige Leibesgefangenschaft," were fraudulently changed by Granvella to read, "not eternal captivity — nit ewige Leibesgefangenschaft." (Marheineke, G. d. Deut. Ref. 4, 438.) The sons of the Landgrave remained in possession of his territory. Thus all of Southern and, barring a few cities, also all of Northern Germany was conquered by Charles. Everywhere the Lutherans were at the tender mercy of the Emperor, whose undisputed power struck terror into all Germany.

## 122. The Augsburg Interim.

The first step to reduce the Lutherans to obedience to the Pope was the so-called Augsburg Interim. It was proclaimed by the Emperor at Augsburg on May 15, 1548, as the law of the Empire under the title: "Der roemischen kaiserlichen Majestaet Erklaerung, wie es der Religion halben im heiligen Reich bis zu Austrag des gemeinen Concilii gehalten werden soll." The people were also forbidden to teach, write, or preach against the document. The Interim had been prepared by the papal bishops Julius Pflug and Michael Helding and the court-preacher of Elector Joachim of Brandenburg, John Agricola, a man with whom Luther had, already since 1540, refused to have any further intercourse owing to his insincerity and duplicity. "I go forth as the Reformer of all Germany," Agricola boasted when he left Berlin to attend the Diet at Augsburg, which was to open September 1, 1547. After the Diet he bragged that in Augsburg he had flung the windows wide open for the Gospel; that he had reformed the Pope and made the Emperor a Lutheran; that a golden time had now arrived, for the Gospel would be preached in all Europe; that he had not only been present, but had presided at the drafting of the Interim; that he had received 500 crowns from the Emperor and 500 from King Ferdinand, etc. (Preger, M. Flacius Illyricus, 1, 119.)

The document, prepared at the command of the Emperor, was called Interim because its object was to regulate the church affairs until the religious controversy would be finally settled by the Council of Trent, to the resolutions of which the Lutherans were required to submit. It was, however, essentially papal. For the time being, indeed, it permitted Protestant clergymen to marry, and to celebrate the Lord's Supper in both kinds, but demanded the immediate restoration of the Romish customs and ceremonies, the acknowledgment of papal supremacy iure divino, as well as the jurisdiction of the bishops, and the adoption of articles in which the doctrines were all explained in the sense of the Catholic dogmas, and in which truth and falsehood, in general, were badly mingled. Transubstantiation, the seven sacraments, and other papal errors were reaffirmed, while Lutheran tenets, such as the doctrine of justification by faith alone, were either denied or omitted.

And from the fact that this Interim was nevertheless condemned by the Pope and the Romanists, who demanded an unqualified, blind, and unconditional submission, the Lutherans could infer what they were to expect after consenting to these interimistic provisions. The general conviction among Catholics as well as Protestants was that the Interim was but the first step to a complete return to Romanism. Indeed, soon after its promulgation, the Catholic Electors of Mainz and Koeln endeavored to rob the Lutherans also of the use of the cup and of the marriage of the priests. The Elector of Mainz declared all such marriages void and their children bastards. (Jaekel, 162.)

In the most important point, the doctrine of justification, the Augsburg Interim not only omitted the *sola fide*, but clearly taught that justification embraces also renewal. When God justifies a man, the Interim declared, He does not only absolve him from his guilt, but also "makes him better by imparting the Holy Ghost, who cleanses his heart and incites it through the love of God which is shed abroad in his heart." (Frank, *Theologie d. Konkordienformel*, 2, 80.) A man "is absolved from the guilt of eternal damnation and renewed through the Holy Spirit, and thus an unjust man becomes just." (143.) Again: "This faith obtains the gift of the Holy Ghost, by which the love of God is shed abroad in our hearts; and after this has been added to faith and hope, we are truly justified by the infused righteousness which is in man; for this righteousness consists in faith, hope, and love." (81.)

In Southern Germany, Charles V and his Italian and Spanish troops, employing brute force, succeeded in rigidly enforcing the Interim outwardly and temporarily. Free cities rejecting it were deprived of their liberties and privileges. Constance, having fallen after a heroic defense, was annexed to Austria. Magdeburg offered the longest resistance and was outlawed three times. Defiantly its citizens declared: "We are saved neither by an Interim nor by an Exterim, but by the Word of God alone." (Jaekel 1, 166.) Refractory magistrates were treated as rebels. Pastors who declined to introduce the Interim were deposed; some were banished, others incarcerated, still others even executed. In Swabia and along the Rhine about four hundred ministers were willing to suffer imprisonment and banishment rather than conform to the Interim. They were driven into exile with their families, and some of them were killed. When Jacob Sturm of Augsburg presented his grievances to Granvella, the latter answered: "If necessary, one might proceed against heretics also with fire." "Indeed," Sturm retorted, "you may kill people by fire, but even in this way you cannot force their faith." (165.) Bucer and Fagius, preachers in Augsburg, left for England. Musculus was deposed because he had preached against the Interim. Osiander was compelled to leave Nuernberg, Erhard Schnepf, Wuerttemberg. Among the fugitives eagerly sought throughout Germany by the

imperial henchmen was Brenz in Schwaebisch-Hall, the renowned theologian of Wuerttemberg, who spoke of the Interim only as "Interitus, Ruin." (*C. R.* 7, 289.) The tombstone of Brenz bears the inscription: "*Voce, stylo, pietate, fide, ardore probatus* — Renowned for his eloquence, style, piety, faithfulness, and ardor." (Jaekel, 164.) A prize of 5,000 gulden was offered for the head of Caspar Aquila, who was one of the first to write against the Interim. (Preger 1, 12.) Of course, by persecuting and banishing their ministers, the Emperor could not and did not win the people. Elector Frederick II of the Palatinate consented to introduce the Interim. But even in Southern Germany the success of the Emperor was apparent rather than real. The churches in Augsburg, Ulm, and other cities stood empty as a silent protest against the Interim and imperial tyranny.

In Northern Germany the Emperor met with more than a mere passive resistance on the part of the people as well as the preachers. The Interim was regarded as a trap for the Lutherans. The slogan ran: "There is a rogue behind the Interim! *O selig ist der Mann, Der Gott vertrauen kann Und willigt nicht ins Interim, Denn es hat den Schalk hinter ihm!*" The Interim was rejected in Brunswick, Hamburg, Luebeck, Lueneburg, Goslar, Bremen, Goettingen, Hannover, Einbeck, Eisleben, Mansfeld, Stolberg, Schwarzburg, Hohenstein, Halle, etc. Joachim of Brandenburg endeavored to introduce it, but soon abandoned these efforts. At a convent of 300 preachers assembled in Berlin for the purpose of subscribing to the Interim, an old minister, whose name was Leutinger, arose and declared in the presence of Agricola, the co-author of the Interim: "I love Agricola, and more than him I love my Elector; but my Lord Jesus Christ I love most," and saying this, he cast the document handed him for subscription into the flames of the fire burning in the hearth. Before this, Margrave Hans, of Kuestrin, had flung away the pen handed him for the subscription of the infamous document, saying: "I shall never adopt this poisonous concoction, nor submit to any council. Rather sword than pen; blood rather than ink!"

The three Counts of Mansfeld, Hans Jorge, Hans Albrecht, and Hans Ernest, declared in a letter of August 20, 1548, to the Emperor: "Most gracious Emperor and Lord! As for our government, the greater part of the people are miners, who have not much to lose and are easily induced to leave. Nor are they willing to suffer much coercion. Yet the welfare of our whole government depends upon them. Besides, we know that, if we should press the matter, all of the preachers would leave, and the result would be a desolation of preaching and of the Sacraments. And after losing our preachers, our own lives and limbs would not be safe among the miners, and we must needs expect a revolt of all the people." (Walther, 19 f.) Thus the Interim before long became a dead letter throughout the greater part of Germany.

## 123. Attitude of John Frederick toward Interim.

In order to obtain his liberty, the vacillating Philip of Hesse, though he had declined to submit to the resolutions of the Council of Trent, declared himself willing to adopt the Interim. "It is better," he is reported to have said, "to hear a mass than to play cards," etc. (Jaekel 1, 130. 162.) Especial efforts were also made by the Emperor to induce John Frederick to declare his submission to the Council and to sanction the Interim. But the Elector solemnly protested that this was impossible for him. All attempts to induce him to abandon his religious convictions met with quiet, but determined resistance. One of the cruel conditions under which the Emperor was willing to rescind the death-sentence passed on the Elector was, that he should consent to everything the Emperor or the Council would prescribe in matters of religion. But the Elector declared: "I will rather lose my head and suffer Wittenberg to be battered down than submit to a demand that violates my conscience. *Lieber will ich meinen Kopf verlieren und Wittenberg zusammenschiessen lassen, als eine Forderung eingehen, die mein Gewissen verletzt.*" (1, 116.) Through Granvella the Emperor promised the Elector liberty if he would sign the Interim. But again the Elector declared decidedly that this was impossible for him.

In a written answer to the Emperor the ex-Elector declared, boldly confessing his faith: "I cannot refrain from informing Your Majesty that since the days of my youth I have been instructed and taught by the servants of God's Word, and by diligently searching the prophetic and apostolic Scriptures I have also learned to know, and (this I testify as in the sight of God) unswervingly to adhere in my conscience to this, that the articles composing the Augsburg Confession, and whatever is connected therewith, are the correct, true, Christian, pure doctrine, confirmed by, and founded in, the writings of the holy prophets and apostles, and of the teachers who followed in their footsteps, in such a manner that no substantial objection can be raised against it. . . . Since now in my conscience I am firmly persuaded of this, I owe this gratefulness and obedience to God, who has shown me such unspeakable grace, that, as I desire to obtain eternal salvation and escape eternal damnation, I do not fall away from the truth of His almighty will which His Word has revealed to me, and which I know to be the truth. For such is the comforting and also the terrible word of God: 'Whosoever therefore shall confess Me before men, him will I confess also before My Father which is in heaven. But whosoever shall deny Me before men, him will I also deny before My Father which is in heaven.' If I should acknowledge and adopt the Interim as Christian and godly, I would have to condemn and deny against my own conscience, knowingly and maliciously, the Augsburg Confession, and whatever I have heretofore held and believed concerning the Gospel of Christ, and approve with my mouth what I regard in my heart and conscience as altogether contrary to the holy and divine Scriptures. This, O my God in heaven, would indeed be misusing and cruelly blaspheming Thy holy name, . . . for which I would have to pay all too dearly with my soul. For this is truly the sin against the Holy Ghost concerning which Christ says that it shall never be forgiven, neither in this nor in the world to come, *i. e.*, in eternity." (Walther, 16.)

The Emperor was small enough to punish the heroic refusal and bold confession of the Elector by increasing the severity of his imprisonment. For now he was deprived of Luther's writings and even of the Bible. But the Elector, who drew the line of submission at his conscience and faith, declared, "that they were able indeed to deprive him of the books, but could not tear out of his heart what he had learned from them." And when Musculus and the Lutheran preachers of Augsburg whom the Emperor had banished because of their refusal to introduce the Interim, took leave of the Elector, the latter said: "Though the Emperor has banished you from the realm, he has not banished you from heaven. Surely, God will find some other country where you may preach His Word." (Jaekel, 164.)

## 124. Melanchthon's Attitude toward the Interim.

In the beginning, Melanchthon, too, assumed an attitude of defiance over against the Augsburg Interim. Especially among his friends and in his private letters he condemned it. In several letters, also to Elector Maurice, he and his Wittenberg colleagues declared that they disapproved of the document, and that the doctrine must not be denied, changed, nor falsified. (*C. R.* 6, 874. 954.) April 25, 1548, he wrote to Camerarius that the Interim corrupted the truth in the doctrine of justification, and that he was unable to assent to its sophisms. (878. 900.) April 29, 1548: "The manifest facts teach that efforts at conciliation with our persecutors are vain. Even though some kind of concord is patched up, still a peace will be established such as exists between wolves and lambs. *Etiam cum sarcitur concordia qualiscumque, tamen pax constituitur, qualis est inter lupos et agnos.*" (*C. R.* 6, 889; Frank 4, 90.) In a letter to Christian, King of Denmark (June 13, 1548), he said that the Interim "confirmed and reestablished many papal errors and abuses," and that the "abominable book would cause many dissensions in the German nation." (*C. R.* 6, 923.) June 20 he wrote with reference to the Interim: "I shall not change the doctrine of our churches, nor assent to those who do." (946.) July 31, to the Margrave John of Brandenburg: "As for my person, I do not intend to approve of this book, called Interim, for which I have many weighty reasons, and will commend my miserable life to God, even if I am imprisoned or banished." (7, 85.) In a letter of August 10 he speaks of the corruptions "which are found in the Augsburg sphinx," and declares that he is determined faithfully to guard the doctrine of the Gospel. (97.) August 13, 1548, he wrote to Medler: "Brenz, Nopus [Noppius], Musculus, learned, pious, and most deserving men, have been driven from their churches, and I hear that everywhere others are being expelled from other places, — and Islebius [Agricola] is shouting that this is the way to spread the Gospel." (102.)

In a criticism of the Augsburg Interim published in the beginning of July, 1548, Melanchthon declared: "Although war and destruction are threatened, it is, nevertheless, our duty to regard the Word of God as higher; that is to say, we must not deny what we know to be the truth of the Gospel." On November 10, 1548, he said before a convention of theologians: "Remember that you are the guardians of truth, and consider what has been entrusted to you for preservation by God through the prophets and the apostles, and, last of all, through Dr. Luther. If that man were still living, the misfortune of a change of doctrine would not be threatening us; but now that there is no one who is clothed with the authority which he had, now that there is no one who warns as he was wont to do, and many are accepting error for truth, the churches are brought to ruin, the doctrine heretofore correctly transmitted is distorted, idolatrous customs are established, fear, doubt, and strife are reigning everywhere." (Walther, 21.)

However, though Melanchthon disapproved of the imperial Interim, he was afraid to antagonize it openly and unflinchingly. Yet it was just such a public and decided testimony that was needed, and everywhere expected of Melanchthon; for he was generally regarded as the logical and lawful successor of Luther and as the theological leader of the Church. July 22, 1548, Aquila wrote: "What shall I say of the arch-knave Eisleben, Agricola? He said: 'The Interim is the best book and work making for unity in the whole Empire and for religious agreement throughout all Europe. For now the Pope is reformed, and the Emperor is a Lutheran.'" Imploring Melanchthon to break his silence and sound the public warning, Aquila continues: "Thou holy man, answer and come to our assistance, defend the Word and name of Christ and His honor (which is the highest good on earth) against that virulent sycophant Agricola, who is an impostor." (7, 78.)

Such were the sentiments of loyal Lutherans everywhere. But Melanchthon, intimidated by threats of the Emperor, and fearing for his safety, turned a deaf ear to these entreaties. While the captive Elector was determined to die rather than submit to the Interim, and while hundreds of Lutheran ministers were deposed, banished, imprisoned, and some of them even executed because of their devotion to the truth, Melanchthon was unwilling to expose himself to the anger of the Emperor. And before long his fear to confess and his refusal to give public testimony to the truth

was followed by open denial. At the behest of Elector Maurice he consented to elaborate, as a substitute for the Augsburg Interim, a compromise document — the so-called Leipzig Interim.

## 125. Melanchthon and the Leipzig Interim.

After the victory of the Emperor and the proclamation of the Augsburg Interim, Maurice, the new-fledged Elector, found himself in a dilemma. Charles V urged him to set a good example in obeying and enforcing the Interim. Indebted as he was to the Emperor for his Electorate, he, to some extent, felt bound to obey him also in religious matters. At the same time, Maurice was personally not at all in agreement with the radical Augsburg Interim and afraid of forfeiting the sympathies of both his old and new subjects on account of it. Nor did he fail to realize the difficulties he would encounter in enforcing it. Accordingly, he notified the Emperor on May 18 that he was not able to introduce the Interim at present. Soon after, he commissioned the Wittenberg and Leipzig theologians to elaborate, as a substitute for the Augsburg Interim, a compromise, more favorable and acceptable to his subjects. At the preliminary discussions, especially at Pegau and Celle, the theologians yielded, declaring their willingness to submit to the will of the Emperor with respect to the reintroduction of Romish ceremonies and to acknowledge the authority of the Pope and bishops if they would tolerate the true doctrine. (Preger 1, 40.) The final upshot of it all was the new Interim, a compromise document, prepared chiefly by Melanchthon and adopted December 22, 1548, at Leipzig. This "Resolution of the Diet at Leipzig" was designated by its opponents the "Leipzig Interim." Schaff remarks: "It was the mistake of his [Melanchthon's] life, yet not without plausible excuses and incidental advantages. He advocated immovable steadfastness in doctrine [?], but submission in everything else for the sake of peace. He had the satisfaction that the University of Wittenberg, after temporary suspension, was restored and soon frequented again by two thousand students. [The school was closed May 19, and reopened October 16, 1547.] But outside of Wittenberg and Saxony his conduct appeared treasonable to the cause of the Reformation, and acted as an encouragement to an unscrupulous and uncompromising enemy. Hence the venerable man was fiercely assailed from every quarter by friend and foe." (*Creeds* 1, 300.)

It is generally held that fear induced Melanchthon to condescend to this betrayal of Lutheranism, — for such the Leipzig Interim amounted to in reality. And, no doubt, there is a good deal of truth in this assumption. For Melanchthon had been told that because of his opposition to the Augsburg Interim the anger of the Emperor was directed against him especially, and that he had already called upon Maurice to banish this "arch-heretic." It certainly served the purpose of Maurice well that he had to deal with Melanchthon, whose fear and vacillation made him as pliable as putty, and not with Luther, on whose unbending firmness all of his schemes would have foundered. However, it cannot have been mere temporary fear which induced Melanchthon to barter away eternal truth for temporal peace. For the theologians of Wittenberg and Leipzig did not only identify themselves with the Leipzig Interim while the threatening clouds of persecution were hovering over them, but also afterwards continued to defend their action. When the representatives of the Saxon cities protested against some of the provisions of the Interim, they declared, on December 28, 1548: "We have learned your request and are satisfied with the articles [Leipzig Interim] delivered, which not we alone, but also several other superintendents and theologians prepared and weighed well; therefore we are unable to change them. For they can well be received and observed without any violence to good conscience." (*C. R.* 7, 270.) It was as late as September, 1556, that Melanchthon, though even then only in a qualified way, admitted that he had sinned in this matter, and should have kept aloof from the insidious counsels of the politicians. (8, 839.) Indeed, in 1557 and 1560 the Leipzig and Wittenberg theologians still defended the position they had occupied during the Interim. Evidently, then, apart from other motives of fear, etc., Melanchthon consented to write the Interim because he still believed in the possibility of arriving at an understanding with the Romanists and tried to persuade himself that the Emperor seriously sought to abolish prevailing errors and abuses, and because the theological views he entertained were not as far apart from those of the Leipzig compromise as is frequently assumed.

### 126. Provisions of Leipzig Interim.

The professed object of the Leipzig Interim was to effect a compromise in order to escape persecution and desolation of the churches by adhering to the doctrine, notably of justification, but yielding in matters pertaining to ceremonies, etc. December 18, 1548, Melanchthon (in the name of George of Anhalt) wrote to Burchard concerning the Interim adopted four days later: "They [Maurice and the estates] hope to be able to ward off dangers if we receive some rites which are not in themselves vicious; and the charge of unjust obstinacy is made if in such things we are unwilling to contribute toward public tranquillity. . . . In order, therefore, to retain necessary things, we are not too exacting with respect to such as are unnecessary, especially since heretofore these rites have, to a great extent, remained in the churches of these regions. . . . We know that much is said against this moderation; but the devastation of the churches, such as is taking place in Swabia, would be a still greater offense." (7, 251 ff.) The plan of Melanchthon therefore was to yield in things which he regarded

as unnecessary in order to maintain the truth and avoid persecution.

As a matter of fact, however, the Leipzig Interim, too, was in every respect a truce over the corpse of true Lutheranism. It was a unionistic document sacrificing Lutheranism doctrinally as well as practically. The obnoxious features of the Augsburg Interim had not been eliminated, but merely toned down. Throughout, the controverted doctrines were treated in ambiguous or false formulas. Tschackert is correct in maintaining that, in the articles of justification and of the Church, "the fundamental thoughts of the Reformation doctrine were catholicized" by the Leipzig Interim. (508.) Even the Lutheran *sola* (*sola fide*, by faith alone) is omitted in the article of justification. The entire matter is presented in terms which Romanists were able to interpret in the sense of their doctrine of "infused righteousness, *iustitia infusa*." Faith is coordinated with other virtues, and good works are declared to be necessary to salvation. "Justification by faith," says Schmauk, "is there [in the Leipzig Interim] so changed as to mean that man is renewed by the Holy Spirit, and can fulfil righteousness with his works, and that God will, for His Son's sake, accept in believers this weak beginning of obedience in this miserable, frail nature." (*Conf. Prin.*, 596.)

Furthermore, the Leipzig Interim indirectly admits the Semi-Pelagian teaching regarding original sin and free will, while other doctrines which should have been confessed are passed by in silence. It recognizes the supremacy of the Pope, restores the power and jurisdiction of the bishops, acknowledges the authority of the council, approves of a number of ceremonies objectionable as such (*e. g.*, the Corpus Christi Festival), and advocates the reintroduction of these and others in order to avoid persecution and to maintain outward peace with the Papists.

Self-evidently, in keeping with the Interim, the Pope also could no longer be, regarded as, and publicly declared to be, the Antichrist. In 1561 Flacius wrote that at that time the suspected Lutherans did not consider the Pope the Antichrist. Simon Musaeus and others were banished because they refused to eliminate the hymn "Erhalt uns, Herr, bei deinem Wort" from their services. (Walther, 25.) — Such, then, being the character of the Leipzig Interim, it stands to reason that this document, adopted as it was by Melanchthon and other Lutheran leaders, was bound to become a fertile source of numerous and violent controversies.

### 127. Flacius and Other Opponents of Interimists.

The Leipzig Interim was imposed upon the churches of Electoral Saxony as a directory for teaching, preaching, and worship. Melanchthon declared that it could be adopted with a good conscience, and hence should be introduced, as demanded by Maurice, in order to insure the peace of the Church. At Wittenberg and other places corresponding efforts were made. But everywhere the result was dissension and strife. The Interim defeated its own purpose. Pastors who declined to conform were deposed, banished, incarcerated, or abused in other ways. And wherever faithful ministers were removed, the people refused to be served by the hirelings who took their places. At the very convention at Leipzig where, the Interim was adopted, Wolfgang Pfentner, Superintendent at Annaberg, declared: "What caused them to reintroduce such tomfooleries [Romish ceremonies]? Were they growing childish again? They might do what they wanted to, but as for himself, he could not consent [to the Interim]. And even if he should permit himself to be deceived, his parishioners would not accept it. For in a letter delivered by a messenger on horseback they had charged him to agree to no ungodly article, or not return to them. Accordingly, he would have his head cut off at Leipzig and suffer this with a good conscience rather than give offense to his church." (Walther, 22.)

December 24, three days after the adoption of the Interim, representatives of the cities in Saxony presented complaints to Elector Maurice and Melanchthon against some of the provisions of the document. They protested particularly against the reinstitution of Extreme Unction, the Festival of Corpus Christi, and the use of chrism at Baptism. (*C. R.* 7, 270.) Even the Wittenberg theologians finally admitted that in consequence of "the Interim the rupture had become so great that there was an agreement neither of one church with another, nor, in the same church, of any deacon, any schoolmaster, or sexton with his pastor, nor of one neighbor with another, nor of members of the household with one another." (Walther, 23.)

Foremost among the champions of true Lutheranism over against the Interimists were John Hermann, Aquila, Nicholas Amsdorf, John Wigand, Alberus, Gallus, Matthias Judex, Westphal, and especially Matthias Flacius Illyricus, then (from 1544 to 1549) a member of the Wittenberg faculty, where he opposed all concessions to the Adiaphorists. It is due, no doubt, to Flacius more than to any other individual that true Lutheranism and with it the Lutheran Church was saved from annihilation in consequence of the Interims. In 1548 he began his numerous and powerful publications against them. In the same year, 1548, the following book of John Hermann appeared: "That during These Dangerous Times Nothing should be Changed in the Churches of God in Order to Please the Devil and the Antichrist." In 1549: "Against the Mean Devil who Now Again is Disguising Himself as an Angel of Light."

In 1549, when he was no longer safe in Wittenberg, Flacius removed to Magdeburg, then the only safe asylum in all Germany for such as were persecuted on account of their Lutheran faith and loyalty, where he was joined by such "exiles of Christ" as Wigand,

Gallus, and others, who had also been banished and persecuted because of their opposition to the Interim. Here they inaugurated a powerful propaganda by publishing broadsides of annihilating pamphlets against the Interim, as well as its authors, patrons, and abettors. They roused the Lutheran consciousness everywhere; and before long the great majority of Lutherans stood behind Flacius and the heroes of Magdeburg. The publications emanating from this fortress caused such an aversion to the Adiaphoristic princes as well as theologians among the people that from the very outset all their plans and efforts were doomed to failure, and the sinister schemes of the Pope and Emperor were frustrated. Because of this able and staunch defense of Lutheranism and the determined opposition to any unionistic compromise, Magdeburg at that time was generally called "God's chancellery, *Gottes Kanzlei.*" Nor did the opposition subside when this Lutheran stronghold, thrice outlawed by the Emperor, was finally, after a siege of thirteen months, captured by Maurice. In their attacks the champions of Magdeburg were joined also by the ministers of Hamburg and other places. Only in Saxony and Brandenburg the policy of Melanchthon was defended.

As the conflict extended, it grew in bitterness, revealing with increasing luridness the insincerity and dishonesty of the Philippists. True Lutherans everywhere were satisfied that the adoption also of the Leipzig Interim was tantamount to a complete surrender, of Lutheranism. Their animosity against this document was all the stronger because it bore the stamp of the Wittenberg and Leipzig theologians and was sponsored by Melanchthon, the very man whom they had regarded as Luther's successor and as the leader of the Church. This, too, was the reason why the Leipzig Interim caused even more resentment among the Lutherans, especially in Northern Germany, than did the Augsburg Interim. In their view, Melanchthon and his colleagues had betrayed the cause of the Reformation and practically joined their forces with those of the Romanists, even as Maurice had betrayed the Lutherans politically when fighting at the side of the Emperor against his own coreligionists. Tschackert remarks: "In view of the fact that at that time about 400 Evangelical pastors in Southern Germany, because of their refusal to adopt the Augsburg Interim, had suffered themselves to be driven from their charges and homes and wandered about starving, many with their wives and children, the yielding of the theologians of Electoral Saxony could but appear as unpardonable and as a betrayal of the Church." (508.)

## 128. Grief over Melanchthon's Inconstancy.

In consequence of his dubious attitude, Melanchthon also, who before this had been generally honored as the leader of the Lutheran Church, completely lost his prestige, even among many of his formerly most devoted friends. The grief and distress experienced by loyal Lutherans at his wavering and yielding is eloquently expressed by Antonius Corvinus, Superintendent at Kalenberg-Goettingen, the Lutheran martyr, who, because of his opposition to the Interim, was incarcerated for three years, in consequence of which he died, 1553. In a letter dated September 25, 1549, he implored his friend to abandon the Interim, and to "return to his pristine candor, his pristine sincerity, and his pristine constancy," and "to think, say, write, and do what is becoming to Philip, the Christian teacher, not the court philosopher." Peace, indeed, was desirable, but it must not be obtained by distracting the churches. Christ had also declared that He did not come to bring peace, but the sword. Even the heathen Horatius Flaccus had said: *"Si fractus illabitur orbis, impavidum ferient ruinae."* How much more should Christians avoid cowardice! One must not court the cross wantonly, but it must be borne courageously when for the sake of truth it cannot be avoided, etc.

In the original, Corvinus's letter reads, in part, as follows: "O mi Philippe, o, inquam, Philippe noster, rede per immortalem Christum ad pristinum candorem, ad pristinam sinceritatem, ad pristinam constantiam! Ne languescito ista tua formidine ac pusillanimitate nostrorum animos tantopere! . . . Non sis tantorum in ecclesia offendiculorum autor! Ne sinas, tua tam egregia scripta, dicta, facta, quibus mirifice hactenus de ecclesia ac scholis meritus es, isto condonationis, novationis, moderationis naevo ad eum modum deformari! Cogita, quantum animi ista vestra consilia et adversariis addant et nostris adimant! . . . Rogamus, ut, professionis tuae memor, talem te cum Vitebergensibus tuis iam geras, qualem te ab initio huius causae gessisti, hoc est, ut ea sentias, dicas, scribas, agas, quae Philippum, doctorem Christianum, non aulicum philosophum decent." (Tschackert, 506.)

In a similar manner Melanchthon was admonished also by Brenz, who preferred exile and misery to the Interim. In a letter written early in 1549 he said: "It is also most manifest that the Interitus [Ruin, a term employed by Brenz for Interim] conflicts with the Word of the Lord. What concord, then, can be found between such conflicting things? You think that one ought to come to the assistance of the churches and pious ministers. Correct, if such can be done without dishonor to Christ. Perhaps you believe that the Interimists will tolerate the pious doctrine if we agree to accept all their ceremonies. But do you not know that it is clearly commanded in the introduction of the Interitus that no one shall speak or write against this book? What kind of liberty in regard to doctrine is this? Therefore, if the Church and the pious ministers cannot be saved in any other way than by dishonoring the pious doctrine, let us commend them to Christ, the Son of God. He will take care of them. Meanwhile let us patiently bear our exile and wait for the Lord." (*C. R.* 7, 289.)

June 18, 1550, Calvin also wrote a letter of warning to Melanchthon, in which he said, in substance: "My grief renders me almost speechless. How the enemies of Christ enjoy your conflicts with the Magdeburgers appears from their mockeries. Nor do I acquit you altogether of all guilt. Permit me to admonish you freely as a true friend. I should like to approve of all your actions. But now I accuse you before your very face (*ego te nunc apud te ipsum accuso*). This is the sum of your defense: If the purity of doctrine be retained, externals should not be pertinaciously contended for (*modo retineatur doctrinae puritas, de rebus externis non esse pertinaciter dimicandum*). But you extend the adiaphora too far. Some of them plainly conflict with the Word of God. Now, since the Lord has drawn us into the fight, it behooves us to struggle all the more manfully (*eo virilius nos eniti decebat*). You know that your position differs from that of the multitude. The hesitation of the general or leader is more disgraceful than the flight of an entire regiment of common soldiers. Unless you set an example of unflinching steadfastness, all will declare that vacillation cannot be tolerated in such a man. By yielding but a little, you alone have caused more lamentations and complaints than a hundred ordinary men by open apostasy (*Itaque plures tu unus paululum cedendo querimonias et gemitus excitasti quam centum mediocres aperta defectione*). I would die with you a hundred times rather than see you survive the doctrine surrendered by you. You will pardon me for unloading into your bosom these pitiable, though useless groans." (Schluesselburg 13, 635; *C. R.* 41 [*Calvini Opera* 13], 593; Frank 4, 88.)

## 129. Interim Eliminated Politically, But Not Theologically.

It was also in the interest of allaying the animosity against his own person that Elector Maurice had prevailed upon Melanchthon to frame the Leipzig Interim. But in this respect, too, the document proved to be a dismal failure. Openly the people, his own former subjects included, showed their contempt for his person and character. Everywhere public sentiment was aroused against him. He was held responsible for the captivity and shameful treatment of Philip of Hesse and especially of John Frederick, whom the people admired as the Confessor of Augsburg and now also as the innocent Martyr of Lutheranism. Maurice, on the other hand, was branded a mameluke, condemned as a renegade and an apostate, despised as the traitor of Lutheranism, and abhorred as the "Judas of Meissen," who had sold his coreligionists for an electorate.

At the same time Maurice was provoked by the arbitrary manner in which the Emperor exploited and abused his victory by a repeated breach of his promises, and by the treacherous and shameful treatment accorded his father-in-law, Philip of Hesse. Chagrined at all this and fully realizing the utter impossibility of enforcing the Interim, Maurice decided to end the matter by a single stroke, which at the same time would atone for his treachery, and turn shame into glory and the vile name of a "traitor" into the noble title of "Champion of Protestantism." Accordingly Maurice, easily the match of Charles in duplicity and cunning, secretly prepared his plans, and, suddenly turning his army against the unsuspecting Emperor, drove him from Innsbruck, scared the "Fathers of Trent" to their homes, and on April 5, 1552, victoriously entered Augsburg, where he was received with great rejoicing. The fruits of this victory were the Treaties of Passau, August 2, 1552, and of Augsburg, 1555, which for the first time granted religious liberty to the Protestants. The latter placed Lutherans and Catholics on an equal footing in the Empire and, according to the rule: *Cuius regio, eius religio,* gave every prince religious control in his own territory, non-conformists being granted the right of emigration. To the great advantage of the Romanists, however, the treaty also provided that territories ruled by bishops must remain Catholic even though the ruler should turn Protestant.

But while the Interim was thus eliminated as a political and practical issue, the theological controversy precipitated by it continued unabated. Its political elimination cleared the situation toward the Romanists, but left conditions within the Lutheran Church unsettled. It neither unified nor pacified the Church. It neither eliminated the false doctrines and unionistic principles and tendencies injected by the Interimists, nor did it restore confidence in the doctrinal soundness, loyalty, and sincerity of the vacillating Philippists, who had caused the first breach in the Lutheran Church. "Does it agree with the character of the Lutheran Church to tolerate and approve the doctrines and principles contained and involved in the Interim, and to harbor and fellowship such indifferentists as framed, indorsed, and defended this document?" such and similar were the questions which remained live issues even after the Interim was politically dead. The theological situation within the Lutheran Church, therefore, was not changed in the least when the annihilation threatening her from without was warded off by the victory of Maurice over the Emperor. The Interim was fraught with doctrinal issues which made unavoidable the subsequent controversies.

# XI. Controversies Following the Interim and Settled by the Formula of Concord.

### 130. Three Theological Parties.

In the theological conflicts after Luther's death three parties may be distinguished. The first party embraced chiefly the Interimists, the Synergists, and the Crypto-Calvinists. They were adherents of Philip Melanchthon, hence called Melanchthonians or, more commonly, Philippists, and were led by the theologians of Electoral Saxony. Their object was to supplant the authority and theology of Luther by the unionistic and liberal views of Melanchthon. Their headquarters were the universities of Wittenberg and Leipzig. Some of their chief representatives were: Joachim Camerarius (born 1500, professor of Greek in Leipzig, a close friend of Melanchthon, died 1574); Paul Eber (born 1511, professor in Wittenberg, died 1568); Caspar Cruciger, Jr. (born 1525, professor in Wittenberg, died at Cassel 1597); Christopher Pezel (born 1539, professor in Wittenberg, died 1600 or 1604); George Major (Meier; born 1502, professor in Wittenberg, died 1574); Caspar Peucer (doctor of medicine, son-in-law of Melanchthon; born 1525, imprisoned from 1574 till 1586, died 1602); Paul Crell (born 1531, professor in Wittenberg, died 1579); John Pfeffinger (born 1493, professor in Leipzig, died 1573); Victorin Strigel (born 1524, 1548 professor in Jena, died in Heidelberg 1569); John Stoessel (born 1524, died in prison 1576); George Cracow (born 1525, professor of jurisprudence in Wittenberg, privy counselor in Dresden, died in prison 1575).

The second party, the so-called Gnesio-Lutherans (genuine Lutherans), was represented chiefly by the theologians of Ducal Saxony and embraced such staunch and loyal men as Amsdorf, Flacius, Wigand, Gallus, Matthias Judex, Moerlin, Tileman Hesshusius, Timann, Westphal, and Simon Musaeus. Though some of these leaders were later discredited by falling into extreme positions themselves, they all proved to be valiant champions of Luther and most determined opponents of the Philippists. The strongholds of this party were Magdeburg and the University of Jena, founded by the sons of John Frederick in 1547. Led by Flacius, this university unflinchingly opposed the modified and unionistic Lutheranism advocated by the Philippists at Wittenberg and Leipzig. Seeberg says, in substance: The Gnesio-Lutherans were opposed to the philosophy of the Philippists and stood for "the simple Biblical truth as Luther had understood it." Even when opposed by the government, they defended the truth, and were willing to suffer the consequences. Strict doctrinal discipline was exercised by them. They opposed with equal determination the errors also of their fellow-combatants: Amsdorf, Flacius, Poach, and others. Intellectually they were superior to the Philippists. Seeberg concludes: "In the forms of their time (which were not outgrown by any one of the Philippists either) they preserved to the Church genuine Luther-treasures — *echtes Luthergut.*" (*Dogmengeschichte* 4, 2, 482.)

·The third, or center-party, was composed of the loyal Lutherans who took no conspicuous part in the controversies, but came to the front when the work of pacification began. They were of special service in settling the

*Martin Chemnitz was second Martin Luther.*
*He had big part in writing Formula of Concord.*

controversies, framing the Formula of Concord, and restoring a true and godly peace to our Church. Prominent among them were Brenz, Andreae, Chemnitz, Selneccer, Chytraeus, Cornerus, Moerlin, and others. These theologians were, on the one hand, opposed to all unnecessary logomachies, *i. e.*, controversies involving no doctrinal differences, and, at the same time, were most careful not to fall into any extreme position themselves. On the other hand, however, they approved of all controversies really necessary in the interest of truth, rejected and condemned all forms of indifferentism and unionism, and strenuously opposed every effort at sacrificing, veiling, or compromising any doctrine by ambiguous formulas for the sake of external peace or any other policy whatsoever. (CONC. TRIGL., 855 f.)

## 131. Various Theological Controversies.

Following is a synopsis and summary of the main controversies within the Lutheran Church after the death of Luther, which were settled in the first eleven articles of the Formula of Concord. The sequence of these articles, however, is not strictly historical and chronological, but dogmatic. In the main, the arrangement of the Augsburg Confession is observed.

The first of these controversies was the so-called Adiaphoristic Controversy, from 1548 to 1555, in which the Wittenberg and Leipzig theologians (Melanchthon, Eber, Pfeffinger, etc.) defended the Leipzig Interim and the reintroduction of Romish ceremonies into the Lutheran Church. They were opposed by the champions of a consistent and determined Lutheranism, led by Flacius, who declared: "*Nihil est adiaphoron in statu confessionis et scandali.* Nothing is an adiaphoron in case of confession and offense." The controversy was decided by Article X.

The second is the Majoristic Controversy, from 1551 to 1562, in which George Major and Justus Menius defended the phrase of Melanchthon that good works are necessary to salvation. They were opposed by the loyal Lutherans, of whom Amsdorf, however, lapsed into the opposite error: Good works are detrimental to salvation. This controversy was settled by Article IV.

The third is the Synergistic Controversy, from 1555 to 1560, in which Pfeffinger, Eber, Major, Crell, Pezel, Strigel, and Stoessel held with Melanchthon that man by his own natural powers cooperates in his conversion. Their opponents (Amsdorf, Flacius, Hesshusius, Wigand, Gallus, Musaeus, and Judex) taught, as formulated by Flacius: "*Solus Deus convertit hominem. . . . Non excludit voluntatem, sed omnem efficaciam et operationem eius.* God alone converts man. . . . He does not exclude the will, but all efficaciousness and operation of the same." This controversy was decided and settled by Article II.

The fourth is the Flacian Controversy, from 1560 to 1575, in which Flacius, supported by Cyriacus Spangenberg, Christian Irenaeus, Matthias Wolf, I. F. Coelestinus, Schneider, and others, maintained that original sin is not an accident, but the very substance of fallen man. The Lutherans, including the Philippists, were practically unanimous in opposing this error. It was decided by Article I.

The fifth was the Osiandristic and the Stancarian Controversy, from 1549 to 1566, in which Andrew Osiander denied the forensic character of justification, and taught that Christ is our righteousness only according to His divine nature, while Stancarus contended that Christ is our righteousness according to His human nature only. Both, Osiander as well as Stancarus, were opposed by Melanchthon, Flacius, and practically all other Lutherans, the Philippists included. This controversy was settled by Article III.

The sixth was the Antinomistic Controversy, from 1527 to 1556, in which various false views concerning the Law and the Gospel were defended, especially by John Agricola, who maintained that repentance (contrition) is not wrought by the Law, but by the Gospel (a view which, in a modified form, was later on defended also by Wittenberg Philippists), and, after Luther's death, by Poach and Otto, who rejected the so-called Third Use of the Law. The questions involved in these Antinomian controversies were decided by Articles V and VI.

The seventh was the Crypto-Calvinistic Controversy, from 1560 to 1574, in which the Philippists in Wittenberg, Leipzig, and Dresden (Peucer, Cracow, Stoessel, etc.) endeavored gradually to supplant Luther's doctrines concerning the Lord's Supper and the majesty of the human nature of Christ by the Calvinistic teachings on these points. These secret and dishonest enemies of Lutheranism were opposed by true Lutherans everywhere, notably by the theologians of Ducal Saxony. In 1574 they were publicly unmasked as deceivers and Calvinistic schemers. The controversy was settled by Articles VII and VIII.

The two last controversies were of a local nature. The first was chiefly confined to Hamburg, the second to Strassburg. In the former city John Aepinus taught that Christ's descent into hell was a part of His suffering and humiliation. He was opposed by his colleagues in Hamburg. In Strassburg John Marbach publicly denounced Zanchi, a Crypto-Calvinist, for teaching that faith, once engendered in a man, cannot be lost. The questions involved in these two articles are dealt with in Articles IX and XI, respectively.

## 132. Conflicts Unavoidable.

When describing the conflicts after Luther's death, historians frequently deplore "the dreadful controversies of these dark days of doctrinal extremists and the polemical spirit of rigid Lutheranism." G. J. Planck, in particular, characterized them all as useless quarrels and personal wranglings of narrow-minded, bigoted adherents of Luther, who vitiated original Lutheranism by making it essentially a matter of "pure doctrine." To the present day indifferentistically inclined historians are wont to mar their pages with similar views.

True, "pure doctrine," "unity in the pure doctrine of the Gospel," such was the shibboleth of the faithful Lutherans over against the Melanchthonians and other errorists. But this was neither reprehensible doctrinalism nor a corruption of original Lutheranism, but the very principle from which it was born and for which Luther contended throughout his life — a principle of life or death for the Lutheran Church. It was the *false* doctrine of justification which made Luther a most miserable man. It was the *pure* doctrine as taught by St. Paul which freed his conscience, transported him into Paradise, as he himself puts it, and made him the Reformer of the Church. Ever since, purity of doctrine was held, by Luther and all true Lutheran theologians, to be of paramount import to Christianity and the Church. Fully realizing that adulteration of any part of the Christian doctrine was bound to infect also the doctrine of faith and justification and thus endanger salvation, they earnestly warned against, and opposed, every deviation from the clear Word of God, no matter how insignificant it might appear. They loved the truth more than external peace, more even than their own lives. Hence they found it impossible to be silent, apathetic, and complacent spectators while the Philippists and others denied, attacked, and corrupted the truth taught by Luther from the Word of God.

Accordingly, since the Leipzig Interim involved and maintained doctrines and principles subversive of genuine Lutheranism and was prepared, introduced, and defended by the very men who were regarded as pillars of the Lutheran Church, it was evident from the outset that this document must of necessity precipitate most serious internal troubles. From the moment the Wittenbergers cast the Interim as a firebrand into the Church, a domestic warfare was unavoidable, — if indeed any true disciples of Luther still remained in the Church of which he, and not Melanchthon, was the founder. While the Augsburg Interim resulted in an external theological warfare of the Lutherans against the Romanists, the Leipzig Interim added a most serious domestic conflict, which conscientious Lutherans could not evade, though it well-nigh brought our Church to the brink of destruction. For now the issue was not merely how to resist the Pope and the Romanists, but, how to purge our own Church from the Interimists and their pernicious principles. And as long as the advocates of the Interim or of other aberrations from the old Lutheran moorings refused to abandon their errors, and nevertheless insisted on remaining in the Church, there was no real unity in the truth. Hence there could also be no true peace and brotherly harmony among the Lutherans. And the way to settle these differences was not indifferently to ignore them, nor unionistically to compromise them by adopting ambiguous formulas, but patiently to discuss the doctrines at issue until an agreement in the truth was reached, which finally was done by means of the Formula of Concord.

True, these controversies endangered the very existence of our Church. But the real cause of this was not the resistance which the loyal Lutherans offered to the errorists, nor even the unseemly severity by which the prosecution of these controversies was frequently marred, but the un-Lutheran spirit and the false principles and doctrines manifested and defended by the opponents. In so far as divine truth was defended and error opposed, these controversies were truly wars to end war, and to establish real peace and true unity within our Church. A cowardly surrender to the indifferentistic spirit, the unionistic policy, the false principles, and the erroneous doctrines of the Interimists would have been tantamount to a complete transformation of our Church and a total annihilation of genuine Lutheranism.

The manner in which these controversies were conducted, it is true, was frequently such as to obstruct, rather than further, mutual understanding and peace. As a rule, it is assumed that only the genuine Lutherans indulged in unseemly polemical invective, and spoke and wrote in a bitter and spiteful tone. But the Melanchthonians were, to say the least, equally guilty. And when censuring this spirit of combativeness, one must not overlook that the ultimate cause of the most violent of these controversies was the betrayal of the Lutheran Church by the Interimists; and that the severity of the polemics of the loyal Lutherans did not, at least not as a rule, emanate from any personal malice toward Melanchthon, but rather from a burning zeal to maintain sound Lutheranism, and from the fear that by the scheming and the indifference of the Philippists the fruits of Luther's blessed work might be altogether lost to the coming generations. The "peace-loving" Melanchthon started a conflagration within his own church in order to obtain a temporal and temporary peace with the Romanists; while the loyal Lutherans, inasmuch as they fought for the preservation of genuine Lutheranism, stood for, and promoted, a truly honorable, godly, and lasting peace on the basis of eternal truth. And while the latter fought honestly and in the open, the Philippists have never fully cleared themselves from the charges of duplicity, dishonesty, and dissimulation.

### 133. Melanchthon Prime Mover of Conflicts.

The Leipzig Interim was the signal for a general and prolonged warfare within the Lutheran Church. It contained the germs of various doctrinal errors, and produced a spirit of general distrust and suspicion, which tended to exaggerate and multiply the real differences. Schmauk says: "The seeds of the subsequent controversies are all to be found in the Leipzig Interim." (595.) At any rate, most of the controversies after Luther's death flowed from, or were in some way or other connected with, this unfortunate document. Such is the view also of the Formula of Concord, which declares that the thirty years' controversies which it settled originated especially in the Interim. (857, 19; 946, 29.)

Yet the Interim was rather the occasion than the ultimate cause of these conflicts. Long before the flames of open discord burst forth, the embers of secret doctrinal dissension had been glowing under the surface. Even during the life of Luther much powder had been secretly stored up for which the Interim furnished the spark. This is proved, among other things, by Luther's predictions (referred to in the preceding chapter) concerning his own colleagues. And above all it was the "peace-loving" Philip who first and most successfully sowed the dragon's teeth of discord. Melanchthon's doctrinal deviations from the teachings of Luther and from his own former position must be regarded as the last cause of both the Leipzig Interim and the lamentable controversies that followed in its wake. Indeed, a tragic sight to behold: The colaborer of Luther, the servant of the Reformation second only to Luther, the Praeceptor Germaniae, the ardent and anxious lover of peace, etc. — untrue to his confiding friend, disloyal to the cause of the Reformation, and the chief cause of strife and dissension in the Lutheran Church! And withal, Melanchthon, mistaking external union for real unity and temporal peace with men for true peace with God, felt satisfied that he had spent the efforts of his entire life in the interest of the true welfare of the Church! Shortly before his death (April 19, 1560) he expressed his joy that now he would be delivered from the "fury of the theologians." On a sheet of paper found on his table were written a number of reasons why he feared death less. One of them was: "*Liberaberis ab aerumnis et a rabie theologorum.* You will be delivered from toils and from the fury of the theologians." (*C. R.* 9, 1098.) Thus even in the face of death he did not realize that he himself was the chief cause of the conflicts that had embittered his declining years!

### 134. Melanchthon's Humanistic and Unionistic Tendencies.

Till about 1530 Melanchthon seems to have been in complete harmony with Luther, and to have followed him enthusiastically. To propagate, coin, and bring into scholastic form the Christian truths once more brought to light by the Reformer he considered to be his peculiar mission. But his secret letters and, with gradually increasing clearness and boldness, also his publications show that later on he began to strike out on paths of his own, and to cultivate and disseminate doctrines incompatible with the Lutheranism of Luther. In a measure, these deviations were known also to the Wittenberg students and theologians, to Cordatus, Stifel, Amsdorf, the Elector John Frederick, Brueck, and Luther, who also called him to account whenever sufficient evidence warranted his doing so. (*Lehre und Wehre* 1908, 61 ff.)

In a letter to Cordatus, dated April 15, 1537, Melanchthon was bold enough to state that he had made many corrections in his writings and was glad of the fact: "*Multa ultro correxi in libellis meis et correxisse me gaudeo.*" (*C. R.* 3, 342.) In discussing the squabble between Cordatus and Melanchthon, whether good works are necessary for salvation, Luther is reported by the former to have said, in 1536: "To Philip I leave the sciences and philosophy and nothing else. But I shall be compelled to chop off the head of philosophy, too." (Kolde, *Analecta,* 266.) Melanchthon, as Luther put it, was always troubled by his philosophy; that is to say, instead of subjecting his reason to the Word of God, he was inclined to balance the former against the latter. The truth is that Melanchthon never fully succeeded in freeing himself from his original humanistic tendencies, a fact which gave his mind a moralistic rather than a truly religious and Scriptural bent. Even during the early years of the Reformation, when he was carried away with admiration for Luther and his work, the humanistic undercurrent did not disappear altogether. January 22, 1525, he wrote to Camerarius: "*Ego mihi conscius sum, non ullam ob causam unquam τεϑεολογηκέναι, nisi ut mores meos emendarem.* I am conscious of the fact that I have never theologized for any other reason than to improve my morals." (*C. R.* 1, 722.) Such, then, being his frame of mind, it was no wonder that he should finally desert Luther in most important points, lapse into synergism and other errors, and, in particular, value indifferentistically doctrinal convictions, notably on the real presence in the Lord's Supper and the person of Christ. "Over against Luther," says Schaff, "Melanchthon represented the unionistic and liberal type of Lutheranism." (*Creeds,* 1, 259.) This is correct; but the stricture must be added that, since unionism and liberalism are incompatible with the very essence of Lutheranism, Melanchthonianism as such was in reality not a "type," but a denial of Lutheranism.

Melanchthon lacked the simple faith in, and the firm adherence and implicit submission to, the Word of God which made Luther the undaunted and invincible hero of the Reformation. Standing four-square on the Bible and deriving from this source of divine power alone all his theological thoughts and convictions, Luther was a rock, firm and immovable. With him every theological question was decided and settled conclusively by quoting a clear passage from the Holy Scriptures, while Melanchthon, devoid of Luther's single-minded and whole-hearted devotion to the Word of God, endeavored to satisfy his reason as well. Consequently he lacked assurance and firm conviction, wavered and vacillated, and was never fully satisfied that the position he occupied was really the only correct one, while, on the other hand, he endeavored to present his views concerning some of the disputed doctrines in ambiguous and indefinite terms. "We have twenty-eight large volumes of Melanchthon's writings," says C. P. Krauth, "and, at this hour, impartial and learned men are not agreed as to what were his views on some of the profoundest questions of church doctrine, on which Melanchthon was writing all his life!" (*Conservative Ref.*, 291; Schmauk, 748.) This indefinite and wavering attitude towards divine truth, the natural consequence of the humanistic bent of his mind, produced in Melanchthon a general tendency and proneness to surrender or compromise doctrinal matters in the interest of policy, and to barter away eternal truth for temporal peace. It made him an indifferentist and a unionist, always ready to strike a bargain also in matters pertaining to Christian faith, and to cover doctrinal differences with ambiguous formulas. While Luther's lifelong attitude on matters of Christian doctrine is characterized by the famous words spoken by him at Worms in 1521: "*Ich kann nicht anders,* I cannot do otherwise," Melanchthon, treating even questions of faith as matters of expediency rather than of conscience, was the man who, as a rule, could also do otherwise, and who was great in manufacturing "Polish boots," as the ambiguous phrases by which he endeavored to unite opposing parties were called by the Lutherans in Reuss.

In order to preserve peace with the Romanists at Augsburg in 1530, he did not hesitate to sacrifice Lutheran truths and to receive into the bargain a number of what he considered minor papal errors. In his subsequent overtures to the Reformed he was more than willing to make similar concessions. The spirit of Melanchthon was the spirit of religious indifference and of unionism, which, though thoroughly eliminated by the Formula of Concord, was from time to time revived within the Lutheran Church by such men as Calixtus, Spener, Zinzendorf, Neander, and, in our own country, by S. S. Schmucker.

The unionistic tendencies and doctrinal corruptions which Melanchthon injected into Lutheranism were all the more dangerous to our Church because they derived special weight and prestige from the fact that Luther had unstintingly praised his gifts, his books, and the services he had rendered the Church (St. L. 18, 1671; 23, 1152), that he was now generally regarded as Luther's successor with regard to theological leadership of the Church; and that he was gratefully admired as the Praeceptor Germaniae by a host of loyal pupils, who made it a point also to cultivate just those theological peculiarities of Master Philip, as they called him, in which he differed from Luther.

### 135. Melanchthon's "Shameful Servitude."

That Melanchthon failed our Church in the Interim emergency as well as in the subsequent controversies is generally ascribed to the fact that he lacked the bracing influence and assistance of Luther. No doubt, there is a good deal of truth in this assumption. But the true reason why he did not measure up to the demands of the times and the expectations of our Church were not mere moral weaknesses, but rather the errors and false principles to which he was wedded. How

could Melanchthon have approved himself a leader of the Lutherans when he was out of sympathy with them, doubted some of their most cherished doctrines, and long ago had struck out on a path deviating from that mapped out by Luther? True, the bracing which he received from Luther in the past had repeatedly kept him from publicly sacrificing the truth; but even in these instances he did not always yield because he was really convinced, but because he feared the uncompromising spirit of Luther.

That fear of an open conflict with Luther, which, he felt, would result in a crushing defeat for himself, bulked large among the motives which prompted him to maintain a semblance of true orthodoxy as long as Luther lived, is clearly admitted by Melanchthon himself. In his notorious and most discreditable letter to Carlowitz (counselor of Elector Maurice), written April 28, 1548, eight days after the meeting at Celle, where he had debauched his conscience by promising submission to the religious demands of the Emperor, Melanchthon, pouring forth his feelings and revealing his true inwardness and his spirit of unionism and indifferentism, as much as admitted that in the past he had been accustomed to hiding his real views. Here he declared in so many words that it was not he who started, and was responsible for, the religious controversy between the Lutherans and Romanists, but rather Luther, whose contentious spirit (he said) also had constantly increased the rupture, and that under Luther he had suffered "a most shameful servitude."

In the original the letter reads, in part, as follows: "Totum enim me tibi [Carlowitz] aperio. . . . Ego, cum decreverit princeps, etiamsi quid non probabo, tamen nihil seditiose faciam, sed vel tacebo, vel cedam, vel feram, quidquid accidet. *Tuli etiam antea servitutem paene deformem,* cum saepe Lutherus magis suae naturae, in qua φιλονεικία erat non exigua, quam vel personae suae vel utilitati communi serviret. Et scio, omnibus aetatibus, ut tempestatum incommoda, ita aliqua in gubernatione vitia modeste et arte ferenda et dissimulanda esse. . . . Fortassis natura sum ingenio servili." (*C. R.* 6, 879 f.)

Even before Melanchthon had, in private letters to his friends, displayed a similar vein of ill will toward Luther, whom he evidently feared because of his own secret doctrinal deviations. (*Lehre und Wehre* 1908, 61. 68.) No doubt, as stated above, fear was also among the motives which induced him to identify himself with the Leipzig Interim. But evidently his own theological attitude, too, differed little from the spirit pervading this document. At any rate, the letter to Carlowitz does not support the assumption that Melanchthon really outraged his own convictions when he wrote and adopted the Interim. As a matter of fact, he also continued to defend the Interim; and it was as late as 1556 before he was ready to make even a qualified admission of one of the errors connected with it.

While, therefore, the Lutheran Church will always gratefully acknowledge the splendid services which Melanchthon rendered in the work of Luther's Reformation, it must at the same time be admitted and cannot be gainsaid that, in the last analysis, Melanchthon, by reason of his deviations from Luther, which will be set forth more fully in the following, was the ultimate cause and originator of most of the dissensions which began to distract the Lutheran Church soon after the death of Luther. Andrew Musculus, who assisted in drafting the *Formula of Concord*, brought out this fact (though in terms too strong) when he characterized Melanchthon as a "philosophical theologian and a patriarch of all heretics." (Meusel, *Handl.* 4, 710.) In a way, Melanchthon may even be regarded as the indirect cause of the Smalcald War and its unfortunate issue, inasmuch, namely, as his vacillating and compromising attitude and his incompetent leadership created conditions of internal weakness among the Lutherans, which invited the aggression of Pope and Emperor.

# XII. The Adiaphoristic Controversy.

## 136. Contents of the Leipzig Interim.

To exhibit the insidious character of the Leipzig Interim more fully, we submit the following quotations. In its Introduction we read: "As far as the doctrine of the state and nature of man before and after the Fall is concerned, there is no controversy" (between the Lutherans and Romanists). The article "Of Justification," in which the Lutheran *sola fide* is omitted, declares: "The merciful God does not work with man as with a block, but draws him, so that his will also cooperates if he be of understanding years." Again: "And they who have thus received the forgiveness of sins and the Holy Ghost, and in whom the Holy Ghost begins faith and trust in the Son of God, love and hope, *then* become heirs of eternal salvation for the Savior's sake." In the article "Of Good Works" we read: "Nevertheless, the new virtues and good works are so highly necessary that, if they were not quickened in the heart, there would be no reception of divine grace." Again: "It is certainly true that these virtues, faith, love, hope, and others, must be in us and are *necessary to salvation.* . . . And since the virtues and good works, as has been said, please God, they merit also a reward in this life, both spiritual and temporal, according to God's counsel, and still more reward in the eternal life, because of the divine promise."

The article "Of Ecclesiastical Power" runs as follows: "What the true Christian Church, gathered in the Holy Ghost, acknowledges, determines, and teaches in regard to matters of faith is to be taught and preached, since it neither should nor can determine anything contrary to the Holy Scriptures." Self-evidently, Romanists construed this as an *a priori* endorsement of the Council and its resolutions. In the article "Of Ecclesiastical Ministers" we read: "And that all other ministers should be subject and obedient to the chief bishop [the Pope] and to other bishops who administer their episcopal office according to God's command, using the same for edification and not for destruction; which ministers should be ordained also by such bishops upon presentation by the patrons." This article conceded the primacy of the Pope and the ecclesiastical jurisdiction of the bishops. The article "Of Ordination" declares: "Also, that, as has been said, upon presentation by patrons, ministers should hereafter be ordained with Christian ceremonies by such bishops as administer their episcopal office, and that no one should be allowed to be in the ministry unless, as has been said, he be presented by the patrons and have the permission of the bishops." That was tantamount to a restoration of the "sacrament" of episcopal ordination.

The Interim furthermore demanded the immediate reintroduction of abolished ceremonies, such as exorcism and other ceremonies of Baptism, confirmation by bishops, auricular confession, extreme unction, episcopal ordination, and the like. We read: "That repentance, confession, and absolution, and what pertains thereto, be diligently taught and preached; that the people confess to the priests, and receive of them absolution in God's stead, and be also diligently admonished and urged to prayer, fasting, and almsgiving; also, that no one be admitted to the highly venerable Sacrament of the body and blood of Christ [in this indirect way only the cup of the laity is referred to in the Interim] unless he have first confessed to the priest and received of him absolution." Again: "Although in this country the unction [Extreme Unction] has not been in use for many years, yet . . . such unction, according to the apostle, may be hereafter observed." Again: "That henceforth the mass be observed in this country with ringing of bells, with lights and vessels, with chants, vestments, and ceremonies." Among the holidays to be observed the Interim mentions also Corpus Christi and the festivals of the holy Virgin Mary. Again we read: "The images and pictures of the sufferings of Christ and of the saints may be also retained in the churches." Again: "In the churches where the canonical hours have been formerly observed, the devout Psalms shall be sung in chapters and towns at the appointed time and on other high festivals, and also on Sundays." "Likewise, that on Fridays and Saturdays, as well as during fasts, the eating of meat be abstained from, and that this be observed as an external ordinance at the command of His Imperial Majesty." The clause, "that this be observed," etc., was regarded by Flacius and Gallus as implying self-deception and hypocrisy on the part of the Interimists. (Frank 4, 72. 119.) Again, as to the apparel of priests, that "a distinction be observed between ministers and secular persons, and that proper reverence be paid the priestly estate." The Introduction of the Interim gives the assurance that the Lutherans would obey the Emperor and be found disposed toward peace and unity. The Conclusion adds the humble promise: "In all other articles we are ready . . . in a friendly and submissive manner to confer with Your Beloved and Princely Graces, and to settle our differences in a Christian way." (*C. R.* 7, 258. Jacobs, *Book of Concord*, 2, 260.)

### 137. Issue in Adiaphoristic Controversy.

From the passages quoted it appears that the Leipzig Interim was inoculated with the germs of many controversies. However, while in the beginning its offensive doctrinal features were not fully and generally recognized and realized, the Emperor's demand for, and approval of, the Wittenberg and Leipzig theologian's reintroduction of the Romish ceremonies immediately created an acute situation and a great commotion everywhere. The resulting theological conflict pertaining to the latter point in particular was called the Adiaphoristic or Interimistic Controversy. And, as explained above, even after the Interim had become a dead letter politically, this controversy did not subside, because its paramount object was not merely to pass a correct judgment on past events during the Interim, nor even to obtain norms for similar situations in the future, but, above all, to eliminate from our Church the spirit of indifferentism, unionism, and of direct as well as indirect denial of the Gospel-truth.

Accordingly, the exact issue in the Adiaphoristic Controversy was: May Lutherans, under conditions such as prevailed during the Interim, when the Romanists on pain of persecution and violence demanded the reinstitution of abolished papal ceremonies, even if the ceremonies in question be truly indifferent in themselves, submit with a good conscience, that is to say, without denying the truth and Christian liberty, without sanctioning the errors of Romanism, and without giving offense either to the enemies or to the friends of the Lutheran Church, especially its weak members? This was affirmed by the Interimists and denied by their opponents.

### 138. Opposition to the Adiaphorists.

Prominent among the theologians who participated in the controversy against the Adiaphorists were Flacius, Wigand, Gallus, and others, who in Magdeburg opened a most effective fire on the authors, sponsors, and advocates of the Interim. Following are some of the chief publications which dealt with the questions involved: "Opinion concerning the Interim, by Melanchthon, June 16, 1548," published by Flacius without the knowledge of Melanchthon. — "Report on the Interim by the Theologians of Meissen," 1548. — "That in These Dangerous Times (in diesen geschwinden Laeuften) Nothing is to be Changed in the Churches of God in Order to Please the Devil and the Antichrist," by John Hermann, 1548. A Latin edition of this publication appeared 1549, mentioning Flacius as its author. — "A Brief Report (Ein kurzer Bericht) on the Interim from which One may Easily Learn the Doctrine and Spirit of That Book," 1548. — "A General Protest and Writ of Complaint (Eine gemeine Protestation und Klageschrift) of All Pious Christians against the Interim and Other Sinister Schemes and Cruel Persecutions by the Enemies of the Gospel, by John Waremund, 1548." Waremund was a pseudonym for Flacius. — "Against the Interim, Papal Mass, Canon, and Master Eisleben," 1549. — "Against the Vile Devil (Wider den schnoeden Teufel), who Now Again Transforms Himself into an Angel of Light, *i. e.*, against the New Interim, by Carolus Azarias Gotsburgensis, 1549." Of this book, too, Flacius was the author. (Preger 1, 67.) — "Apology (Entschuldigung) of Matthias Flacius Illy. to a Certain Pastor," 1549. — "Several Letters of the Venerable D. M. Luther concerning the Union of Christ and Belial, Written 1530 to the Theologians at the Diet in Augsburg," 1549, with a preface by Flacius. — "Apology of Matthias Flacius Illy., Addressed to the University of Wittenberg, regarding the Adiaphora," 1549. — "Writing of Matthias Flacius Illy. against a Truly Heathen, yea, Epicurean Book of the Adiaphorists (in which the Leipzig Interim is Defended) in Order to Guard Oneself against the Present Counterfeiters of the True Religion," 1549. — "Answer of Magister Nicolas Gallus and Matthias Flacius Illy. to the Letter of Some Preachers in Meissen regarding the Question whether One should Abandon His Parish rather than Don the Cassock" (*linea vestis, Chorrock*). — "Against the Extract of the Leipzig Interim, or the Small Interim," by Flacius, 1549. — "Book concerning True and False Adiaphora (*Liber de Veris et Falsis Adiaphoris*), in which the Adiaphoristic Controversy is Explained Almost in Its Entirety, by Flacius, 1549." This book, which is most frequently quoted and deals most thoroughly with the questions involved, is found in Schluesselburg's *Catalogus Haereticorum*, 13, 154 ff. — "An Admonition (Vermahnung) to be Constant in the Confession of the Truth, in Cross and Prayer, by Flacius," 1549. — "A Christian Admonition by Matthias Flacius Illy. to be Constant in the True, Pure Religion of Jesus Christ and in the Augsburg Confession," 1550. — "Against the Alleged Power and Primacy of the Pope, Useful to Read at This Time, when the Whole World Endeavors again to Place the Expelled Antichrist into the Temple of Christ, by Matthias Flacius Illy." — "Against the Evangelist of the Holy Chorrock, D. Geitz Major, by Matthias Flacius Illy., 1552." — For a complete list of the writings of Flacius against the Interim, see Preger's *Matthias Flacius Illyricus*, 2, 540 ff.

Even the titles of these publications indicate that the Adiaphoristic Controversy did not lack violence and virulence. This animosity against the Interimists was chiefly due to the fear that their policy would finally lead to the complete undoing of the Reformation. For while Melanchthon still believed in, and hoped for, an understanding with the Romanists, Flacius saw through their schemes and fully realized the impending danger. In the reintroduction of Catholic ceremonies, which Melanchthon regarded as entirely harmless, Flacius beheld nothing but the entering wedge, which would gradually be followed by the entire mass of Romish errors and abuses and the absolute dominance of Pope and Emperor over the Lutheran Church. The obedience demanded by the Emperor, said Flacius, consists in this, that "we abandon our true doctrine and adopt the godless Papacy." In all its details, he explained, the ultimate purpose of the Interim is none other than the reestablishment of Popery, of which even such seemingly trifling matters as the reintroduction of the *Chorrock* (*linea vestis*) were but the beginning, as it were, the breach in the dam which was bound ultimately to result in a complete submersion of Lutheranism. (Frank 4, 74. 76. 119.)

Since the loyal Lutherans, in keeping with the teaching of Luther and the Lutheran Confessions, regarded the Papacy as antichristendom, they could not but abhor the concessions made by the Interimists as treachery against the truth. From the very outset Flacius and Gallus insisted that their opponents answer the question, "whether the Pope with his government is the true Antichrist in the Church as according to the Word of God he has been publicly declared to be in our churches, and whether he still should and must be regarded and confessed as such." And if Luther's doctrine was to stand, how, then, they argued, could a union be effected between the enemies of the Gospel (the Antichrist and his bishops) and the Lutherans without idolatry and denial of the religion of Christ? (53. 107.) On the title-page of his *Apology*, of 1549, Flacius declares: "The upshot [of the Interim] is the establishment of the Papacy and the installation of the Antichrist in the temple of Christ, the encouragement of the wicked to flaunt their victory over the Church of Christ and to grieve the godly, likewise weakening, leading into doubt, separation and innumerable offenses." (Schaff 1, 301.) Regarding the acknowledgment of the Pope and bishops by the Interim, Flacius remarked: "Mark well, here the werwolf (*Baerwolf*), together with his fellow-wolves, is placed over the little flock of Christ. There is, however, no danger whatever; for, as is added [in the Interim: "The Pope should use his power not for destruction, but for edification"], they have counted the sheep and commanded the wolves to be gentle. In my opinion this is certainly a good adiaphoron to restore Antichrist to the temple from which he has been expelled by the Finger of God." (Preger 1, 191.) Accordingly, burning with shame and indignation, and trembling with fear for the future of Lutheranism, Flacius charged Melanchthon with want of faith and with treason against the truth, and characterized the Leipzig Interim as an unholy union of Christ and Belial, of light and darkness, of Christ and Antichrist.

While Flacius thus denounced the Interim as well as its authors and abettors, he at the same time admonished and encouraged the Lutheran pastors to be steadfast in confessing the truth, in spite of cross and persecution, and to stand by their flocks as true shepherds. That minister, he said, who denies or fails to confess the truth, or who yields to a tyrant, deserts his Church. We must not only confess with our mouths, but by deeds and actions as well. Not abandonment of the flock, but suffering is the best way to win the victory over a tyrant. Flacius also earnestly warned the people against yielding to the princes and acknowledging, hearing, and following their own ministers if they advocated and introduced the Interim. Moreover, he encouraged both pastors and laymen to resist the tyranny of princes demanding the reinstitution of the Roman ceremonies. "A government," said he in his *Admonition*, "no matter which, has not the authority to forbid a pastor to preach the pure doctrine." When the government presecutes the truth, we must not yield, no matter what the consequences may be. Christians will sacrifice everything to a tyrannical prince, but not "the truth, not the consolation of divine grace, nor the hope of eternal life." (Frank 4, 68. 117.)

### 139. Doctrinal Position of Anti-Adiaphorists.

The theological position occupied by the opponents of the Adiaphorists may be summarized as follows: Ceremonies which God has neither commanded nor prohibited are adiaphora (*res mediae, Mitteldinge*) and, *ceteris paribus* (other things being equal), may be observed or omitted, adopted or rejected. However, under circumstances testing one's faith they may become a matter of principle and conscience. Such is the case wherever and whenever they are demanded as necessary, or when their introduction involves a denial of the truth, an admission of error, an infringement of Christian liberty, an encouragement of errorists and of the enemies of the Church, a disheartening of the confessors of the truth, or an offense to Christians, especially the weak. Such conditions, they maintained, prevailed during the time of the Interim, when both Pope and Emperor plainly declared it to be their object to reestablish the Romish religion in Lutheran churches; when the adoption of the Interim and the reinstitution of the papal ceremonies were universally regarded, by Catholics as well as Protestants, as the beginning of just such a reestablishment of the Papacy; when the timid Wittenberg and Leipzig theologians, instead of boldly confessing the Gospel and trusting to God for the protection of His Church, compromised the truth and yielded to the demands of the Romanists in order to escape persecution; when the consciences of Lutherans were perplexed and confused wherever the abolished rites were reinstituted. Accordingly, they declared that under the prevailing circumstances the reintroduction of the Romish ceremonies was nothing short of a denial of Christian faith and of Christian love as well.

Flacius, in particular, maintained that under the prevailing circumstances even such ceremonies as were in themselves true adiaphora ceased to be adiaphora and could not be reintroduced with a good conscience, because they were forced upon the Lutherans by the enemies of the Gospel, because they were accepted for reprehensible reasons, such as fear of persecution and desire for external peace, and because their reintroduction confounded the consciences, offended the weak, and gave comfort and encouragement to the enemies of Christ. The people, Protestants as well as Catholics, said Flacius, would regard such reintroduction both as an admission on the part of the Lutherans that they had been in the wrong and the Romanists in the right, and as the beginning of a general restoration of the Papacy. Explain the reintroduction of the ceremonies as piously as you may, said he to the Interimists, the common people, especially the Romanists, always impressed by ceremonies much more than by the doctrine, will infer that those teachers who reintroduce the ceremonies approve of the Papacy in every respect and reject the Evangelical doctrine. In his book *De Veris et Falsis Adiaphoris* we read: "Adversarii totum suum cultum, vel certe praecipua capita suae religionis in ceremoniis collocant, quas cum in nostris ecclesiis in eorum gratiam restituimus, an non videmur tum eis, tum aliis eorum impiis cultibus assentiri? Nec dubitant, quin quandoquidem in tantis rebus ipsis cesserimus, etiam in reliquis cessuri simus, nostrum errorem agnoscamus, eorumque religionem veram esse confiteamur." (Schluesselburg 13, 217.) Accordingly, Flacius contended that under the prevailing circumstances a concession to the Romanists, even in ceremonies harmless in themselves, was tantamount to a denial of Lutheranism. The entire argument of the Anti-Adiaphorists was by him reduced to the following principle or axiom: "*Nihil est adiaphoron in casu confessionis et scandali.* Nothing is an adiaphoron when confession and offense are involved." And wherever the Interim was enforced, the consequences foretold by Flacius showed themselves: consciences were confused, simple Christians were offended, and the enemies were strengthened in their error and emboldened in their attacks and in further demands made upon the Lutherans.

### 140. Sophistries of Adiaphorists Refuted.

The Wittenberg Interimists endeavored to justify their attitude by a series of sophisms to which they also adhered in the "Final Report (Endlicher Bericht) of the Theologians of Both Universities of Leipzig and Wittenberg," 1570. (Frank 4, 87. 2.) By adopting the Interim, the Wittenbergers, in reality, had assented also to doctrinally false and dubious statements and to a number of ceremonies objectionable as such. Yet they pleaded the

guilelessness of their intentions and the harmlessness of their procedure. They maintained that they had yielded merely in minor matters and ceremonies, which were neither commanded nor prohibited by the Word of God; that this was done in order to preserve intact the central Christian truth of justification; to preserve political peace and to save the Church from ruin; to protect the weak, whose shoulders were not strong enough to suffer persecution; that in their concessions they had been guided by the dictates of true wisdom, which always chooses the lesser of two evils; and that in all this they had merely followed the example set by Luther himself. They minimized the entire affair, and endeavored to explain away the seriousness of the situation. In particular they ridiculed Flacius for shouting and sounding the fire-alarm, when in reality, they said, he had discovered nothing but a little smoke coming from a Wittenberg chimney.

But in the ears of all genuine and earnest Lutherans their sophistries and apologies rang neither true nor sincere. The arguments which they employed merely served to defeat their own purpose. What else, for example, than disgust, indignation, and distrust could be the effect on all honest Lutherans when the Wittenberg theologians, dishonestly veiling the real facts, declared in their official "Exposition" of 1559 (when danger of persecution had passed long ago) concerning the reintroduction of Corpus Christi that they had reintroduced this festival all the more readily in order that they might be able to instruct the people in the right use of the Sacrament and in the horrible abuses and profanations of the most holy Supper of the Lord in the circumgestation and adoration of the bread which their critics [the Lutheran opponents of the Interimists, by their doctrine concerning the Lord's Supper] strengthened, and that they might thank God for the purification of the temple from the Romish idol Maozim, Dan. 11, 38. (Tschackert, 510.) Frank remarks: "One must see this passage black on white in order to believe the Wittenbergers really capable of stultifying themselves in such an incredible manner. It is a monstrosity, a defense unworthy of an honest man, let alone an Evangelical Christian." (4, 61. 113.)

The weak and insincere arguments of the Adiaphorists were thoroughly and convincingly refuted by their opponents. To the assertion of the Wittenbergers that the dispute was concerning mere unimportant ceremonies, which were neither commanded nor prohibited by God, Flacius and Gallus replied (in their answer to the question of the ministers of Meissen whether they should leave their charges rather than don the *Chorrock, lineam vestem induere*) that even with respect to such seemingly most trifling adiaphora as the cope (*Chorrock, vestis alba*) one must not overlook what is attached to it. "We do not believe," they said, "that the robber will let the traveler keep his money, although first he only asks for his coat or similar things, at the same time, however, not obscurely hinting that, after having taken these, he will also demand the rest. We certainly do not doubt that you yourselves, as well as all men endowed with a sound mind, believe that, since the beginning is always hardest, these small beginnings of changes are at present demanded only that a door may be opened for all the other impieties that are to follow — *quod tantum ideo parva ista mutationum initia iam proponantur, ut quia principia semper sunt difficillima per ea aditus reliquis omnibus secuturis impietatibus patefiat.*" (Schluesselburg 13, 644.)

The Adiaphorists pretended that they had consented to the Interim in the interest of the weak, who were unable to bear persecution. But the Lutherans answered that weak Christians could not be strengthened in their faith by teaching and persuading them to deny it, and that the enemies and persecutors of the Gospel could certainly not be regarded as weak. (Frank 4, 78.) The protestations of the Adiaphorists that they had made the changes in ceremonies with the very best of intentions were answered by Flacius in *De Veris et Falsis Adiaphoris* as follows: Hardly ever has a Christian denied Christ without endeavoring to deceive both God and himself as to his motives. "But one must also consider, as maybe clearly shown from 1 Cor. 10, with what design (*quo animo*) the adversaries propose such things to us, likewise, how they as well as others interpret our act." (Schl. 13, 217.) "Even though the intention of those who receive and use the adiaphora be not an evil one, the question is," said Martin Chemnitz in his *Iudicium de Adiaphoris*, "whether the opinion of the one who commands, imposes, and demands the adiaphora is impious or wicked, whether such reception and observation is interpreted and understood as a turning away from the confession of the true doctrine, and whether the weak are offended and grow faint thereby." (717.)

To the claims of the Interimists that they were but following the example of Luther, who, for the sake of the weak, had tolerated Romish ceremonies, etc., the Lutherans replied: Distinguish times and conditions! Luther was dealing with Christians who in their consciences still felt bound to the Roman usages, while the "weakness" spoken of by Adiaphorists is not an erring conscience, but fear of persecution. Moreover, Luther tolerated existing Romish ceremonies as long as there was hope of arriving at an agreement with the Romanists in doctrine, while the Adiaphorists reinstitute ceremonies which have been abolished, and this, too, in deference and obedience to irreconcilable adversaries of the truth. Accordingly, Luther's attitude in this matter flowed from pure love for truth and from compassion with the weak, whom he endeavored to win for the truth, while the submission of the Adiaphorists to the demands of their adversaries is nothing short of unchristian denial of both true love and faith. (Frank 4, 55.) Brenz declared: "*Adiaphora ex suis conditionibus iudicanda*

*sunt.* Adiaphora must be judged from their conditions. For if the condition is good, the adiaphoron, too, is good, and its observance is commanded. If, however, the condition is evil, the adiaphoron, too, is evil, and the observance of it is prohibited." (Schl. 13, 562.)

Furthermore, when the Wittenberg and Leipzig theologians maintained that, in preferring the lesser evil (the Roman ceremonies) to the greater (persecution), they had merely listened to, and followed, the voice of true wisdom, the Lutherans replied that moral evils must not be placed on a level with physical evils, nor guilt be incurred in order to avoid suffering and persecution. Westphal declared in his *Explicatio Generalis Sententiae, quod a Duobus Malis Minus sit Eligendum:* "*Impium est, amoliri pericula per peccata, nec ita removentur aut minuuntur, sed accersuntur et augentur poenae.* It is wicked to avert dangers by sins, nor are they removed or diminished in this way, but rather superinduced and increased." (13, 251.) "It is better to take upon oneself punishments and great dangers than to offend God and to provoke His wrath by such offense." (250.) "It is better and easier to bear many evils and to undergo many dangers than to be unfaithful in the least commandment of God, and burden oneself with the guilt of even a single sin." (251.) Our paramount duty is not to escape persecution, but to retain a good conscience. Obey the Lord and await His help! Such was the counsel of Flacius and the loyal Lutherans. (Frank 4, 65.)

But our Wittenberg school will be closed, our churches will be desolated, and our preachers will be banished, exclaimed the faint-hearted Wittenbergers. The Lutherans answered: It is our duty to confess the truth regardless of consequences, and, at the same time, to look to God for the protection of His Church. Flacius said, in *De Veris et Falsis Adiaphoris:* Confess the truth and suffer the consequences! A Christian cannot obtain peace by offending God and serving and satisfying tyrants. Rather be drowned by the Spaniards in the Elbe with a millstone about one's neck than offend a Christian, deny the truth, and surrender the Church to Satan. "*Longe satius esset teste Christo pati, ut alligata mola asinaria in medium Albis ab Hispanis proiiceremur, quam unicum parvulum Christi scandalizaremus, multo vero magis haec et quaevis gravissima pati deberemus, quam tam infinitis* (ut iam fit) *Christi parvulis offendiculum daremus, ecclesiam Satanae proderemus et salvificam confessionem veritatis abiiceremus.*" (Schl. 13, 227.)

As to the Wittenberg School, Flacius said: "It would certainly be better that the school were closed not one, but many years than that we, by avoiding confession, extremely weaken our own religion as well as strengthen the one opposed to it." (13, 231.) "As for myself, I do not doubt that, if only the theologians had been steadfast, the Wittenberg School would have been to-day much firmer than it is. . . . The Interim sprang from the timidity of the Wittenberg theologians. . . . Even a thousand Wittenberg schools ought certainly not to be valued so highly by pious men that, in order to preserve them unimpaired, they would rather suffer the world to be deprived of the light of the Gospel. *Certe non tanti mille Wittenbergenses scholae piis esse debent, ut propter earum incolumitatem velint pati orbem terrarum Evangelii luce privari.*" (232.) In a letter to Melanchthon, written in the beginning of 1549, Brenz said: "If therefore the Church and pious ministers cannot be preserved in any other way than by bringing reproach upon the pious doctrine, then let us commend them to Christ, the Son of God; He will take care of them; and in the mean time let us patiently bear our banishment and wait for the Lord." (*C. R.* 7, 290.)

June 30, 1530, Luther had written to Melanchthon, who was then in Augsburg: "You want to govern things according to your philosophy; you torment yourself and do not see that this matter is not within your power and wisdom. . . . If we fall, Christ, that is to say, the Ruler of the world, falls with us; and even though He should fall, I would rather fall with Christ than stand with the Emperor." This passage is contained in one of the letters of Luther which Flacius published 1548 in order to dispel Melanchthon's timidity, rouse his Lutheran consciousness, and cure him of his vain and most dangerous disposition to save the Church by human wisdom and shrewdness, instead of, as Luther believed, solely by a bold confession of the truth of God's Word.

### 141. Theological Attitude of Flacius Sanctioned.

The theological position which Flacius and his fellow-combatants occupied over against the Adiaphorists was embodied in the Tenth Article of the *Formula of Concord,* and thus endorsed by the Lutheran Church as a whole. Frank says concerning this most excellent article which our Church owes to the faithfulness of the Anti-Melanchthonians, notably Flacius: "The theses which received churchly recognition in the *Formula of Concord* were those of Flacius." The entire matter, too, concerning the adiaphora had been discussed so thoroughly and correctly that the subsequent formulation and recognition of the Tenth Article caused but little difficulties. (Frank 4, 3 f.)

Even Melanchthon, though refusing to confess that he was guilty of any doctrinal deviations, finally yielded to the arguments of his opponents and admitted that they were right in teaching as they did regarding the adi-

aphora. In his famous letter to Flacius (who, however, was not satisfied with the manner of Melanchthon's retraction), dated September 5, 1556, he wrote with respect to the Adiaphoristic Controversy: "I knew that even the least changes [in ceremonies] would be unwelcome to the people. However, since the doctrine [?] was retained, I would rather have our people submit to this servitude than forsake the ministry of the Gospel. *Cum doctrina retineretur integra, malui nostros hanc servitutem subire quam deserere ministerium evangelii.* And I confess that I have given the same advice to the Francans (*Francis*). This I have done; the doctrine of the Confession I have never changed. . . . Afterwards you began to contradict. I yielded; I did not fight. In Homer, Ajax fighting with Hector is satisfied when Hector yields and admits that the former is victor. You never come to an end with your accusations. Where is the enemy that does such a thing as striking those who yield and cast their arms away? Win! I yield. I do not contend concerning those rites, and I most earnestly wish that the churches would enjoy sweet concord. I also admit that I have sinned in this matter, and ask forgiveness of God, that I did not flee far from those insidious deliberations [in which the Interim was framed]. *Fateor hac in re a me peccatum esse, et a Deo veniam peto, quod non procul fugi insidiosas illas deliberationes.*" (*C. R.* 8, 839.)

On January 17, 1557, Melanchthon wrote to the Saxon pastors: "I was drawn into the insidious deliberations of the courts. Therefore, if in any way I have either fallen or been too weak, I ask forgiveness of God and of the Church, and I shall submit to the judgments of the Church." (9, 61.) In the *Formula Consensus,* written by Melanchthon at Worms, in 1557, the Interim is expressly condemned. For here we read: "With the help of God we retain, and shall retain, the entire doctrine of justification, agreeing with the Augsburg Confession and with the confessions which were published in the church of Hamburg against the book called Interim. Nor do we want any corruptions or ambiguities to be mixed with it; and we desire most earnestly that the true doctrine in all its articles be set forth, as far as possible, in identical and proper forms of speech, and that ambitious innovations be avoided." (9, 369.) The *Frankfurt Recess* of 1558, also written by Melanchthon and signed by the princes, maintains: "Where the true Christian doctrine of the holy Gospel is polluted or persecuted, there the adiaphora as well as other ceremonies are detrimental and injurious." (9, 501.)

# XIII. The Majoristic Controversy.

### 142. Early Origin of This Error.

Though not personally mentioned and attacked by the opponents of Majorism, Melanchthon must be regarded as the real father also of this controversy. He was the first to introduce and to cultivate the phrase: "Good

works are necessary to salvation." In his *Loci* of 1535 he taught that, in the article of justification, good works are the *causa sine qua non* and are necessary to salvation, *ad vitam aeternam, ad salutem.* (Herzog, *R. E.,* 1903, 12, 519; Galle, *Melanchthon,* 345. 134.)

Melanchthon defined: *"Causa sine qua non* works nothing, nor is it a constituent part, but merely something without which the effect does not occur, or by which, if it were not present, the working cause would be hindered because it was not added. *Causa sine qua non nihil agit, nec est pars constituens, sed tantum est quiddam, sine quo non fit effectus, seu quo, si non adesset, impediretur agens, ideo quia illud non accessisset."* (Preger 1, 356.) According to Melanchthon, therefore, justification cannot occur without the presence of good works. He explained: *"Et tamen bona opera ita necessaria sunt ad vitam aeternam, quia sequi reconciliationem necessario debent.* Nevertheless good works are necessary to eternal life, inasmuch as they must necessarily follow reconciliation." (*C. R.* 21, 429. 775.) According to the context in which it is found, this statement includes that good works are necessary also to justification; for Melanchthon, too, correctly held "that the adoption to eternal life or the gift of eternal life was connected with justification, that is, the reconciliation imparted to faith." (453.)

At Wittenberg Melanchthon's efforts to introduce the new formula met with energetic opposition, especially on the part of Cordatus and Amsdorf. The formula: *"Bona opera non quidem esse causam efficientem salutis, sed tamen causam sine qua non —* Good works are indeed not the efficient cause of salvation, but nevertheless an indispensable cause," a necessary antecedent, was launched in a lecture delivered July 24, 1536, by a devoted pupil of Melanchthon, Caspar Cruciger, Sr. [born at Leipzig, January 1, 1504; professor in Wittenberg; assisted Luther in translating the Bible and in taking down his lectures and sermons; present at colloquies in Marburg 1529, in Wittenberg 1536, in Smalcald 1537, in Worms and Hagenau 1540, in Regensburg 1541, in Augsburg 1548; died November 16, 1548]. According to Ratzeberger, Cruciger had dictated: *"Bona opera requiri ad salutem tamquam causam sine qua non."* Cordatus reports Cruciger's dictation as follows: *"Tantum Christus est causa propter quem; interim tamen verum est, homines agere aliquid oportere; oportere nos habere contritionem et debere Verbo erigere conscientiam, ut fidem concipiamus, ut nostra contritio et noster conatus sunt causae iustificationis sine quibus non —* our contrition and our endeavor are causes of justification without which it does not take place." (3, 350.)

Cordatus immediately attacked the new formula as false. "I know," said he, "that this duality of causes cannot stand with the simple article of justification." (3, 350.) He demanded a public retraction from Cruciger. Before long Amsdorf also entered the fray. September 14, 1536, he wrote to Luther about the new-fangled teaching of Melanchthon, "that works are necessary to eternal life." (3, 162; Luther, St. L. 21 b, 4104.) Pressed by Cordatus, Cruciger finally admitted that Melanchthon was back of the phrases he had dictated. He declared that he was the pupil of

Mr. Philip; that the entire dictation was Mr. Philip's; that by him he had been led into this matter; and that he did not know how it happened. *Se esse D. Philippi discipulum, et dictata omnia esse D. Philippi, se ab eo in illam rem traductum, et nescire quomodo."* (*C. R.* 3, 162.)

That Melanchthon had been making efforts to introduce the new phrases in Wittenberg appears from the passage in his *Loci* of 1535 quoted above, and especially from his letters of the two following years. November 5, 1536, he wrote to Veit Dietrich: "Cordatus incites the city, its neighborhood, and even the Court against me because in the explanation of the controversy on justification I have said that new obedience is necessary to salvation, *novam obedientiam necessariam esse ad salutem."* (185. 179.) May 16, 1537, Veit Dietrich wrote to Foerster: "Our Cordatus, driven, I know not, by what furies, writes against Philip and Cruciger as against heretics, and is determined to force Cruciger to retract because he has said that good works are necessary to salvation. . . . This matter worries Philip very much, and if certain malicious men do not control themselves, he threatens to leave." (372.) As for Melanchthon, he made no efforts to shirk the responsibility for Cruciger's dictation. *"Libenter totam rem in me transfero —* I cheerfully transfer the entire affair to myself," he wrote April 15, 1537. Yet he was worried much more than his words seem to indicate. (342.)

Complaints against the innovations of Melanchthon and Cruciger were also lodged with Luther by Cordatus, Amsdorf, and Stiefel. Cordatus reports Luther as saying after the matter had been related to him, October 24, 1536: "This is the very theology of Erasmus, nor can anything be more opposed to our doctrine. *Haec est ipsissima theologia Erasmi, neque potest quidquam nostrae doctrinae esse magis adversum."* To say that new obedience is the *"causa sine qua non — sine qua non contingit vita aeterna,"* Luther declared, was tantamount to treading Christ and His blood under our feet. *"Cruciger autem haec, quae publice dictavit, publice revocabit.* What he has publicly dictated, Cruciger shall publicly retract." (Kolde, *Analecta,* 266.)

According to Ratzeberger, Luther immediately warned and censured Cruciger "in severe terms." (*C. R.* 4, 1038.) Flacius reports that Luther had publicly declared more than five times: *"Propositionem: Bona opera esse necessaria ad salutem, volumus damnatam, abrogatam, ex ecclesiis et scholis nostris penitus explosam."* (Schluesselburg 7, 567.) After his return from Smalcald, where he had expressed grave fears as to the future doctrinal soundness of his Wittenberg colleagues, Luther, in a public disputation on June 1, 1537, "exploded and condemned" the teaching that good works are necessary to salvation, or necessary to salvation as a *causa sine qua non.* (*Lehre u. Wehre* 1908, 65.) Both parties were present at the disputation, Cordatus as well as Melanchthon and Cruciger. In a letter to

Veit Dietrich, June 27, 1537, Cruciger reports: Luther maintained that new obedience is an "effect necessarily following justification," but he rejected the statement: "New obedience is necessary to salvation, *necessariam ad salutem.*" He adds: "*Male hoc habuit nostrum* [Melanchthon], *sed noluit eam rem porro agitare.* Melanchthon was displeased with this, but he did not wish to agitate the matter any further." (*C. R.* 3, 385.) After the disputation Cruciger was handed an anonymous note, saying that his "Treatise on Timothy" was now branded as "heretical, sacrilegious, impious, and blasphemous (*haeretica, sacrilega, impia et blasphema*)," and unless he retracted, he would have to be regarded as a Papist, a teacher and servant of Satan and not of Christ, and that his dictations would be published. (387.) In a letter to Dietrich, Cruciger remarks that Luther had disapproved of this anonymous writing, but he adds: "I can't see why he [Luther] gives so much encouragement to Cordatus." (385.)

In private, Luther repeatedly discussed this matter also with Melanchthon. This appears from their Disputation of 1536 on the question: "Whether this proposition is true: The righteousness of works is necessary to salvation." (E. 58, 353.) In a letter to Dietrich of June 22, 1537, Melanchthon, in substance, refers as follows to his discussions with Luther: I am desirous of maintaining the unity of the Wittenberg Academy; in this matter I also employ some art; nor does Luther seem to be inimical; yesterday he spoke to me in a very kind manner on the questions raised by Quadratus [Cordatus]. What a spectacle if the Lutherans would oppose each other as the Cadmean brethren! I will therefore modify whatever I can. Yet I desire a more thorough exposition of the doctrines of predestination, of the consent of the will, of the necessity of our obedience, and of the sin unto death. (*C. R.* 3, 383.)

A number of private letters written by Melanchthon during and immediately after his conflict with Cordatus, however, reveal much animosity, not only against Cordatus, but against Luther as well. Nor do those written after Luther's disputation, June 1, 1537, indicate that he was then fully cured of his error. (357. 392. 407.) Moreover, in his *Loci* of 1538 we read: "*Et tamen haec nova spiritualis obedientia* (*nova spiritualitas*) *necessaria est ad vitam aeternam.* And nevertheless this new spiritual obedience is necessary to eternal life." (21, 429.) Evidently, then, Melanchthon did not grasp the matter, and was not convinced of the incorrectness of his phraseology. Yet he made it a point to avoid and eliminate from his publications the obnoxious formula: "*Bona opera necessaria esse ad salutem.*" At any rate, his essay on Justification and Good Works, of October, 1537, as well as subsequent publications of his, do not contain it. In the *Loci* of 1538, just referred to, he replaced the words *bona opera* by the phrase *obedientia haec nova spiritualis,* — indeed, a purely verbal rather than a doctrinal change. Nor did it reappear even in the

*Variata* of 1540. In 1541, at Regensburg, Melanchthon consented to the formula "that we are justified by a living and efficacious faith — *iustificari per fidem vivam et efficacem.*" But when Luther deleted the words "*et efficacem,* and efficacious," Melanchthon acquiesced. (4, 499.) In the *Loci* of 1543 he expunged the appendix "*ad salutem,* to salvation." At the same time, however, he retained the error in a more disguised form, viz., that good works are necessary to retain faith. For among the reasons why good works are necessary he here enumerates also "the necessity of retaining the faith, since the Holy Spirit is expelled and grieved when sins against the conscience are admitted." (21, 775.)

### 143. Formula Renewed — Abandoned.

Under the duress of the Augsburg Interim, Melanchthon relapsed into his old error. July 6, 1548, he (together with Caspar Cruciger, John Pfeffinger, Daniel Gresser, George Major, and John Foerster) agreed to the statement: "For this proposition is certainly true, that no one can be saved without love and good works. Yet we are not justified by love and good works, but by grace for Christ's sake." (7, 22.) In the Leipzig Interim, adopted several months later, the false teaching concerning the necessity of good works to salvation was fully restored, as appears from the quotations from this document cited in the chapter on the Adiaphoristic Controversy. According to the *Formula of Concord* this renewal of the obnoxious formula at the time of the Interim furnished the direct occasion for the Majoristic Controversy. For here we read: "The aforesaid modes of speech and false expressions [concerning the necessity of good works to salvation] were renewed by the Interim, just at a time when there was special need of a clear, correct confession against all sorts of corruptions and adulterations of the article of justification." (947, 29.) However, when the controversy on good works began, and George Major zealously championed the restored formula, Melanchthon, probably mindful of his former troubles in this matter, signally failed to support and endorse his friend and colleague. Moreover, he now advised Major and others to abstain from using the phrase: Good works are necessary to salvation, "because," said he, "this appendix [to salvation, *ad salutem*] is interpreted as merit, and obscures the doctrine of grace."

In an opinion of December, 1553, Melanchthon explains: "New obedience is necessary; . . . but when it is said: New obedience is necessary to salvation, the Papists understand that good works merit salvation. This proposition is false; therefore I relinquish this mode of speech." (*C. R.* 8, 194.) January 13, 1555, he wrote to the Senate of Nordhausen that their ministers "should not preach, defend, and dispute the proposition [Good works are necessary to salvation], because it would immediately be interpreted to mean that good works merit salvation — *weil doch alsbald diese Deutung angehaengt wird, als sollten*

*gute Werke Verdienst sein der Seligkeit.*"
(410.) September 5, 1556, he said in his letter to Flacius: "I have always admonished
George [Major] not only to explain his sentence (which he did), but to abandon that
form of speech. And he promised that he
would not use it. What more can I ask? The
same I did with others." (842.)

In the Frankfurt Recess of 1558, written
by Melanchthon and signed by the Lutheran
princes, we read: "Although therefore this
proposition, 'New obedience is necessary
(*Nova obedientia est necessaria, nova obedientia est debitum*),' must be retained, we
nevertheless do not wish to attach these
words, '*ad salutem*, to salvation,' because this
appendix is interpreted as referring to merit
and obscures the doctrine of grace; for this
remains true that man is justified before God
and is an heir of eternal salvation by grace,
for the sake of the Lord Christ, by faith in
Him only." (9, 497. 405.) In an opinion written November 13, 1559, Melanchthon (together
with Paul Eber, Pfeffinger, and H. Salmut)
again declared: "I say clearly that I do not
employ the phrase, 'Good works are necessary
to salvation.'" (969.) In his *Responsiones ad
Articulos Bavaricos* of 1559 he wrote: "*Ego
non utor his verbis: Bona opera sunt necessaria ad salutem, quia hac additione 'ad salutem' intelligitur meritum.* I do not use these
words: Good works are necessary to salvation, because by the addition 'to salvation'
a merit is understood." In his lectures, too,
Melanchthon frequently rejected the appendix
(to salvation), and warned his pupils not to
use the phrase. (4, 543; *Lehre und Wehre*
1908, 78.)

Thus Melanchthon, time and again, disowned the proposition which he himself had
first introduced. Nowhere, however, did he
reject it or advise against its use because it
was inherently erroneous and false as such,
but always merely because it was subject to
abuse and misapprehension,— a qualified rejection which self-evidently could not and did
not satisfy his opponents. In an opinion,
dated March 4, 1558, Melanchthon refuses to
reject flatly the controverted formula, and endeavors to show that it is not in disagreement
with the mode of speech employed in the
Bible. We read: "Illyricus and his compeers are not satisfied when we say that the
appendix [to salvation] is to be omitted on
account of the false interpretation given it, but
demand that we simply declare the proposition, 'Good works are necessary to salvation,'
to be wrong. Against this it must be considered what also Paul has said, Rom. 10:
Confession is made to salvation (*Confessio fit
ad salutem*), which Wigand maliciously alters
thus: Confession is made concerning salvation
(*Confessio fit de salute*). Again, 2 Cor. 7:
'For godly sorrow worketh repentance to salvation.' Likewise Phil. 2: 'Work out your
own salvation with fear and trembling.' Nor
do these words sound any differently: 'Whosoever shall call upon the name of the Lord
will be saved,' Acts 2, 21. But, they say, one
must understand these expressions correctly!

That is what we say, too. This disputation,
however, would be ended if we agreed to eliminate the appendix and rack our brains no
further — *dass wir den Anhang ausschliessen
und nicht weiter gruebelten.*" (9, 474.)

### 144. Major Champions Error.

The immediate cause of the public controversy concerning the question whether good
works are necessary to salvation was George
Major, a devoted pupil and adherent of Melanchthon and a most active member of the
Wittenberg faculty [Major was born April 25,
1502; 1529 Rector of the school in Magdeburg; 1536 Superintendent in Eisleben; soon
after, preacher and professor in Wittenberg;
1544 Rector of the University of Wittenberg;
in 1548, at Celle, he, too, submitted to the
demands of Maurice; in the Leipzig Interim
he merely objected to the insertion of Extreme
Unction; 1552 Superintendent in Eisleben;
professor in Wittenberg from 1553 until his
death in 1574].

"*That Dr. Pommer* [Bugenhagen] *and Dr.
Major have Caused Offense and Confusion.
Nicholas Amsdorf, Exul Christi. Magdeburg,
1551,*" — such was the title of a publication
which appeared immediately prior to Major's
appointment as Superintendent in Eisleben.
In it Bugenhagen (who died 1558) and Major
(of course, Melanchthon could and should
have been included) were denounced for their
connection with the Leipzig Interim. Major,
in particular, was censured for having, in the
Interim, omitted the word *sola*, "alone," in
the phrase "*sola fide iustificamur,* we are justified by faith alone," and for having emphasized instead that Christian virtues and good
works are meritorious and necessary to salvation. When, as a result of this publication,
the preachers of Eisleben and Mansfeld refused to recognize Major as their superior,
the latter promised to justify himself publicly. He endeavored to do so in his *Answer*,
published 1552 at Wittenberg, after he had
already been dismissed by Count Albrecht as
Superintendent of Eisleben. The *Answer* was
entitled: *Auf des ehrenwuerdigen Herrn Niclas von Amsdorfs Schrift, so jetzund neulich
mense Novembri 1551 wider Dr. Major oef-
fendtlich im Druck ausgegangen. Antwort
Georg Majors.* In it Major disclaimed responsibility for the Interim (although he had
been present at Celle, where it had been
framed), and declared that he had never
doubted the "*sola fide,* by faith alone."
"But," continued Major, "I do confess that
I have hitherto taught, and still teach, and
henceforth will teach all my life: that good
works are necessary to salvation. And I declare publicly and with clear and plain words
that no one is saved by evil works, and also,
that no one is saved without good works.
Furthermore I say, let him who teaches otherwise, even though an angel from heaven, be accursed (*der sei verflucht*)!" Again: "Therefore it is impossible for a man to be saved
without good works." Major explained that
good works are necessary to salvation, not because they effect or merit forgiveness of sins,

justification, the gift of the Holy Spirit, and eternal life (for these gifts are merited alone by the death of our only Mediator and Savior Jesus Christ, and can be received only by faith), "but nevertheless good works *must be present*, not as a merit, but as due obedience toward God." (Schlb. 7, 30.)

In his defiant attitude Major was immediately and firmly opposed by Amsdorf, Flacius, Gallus, and others. Amsdorf published his "*Brief Instruction Concerning Dr. Major's Answer, that he is not innocent, as he boasts.* Ein kurzer Unterricht auf Dr. Majoris Antwort, dass er nicht unschuldig sei, wie er sich ruehmet," 1552. Major's declaration and anathema are here met by Amsdorf as follows: "First of all, I would like to know against whom Dr. George Major is writing when he says: Nobody merits heaven by evil works. Has even the angry and impetuous Amsdorf ever taught and written thus? . . . We know well, praise God, and confess that a Christian should and must do good works. Nobody disputes and speaks concerning that; nor has anybody doubted this. On the contrary, we speak and dispute concerning this, whether a Christian earns salvation by the good works which he should and must do. . . . For we all say and confess that after his renewal and new birth a Christian should love and fear God and do all manner of good works, but not that he may be saved, for he is saved already by faith (*aber nicht darum, dass er selig werde, denn er ist schon durch den Glauben selig*). This is the true prophetic and apostolic doctrine, and whoever teaches otherwise is already accursed and damned. I, therefore, Nicholas von Amsdorf, declare: Whoever teaches and preaches these words as they read (Good works are necessary to salvation), is a Pelagian, a mameluke, and a denier of Christ, and he has the same spirit which prompted Drs. Mensing and Witzel to write against Dr. Luther, of blessed memory, that good works are necessary to salvation." (Schlb. 7, 210.)

Another attack was entitled: "Against the Evangelist of the Holy Gown, Dr. Miser Major. *Wider den Evangelisten des heiligen Chorrocks, Dr. Geitz Major,*" 1552. Here Flacius — for he was the author of this publication — maintained that neither justification, nor salvation, nor the preservation of the state of grace is to be based on good works. He objected to Major's propositions because they actually made good works the antecedent and cause of salvation and robbed Christians of their comfort. He declared: "When we say: That is necessary for this work or matter, it means just as much as if we said: It is a cause, or, by this or that work one effects this or that." As to the practical consequences of Major's propositions, Flacius remarks: "If therefore good works are necessary to salvation, and if it is impossible for any one to be saved without them, then tell us, Dr. Major, how can a man be saved who all his life till his last breath has led a sinful life, but now, when about to die, desires to apprehend Christ (as is the case with many on their death-bed

or on the gallows)? How will Major comfort such a poor sinner? The poor sinner, Flacius continues, would declare: "Major, the great theologian, writes and teaches as most certain that no one can be saved without good works, and that good works are absolutely necessary (*ganz notwendig*) to salvation; therefore I am damned, for I have heretofore never done any good works." "Furthermore Major will also have to state and determine the least number of ounces or pounds of good works one is required to have to obtain salvation." (Preger 1, 363 f.)

In his "Explanation and Answer to the New Subtle Corruption of the Gospel of Christ — *Erklaerung und Antwort auf die neue subtile Verfaelschung des Evangelii Christi,*" 1554, Nicholas Gallus maintained that, if the righteousness presented by Christ alone is the cause of our justification and salvation, then good works can only be the fruits of it. In a similar way Schnepf, Chemnitz, and others declared themselves against Majorism. (Schlb. 7, 55. 162. 205. 534. 572; *C. R.* 9, 475; Seeberg, *Dogg.* 4, 486.)

### 145. Major's Modifications.

Major answered his opponents in his book of 1553 entitled, *A Sermon on the Conversion to God of St. Paul and All God-fearing Men.*" In it he most emphatically denied that he had ever taught that good works are necessary in order to earn salvation, and explained more fully "whether, in what way, which, and why good works are nevertheless necessary to salvation." Here he also admits: "This proposition would be dangerous and dark if I had said without any distinction and explanation: Good works are necessary to salvation. For thus one might easily be led to believe that we are saved by good works without faith, or also by the merit of good works, not by faith alone." "We are not just and saved by renewal, and because the fulfilment of the Law is begun in us, as the Interim teaches, but in this life we always remain just and saved by faith *alone*." (Preger 1, 364 ff.)

Major explains: "When I say: The new obedience or good works which follow faith are necessary to salvation, this is not to be understood in the sense that one must earn salvation by good works, or that they constitute, or could effect or impart the righteousness by which a man may stand before the judgment-seat of God, but that good works are effects and fruits of true faith, which are to follow it [faith] and are wrought by Christ in believers. For whoever believes and is just, he, at the risk of losing his righteousness and salvation, is in duty bound and obliged to begin to obey God as his Father, to do that which is good, and to avoid evil." (370.)

Major furthermore modified his statement by explaining: Good works are necessary to salvation, not in order to obtain, but to retain, salvation. "In order to retain salvation and not to lose it again," he said, "they are necessary to such an extent that, if you fail to do them, it is a sure indication that your faith is dead and false, a painted faith, an

*Here's the error*

opinion existing only in your imagination." The reason, said Major (Menius, too, later on expressed his agreement in this point with Major), why he had urged his proposition concerning the necessity of good works to salvation, was the fact that the greater number also of those who claim to be good evangelical Christians "imagine that they believe, and imagine and fabricate a faith which may exist without good works, though this is just as impossible as that the sun should not emit brightness and splendor." (Tschackert 515; Frank 2, 162. 373.)

Reducing his teaching to a number of syllogisms, Major argued, in substance, as follows: Eternal life is given to none but the regenerate; regeneration, however, is new obedience and good works in the believers and the beginning of eternal life: hence the new life, which consists in good works, is necessary to believers for salvation. Again: No one is saved unless he confesses with his mouth the faith of his heart in Christ and remains steadfast in such faith, Rom. 10, 9. 10; Matt. 22, 13; hence the works of confessing and persevering faith are necessary to salvation as fruits of faith, in order that salvation, obtained by faith, may not be lost by denial and apostasy. (Frank 2, 162.) Again: The thing without which salvation cannot be preserved is necessary to salvation; without obedience toward God salvation, received by grace through faith, cannot be preserved; hence obedience toward God is necessary in order that by it salvation, received by grace, may be preserved and may not be lost by disobedience. At the conclusion of his "Sermon on Paul's Conversion," Major also repeated his anathema against all those who teach otherwise, and added: "Hiewider moegen nun Amseln [Amsdorf] oder Drosseln singen und schreien, Haehne [Gallus] kraehen oder gatzen [gakkern], verloffene und unbekannte Wenden und Walen [Flacius] laestern, die Schrift verwenden, verkehren, kalumniieren, schreiben und malen, wie sie wollen, so bin ich doch gewiss, dass diese Lehre, so in diesem Sermon steht, die rechte goettliche Wahrheit ist, wider welche auch alle hoellischen Pforten nichts Bestaendiges oder Gruendliches koennen aufbringen, wie boese sie sich auch machen." (Preger 1, 371. 380.)

Schluesselburg charges Major also with confounding justification with sanctification. In proof of this he quotes the following from Major's remarks on Rom. 8: "Salvation or justification is twofold: one in this life and the other in eternal life. The salvification in this life consists, first, in the remission of sins and in the imputation of righteousness; secondly, in the gift and renewing of the Holy Spirit and in the hope of eternal life bestowed freely for the sake of Christ. This salvification and justification is only begun [in this life] and imperfect; for in those who are saved and justified by faith there still remains sin, the depravity of nature; there remain also the terrors of sin and of the Law, the bite of the old Serpent, and death, together with all miseries that flesh is heir to. Thus

by faith and the Holy Ghost we, indeed, *begin to be justified*, sanctified, and saved, but we are not yet *perfectly justified*, sanctified, and saved. It remains, therefore, that we become *perfectly just and saved*. Sic per fidem et Spiritum Sanctum *coepimus quidem iustificari*, sanctificari, et salvari, nondum tamen perfecte iusti et salvi sumus. Reliquum igitur est, ut perfecte iusti et salvi fiamus." (7, 348.)

## 146. Menius Sides with Major.

Prominent among the theologians who were in essential agreement with Major was Justus Menius. He was born 1499; became Superintendent in Gotha 1546; was favorably disposed toward the Leipzig Interim; resigned his position in Gotha 1557; removed to Leipzig, where he published his polemical writings against Flacius; died August 11, 1558. In 1554 he was entangled in the Majoristic controversy. In this year Amsdorf demanded that Menius, who, together with himself, Schnepf, and Stolz, had been appointed visitors of Thuringia, declare himself against the Adiaphorists, and, in particular, reject the books of Major, and his doctrine that good works are necessary to salvation. Menius declined, because, he said, he had not read these books. As a result Menius was charged with being a secret adherent of Majorism.

In 1556, however, Menius himself proved by his publications that this suspicion was not altogether unwarranted. For in his *Preparation for a Blessed Death* and in a *Sermon on Salvation*, published in that year, Menius taught that the beginning of the new life in believers is "necessary to salvation" (Tschackert, 517; *Herzog, R.* 12, 89.) This caused Flacius to remark in his book, *Concerning the Unity of Those who in the Past Years have Fought for and against the Adiaphora*, 1556: "Major and Menius, in their printed books, are again reviving the error that good works are necessary to salvation; wherefore it is to be feared that the latter misfortune will be worse than the former." (Preger 1, 382.) Soon after, Menius was suspended from office and required to clear himself before the Synod in Eisenach, 1556. Here he subscribed seven propositions in which the doctrine that good works are necessary to salvation, or to retain salvation, was rejected.

The seven Eisenach propositions, signed by Menius, read as follows: "1. Although this proposition, Good works are necessary to salvation, may be tolerated in the doctrine of the Law abstractly and ideally (*in doctrina legis abstractive et de idea tolerari potest*), nevertheless there are many weighty reasons why it should be avoided and shunned no less than the other: Christ is a creature. 2. In the forum of justification and salvation this proposition, Good works are necessary to salvation, is not at all to be tolerated. 3. In the forum of new obedience, after reconciliation, good works are not at all necessary to salvation, but for other causes. 4. Faith alone justifies and saves in the beginning, middle, and end. 5. Good works are not necessary to

*Major confuses justification with sanctification*

retain salvation (*ad retinendam salutem*). 6. Justification and salvation are synonyms and equipollent or convertible terms, and neither can nor must be separated in any way (*nec ulla ratione distrahi aut possunt aut debent*). 7. May therefore the papistical buskin be banished from our church on account of its manifold offenses and innumerable dissensions and other causes of which the apostles speak Acts 15." (Preger 1, 383.)

In his subscription to these theses Menius declared: "I, Justus Menius, testify by my present signature that this confession is true and orthodox, and that, according to the gift given me by God, I have heretofore by word and writing publicly defended it, and shall continue to defend it." In this subscription Menius also promised to correct the offensive expressions in his *Sermon on Salvation*. However, dissatisfied with the intolerable situation thus created, he resigned, and soon after became Superintendent in Leipzig. In three violently polemical books, published there in 1557 and 1558, he freely vented his long pent-up feelings of anger and animosity, especially against Flacius. (384 f.)

In these publications, Menius denied that he had ever used the proposition of Major. However, he not only refused to reject it, but defended the same error, though in somewhat different terms. He merely replaced the phrase "good works" by "new life," "new righteousness," "new obedience," and affirmed "that it is necessary to our salvation that such be wrought in us by the Holy Ghost." He wrote: The Holy Spirit renews those who have become children of God by faith in Christ, and that this is performed in them, "this, I say, they need for their salvation — *sei ihnen zur Seligkeit vonnoeten.*" (Frank 2, 223.) Again: "He [the Holy Spirit] begins righteousness and life in the believers, which beginning is in this life (as long as we dwell on earth in this sinful flesh) very weak and imperfect, *but nevertheless necessary to salvation,* and will be perfect after the resurrection, that we may walk in it before God eternally and be saved." (222.) Works, said Menius, must not be introduced into the article of justification, reconciliation, and redemption; but when dealing with the article of sanctification, "then it is correct to say: Sanctification, or renewal of the Holy Spirit, is necessary to salvation." (Preger 1, 388.)

With respect to the proposition, Good works are necessary to salvation, Menius stated that he could not simply condemn it as altogether false and heretical. Moreover, he argued: "If it is correct to say: Sanctification, or renewal by the Holy Spirit, is necessary to salvation, then it cannot be false to say: Good works are necessary to salvation, since it is certain and cannot be gainsaid that sanctification and renewal do not and cannot exist without good works." (386.) Indeed, he himself maintained that "good works are necessary to salvation in order that we may not lose it again." (387. 391.) At the same time Menius, as stated above, claimed that he had never employed Major's proposition, and coun-

seled others to abstain from its use in order to avoid misinterpretation. The same advice he gave with respect to his own formula, that new obedience is necessary to salvation. (Frank 2, 165. 223.)

Menius also confounded justification and sanctification. He wrote: "By faith in Christ alone we become just before God and are saved. Why? Because by faith one receives, first, forgiveness of sins and the righteousness or obedience of Christ, with which He fulfilled the Law for us; thereupon, one also receives the Holy Spirit, who effects and fulfils in us the righteousness required by the Law, here in this life imperfectly, and perfectly in the life to come." (Preger 1, 387.) At the synod of Eisenach, 1556, the theologians accordingly declared: "Although it is true that grace and the gift through grace cannot be separated, but are always together, nevertheless the gift of the Holy Spirit is not a piece or part, much less a co-cause of justification and salvation, but an appendix, a consequence, and an additional gift of grace. — *Wiewohl es wahr ist, dass gratia und donum per gratiam nicht koennen getrennt werden, sondern allezeit beieinander sind, so ist doch die Gabe des Heiligen Geistes nicht ein Stueck oder Teil, viel weniger eine Mitursache der Justifikation und Salvation, sondern ist ein Anhang, Folge und Zugabe der Gnade.*" (Seeberg 4, 487.)

### 147. Attitude of Anti-Majorists.

With the exception of Menius and other adherents in Electoral Saxony, Major was firmly opposed by Lutheran ministers and theologians everywhere. Even when he was still their superintendent, the ministers of Mansfeld took issue with him; and after he was dismissed by Count Albrecht, they drafted an *Opinion,* in which they declared that Major's proposition obscures the doctrine of God's grace and Christ's merit. Also the clergy of Luebeck, Hamburg, Lueneburg, and Magdeburg united in an *Opinion,* in which they rejected Major's proposition. Chief among the theologians who opposed him were, as stated, Amsdorf, Flacius, Wigand, Gallus, Moerlin, and Chemnitz. In their publications they unanimously denounced the proposition that good works are necessary to salvation, and its equivalents, as dangerous, godless, blasphemous, and popish. Yet before the controversy they themselves had not all nor always been consistent and correct in their terminology.

The *Formula of Concord* says: "Before this controversy quite a few pure teachers employed such and similar expressions [that faith is preserved by good works, etc.] in the exposition of the Holy Scriptures, in no way, however, intending thereby to confirm the above-mentioned errors of the Papists." (949, 36.) Concerning the word "faith," 1549, Flacius, for example had said that our effort to obey God might be called a "*causa sine qua non,*" or something which serves salvation." His words are: "*Atque hinc apparet, quatenus nostrum studium obediendi Deo dici possit causa sine qua non, seu ὑπηρετικόν τι, id est, quiddam subserviens ad salutem.*" But when his attention was called to this passage, he first eliminated the *causa sine qua non* and substituted *ad vitam aeternam* for *ad salutem*, and afterwards changed this phrase into *ad veram pietatem*. (Frank 2, 218. 169.) However, as soon as the controversy began, the Lutherans, notably Flacius, clearly saw the utter falsity of Major's statements.

Flacius wrote: "Salvation is forgiveness of sins, as Paul testifies, Rom. 4, and David, Ps. 32: 'Blessed are they whose sins are forgiven.' 'Thy faith hath made thee whole.' Matt. 9; Mark 5. 10; Luke 7. 8. 18. Jesus saves sinners and the lost. Matt. 1, 18; 1 Tim. 1. Since, now, salvation and forgiveness of sins are one and the same thing, consider, dear Christian, what kind of doctrine this is: No one has received forgiveness of sins without good works; it is impossible for any one to receive forgiveness of sins or to be saved without good works; good works are necessary to forgiveness of sins." (Preger 1, 375.) Again: "Young children and those who are converted in their last hour (who certainly constitute the greater part), must confess that they neither possess, nor will possess, any good works, for they die forthwith. Indeed, St. Bernard also wrote when on his deathbed: *Perdite vixi* — I have led a wicked life! And what is still more, all Christians, when, in their dying moments, they are striving with sins, must say: 'All our good works are like filthy rags'; in my life there is nothing good'; and, as David says, Ps. 51: 'Before Thee I am nothing but sin,' as Dr. Luther explains it." (376.) Again: "We are concerned about this, that poor and afflicted consciences may have a firm and certain consolation against sin, death, devil, and hell, and thus be saved. For if a condition or appendix concerning our good works and worthiness is required as necessary to salvation, then, as Dr. Major frequently discusses this matter very excellently, it is impossible to have a firm and solid consolation." (376.)

Flacius showed that Major's proposition, taken as it reads, can be interpreted only in a papistical sense, and that no amount of explanations is able to cure it of its ingrained falsity. Major, said he, must choose between his proposition, or the interpretations which he places upon it; for the former does not admit of the latter. He added that a proposition which is in constant need of explanations in order not to be misunderstood, is not adapted for religious instruction. From the fact, says Flacius, that the justified are obliged to obey the Law, it follows indeed that good works are necessary, but not that they are necessary to salvation (as Major and Menius inferred). "From the premises [that Christians are in duty bound to obey the Law and to render the new obedience] it merely follows that this obedience is necessary; but nothing is here said of salvation." (392.) Flacius showed that Major's proposition, even with the proviso that each and every merit of works was to be excluded, remained objectionable. The words "necessary to, *necessaria ad*," always, he insisted, designate something that precedes, moves, works, effects. The proposition: Justification, salvation, and faith are necessary to good works, cannot be reversed, because good works are not antecedents, but consequents of justification, salvation, and faith.

For the same reason Flacius objected to the phrase that good works are necessary as *causa sine qua non*. "Dear Dr. G." (Major), says he, "ask the highly learned Greek philosophers for a little information as to what they say *de causa sine qua non, ὦν οὐκ ἄνευ*. Ask, I say, the learned and the unlearned, ask philosophy, reason, and common languages, whether it is not true that it [*causa sine qua non*] must precede." (377.) No one, said he, would understand the propositions of Major and Menius correctly. Illustrating this point, Flacius wrote: "Can one become a carpenter without the house which he builds afterwards? Can one make a wagon or ship without driving or sailing? I say, yes! Or, dear Doctor, are we accustomed to say: Driving and sailing is necessary to the wagon and ship, respectively, and it is impossible for a wagon or ship to be made without driving or sailing? I hear: No!" (375.) "Nobody says: Fruits and leaves are necessary to the tree; wine and grapes are necessary to the vineyard; or, dwelling is necessary to a house; driving and sailing, to a wagon and ship; riding is necessary to a horse; but thus they speak: Wagons and horses are necessary to riding, a ship is necessary to sailing." (391.)

The charge that Major's proposition robbed Christians of their assurance of salvation was urged also by Nicholas Gallus. He says: It is giving with one hand and taking again with the other when Major adds [to his proposition concerning the necessity of good works to salvation] that our conscience is not to look upon our works, but on Christ alone. (Frank 2, 224.) The same point was stressed in the *Opinion* of the ministers of Luebeck, Hamburg, Lueneburg, and Magdeburg, published by Flacius and Gallus in 1553. (220.) The Hamburg theologians declared: "This appendix [necessary to salvation, *ad salutem*] indicates a cause and a merit." They added that in this sense also the phrase is generally understood by the Papists. (Planck, *Geschichte des prot. Lehrbegriffes* 5, 505. 497.) Gallus also explained that it was papistical to infer: By sins we lose salvation, hence it is retained by good works; or, Sins condemn, hence good works save. (Frank 2, 171.) Hesshusius wrote to Wigand: "I regard Eber's assertion that good works are necessary to justification *because they must be present*, as false and detrimental. For Paul expressly excludes good works from the justification of a sinner before God, not only when considered a merit, cause, glory, dignity, price, object or trust, and medium of application, etc., but also as to the necessity of their presence (*verum etiam quoad necessitatem praesentiae*). If it is necessary that good works be present with him who is to be justified, then Paul errs when he declares that a man is justified without the works of the Law." (172.)

Regarding this point, that good works are necessary to justification in so far as they must be present, the Majorists appealed to Luther, who, however, had merely stated that faith is never alone, though it alone justifies. His axiom was: "Faith alone justifies, but it is not alone — *Fides sola iustificat, sed non est sola.*" According to Luther good works, wherever they are found, are present in virtue of faith; where they are not present, they are absent because faith is lacking; nor can they preserve the faith by which alone they are produced. At the Altenburg Colloquy (1568 to 1569) the theologians of Electoral Saxony insisted that, since true faith does not and cannot exist in those who persevere in sins against their conscience, good works must not be altogether and absolutely excluded from justification, at least their necessity and presence must not be regarded as unnecessary. (189.) The theologians of Ducal Saxony, however, denied "that in the article and act of justification our good works are necessary by necessity of presence. *Sed impugnamus istam propositionem, in articulo et actu iustificationis bona nostra opera necessaria esse necessitate praesentiae.*" On the other hand, however, they, too, were solicitous to affirm the impossibility of faith's coexisting with an evil purpose to sin against God in one and the same mind at the same time." (237; Gieseler 3, 2, 251.) In the *Apology of the Book of Concord* the Lutheran theologians declared: "The proposition (Justification of faith requires the presence of good works) was rejected [in the *Formula of Concord*] because it cannot be understood otherwise than of the cause of justification. For whatever is present in justification as necessary in such a manner that without its presence justification can neither be nor occur, that must indeed be understood as being a cause of justification itself." (238.)

### 148. Major's Concessions Not Satisfactory.

In order to put an end to the controversy, Major offered a concession in his *"Confession concerning the Article of Justification,"* that is, concerning the doctrine that by faith alone, without any merit, for the sake of Christ, a man has forgiveness of sins, and is just before God and an heir of eternal salvation," 1558. Here he states that he had not used the controverted formula for several years and, in order not to give further cause for public contention, he promised "not to employ the words, 'Good works are necessary to salvation,' any more, on account of the false interpretations placed upon it." (Preger 1, 396.) In making this concession, however, Major did not at all intend to retract his teaching or to condemn his proposition as false. He promised to abstain from its use, not because he was now convinced of his error and viewed his propositions as false and incorrect as such, but merely because it was ambiguous and liable to abuse, and because he wished to end the conflict. (Frank 2, 166 f. 223.)

Nor did Major later on ever admit that he had erred in the matter. In an oration delivered 1567 he boasted of his intimate relation and doctrinal agreement with Luther and Melanchthon, adding: "Neither did I ever deviate, nor, God assisting me, shall I ever deviate, from the truth once acknowledged. *Nec discessi umquam nec Deo iuvante discedam ab agnita semel veritate.*" He had never thought or taught, said he, that good works are a cause of justification. And concerning the proposition, "Good works are necessary to salvation," he had expressly declared that he intended to abstain from its use "because it had offended some on account of its ambiguity, *cum propter ambiguitatem offenderit aliquos.*" He continued: "The facts show that we [the professors of Wittenberg University] are and have remained guardians of that doctrine which Luther and Melanchthon . . . delivered to us, in whose writings from the time of the [Augsburg] Confession there is neither a dissonance nor a discrepancy, either among themselves or from the foundation, nor anything obscure or perplexing." (Frank 2, 224. 167.)

Also in his *Testament* (*Testamentum Doctoris Georgii Majoris*), published 1570, Major emphatically denied that he had ever harbored or taught any false views concerning justification, salvation, and good works. Of his own accord he had also abandoned the phrases: "Good works are necessary to salvation; it is impossible to be saved without good works; no one has ever been saved without good works — *Bona opera sunt necessaria ad salutem; impossibile est, sine bonis operibus salvum fieri; nemo umquam sine bonis operibus salvatus est.*" He had done this in order to obviate the misapprehension as though he taught that good works are a cause of salvation which contribute to merit and effect salvation. According to this *Testament*, he desired his doctrines and writings to be judged. In future he would not dispute with anybody about these phrases. (168.) Thus in his *Testament*, too, Major withdrew his statements not because they were simply false, but only because they had been interpreted to mean that good works are the efficient cause of justification and salvation. And while Major in later writings did eliminate the appendix *"ad salutem,* to salvation," or *"ad vitam aeternam,* to eternal life," he retained, and continued to teach, essentially the same error in another garb, namely, that good works are necessary in order to retain faith. Enumerating, in his *Explanation of the Letter to the Galatians,* of 1560, the purposes on account of which good works ought to be rendered, he mentions as the "first, in order to retain faith, the Holy Spirit, the grace bestowed, and a good conscience." (218.)

Thus Major was willing to abandon as dangerous and ambiguous, and to abstain from the use of, the formula, "Good works are necessary to salvation," but refused to reject it as false and to make a public admission and confession of his error. This, however, was precisely what his opponents demanded; for they were convinced that they could be satisfied with nothing less. As a result the controversy continued till Major's death, in

1574. The Jena professors, notably Flacius, have been charged with prolonging the controversy from motives of personal revenge. (Schaff, 276.) No doubt, the Wittenbergers had gone to the very limit of rousing the animosity and resentment of Flacius (who himself, indeed, was not blameless in the language used against his opponents). Major had depicted Flacius as a most base and wicked man; as a cunning and sly adventurer; as a tyrant, who, after having suppressed the Wittenbergers, would, as a pope, lord it over all Germany; as an Antinomian and a despiser of all good works, etc. (Preger 1, 397.) In the address of October 18, 1567, already referred to, Major said: "There was in this school [Wittenberg] a vagabond of uncertain origin, fatherland, religion, and faith, who called himself Flacius Illyricus. . . . He was the first one to spew out against this school, against its principal Doctors, against the churches of these regions, against the princes themselves, the poison which he had brewed and imbibed some time ago, and, having gnawed and consumed with the bite of a serpent the womb of his mother, to destroy the harmony of these churches, at first by spreading his dreams, fables, and gossip, but now also by calumnies and manifest lies." (Frank 2, 217.) Melanchthon, too, had repeatedly written in a similar vein. In an *Opinion* of his, dated March 4, 1558, we read: "Even if they [Flacius and his adherents] condemn and banish me, I am well satisfied; for I do not desire to associate with them, because I well know that the said Illyricus with his adherents does not seek the honor of God, but publicly opposes the truth, and as yet has never declared himself concerning the entire sum of Christian doctrine." (*C. R.* 9, 463. 476. 311.) In an *Opinion* of March 9, 1559, Melanchthon even insinuated that Flacius denied the Trinity. (763.) Before this, August, 1549, he had written to Fabricius: "The Slavic runagate (Slavus δραπέτης) received many benefits from our Academy and from me. But we have nursed a serpent in our bosom. He deserves to be branded on his forehead as the Macedonian king did with a soldier: 'Ungrateful stranger, ξένος ἀχάριστος.' Nor do I believe that the source of his hatred is any other than that the place of Cruciger was not given to him. But I omit these disagreeable narrations." (7, 449. 478 ff.) This personal abuse, however, was not the reason why Flacius persisted in his opposition despite the concessions made by Major and Menius, — concessions with which even such moderate men as Martin Chemnitz were not satisfied.

Flacius continued his opposition because he could not do otherwise without sacrificing his own principles, compromising the truth, and jeopardizing the doctrine of justification. He did not yield because he was satisfied with nothing less than a complete victory of the divine truth and an unqualified retraction of error. The truly objective manner in which he dealt with this matter appears from his *Strictures on the Testament of Dr. Major* (*Censura de Testamento D. Majoris*). Here we

read, in substance: In his *Testament* Major covers his error with the same sophism which he employed in his former writings. For he says that he ascribes the entire efficient cause, merit, and price of our justification and salvation to Christ alone, and therefore excludes and removes all our works and virtues. This he has set forth more fully and more clearly in his previous writings, saying that the proposition, "Good works are necessary to salvation," can be understood in a double sense; *viz.*, that they are necessary to salvation as a certain merit, price, or efficient cause of justification or salvation (as the Papists understand and teach it), or that they are necessary to salvation as a certain debt or an indispensable cause (*causa sine qua non*), or a cause without which it is impossible for the effect of salvation to follow or for any one to obtain it. He now confesses this same opinion. He does not expressly eliminate "the indispensable cause, or the obligation without the fulfilment of which it is impossible for any one to be preserved, as he asserted repeatedly before this, from which it appears that he adheres to his old error. *Et non diserte tollit causam sine qua non seu debitum, sine cuius persolutione sit impossibile quemquam servari, quod toties antea asseruit; facile patet, eum pristinum illum suum errorem retinere."* (Schlb. 7, 266; Preger 1, 398.) Flacius demanded an unqualified rejection of the statement, "Good works are necessary to salvation" — a demand with which Major as well as Melanchthon refused to comply. (*C. R.* 9, 474 f.)

The *Formula of Concord*, however, sanctioned the attitude of Flacius. It flatly rejected the false and dubious formulas of Melanchthon, Major, and Menius concerning the necessity of good works to salvation, and fully restored Luther's doctrine. Luther's words concerning "good works" are quoted as follows: "We concede indeed that instruction should be given also concerning love and good works, yet in such a way that this be done when and where it is necessary, namely, when otherwise and outside of this matter of justification we have to do with works. But here the chief matter dealt with is the question, not whether we should also do good works and exercise love, but by what means we can be justified before God and saved. And here we answer with St. Paul: that we are justified by faith in Christ alone, and not by the deeds of the Law or by love. Not that we hereby entirely reject works and love, as the adversaries falsely slander and accuse us, but that we do not allow ourselves to be led away, as Satan desires, from the chief matter, with which we have to do here, to another and foreign affair, which does not at all belong to this matter. Therefore, whereas and as long as we are occupied with this article of justification, we reject and condemn works, since this article is so constituted that it can admit of no disputation or treatment whatever regarding works. Therefore in this matter we cut short all Law and works of the Law." (925, 29.)

The *Formula of Concord* rejects the Majoristic formula, not because it is ambiguous, but because it is false. Concerning ambiguous phrases it declares: "To avoid strife about words, *aequivocationes vocabulorum, i. e.,* words and expressions which are applied and used in various meanings, should be carefully and distinctly explained." (874, 51.) An ambiguous phrase or statement need not be condemned, because it may be made immune from error and misapprehension by a careful explanation. The statement, "Good works are necessary to salvation," however, does not admit of such treatment. It is inherently false and cannot be cured by any amount of explanation or interpretation. Because of this inherent falsity it must be rejected as such. Logically and grammatically the phrase, "Good works are necessary to salvation," reverses the correct theological order, by placing works before faith and sanctification before justification. It turns things topsy-turvy. It makes the effect the cause; the consequent, the antecedent; and *vice versa.*

Not personal animosity, but this fundamental falsity of the Majoristic formula was, in the last analysis, the reason why the explanations and concessions made by Major and Menius did not and could not satisfy their opponents. They maintained, as explained above, that the words "necessary to" always imply "something that precedes, moves, effects, works," and that, accordingly, the obnoxious propositions of Major "place good works before the remission of sins and before salvation." (Preger 1, 377.) Even Planck admits that only force could make the proposition, "Good works are necessary to salvation," say, "Good works must follow faith and justification." "According to the usage of every language," says he, "a phrase saying that one thing is necessary to another designates a causal connection. Whoever dreamt of asserting that heat is necessary to make it day, because it is a necessary effect of the rays of the sun, by the spreading of which it becomes day." (4, 542. 485.) Without compromising the truth and jeopardizing the doctrine of justification, therefore, the Lutherans were able to regard as satisfactory only a clear and unequivocal rejection of Majorism as it is found in the *Formula of Concord.*

### 149. Absurd Proposition of Amsdorf.

Nicholas Amsdorf, the intimate and trusted friend of Luther, was among the most zealous of the opponents of Majorism. He was born December 3, 1483; professor in Wittenberg; 1521 in Worms with Luther; superintendent in Magdeburg; 1542 bishop at Naumburg; banished by Maurice in 1547, he removed to Magdeburg; soon after professor and superintendent in Jena; opposed the Interimists, Adiaphorists, Osiandrists, Majorists, Synergists, Sacramentarians, Anabaptists, and Schwenckfeldians; died at Eisenach May 14, 1565. Regarding the bold statements of Major as a blow at the very heart of true Lutheranism, Amsdorf antagonized his teaching as a "most pernicious error," and de-

nounced Major as a Pelagian and a double Papist. But, alas, the momentum of his uncontrolled zeal carried him a step too far — over the precipice. He declared that good works are detrimental and injurious to salvation, *bona opera perniciosa (noxia) esse ad salutem.* He defended his paradoxical statement in a publication of 1559 against Menius, with whose subscription to the Eisenach propositions, referred to above, he was not satisfied; chiefly because Menius said there that he had taught and defended them also in the past. The flagrant blunder of Amsdorf was all the more offensive because it appeared on the title of his tract, reading as follows: "*Dass diese Propositio: 'Gute Werke sind zur Seligkeit schaedlich,' eine rechte, wahre, christliche Propositio sei,* durch die heiligen Paulum und Lutherum gelehrt und gepredigt. Niclas von Amsdorf, 1559. That this proposition, 'Good works are injurious to salvation,' is a correct, true, Christian proposition, taught and preached by Sts. Paul and Luther." (Frank 2, 228.)

Luther, to whose writings Amsdorf appealed, had spoken very guardedly and correctly in this matter. He had declared: Good works are detrimental to the righteousness of faith, "if one presumes to be justified by them, *si quis per ea praesumat iustificari.*" Wherever Luther speaks of the injuriousness of good works, it is always *sub specie iustificationis,* that is to say, viewing good works as entering the article of justification, or the forgiveness of sins. (Weimar 7, 59; 10, 3, 373. 374. 387; E. 16, 465. 484; Tschackert, 516.) What vitiated the proposition as found in Amsdorf's tract was the fact that he had omitted the modification added by Luther. Amsdorf made a flat statement of what Luther had asserted, not flatly, *nude et simpliciter,* but with a limitation, *secundum quid.*

Self-evidently the venerable Amsdorf, too, who from the very beginning of the Reformation had set an example in preaching as well as in living a truly Christian life, did not in the least intend to minimize, or discourage the doing of, good works by his offensive phrase, but merely to eliminate good works from the article of justification. As a matter of fact, his extravagant statement, when taken as it reads, flatly contradicted his own clear teaching. In 1552 he had declared against Major, as recorded above: "Who has ever taught or said that one should or need not do good works?" "For we all say and confess that after his renewal and new birth a Christian should love and fear God and do all manner of good works," etc. What Amsdorf wished to emphasize was not that good works are dangerous in themselves and as such, but in the article of salvation. For this reason he added: "*ad salutem,* to salvation." By this appendix he *meant* to emphasize that good works are dangerous when introduced as a factor in justification and trusted for one's salvation.

Melanchthon refers to the proposition of Amsdorf as "filthy speech, *unflaetige Rede.*" In 1557, at Worms, he wrote: "Now Amsdorf writes: Good works are detrimental to salvation. . . . The Antinomians and their like must avoid the filthy speech, 'Good works are detrimental to salvation.'" (*C. R.* 9, 405 ff.) Though unanimously rejecting his blundering proposition, Amsdorf's colleagues treated the venerable veteran of Lutheranism with consideration and moderation. No one, says Frank, disputed the statement in the sense in which Amsdorf took it, and its form was so apparently false that it could but be generally disapproved. (2, 176.) The result was that the paradox assertion remained without any special historical consequences.

True, Major endeavored to foist Amsdorf's teaching also on Flacius. He wrote: Flacius "endeavors with all his powers to subvert this proposition, that good works are necessary to those who are to be saved; and tries to establish the opposite blasphemy, that good works are dangerous to those who are to be saved, and that they are a hindrance to eternal salvation — *evertere summis viribus hanc propositionem conatur: bona opera salvandis esse necessaria. Ac contra stabilire oppositam blasphemiam studet: Bona opera salvandis periculosa sunt et aeternae saluti officiunt.*" Major continues: "Let pious minds permit Flacius and his compeers, at their own risk, to prostitute their eternal salvation to the devils, and by their execrations and anathemas to sacrifice themselves to the devil and his angels." (Frank 2, 221.) This, however, was slander pure and simple, for Flacius was among the first publicly to disown Amsdorf when he made his extravagant statement against Menius. (Preger 1, 392. 384.)

The *Formula of Concord* most emphatically rejects the error of Amsdorf (the bare statement that good works are injurious to salvation) "as offensive and detrimental to Christian discipline." And justly so; for the question was not what Amsdorf meant to say, but what he really did say. The *Formula* adds: "For especially in these last times it is no less needful to admonish men to Christian discipline and good works, and remind them how necessary it is that they exercise themselves in good works as a declaration of their faith and gratitude to God, than that works be not mingled in the article of justification; because men may be damned by an Epicurean delusion concerning faith, as well as by papistic and Pharisaical confidence in their own works and merits." (801, 18.)

## 150. Other Points of Dispute.

Is it correct to say: God requires good works, or, Good works are necessary, and, Christians are obliged or in duty bound to do good works (*bona opera sunt necessaria et debita*)? This question, too, was a point of dispute in the Majoristic controversy. Originally the controversy concerning these terms and phrases was a mere logomachy, which, however, later on (when, after the error lurking in the absolute rejection of them had been pointed out, the phrases were still flatly condemned), developed into a violent controversy.

The *Formula of Concord* explains: "It has also been argued by some that good works are not *necessary* (*noetig*), but are *voluntary* (*freiwillig*), because they are not extorted by fear and the penalty of the Law, but are to be done from a voluntary spirit and a joyful heart. Over against this the other side contended that good works are *necessary*. This controversy was originally occasioned by the words *necessitas* and *libertas* ["*notwendig*" und "*frei*"], that is, necessary and free, because especially the word *necessitas*, necessary, signifies not only the eternal, immutable order according to which all men are obliged and in duty bound to obey God, but sometimes also a coercion, by which the Law forces men to good works. But afterwards there was a disputation not only concerning the words, but the doctrine itself was attacked in the most violent manner, and it was contended that the new obedience in the regenerate is not necessary because of the above-mentioned divine order." (939, 4 f.)

From the very beginning of the Reformation the Romanists had slandered Luther also by maintaining that he condemned good works and simply denied their necessity. A similar charge was made by the Majorists against their opponents generally. And Melanchthon's writings, too, frequently create the same impression. But it was an inference of their own. They argued: If good works are not necessary to salvation, they cannot be necessary at all. Wigand wrote: "It is a most malicious and insidious trait in the new teachers [the Majorists] that they, in order to gloss over their case, cry out with the Papists that the controversy is whether good works are necessary. But this is not in dispute, for no Christian ever denied it. Good works are necessary; that is certainly true. But the conflict arises from the appendix attached to it, and the patch pasted to it, *viz.*, 'to salvation.' And here all God-fearing men say that it is a detrimental, offensive, damnable, papistic appendix." (Planck 4, 498. 544.)

It is true, however, that the Antinomians (who will be dealt with more extensively in a following chapter) as well as several other opponents of the Majorists were unwilling to allow the statement, "Good works are necessary." Falsely interpreting the proposition as necessarily implying, not merely moral obligation, but also compulsion and coercion, they rejected it as unevangelical and semipopish. The word "must" is here not in place, they protested. Agricola, as well as the later Antinomians (Poach and Otto), rejected the expressions "*necessarium*, necessary" and "duty, *debitum*," when employed in connection with good works. January 13, 1555, Melanchthon wrote: "Some object to the words, 'Good works are *necessary*,' or, 'One *must* do good works.' They object to the two words *necessitas* and *debitum*. And the Court-preacher [Agricola] at that time juggled with the word *must*: 'das Muss ist versalzen.' He understood *necessarium* and *debitum* as meaning, coerced by fear of punishment, *extortum co-*

*actione* (extorted by coercion), and spoke high-sounding words, such as, how good works came without the Law. Yet the first meaning of *necessarium* and *debitum* is not *extortum coactione*, but the eternal and immutable order of divine wisdom; and the Lord Christ and Paul themselves employ these words *necessarium* and *debitum*." In December, 1557, he wrote: "They [the Antinomians] object to the proposition: 'New obedience is necessary'; again: 'New obedience is a debt (*debitum*).' And now Amsdorf writes: 'Good works are detrimental to salvation,' and it was Eisleben's [Agricola's] slogan: 'Das Muss ist versalzen.' In Nordhausen some one has publicly announced a disputation which contains the proposition: '*Summa ars Christianorum est nescire legem* — The highest art of a Christian is not to know the Law.'" March 4, 1558: "Some, for instance, Amsdorf and Gallus, object to the word *debitum*." (*C. R.* 8, 411. 194. 842; 9, 405. 474.)

Andrew Musculus, professor in Frankfurt on the Oder, is reported to have said in a sermon, 1558: "They are all the devil's own who teach: 'New obedience is necessary (*nova obedientia est necessaria*)'; the word 'must (necessary)' does not belong here. 'Good works are necessary to salvation,' and, 'Good works are necessary, but not to salvation' — these are both of a cloth — *das sind zwei Hosen aus* EINEM *Tuch*." (Meusel, *Handlexikon* 4, 710; Gieseler 3, 2, 216.)

Over against this extreme position, Melanchthon, Flacius, Wigand, Moerlin, and others held that it was entirely correct to say that good works are necessary. In the *Opinion* of November 13, 1559, referred to above, Melanchthon, after stating that he does not employ the phrase, "Good works are necessary to salvation," continues as follows: "But I do affirm that these propositions are true, and that one may properly and without sophistry say, 'The new obedience or good works are necessary,' because obedience is due to God, . . . and because it is necessary that, after the Holy Spirit has been received, regeneration or conversion be followed by motions corresponding to the Holy Spirit. . . . And the words 'duty' and 'necessity' signify the order of God's wisdom and justice; they do not signify an obedience which is compelled or extorted by fear." (*C. R.* 9, 969.) The Frankfurt *Rezess* of 1558 [Rezess, Rueckzug, Vergleich = Agreement], written by Melanchthon and signed by the Lutheran princes, declared: "These propositions, '*Nova obedientia est necessaria, nova obedientia est debitum*, New obedience is necessary, is a debt,' shall

not be rejected." The *Rezess* explained: "It is certainly a divine, immovable truth that new obedience is necessary in those who are justified, and these words are to be retained in their true meaning. 'Necessary' signifies divine order. New obedience is necessary and is a debt for the very reason that it is an immutable divine order that the rational creature obeys God." (*C. R.* 9, 496. 498.)

In a similar way this matter was explained by Flacius and other theologians. They all maintained that it is correct to say, Good works are necessary. Even Amsdorf wrote 1552 in his *Brief Instruction* against Major: "For we all say and confess that a Christian after his renewal and new birth *should* and must (*soll und muss*) love and fear God and do all manner of good works, but not in order to be saved thereby, for he is saved already by faith." (Schlb. 7, 210.) This view, which was also plainly taught in the *Augsburg Confession*, prevailed and received the sanction of our Church in Article IV of the *Formula of Concord*. When a Christian spontaneously and by the free impulse of his own faith does (and would do, even if there were no law at all) what, according to the holy will of God, revealed in the Ten Commandments, he is obliged and in duty bound to do — such works, and such only, are, according to the *Formula of Concord*, truly good works, works pleasing to God. It was the doctrine of Luther, who had written, *e. g.*, in his *Church Postil* of 1521: "No, dear man, you [cannot earn heaven by your good works, but you] must have heaven and already be saved before you do good works. Works do not merit heaven, but, on the contrary, heaven, imparted by pure grace, does good works spontaneously, seeking no merit, but only the welfare of the neighbor and the glory of God. *Nein, lieber Mensch, du musst den Himmel haben und schon selig sein, ehe du gute Werke tust. Die Werke verdienen nicht den Himmel, sondern wiederum [umgekehrt], der Himmel, aus lauter Gnaden gegeben, tut die guten Werke dahin, ohne Gesuch des Verdienstes, nur dem Naechsten zu Nutz und Gott zu Ehren.*" (E. 7, 174.) Again, in *De Servo Arbitrio* of 1525: "The children of God do good entirely voluntarily, seeking no reward, but only the glory and will of God, ready to do the good even if, assuming the impossible, there were neither heaven nor hell. *Filii autem Dei gratuita voluntate faciunt bonum, nullum praemium quaerentes, sed solam gloriam et voluntatem Dei, parati bonum facere, si per impossibile neque regnum neque infernus esset.*" (E. v. a. 7, 234.)

# XIV. The Synergistic Controversy.

### 151. Relation of Majorism and Synergism.

The theological connection between Majorism and synergism is much closer than is generally realized. Both maintain that, in part, or in a certain respect, salvation depends not on grace alone, but also on man and his

efforts. The Majorists declared good works to be necessary to salvation, or at least to the preservation of faith and of salvation. Thus salvation would, in a way, depend on the right conduct of a Christian after his conversion. The Synergists asserted: Man, too, must do his bit and cooperate with the Holy Spirit if he desires to be saved. Conversion and salvation, therefore, would depend, at least in part, on man's conduct toward converting grace, and he would be justified and saved, not by grace alone, but by a faith which to a certain extent is a work of his own. The burden of both, Majorism and synergism, was the denial of the *sola gratia.* Both coordinated man and God as the causes of our salvation. Indeed, consistently carried out, both destroyed the central Christian truth of justification by grace alone and, with it, the assurance of a gracious God and of eternal salvation — the supreme religious concern of Luther and the entire Lutheran theology.

Majorists and Synergists employed also the same line of argument. Both derived their doctrine, not from any clear statements of the Bible, but by a process of anti-Scriptural and fallacious reasoning. The Majorists inferred: Since evil works and sins against conscience destroy faith and justification, good works are required for their preservation. The Synergists argued: Since all who are not converted or finally saved must blame, not God, but themselves for rejecting grace, those, too, who are converted must be credited with at least a small share in the work of their salvation, that is to say, with a better conduct toward grace than the conduct of those who are lost.

However, while Majorism as well as synergism, as stated, represented essentially the same error and argued against the doctrine of grace in the same unscriptural manner, the more subtle, veiled, and hence the more dangerous of the two, no doubt, was synergism, which reduced man's cooperation to a seemingly harmless minimum and, especially in the beginning, endeavored to clothe itself in ambiguous phrases and apparently pious and plausible formulas. Perhaps this accounts also for the fact that, though Melanchthon and the Majorists felt constrained to abandon, as described in the preceding chapter, the coarser and more offensive Majoristic propositions, they had at the same time no compunctions about retaining and defending essentially the same error in their doctrine of conversion; and that, on the other hand, their opponents, who by that time fully realized also the viciousness of synergism, were not satisfied with Major's concessions in the controversy on good works, because he and his colleagues in Wittenberg were known to identify themselves with the Synergists. For the same reason the dangerous error lurking in the synergistic phrases does not seem from the first to have been recognized by the Lutherans in the same degree as was the error contained in the Majoristic propositions, which indeed had even during Luther's life to some extent become a subject of dispute. Yet it seems hardly possible that for years they should not have detected the synergistic deviations in Wittenberg from Luther's doctrine of free will. Perhaps the fact that at the time when Melanchthon came out boldly with his synergism, 1548, the Lutherans were engrossed with the Adiaphoristic and Majoristic controversies may help to explain, at least to some extent, why the synergistic error caused small concern, and was given but little consideration in the beginning. As a matter of fact, although a considerable amount of synergistic material had been published by 1548, the controversy did not begin till 1556, while the error that good works are necessary to salvation was publicly opposed soon after its reappearance in the Leipzig Interim. At the Weimar Disputation, 1560, Strigel referred to this silence, saying: "I am astonished that I am pressed so much in this matter [concerning synergism], since three years ago at Worms no mention whatever [?] was made of this controversy, while many severe commands were given regarding others." (Richard, *Conf. Prin.*, 349.) The matter was mentioned at Worms, but Melanchthon is reported to have satisfied Brenz and others by declaring that in the passages of his *Loci* suspected of synergism he meant "the regenerated will."

## 152. Luther's Monergism.

According to Lutheran theology, the true opposite of synergism is not Calvinism with its double election, irresistible grace, denial of universal redemption, etc., but the monergism of grace, embracing particularly the tenets that in consequence of Adam's fall man is spiritually dead and utterly unable to contribute in any degree or manner toward his own justification and conversion; moreover, that, being an enemy of God, man, of his own natural powers, is active only in resisting the saving efforts of God, as well as able and prone only to do so; that God alone and in every respect is the Author of man's conversion, perseverance, and final salvation; and that, since the grace of God is universal and earnestly proffered, man alone is responsible for, and the cause of, his own damnation. *"Sola fides iustificat,* Faith alone justifies" — that was the great slogan of the Reformation sounded forth by Luther and his followers with ever increasing boldness, force, and volume. And the distinct meaning of this proposition, which Luther called *"hoc meum dogma,* this my dogma," was just this, that we are saved not by any effort or work of our own, but in every respect by God's grace alone. The restoration of this wonderful truth, taught by St. Paul, made Luther the Reformer of the Church. This truth alone, as Luther had experienced, is able to impart solid comfort to a terror-stricken conscience, engender divine assurance of God's pardon and acceptance, and thus translate a poor miserable sinner from the terrors of hell into paradise.

In the *Seven Penitential Psalms,* written 1517, Luther says: "If God's mercy is to be praised, then all [human] merits and worthiness must come to naught." (Weimar 1, 161.) "Not such are blessed as have no sins or extricate themselves by their own labors, but only those whose sins are graciously forgiven by God." (167.) It is characteristic of God (*es ist Gottes Natur*) to make something out of nothing. Hence God cannot make anything out of him who is not as yet nothing. . . . Therefore God receives none but the forsaken, heals none but the ill, gives sight to none but the blind, quickens none but the dead, makes pious none but the sinners, makes wise none but the ignorant, — in short, He has mercy on none but the miserable, and gives grace to none but those who are in disgrace. Whoever, therefore, is a proud saint, wise or just, cannot become God's material and receive God's work within himself, but remains in his own work and makes an imaginary, seeming, false, and painted saint of himself, i. e., a hypocrite." (183.) "For he whom Thou [God] dost justify will never become righteous by his works; hence it is called Thy righteousness, since Thou givest it to us by grace, and we do not obtain it by works." (192.) "Israel, the true [new] man, does not take refuge in himself, nor in his strength, nor in his righteousness and wisdom. . . . For help and grace is not with themselves. They are sinners and damned in themselves, as He also says through Hosea: O Israel, with thee there is nothing but damnation, but with Me is thine help." (210.) "He, He, God Himself, not they themselves, will deliver the true Israel. . . . Mark well, Israel has sin and cannot help itself." (211.)

In his explanation of Ps. 109 (110), 1518, Luther says: "He calls these children [conceived from spiritual seed, the Word of God] dew, since no soul is converted and transformed from Adam's sinful childhood to the gracious childhood of Christ by human work, but only by God, who works from heaven like the dew, as Micah writes: 'The children of Israel will be like the dew given by God which does not wait for the hands of men.'" (701.) Again: "In every single man God precedes with grace and works before we pray for grace or cooperate. The Doctors call this gratiam primam et praevenientem, that is, the first and prevenient grace. Augustine: Gratia Dei praevenit, ut velimus, ne frustra velimus. God's grace prevenes that we will, lest we will in vain." (710.)

In his 40 theses for the Heidelberg disputation, also of 1518, Luther says of man's powers in spiritual matters: "13. Free will after sin [the Fall] is a mere titular affair [an empty title only], and sins mortally when it does what it is able to do. Liberum arbitrium post peccatum res est de solo titulo, et dum facit, quod in se est, peccat mortaliter." 16. A man desirous of obtaining grace by doing what he is able to do adds sin to sin, becoming doubly guilty. Homo putans, se ad gratiam velle pervenire faciendo, quod est in se, peccatum addit peccato, ut duplo reus fiat." "18. It is certain that a man must utterly despair of himself in order to become apt to acquire the grace of Christ. Certum est, hominem de se penitus oportere desperare, ut aptus fiat ad consequendam gratiam Christi." (W. 1, 354.) By way of explanation Luther added to thesis 13: "The first part [of this thesis, that free will is a mere empty title] is apparent, because the will is a cap-

tive and a servant to sin; not that it is nothing, but that it is free only to [do] evil — non quod sit nihil, sed quod non sit liberum nisi ad malum. John 8, 34. 36: 'Whosoever committeth sin is the servant of sin. If the Son shall make you free, ye shall be free indeed.' Hence St. Augustine says in his book De Spiritu et Litera: Free will without grace can only sin — non nisi ad peccandum valet. And in his second book against Julianus: You call that a free will which in truth is captive, etc." To thesis 16 Luther added: "When man does what he is able to do (dum facit, quod est in se), he sins, seeking altogether his own. And if he is minded to become worthy of, and apt for, grace by a sin, he adds proud presumption."

In his sermon of 1519 on Genesis 4, Luther remarked: "This passage ['The Lord had respect unto Abel'] subverts the entire liberty of our human will. Hic locus semel invertit universam libertatem voluntatis nostrae." (Weimar 9, 337.) In a sermon of September 8, 1520, we read: "By nature we are born accursed; . . . through Christ we are born again children of life. Thus we are born not by free will, not by works, not by our efforts. As a child in the womb . . . is not born by its own works, but suffers itself to be carried and to be given birth, so we are justified by suffering, not by doing." (474.) "Where, then," Luther exclaimed about the same time in his Operationes in Psalmos, "will free will remain? where the doing what one can? Ubi ergo manebit liberum arbitrium, ubi facere, quod in se?" (5, 544. 74.) In a sermon of February 2, 1521, he said: "Whatever grace is in us comes from God alone. Here free will is entirely dead. All that we attempt to establish with our powers is lost, unless He prevenes and makes us alive through His grace. Grace is His own work, which we receive in our hearts by faith. This grace the soul did not possess before, for it is the new man. . . . The great proud saints will not do this [ascribe everything to God and His mercy]. They, too, would have a share in it, saying to our Lord: 'This I have done by my free will, this I have deserved.'" (9, 573; 5, 544.)

Thus Luther, from the very beginning of the Reformation, stood for the doctrine of justification, conversion, and salvation by grace alone. Most emphatically he denied that man, though free to a certain extent in human and temporal affairs, is able to cooperate with the powers of his natural, unregenerate will in matters spiritual and pertaining to God. This was also the position which Luther victoriously defended against Erasmus in his De Servo Arbitrio of 1525. Goaded on by the Romanists to come out publicly against the German heretic, the great Humanist, in his Diatribe of 1524, had shrewdly planned to attack his opponent at the most vulnerable point. As such he regarded Luther's monergistic doctrine, according to which it is God alone who justifies, converts, preserves, and saves men, without any works of their own. In reality, however, as presently appeared from his glorious classic on the *sola-gratia*-doctrine, Erasmus had assaulted the strongest gate of Luther's fortress. For the source of the wonderful power which Luther displayed throughout the Reformation was none other than the divine conviction born of the Word of God that in every respect grace alone is the cause of our justification and salvation. And if ever this blessed doctrine was firmly established, successfully defended, and greatly glorified, it was in Luther's book against Erasmus.

Justification, conversion, perseverance in faith, and final salvation, obtained not by any effort of ours, but in every respect received as a gracious gift of God alone — that was the teaching also to which Luther faithfully, most determinedly, and without any wavering adhered throughout his life. In his *Large Confession* of 1528, for example, we read: "Herewith I reject and condemn as nothing but error all dogmas which extol our free will, as they directly conflict with this help and grace of our Savior Jesus Christ. For since outside of Christ death and sin are our lords, and the devil our god and prince, there can be no power or might, no wisdom or understanding, whereby we can qualify ourselves for, or strive after, righteousness and life; but we must be blinded people and prisoners of sin and the devil's own, to do and to think what pleases them and is contrary to God and His commandments." (CONC. TRIGL. 897, 43.)

### 153. Luther's Doctrine Endorsed.

To adhere faithfully to Luther's doctrine of conversion and salvation by grace alone was also the determination of the loyal Lutherans in their opposition to the Synergists. Planck correctly remarks that the doctrine which Flacius and the Anti-Synergists defended was the very doctrine which "Luther advocated in his conflict with Erasmus." (*Prot. Lehrbegriff* 4, 667.) This was substantially conceded even by the opponents. When, for example, at the colloquy in Worms, 1557, the Romanists demanded that Flacius's doctrine of free will be condemned by the Lutherans, Melanchthon declared that herein one ought not to submit to the Papists, who slyly, under the name of Illyricus [Flacius], demanded the condemnation of Luther, whose opinion in the doctrine of free will he [Melanchthon] was neither able nor willing to condemn. (Gieseler 3, 2, 232.) In their *Confession*, published in March, 1569, the theologians of Ducal Saxony (Wigand, Coelestin, Irenaeus, Kirchner, etc.) declared: "We also add that we embrace the doctrine and opinion of Dr. Luther, the Elias of these latter days of the world, as it is most luminously and skilfully set forth in the book *De Servo Arbitrio*, against Erasmus, in the *Commentary on Genesis*, and in other books; and we hold that this teaching of Luther agrees with the eternal Word of God." (Schluesselburg, *Catalogus* 5, 133.) Luther's *sola-gratia*-doctrine was embodied also in the *Formula of Concord*, and this with a special endorsement of his book *De Servo Arbitrio*. For here we read: "Even so Dr. Lu-

ther wrote of this matter [the doctrine that our free will has no power whatever to qualify itself for righteousness, etc.] also in his book *De Servo Arbitrio; i. e.*, Of the Captive Will of Man, in opposition to Erasmus, and elucidated and supported this position well and thoroughly [*egregie et solide*]; and afterward he repeated and explained it in his glorious exposition of the book of Genesis, especially of chapter 26. There likewise his meaning and understanding of some other peculiar disputations introduced incidentally by Erasmus, as of absolute necessity, etc., have been secured by him in the best and most careful way against all misunderstanding and perversion; to which we also hereby appeal and refer others." (897, 44; 980, 28.) In the passage of his *Commentary on Genesis* referred to by the *Formula*, Luther does not, as has been claimed, retract or modify his former statements concerning the inability of the human will and the monergism of grace, but emphasizes that, in reading *De Servo Arbitrio*, one must heed and not overlook his frequent admonitions to concern oneself with God as He has revealed Himself in the Gospel, and not speculate concerning God in His transcendence, absoluteness, and majesty, as the One in whom we live and move and have our being, and without whom nothing can either exist or occur, and whose wonderful ways are past finding out. (CONC. TRIGL., 898.) And the fact that the Lutheran theologians, living at the time and immediately after the framing of the *Formula of Concord*, objected neither to the book *De Servo Arbitrio* itself nor to its public endorsement by the *Formula of Concord*, is an additional proof of the fact that they were in complete agreement with Luther's teaching of conversion and salvation by grace alone. (Frank 1, 120.)

This *sola-gratia*-doctrine, the vital truth of Christianity, rediscovered and proclaimed once more by Luther, was, as stated, the target at which Erasmus directed his shafts. In his *Diatribe* he defined the power of free will to be the faculty of applying oneself to grace (*facultas applicandi se ad gratiam*), and declared that those are the best theologians who, while ascribing as much as possible to the grace of God, do not eliminate this human factor. He wrote: Free will is "the ability of the human will according to which man is able either to turn himself to what leads to eternal salvation or to turn away from it." (St. L. 18, 1612.) Again: "Those, therefore, who are farthest apart from the views of Pelagius ascribe to grace the most, but to free will almost nothing; yet they do not abolish it entirely. They say that man cannot will anything good without special grace, cannot begin anything good, cannot continue in it, cannot complete anything without the chief thing, the constant help of divine grace. This opinion seems to be pretty probable because it leaves to man a striving and an effort, and yet does not admit that he is to ascribe even the least to his own powers." (1619.) One must avoid extremes, and seek the middle of the road, said Erasmus. Pelagius had fallen into Scylla, and Luther into Charybdis. "I am pleased with the opinion of those who ascribe to free will something, but to grace by far the most." (1666.) Essentially, this was the error held, nursed, and defended also by the Synergists, though frequently in more guarded and ambiguous phrases. But their theory of conversion also involved, as Schaff and Schmauk put it, "the idea of a partnership between God and man, and a corresponding division of work and merit." (*Conf. Principle*, 600.)

However, these attempts to revamp the Semi-Pelagian teaching resulted in a controversy which more and longer than any other endangered and disquieted the Lutheran Church, before as well as after the adoption of the *Formula of Concord*. Whether the unregenerate man, when the Word of God is preached, and the grace of God is offered him, is able to prepare himself for grace, accept it, and assent thereto, was, according to the *Formula of Concord*, "the question upon which, *for quite a number of years now*, there has been a controversy among some theologians in the churches of the Augsburg Confession." (881, 2.) And of all the controversies after Luther's death the synergistic controversy was most momentous and consequential. For the doctrine of grace with which it dealt is the vital breath of every Christian. Without it neither faith nor the Christian religion can live and remain. "If we believe," says Luther in *De Servo Arbitrio*, "that Christ has redeemed men by His blood, then we must confess *that the entire man was lost*; otherwise we make Christ superfluous or the Redeemer of but the meanest part of us, which is blasphemous and sacrilegious." Reading the book of Erasmus, in which he bent every effort toward exploding the doctrine of grace, Luther felt the hand of his opponent clutching his throat. In the closing paragraph of *De Servo Arbitrio* Luther wrote: "I highly laud and extol you for this thing also, that of all others you alone have gone to the heart of the subject. . . . You alone have discerned the core of the matter and have aimed at the throat, for which I thank you heartily. — *Unus tu et solus cardinem rerum vidisti, et ipsum iugulum petisti, pro quo ex animo tibi gratias ago, in hac enim causa libentius versor, quantum favet tempus et otium.*" (E. v. a. 7, 367. 137; St. L. 18, 1967; Pieper, *Dogm.* 2, 543.) And so the Synergists, who renewed the doctrine of Erasmus, also flew at the throat of Christianity. Genuine Lutheranism would have been strangled if synergism had emerged victorious from this great controversy of grace *versus* free will.

### 154. The Father of Synergism.

During the first period of his activity in Wittenberg, Melanchthon was in perfect agreement with Luther also on the question of man's inability in spiritual matters and the sole activity, or monergism, of grace in the work of his salvation. As late as 1530 he incorporated these views in the *Augsburg Confession*, as appears, in particular, from Articles II, V, XVIII, and XIX. His later doctrine concerning the three concurring causes of conversion (the Holy Spirit, the Word, and the consenting will of man), as well as his theory explaining synergistically, from an alleged dissimilar action in man, the difference why some are saved while others are lost, is not so much as hinted at in the Confession. But even at this early date (1530) or soon after, Melanchthon also does not seem any longer to have agreed whole-heartedly with Luther in the doctrine of grace and free will. And in the course of time his theology drifted farther and farther from its original monergistic moorings. Nor was Luther wholly unaware of the secret trend of his colleague and friend toward — Erasmus. In 1536, when the deviations of Melanchthon and Cruciger, dealt with in our previous chapter, were brought to his notice, Luther exclaimed: "*Haec est ipsissima theologia Erasmi.* This is the identical theology of Erasmus, nor can there be anything more opposed to our doctrine." (Kolde, *Analecta*, 266.)

That Melanchthon's theology was verging toward Erasmus appears from his letter of June 22, 1537, to Veit Dietrich, in which he said that he desired a more thorough exposition also of the doctrines of predestination and of the *consent of the will.* (*C. R.* 3, 383.) Before this, in his *Commentary on Romans* of 1532, he had written that there is some cause of election also in man; *viz.*, in as far as he does not repudiate the grace offered — "*tamen eatenus aliquam causam in accipiente esse, quatenus promissionem oblatam non repudiat.*" (Seeberg 4, 442.) In an addition to his *Loci* of 1533 he also spoke of a cause of justification and election residing in man. (*C. R.* 21, 332.) In the revised editions of 1535 and 1543 he plainly began to prepare the way for his later bold and unmistakable deviations. For even though unable to point out a clearcut and unequivocal synergistic statement, one cannot read these editions without scenting a Semi-Pelagian and Erasmian atmosphere. What Melanchthon began to teach was the doctrine that man, when approached by the Word of God, is able to assume either an attitude of *pro* or *con*, *i. e.*, for or against the grace of God. The same applies to the *Variata* of 1540 in which the frequent "*adiuvari*" there employed, though not incorrect as such, was not without a synergistic flavor.

Tschackert remarks of the *Loci* of 1535: "Melanchthon wants to make man responsible for his state of grace. Nor does the human will in consequence of original sin lose the ability to decide itself when incited; the will produces nothing new by its own power, but assumes an attitude toward what approaches it. When man hears the Word of God, and the Holy Spirit produces spiritual affections in his heart, the will can either assent or turn against it. In this way Melanchthon arrives at the formula, ever after stereotype with him, that there are three concurring causes in the process of conversion: 'the Word of God, the Holy Spirit, and the human will, which, indeed, is not idle, *but strives against its infirmity.*'" (520.)

However, during the life of Luther, Melanchthon made no further measurable progress towards synergism. Perhaps the unpleasant experiences following upon his innovations in the doctrine of good works acted as a check also on the public development of his synergistic tendencies. During Luther's life Melanchthon, as he himself admitted to Carlowitz (106), dissimulated, keeping his deviating views to himself and his intimate friends. After Luther's death, however, he came out unmistakably and publicly, also in favor of synergism, endorsing even the Erasmian definition of free will as "the power in man to apply himself to grace." He plainly taught that, when drawn by the Holy Spirit, the will is able to decide *pro* or *con*, to obey or to resist. Especially in his lectures, Melanchthon — not indeed directly, but mentioning the name of Flacius — continually lashed such phrases of Luther as "purely passive," "block," "resistance," — a fact to which Schluesselburg, who had studied in Wittenberg, refers in support of his assertion that Melanchthon had departed from Luther's teaching on free will. (*Catalogus* 5, 32.) While Melanchthon formerly (in his *Loci* of 1543) had spoken of three causes of a good *action* (*bonae actionis*), he now publicly advocated the doctrine of three concurring causes of *conversion*. Now he boldly maintained that, since the grace of God is universal, one must assume, and also teach, that there are different actions in different men, which accounts for the fact that some are converted and saved while others are lost. According to the later Melanchthon, therefore, man's eternal salvation evidently does not depend on the gracious operations of God's Holy Spirit and Word alone, but also on his own correct conduct toward grace. In his heart, especially when approaching the mercy-seat in prayer, Melanchthon, no doubt, forgot and disavowed his own teaching, and believed and practised Luther's *sola-gratia*-doctrine. But it cannot be denied that, in his endeavors to harmonize universal grace with the fact that not all, but some only, are saved, Melanchthon repudiated the monergism of Luther, espoused and defended the powers of free will in spiritual matters, and thought, argued, spoke, and wrote in terms of synergism. Indeed, Melanchthon must be regarded as the father of both synergism and the rationalistic methods employed in its defense, and as the true father also of the modern rationalistico-synergistic theology represented by such distinguished men as Von Hofmann, Thomasius, Kahnis, Luthardt, etc. (Pieper 2, 582; Frank 1, 231.)

## 155. Unsound Statements of Melanchthon.

Following are some of the ambiguous and false deliverances of Melanchthon: In the *Loci* of 1535 the so-called human cause of conversion which must be added to the Word and Spirit is described as endeavoring, striving, and wishing to obey and believe. We read: "We do not say this to ensnare the consciences, or to deter men from the endeavor to obey and believe, or 'from making an effort. On the contrary, since we are to begin with the Word, we certainly must not resist the Word of God, but strive to obey it. . . . We see that these causes are united: the Word, the Holy Spirit, and the will, which is certainly not idle, but strives against its infirmity. In this manner ecclesiastical writers are accustomed to join these causes. Basil says: 'Only will, and God will precede.' God precedes, calls, moves, assists us; but let us beware lest we resist. . . . Chrysostom says: He who draws, draws him who is willing." (*C. R.* 21, 376.)

In conversion and salvation God certainly must do and does His share, but man must beware lest he fail to do what is required of him. This is also the impression received from Melanchthon's statements in the third elaboration of his *Loci*, 1543. We read: "Here three causes of a good action concur (*hic concurrunt tres causae bonae actionis*): the Word of God, the Holy Spirit, and the human will assenting to and not resisting the Word of God (*humana voluntas assentiens, nec repugnans Verbo Dei*). For it could expel [the Spirit], as Saul expelled [Him] in his own free will. But when the mind hearing and sustaining itself does not resist, does not give way to diffidence, but, the Holy Spirit assisting, endeavors to assent, — in such a struggle the will is not inactive (*in hoc certamine voluntas non est otiosa*). The ancients have said that good works are done when grace precedes and the will follows. So also Basil says: Μόνον θέλησον, καὶ θεὸς προαπαντᾷ, Only will, and God anticipates. God precedes, calls, moves, assists us; but as for us, let us see to it that we do not resist. *Deus antevertit nos, vocat, movet, adiuvat,* SED NOS VIDERIMUS, *ne repugnemus.*" (21, 658.) "And Phil. 1, 6: 'He which hath begun a good work in you will perform it until the day of Jesus Christ,' *i. e.*, we are assisted by God (*adiuvamur a Deo*), but we must hear the Word of God and not resist the drawing God." (916.) "God draws our minds that they will, but we must assent, not resist. *Deus trahit mentes, ut velint, sed assentiri nos, non repugnare oportet.*" (917.) Here we also meet the remark: "But the will, when assisted by the Holy Spirit, becomes more free. *Fit autem voluntas adiuvata Spiritu Sancto magis libera.*" (663.) Frank comments pertinently that the *magis* presupposes a certain degree of liberty of the will before the assistance of the Holy Spirit. (1, 198.)

The boldest synergistic statements are found in the *Loci* of 1548. It was the year of the Leipzig Interim, in which the same error was embodied as follows: "The merciful God does not deal with man as with a block, but draws him in such a way that his will, too, cooperates." (*C. R.* 7, 51. 260.) As to the *Loci* of this year, Bindseil remarks in the *Corpus Reformatorum:* "This edition is famous on account of certain paragraphs inserted by the author in the article on Free Will. For these additions contain the Erasmian definition of free will (that it is the faculty of applying oneself to grace), on account of which Melanchthon was charged with synergism by the Flacians. . . . For this reason the edition is called by J. T. Mayer 'the worst of all (*omnium pessima*).'" At the Weimar colloquy, 1560, even Strigel was not willing to identify himself openly with the Erasmian definition of free will (*facultas applicandi se ad gratiam*) as found in one of these sections. When Flacius quoted the passage, Strigel retorted excitedly: "I do not defend that definition which you have quoted from the recent edition [1548]. When did you hear it from me? When have I undertaken to defend it?" (Frank 1, 199. 135.) At the Herzberg colloquy Andreae remarked: "The *Loci Communes* of Melanchthon are useful. But whoever reads the *locus de libero arbitrio* must confess, even if he judges most mildly, that the statements are dubious and ambiguous. And what of the four paragraphs which were inserted after Luther's death? For here we read: 'There must of necessity be a cause of difference in us why a Saul is rejected, a David received.'" (Pieper 2, 587.)

From these additions of 1548 we cite: "Nor does conversion occur in David in such a manner as when a stone is turned into a fig; but free will does something in David; for when he hears the rebuke and the promise, he willingly and freely confesses his fault. And his will does something when he sustains himself with this word: The Lord hath taken away your sin. And when he endeavors to sustain himself with this word, he is already assisted by the Holy Spirit." (*C. R.* 21, 659.) Again: "I therefore answer those who excuse their idleness because they think that free will does nothing, as follows: It certainly is the eternal and immovable will of God that you obey the voice of the Gospel, that you hear the Son of God, that you acknowledge the Mediator. How black is that sin which refuses to behold the Mediator, the Son of God, presented to the human race! You will answer: 'I cannot.' But in a manner you can (*immo aliquo modo potes*), and when you sustain yourself with the voice of the Gospel, then pray that God would assist you, and know that the Holy Spirit is efficacious in such consolation. Know that just in this manner God intends to convert us, when we, roused by the promise, wrestle with ourselves, pray and resist our diffidence and other vicious affections. For this reason some of the ancient Fathers have said that free will in man is the faculty to apply himself to grace (*liberum arbitrium in homine facultatem esse applicandi se ad gratiam*); i. e., he hears the promise, endeavors to assent, and abandons sins against conscience. Such things do not occur in devils. The difference therefore between the devils and the human race ought to be considered. These matters, however, become still clearer when the promise is considered. For since the promise is universal, and since there are no contradictory wills in God, there must of necessity be in us some cause of difference why Saul is rejected and David is received; i. e., there must of necessity be some dissimilar action in these two. *Cum promissio sit uni-*

*versalis, nec sint in Deo contradictoriae voluntates, necesse est in nobis esse aliquam discriminis causam, cur Saul abiiciatur, David recipiatur, id est, necesse est aliquam esse actionem dissimilem in his duobus.* Properly understood, this is true, and the use [*usus*] in the exercises of faith and in true consolation (when our minds acquiesce in the Son of God, shown in the promise) will illustrate this copulation of causes: the Word of God, the Holy Spirit, and the will." (*C. R.* 21, 659 f.)

At the colloquy of Worms, 1557, Melanchthon, interpellated by Brenz, is reported to have said that the passage in his *Loci* of 1548 defining free will as the faculty of applying oneself to grace referred to the regenerated will (*voluntas renata*), as, he said, appeared from the context. (Gieseler 3, 2, 225; Frank 1, 198.) As a matter of fact, however, the context clearly excludes this interpretation. In the passage quoted, Melanchthon, moreover, plainly teaches: (1) that in conversion man, too, can do, and really does, something by willingly confessing his fault, by sustaining himself with the Word, by praying that God would assist him, by wrestling with himself, by striving against diffidence, etc.; (2) that the nature of fallen man differs from that of the devils in this, that his free will is still able to apply itself to grace, endeavor to assent to it, etc.; (3) that the dissimilar actions resulting from the different use of this natural ability accounts for the fact that some are saved while others are lost. Such was the plain teaching of Melanchthon from which he never receded, but which he, apart from other publications, reaffirmed in every new edition of his *Loci*. For all, including the last one to appear during his life (1559), contain the additions of 1548. "The passage added by the author [Melanchthon, 1548] after Luther's death is repeated in all subsequent editions," says Bindseil. (*C. R.* 21, 570.)

The sections which were added to the *Loci* after 1548 also breathe the same synergistic spirit. In 1553 Melanchthon inserted a paragraph which says that, when approached by the Holy Spirit, the will can obey or resist. We read: "The liberty of the human will after the Fall, also in the non-regenerate, is the faculty by virtue of which man is able to govern his motions; i. e., he can enjoin upon his external members such actions as agree, or such as do not agree, with the Law of God. But he cannot banish doubts from his mind and evil inclinations from his heart without the light of the Gospel and without the Holy Spirit. But when the will is drawn by the Holy Spirit, it can obey or resist. *Cum autem trahitur a Spiritu Sancto, potest obsequi et repugnare.*" (21, 1078; 13, 162.)

Other publications contain the same doctrine. While in his *Loci* of 1543 he had spoken only of three causes of a good action (*bonae actionis*), Melanchthon, in his *Enarratio Symboli Nicaeni* of 1550, substituted "conversion" for "good action." We read: In conversion these causes concur: the Holy Spirit, the voice of the Gospel, "and the will of man, which does not resist the divine voice, but somehow, with trepidation, assents. *Concurrunt in conversione hae causae: Spiritus Sanctus . . . vox Evangelii . . . et voluntas hominis, quae non repugnat voci divinae, sed inter trepidationem utcumque assentitur.*" Again: "And concerning this copulation of causes it is said: The Spirit comes to the assistance of our infirmity. And Chrysostom truly says: God draws, but He draws him who is willing." Again: God's promise is universal, and there are no contradictory wills in God; hence, though Paul is drawn in a different manner than Zacchaeus, "nevertheless there is some assent of the will (*tamen aliqua est voluntatis assensio*)." "God therefore begins and draws by the voice of the Gospel, but He draws him who is willing, and assists him who assents." "Nor is anything detracted from the glory of God, but it is truly affirmed that the assistance of God always concurs in the beginning and afterwards (*auxilium Dei semper initio et deinceps concurrere*)." (23, 280 ff.) Accordingly, God merely concurs as one of three causes, among which the will of man is the third. In his *Examen Ordinandorum* of 1554, Melanchthon again replaced the term "good action" by "conversion." He says: "In conversion these causes concur: the Word of God, the Holy Spirit, whom the Father and Son send to kindle our hearts, and our will, assenting and not resisting the Word of God (*et nostra voluntas assentiens et non repugnans Verbo Dei*). And lest we yield to diffidence, we must consider that both preachings are universal, the preaching of repentance as well as the promise of grace. . . . Let us therefore not resist, but assent to the promise, and constantly repeat this prayer: I believe, O Lord, but come to the help of my weakness." (23, 15.) Finally in his *Opinion on the Weimar Book of Confutation*, March 9, 1559, Melanchthon remarks: "Again, if the will is able to turn from the consolation, it must be inferred that it works something and follows the Holy Spirit when it accepts the consolation. *Item, so sich der Wille vom Trost abwenden mag, so ist dagegen zu verstehen, dass er etwas wirket und folget dem Heiligen Geist, so er den Trost annimmt.*" (9, 768.) W. Preger is right when he says: "According to Melanchthon's view, natural man is able to do the following [when the Word of God is preached to him]: he is able not to resist; he is able to take pains with respect to obedience; he is able to comfort himself with the Word. . . . This [according to Melanchthon] is a germ of the positive good will still found in natural man which prevenient grace arouses." (*Flacius Illyricus* 2, 189 f.) Schmauk writes: Melanchthon found "the cause for the actual variation in the working of God's grace in man, its object. This subtle synergistic spirit attacks the very foundation of Lutheranism, flows out into almost every doctrine, and weakens the Church at every point. And it was particularly this weakness which the great multitude of Melanchthon's scholars, who became the leaders of the generation of which we are speaking, absorbed,

and which rendered it difficult to return, finally, after years of struggle, to the solid ground, once more recovered in the *Formula of Concord*." (*Conf. Principle*, 601.)

R. Seeberg characterizes Melanchthon's doctrine as follows: "A synergistic trait therefore appears in his doctrine. In the last analysis, God merely grants the outer and inner possibility of obtaining salvation. Without man's cooperation this possibility would not become reality; and he is able to refuse this cooperation. It is, therefore, in conversion equally a cause with the others. *Sie [die Mitwirkung des Menschen] ist also freilich eine den andern Ursachen gleichberechtigte Ursache in der Bekehrung.*" God makes conversion possible, but only the decision of man's free will makes it actual, — such, according to Seeberg, was the "synergism" of Melanchthon. (Seeberg, *Dogg.*, 4, 444. 446.)

Frank says of Melanchthon's way of solving the question why some are converted and saved while others are lost: "The road chosen by Melanchthon has indeed led to the goal. The contradictions are solved. But let us look where we have landed. We are standing — in the Roman camp!" After quoting a passage from the *Tridentinum*, which speaks of conversion in terms similar to those employed by Melanchthon, Frank continues: "The foundation stone of Luther's original Reformation doctrine of salvation by grace alone; *viz.*, that nothing in us, not even our will moved and assisted by God, is the *causa meritoria* of salvation, is subverted by these propositions; and it is immaterial to the contrite heart whether much or little is demanded from free will as the faculty of applying oneself to grace." Frank adds: "What the Philippists, synchronously [with Melanchthon] and later, propounded regarding this matter [of free will] are but variations of the theme struck by Melanchthon. Everywhere the sequence of thought is the same, with but this difference, that here the faults of the Melanchthonian theory together with its consequences come out more clearly." (1, 134 f.) The same is true of modern synergistic theories. Without exception they are but variations of notes struck by Melanchthon, — the father of all the synergists that have raised their heads within the Lutheran Church.

## 156. Pfeffinger Champions Synergistic Doctrine.

Prior to 1556 references to the unsound position of the Wittenberg and Leipzig theologians are met with but occasionally. (Planck 4, 568.) The unmistakably synergistic doctrine embodied in the *Loci* of 1548, as well as in the Leipzig Interim, did not cause alarm and attract attention immediately. But when, in 1555, John Pfeffinger [born 1493; 1539 superintendent, and 1543 professor in Leipzig; assisted 1548 in framing the Leipzig Interim; died January 1, 1573] published his "Five Questions Concerning the Liberty of the Human Will — *De Libertate Voluntatis Humanae, Quaestiones Quinque. D. Johannes Pfeffinger Lipsiae Editae in Officina Georgii*

Hantschi 1555," the controversy flared up instantly. It was a little booklet containing, besides a brief introduction, only 41 paragraphs, or theses. In these Pfeffinger discussed and defended the synergistic doctrine of Melanchthon, maintaining that in conversion man, too, must contribute his share, though it be ever so little.

Early in the next year Pfeffinger was already opposed by the theologians of Thuringia, the stanch opponents of the Philippists, John Stolz, court-preacher at Weimar, composing 110 theses for this purpose. In 1558 Amsdorf published his *Public Confession of the True Doctrine of the Gospel and Confutation of the Fanatics of the Present Time*, in which he, quoting from memory, charged Pfeffinger with teaching that man is able to prepare himself for grace by the natural powers of his free will, just as the godless sophists, Thomas Aquinas, Scotus, and their disciples, had held. (Planck 4, 573. 568.) About the same time Stolz published the 110 theses just referred to with a preface by Aurifaber (*Refutatio Propositionum Pfeffingeri de Libero Arbitrio*). Flacius, then professor in Jena, added his *Refutation of Pfeffinger's Propositions on Free Will* and *Jena Disputation on Free Will*.

In the same year, 1558, Pfeffinger, in turn, published his *Answer to the Public Confession of Amsdorf*, charging the latter with falsification, and denouncing Flacius as the "originator and father of all the lies which have troubled the Lutheran Church during the last ten years." But at the same time Pfeffinger showed unmistakably that the charges of his opponents were but too well founded. Says Planck: "Whatever may have moved Pfeffinger to do so, he could not (even if Flacius himself had said it for him) have confessed synergism more clearly and more definitely than he did spontaneously and unasked in this treatise." (4, 574.) Frank: "Pfeffinger goes beyond Melanchthon and Strigel; for the action here demanded of, and ascribed to, the natural will is, according to him, not even in need of liberation by prevenient grace. . . . His doctrine may without more ado be designated as Semi-Pelagianism." (1, 137.)

At Wittenberg, Pfeffinger was supported by George Major, Paul Eber, and Paul Crell; and before long his cause was espoused also by Victorin Strigel in Jena. Disputations by the Wittenberg and Leipzig synergists (whom Schluesselburg, 5, 16, calls "cooperators" and "die freiwilligen Herren") and by their opponents in Jena increased the animosity. Both parties cast moderation to the winds. In a public letter of 1558 the Wittenberg professors, for example, maligned Flacius in every possible way, and branded him as "der verloffene undeutsche Flacius Illyricus" and as the sole author of all the dissensions in the churches of Germany. (Planck 4, 583.)

### 157. Statements of Pfeffinger.

Following are some of the synergistic deliverances made by Pfeffinger in his *Five Questions Concerning the Liberty of the Human Will*. § 11 reads: "Thirdly, when we inquire concerning the spiritual actions, it is correct to answer that the human will has not such a liberty as to be able to effect the spiritual motions without the help of the Holy Spirit (*humanam voluntatem non habere eiusmodi libertatem, ut motus spirituales* SINE AUXILIO *Spiritus Sancti efficere possit*)." § 14: "Therefore some assent or apprehension on our part must concur (*oportet igitur nostram aliquam assensionem seu apprehensionem concurrere*) when the Holy Spirit has aroused (*accenderit*) the mind, the will, and the heart. Hence Basil says: Only will, and God anticipates; and Chrysostom: He who draws, draws him who is willing; and Augustine: He assists those who have received the gift of the call with becoming piety, and preserve the gifts of God as far as man is able. Again: When grace precedes, the will follows — *praeeunte gratia, comitante voluntate*." In § 16 we read: "The will, therefore, is not idle, but assents faintly. *Voluntas igitur non est otiosa, sed languide assentitur*."

Paragraph 17 runs: "If the will were idle or purely passive, there would be no difference between the pious and the wicked, or between the elect and the damned, as, between Saul and David, between Judas and Peter. God would also become a respecter of persons and the author of contumacy in the wicked and damned; and to God would be ascribed contradictory wills, — which conflicts with the entire Scripture. Hence it follows that there is in us a cause why some assent while others do not. *Sequitur ergo in nobis esse aliquam causam, cur alii assentiantur, alii non assentiantur*." § 24: "Him [the Holy Spirit], therefore, we must not resist; but on the part of our will, which is certainly not like a stone or block, some assent must be added — *sed aliquam etiam assensionem accedere nostrae voluntatis, quam non sicut saxum aut incudem se habere certum est*." § 30: "But apprehension on our part must concur. For, since the promise of grace is universal, and since we must obey this promise, some difference between the elect and the rejected must be inferred from our will (*sequitur, aliquod discrimen inter electos et reiectos a voluntate nostra sumendum esse*), viz., that those who resist the promise are rejected, while those who embrace the promise are received. . . . All this clearly shows that our will is not idle in conversion or like a stone or block in its conduct. *Ex quibus omnibus manifestissimum apparet, voluntatem nostram non esse otiosam in conversione, aut se ut saxum aut incudem habere*."

§ 34 reads: "Some persons, however, shout that the assistance of the Holy Spirit is extenuated and diminished if even the least particle be attributed to the human will. Though this argument may appear specious and plausible, yet pious minds understand that by our doctrine — according to which we ascribe some cooperation to our will; viz., some assent and apprehension (*qua tribuimus aliquam* SYNERGIAM *voluntati nostrae, videlicet qualemcumque assensionem et apprehensionem*) — absolutely nothing is taken away from the assistance rendered by the Holy Spirit. For we affirm that the first acts (*primas partes*) must be assigned and attributed to Him who first and primarily, through the Word or the voice of the Gospel, moves our hearts to believe, to which thereupon we, too, ought to assent as much as we are able (*cui deinde et* NOS, QUANTUM IN NOBIS EST, ASSENTIRI *oportet*), and not resist the Holy Spirit, but submit to the Word, ponder, learn, and hear it, as Christ says: 'Whosoever hath heard of the Father and learned, cometh to Me.'" § 36: "And although original sin has brought upon our nature a ruin so sad and horrible that we can hardly imagine it, yet we must not think that absolutely all the knowledge (*notitiae*) which was found in the minds of our first parents before the Fall has on that account been destroyed and extinguished after the Fall, or that the human will does not in any way differ from a stone or a block; for we are, as St. Paul has said most seriously, *coworkers with God*, which coworking, indeed, is assisted and strengthened by the Holy Spirit — *sumus synergi Dei, quae quidem synergia adiuvatur a Spiritu Sancto et confirmatur*." Evidently no comment is necessary to show that the passages cited from Pfeffinger are conceived, born, and bred in Semi-Pelagianism and rationalism.

Planck furthermore quotes from Pfeffinger's *Answer* to Amsdorf, 1558: "And there is no other reason why some are saved and some are damned than this one alone, that some, when incited by the Holy Spirit, do not resist, but obey Him and accept the grace and salvation offered, while others will not accept it, but resist the Holy Spirit, and despise the grace." (4, 578.) Again: "Although the will cannot awaken or incite itself to spiritually good works, but must be awakened and incited thereto by the Holy Ghost, yet man is *not altogether excluded* from such works of the Holy Ghost, as if he were not engaged in it and were not to contribute his share to it — *dass er nicht auch dabei sein und das Seine nicht auch dabei tun muesse*." (576.) Again: In the hands of the Holy Spirit man is not like a block or stone in the hands of a sculptor, which do not and cannot "know, understand, or feel what is done with them, nor *in the least further* or hinder what the artist endeavors to make of them." (576.) "But when the heart of man is touched, awakened, and moved by the Holy Ghost, man must not be like a dead stone or block, . . . but must obey and follow Him. And although he perceives his great weakness, and, on the other hand, how powerfully sin in his flesh opposes, he must nevertheless not desist, but ask and pray God for grace and assistance against sin and flesh." (577.) Planck remarks: According to Pfeffinger, the powers for all this are still found in natural man, and the only thing required is, not to recreate them, but merely to incite them to action. (579.)

In 1558, in an appendix to his disputation of 1555, Pfeffinger explained and illustrated his position, in substance, as follows: I was to prove nothing else than that some use of the will [in spiritual matters] was left, and that our nature is not annihilated or extinguished, but corrupted and marvelously depraved after the Fall. Now, to be sure, free will cannot by its own natural powers regain its integrity nor rise after being ruined; yet, as the doctrine [the Gospel] can be understood by paying attention to it, so it can also in a manner (*aliquo modo*) be obeyed by assenting to it. But it is necessary for all who would dwell in the splendor of the eternal light and in the sight of God to look up to, and not turn away from, the light. Schluesselburg adds: "*Haec certe est synergia* — This is certainly synergism." (*Catalogus 5*, 161.)

Tschackert summarizes Pfeffinger's doctrine as follows: "When the Holy Spirit, through the Word of God, influences a man, then the assenting will becomes operative as a factor of conversion. The reason why some assent while others do not must lie in themselves. . . . Evidently Pfeffinger's opinion was that not only the regenerate, but even the natural will of man possesses the ability either to obey the divine Spirit or to resist Him." (521.) According to W. Preger, Pfeffinger taught "that the Holy Spirit must awaken and incite our nature that it may understand, think, will, and do what is right and pleasing to God," but that natural free will is able "to obey and follow" the motions of the Spirit. (2, 192. 195.)

No doubt, Pfeffinger advocated, and was a candid exponent and champion of, nothing but the three-concurring-causes doctrine of Melanchthon, according to which God never fails to do His share in conversion, while we must beware (*sed nos viderimus, C. R.* 21, 658) lest we fail to do our share. Pfeffinger himself made it a special point to cite Melanchthon as his authority in this matter. The last (41st) paragraph in his *Five Questions* begins as follows: "We have briefly set forth the doctrine concerning the liberty of the human will, agreeing with the testimonies of the prophetic and apostolic Scriptures, a fuller explanation of which students may find in the writings of our preceptor, Mr. Philip (*prolixiorem explicationem requirant studiosi in scriptis D. Philippi, praeceptoris nostri*)." And when, in the subsequent controversy, Pfeffinger was publicly assailed by Amsdorf, Flacius, and others, everybody knew that their real target was none other than — Master Philip. Melanchthon, too, was well aware of this fact. In his *Opinion on the Weimar Confutation*, of March 9, 1559, in which the synergism of the Philippists is extensively treated, he said: "As to free will, it is apparent that they attack me, Philip, in particular." (*C. R.* 9, 763.)

### 158. Strigel and Huegel Entering Controversy.

The synergistic controversy received new zest and a new impetus when, in 1559, Victorin Strigel and Huegel (Hugelius), respectively professor and pastor at Jena, the stronghold of the opponents of the Wittenberg

Philippists, opposed Flacius, espoused the cause of Pfeffinger, championed the doctrine of Melanchthon, and refused to endorse the so-called *Book of Confutation* which Flacius had caused to be drafted particularly against the Wittenberg Philippists and Synergists, and to be introduced. The situation thus created was all the more sensational, because, in the preceding controversies, Strigel had, at least apparently, always sided with the opponents of the Philippists.

The "*Konfutationsbuch* — Book of Confutation and Condemnations of the Chief Corruptions, Sects, and Errors Breaking in and Spreading at this Time" was published in 1559 by Duke John Frederick II as a doctrinal norm of his duchy. In nine chapters this Book, a sort of forerunner of the *Formula of Concord*, dealt with the errors 1. of Servetus, 2. of Schwenckfeld, 3. of the Antinomians, 4. of the Anabaptists, 5. of the Zwinglians, 6. of the Synergists, 7. of Osiander and Stancarus, 8. of the Majorists, 9. of the Adiaphorists. Its chief object, as expressly stated in the Preface, was to warn against the errors introduced by the Philippists, whose doctrines, as also Planck admits, were not in any way misrepresented in this document. (4, 597. 595.) The sixth part, directed against synergism, bore the title: "*Confutatio Corruptelarum in Articulo de Libero Arbitrio sive de Viribus Humanis* — Confutation of the Corruptions in the Article Concerning Free Will or Concerning the Human Powers." The *Confutation* was framed by the Jena theologians, Strigel and Huegel also participating in its composition. However, some of the references to the corruptions of the Philippists must have been rather vague and ambiguous in the first draft of the book; for when it was revised at the convention in Weimar, Flacius secured the adoption of additions and changes dealing particularly with the synergism of the Wittenbergers, which were energetically opposed by Strigel.

Even before the adoption of the *Book of Confutation*, Strigel had been polemicizing against Flacius. But now (as Flacius reports) he began to denounce him at every occasion as the "architect of a new theology" and an "enemy of the *Augsburg Confession*." At the same time he also endeavored to incite the students in Jena against him. Flacius, in turn, charged Strigel with scheming to establish a Philippistic party in Ducal Saxony. The public breach came when the *Book of Confutation* was submitted for adoption and publication in the churches and schools. Pastor Huegel refused to read and explain it from the pulpit, and Strigel presented his objections to the Duke, and asked that his conscience be spared. But when Strigel failed to maintain silence in the matter, he as well as Pastor Huegel were summarily dealt with by the Duke. On March 27, 1559, at two o'clock in the morning, both were suddenly arrested and imprisoned. Flacius, who was generally regarded as the secret instigator of this act of violence, declared publicly that the arrest had been made without

his counsel and knowledge. About six months later (September 5, 1569) Strigel and Huegel, after making some doctrinal concessions and promising not to enter into any disputation on the Confutation, were set at liberty. (Planck 4, 591. 604.)

## 159. Weimar Disputation.

In order to settle the differences, Flacius and his colleagues (Wigand, Judex, Simon Musaeus), as well as Strigel, asked for a public disputation, which John Frederick, too, was all the more willing to arrange because dissatisfaction with his drastic procedure against Strigel and Huegel was openly displayed everywhere outside of Ducal Saxony. The disputation was held at Weimar, August 2 to 8, 1560. It was attended by the Saxon Dukes and their entire courts, as well as by a large number of other spectators, not only from Jena, but also from Erfurt, Wittenberg, and Leipzig. The subjects of discussion, for which both parties had submitted theses, were: Free Will, Gospel, Majorism, Adiaphorism, and Indifferentism (*academica epoche*, toleration of error). The disputing parties (Flacius and Strigel) agreed that "the only rule should be the Word of God, and that a clear, plain text of the Holy Scriptures was to weigh more than all the inferences and authorities of interpreters." (Planck 4, 606.)

According to the proceedings of the Weimar Disputation, written by Wigand and published by Simon Musaeus 1562 and 1563 under the title: "*Disputatio de Originali Peccato et Libero Arbitrio inter M. Flacium Illyr. et Vict. Strigelium Publice Vinariae Anno 1560 Habita,*" the only questions discussed were free will and, incidentally, original sin. Strigel defended the Melanchthonian doctrine, according to which the causes of conversion are the Holy Spirit, the Word of God, and the will of man feebly assenting to the Gospel and, at the same time, seeking strength from God. He repeated the formula: "Concurrunt in conversione haec tria: Spiritus Sanctus movens corda, vox Dei, voluntas hominis, quae voci divinae assentitur." Flacius, on the other hand, defended the *mere passive* of Luther, according to which man, before he is converted and endowed with faith, does not in any way cooperate with the Holy Spirit, but merely suffers and experiences His operations. At the same time, however, he seriously damaged and discredited himself as well as the sacred cause of divine truth by maintaining that original sin is not a mere accident, such as Strigel maintained, but the very substance of man. The discussions were discontinued after the thirteenth session. The Duke announced that the disputation would be reopened later, charging both parties in the mean time to maintain silence in public, — a compromise to which Flacius and his adherents were loath to consent.

John Wigand and Matthias Judex, however, continued to enforce the *Book of Confutation*, demanding an unqualified adoption in every point, *per omnia*. When the jurist Matthew

Wesenbecius declined to accept the book in this categorical way, he was not permitted to serve as sponsor at a baptism. John Frederick was dissatisfied with this procedure and action of the ministers; and when they persisted in their demands, the autocratic Duke deprived them of the right to excommunicate, vesting this power in a consistory established at Weimar. Flacius and his adherents protested against this measure as tyranny exercised over the Church and a suppression of the pure doctrine. As a result Musaeus, Judex, Wigand, and Flacius were suspended and expelled from Jena, December, 1561. (Gieseler 3, 2, 244. 247.) Their vacant chairs at the university were filled by Freihub, Salmuth, and Selneccer, who had been recommended by the Wittenberg Philippists at the request of the Duke, who now evidently favored a compromise with the Synergists. Strigel, too, was reinstated at Jena after signing an ambiguous declaration.

Amsdorf, Gallus, Hesshusius, Flacius, and the other exiled theologians denounced Strigel's declaration as insincere and in conflict with Luther's book *De Servo Arbitrio*, and demanded a public retraction of his synergistic statements. When the ministers of Ducal Saxony also declined to acknowledge Strigel's orthodoxy, a more definite "Superdeclaration," framed by Moerlin and Stoessel (but not signed by Strigel), was added as an interpretation of Strigel's declaration. But even now a minority refused to submit to the demands of the Duke, because they felt that they were being deceived by ambiguous terms, such as "capacity" and "aptitude," which the wily Strigel and the Synergists used in the active or positive, and not in the passive sense. These conscientious Lutherans, whom the rationalist Planck brands as "almost insane, *beinahe verrueckt*," were also deposed and banished, 1562. Strigel's declaration of March, 1562, however, maintaining that "the will is passive in so far as God alone works all good, but active in so far as it must be present in its conversion, must consent, and not resist, but accept," showed that he had not abandoned his synergism. In the same year he applied for, and accepted, a professorship in Leipzig. Later on he occupied a chair at the Reformed university in Heidelberg, where he died 1569, at the age of only forty-five years.

In 1567, when John William became ruler of Ducal Saxony, the Philippists were dismissed, and the banished Lutheran pastors and professors (with the exception of Flacius) were recalled and reinstated. While this rehabilitation of the loyal Lutherans formally ended the synergistic controversy in Ducal Saxony, occasional echoes of it still lingered, due especially to the fact that some ministers had considered Strigel's ambiguous declaration a satisfactory presentation of the Lutheran truth with regard to the questions involved. That the synergistic teaching of Melanchthon was continued in Wittenberg appears, for example, from the *Confessio Wittenbergica* of 1570.

## 160. Strigel's Rationalistic Principle.

Although at the opening of the disputation the debaters had agreed to decide all questions by clear Scripture-passages alone, Strigel's guiding principle was in reality not the Bible, but philosophy and reason. His real concern was not, What does Scripture teach concerning the causes of conversion? but, How may we harmonize the universal grace of God with the fact that only some are converted and saved? Self-evidently Strigel, too, quoted Bible-passages. Among others, he appealed to such texts as John 6, 29; Rom. 1, 16; 10, 17; Luke 8, 18; Heb. 4, 2; Rev. 3, 20; Luke 11, 13; Mark 9, 24; 1 Thess. 2, 13; Jas. 1, 18. But as we shall show later, his deductions were philosophical and sophistical rather than exegetical and Scriptural. Preger remarks: In his disputation Strigel was not able to advance a single decisive passage of Scripture for the presence and cooperation of a good will at the moment when it is approached and influenced (*ergriffen*) by grace. (2, 211.) And the clear, irrefutable Bible-texts on which Flacius founded his doctrine of the inability of natural will to cooperate in conversion, Strigel endeavored to invalidate by philosophical reasoning, indirect arguing, and alleged necessary logical consequences.

At Weimar and in his *Confession* of December 5, 1560, delivered to the Duke soon after the disputation, Strigel argued: Whoever denies that man, in a way and measure, is able to cooperate in his own conversion is logically compelled also to deny that the rejection of grace may be imputed to man; compelled to make God responsible for man's damnation; to surrender the universality of God's grace and call; to admit contradictory wills in God; and to take recourse to an absolute decree of election and reprobation in order to account for the fact that some reject the grace of God and are lost while others are converted and saved. At Weimar Strigel declared: "I do not say that the will is able to assent to the Word without the Holy Spirit, but that, being moved and assisted by the Spirit, it assents with trepidation. If we were unable to do this, we would not be responsible for not having received the Word. *Si hoc [utcumque assentiri inter trepidationes] non possemus, non essemus rei propter Verbum non receptum.*" Again, also at Weimar: "If the will is not able to assent in some way, even when assisted, then we cannot be responsible for rejecting the Word, but the blame must be transferred to another, and others may judge how religious that is. *Si voluntas ne quidem adiuta potest aliquo modo annuere, non possumus esse rei propter Verbum reiectum, sed culpa est in alium transferenda, quod quam sit religiosum, alii iudicent.*" (Planck 4, 689. 719; Luthardt, *Lehre vom freien Willen*, 222.)

Over against this rationalistic method of Strigel and the Synergists generally, the Lutherans adhered to the principle that nothing but a clear passage of the Bible can decide a theological question. They rejected as false philosophy and rationalism every argument directed against the clear sense of a clear Word of God. They emphatically objected to the employment of reason for establishing a Christian doctrine or subverting a statement of the Bible. At Weimar, Flacius protested again and again that human reason is not an authority in theological matters. "Let us hear the Scriptures! *Audiamus Scripturam!*" "Let the woman be silent in the Church! *Mulier taceat in ecclesia!*" With such slogans he brushed aside the alleged necessary logical inferences and deductions of Strigel. "You take your arguments from philosophy," he said in the second session, "which ought not to be given a place in matters of religion. *Disputas ex philosophia, cui locus in rebus religionis esse non debet.*" Again, at Weimar: "It is against the nature of inquiring truth to insist on arguing from blind philosophy. What else corrupted such ancient theologians as Clement, Origen, Chrysostom, and afterwards also the Sophists [scholastic theologians] but that they endeavored to decide spiritual things by philosophy, which does not understand the secret and hidden mysteries of God. *Est contra naturam inquirendae veritatis, si velimus ex caeca philosophia loqui. Quid aliud corrupit theologos veteres, ut Clementem, Originem, Chrysosthomum et postea etiam Sophistas, nisi quod de rebus divinis ex philosophia voluerunt statuere, quae non intelligit abstrusissima et occultissima mysteria Dei.*" "May we therefore observe the rule of Luther: Let the woman be silent in the Church! For what a miserable thing would it be if we had to judge ecclesiastical matters from logic! *Itaque observemus legem Lutheri: Taceat mulier in ecclesia! Quae enim miseria, si ex dialectica diiudicandae nobis essent res ecclesiae!*" (Planck 4, 709.)

In an antisynergistic confession published by Schluesselburg, we read: "This doctrine [of conversion by God's grace alone] is simple, clear, certain, and irrefutable if one looks to God's Word alone and derives the *Nosce teipsum*, Know thyself, from the wisdom of God. But since poor men are blind, they love their darkness more than the light, as Christ says John 3, and insist on criticizing and falsifying God's truth by means of blind philosophy, which, forsooth, is a shame and a palpable sin, if we but had eyes to see and know. . . . Whatsoever blind reason produces in such articles of faith against the Word of God is false and wrong. For it is said: *Mulier in ecclesia taceat!* Let philosophy and human wisdom be silent in the Church." (*Catalogus* 5, 665 f.) Here, too, the sophistical objections of the Synergists are disposed of with such remarks as: "In the first place, this is but spun from reason, which thus acts wise in these matters. *Denn fuers erste ist solches nur aus der Vernunft gesponnen, die weiss also hierin zu kluegeln.*" (668.) "This is all spun from reason; but God's Word teaches us better. *Dies ist alles aus der Vernunft spintisiert; Gottes Wort aber lehrt es besser.*" (670.)

Evidently Strigel's rationalistic method was identical with that employed by Melanchthon in his *Loci*, by Pfeffinger, and the Synergists generally. Accordingly, his synergism also could not differ essentially from Melanchthon's. Planck pertinently remarks: "It is apparent from this [argument of Strigel that natural man must have power to cooperate in his conversion because otherwise God would be responsible for his resistance and damnation] that his synergism was none other than that of the Wittenberg school; for was not this the identical foundation upon which Melanchthon had reared his [synergism]?" (4, 690.) Like methods lead to the same results, and *vice versa.* Besides, Strigel had always appealed to the Wittenbergers; and in his *Opinion on the Weimar Confutation,* 1559, Melanchthon, in turn, identified himself with Strigel's arguments. (*C. R.* 9, 766.) The "Confession and Opinion of the Wittenbergers Concerning Free Will — *Confessio et Sententia Wittebergensium de Libero Arbitrio*" of 1561 also maintained the same attitude.

### 161. Strigel's Theory.

Strigel's views concerning the freedom of man's will in spiritual matters may be summarized as follows: Man, having a will, is a free agent, hence always able to decide for or against. This ability is the "mode of action" essential to man as long as he really is a man and in possession of a will. Even in matters pertaining to grace this freedom was not entirely lost in the Fall. It was impeded and weakened by original sin, but not annihilated. To be converted, man therefore requires that these residual or remaining powers be excited and strengthened rather than that new spiritual powers be imparted or a new will be created. Accordingly, persuasion through the Word is the method of conversion employed by the Holy Spirit. When the will is approached by the Word, incited and assisted by the Spirit, it is able to admit the operations of the Spirit and assent to the Word, though but feebly. Hence, no matter how much of the work of conversion must be ascribed to the Holy Spirit and the Word, the will itself, in the last analysis, decides for or against grace. Man is, therefore, not purely passive in his conversion, but cooperates with the Holy Spirit and the Word, not merely after, but also in his conversion, before he has received the gift of faith.

"God who, outside of His essence in external actions, is the freest agent," said Strigel, "created two kinds of natures, the one free, the other acting naturally (*naturaliter agentes*). The free natures are the angels and men. Those acting naturally embrace all the rest of the creatures. A natural agent is one that cannot do anything else [than it does], nor suspend its action; *e. g.,* fire. Men and angels were created differently, after the image of God, that they might be free agents. *Homines et angeli aliter conditi sunt ad imaginem Dei, ut sint liberum agens.*" (Planck 4, 669.) This freedom, which distinguishes man essentially from all other creatures, according to Strigel, always implies the power to will or not to will with respect to any object. He says: The act of willing, be it good or evil, always belongs to the will, because the will is so created *that it can will or not*, without coercion. "*Ipsum velle, seu bonum seu malum, quod ad substantiam attinet, semper est voluntatis; quia voluntas sic est condita,* UT POSSIT VELLE AUT NON; *sed etiam hoc habet voluntas ex opere creationis, quod adhuc reliquum, et non prorsus abolitum et extinctum est,* UT POSSIT VELLE AUT NON, SINE COACTIONE." (674.) According to Strigel, the very essence of the will consists in being able, in every instance, to decide in either direction, for or against. Hence the very idea of will involves also a certain ability to cooperate in conversion. (689.)

This freedom or ability to decide *pro* or *con*, says Strigel, is the mode of action essential to man, his mode of action also in conversion. And in the controversy on free will he sought to maintain that this alleged mode of action was a part of the very essence of the human will and being. At Weimar Strigel declared: "I do not wish to detract from the will the mode of action which is different from other natural actions. *Nolo voluntati detrahi modum agendi, qui est dissimilis aliis actionibus naturalibus.*" (Planck 4, 668.) Again: "The will is not a natural, but a free agent; hence the will is converted not as a natural agent, but as a free agent. . . . In conversion the will acts in its own mode; it is not a statue or a log in conversion. Hence conversion does not occur in a purely passive manner. *Voluntas non est agens naturale, sed liberum; ergo convertitur voluntas non ut naturalitur agens, sed ut liberum agens. . . . Et voluntas suo modo agit in conversione, nec est statua vel truncus in conversione. Et per consequens non fit conversio pure passive.*" (Luthardt, 217. 219. 209.)

What Strigel means is that man, being a free agent, must, also in conversion, be accorded the ability somehow to decide for grace. According to the *Formula of Concord* the words, "man's mode of action," signify "a way of working something good and salutary in divine things." (905, 61.) The connection and the manner in which the phrase was employed by Strigel admitted of no other interpretation. Strigel added: This mode of action marks the difference between the will of man and the will of Satan; for the devil neither endeavors to assent, nor prays to God for assistance, while man does. (Luthardt, 220.) Natural man is by Strigel credited with the power of "endeavoring to assent, *conari assentiri,*" because he is endowed with a will. But shrewd as Strigel was, it did not occur to him that, logically, his argument compelled him to ascribe also to the devils everything he claimed for natural man, since they, too, have a will and are therefore endowed with the same *modus agendi*, which, according to Strigel, belongs to the very idea and essence of will. Yet this palpable truth, which overthrew his entire theory, failed to open the eyes of Strigel.

If, as Strigel maintained, the human will, by virtue of its nature as a free agent, is, in

a way, *able* to cooperate in conversion, then the only question is how to elevate this ability to an actuality, in other words, how to influence the will and rouse its powers to move in the right direction. Strigel answered: Since the will cannot be forced, moral suasion is the true method required to convert a man. "The will," says he, "cannot be forced, hence it is by persuasion, *i. e.*, by pointing out something good or evil, that the will is moved to obey and to submit' to the Gospel; not coerced, *but somehow willing. Voluntas non potest cogi, ergo voluntas persuadendo, id est, ostensione alicuius boni vel mali flectitur ad obediendum et obtemperandum evangelio, non coacta, sed* ALIQUO MODO VOLENS." (Seeberg 4, 491.) Again: "Although God is efficacious through the Word, drawing and leading us efficaciously, yet He does not make assenting necessary for such a nature as the will, — a nature so created that it is able not to assent, if it so wills, and to expel Him who dwells in us. This assent therefore is the work of God and the Holy Spirit, but in so far as it is a free assent, not coerced and pressed out by force, *it is also the work of the will. Etiamsi Deus est efficax per Verbum et efficaciter nos trahit et ducit, tamen non affert necessitatem assentiendi tali naturae, qualis est voluntas, id est, quae sic est condita, ut possit non assentiri, si velit, et excutere sessorem. Est igitur hic assensus opus Dei et Spiritus Sancti, sed quatenus est liber assensus, non coactus, expressus vi,* EST ETIAM VOLUNTATIS." (491.) Strigel evidently means: The fact that man is able not to assent to grace of necessity involves that somehow (*aliquo modo*) he is able also to assent; according to man's peculiar mode of action (freedom), he must himself actualize his conversion by previously (in the logical order) willing it, deciding for it, and assenting to it; he would be converted by coercion if his assent to grace were an act of the will engendered and created solely by God, rather than an act effected and produced by the powers of the will when incited and assisted by the Spirit. Man is converted by persuasion only, because God does not create assent and faith in him, but merely elicits these acts from man by liberating and appealing to the powers of his will to effect and produce them.

In defending this freedom of the will, Strigel appealed also to the statement of Luther: "The will cannot be coerced; . . . if the will could be coerced, it would not be volition, but rather nolition. *Voluntas non potest cogi; . . . si posset cogi voluntas, non esset voluntas, sed potius noluntas.*" However, what Luther said of the form or nature of the will, according to which it always really wills what it wills, and is therefore never coerced, was by Strigel transferred to the spiritual matters and objects of the will. According to Strigel's theory, says Seeberg, "the will must be free even in the first moment of conversion, free not only in the psychological, but also in the moral sense." (4, 492.) Tschackert, quoting Seeberg, remarks that Strigel transformed the natural formal liberty into an ethical material liberty — *"indem die natuerliche for-male Freiheit sich ihm unter der Hand [?] verwandelte in die ethische materiale Frei-heit."* (524.)

### 162. Strigel's Semi-Pelagianism.

Strigel's entire position is based on the error that a remnant of spiritual ability still remains in natural man. True, he taught that in consequence of original sin the powers of man and the proper use and exercise of these powers are greatly impeded, weakened, checked, and insulated, as it were, and that this impediment can be removed solely by the operation of the Holy Spirit. "Through the Word the Holy Spirit restores to the will the power and faculty of believing," Strigel declared. (Luthardt, 250.) But this restora-tion, he said, was brought about by liberat-ing, arousing, inciting, and strengthening the powers inherent in man rather than by divine impartation of new spiritual powers or by the creation of a new good volition.

Strigel plainly denied that natural man is truly spiritually dead. He declared: "The will is so created that it can expel the Holy Spirit and the Word, or, when assisted by the Holy Spirit, can in some manner will and obey — to receive is the act of the will; in this I cannot concede that man is simply *dead — accipere est hominis; in hoc non pos-sum concedere simpliciter mortuum esse homi-nem."* (Frank 1, 199.) Natural man, Strigel explained, is indeed not able to grasp the helping hand of God with his own hand; yet the latter is not dead, but still retains a minimum of power. (678.) Again: Man is like a new-born child, whose powers must first be strengthened with nourishment given it by its mother, and which, *though able to draw this nourishment out of its mother's breast,* is yet unable to lift itself up to it, or to take hold of the breast, unless it be given it. (Preger 2, 209.)

With special reference to the last illustra-tion, Flacius declared: "Strigel, accordingly, holds that we have the faculty to desire and receive the food, *i. e.,* the benefits of God. For-sooth, you thereby attribute to corrupt man a very great power with respect to spiritual things. Now, then, deny that this opinion is Pelagian." (209.) "Your statements agree with those of Pelagius; yet I do not simply say that you are a Pelagian; for a good man may fall into an error which he does not see." Pelagius held that man, by his natural powers, is able to begin and complete his own conversion; Cassianus, the Semi-Pelagian, taught that man is able merely to begin this work; Strigel maintained that man can ad-mit the liberating operation of the Holy Spirit, and that after such operation of the Spirit he is able to cooperate with his natural powers. Evidently, then, the verdict of Fla-cius was not much beside the mark. Planck, though unwilling to relegate Strigel to the Pelagians, does not hesitate to put him down as a thoroughgoing Synergist. (Planck 4, 683 f.) Synergism, however, always includes at least an element of Pelagianism.

Strigel illustrated his idea by the following analogy. When garlic-juice is applied to a magnet, it loses its power of attraction, but remains a true magnet, and, when goat's blood is applied, immediately regains its efficacious-ness. So the will of man is hindered by origi-nal sin from beginning that which is good; but when the impediment has been removed through the operation of the Holy Spirit, the native powers of the will again become effica-cious and active. (Tschackert, 524; Planck 4, 672; Preger 2, 198; Luthardt, 211.) Frank remarks: "The example of the temporarily impeded power of the magnet, which was re-peated also at this juncture [in the disputa-tion at Weimar], immediately points to the related papal doctrine; for the Catholic An-dradius explains the dogma of the *Tridenti-num* to this effect: The free will of natural man may be compared to a chained prisoner, who, though still in possession of his loco-motive powers, is nevertheless impeded by his fetters." (1, 136.) Also the *Formula of Con-cord,* evidently with a squint at Strigel, re-jects as a Pelagian error the teaching "that original sin is not a despoliation or deficiency, but only an external impediment to these spir-itual good powers, as when a magnet is smeared with garlic-juice, whereby its natu-ral power is not removed, but only hindered; or that this stain can be easily washed away, as a spot from the face or a pigment from the wall." (865, 22.)

### 163. Strigel's "Cooperation."

When the impediment caused by original sin has been removed, and the will liberated and aroused to activity, man, according to Strigel, is able also to cooperate in his con-version. At Weimar he formulated the point at issue as follows: "The question is whether [in conversion] the will is present idle, as an inactive, indolent subject, or, as the common saying is, in a purely passive way; or whether, when grace precedes, the will follows the efficacy of the Holy Spirit, and in some manner assents — *an vero praeeunte gratia voluntas comitetur efficaciam Spiritus Sancti et aliquo modo annuat."* (Luthardt, 222.) Following are some of his answers to this question: When incited by the Spirit, the will is able to assent somewhat and to pray for assistance. *Inter trepidationem utcumque assentitur, simul petens auxilium.* Contrition and faith, as well as other virtues, are gifts of God, "but they are given to those only who hear and contemplate God's Word, embrace it by assenting to it, strive against their doubts, and in this conflict pray for the help of God." (230.) The Holy Ghost converts those "who hear the Word of God and do not resist stub-bornly, but consent," and God assists such only "as follow His call and pray for assist-ance." (229.) "The will and heart do not re-sist altogether, but desire divine consolation, when, indeed, they are assisted by the Holy Ghost." "The will is neither idle nor con-tumacious; but, in a manner, desires to obey." (Planck 4, 682.) "Man is dead [spir-itually] in as far as he is not able to heal his wounds with his own powers; but when the remedy is offered him by the Holy Spirit and the Word, then he, at least in receiving the benefit, is not altogether dead; for otherwise a conversion could not occur. For I cannot conceive a conversion where the process is that of the flame consuming straw (*denn ich kann mir keine Bekehrung vorstellen, bei der es zugeht, wie wenn die Flamme das Stroh ergreift*). The nature of the will is such that it can reject the Holy Spirit and the Word; or, being supported by the Holy Spirit, can in a manner will and obey. The remedy is heavenly and divine; but the will — not the will alone, but the will supported by the Holy Spirit — is able to accept it. One must ascribe at least a feeble consent and an 'Aye' to the will, which is already supported by the Holy Spirit." (Preger 2, 208.) "In a betrothal, consent is necessary; conversion is a betrothal of Christ to the Church and its individual members; hence consent is required," which the will is able to give when assisted by the Holy Spirit. (Luthardt, 224.)

It is, however, only a languid, wavering, and weak consent which man is able to render (*qualiscumque assensio languida, trepida et imbecilla*). "Compared with the divine operation," Flacius reports Strigel as having said, "the cooperation of our powers in conversion is something extremely small (*quiddam pertenue prorsus*). If, after drinking with a rich man, he paying a *taler* and I a *heller*, I would afterwards boast that I had been drinking and paying with him — such is cooperation, *talis est synergia*." (Planck 4, 677; Luthardt, 220. 222.) According to Strigel, therefore, man is not purely passive, but plays an active part in his conversion. With Melanchthon and Pfeffinger he maintained: "These three concur in conversion: the Holy Spirit, who moves the hearts; the voice of God; the will of man, which assents to the divine voice. *Concurrunt in conversione haec tria: Spiritus Sanctus movens corda, vox Dei, voluntas hominis, quae voci divinae assentitur.*" (Tschackert, 524.)

Flacius declared with respect to the issue formulated by Strigel: "I explain my entire view as follows: "Man is purely passive (*homo se habet pure passive*). If you consider the native faculty of the will, its willing and its powers, then he is purely passive when he receives (*in accipiendo*). But if that divinely bestowed willing or spark of faith kindled by the Spirit is considered, then this imparted willing and this spark is not purely passive. But the Adamic will does not only not operate or cooperate, but, according to the inborn malice of the heart, even operates contrarily (*verum etiam pro nativa malitia cordis sui contra operatur*)." (Planck 4, 697.) Thus Flacius clearly distinguished between cooperation *before* conversion (which he rejected absolutely) and cooperation *after* conversion (which he allowed). And pressing this point, he said to Strigel: "I ask whether you say that the will cooperates *before* the gift of faith or *after* faith has been received; whether you say that the will cooperates from

natural powers, or in so far as the good volition has been bestowed by the renovation of the Holy Spirit. *Quaero, an dicas, voluntatem cooperari ante donum fidei aut post acceptam fidem; an dicas, cooperari ex naturalibus viribus aut quatenus ex renovatione Spiritus Sancti datum est bene velle.*" (Seeberg 4, 492.) Again: I shall withdraw the charge of Pelagianism if you will declare it as your opinion "that only the regenerated, sanctified, renewed will cooperates, and not the other human, carnal, natural will." "Confess openly and expressly and say clearly: 'I affirm that man cooperates from faith and the good will bestowed by God, not from the will he brings with him from his natural Adam — *quod homo cooperetur ex fide et bono velle divinitus donato, non ex eo, quod attulit ex suo naturali Adamo.*'" "We say, Only the regenerate will cooperates; if you [Strigel] say the same, the controversy is at an end." Strigel, however, who, to use a phrase of Luther (St. L. 18, 1673), was just as hard to catch as Proteus of old, did not reply with a definite *yes* or *no*, but repeated that it was only a weak assent (*qualiscumque assensio languida trepida et imbecilla*) which man was able to render when his will was incited and supported by the prevenient grace of the Holy Spirit. (Preger 2, 217; Luthardt, 217. 222. 227; Frank 1, 115.)

### 164. Objections Answered.

At Weimar, Strigel insisted: The human will must not be eliminated as one of the causes of conversion; for without man's will and intellect no conversion is possible. Flacius replied: The will, indeed, is present in conversion, for it is the will that is converted and experiences conversion; but the inborn power of the natural will contributes nothing to conversion, and therefore the will "is purely passive in the reception of grace." (Preger 2, 217.) "We are pressed hard with the sophistical objection that man is not converted without his knowledge and will. But who doubts this? The entire question is: Whence does that good knowledge originate? Whence does that good volition originate?" (216.) "We certainly admit that in conversion there are many motions of the intellect and will, good and bad. But the dispute among us is not whether in conversion the intellect understands and the will wills; but whence is the capability to think right, and whence is that good willing of the will? Is it of us, as of ourselves, or is this sufficiency of willing and thinking of God alone?" (Planck 4, 711.) The fact that God alone converts man, said Flacius, "does not exclude the presence of the will; but it does exclude all efficaciousness and operation of the natural will in conversion (*non excludit voluntatem, ne adsit, sed excludit omnem efficaciam et operationem naturalis voluntatis in conversione*)." (Seeberg 4, 492.)

In order to prove man's cooperation in conversion, Strigel declared: "Both [to will and to perform] are in some way acts of God and of ourselves; for no willing and performing takes place unless we will. *Utrumque* [*velle et perficere*] *aliquo modo Dei et nostrum est; non fit velle aut perficere nisi nobis volentibus*." Charging Strigel with ambiguity, Flacius replied: "You speak of one kind of synergism and we of another. You cannot affirm with a good conscience that these questions are unknown to you." Strigel, protesting that he was unable to see the difference, answered: "For God's sake, have a little forbearance with me; I cannot see the difference. If that is to my discredit, let it be to my discredit. — *Bitte um Gottes willen, man wolle mir's zugut halten; ich kann's nicht ausmessen. Ist mir's eine Schand', so sei mir's eine Schand'.*" (Frank 1, 136.) Strigel, however, evidently meant that man, too, has a share in *producing* the good volition, while Flacius understood the phraseology as Luther and Augustine explained it, the latter, *e. g.*, writing in *De Gratia et Libero Arbitrio*: "It is certain that we will when we will; but He who makes us will is He of whom it is written: It is God who worketh in us to will. *Certum est, nos velle cum volumus; sed ille facit, ut velimus, de quo dictum est: Deus est, qui operatur in nobis velle.*" (Frank 1, 238.)

In his objections to the doctrine that man is purely passive in his conversion, Strigel protested again and again that man is not like a block or stone when he is converted. "That is true," said Flacius, "for a block can neither love nor hate God, while man by nature hates God, and scoffs at Him. Rom. 8, 1; 1 Cor. 2. Thus God is dealing with one whose will and heart is altogether against Him. But here [in the denial that man is purely passive in conversion] is buried a popish *meritum de congruo* and a particle of free will." (Preger 2, 191.) Flacius furthermore explained that in his conversion man is able to cooperate just as little as a stone can contribute to its transformation into a statue. Indeed, man's condition is even more miserable than that of a stone or block (*miserior trunco*), because by his natural powers he resists, and cannot but resist, the operations of the Spirit. (Planck 4, 696 f.)

Strigel reasoned: If man is converted without his consent, and if he cannot but resist the operations of the Holy Spirit, conversion is an impossibility, a contradiction. He said: "If the will, even when assisted by the Holy Spirit, is unable to assent, it must of necessity resist Him perpetually, drive out, reject, and repudiate the Word and Holy Spirit; for it is impossible that motions extremely conflicting and contradictory, the one embracing, the other repudiating and persistently rejecting, should be in the same will. *Si voluntas etiam adiuta a Spiritu Sancto non potest assentiri, necesse est, ut perpetuo ei repugnet, ut excutiat, reiiciat et repudiet Verbum et Spiritum Sanctum. Nam impossibile est in eadem voluntate esse motus extreme pugnantes et contradictorios, quorum alter sit amplecti, alter repudiare et quidem perstare in reiectione.*" Flacius replied: You need but distinguish between the sinful natural will inherited from Adam, which always resists, and

the new consenting will implanted by God in conversion. "Man consents with the faith given by God, but he resists with the inborn wickedness of his Old Adam." Your error is that you acknowledge only an inciting grace, which mere incitation presupposes powers of one's own to do and to perform (*talis incitatio includit proprias vires ad perficiendum*). "I plead," said Flacius, "that by original sin man is not only wounded, but, as the Scriptures affirm, entirely dead, and his faculties to do that which is good have been destroyed; on the other hand, however, he is alive and vigorous toward evil (*hominem . . . penitus esse mortuum, extinctum et interfectum ad bonum et contra insuper vivum et vigentem ad malum*)." "The will is free with respect to things beneath itself, but not with respect to things above itself. In spiritual matters it is a servant of Satan." Hence, said Flacius, in order to cooperate, new spiritual life must first be imparted to, and created in, man by the grace of God. (Planck 4, 693 ff.; Frank 1, 224 ff.; Luthardt, 224; Preger 2, 216.)

Strigel argued: If man is able only to sin and to resist the grace of God, he cannot be held accountable for his actions. But Flacius replied: "Also the non-regenerate are justly accused [made responsible for their actions]; for with the remnant of the carnal liberty they are able at least to observe external decency (*Zucht*), which God earnestly demands of us, for example, to hear God's Word, to go to church more frequently than into the tavern." "Furthermore, there are many carnal transgressions in which natural man could have done something which he has not done." "God may justly hold us responsible also with respect to things which we are unable to do, because He has bestowed uninjured powers upon the human race, which, though forewarned, man has shamefully lost through his own fault." (Preger 2, 214 f.)

Time and again Strigel told Flacius that according to his doctrine man is coerced to sin and compelled to resist the grace of God. But the latter replied: As far as his own powers are concerned, the natural will of man indeed sins and resists inevitably and of necessity (*voluntas repugnat necessario et inevitabiliter*), but not by coercion or compulsion. Necessity to resist (*necessitas repugnandi*), Flacius explained, does not involve coercion to resist (*coactio repugnandi*), since there is such a thing as a necessity of immutability (*necessitas immutabilitatis*), that is to say, man may be unable to act otherwise and yet act willingly. The impossibility of being able to will otherwise than one really wills, does, according to Flacius, not at all involve coercion or compulsion. The holy angels are free from compulsion, although they cannot sin or fall any more. It is the highest degree of freedom and Christian perfection when, in the life to come, our will to remain in union with God is elevated to immutability of so willing. Again, though Satan cannot but sin, yet he is not coerced to sin. Thus, too, of his own powers, natural man is able only to resist grace, yet there is no compulsion involved. The fact, therefore, that natural man cannot but sin and resist grace does not warrant the inference that he is compelled to sin; nor does the fact that natural man is not coerced to resist prove that he is able also to assent to grace. The fact, said Flacius, that the wicked *willingly* will, think, and do only what pleases Satan does not prove an ability to will in the opposite spiritual direction, but merely reveals the terrible extent of Satan's tyrannical power over natural man. (Luthardt, 224. 231.) According to Flacius, the will always wills willingly when it wills and what it wills. In brief: The categories "coercion" and "compulsion" cannot be applied to the will. This, however, does not imply that God is not able to *create* or restore a good will without coercion or compulsion. There was no coercion or compulsion involved when God, creating Adam, Eve, and the angels, endowed them with a good will. Nor is there any such thing as coercion or compulsion when God, in conversion, bestows faith and a good will upon man.

In his statements on the freedom of the will, Flacius merely repeated what Luther had written before him, in *De Servo Arbitrio:* "For if it is not we, but God alone, who works salvation in us, then nothing that we do previous to His work, whether we will or not, is salutary. But when I say, 'by necessity,' I do not mean by coercion, but, as they say, by the necessity of immutability, not by necessity of coercion, *i. e.*, man, destitute of the Spirit of God, does not sin perforce, as though seized by the neck [stretched upon the rack], nor unwillingly, as a thief or robber is led to his punishment, but spontaneously and willingly. And by his own strength he cannot omit, restrain, or change this desire or willingness to sin, but continues to will it and to find pleasure in it. For even if he is compelled by force, outwardly to do something else, within, the will nevertheless remains averse, and rages against him who compels or resists it. For if it were changed and willingly yielded to force, it would not be angry. And this we call the necessity of immutability, *i. e.*, the will cannot change itself and turn to something else, but is rather provoked to will more intensely by being resisted, as is proved by its indignation. *Si enim non nos, sed solus Deus operatur salutem in nobis, nihil ante opus eius operamur salutare, velimus nolimus. Necessario vero dico,* NON COACTE, *sed, ut illi dicunt, necessitate immutabilitatis,* NON COACTIONIS; *id est, homo cum vacat Spiritu Dei,* NON QUIDEM VIOLENTIA, *velut raptus obtorto collo,* NOLENS *facit peccatum, quemadmodum fur aut latro nolens ad poenam ducitur, sed sponte et libenti voluntate facit. Verum hanc libentiam seu voluntatem faciendi non potest suis viribus omittere, coercere aut mutare, sed pergit volendo et lubendo; etiamsi ad extra cogatur aliud facere per vim, tamen voluntas intus manet aversa et indignatur cogenti aut resistenti. Non enim indignaretur, si mutaretur ac volens vim sequeretur. Hoc vocamus modo necessitatem immutabilitatis, id est, quod*

*voluntas sese mutare et vertere alio non possit, sed potius irritetur magis ad volendum, dum ei resistitur, quod probat eius indignatio."* (E. v. a. 7, 155 f. 134. 157; St. L. 18, 1717. 1692. 1718.)

Flacius was also charged with teaching that "man is converted resisting (*hominem converti repugnantem*). "In their *Confession and Opinion Concerning Free Will*, of 1561, the Wittenberg theologians repeated the assertion that Flacius taught "*converti hominem . . . repugnantem et hostiliter Deo convertenti adversantem.*" (Planck 4, 688.) But Flacius protested: "I do not simply say that man is converted resisting (*hominem repugnantem converti*). But I say that he resists with respect to his natural and carnal free will." "It is not denied that God converts us as willing and understanding (*quin Deus nos convertat volentes et intelligentes*), but willing and understanding not from the Old Adam, but from the light given by God and from the good volition bestowed through the Word and the Holy Spirit." (692.) "Man is converted or drawn by the Father to the Son not as a thief is cast into prison, but in such a manner that his evil will is changed into a good will by the power of the Holy Spirit." (Preger 2, 218.) It is the very essence of conversion that by the grace of God unwilling men are made willing.

In support of his error that natural man is able to cooperate in his conversion Strigel appealed to Rom. 8, 26: "Likewise the Spirit also helpeth our infirmities," etc.; and appealing to the *Augustana* for the correctness of his interpretation, he declared that this passage proves that one may speak of a languid and weak assent in man even before he is endowed with faith. Flacius replied that this Bible-passage referred to such only as are already converted, and that Strigel's interpretation was found not in the original *Augustana*, but in the *Variata.* — From the admonition 2 Cor. 5, 20: "Be ye reconciled to God," Strigel inferred that free will must to a certain extent be capable of accepting the grace offered by God. Flacius answered that it was a logical fallacy, conflicting also with the clear Word of God, to conclude that man by his own powers is able to perform something because God demands it and admonishes and urges us to do it. — From Acts 5, 32: ". . . the Holy Ghost, whom God hath given to them that obey Him," Strigel argued that the will is able to consent to the Holy Spirit. But Flacius rejoined that this passage refers to special gifts bestowed upon such as are already converted. — In support of his synergism, Strigel also appealed to the Parable of the Prodigal Son, who himself repented and returned to his father. But Flacius answered: If every detail of this parable taken from every-day life were to be interpreted in such a manner, Strigel would have to abandon his own teaching concerning prevenient grace, since according to the parable the repentance and return of the son precedes the grace bestowed by the father. (Preger 2, 210 f.)

### 165. Teaching of the Anti-Synergists.

While the Philippists, also in the Synergistic Controversy, endeavored to supplant the authority and doctrine of Luther by that of Melanchthon, their opponents, Amsdorf, Flacius, Wigand, Hesshusius, and others (though not always fortunate in the choice of their phraseology), stood four-square on Luther's teaching of the *sola gratia*, which, they were fully convinced, was nothing but the pure truth of the Gospel itself. They maintained that, as a result of the Fall, man has lost his original holiness and righteousness, or the image of God; that both as to his intellect and will he is totally corrupt spiritually; that of his own powers he is utterly unable to think or will anything that is truly good; that not a spark of spiritual life is found in natural man by virtue of which he might assent to the Gospel or cooperate with the Holy Spirit in his conversion; that his carnal mind is enmity toward God; that of his own powers he is active only in resisting the work of the Holy Spirit, nor is he able to do otherwise; that such resistance continues until he is converted and a new will and heart have been created in him; that conversion consists in this, that men who by nature are unwilling and resist God's grace become such as willingly consent and obey the Gospel and the Holy Spirit; that this is done solely by God's grace, through Word and Sacrament; that man is purely passive in his conversion, inasmuch as he contributes nothing towards it, and merely suffers and experiences the work of the Holy Spirit; that only after his conversion man is able to cooperate with the Holy Spirit; that such cooperation, however, flows not from innate powers of the natural will, but from the new powers imparted in conversion; that also in the converted the natural sinful will continues to oppose whatever is truly good, thus causing a conflict between the flesh and the spirit which lasts till death; in brief, that man's conversion and salvation are due to grace alone and in no respect whatever to man and his natural powers.

The *Book of Confutation*, of 1559, drafted, as stated above, by the theologians of Jena, designates the synergistic dogma as a "rejection of grace." Here we also meet with statements such as the following: Human nature "is altogether turned aside from God, and is hostile toward Him and subject to the tyranny of sin and Satan (*naturam humanam prorsus a Deo aversam eique inimicam et tyrannidi peccati ac Satanae subiectam esse*)." It is impossible for the unregenerate man "to understand or to apprehend the will of God revealed in the Word, or by his own power to convert himself to God and to will or perform anything good (*homini non renato impossibile esse intelligere aut apprehendere voluntatem Dei in Verbo patefactam aut sua ipsius voluntate ad Deum se convertere, boni aliquid velle aut perficere*)." "Our will to obey God or to choose the good is utterly extinguished and corrupted. *Voluntas nostra ad Dei obedientiam aut ad bonum eligendum prorsus extincta et depravata est.*" (Tschackert, 523; Gieseler 3, 2, 229.)

The second of the Propositions prepared by Simon Musaeus and Flacius for the Disputation at Weimar, 1560, reads: "Corrupt man cannot operate or cooperate toward anything good by true motions, and such as proceed from the heart; for his heart is altogether dead spiritually; and has utterly lost the image of God, or all powers and inclinations toward that which is good. *Homo corruptus nihil boni potest veris ac ex corde proficiscentibus motibus operari aut cooperari, nam plane est spiritualiter mortuus et Dei imaginem seu omnes bonas vires et inclinationes prorsus amisit.*" The third: Not only "has he lost entirely all good powers, but, in addition, he has also acquired contrary and most evil powers, . . . so that, of necessity or inevitably, he constantly and vehemently opposes God and true piety (*ita ut necessario seu inevitabiliter Deo ac verae pietati semper et vehementer adversetur.*" The fourth thesis states that God alone, through His Word and the Holy Spirit, converts, draws, and illumines man, kindles faith, justifies, renews, and creates him unto good works, while natural or Adamic free will is of itself not only inactive, but resists (*non solum non cooperante ex se naturali aut Adamico libero arbitrio, sed etiam contra furente ac fremente*). (Planck 4, 692; Gieseler 3, 2, 245.)

The same position was occupied by the Mansfeld ministers in a statement of August 20, 1562, and by Hesshusius in his *Confutation of the Arguments by which the Synergists Endeavor to Defend Their Error Concerning the Powers of the Dead Free Will.* They held that in his conversion man is purely passive and has no mode of action whatever; that he is but the passive subject who is to be converted (*subiectum patiens, subiectum convertendum*); that he contributes no more to his conversion than an infant to its own formation in the womb of its mother; that he is passive, like a block, inasmuch as he does not in any way cooperate, but at the same time differs from, and is worse than, a block, because he is active in resisting the Holy Spirit until he has been converted. The *Confession* presented by the theologians of Ducal Saxony (Wigand, Coelestinus, Irenaeus, Rosinus, Kirchner, etc.) at the Altenburg Colloquy, March, 1569, occupies the same doctrinal position. As stated before, these theologians made it a special point also to declare their agreement with Luther's book *De Servo Arbitrio.* (Schluesselburg 5, 316. 133.)

### 166. Attitude of Formula of Concord.

The second article of the *Formula of Concord*, which decided the questions involved in the Synergistic Controversy, takes a clear, determined, and consistent stand against all forms and formulas of synergism. At the same time it avoids all extravagant, improper, offensive, and inadequate terms and phrases, as well as the numerous pitfalls lurking everywhere in the questions concerning free will, against which also some of the opponents of the Synergists had not always sufficiently been on their guard. Article II teaches "that original sin is an unspeakable evil and such an entire corruption of human nature that in it and all its internal and external powers nothing pure or good remains, but everything is entirely corrupt, so that on account of original sin man is in God's sight truly spiritually dead, with all his powers dead to that which is good (*dass der Mensch durch die Erbsuende wahrhaftig vor Gott geistlich tot und zum Guten mit allen seinen Kraeften erstorben sei*)" (CONC. TRIGL. 879, 60); "that in spiritual and divine things the intellect, heart, and will of the unregenerate man are utterly unable, by their own natural powers, to understand, believe, accept, think, will, begin, effect, work, or concur in working, anything, but they are entirely dead to what is good, and corrupt, so that in man's nature since the Fall, before regeneration, there is not the least spark of spiritual power remaining, nor present, by which, of himself, he can prepare himself for God's grace, or accept the offered grace, nor be capable of it for and of himself, or apply or accommodate himself thereto, or by his own powers be able of himself, as of himself, to aid, do, work, or concur in working anything towards his conversion, either wholly, or half, or in any, even the least or most inconsiderable part; but that he is the servant [and slave] of sin, John 8, 34, and a captive of the devil, by whom he is moved, Eph. 2, 2; 2 Tim. 2, 26. Hence natural free will according to its perverted disposition and nature is strong and active only with respect to what is displeasing and contrary to God" (883, 7; 887, 17); that "before man is enlightened, converted, regenerated, renewed, and drawn by the Holy Spirit, he can of himself and of his own natural powers begin, work, or concur in working in spiritual things and in his own conversion or regeneration just as little as a stone or a block or clay." (891, 24); that, moreover, "in this respect" [inasmuch as man resists the Holy Spirit] "it may well be said that man is not a stone or block, for a stone or block does not resist the person who moves it, nor does it understand and is sensible of what is being done with it, as man with his will so long resists God the Lord until he is converted (*donec ad Deum conversus fuerit*)" (905, 59); that "the Holy Scriptures ascribe conversion, faith in Christ, regeneration, renewal, and all that belongs to their efficacious beginning and completion, not to the human powers of the natural free will, neither entirely, nor half, nor in any, even the least or most inconsiderable part, but *in solidum*, that is, entirely and solely, to the divine working and the Holy Spirit" (891, 25); that "the preaching and hearing of God's Word are instruments of the Holy Ghost, by, with, and through which He desires to work efficaciously, and to convert men to God, and to work in them both to will and to do" (901, 52); that "as soon as the Holy Ghost . . . has begun in us this His work of regeneration and renewal, it is certain that through the power of the Holy Ghost we can and should cooperate (*mitwirken*), although still in great weakness" (907, 65); that this cooperation, however, "does not occur from

our carnal natural powers, but from the new powers and gifts which the Holy Ghost has begun in us in conversion," and "is to be understood in no other way than that the converted man does good to such an extent and so long as God by His Holy Spirit rules, guides, and leads him, and that as soon as God would withdraw His gracious hand from him, he could not for a moment persevere in obedience to God," and that hence it is not a power independent from, and coordinated with, the Holy Spirit, as though "the converted man cooperated with the Holy Ghost in the manner as when two horses together draw a wagon" (907, 66); and finally, that as to the three-concurring-causes doctrine it is "manifest, from the explanations presented, that conversion to God is a work of God the Holy Ghost alone, who is the true Master that alone works this in us, for which He uses the preaching and hearing of His holy Word as His ordinary means and instrument. But the intellect and will of the unregenerate man are nothing else than *subiectum convertendum*, that is, that which is to be converted, it being the intellect and will of a spiritually dead man, in whom the Holy Ghost works conversion and renewal, towards which work man's will that is to be converted does nothing, but suffers God alone to work in him until he is regenerated and then he [cooperates] works also with the Holy Ghost that which is pleasing to God in other good works that follow, in the way and to the extent fully set forth above" (915, 90).

It has been said that originally also the *Formula of Concord* in its Torgau draft (*Das Torgausche Buch, i. e.*, the draft preceding the Bergic Book = *Formula of Concord*) contained the three-concurring-causes doctrine of Melanchthon and the Synergists. As a matter of fact, however, the Torgau Book does not speak of three causes of conversion, but of three causes in those who are already converted, — a doctrine entirely in agreement with the *Formula of Concord*, which, as shown, plainly teaches that *after* conversion the will of man also cooperates with the Holy Spirit. In the Torgau Book the passage in question reads: "Thus also three causes concur to effect this internal new obedience in the *converted*. The first and chief cause is God Father, Son, and Holy Ghost. . . . The second is God's Word. . . . The third is man's intellect, enlightened by the Holy Spirit, which ponders and understands God's command [threat and promise], and our new and regenerate will, which is governed by the Holy Spirit, and now desires with a glad and willing heart (*herzlich gern und willig*), though in great weakness, to submit to, and obey, the Word and will of God." In the same sense, at the colloquy in Altenburg, 1568 to 1569, the Jena theologians also mentioned as a "third cause" "the mind of man, which is regenerated and renewed, and yields to, and obeys, the Holy Spirit and the Word of God (*des Menschen Gemuet, so wiedergeboren und erneuert ist und dem Heiligen Geiste und Gottes Wort Folge tut und gehorsam ist*)." (Frank 1, 214 f.)

# XV. The Flacian Controversy.

### 167. Flacius Entrapped by Strigel.

Matthias Flacius Illyricus, one of the most learned and capable theologians of his day and the most faithful, devoted, stanch, zealous, and able exponent and defender of genuine Lutheranism, was the author of the malignant controversy which bears his name. Flacius was born March 3, 1520, in Illyria, hence called Illyricus. He studied in Basel, Tuebingen, and Wittenberg. At Wittenberg he was convinced that the doctrine of the Lutheran Church is in complete agreement with the Word of God. Here, too, he was appointed Professor of Hebrew in 1544. In April, 1549, he left the city on account of the Interim. He removed to Magdeburg, where he became the energetic and successful leader of the opponents of the Interimists and Adiaphorists. He was appointed professor at the University of Jena, founded 1547, partly in opposition to Philippism. In December, 1561, he and his adherents were banished from Jena. When the latter returned in 1567, he was not recalled. Persecuted by his enemies (especially Elector August of Saxony) and forsaken by his friends, he now moved from one place to another: from Jena to Regensburg, thence to Antwerp, to Frankfort-on-the-Main, to Strassburg (from where he was expelled in the spring of 1573), and again to Frankfort-on-the-Main, where he found a last asylum for himself and his family (wife and eight children), and where he also died in a hospital, March 11, 1575.

In the Adiaphoristic Controversy Flacius had time and again urged the Lutherans to die rather than deny and surrender the truth. And when in the controversy about original sin all shunned him and turned against him, he gave ample proof of the fact that he himself was imbued with the spirit he had endeavored to kindle in others, being willing to suffer and to be banished and persecuted rather than sacrifice what he believed to be the truth. — The most important of his numerous books are: *Catalogus Testium Veritatis, qui ante nostram aetatem reclamarunt Papae,* 1556; *Ecclesiastica Historia,* or the so-called Magdeburg Centuries (*Centuriones*), comprising the history of the first thirteen centuries, and published 1559—1574; *Clavis Scripturae,* of 1567; and *Glossa Novi Testamenti.* Walther remarks: "It was a great pity that Flacius, who had hitherto been such a faithful champion of the pure doctrine, exposed himself to the enemies in such a manner. Henceforth the errorists were accustomed to brand all those as Flacianists who were zealous in defending the pure doctrine of Luther." (*Kern und Stern,* 34.)

The Flacian Controversy sprang from, and must be regarded as an episode of, the Synergistic Controversy, in which also some champions of Luther's theology (Amsdorf, Wigand, Hesshusius, and others) had occasionally employed unguarded, extreme, and inadequate expressions. Following are some of the immoderate and extravagant statements made by

Flacius: God alone converts man, the Adamic free will not only not cooperating, "but also raging and roaring against it (*sed etiam contra furente ac fremente*)." (Preger 2, 212.) The malice of our free will is a "diabolical malice (*nostra diabolica malitia carnis aut liberi arbitrii*)." By original sin man is "transformed into the image of Satan (*ad imaginem Satanae transformatus, eiusque charactere [foeda Satanae imagine] signatus*)." (Gieseler 3, 2, 245.) By original sin "the substance of man is destroyed (*substantiam hominis ablatam esse*)"; after the Fall original sin is the substance of man; man's nature is identical with sin; in conversion a new substance is created by God. In particular, the assertions concerning the substantiality of original sin gave rise to the so-called Flacian Controversy. After Strigel, at the second session of the disputation in Weimar, had dilated on the philosophical definitions of the terms "substance" and "accident" ("*accidens, quod adest vel abest praeter subiecti corruptionem*"), and had declared that original sin was an accident which merely impeded free will in its activity, Flacius, in the heat of the controversy, exclaimed: "*Originale peccatum non est accidens.* Original sin is not an accident, for the Scriptures call it flesh, the evil heart," etc. Thus he fell into the pitfall which the wily Strigel had adroitly laid for him. Though Flacius seemed to be loath to enter upon the matter any further, and protested against the use of philosophical definitions in theology, Strigel now was eager to entangle him still further, plying him with the question: "*An negas peccatum originis esse accidens?* Do you deny that original sin is an accident?" Flacius answered: "*Lutherus diserte negat esse accidens.* Luther expressly denies that it is an accident." Strigel: "*Visne negare peccatum esse accidens?* Do you mean to deny that sin is an accident?" Flacius: "*Quod sit substantia, dixi Scripturam et Lutherum affirmare.* I have said that Scripture and Luther affirm that it is a substance." (Luthardt, 213. 216.)

After the session in which the fatal phrase had fallen from his lips, Wigand and Musaeus expostulated with Flacius, designating (according to later reports of theirs) his statement as "this new, perilous, and blasphemous proposition of the ancient Manicheans (*haec nova, periculosa et blasphema veterum Manichaeorum propositio*)." (Planck 4, 611.) Flacius declared that, "in the sudden and pressing exigency, in the interest of truth, and against Pelagian enthusiasm, he had taken this expression [concerning the substantiality of original sin] from Luther's doctrine and books." (Preger 2, 324.) In the following (third) session, however, he repeated his error, declaring: I must stand by my statement that original sin is not an accident, but a substance, "because the testimonies of the Holy Scriptures which employ terms denoting substance (*quae verbis substantialibus utuntur*) are so numerous." (Planck 4, 610; Luthardt, 216.) Also later on Flacius always maintained that his doctrine was nothing but the teaching of the Bible and of Luther. As to Scripture-proofs, he referred to passages in which the Scriptures designate sin as "flesh," "stony heart," etc. Regarding the teaching of Luther, he quoted statements in which he describes original sin as "man's nature," "essence," "substantial sin," "all that is born of father and mother," etc. (Preger 2, 318.)

However, the palpable mistake of Flacius was that he took the substantial terms on which he based his theory in their original and proper sense, while the Bible and Luther employ them in a figurative meaning, as the *Formula of Concord* carefully explains in its first article, which decided and settled this controversy. (874, 50.) Here we read: "Also, to avoid strife about words, *aequivocationes vocabulorum*, that is, words and expressions which are applied and used in various meanings, should be carefully and distinctly explained; as when it is said: God creates the nature of men, there by the term *nature* the essence, body, and soul of men are understood. But often the disposition or vicious quality of a thing is called its nature, as when it is said: It is the nature of the serpent to bite and poison. Thus Luther says that sin and sinning are the disposition and nature of corrupt man. Therefore original sin properly signifies the deep corruption of our nature as it is described in the *Smalcald Articles*. But sometimes the concrete person or the subject, that is, man himself with body and soul, in which sin is and inheres, is also comprised under this term, for the reason that man is corrupted by sin, poisoned and sinful, as when Luther says: 'Thy birth, thy nature, and thy entire essence is sin,' that is, sinful and unclean. Luther himself explains that by nature-sin, person-sin, essential sin he means that not only the words, thoughts, and works are sin, but that the entire nature, person, and essence of man are altogether corrupted from the root by original sin." (875, 51 f.)

## 168. Context in which Statement was Made.

In making his statement concerning the substantiality of original sin, the purpose of Flacius was to wipe out the last vestige of spiritual powers ascribed to natural man by Strigel, and to emphasize the doctrine of total corruption, which Strigel denied. His fatal blunder was that he did so in terms which were universally regarded as savoring of Manicheism. As was fully explained in the chapter of the Synergistic Controversy, Strigel taught that free will, which belongs to the substance and essence of man, and hence cannot be lost without the annihilation of man himself, always includes the capacity to choose in both directions; that also with respect to divine grace and the operations of the Holy Spirit man is and always remains a *liberum agens* in the sense that he is able to decide *in utramque partem;* that this ability, constituting the very essence of free will, may be weakened and impeded in its

activity, but never lost entirely. If it were lost, Strigel argued, the very substance of man and free will as such would have to be regarded as annihilated. But now man, also after the Fall, is still a real man, possessed of intellect and will. Hence original sin cannot have despoiled him of this liberty of choosing *pro* or *con* also in matters spiritual. The loss of original righteousness does not, according to Strigel, involve the total spiritual disability of the will and its sole tendency and activity toward what is spiritually evil. Moreover, despite original corruption, it is and remains an indestructible property of man to be able, at least in a measure, to assent to, and to admit, the operations of the Holy Spirit, and therefore and in this sense to be converted *"aliquo modo volens."* (Planck 4, 667. 675. 681.)

It was in opposition to this Semi-Pelagian teaching that Flacius declared original sin to be not a mere accident, but the substance of man. Entering upon the train of thought and the phraseology suggested by his opponent, he called substance what in reality was an accident, though not an accident such as Strigel contended. From his own standpoint it was therefore a shrewd move to hide his own synergism and to entrap his opponent, when Strigel plied Flacius with the question whether he denied that original sin was an accident. For in the context and the sense in which it was proposed the question involved a vicious dilemma. Answering with yes or no, Flacius was compelled either to affirm Strigel's synergism or to expose himself to the charge of Manicheism. Instead of replying as he did, Flacius should have cleared the sophistical atmosphere by explaining: "If I say, 'Original sin is an accident,' you [Strigel] will infer what I reject, *viz.,* that the corrupt will of man retains the power to decide also in favor of the operations of the Holy Spirit. And if I answer that original sin is not an accident (such as you have in mind), you will again infer what I disavow, *viz.,* that man, who by the Fall has lost the ability to will in the spiritual direction, has *eo ipso* lost the will and its freedom entirely and as such. As it was, however, Flacius, instead of adhering strictly to the real issue — the question concerning man's cooperation in conversion — and exposing the sophistry implied in the question put by Strigel, most unfortunately suffered himself to be caught on the horns of the dilemma. He blindly walked into the trap set for him by Strigel, from which also later on he never succeeded in fully extricating himself.

With all his soul Flacius rejected the synergism involved in Strigel's question. His blunder was, as stated, that he did so in terms universally regarded as Manichean. He was right when he maintained that original sin is the inherited tendency and motion of the human mind, will, and heart, not toward, but against God, — a direction, too, which man is utterly unable to change. But he erred fatally by identifying this inborn evil tendency with the substance of fallen man and the essence of his will as such. It will always be regarded as a redeeming feature that it was in antagonizing synergism and championing the Lutheran *sola gratia* that Flacius coined his unhappy proposition. And in properly estimating his error, it must not be overlooked that he, as will be shown in the following, employed the terms "substance" and "accident" not in their generally accepted meaning, but in a sense, and according to a philosophical terminology, of his own.

### 169. Formal and Material Substance.

The terms "substance" and "accident" are defined in Melanchthon's *Erotemata Dialectices* as follows: "*Substantia est ens, quod revera proprium esse habet, nec est in alio, ut habens esse a subiecto.* Substance is something which in reality has a being of its own and is not in another as having its being from the subject." (*C. R.* 13, 528.) "*Accidens est, quod non per sese subsistit, nec est pars substantiae, sed in alio est mutabiliter.* Accident is something which does not exist as such nor is a part of the substance, but is changeable in something else." (522.) Melanchthon continues: "*Accidentium alia sunt separabilia, ut frigus ab aqua, notitia a mente, laetitia, tristitia a corde. Alia accidentia sunt inseparabilia, ut quantitas seu magnitudo a substantia corporea, calor ab igni, humiditas ab aqua, non separantur. . . . Et quia separabilia accidentia magis conspicua sunt, ideo inde sumpta est puerilis descriptio: Accidens est, quod adest et abest praeter subiecti corruptionem.* Whatever is present or absent without the corruption of the subject is an accident." (*C. R.* 13, 523; Preger 2, 396. 407; Seeberg 4, 494.)

Evidently this last definition, which was employed also by Strigel, is ambiguous, inasmuch as the word "corruption" may signify an annihilation, or merely a perversion, or a corruption in the ordinary meaning of the word. In the latter sense the term applied to original sin would be tantamount to a denial of the Lutheran doctrine of *total* corruption. When Jacob Andreae, in his disputation with Flacius, 1571, at Strassburg, declared that accident is something which is present or absent without *corruption* of the subject, he employed the term in the sense of destruction or annihilation. In the same year Hesshusius stated that by original sin "the whole nature, body and soul, substance as well as accidents, are defiled, corrupted, and dead," of course, spiritually. And what he understood by substance appears from his assertion: "The being itself, the substance and nature itself, in as far as it is nature, is not an evil conflicting with the Law of God. . . . Not even in the devil the substance itself, in as far as it is substance, is a bad thing, a thing conflicting with the Law." (Preger 2, 397.)

The *Formula of Concord* carefully and correctly defines: "Everything that is must be either *substantia*, that is, a self-existent essence, or *accidens*, that is, an accidental matter, which does not exist by itself essentially, but is in another self-existent essence and can be distinguished from it." "Now, then, since it is the indisputable truth that everything that is, is either a substance or an *accidens*, that is, either a self-existing essence or something accidental in it (as has just been shown and proved by testimonies of the church-teachers, and no truly intelligent man has ever had any doubts concerning this), necessity here constrains, and no one can evade it, if the question be asked whether original sin is a substance, that is, such a thing as exists by itself, and is not in another, or whether it is an *accidens*, that is, such a thing as does not exist by itself, but is in another, and cannot exist or be by itself, he must confess straight and pat that original sin is no substance, but an accident." (877, 54. 57.)

Flacius, however, took the words "substance" and "accident" in a different sense. He distinguished between the material and formal substance, and the latter he regarded as man's true original essence. This essence, he explained, consisted in the original righteousness and holiness of man, in the image of God or the will as truly free and in proper relation toward God. He said: "Ipsum hominem *essentialiter* sic esse formatum, ut recta voluntas esset imago Dei, non tantum eius accidens." (Seeberg 4, 494.) He drew the conclusion that original sin, by which the image of God (not the human understanding and will as such) is lost, cannot be a mere accident, but constitutes the very essence and substance of fallen man. He argued: The image of God is the formal essence of man, or the soul itself according to its best part; by original sin this image is changed into its opposite: hence the change wrought by original sin is not accidental, but substantial, — just as substantial and essential as when wine is changed into vinegar or fire into frost. What man has lost, said Flacius, is not indeed his material substance (*substantia materialis*), but his true formal substance or substantial form (*substantia formalis* or *forma substantialis*). Hence also original sin, or the corruption resulting from the Fall, in reality is, and must be designated, the formal substance or substantial form of natural man. Not all gifts of creation were lost to man by his Fall; the most essential boon, however, the image of God, was destroyed and changed into the image of Satan. "In homine," said Flacius, "et mansit aliquid, et tamen quod optimum in ratione et essentia fuit, nempe imago Dei, non tantum evanuit, sed etiam in contrarium, nempe in imaginem diaboli, commutatum est." The devil, Flacius continued, has robbed man of his original form (*forma*), the image of God, and stamped him with his own diabolical form and nature. (Luthardt 215; Gieseler 3, 2, 253.)

### 170. Further Explanations of Flacius.

The manner in which Flacius distinguished between material and formal substance appears from the tract on original sin (*De Peccati Originalis aut Veteris Adami Appellationibus et Essentia*), which he appended to his *Clavis Scripturae* of 1567. There we read:

"In this disputation concerning the corruption of man I do not deny that this meaner matter (*illam viliorem materiam*) or mass of man created in the beginning has indeed remained until now, although it is exceedingly vitiated, as when in wine or aromas the spirituous (*airy*) or fiery substance escapes, and nothing remains but the earthy and watery substance; but I hold that the substantial form or the formal substance (*formam substantialem aut substantiam formalem*) has been lost, yea, changed into its opposite. But I do not speak of that external and coarse form (although it, too, is corrupted and weakened very much) which a girl admires in a youth, or philosophy also in the entire man, according to which he consists of body and soul, has an erect stature, two feet, hands, eyes, ears, and the like, is an animal laughing, counting, reasoning, etc.; but I speak of that most noble substantial form (*nobilissima substantialis forma*) according to which especially the heart itself, or rather the rational soul, was formed in such a manner that his very essence might be the image of God and represent Him, and that his substantial powers, intellect and will, and his affections might be conformed to the properties of God, represent, truly acknowledge, and most willingly embrace Him." (Preger 2, 314; Gieseler 3, 2, 254.)

Again: "In this manner, therefore, I believe and assert that original sin is a substance, because the rational soul (as united with God) and especially its noblest substantial powers, namely, the intellect and will, which before had been formed so gloriously that they were the true image of God and the fountain of all justice, uprightness, and piety, and altogether essentially like unto gold and gems, are now, by deceit of Satan, so utterly perverted that they are the true and living image of Satan, and, as it were, filthy or rather consisting of an infernal flame, not otherwise than when the sweetest and purest mass, infected with the most venomous ferment, is altogether and substantially changed and transformed into a lump of the same ferment." (Gieseler 3, 2, 254.) Original sin "is not a mere accident in man, but his inverted and transformed essence or new form itself, just as when a most wholesome medicine is changed into the most baneful poison." "The matter remains, but it receives a new form, namely, the image of Satan." "Man, who in his essential form was the image of God, has in his essential form become the image of Satan." "This change may be compared to the change which the golden image of a beautiful man undergoes when it is transformed into the image of a dragon, the matter at the same time being corrupted." (Preger 2, 214. 217. 325.)

Dilating on the substantiality of original sin, Flacius furthermore declared: "Original malice in man is not something different from the evil mind or stony heart itself, not something that destroys him spiritually as a disease consumes him bodily, but it is ruined and destroyed nature itself (*sed est tantum ipsa perditissima· et iam destructissima natura*).

Original malice was not, as many now think, infused from without into Adam in such a way as when poison or some other bad substance is thrown or poured into good liquor, so that by reason of the added bad substance also the rest becomes noxious, but in such a way as when good liquor or bread itself is perverted so that now it is bad as such and poisonous or rather poison (*ut illud per se iam malum ac venenatum aut potius venenum sit*)." (Preger 2, 313.)

Also concerning the body and soul of fallen man Flacius does not hesitate to affirm that, since they are permeated and corrupted by original sin, "these parts themselves are sin, *eas ipsas* [*pártes, corpus et animam*] *esse illud nativum malum, quod cum Deo pugnat.*" "Some object," says Flacius, "that the creature of God must be distinguished from sin, which is not of God. I answer: Now do separate, if you can, the devil from his inherent wickedness! . . . How can the same thing be separated from itself! We therefore cannot distinguish them in any other way than by stating that with respect to his first creation and also his present preservation, man, even as the devil himself, is of God, but that with respect to this horrible transformation (*ratione istius horrendae metamorphoseos*) he is of the devil, who, by the force of the efficacious sentence and punishment of angry God: 'Thou shalt die,' not only captured us to be his vilest slaves, but also recast, rebaked, and changed, or, so to speak, metamorphosed us into another man, as the Scripture says, even as he [the devil] himself is inverted." All parts, talents, and abilities of man, Flacius contends, are "evil and mere sins," because they all oppose God. "What else are they than armed unrighteousness!" he exclaims. Even the natural knowledge of God "is nothing but the abominable source of idolatry and of all superstitions." (Preger 316 f.; Gieseler 3, 2, 255.)

That the fundamental view of Flacius, however, was much farther apart from Manicheism than some of his radical phrases imply, appears from his „Γνῶθι σεαυτόν, *De Essentia Originalis Iustitiae*," of 1568. After admitting that Augustine, Luther, and the *Apology of the Augsburg Confession* are correct when they define original sin as an inordinate disposition, a disorder (ἀταξία), perversion, and confusion of the parts of man, Flacius proceeds: "The substantial form of a certain thing, for the most part, consists in the right position and disposition of the parts; as, for example, if a human body were born which had its eyes, ears, and mouth on the belly or feet, and, *vice versa*, the toes on the head, no one would say that it was properly a man, but rather a monster. . . . It appears, therefore, that the inordinate disposition of the parts produces an altogether new body or thing. Thus, forsooth, the horrible perturbation of the soul has also produced, as it were, a new kind of monster fighting against God." (Preger 2, 409.) Accordingly, it was not man's body and soul as such, but the alteration of the relation of his powers toward one another and the consequent corruption of these powers, that Flacius had in mind when he designated original sin as the new substantial form, or substance, of sinful man.

Flacius expressly denied that the fall of man or his conversion involved a physical change. "I do not teach a physical regeneration," he declared, "nor do I say that two hearts are created, but I say that this most excellent part of the soul or of man is once more established, or that the image of God is recast and transformed out of the image of Satan, even as before the image of God was transformed into the image of Satan. *Physicam renascentiam non assero nec dico duo corda creari, sed dico istam praestantissimam animae aut hominis partem denuo condi aut ex imagine Satanae refundi aut transformari imaginem Dei, sicut antea imago Dei fuit transformata in imaginem Satanae.*" (Seeberg 4, 495.) Gieseler pertinently remarks: "It is apparent that Flacius did not deviate from the common concept of original sin, but from the concepts of substance and accident, but that here, too, he was uncertain, inasmuch as he employed the terms *substantia, forma substantialis*, and *substantia formalis* promiscuously." (3, 2, 255.)

If not necessarily involved in, it was at least in keeping with his extreme position and extravagant phraseology concerning original sin when Flacius, in his *De Primo et Secundo Capite ad Romanos, quatenus Libero Arbitrio Patrocinari Videntur*, rejected the doctrine of an inborn idea of God and of His Law inscribed in the heart of natural man. On Rom. 1, 19 he comments: It is only from the effects in the world that man infers the existence of a supreme cause. And with respect to Rom. 2, 15 he maintains that Paul's statements were to be understood, not of a law written in the heart of man, but of a knowledge which the heathen had derived by inference, from experience, or from tradition of the fathers. On this point Strigel, no doubt, was correct when he objected: If the knowledge of God's existence were really extinguished from the heart, there could be no discipline among men; and if man had no inborn knowledge of the Law, then there could be no such thing as conscience which condemns him when he sins. The fact that man fears punishments even when there is no government to fear, as was the case with Alexander when he had murdered Clitus, proves that in the heart there is a certain knowledge both of God and of His Law. (Preger 2, 213.) However, Flacius did not, as Strigel seems to insinuate, deny that natural man has an obscure knowledge of God's existence and Law, but merely maintained that this knowledge was not inborn or inherited, but acquired from without.

## 171. Controversy Precipitated by Flacius.

Though Flacius, when he first made his statement concerning the substantiality of original sin may not have felt absolutely sure of the exact meaning, bearing, and correctness of his position, yet the facts do not warrant the assumption that afterwards he was in any way diffident or wavering in his attitude. Whatever his views on this subject may have been before 1560 — after the fatal phrase had fallen from his lips, he never flinched nor flagged in zealously defending it. Nor was he ever disposed to compromise the matter as far as the substance of his doctrine was concerned. In 1570 Spangenberg of Mansfeld, who sided with Flacius, suggested that he retain his meaning, but change his language: "*Teneat Illyricus mentem, mutet linguam.*" To this Flacius consented. On September 28, 1570, he published his *Brief Confession*, in which he agreed to abstain from the use of the term "substance." However, what he suggested as a substitute, viz., that original sin be defined as the nature of man (the word "nature," as he particularly emphasized, to be taken not in a figurative, but in its proper meaning), was in reality but another way of repeating his error.

The same was the case in 1572, when Flacius, opposed and sorely pressed by the ministerium of Strassburg (whence he was banished the following year), offered to substitute for the word "substance" the phrase "essential powers." (Preger 2, 371.) Two years later, at the public disputation in Langenau, Silesia, where Flacius defended his doctrine with favorable results for himself against Jacob Coler [born 1537; studied in Frankfort-in-the-Oder; 1564 pastor in Lauban, Upper Lausatia (Oberlausitz); 1573 in Neukirch; 1574 he opposed Leonard Crentzheim and Flacius; 1575 professor in Frankfort; afterwards active first as Praepositus in Berlin and later on as Superintendent in Mecklenburg; published *Disputatio De Libero Arbitrio;* died March 7, 1612], he declared that he did not insist on his phrase as long as the doctrine itself was adopted and original sin was not declared to be a mere accident. But this, too, was no real retraction of his error. (Preger 2, 387.) In a similar way Flacius repeatedly declared himself willing to abstain from the use of the word "substance" in connection with his doctrine concerning original sin, but with conditions and limitations which made his concessions illusory, and neither did nor could satisfy his opponents.

At the disputation in Weimar, 1560, Wigand and Musaeus, as stated, warned Flacius immediately after the session in which he had made his statement. Schluesselburg relates: "Immediately during the disputation, as I frequently heard from their own lips, Dr. Wigand, Dr. Simon Musaeus, and other colleagues of his who attended the disputation . . . admonished Illyricus in a brotherly and faithful manner to abstain from this new, perilous, and blasphemous proposition of the ancient Manicheans, which would cause great turmoil in the Church of God, and to refute the error of Victorin [Strigel] concerning free will not by means of a false proposition, but with the Word of God. However, intoxicated with ambition, and relying, in the heat of the conflict, too much on the acumen and sagacity of his own mind, Illyricus haughtily spurned the brotherly and faithful admonitions of all his colleagues." (*Catalogus* 2, 4.) In his book *De Manichaeismo Renovato* Wigand himself reports: "Illyricus answered [to the admonition of his colleagues to abstain from the Manichean phrase] that he had been drawn into this discussion by his opponent against his own will. But what happened? Contrary to the expectations of his colleagues, Illyricus in the following session continued, as he had begun, to defend this insanity." (Preger 2, 324; Planck 4, 611.) However, it does not appear that after the disputation his friends pressed the matter any further, or that they made any efforts publicly to disavow the Flacian proposition.

In 1567 Flacius published his tract *De Peccati Originalis aut Veteris Adami Appellationibus et Essentia,* "On the Appellations and Essence of Original Sin or the Old Adam," appending it to his famous *Clavis Scripturae* of the same year. He had written this tract probably even before 1564. In 1566 he sent it to Simon Musaeus, requesting his opinion and the opinion of Hesshusius, who at that time was celebrating his marriage with the daughter of Musaeus. In his answer, Musaeus approved the tract, but desired that the term "substance" be explained as meaning not the matter, but the form of the substance, to which Hesshusius also agreed. After the tract had appeared, Musaeus again wrote to Flacius, June 21, 1568, saying that he agreed with his presentation of original sin. At the same time, however, he expressed the fear that the bold statement which Flacius had retained, "Sin is substance," would be dangerously misinterpreted. (Preger 2, 327.) And before long a storm was brewing, in which animosity registered its highest point, and a veritable flood of controversial literature (one publication following the other in rapid succession) was poured out upon the Church, which was already distracted and divided by numerous and serious theological conflicts.

By the publication of this treatise Flacius, who before long also was harassed and ostracized everywhere, had himself made a public controversy unavoidable. In the conflict which it precipitated, he was opposed by all parties, not only by his old enemies, the Philippists, but also by his former friends. According to the maxim: *Amicus Plato, amicus Socrates, sed magis amica veritas,* they now felt constrained, in the interest of truth, to turn their weapons against their former comrade and leader. Flacius himself had made it impossible for his friends to spare him any longer. Nor did he deceive himself as to the real situation. In a letter written to Wigand he reveals his fear that the Lutherans and Philippists, then assembled at the Colloquium in Altenburg (held from October 21, 1568, to March, 1569, between the theologians of Thuringia and those of Electoral Saxony), would unite in a public declaration against his teaching. Wigand, whose warning Flacius had disregarded at Weimar, wrote to Gallus: Flacius has forfeited the right to request that nothing be published against him, because he himself has already spread his views in print. And before long Wigand began to denounce publicly the Flacian doctrine as "new and prolific monsters, *monstra nova et fecunda.*"

## 172. Publications Pro and Con.

According to Preger the first decided opposition to the Flacian teaching came from Moerlin and Chemnitz, in Brunswick, to whom Flacius had also submitted his tract for approval. Chemnitz closed his criticism by saying: It is enough if we are able to retain what Luther has won (*parta tueri*); let us abandon all desires to go beyond (*ulterius quaerere*) and to improve upon him. (Preger 2, 328.) Moerlin characterized Flacius as a vain man, and dangerous in many respects. Flacius answered in an objective manner, betraying no irritation whatever. (332.) In a letter of August 10, 1568, Hesshusius, who now had read the tract more carefully, charged Flacius with teaching that Satan was a creator of substance, and before long refused to treat with him any further. In September of the same year Flacius published his Γνῶθι σεαυτόν against the attacks of the Synergists and Philippists, notably Christopher Lasius [who studied at Strassburg and Wittenberg; was active in Goerlitz, Greussen, Spandau, Kuestrin, Cottbus, and Senftenberg; wrote *Praelibationes Dogmatis Flaciani de Prodigiosa Hominis Conversione;* died 1572]. In the same year Hesshusius prepared his *Analysis,* which was approved by Gallus and the Jena theologians.

Realizing that all his former friends had broken with him entirely, Flacius, in January, 1570, *published* his *Demonstrations Concerning the Essence of the Image of God and the Devil,* in which he attacked his opponents, but without mentioning their names. His request for a private discussion was bluntly rejected by the Jena theologians. Wigand, in his *Propositions on Sin* of May 5, 1570, was the first publicly to attack Flacius by name. About the same time Moerlin's *Themata de Imagine Dei* and Chemnitz's *Resolutio* appeared. The former was directed "against the impious and absurd proposition that sin is a substance"; the latter, against the assertion "that original sin is the very substance of man, and that the soul of man itself is original sin." Hesshusius also published his *Letter to M. Flacius Illyricus in the Controversy whether Original Sin is a Substance.* Flacius answered in his *Defense of the Sound Doctrine Concerning Original Righteousness and Unrighteousness, or Sin,* of September 1, 1570. Hesshusius published his *Analysis,* in which he repeated the charge that Flacius made the devil a creator of substance.

In his *Brief Confession,* of September 28, 1570, Flacius now offered to abstain from the use of the term "substance" in the manner indicated above. A colloquium, however, requested by Flacius and his friends on the basis of this *Confession,* was declined by the theologians of Jena. Moreover, in answer to the *Brief Confession,* Hesshusius published

(April 21, 1571) his *True Counter-Report*, in which he again repeated his accusation. that Flacius made the devil a creator of substance. He summarized his arguments as follows: "I have therefore proved from one book [Flacius's tract of 1567] more than six times that Illyricus says: *Satan condidit, fabricavit, transformavit veterem hominem, Satan est figulus,* that is: The devil created and made man, the devil is man's potter." The idea of a creation out of nothing, however, was not taught in the statements to which Hesshusius referred. (Preger 2, 348.)

Further publications by Andrew Schoppe [died after 1615], Wigand, Moerlin, Hesshusius, and Chemnitz, which destroyed all hopes of a peaceful settlement, caused Flacius to write his *Orthodox Confession Concerning Original Sin.* In this comprehensive answer, which appeared August 1, 1571, he declares "that either image, the image of God as well as of Satan, is an essence, and that the opposite opinion diminishes the merit of Christ." At the same time he complained that his statements were garbled and misinterpreted by his opponents; that his was the position of the man who asked concerning garlic and received an answer concerning onions; that his opponents were but disputing with imaginations of their own. (349 f.)

In the same year, 1571, Wigand published a voluminous book, *On Original Sin,* in which he charged Flacius with teaching that original sin is the entire carnal substance of man according to both his body and soul. In his description of the Flacian doctrine we read: "Original sin is a substance, as they teach. Accordingly, original sin is an animal, and that, too, an intelligent animal. You must also add ears, eyes, mouth, nose, arms, belly, and feet. Original sin laughs, talks, sews, sows, works, reads, writes, preaches, baptizes, administers the Lord's Supper, etc. For it is the substance of man that does such things. Behold, where such men end!" Flacius replied in his *Christian and Reliable Answer to All Manner of Sophistries of the Pelagian Accident,* 1572, protesting that the doctrine ascribed to him was a misrepresentation of his teaching. In the same year Wigand published *Reasons Why This Proposition, in Controversy with the Manicheans: "Original Sin Is the Corrupt Nature," Cannot Stand.* Here Wigand truly says: "Evil of the substance and evil substance are not identical. *Malum substantiae et mala substantia non sunt idem.*" (Preger 2, 353. 410.)

In several publications of the same year Hesshusius asserted (quoting testimonies to this effect from Augustine), that the Flacian doctrine was identical with the tenets of the Manicheans, in substance as well as terms. Flacius answered in *De Augustini et Manichaeorum Sententia, in Controversia Peccati,* 1572, in which he declared: "I most solemnly condemn the Manichean insanity concerning two creators. I have always denied that original sin is something, or has ever been something, outside of man; I have never ascribed to this sin any materiality of its own." (355.)

This book was followed by another attack by Hesshusius and an answer, in turn, by Flacius.

In the same year Hesshusius, in order to prevent further accessions to Flacianism, published his *Antidote (Antidoton) against the Impious and Blasphemous Dogma of Matthias Flacius Illyricus by which He Asserts that Original Sin Is Substance.* In this book, which was republished in 1576 and again in 1579, Hesshusius correctly argued: "If original sin is the substance of the soul, then we are compelled to assert one of two things, viz., either that Satan is the creator of substances, or that God is the creator and preserver of sin. *Si substantia animae est peccatum originis, alterum a duobus necesse est poni, videlicet, aut Satanam esse conditorem substantiarum, aut Deum esse peccati creatorem et sustentatorem.*" (Gieseler 3, 2, 256.) At this late hour, 1572, Simon Musaeus, too, entered the arena with his *Opinion Concerning Original Sin, Sententia de Peccato Originali.* In it he taught "that original sin is not a substance, but the utmost corruption of it, in matter as well as form," and that therefore "Pelagianism no less than Manicheism is to be excluded and condemned."

When the ministerium of Strassburg turned against Flacius, he again published several books defending his position on the controverted questions, which resulted in his expulsion from the city. In 1573 Flacius published an answer to Hesshusius's *Antidote* entitled, *Solid Refutation of the Groundless Sophistries, Calumnies, and Figments, as also of the Most Corrupt Errors of the "Antidote" and of Other Neopelagian Writers.* Flacius charged Hesshusius with misrepresentation, and demanded that he swear whether he really believed to have found the alleged errors in his writings. (Preger 2, 364 ff.)

Till his death, on March 11, 1575, at Frankfort-on-the-Main, Flacius consistently adhered to his false terminology as well as teaching, apparently never for a moment doubting that he was but defending Luther's doctrine. One of his last books was entitled, *Some Clear and Splendid Testimonies of Martin Luther Concerning the Evil Essence, Image, Form, or Shape* (Wesen, essentia, Bild, Form oder Gestalt) *of the Earthly Dead Adam and Concerning the Essential Transformation of Man.* (389.) As stated above, the mistake of Flacius was that he took literally terms denoting substance which the Bible and Luther employ in a figurative sense.

### 173. Adherents of Flacius.

The chief supporters of Flacius were the Mansfeldians, Count Vollrath and Cyriacus Spangenberg [born 1528; studied in Wittenberg; served in Eisleben, then in Mansfeld; died in Strassburg February 10, 1604]. In the serious dissensions which arose in Mansfeld in consequence of the controversy on original sin, the Count and Spangenberg were opposed by the Jena theologians and Superintendent Menzel [Jerome Menzel, born 1517; studied in Wittenberg; wrote against Spangenberg; died 1590]. As stated above, it was

Spangenberg who endeavored to bring about an understanding between the contending parties on the principle: *"Teneat Illyricus mentem, mutet linguam."* A colloquy was held 1572 at Castle Mansfeld, in which Flacius and his adherents were pitted against Menzel, Rhode, Fabricius, and others. When Fabricius declared in the discussions: "Only in so far as our nature is not in conformity with the Law of God is it corrupt," Flacius exclaimed: *"Non quantum,* not in as far; but I say it is not in conformity *because* it is corrupt, *quia corrupta est."* (Preger 2, 375.) Count Vollrath and his adviser, Caspar Pflug, gave Flacius a written testimony that at the colloquy he had not been convinced, but found to be correct in the controversy on original sin. The publication of this testimony by Flacius as also of the minutes of the Colloquy by Count Vollrath, in 1573, resulted in a number of further publications by Flacius and his friends as well as his opponents. At Mansfeld the animosity against the Flacians did not subside even after the death of Flacius in 1575. They were punished with excommunication, ·incarceration, and the refusal of a Christian burial. Count Vollrath left 1577, and died at Strassburg 1578. Spangenberg, who also had secretly fled from Mansfeld, defended the doctrine of Flacius in a tract, *De Peccato Originali, Concerning Original Sin,* which he published 1586 under a pseudonym. He died without retracting or changing his views.

Another adherent of Flacius was F. Coelestinus, professor at Jena. After his suspension he left the city and participated in the controversy. He published *Colloquium inter Se et Tilem. Hesshusium.* He died 1572. In August, 1571, Court-preacher Christopher Irenaeus and Pastors·Guenther and Reinecker were dismissed in Weimar because of Flacianism. Irenaeus published *Examen Libri Concordiae* and many other books, in which he contends that original sin is a substance. Pastors Wolf in Kahla, Schneider in Altendorf, and Franke in Oberrosla were dismissed in 1572 for the same reason. They, too, entered the public arena in favor of Flacius. At Lindau four preachers, who had identified themselves with Flacius, were also deposed. One of them, Tobias Rupp, held a public disputation with Andreae. In Antwerp the elders forbade their ministers to indulge in any public polemics against Flacius. Among the supporters of Flacius were also his son, Matthias Flacius, and Caspar Heldelin. It may be noted here that Saliger (Beatus) and Fredeland, who were deposed at Luebeck in 1568, also taught "that original sin is the very substance of the body and soul of man," and that Christ had assumed "the flesh of another species" than ours. (Gieseler 3, 2, 257.)

In Regensburg four adherents of Flacius were dismissed in 1574, among them Joshua Opitz [born 1543; died 1585]. These and others emigrated to the Archduchy of Austria, where the Lutherans were numerous and influential, Opitz frequently preaching to an audience of 7,000. No less than 40 of the Lutheran ministers of Austria are said to have shared the views of Flacius. (Preger 2, 393.) Only a few of them revealed symptoms of fanaticism, which resulted in their dismissal. Among the latter was Joachim Magdeburgius, then an exile at Efferding. He taught "that the bodies of believing Christians after their death were still essential original sin, and that God's wrath remained over them till the Day of Judgment." (Joecher, *Lexicon* 3, 32.) At the same time he branded as errorists Spangenberg, Opitz, and Irenaeus, who declared their dissent. In 1581 the Flacians in Austria issued a declaration against the *Formula of Concord,* charging its teaching to be inconsistent with Luther's doctrine on original sin. As late as 1604 there were numerous Flacianists in German Austria.

## 174. Decision of Formula of Concord.

Seeberg remarks: "Flacius was not a heretic, but in the wrangle of his day he was branded as such, and this has been frequently repeated." (4, 2, 495.) A similar verdict is passed by Gieseler and other historians. But whatever may be said in extenuation of his error, it cannot be disputed that the unfortunate phrases of Flacius produced, and were bound to produce, most serious religious offense, as well as theological strife, and hopeless doctrinal confusion. Even when viewed in the light of his distinction between formal substance (man as endowed with the image of God) and material substance (man as possessed of body and soul, together with will and intellect), the odiousness of his terminology is not entirely removed. It was and remained a form of doctrine and trope or mode of teaching which the Lutherans were no more minded to tolerate than the error of Strigel.

Accordingly, the first article of the *Formula of Concord* rejects both the synergistic as well as the Manichean aberrations in the doctrine of original sin. In its Thorough Declaration we read: "Now this doctrine [of original sin] must be so maintained and guarded that it may not deflect either to the Pelagian or the Manichean side. For this reason the contrary doctrine . . . should also be briefly stated." (865, 16.) Accordingly, in a series of arguments, the Flacian error is thoroughly refuted and decidedly rejected. At the same time the *Formula of Concord* points out the offensiveness of the Flacian phraseology. It refers to the controversy regarding this question as "scandalous and very mischievous," and declares: "Therefore it is unchristian and horrible to hear that original sin is baptized in the name of the Holy Trinity, sanctified, and saved, and other similar expressions found in the writings of the recent Manicheans, with which we will not offend simple-minded people." (873, 45. 59.)

On the other hand, the *Formula of Concord* is just as determined in opposing every effort at extenuating the corruption wrought by original sin. It is solicitous to explain that, in designating original sin as an accident, its corruption is not minimized in the least, if the answer concerning the nature of this accident is not derived from philosophy or human reason, but from the Holy Scriptures. "For the Scriptures," says the *Formula*, "testify that original sin is an unspeakable evil and such an entire corruption of human nature that in it and all its internal and external powers nothing pure or good remains, but everything is entirely corrupt, so that on account of original sin man in God's sight is truly spiritually dead (*plane sit emortuus*), with all his powers dead to that which is good." (879, 60.)

Accordingly, the *Formula of Concord* rejects the errors of Strigel and the Semi-Pelagians, "that original sin is only external, a slight, insignificant spot sprinkled, or a stain dashed upon the nature of man . . . along with and beneath which the nature nevertheless possesses and retains its integrity and power even in spiritual things. Or that original sin is not a despoliation or deficiency, but only an external impediment to these spiritual good powers. . . . They are rebuked and rejected likewise who teach that the nature has indeed been greatly weakened and corrupted through the Fall, but that nevertheless it has not entirely lost all good with respect to divine, spiritual things, and that what is sung in our churches, '*Through Adam's fall is all corrupt, nature and essence human,*' is not true, but from natural birth it still has something good, small, little, and inconsiderable though it be, namely, capacity, skill, aptness, or ability to begin, to effect, or to help effect something in spiritual things." (865, 21 ff.)

While the *Formula of Concord* does not deny the capacity of fallen man for salvation, it is careful in defining that this is not an active, but a passive capacity. That is to say: Man is utterly incapable of qualifying himself for, or of contributing in the least toward, his own spiritual restoration; but what is impossible for man is not impossible with God, who, indeed, is able to convert man, endow him with new spiritual powers, and lead him to eternal salvation, — a goal for the attainment of which, in contradistinction from inanimate and other creatures, man, being a rational creature, endowed with intellect and will, was created by God and redeemed by Christ. In the *Formula of Concord*, we read: "And although God, according to His just, strict sentence, has utterly cast away the fallen evil spirits forever, He has nevertheless, out of special, pure mercy, willed that poor fallen human nature might again become and be capable and participant of conversion, the grace of God, and eternal life; not from its own natural, active [or effective] skill, aptness, or capacity (for the nature of man is obstinate enmity against God), but from pure grace, through the gracious efficacious working of the Holy Ghost. And this Dr. Luther calls *capacitatem* (*non activam, sed passivam*), which he explains thus: *Quando patres liberum arbitrium defendunt, capacitatem libertatis eius praedicant, quod scilicet verti potest ad bonum per gratiam Dei et fieri revera liberum, ad quod creatum est.* That is: When the Fathers defend the free will, they are speaking of this, that it is capable of freedom in this sense, that by God's grace it can be converted to good, and become truly free, for which it was created in the beginning." (889, 20.)

This accords with Luther's words in *De Servo Arbitrio*: "It would be correct if we should designate as the power of free will that [power] by which man, who is created for life or eternal death, is apt to be moved by the Spirit and imbued with the grace of God. For we, too, confess this power, *i. e.,* aptitude or, as the Sophists [Scholastic theologians] say, disposition and passive aptitude. And who does not know that trees and animals are not endowed with it? For, as the saying goes, heaven is not created for geese. *Hanc enim vim, hoc est, aptitudinem, seu, ut Sophistae loquuntur, dispositivam qualitatem et passivam aptitudinem, et nos confitemur; quam non arboribus neque bestiis inditam esse, quis est, qui nesciat? Neque enim pro anseribus, ut dicitur, coelum creavit.*" (E. v. a. 158; St. L. 18, 1720.)

## XVI. The Osiandrian and Stancarian Controversies.

### 175. Osiander in Nuernberg and in Koenigsberg.

In the writings of Luther we often find passages foreboding a future corruption of the doctrine of justification, concerning which he declared in the *Smalcald Articles*: "Of this article nothing can be yielded or surrendered, even though heaven and earth, and whatever will not abide, should sink to ruin. . . . And upon this article all things depend which we teach and practise in opposition to the Pope, the devil, and the world. Therefore we must be sure concerning this doctrine, and not doubt; for otherwise all is lost, and the Pope and devil and all things gain the victory and suit over us." (461, 5.) Martin Chemnitz remarks: "I frequently shudder, because Luther — I do not know by what kind of presentiment — in his commentaries on the Letter to the Galatians and on the First Book of Moses so often repeats the statement: 'This doctrine [of justification] will be obscured again after my death.'" (Walther, *Kern und Stern*, 26.)

Andrew Osiander was the first to fulfil Luther's prophecy. In 1549 he began publicly to propound a doctrine in which he abandoned the forensic conception of justification by imputation of the merits of Christ, and returned to the Roman view of justification by infusion, *i. e.,* by infusion of the eternal essential righteousness of the divine nature of Christ. According to his own statement, he had harbored these views ever since about 1522. He is said also to have presented them in a sermon delivered at the convention in Smalcald, 1537.

(Planck 4, 257.) Yet he made no special effort to develop and publicly to disseminate his ideas during the life of Luther. After the death of the Reformer, however, Osiander is reported to have said: "Now that the lion is dead, I shall easily dispose of the foxes and hares" — i. e., Melanchthon and the other Lutheran theologians. (257.) Osiander was the originator of the controversy "Concerning the Righteousness of Faith before God," which was finally settled in Article III of the *Formula of Concord.*

Osiander, lauded by modern historians as the only real "systematizer" among the Lutherans of the first generation, was a man as proud, overbearing, and passionate as he was gifted, keen, sagacious, learned, eloquent, and energetic. He was born December 19, 1498, at Gunzenhausen, Franconia, and died October 17, 1552, at Koenigsberg, where he was also buried with high honors in the Old City Church. In 1522 he was appointed priest at St. Lawrence's Church in the Free City of Nuernberg. Here he immediately acted the part of a determined champion of the Reformation. Subsequently he also participated in some of the most important transactions of his day. He was present at the Marburg Colloquy, 1529, where he made the personal acquaintance of Luther and the Wittenbergers. He also took part in the discussions at the Diet in Augsburg, 1530; at Smalcald, 1537; at Hagenau and Worms, 1540. Nor were his interests confined to theological questions. When, at Nuernberg, 1543, the work of Copernicus, *De Revolutionibus Orbium Coelestium,* "Concerning the Revolutions of the Heavenly Bodies," was published for the first time, Osiander read the proof-sheets and wrote the Preface, in which he designated the new theory as "hypotheses," thus facilitating its circulation also among the Catholics, until in the 17th century the book was placed on the *Index Librorum Prohibitorum,* where it remained till the 18th century.

When the Augsburg Interim was introduced in Nuernberg, Osiander resigned, and with words of deep emotion (in a letter of November 22, 1548, addressed to the city council), he left the place where he had labored more than a quarter of a century. January 27, 1549, he arrived in Koenigsberg. Here he was joyously received by Count Albrecht of Prussia, whom he had gained for the Reformation in 1523. Moved by gratitude toward Osiander, whom he honored as his "spiritual father," Count Albrecht appointed him pastor of the Old City Church and, soon after, first professor of theology at the University of Koenigsberg, with a double salary, though Osiander had never received an academic degree. The dissatisfaction which this unusual preferment caused among his colleagues, Briessman, Hegemon, Isinder, and Moerlin, soon developed into decided antipathy against Osiander, especially because of his overbearing, domineering ways as well as his intriguing methods. No doubt, this personal element added largely to the animosity and violence of the controversy that was soon to follow, and

during which the professors in Koenigsberg are said to have carried firearms into their academic sessions. (Schaff, *Creeds* 1, 273.) Yet it cannot be regarded as the real cause, or even as the immediate occasion, of the conflict, which was really brought about by the unsound, speculative, and mystical views of Osiander on the image of God and, particularly, on justification and the righteousness of faith, — doctrinal points on which he deviated from the Lutheran teaching to such an extent that a controversy was unavoidable. Evidently, his was either a case of relapse into Romanism, or, what seems to be the more probable alternative, Osiander never attained to a clear apprehension of the Lutheran truth, nor ever fully freed himself from the Roman doctrine, especially in its finer and more veiled form of mysticism.

## 176. Opposed by Moerlin and Lutherans Generally.

Osiander, as stated, had conceived the fundamental thoughts of his system long before he reached Koenigsberg. In 1524, when only twenty-six years of age, he laid down the outlines of his theory in a publication entitled: "*A Good Instruction (Ein gut Unterricht) and Faithful Advice from the Holy Divine Scriptures What Attitude to Take in These Dissensions Concerning Our Holy Faith and Christian Doctrine,* dealing especially with the questions what is God's Word and what human doctrine, what Christ and what Antichrist." Here he says: "Whoever hears, retains, and believes the Word, receives God Himself, for God is the Word. If, therefore, the Word of God, Christ, our Lord, dwells in us by faith and we are one with Him, we may say with Paul: 'I live, though not I, but Christ lives in me,' and then we are justified by faith." (Gieseler 3, 2, 270.) In the following year, 1525, he wrote in his *Action of the Honorable Wise Council in Nuernberg with their Preachers (Handlung eines ehrsamen weisen Rats zu Nuernberg mit ihren Praedikanten):* "The one and only righteousness availing before God is God Himself. But Christ is the Word which we apprehend by faith, and thus Christ in us, God Himself, is our Righteousness which avails before God." "The Gospel has two parts: the first, that Christ has satisfied the justice of God; the other, that He has cleansed us from sin, and justifies us by dwelling in us (*und uns rechtfertigt, so er in uns wohnet*)." (271.) The embryonic ideas of these early publications concerning the image of God and justification were fully developed by Osiander in his book of 1550, *Whether the Son of God would have had to be Incarnated (An Filius Dei fuerit Incarnandus), if Sin had Not Entered the World;* and especially in his confession of September, 1551, *Concerning the Only Mediator Jesus Christ (Von dem einigen Mittler Jesu Christo) and Justification of Faith,* which appeared also in Latin under the title, *De Unico Mediatore,* in October of the same year.

The public conflict began immediately after Osiander had entered upon his duties at the university. In his inaugural disputation of April 5, 1549, "Concerning the Law and Gospel (De Lege et Evangelio)," Osiander's vanity prompted him at least to hint at his peculiar views, which he well knew were not in agreement with the doctrine taught at Wittenberg and in the Lutheran Church at large. His colleague, Matthias Lauterwald, a Wittenberg master, who died 1555, immediately took issue with him. On the day following the disputation, he published theses in which he declared: "Osiander denied that faith is a part of repentance." October 24 of the following year Osiander held a second disputation ("On Justification, De Iustificatione"), in which he came out clearly against the doctrine hitherto taught in the Lutheran Church. But now also a much more able and determined combatant appeared in the arena, Joachim Moerlin, who henceforth devoted his entire life to defeat Osiandrism and to vindicate Luther's forensic view of justification.

Moerlin (Moehrlein) was born at Wittenberg April 6, 1514; he studied under Luther, and was made Master in 1537 and Doctor in 1540; till 1543 he was superintendent in Arnstadt, Thuringia, and superintendent in Goettingen till 1549, when he was compelled to leave because of his opposition to the Augsburg Interim. Recommended by Elizabeth, Duchess of Braunschweig - Lueneburg, the mother-in-law of Duke Albrecht, he was appointed preacher at the Dome of Koenigsberg in 1550. Clearly understanding that solid comfort in life and death is possible only as long as our faith rests solely on the *aliena iustitia,* on the objective righteousness of Christ, which is without us, and is offered in the Gospel and received by faith; and fully realizing also that Christian assurance is incompatible with such a doctrine as Osiander taught, according to which our faith is to rely on a righteous condition within ourselves, Moerlin publicly attacked Osiander from his pulpit, and in every way emphasized the fact that his teaching could never be tolerated in the Lutheran Church. Osiander replied in his lectures. The situation thus created was most intolerable. At the command of the Duke discussions were held between Moerlin and Osiander, but without result.

In order to settle the dispute, Duke Albrecht, accordingly, on October 5, 1551, placed the entire matter before the evangelical princes and cities with the request that the points involved be discussed at the various synods and their verdicts forwarded to Koenigsberg. This aroused the general interest and the deepest concern of the entire Lutheran Church in Germany. Numerous opinions of the various synods and theologians arrived during the winter of 1551 to 1552. With the exception of the Wuerttemberg *Response* (*Responsum*), written by John Brenz, and the *Opinion* of Matthew Vogel, both of whom regarded Osiander's teaching as differing from the doctrine received by the Lutheran Church in terms and phrases rather than in substance,

they were unfavorable to Osiander. At the same time all, including the opinions of Brenz and Vogel, revealed the fact that the Lutherans, the theologians of Wittenberg as well as those of Jena, Brandenburg, Pomerania, Hamburg, etc., were firmly united in maintaining Luther's doctrine, *viz.,* that the righteousness of faith is not the essential righteousness of the Son of God, as Osiander held, but the obedience of Christ the God-man imputed by grace to all true believers as their sole righteousness before God.

Feeling safe under the protection of Duke Albrecht, and apparently not in the least impressed by the general opposition which his innovations met with at the hands of the Lutherans, Osiander continued the controversy by publishing his *Proof* (*Beweisung*) *that for Thirty Years I have Always Taught the Same Doctrine.* And irritated by an opinion of Melanchthon (whom Osiander denounced as a pestilential heretic), published with offensive explanations added by the Wittenbergers, he in the same year (April, 1552) wrote his *Refutation* (*Widerlegung*) *of the Unfounded, Unprofitable Answer of Philip Melanchthon.* In this immoderate publication Osiander boasted that only the Philippian rabble, dancing according to the piping of Melanchthon, was opposed to him.

Before long, however, also such opponents of the Philippists as Flacius, Gallus, Amsdorf, and Wigand were prominently arraigned against Osiander. Meanwhile (May 23, 1552) Moerlin published a large volume entitled: *Concerning the Justification of Faith.* Osiander replied in his *Schmeckbier* of June 24, 1552, a book as keen as it was coarse. In 1552 and 1553 Flacius issued no less than twelve publications against Osiander, one of them bearing the title: *Zwo fuernehmliche Gruende Osiandri verlegt, zu einem Schmeckbier;* another: *Antidotum auf Osiandri giftiges Schmeckbier.* (Preger 2, 551.)

When the controversy had just about reached its climax, Osiander died, October 17, 1552. Soon after, the Duke enjoined silence on both parties, and Moerlin was banished. He accepted a position as superintendent in Brunswick, where he zealously continued his opposition to Osiandrism as well as to other corruptions of genuine Lutheranism. At Koenigsberg the Osiandrists continued to enjoy the protection and favor of Duke Albrecht, and gradually developed into a quasi-political party. The leader of the small band was John Funck, the son-in-law of Osiander and the chaplain of the Duke. In 1566, however, the king of Poland intervened, and Funck was executed as a disturber of the public peace. Moerlin was recalled and served as bishop of Samland at Koenigsberg from 1567 till his death in 1571. The *Corpus Doctrinae Pruthenicum,* or *Borussicum,* framed by Moerlin and Chemnitz and adopted 1567 at Koenigsberg, rejected the doctrines of Osiander. Moerlin also wrote a history of Osiandrism entitled: *Historia, welchergestalt sich die Osiandrische Schwaermerei im Lande zu Preussen erhaben.*

## 177. Corruptions Involved in Osiander's Teaching.

Osiander's theory of justification, according to which the righteousness of faith is the eternal, essential holiness of the divine nature of Christ inhering and dwelling in man, consistently compelled him to maintain that justification is not an act by which God declares a man just, but an act by which He actually makes him inherently just and righteous; that it is not an imputation of a righteousness existing outside of man, but an actual infusion of a righteousness dwelling in man; that it is not a mere acquittal from sin and guilt, but regeneration, renewal, sanctification, and internal, physical cleansing from sin; that it is not a forensic or judicial act outside of man or a declaration concerning man's standing before God and his relation to Him, but a sort of medicinal process within man; that the righteousness of faith is not the alien (strange, foreign) righteousness, *aliena iustitia* (a term employed also by Luther), consisting in the obedience of Christ, but a quality, condition, or change effected in believers by the essential righteousness of the divine nature dwelling in them through faith in Christ; that faith does not justify on account of the thing outside of man in which it trusts and upon which it relies, but by reason of the thing which it introduces and produces in man; that, accordingly, justification is never instantaneous and complete, but gradual and progressive.

Osiander plainly teaches that the righteousness of faith (our righteousness before God) is not the obedience rendered by Christ to the divine Law, but the indwelling righteousness of God (*iustitia Dei inhabitans*), — essentially the same original righteousness or image that inhered in Adam and Eve before the Fall. It consists, not indeed in good works or in "doing and suffering," but in a quality (*Art*) which renders him who receives it just, and moves him to do and to suffer what is right. It is the holiness (*Frommkeit*) which consists in the renewal of man, in the gifts of grace, in the new spiritual life, in the regenerated nature of man. By His suffering and death, said Osiander, Christ made satisfaction and acquired forgiveness for us, but He did not thereby effect our justification. His obedience as such does not constitute our righteousness before God, but merely serves to restore it. It was necessary that God might be able to dwell in us, and so become our life and righteousness. Faith justifies, not inasmuch as it apprehends the merits of Christ, but inasmuch as it unites us with the divine nature, the infinite essential righteousness of God, in which our sins are diluted, as it were, and lost, as an impure drop disappears when poured into an ocean of liquid purity.

According to the teaching of Osiander, therefore, also the assurance that we are justified and accepted by God does not rest exclusively on the merits of Christ and the pardon offered in the Gospel, but must be based on the righteous quality inhering in us. Our assurance is conditioned not alone upon what Christ has done outside of us and for us, but rather upon what He is in us and produces in us. The satisfaction rendered by Christ many centuries ago is neither the only ground on which God regards us as just, nor a sufficient basis of our certainty that we are accepted by God. Not the Christ for us, but rather the Christ in us, is the basis both of our justification and assurance. Accordingly, in order to satisfy an alarmed sinner, it is not sufficient to proclaim the Gospel-promise of divine absolution. In addition, an investigation is required whether the righteousness and holiness of God is also really found dwelling in him. While Luther had urged alarmed consciences to trust in the merits of Christ alone for their justification and salvation, Osiander led them to rely on the new life of divine wisdom, holiness, and righteousness dwelling in their own hearts. From the very beginning of the controversy, Moerlin, Melanchthon, and the Lutherans generally were solicitous to point out that Osiander's doctrine robs Christians of this glorious and only solid comfort, that it is not a subjective quality in their own hearts, but solely and only the objective and absolutely perfect obedience rendered by Christ many hundred years ago, which God regards when He justifies the wicked, and upon which man must rely for the assurance of his acceptance and salvation.

Consistently developed, therefore, the innovation of Osiander was bound to vitiate in every particular the doctrine of justification restored once more by Luther. In fact, his theory was but a revamping of just such teaching as had driven the Lutherans out of the Church of Rome. True, Osiander denied that by our own works we merit justification; that our righteousness consists in our good works; that our good works are imputed to us as righteousness. But the fact that he held a subjective condition to be our righteousness before God gives to his doctrine an essentially Roman stamp, no matter how widely it may differ from it in other respects. Moehler, the renowned Catholic apologist, declared that, properly interpreted and illucidated, Osiander's doctrine was "identical with the Roman Catholic doctrine." (Frank 2, 5. 91.) As stated before, his teaching was Romanism in its finer and more veiled form of mysticism.

## 178. Excerpts from Osiander's Writings.

In his publication of January 10, 1552, *Wider den lichtfluechtigen Nachtraben*, Osiander endeavors to prove that he is in complete doctrinal agreement with Luther. In it he gives the following summary, but guarded, presentation of his views. "I understand it this way," says he. "1. It flowed from His pure grace and mercy that God sacrificed His only Son for us. 2. The Son became man and was made under the Law, and He has redeemed us from the Law and from the curse of the Law. 3. He took upon Himself the sins of the whole world, for which He suffered, died, shed His blood, descended into hell, rose again, and thus overcame sin, death, and hell, and merited for us forgiveness of sin, reconciliation with God, the grace and gift of justification, and eternal life. 4. This is to be preached in all the world. 5. Whoever believes this and is baptized, is justified and blessed (*selig*) by virtue of such faith. 6. Faith apprehends Christ so that He dwells in our hearts through faith, Eph. 3, 17. 7. Christ, living in us through faith, is our Wisdom, Righteousness, Holiness, and Redemption, 1 Cor. 1, 30; Jer. 23, 6; 33, 16. 8. Christ, true God and man, dwelling in us through faith, is our Righteousness according to His divine nature, as Dr. Luther says: 'I rely on the righteousness which is God Himself; this He cannot reject. Such is, says Luther, the simple, correct understanding; do not suffer yourself to be led away from it.'" (Frank 2, 7 f.) Seeberg cites the following passage: "But if the question be asked what is righteousness, one must answer: Christ dwelling in us by faith is our Righteousness according to His divinity; and the forgiveness of sins, which is not Christ Himself, but merited by Christ, is a preparation and cause that God offers us His righteousness, which He is Himself." (*Dogg.* 4, 498.) Incidentally, Osiander's appeal to Luther is unwarranted. For according to him Christ is our Righteousness because His obedience is God's obedience, the work not only of His human nature, but, at the same time, also of His divine nature, while according to Osiander everything that Christ did for us merely serves to bring about the indwelling of the divine nature of Christ, whose essential holiness is our righteousness before God. That Osiander was not in agreement with Luther, as he claimed, appears also from his assertion that such statements of Luther as: Christ's death is our life, forgiveness of sins is our righteousness, etc., must be explained figuratively, as words flowing from a joyous heart. (2, 23.)

The manner in which Osiander maintained that Christ is our Righteousness only according to His divine nature appears from the following excerpts: "If the question be asked according to what nature Christ, His whole undivided person, is our Righteousness, then, just as when one asks according to what nature He is the Creator of heaven and earth, the clear, correct, and plain answer is that He is our Righteousness according to His divine, and not according to His human nature, although we are unable to find, obtain, or apprehend such divine righteousness apart from His humanity." (Frank 2, 12.) Again: "When we say: Christ is our Righteousness, we must understand His deity, which enters us through His humanity. When Christ says: I am the Bread of Life, we must understand His deity which comes into us through His humanity and is our life. When He says: My flesh is meat indeed, and My blood is drink indeed, we must take it to mean His deity which is in the flesh and blood and is meat and drink for us. Thus, too, when John says, 1 John 1, 7: The blood of Christ cleanseth us from all sin, we must understand the deity of Christ which is in the blood; for John does

not speak of the blood of Christ as it was shed on the cross, but as it, united with the flesh of Christ, is our heavenly meat and drink by faith." (23.) Osiander, therefore, is but consistent when he reiterates that the Son of God, the Holy Spirit, and the Father are our Righteousness, because their divine essence, which by faith dwells in Christians, is one and the same.

Osiander emphasizes that the essential righteousness of the divine nature of Christ alone is able to save us. He says: "For of what help would it be to you if you had all the righteousness which men and angels can imagine, but lacked this eternal righteousness which is itself the Son of God, according to His divine nature, with the Father and the Holy Ghost? For no other righteousness can lift you up to heaven and bring you to the Father. But when you apprehend this righteousness through faith, and Christ is in you, what can you then be lacking which you do not possess richly, superabundantly, and infinitely in His deity?" Again: "Since Christ is ours and is in us, God Himself and all His angels behold nothing in us but righteousness on account of the highest, eternal, and infinite righteousness of Christ, which is His deity itself dwelling in us. And although sin still remains in, and clings to, our flesh, it is like an impure little drop compared with a great pure ocean, and on account of the righteousness of Christ which is in us God does not want to see it." (Frank 2, 100. 102.)

To this peculiarity of Osiander, according to which he seems to have had in mind a justification by a sort of mystico-physical dilution rather than by imputation, the *Formula of Concord* refers as follows: "For one side has contended that the righteousness of faith, which the apostle calls the righteousness of God, is God's essential righteousness, which is Christ Himself as the true, natural, and essential Son of God, who dwells in the elect by faith and impels them to do right, and thus is their righteousness, compared with which righteousness the sins of all men are as a drop of water compared with the great ocean." (917, 2; 790, 2.)

In his confession *Concerning the Only Mediator*, of 1551, Osiander expatiates on justification, and defines it as an act by which righteousness is "infused" into believers. We read: "It is apparent that whatever part Christ, as the faithful Mediator, acted with regard to God, His heavenly Father, for our sakes, by fulfilling the Law and by His suffering and death, was accomplished more than 1,500 years ago, when we were not in existence. For this reason it cannot, properly speaking, have been, nor be called, our justification, but only our redemption and the atonement for us and our sins. For whoever would be justified must believe; but if he is to believe, he must already be born and live. Therefore Christ has not justified us who *now* live and die; but we are redeemed by it [His work 1,500 years ago] from God's wrath, death, and hell. . . . This, however, is true and undoubted that by the fulfilment of the Law and by His suffering and death He merited and earned from God, His heavenly Father, this great and superabounding grace, namely, that He not only has forgiven our sin and taken from us the unbearable burden of the Law, but that He also *wishes to justify us by faith in Christ, to infuse justification or the righteousness (sondern auch uns durch den Glauben an Christum will rechtfertigen, die Gerechtmachung eingiessen)*, and, if only we obey, through the operation of His Holy Spirit and through the death of Christ, in which we are embodied by the baptism of Christ, *to mortify, purge out, and entirely destroy sin* which is already forgiven us, but nevertheless still dwells in our flesh and adheres to us. Therefore the *other part* of the office of our dear faithful Lord and Mediator Jesus Christ is now to turn toward us in order to deal also with us poor sinners, as with the guilty party, that we acknowledge such great grace and gratefully receive it by faith, *in order that He by faith may make us alive and just from the guilt of sin, and that sin, which is already forgiven, but nevertheless still dwells and inheres in our flesh, may be altogether mortified and destroyed in us. And this, first of all, is the act of our justification.*" (Tschackert, 492 f.; Planck 4, 268.)

That Osiander practically identified justification with regeneration, renewal, and gradual sanctification appears from the following quotations. To justify, says he, means "to make a just man out of an unjust one, that is to recall a dead man to life — *ex impio iustum facere, hoc est, mortuum ad vitam revocare.*" (Seeberg 4, 499.) Again: "Thus the Gospel further shows its power and also justifies us, *i. e.,* it makes us just, even as, and in the same degree as, He also makes us alive (*eben und in aller Masse, wie er uns auch lebendig macht*)." (Frank 2, 18.) "And here you see again how terribly those err who endeavor to prove by this passage of David and Paul that our righteousness is nothing else than forgiveness of sin; for they have overlooked the covering of sin with the [essential] righteousness of Christ whom we put on in Baptism; *they have also removed from justification the renewal of the inner man effected by regeneration.*" (102.)

Osiander was fanatical in denouncing those who identified justification with the forgiveness of sins. In his Disputation of October 24, 1550, he declared: "The entire fulness of the deity dwells in Christ bodily, hence in those also in whom Christ dwells. . . . Therefore we are just by His essential righteousness. . . . Whoever does not hold this manner of our justification is certainly a Zwinglian at heart, no matter what he may confess with his mouth. . . . They also teach things colder than ice [who hold] that we are regarded as righteous only on account of the forgiveness of sins, and not on account of the [essential] righteousness of Christ who dwells in us through faith. *Glacie frigidiora docent nos tantum propter remissionem peccatorum reputari iustos, et non etiam propter iustitiam Christi per fidem in nobis inhabitantis. Non*

*enim tam iniquus Deus est, ut eum pro iusto habeat, in quo verae iustitiae prorsus nil est.*" (Frank 2, 97; Tschackert, 494; Seeberg 4, 497.) They are errorists, Osiander declared, "who say, teach, and write that the righteousness is outside of us." (Frank 2, 100.) "The [essential] righteousness of Christ is, indeed, imputed to us, but only when it is in us." "For God is not so unrighteous, nor such a lover of unrighteousness that He regards him as just in whom there is absolutely nothing of the true righteousness; as it is written, Ps. 5, 4: 'For Thou art not a God that hath pleasure in wickedness; neither shall evil dwell with Thee.'" (Planck 4, 273.) Evidently, Osiander rejected or had never fully grasped Paul's clear statement and teaching concerning the God who justifies the ungodly, Rom. 4, 5: "But to him that worketh not, but believeth on Him that justifieth the ungodly, his faith is counted for righteousness."

### 179. Attitude of Brenz and Melanchthon.

With the exception of Brenz and Vogel, who, as stated before, regarded Osiander's doctrine as differing from the generally received view in phraseology and mode of presentation rather than in substance, the Lutherans everywhere were unanimous in rejecting Osiander's theory as a recrudescence of the Romish justification not by imputation, but by infusion. And as to Brenz, who put a milder construction on the statements of Osiander, Melanchthon wrote October 1, 1557: "Concerning the affair with Osiander, my writings are publicly known, which I hope will be of benefit to many. Brenz also is agreed with us doctrinally. He said he had advised peace, for he did not take Osiander's expressions to be as dangerous as the opponents did, and for this reason could not as yet condemn his person; but in doctrine he was agreed with us and would unite in condemning Osiander if the charges made against him were proved." Melanchthon himself realized the viciousness of Osiander's error, although at the colloquy in Worms, 1557, he, too, was opposed to condemning Osiandrism together with Zwinglianism, Majorism, and Adiaphorism, as the theologians of Ducal Saxony demanded. (*C. R.* 9, 311. 402.)

In May, 1551, Melanchthon wrote to Osiander that by the essential righteousness of Christ renewal is effected in us, but that we have forgiveness of sins and are reputed to be righteous on account of the merit of Christ, whose blood and death appeased the wrath of God. In his confutation of the Osiandric doctrine, written in September, 1555, we read: "Osiander's definition of righteousness is: Righteousness is that which makes us do what is righteous. . . . Hence man is righteous by doing what is righteous. . . . Thereupon Osiander, in order to say something also concerning forgiveness of sins, tears remission of sins from righteousness. He expressly declares that the sins are forgiven to all men; Nero, however, is damned because he does not possess the essential righteousness; and this, he says, is God Himself, Father, Son, and Holy Spirit. . . . Osiander contends that man is just on account of the indwelling of God, or on account of the indwelling God, not on account of the obedience of the Mediator, not by the imputed righteousness of the Mediator through grace. And he corrupts the proposition, 'By faith we are justified,' into, By faith we are prepared that we may become just by something else, *viz.*, the inhabiting God. Thus he in reality says what the Papists say: 'We are righteous by our renewal,' except that he mentions the cause where the Papists mention the effect. *Ita re ipsa dicit, quod Papistae dicunt, sumus iusti novitate, nisi quod nominat causam, ubi nominant Papistae effectum.* We are just when God renews us. He therefore detracts from the honor due to the Mediator, obscures the greatness of sin, destroys the chief consolation of the pious, and leads them into perpetual doubt. For faith cannot exist unless it looks upon the promise of mercy concerning the Mediator. Nor is there an inhabitation unless the consolation is received by this faith. And it is a preposterous way of teaching that one is to believe first the inhabitation, afterwards forgiveness of sins (*prius credere inhabitationem, postea remissionem peccatorum*). Since therefore this dogma of Osiander is both false and pernicious to consciences, it must be shunned and damned." (*C. R.* 7, 781; 8, 579 ff.)

In another essay, of September, 1555, signed also by Melanchthon, the following propositions are rejected: 1. Man becomes righteous on account of the essential righteousness. 2. Man becomes righteous on account of the essential righteousness of God the Father, Son, and Holy Spirit. 3. Man becomes righteous before God on account of the indwelling of God. 4. Righteousness consists in the indwelling of Christ, on account of which God imputes righteousness to us. . . . 5. Nor must one say there are two or more parts of justification: faith, inhabitation, good works, etc. For justification before God is to receive forgiveness of sins and to become acceptable to God on account of Christ. . . . 6. This proposition, too, is false: The regenerate after the Fall are righteous in the same manner as Adam was before the Fall, namely, not by imputation, but by inhabitation or original righteousness. . . . 8. It is also false when some say we are righteous by faith, namely, in a preparative way in order afterwards to be righteous by the essential righteousness. At bottom this is Popish and destructive of faith. . . . 9. The following propositions must be rejected altogether: The obedience of Christ is called righteousness in a tropical sense; Christ justifies accidentally (*per accidens*). (*C. R.* 8, 561 f.; 9, 319. 451. 455. 457.)

### 180. Osiander's Views on Image of God.

Osiander's corruption of the doctrine of justification was closely connected with his peculiar view concerning the image of God (the central idea of his entire system), of which, however, he declared that he did not consider it essential, and would not contend with anybody about it. Nor were the questions involved disputed to any extent or dealt with in the *Formula of Concord*. As to Osiander, however, the train of his thoughts runs as follows: —

The Logos, the divine Word, is the image of God, into whom His entire essence flows in a manner and process eternal. In a temporal and historical way the same image is destined to be realized in the nature of man. Divine essential righteousness indwelling and efficacious in humanity — such was the eternal plan of God. For the realization of this purpose the Logos, God's image, was to become man, even if the human race should not have fallen. This was necessary because in finite man there is absolutely no similarity with the infinite essence of the non-incarnate Logos. Without the incarnation, therefore, this infinite dissimilarity would have remained forever (*esset et maneret simpliciter infinita dissimilitudo inter hominem et Verbum Dei*). And in order that man might be capable of God and share His divine nature (*capax Dei et divinae naturae consors*), God created him according to His image; *i. e.*, according to the idea of the incarnate Logos. "God formed the body of man," said Osiander, "that it should be altogether like unto the future body of Christ. Thereupon He breathed into it the breath of life, *i. e.*, a rational soul together with the human spirit, adorned with the proper powers, in such a manner that it, too, should be like unto the future soul of Christ in everything." (Frank 2, 104.)

In the incarnate Logos, however, according to whom man was created, humanity and divinity are personally united. When the Word was made flesh, the divine essence was imparted to His human nature. And Christ, in turn, imparts the same essence to all who by faith are one with Him. From eternity the incarnate Word was destined to be the head of the congregation in order that the essential righteousness of God might flow from Him into His body, the believers. Before the Fall the Son of God dwelled in Adam, making him just by God's essential righteousness. By the Fall this righteousness was lost. Hence the redemption and atonement of Christ were required in order again to pave the way for the renewal of the lost image or the indwelling of God's essential righteousness in man. The real source of this righteousness and divine life in man, however, is not the human, but the divine nature of Christ. In the process of justification or of making man righteous, the human nature of Christ merely serves as a medium, or, as it were, a canal, through which the eternal essential wisdom, holiness, and righteousness of Christ's divine nature flows into our hearts.

Christ, the "inner Word" (John 1), says Osiander, approaches man in the "external Word" (the words spoken by Jesus and His apostles), and through it enters the believing soul. For through Word, Sacrament, and faith we are united with His humanity. In the Lord's Supper, for instance, we become the flesh and blood of Christ, just as we draw the nourishment out of natural food and transform it into our flesh and blood. And since the humanity of Christ, with which we become one in the manner described, is personally united with the deity, it imparts to us also the divine essence, and, as a result, we, too, are the abode of the essential righteousness of God. "We cannot receive the divine nature from Christ," says Osiander, "if we are not embodied in Him by faith and Baptism, thus becoming flesh and blood and bone of His flesh, blood, and bone." As the branches could not partake of the nature of the vine if they were not of the wood of the vine, even so we could not share the divine nature of Christ if we had not, incorporated in Him by faith and Baptism, become flesh, blood, and bone of His flesh, blood, and bone. Accordingly, as Christ's humanity became righteous through the union with God, the essential righteousness which moved Him to obedience toward God, thus we also become righteous through our union with Christ and in Him with God. (Frank 2, 104. 20 ff.; Seeberg 4, 497 f.)

In view of such speculative teaching, in which justification is transformed into a sort of mystico-physical process, it is not surprising that the charge of pantheism was also raised against Osiander. The theologians of Brandenburg asserted that he inferred from his doctrine that the believers in Christ are also divine persons, because the Father, Son, and Holy Ghost, dwell in them essentially. But Osiander protested: "Creatures we are and creatures we remain, no matter how wonderfully we are renewed; but the seed of God and the entire divine essence which is in us by grace in the same manner as it is in Christ by nature and remains eternally in us (das also aus Gnaden in uns ist wie in Christo von Natur und bleibt ewiglich in uns) is God Himself, and no creature, and will not become a creature in us or on account of us, but will eternally remain in us true God." Frank says concerning the doctrine of Osiander: It is not pantheism or a mixture of the divine and human nature, "but it is a subjectivism by which the objective foundation of salvation as taught by the Lutheran Church is rent to the very bottom. It is a mysticism which transforms the Christ for us into the Christ in us, and, though unintentionally, makes the consciousness of the inhabitatio essentialis iustitiae (indwelling of the essential righteousness) the basis of peace with God." (2, 19. 10. 13. 95. 103.) In his teaching concerning the image of God and justification, Osiander replaced the comforting doctrine of the Bible concerning the substitutionary and atoning work of Christ in His active and passive obedience unto death with vain philosophical speculations concerning divinity and humanity or the two natures of Christ. It was not so very far beside the mark, therefore, when Justus Menius characterized his theory as "a new alchemistic theology." (Planck 4, 257.)

## 181. Error of Stancarus.

The Stancarian dispute was incidental to the Osiandric conflict. Its author was Francesco Stancaro (born in Mantua, 1501), an Italian ex-priest, who had emigrated from Italy on account of his Protestant views. Vain, opinionated, haughty, stubborn, and insolent as he was, he roamed about, creating trouble wherever he appeared, first in Cracow as professor of Hebrew, 1551 in Koenigsberg, then in Frankfort-on-the-Oder, next at various places in Poland, Hungary, and Transylvania. He died in Stobnitz, Poland, November 12, 1574. Stancarus treated all of his opponents as ignoramuses and spoke contemptuously of Luther and Melanchthon, branding the latter as an antichrist. In Koenigsberg he immediately felt called upon to interfere in the controversy which had just flared up. He opposed Osiander in a fanatical manner, declaring him to be the personal antichrist. The opponents of Osiander at Koenigsberg, however, were not elated over his comradeship, particularly because he fell into an opposite error. They were glad when he resigned and left for Frankfort the same year he had arrived at Koenigsberg. In Frankfort, Stancarus continued the controversy, publishing, 1552, his Apology against Osiander — Apologia contra Osiandrum. But he was ignored rather than opposed by the Lutheran theologians. In 1553 Melanchthon wrote his Answer (Responsio) Concerning Stancar's Controversy. Later on, 1561, when Stancarus was spreading his errors in Poland, Hungary, and Transylvania, Calvin and the ministers of Zurich also wrote against him. The chief publication in which Stancarus set forth and defended his views appeared 1562, at Cracow, under the title: Concerning the Trinity (De Trinitate) and the Mediator, Our Lord Jesus Christ. As late as 1585 Wigand published his book Concerning Stancarism — De Stancarismo.

Stancarus had been trained in scholastic theology and was a great admirer of Peter Lombard. In his book De Trinitate et Mediatore he says: "One Peter Lombard is worth more than a hundred Luthers, two hundred Melanchthons, three hundred Bullingers, four hundred Peter Martyrs, five hundred Calvins, out of whom, if they were all brayed in a mortar, not one drop of true theology would be squeezed. Plus valet unus Petrus Lombardus quam centum Lutheri, ducenti Melanchthones, trecenti Bullingeri, quadringenti Petri Martyres et quingenti Calvini, qui omnes, si in mortario contunderentur, non exprimeretur una mica verae theologiae." (J. G. Walch, Religionsstreitigkeiten 4, 177.) Concerning Christ's obedience Peter Lombard taught: "Christus Mediator dicitur secundum humanitatem, non secundum divinitatem. . . . Mediator est ergo, in quantum homo, et non in quantum Deus. Christ is called Mediator according to His humanity, not according to His divinity. . . . He is therefore Mediator inasmuch as He is man, and not inasmuch as He is God." (Planck 4, 451; Seeberg 4, 507.) In accordance with this teaching, Stancarus maintained, in pointed opposition to Osiander, that Christ is our Righteousness only according to His human nature, and not according to His divine nature. The divine nature of Christ, Stancarus declared, must be excluded from the office of Christ's mediation and priesthood; for if God the Son were Mediator and would do something which the Father and the Holy Spirit could not do, then He would have a will and an operation and hence also a nature and essence different from that of the Father and the Holy Spirit. He wrote: "Christ, God and man, is Mediator [and Redeemer] only according to the other nature, namely, the human, not according to the divine; Christ made satisfaction for us according to His human nature, but not according to His divine nature; according to His divine nature Christ was not under the Law, was not obedient unto death, etc." (Frank 2, 111.) Stancarus argued: "Christ is one God with the Father and the Holy Spirit. Apart from the three personal properties of *'paternitas, filiatio,* and *spiratio passiva'* the three divine persons are absolutely identical in their being and operation. Their work is the sending of the Mediator, whose divine nature itself, in an active way, participates in this sending; hence only the human nature of the God-man *is* sent, and only the human nature of the Mediator acts in a reconciling way. Men are reconciled by Christ's death on the cross; but the blood shed on the cross and death are peculiar to the human nature, not to the divine nature; hence we are reconciled by the human nature of Christ only, and not by His divine nature (*ergo per naturam humanam Christi tantum sumus reconciliati et non per divinam*)." (Schluesselburg 9, 216 ff.)

Consistently, the Stancarian doctrine destroys both the unity of the person of Christ and the sufficiency of His atonement. It not only corrupts the doctrine of the infinite and truly redeeming value of the obedience of the God-man, but also denies the personal union of the divine and human natures in Christ. For if the divine nature is excluded from the work of Christ, then it must be excluded also from His person, since works are always acts of a person. And if it was a mere human nature that died for us, then the price of our redemption is altogether inadequate, and we are not redeemed, as Luther so earnestly emphasized against Zwingli. (CONC. TRIGL. 1028, 44.) True, Stancarus protested: "Christ is Mediator according to the human nature *only;* this exclusive 'only' does not exclude the divine nature from the person of Christ, but from His office as Mediator." (Frank 2, 111.) However, just this was Luther's contention, that Christ is our Mediator also according to His divine nature, and that the denial of this truth both invalidates His satisfaction and divides His person.

The Third Article of the *Formula of Concord,* therefore, rejects the error of Stancarus as well as that of Osiander. Against the latter it maintains that the active and passive obedience of Christ is our righteousness before God; and over against the former, that this obedience was the act of the entire person of Christ, and not of His human nature alone. We read: "In opposition to both these parties [Osiander and Stancarus] it has been unanimously taught by the other teachers of the *Augsburg Confession* that Christ is our Righteousness not according to His divine nature alone, nor according to His human nature alone, but according to both natures; for He has redeemed, justified, and saved us from our sins as God and man, through His complete obedience; that therefore the righteousness of faith is the forgiveness of sins, reconciliation with God, and our adoption as God's children only on account of the obedience of Christ, which through faith alone, out of pure grace, is imputed for righteousness to all true believers, and on account of it they are absolved from all their unrighteousness." (916, 4.)

## 182. Deviations of Parsimonius and Hamburg Ministers.

In 1563 a collateral controversy concerning the obedience of Christ was raised by Parsimonius (George Karg). He was born 1512; studied under Luther in Wittenberg; 1547 he became pastor in Schwabach, and 1556 superintendent in Ansbach; 1563 he was deposed because of erroneous theses published in that year; he was opposed by Hesshusius and Ketzmann in Ansbach; 1570, having discussed his difference with the theologians in Wittenberg, Karg retracted and was restored to his office; he died 1576. In his theses on justification Parsimonius deviated from the Lutheran doctrine by teaching that Christ redeemed us by His passive obedience only, and by denying that His active obedience had any vicarious merit, since as man He Himself owed such obedience to the Law of God, — a view afterwards defended also by such Reformed divines as John Piscator, John Camero, and perhaps Ursinus. (Schaff 1, 274.)

Over against this error the *Formula of Concord* explains and declares: "Therefore the righteousness which is imputed to faith or to the believer out of pure grace is the obedience, suffering, and resurrection of Christ, since He has made satisfaction for us to the Law, and paid for our sins. For since Christ is not man alone, but God and man in one undivided person, He was as little subject to the Law (because He is the Lord of the Law) as He had to suffer and die as far as His person is concerned. For this reason, then, His obedience, not only in suffering and dying, but also in this, that He in our stead was voluntarily made under the Law and fulfilled it by this obedience, is imputed to us for righteousness, so that, on account of this complete obedience, which He rendered His heavenly Father for us, by doing and suffering, in living and dying, God forgives our sins, regards us as godly and righteous, and eternally saves us." (919, 16.) —

In their zealous opposition to the doctrine of Osiander, according to which the indwelling essential holiness of the divine nature of Christ is our righteousness before God, also the Hamburg ministers went a step too far in the opposite direction. They denied, or at any rate seemed to deny, the indwelling of the Holy Trinity as such in believers. In their *Response* (*Responsio*) of 1552 they declared: "God is said to dwell where He is present by His grace and benevolence, where He gives the Word of His grace, and reveals His promises concerning His mercy and the remission of sins, where He works by His Spirit, etc." (Frank 2, 107.) Again: "That His indwelling pertains to His efficacy and operation appears from many passages which describe without a figure the efficacy and operation of Christ and of the Holy Spirit dwelling in believers." "The dwelling of the Holy Spirit in believers signifies that they are led by the Spirit of God." "But it cannot be proved by the Scripture that the fulness of God dwells bodily in us as it dwells in Christ Jesus. The inhabitation of God in us is a matter of grace, not of nature; of gift, not of property." (107.)

In 1551 Melanchthon had written: "It must be admitted that God dwells in our hearts, not only in such a manner that He there is efficacious, though not present with His own essence, but that He is both present and efficacious. A personal union, however, does not take place in us, but God is present in us in a separable manner as in a separable domicile." (*C. R.* 7, 781.) This was the view of the Lutheran theologians generally. Article III of the *Formula of Concord*, too, is emphatic in disavowing a personal union of the deity and humanity in believers, as well as in asserting that God Himself, not merely His gifts, dwell in Christians. (935, 54; 937, 65.) In addition to the aberrations enumerated, Article III rejects also some of the Roman and the Romanizing errors concerning justification in the Leipzig Interim, and some views entertained by Majorists which are extensively and *ex professo* dealt with in Article IV. (CONC. TRIGL. 917, 5.)

# XVII. The Antinomistic Controversy.

### 183. Distinction between Law and Gospel of Paramount Import.

Zwingli, who was a moralist and a Humanist rather than a truly evangelical reformer, taught: "In itself the Law is nothing else than a Gospel; that is, a good, certain message from God by means of which He instructs us concerning His will." (Frank 2, 312.) While Zwingli thus practically identified Law and Gospel, Luther, throughout his life, held that the difference between both is as great as that between life and death or the merits of Christ and our own sinful works; and that no one can be a true minister of the Christian Church who is unable properly to distinguish and apply them. For, according to Luther, a commingling of the Law and the Gospel necessarily leads to a corruption of the doctrine of justification, the very heart of Christianity. And as both must be carefully distinguished, so both must also be upheld and preached in the Church; for the Gospel presupposes the Law and is rendered meaningless without it. Wherever the Law is despised, disparaged, and corrupted, the Gospel, too, cannot be kept intact. Whenever the Law is assailed, even if this be done in the name of the Gospel, the latter is, in reality, hit harder than the former. The cocoon of antinomianism always bursts into antigospelism. Majorism, the mingling of sanctification and justification, and synergism, the mingling of nature and grace, were but veiled efforts to open once more the doors of the Lutheran Church to the Roman work-righteousness, which Luther had expelled. The same is true of antinomianism in all its forms. It amounts to nothing less than apostasy from true Evangelicalism and a return to Romanism. When Luther opposed Agricola, the father of the Antinomians in the days of the Reformation, he did so with the clear knowledge that the Gospel of Jesus Christ with its

doctrine of justification by grace and faith alone was at stake and in need of defense. "By these spirits," said he, "the devil does not intend to rob us of the Law, but of Christ, who fulfilled the Law." (St. L. 20, 1614; Pieper, *Dogm.* 3, 279; Frank 2, 268. 325.)

With the same interest in view, to save the Gospel from corruption, the *Formula of Concord* opposes antinomianism and urges that the distinction between the Law and the Gospel be carefully preserved. The opening paragraph of Article V, "Of the Law and the Gospel," reads: "As the distinction between the Law and Gospel *is a special brilliant light* which serves to the end that God's Word may be rightly divided, and the Scriptures of the holy prophets and apostles may be properly explained and understood, we must guard it with especial care, in order that these two doctrines may not be mingled with one another, or a Law be made out of the Gospel, whereby the merit of Christ is obscured and troubled consciences are robbed of their comfort, which they otherwise have in the holy Gospel when it is preached genuinely and in its purity, and by which they can support themselves in their most grievous trials against the terrors of the Law." (951, 1.) The concluding paragraph of this article declares that the proper distinction between the Law and the Gospel must be preserved, "in order that both doctrines, that of the Law and that of the Gospel, be not mingled and confounded with one another, and what belongs to the one may not be ascribed to the other, *whereby the merit and benefits of Christ are easily obscured and the Gospel is again turned into a doctrine of the Law,* as has occurred in the Papacy, and thus Christians are deprived of the true comfort which they have in the Gospel against the terrors of the Law, and the door is again opened in the Church of God to the Papacy." (961, 27.) The blessed Gospel, our only comfort and consolation against the terrors of the Law, will be corrupted wherever the Law and the Gospel are not properly distinguished, — such, then, was the view also of the *Formula of Concord.*

Articles V and VI of the *Formula* treat and dispose of the issues raised by the Antinomians. In both Luther's doctrine is maintained and reaffirmed. Article V, "Of the Law and Gospel," teaches that, in the proper sense of the term, everything is Law that reveals and rebukes sin, the sin of unbelief in Christ and the Gospel included; that Gospel, in the proper and narrow sense, is nothing but a proclamation and preaching of grace and forgiveness of sin; that, accordingly, the Law as well as the Gospel are needed and must be retained and preached in the Church. This was precisely what Luther had taught. In one of his theses against Agricola he says: "Whatever discloses sin, wrath, or death exercises the office of the Law; Law and the disclosing of sin or the revelation of wrath are convertible terms. *Quidquid ostendit peccatum, iram seu mortem, id exercet officium legis; lex et ostensio peccati seu revelatio irae sunt termini convertibiles.*" Article VI, "Of the Third Use of the Law," teaches that, although Christians, in as far as they are regenerate, do the will of God spontaneously, the Law must nevertheless be preached to them on account of their Old Adam, not only as a mirror revealing their sins and as a check on the lusts of the flesh, but also as a rule of their lives. This, too, is precisely what Luther had maintained against Agricola: "The Law," said he, "must be retained [in the Church], that the saints may know which are the works God requires." (Drews, *Disputationen Dr. Martin Luthers,* 418; *Herzog R.* 1, 588; *Frank* 2, 272; *Tschackert,* 482.)

### 184. Agricola Breeding Trouble.

In the Lutheran Church antinomianism appeared in a double form: one chiefly before, the other after the death of Luther. The first of these conflicts was originated by Agricola, who spoke most contemptuously and disparagingly of the Law of God, teaching, in particular, that true knowledge of sin and genuine contrition is produced, not by the Law, but by the Gospel only, and that hence there is in the Church no use whatever for the Law of God. After Luther's death similar antinomistic errors were entertained and defended by the Philippists in Wittenberg, who maintained that the sin of unbelief is rebuked not by the Law, but by the Gospel. Poach, Otto, and others denied that, with respect to good works, the Law was of any service whatever to Christians after their conversion.

Barring Carlstadt and similar spirits, John Agricola (Schnitter, Kornschneider, Magister Islebius — Luther called him Grickel) was the first to strike a discordant note and breed trouble within the Lutheran Church. Born April 20, 1492, at Eisleben, he studied at Leipzig, and from 1515 to 1516 at Wittenberg.

Here he became an enthusiastic adherent and a close friend of Luther and also of Melanchthon, after the latter's arrival in 1518. In 1539 Luther himself declared that Agricola had been "one of his best and closest friends." (St. L. 20, 1612.) In 1519 he accompanied both to the great debate in Leipzig. In 1525 he became teacher of the Latin school and, though never ordained, pastor of the church in Eisleben. Being a speaker of some renown, he was frequently engaged by the Elector of Saxony, especially on his journeys — to Speyer 1526 and 1529, to Augsburg 1530, to Vienna 1535. At Eisleben, Agricola was active also in a literary way, publishing sermons, a catechism, and, 1526, a famous collection of 300 German proverbs (the Wittenberg edition of 1592 contains 750 proverbs).

When the new theological professorship, created 1526 at Wittenberg, was given to Melanchthon, Agricola felt slighted and much disappointed. In the following year he made his first antinomian attack upon Melanchthon. The dispute was settled by Luther, but only for a time. In 1536 Agricola, through the influence of Luther (whose hospitality also he and his large family on their arrival in Wittenberg enjoyed for more than six weeks), received an appointment at the university. He rewarded his generous friend with intrigues and repeated renewals of the antinomian quarrels, now directing his attacks also against his benefactor. By 1540 matters had come to such a pass that the Elector felt constrained to institute a formal trial against the secret plotter, which Agricola escaped only by accepting a call of Joachim II as courtpreacher and superintendent at Berlin. After Luther's death, Agricola, as described in a preceding chapter, degraded and discredited himself by helping Pflug and Sidonius to prepare the Augsburg Interim (1547), and by endeavoring to enforce this infamous document in Brandenburg. He died September 22, 1566.

Vanity, ambition, conceit, insincerity, impudence, arrogance, and ungratefulness were the outstanding traits of Agricola's character. Luther said that Agricola, swelled with vanity and ambition, was more vexatious to him than any pope; that he was fit only for the profession of a jester, etc. December 6, 1540, Luther wrote to Jacob Stratner, courtpreacher in Berlin: "Master Grickel is not, nor ever will be, the man that he may appear, or the Margrave may consider him to be. For if you wish to know what vanity itself is, you can recognize it in no surer image than that of Eisleben. *Si enim velis scire, quidnam ipsa vanitas sit, nulla certiore imagine cognosces quam Islebii.*" (St. L. 21 b, 2536.) Flacius reports that shortly before Luther's death, when some endeavored to excuse Agricola, the former answered angrily: "Why endeavor to excuse Eisleben? Eisleben is incited by the devil, who has taken possession of him entirely. You will see what a stir he will make after my death! *Ihr werdet wohl erfahren, was er nach meinem Tod fuer einen Laerm wird anrichten!*" (Preger 1, 119.)

## 185. Agricola's Conflict with Melanchthon.

The antinomian views that repentance (contrition) is not wrought by the Law, but by the Gospel, and that hence there is no room for the Law and its preaching in the Christian Church, were uttered by Agricola as early as 1525. In his *Annotations to the Gospel of St. Luke* of that year he had written: "The Decalog belongs in the courthouse, not in the pulpit. All those who are occupied with Moses are bound to go to the devil. To the gallows with Moses!" (Tschackert, 481; *Herzog R.* 1, 588; E. 4, 423.) The public dispute began two years later when Agricola criticized Melanchthon because in the latter's "Instructions to the Visitors of the Churches of Saxony" (Articles of Visitation, *Articuli, de quibus Egerunt per Visitatores in Regione Saxoniae*, 1527) the ministers were urged first to preach the Law to their spiritually callous people in order to produce repentance (contrition), and thus to prepare them for saving faith in the Gospel, the only source of truly good works. Melanchthon had written: "Pastors must follow the example of Christ. Since He taught repentance and remission of sins, pastors also must teach these to their churches. At present it is common to vociferate concerning faith, and yet one cannot understand what faith is, unless repentance is preached. Plainly they pour new wine into old bottles who preach faith without repentance, without the doctrine of the fear of God, without the doctrine of the Law, and accustom the people to a certain carnal security, which is worse than all former errors under the Pope have been." (*C. R.* 26, 9.) Agricola considered these and similar exhortations of Melanchthon unfriendly and Romanizing, and published his dissent in his *130 Questions for Young Children*, where he displayed a shocking contempt for the Old Testament and the Law of God. In particular, he stressed the doctrine that genuine repentance (contrition) is wrought, not by the Law, but by the Gospel only. In letters to his friends, Agricola at the same time charged Melanchthon with corrupting the evangelical doctrine. (Frank 2, 252.)

At a meeting held at Torgau, November 26 to 28, 1527, the differences were discussed by Agricola and Melanchthon in the presence of Luther and Bugenhagen. The exact issue was: Does faith presuppose contrition? Melanchthon affirmed the question, and Agricola denied it. Luther finally effected an agreement by distinguishing between general and justifying faith, and by explaining that repentance (contrition), indeed, presupposes a general faith in God, but that justifying faith presupposes the terrors of conscience (contrition) wrought by the Law. His decision ran "that the term faith should be applied to justifying faith which consoles us in these terrors [produced by the threats of the Law], but that the word repentance correctly includes a general faith," viz., that there is a God who threatens transgressors, etc. (*C. R.* I, 916.)

In agreement herewith Melanchthon wrote in the German *Unterricht der Visitatoren*, published 1528 at Wittenberg, that, in the wider and more general sense, the term "faith" embraces contrition and the Law, but that in the interest of the common people the word "faith" should be reserved for the special Christian or justifying faith in Christ. We read: "Denn wiewohl etliche achten, man solle nichts lehren vor dem Glauben, sondern die Busse aus und nach dem Glauben folgend lehren, auf dass die Widersacher [Papisten] nicht sagen moegen, man widerrufe unsere vorige Lehre, so ist aber doch anzusehen, weil [dass] die Busse und Gesetz auch zu dem gemeinen Glauben gehoeren. Denn man muss ja zuvor glauben, dass Gott sei, der da drohe, gebiete, schrecke usw. So sei es fuer den gemeinen, groben Mann, dass man solche Stuecke des Glaubens lasse bleiben unter dem Namen Busse, Gebot, Gesetz, Furcht usw., auf dass sie desto unterschiedlicher den Glauben Christi verstehen, welchen die Apostel *iustificantem fidem*, das ist, der da gerecht macht und Suende vertilgt, nennen, welches der Glaube von dem Gebot und Busse nicht tut, und doch der gemeine Mann ueber dem Wort Glauben irre wird und Fragen aufbringt ohne Nutzen." (*C. R.* 26, 51 f.)

## 186. Luther's First Disputation against the Antinomians.

At Wittenberg, in 1537, Agricola renewed his antinomianism by secretly and anonymously circulating a number of propositions (*Positiones inter Fratres Sparsae*) directed against both Luther and Melanchthon, whom he branded as "contortors of the words of Christ," urging all to resist them in order to preserve the pure doctrine. Quotations from Luther and Melanchthon were appended to the theses in order to show that their teaching concerning the "mode of justification (*modus iustificationis*)" was sometimes "pure," sometimes "impure." Agricola wrote: "Impure [among the statements of Melanchthon and Luther] are: 1. In the *Saxon Visitation:* 'Since Christ commands that repentance and remission of sins is to be preached in His name, hence the Decalog is to be taught.' 2. Again ...: 'As the Gospel therefore teaches that the Law has been given to humiliate us, in order that we may seek Christ,' etc. 3. In his *Commentary on the Epistle to the Galatians* Luther says that it is the office of the Law to torment and to terrify the conscience, that it may know Christ more readily. Many similar passages are found in this commentary, which we reject as false, in order to maintain the purity of the doctrine." (E., v. a. 4, 422 f.; St. L. 20, 1627.)

Luther answered by publishing, December 1, 1537, the theses of Agricola together with *Other Antinomian Articles* (*Alii Articuli Antinomi*), compiled from written and verbal expressions of Agricola and his followers. In his introductory remarks Luther not only disowned and emphatically condemned (*nos ab eiusmodi portentis prorsus abhorrere*) Agricola's *Positiones inter Fratres Sparsae*, but also announced a number of disputations against antinomianism. (E. 4, 420.) The first was held December 18, 1537, in which Luther maintained: Contrition is wrought by the preaching of the Law; but a man is able to make a good resolution and to hate sin out of love toward God only after the Gospel has comforted his alarmed conscience.

Following are some of the 39 theses discussed by Luther in his first disputation against the Antinomians: "4. The first part of repentance, contrition, is [wrought] by the Law alone. The other part, the good purpose, cannot be [wrought] by the Law. 24. And they [the Antinomians] teach perniciously that the Law of God is simply to be removed from the church, which is blasphemous and sacrilegious. 25. For the entire Scripture teaches that repentance must begin from the Law, which also the order of the matter itself as well as experience shows. 31. Necessarily, then, sin and death cannot be revealed by the Word of Grace and Solace, but by the Law. 32. Experience teaches that Adam is first reproved as a transgressor of the Law, and afterwards cheered by the promised Seed of the woman. 33. Also David is first killed by the Law through Nathan, saying: 'Thou art the man,' etc.; afterwards he is saved by the Gospel, declaring: 'Thou shalt not die,' etc. [2 Sam. 12, 7. 13.] 34. Paul, prostrated by the Law, first hears: 'Why persecutest thou Me?' Afterwards he is revived by the Gospel: 'Arise,' etc. [Acts 9, 4. 6.] 35. And Christ Himself says, Mark 1, 15: 'Repent ye and believe the Gospel, for the kingdom of God is at hand.' 36. Again: 'Repentance and remission of sins should be preached in His name.' [Luke 24, 47.] 37. Likewise the Spirit first reproves the world of sin, in order to teach faith in Christ, i. e., forgiveness of sin. [John 16, 8.] 38. In the Epistle to the Romans Paul observes this method, first to teach that all are sinners, and thereupon, that they are to be justified solely through Christ." (Drews, 253 ff.; St. L. 20, 1628 ff.)

### 187. Luther's Second Disputation against the Antinomians.

Since Agricola did not appear at the first public disputation against the Antinomians, moreover secretly ["im Winkel"] continued his opposition and intrigues, Luther insisted that his privilege of lecturing at the university be withdrawn. Thus brought to terms, Agricola, through his wife, sued for reconciliation. Luther demanded a retraction to be made at his next disputation, which was held January 12, 1538. (Drews, 248. 334 f.; C. R. 25, 64; 3, 482 f.) Here Luther explained that, though not necessary to justification, the Law must not be cast out of the church, its chief object being to reveal the guilt of sin; moreover, that the Law must be taught to maintain outward discipline, to reveal sin, and to show Christians what works are pleasing to God. (Drews, 418.)

Following are some of the 48 theses discussed by Luther in his second disputation:

"3. When treating of justification, one cannot say too much against the inability of the Law [to save] and against the most pernicious trust in the Law. 4. For the Law was not given to justify or vivify or help in any way toward righteousness. 5. But to reveal sin and work wrath, i. e., to render the conscience guilty. [Rom. 3, 20; 4, 15.] 8. In brief, as far as heaven is from the earth, so far must the Law be separated from justification. 9. And nothing is to be taught, said, or thought in the matter of justification but only the word of the grace exhibited in Christ. 10. From this, however, it does not follow that the Law is to be abolished and excluded from the preaching of [done in] the church. 11. Indeed, just for the reason that not only is it not necessary to justification, but also cannot effect it, it is the more necessary to teach and urge it. 12. In order that man, who is proud and trusts in his own powers, may be instructed that he cannot be justified by the Law. 18. Whatever reveals sin, wrath, or death exercises the office of the Law, whether it be in the Old or in the New Testament. 19. For to reveal sin is nothing else, nor can it be anything else, than the Law or an effect and the peculiar power of the Law. 20. Law and revelation of sin or of wrath are convertible terms. 24. So that it is impossible for sin to be, or to be known, without the Law, written or inscribed [in the heart]. 27. And since the Law of God requires our obedience toward God, these Antinomians (nomomachi) abolish also obedience toward God. 28. From this it is manifest that Satan through these his instruments teaches about sin, repentance, and Christ in words only (verbaliter tantum). 29. But in reality he takes away Christ, repentance, sin, and the entire Scripture, together with God, its Author. 45. For the Law, as it was before Christ, did indeed accuse us; but under Christ it is appeased through the forgiveness of sins, and thereafter it is to be fulfilled through the Spirit. 47. Therefore the Law will never, in all eternity, be abolished, but will remain, either to be fulfilled by the damned, or already fulfilled by the blessed. 48. These pupils of the devil, however, seem to think that the Law is temporary only, which ceased under Christ even as circumcision did." (Drews, 336 ff.; St. L. 20, 1632 ff.)

Following is a summary of the views expressed by Luther in his second disputation: "Why is the Law to be taught? The Law is to be taught on account of discipline, according to the word of Paul, 1 Tim. 1, 9: 'The Law is made for the lawless,' and that by this pedagogy men might come to Christ as Paul says to the Galatians (3, 24): 'The Law was our schoolmaster to bring us to Christ.' In the second place, the Law is to be taught to reveal sin, to accuse, terrify, and damn the consciences, Rom. 3, 20: 'By the Law is the knowledge of sin'; again, chapter 4, 15: 'The Law worketh wrath.' In the third place, the Law is to be retained that the saints may know what kind of works God requires in which they may exercise their obedience toward God. *Lex est retinenda, ut sciant sancti, quaenam opera requirat Deus, in quibus obedientiam exercere erga Deum possint."* (Drews, 418; *Herzog R.* 1, 588.)

## 188. Third and Fourth Series of Luther's Theses against Antinomianism.

Having complied with the conditions, and publicly (also in two sermons delivered April 23) retracted his error, and declared his assent to the views expressed in Luther's second disputation, Agricola was again permitted to preach and teach. As a result, Luther also, though he had no faith in the sincerity of Agricola's retraction, did not carry out his original plan of discussing a third and fourth series of theses which he had prepared against antinomianism. (Drews, 419 ff.; E. 4, 430 ff.)

From the third series, comprising 40 theses, we quote the following: "1. The repentance of the Papists, Turks, Jews, and of all unbelievers and hypocrites is alike in every respect. 2. It consists in this, that they are sorry and make satisfaction for one or several sins, and afterwards are secure as to other sins or original sin. 5. The repentance of believers in Christ goes beyond the actual sins, and continues throughout life, till death. 8. For the sin in our flesh remains during the entire time of our life, warring against the Spirit, who resists it. [Rom. 7, 23.] 9. Therefore all works after justification are nothing else than a continuous repentance, or a good purpose against sin. 10. For nothing else is done than that sin, revealed by the Law and forgiven in Christ, is swept out. 17. The Lord's Prayer, taught by the Lord Himself to the saints and believers, is a part of repentance, containing much of the doctrine of the Law. • 18. For whoever prays it aright confesses with his own mouth that he sins against the Law and repents. 27. Therefore also the Lord's Prayer itself teaches that the Law is before, below, and after the Gospel (*legem esse ante, sub et post evangelium*), and that from it repentance must begin. 30. From this it follows that these enemies of the Law [Antinomians] must abolish also the Lord's Prayer if they abolish the Law. 31. Indeed, they are compelled to expunge the greatest part of the sermons of Christ Himself from the Gospel-story. 32. For Matt. 5, 17 ff. He does not only recite the Law of Moses, but explains it perfectly, and teaches that it must not be destroyed. 34. Everywhere throughout the Gospel He also reproves, rebukes, threatens, and exercises similar offices of the Law. 35. So that there never has been nor ever will be more impudent men than those who teach that the Law should be abolished." (St. L. 20, 1636 ff.; E. 4, 430 ff.)

From the fourth series of 41 theses directed by Luther against the Antinomians we quote: "12. Therefore we must beware of the doctrine of the Papists concerning repentance as of hell and the devil himself. 13. Much more, however, must we avoid those who leave no repentance whatever in the Church. 14. For those who deny that the Law is to be taught in reality simply wish that there be no re-

pentance. 15. The argument: 'Whatever is not necessary to justification, neither in the beginning, nor in the middle, nor in the end, must not be taught,' etc., amounts to nothing. 17. It is the same as though you would argue: The truth that man is dead in sin is not necessary to justification, neither in the beginning, nor in the middle, nor in the end; hence it must not be taught. 18. To honor parents, to live chaste, to abstain from murders, adulteries, and thefts is not necessary to justification; hence such things must not be taught. 22. Although the Law helps nothing toward justification, it does not follow therefrom that it ought to be abolished and not to be taught. 26. Everywhere in Paul [the phrase] 'without the Law' must be understood (as Augustine correctly explains) 'without the assistance of the Law,' as we have always done. 27. For the Law demands fulfilment, but helps nothing toward its own fulfilment. 35. But faith in Christ alone justifies, alone fulfils the Law, alone does good works, without the Law. 37. It is true that after justification good works follow spontaneously, without the Law, *i. e.*, without the help or coercion of the Law. 38. In brief, the Law is neither useful nor necessary for justification, nor for any good works, much less for salvation. 39. On the contrary, justification, good works, and salvation are necessary for the fulfilment of the Law. 40. For Christ came to save that which was lost [Luke 19, 10], and for the restitution of all things, as St. Peter says [Acts 3, 21]. 41. Therefore the Law is not destroyed by Christ, but established, in order that Adam may become such as he was, and even better." (St. L. 20, 1639 ff.; E. 4, 433.)

## 189. Luther's Third Public Disputation against the Antinomians.

Soon after his second disputation Luther obtained evidence of Agricola's relapse into his former errors and ways. The upshot was another disputation on a fifth series of theses, held September 13, 1538, in which Luther denounced the Antinomians as deceivers, who lulled their hearers into carnal security. He also explained that the passages culled from his own writings were torn from their historical context, and hence misinterpreted. His former statements, said Luther, had been addressed to consciences already alarmed, and therefore in immediate need of the consolation of the Gospel; while now the Antinomians applied them to secure consciences, who, first of all, were in need of the terrifying power of the Law. (Drews, 421 f.; Tschackert, 482.)

From the 70 theses treated by Luther in his third disputation, we submit the following: "1. The Law has dominion over man as long as he lives. [Rom. 7, 1.] 2. But he is freed from the Law when he dies. 3. Necessarily, therefore, man must die if he would be free from the Law. 7. These three: Law, sin, and death, are inseparable. 8. Accordingly, so far as death is still in man, in so far sin and the Law are in man. 9. Indeed, in Christ the Law is fulfilled, sin abolished, and death destroyed. 11. That is, when, through faith

we are crucified and have died in Christ, such
things [the Law fulfilled, sin abolished, and
death destroyed] are true also in us. 13. But
the fact itself and experience testify that
the just are still daily delivered to death.
14. Necessarily, therefore, in as far as they
are under death, they are still also under the
Law and sin. 15. They [the Antinomians]
are altogether inexperienced men and deceivers of souls who endeavor to abolish the
Law from the church. 16. For this is not
only foolish and wicked, but also absolutely
impossible. 17. For if you would abolish the
Law, you will be compelled to abolish also
sin and death. 18. For death and sin are
present by virtue of the Law, as Paul says
[2 Cor. 3, 6]: 'The letter killeth,' and [1 Cor.
15, 56]: 'The strength of sin is the Law.'
19. But since you see that the just die daily,
what a folly is it to imagine that they are
without the Law! 20. For if there were no
Law, there would be neither sin nor death.
21. Hence they should have first proved that
the just are altogether without sin and death.
22. Or that they no longer live in the flesh,
but are removed from the world. 23. Then it
might justly be taught that also the Law is
altogether removed from them and must not
be taught in any way. 24. This they cannot
prove, but experience itself shows the contrary to their very faces. 25. So, then, the
impudence of the teachers who wish to remove
the Law from the church is extraordinary.
26. Yet it is a much greater impudence, or
rather insanity, when they assert that even
the wicked should be freed from the Law, and
that it should not be preached to them.
29. If, however, they pretend that their church
or their hearers simply are all pious men and
Christians, without the Law, 30. Then it is
evident that they are altogether of unsound
mind and do not know what they say or
affirm. 31. For this is nothing else than to
imagine that all their hearers have been removed from this life. 35. Thus it [the Law]
is also given to the pious, in so far as they
are not yet dead and still live in the flesh.
40. Now, in as far as Christ is raised in us,
in so far we are without Law, sin, and death.
41. But in as far as He is not yet raised in
us, in so far we are under the Law, sin, and
death. 42. Therefore the Law (as also the
Gospel) must be preached, without discrimination, to the righteous as well as to the wicked.
44. To the pious, that they may thereby be
reminded to crucify their flesh with its affections and lusts, lest they become secure. [Gal.
5, 24.] 45. For security abolishes faith and
the fear of God, and renders the latter end
worse than the beginning. [2 Pet. 2, 20.]
46. It appears very clearly that the Antinomians imagine sin to have been removed
through Christ essentially and philosophically
or juridically (formaliter et philosophice seu
iuridice). 47. And that they do not at all
know that sin is removed only inasmuch as
the merciful God does not impute it [Ps. 32, 2],
and forgives it (solum reputatione et ignoscen-
tia Dei miserentis). 61. For if the Law is removed, no one knows what Christ is, or what

He did when He fulfilled the Law for us.
66. The doctrine of the Law, therefore, is
necessary in the churches, and by all means
is to be retained, as without it Christ cannot
be retained. 67. For what will you retain of
Christ when (the Law having been removed
which He fulfilled) you do not know what He
has fulfilled? 69. In brief, to remove the Law
and to let sin and death remain, is to hide the
disease of sin and death to men unto their
perdition. 70. When death and sin are abolished (as was done by Christ), then the Law
would be removed happily; moreover, it
would be established, Rom. 3, 31." (Drews,
423 ff.; St. L. 20, 1642 ff.; E. 4, 436 ff.)

## 190. Agricola's Retraction Written and Published by Luther.

Seeing his position in the Wittenberg University endangered, Agricola was again ready
to submit. And when a public retraction was
demanded, he even left it to Luther to formulate the recantation. Luther did so in a public letter to Caspar Guettel in Eisleben, entitled, Against the Antinomians — Wider die
Antinomer, which he published in the beginning of January, 1539. (St. L. 20, 1610.) In
a crushing manner Luther here denounced
"the specter of the new spirits who dare
thrust the Law or the Ten Commandments
out of the church and relegate it to the court-
house."

Complaining of "false brethren," Luther
here says: "And I fear that, if I had died at
Smalcald [1537], I should forever have been
called the patron of such [antinomian] spirits, because they appeal to my books. And all
this they do behind my back, without my
knowledge and against my will, not even considering it worth while to inform me with as
much as a word or syllable, or at least to ask
me regarding the matter. Thus I am compelled to proceed against Magister John Agricola," etc. (1611.) "But since he was afraid
that he might not express it in a manner such
as would be considered satisfactory, he has
fully authorized and also requested me to do
it [write the retraction for Agricola] as well
as I could, which, he being satisfied, I agreed
to do, and herewith have done, especially for
the reason that after my death neither Master
Eisleben himself nor anybody else might be
able to pretend that I had done nothing in
this matter and simply allowed everything to
pass and go on as fully satisfactory to me."
(1612.)

Referring to his former statements appealed
to by Agricola, Luther continues: "I have indeed taught, and still teach, that sinners
should be led to repentance by the preaching
of, and meditation upon, the suffering of
Christ, so that they may realize how great
God's wrath is over sin, seeing that there is
no other help against it than that God's Son
must die for it. . . . But how does it follow
from this that the Law must be abandoned?
I am unable to discover such an inference in
my logic, and would like to see and hear the
master who would be able to prove it. When
Isaiah says, chap. 53, 8: 'For the transgres-

sion of My people was He stricken,' tell me, dear friend, is the Law abandoned when here the suffering of Christ is preached? What does 'for the transgression of My people' mean? Does it not mean: because My people have sinned against, and not kept, My Law? Or can any one imagine that sin is something where there is no law? Whoever abolishes the Law must with it also abolish sins. If he would allow sins to remain, he must much more allow the Law to remain. For Rom. 5, 13 [4, 15] we read: 'Sin is not imputed where there is no law.' If there is no sin, Christ is nothing. For why does He die if there be neither Law nor sin for which He was to die? From this we see that by this spiritism [*Geisterei*] the devil does not mean to take away the Law, but Christ, who fulfilled the Law. [Matt. 5, 17.] For he well knows that Christ may well and easily be taken away, but not so the Law, which is written in the heart." (1613 f.) "Therefore I request of you, my dear Doctor [Guettel], that, as you have done heretofore, you would continue in the pure doctrine and preach that sinners should and must be led to repentance not only by the sweet grace and suffering of Christ, who has died for us, but also by the terrors of the Law." (1615.) "For whence do we know what sin is if there is no Law and conscience? And whence shall we learn what Christ is, what He has done for us, if we are not to know what the Law is which He has fulfilled for us, or what sin is, for which He has atoned? And even if we did not need the Law for us and were able to tear it out of our hearts (which is impossible), we nevertheless must preach it for the sake of Christ (as also is done and must be done), in order that we may know what He has done and suffered for us. For who could know what and for what purpose Christ has suffered for us if no one were to know what sin or the Law is? Therefore the Law must certainly be preached if we would preach Christ." (1616.) "This, too, is a peculiar blindness and folly, that they imagine the revelation of wrath to be something else than the Law (which is impossible); for the revelation of wrath is the Law when realized and felt, as Paul says [Rom. 4, 15]: '*Lex iram operatur.* The Law worketh wrath.'" (1618.) By way of conclusion Luther remarked: "Let this suffice at present, for I hope that, since Master Eisleben is converted and retracts, the others, too, who received it [the antinomian error] from him, will abandon it, which God may help them to do! Amen." (1619.) At the same time, however, he did not withhold the opinion that Agricola's self-humiliation would hardly be of long duration. "If he continues in such humility," said Luther, "God certainly can and will exalt him; if he abandons it, then God is able to hurl him down again." (1612.)

## 191. Luther's Fourth Disputation against the Antinomians.

Luther's distrust was not unfounded, for Agricola continued secretly to teach his antinomianism, abetted in his sentiments among others also by Jacob Schenck [since 1536 first Lutheran pastor in Freiberg, Saxony; 1538 dismissed on account of his antinomianism; 1540 professor in Leipzig; later on deposed, and finally banished from Saxony]. Indeed, in March, 1540, Agricola even lodged a complaint with the Elector, charging Luther with "calumnies." In the first part of the following month Luther answered these charges in a *Report to Doctor Brueck Concerning Magister John Eisleben's Doctrine and Intrigues.* (St. L. 20, 1648 ff.) About the same time, Count Albrecht of Mansfeld denounced Agricola to the Elector as a dangerous, troublesome man. Hereupon the Elector, on June 15, 1540, opened formal legal proceedings against Agricola, who, as stated above, removed to Berlin in August without awaiting the trial, although he had promised with an oath not to leave before a legal decision had been rendered. (Drews, 611.) Incensed by the treacherous conduct of Agricola, Luther, September 10, 1540, held a final disputation on a sixth series of theses against the Antinomians, charging them with destroying all order, human as well as divine. (St. L. 20, 1647; E. 4, 441.)

Regarding Agricola's duplicity, Luther, in his *Report* to Brueck, said in substance: According to the statements of Caspar Guettel and Wendelin Faber, Agricola had for years secretly agitated against the Wittenbergers and founded a sect at Eisleben calling themselves Minorish [Minorists]; he had branded and slandered their doctrine as false and impure, and this, too, without conferring with them or previously admonishing them; he had come to Wittenberg for the purpose of corrupting and distracting the Church; his adherents had made the statement that Eisleben would teach the Wittenbergers theology and logic; he had inveigled Hans Lufft into printing his Postil by falsely stating that it had been read and approved by Luther; in his dealings with the Wittenbergers he had acted, not as an honest man, let alone a pious Christian and theologian, but treacherously and in keeping with his antinomian principles; parading as a loyal Lutheran at public conventions and laughing and dining with them, he had misled "his old, faithful friend" [Luther] to confide in him, while secretly he was acting the traitor by maligning him and undermining his work. In the *Report* we read: "Agricola blasphemes and damns our doctrine as impure and false (*i. e.,* the Holy Spirit Himself in His holy Law); he slanders and defames us Wittenbergers most infamously wherever he can; and all this he does treacherously and secretly, although we have done him no harm, but only did well by him, as he himself must admit. He deceives and attacks us [me], his best friend and father, making me believe that he is our true friend. Nor does he warn me, but, like a desperate treacherous villain, secretly works behind our back to cause the people to forsake our doctrine and to adhere to him, thus treating us with an ungratefulness, pride, and haughtiness such as I have not frequently met with before." (1656.)

In his charge against Luther, Agricola had said that it was dangerous to preach the Law without the Gospel, because it was a ministry of death (*ministerium mortis*). Luther answered in his *Report* to Brueck: "Behold now what the mad fool does. God has given His Law for the very purpose that it should bite, cut, strike, kill, and sacrifice the old man. For it should terrify and punish the proud, ignorant, secure Old Adam and show him his sin and death, so that, being humiliated, he may despair of himself, and thus become desirous of grace, as St. Paul says: 'The strength of sin is the Law; the sting of death is sin.' [1 Cor. 15, 56.] For this reason he also calls it *bonam, iustam, sanctam* — good, just, holy. Again, Jeremiah [23, 29]: 'My Word is like a hammer that breaketh the rock to pieces.' Again: '*Ego ignis consumens*, etc. — I am a consuming fire.' Ps. 9, 21 [20]: '*Constitue legislatorem super eos, ut sciant gentes, se esse homines, non deos, nec Deo similes* — Put them in fear, O Lord, that the nations may know themselves to be but men.' Thus St. Paul does Rom. 1 and 2 and 3, making all the world sinners by the Law, casting them under the wrath of God, and entirely killing them before God. But here our dear Master Grickel appears on the scene and invents a new theology out of his own mad and reckless fool's head and teaches: One must not kill and reprove the people, *i. e.*, one must not preach the Law. Here he himself confesses publicly in his suit [against Luther] that he has condemned and prohibited the preaching of the Law." (St. L. 20, 1657.)

The *Report* continues: "Since, now, the little angry devil who rides Master Grickel will not tolerate the Law, *i. e., mortificantem, irascentem, accusantem, terrentem, occidentem legem,* — the mortifying, raging, accusing, terrifying, killing Law, — it is quite evident what he intends to do through Master Grickel's folly (for he nevertheless wishes to be praised as preaching the Law after and under the Gospel, etc.), *viz.*, to hide original sin and to teach the Law no further than against future actual sins, for such is the manner of his entire Postil; even as the Turks, Jews, philosophers, and Papists teach, who regard our nature as sound; but Master Grickel does not see that it is just this which his little spirit [devil] aims at by his bragging and boasting, that he, too, is preaching the Law. . . . Thus Christ and God are altogether vain and lost. And is not this blindness beyond all blindness that he does not want to preach the Law without and before the Gospel? For are these not impossible things? How is it possible to preach of forgiveness of sins if previously there have been no sins? How can one proclaim life if previously there is no death? Are we to preach to angels who have neither sin nor death concerning forgiveness of sins and redemption from death? But how can one preach of sins, or know that there are sins, if the Law does not reveal them? For according to its proper office the Gospel does not say who [is a sinner] and what is sin; it does, however, indicate that there must be some great hurt, since

so great a remedy is required; but it does not say how the sin is called, or what it is. The Law must do this. Thus Master Eisleben must in fact (*re ipsa*) allow the Law to perform its duty (*occidere*, to kill, etc.) prior to the [preaching of the] Gospel, no matter how decidedly he, with words only, denies it, to spite the Wittenbergers, in order that he also, as *novus autor* (new author), may produce something of his own and confuse the people and aggravate the churches." (1658.)

From the 20 theses which Luther treated in his last disputation against the Antinomians we cull the following: "1. The inference of St. Paul: 'For where no law is, there is no transgression' [Rom. 4, 15] is valid not only theologically, but also politically and naturally (*non solum theologice, sed etiam politice et naturaliter*). 2. Likewise this too: Where there is no sin, there is neither punishment nor remission. 3. Likewise this too: Where there is neither punishment nor remission, there is neither wrath nor grace. 4. Likewise this too: Where there is neither wrath nor grace, there is neither divine nor human government. 5. Likewise this too: Where there is neither divine nor human government, there is neither God nor man. 6. Likewise this too: Where there is neither God nor man, there is nothing except perhaps the devil. 7. Hence it is that the Antinomians, the enemies of the Law, evidently are either devils themselves or the brothers of the devil. 8. It avails the Antinomians nothing to boast that they teach very much of God, Christ, grace, Law, etc. 10. This confession of the Antinomians is like the one when the devils cried: 'Thou art the Son of the living God.' [Luke 4, 34; 8, 28.] 12. Whoever denies that the damning Law must be taught, in reality simply denies the Law. 14. A law which does not damn is an imagined and painted law as the chimera or tragelaphus. 15. Nor is the political or natural law anything unless it damns and terrifies sinners, Rom. 13, 1. 5; 1 Pet. 2, 13 ff. 17. What the Antinomians say concerning God, Christ, faith, Law, grace, etc., they say without any meaning as the parrot says its '*χαῖρε*, Good day!' 18. Hence it is impossible to learn theology or civil polity (*theologiam aut politiam*) from the Antinomians. 19. Therefore they must be avoided as most pestilential teachers of licentious living who permit the perpetration of all crimes. 20. For they serve not Christ, but their own belly [Rom. 16, 18], and, madmen that they are, seek to please men, in order that from them, as a man's judgment, they may gain glory." (Drews, 613; St. L. 20, 1647; E. 4, 441.) — Regarding Luther's disputations against the Antinomians Planck pertinently remarks that they compel admiration for his clear and penetrating mind, and rank among the very best of his writings. (1, 18; Frank 2, 311.)

### 192. "Grickel" Remained Grickel.

At the instance of Elector Joachim, negotiations were begun with Luther, which finally led to a sort of peaceful settlement. Agricola was required to send (which he also did) a revocation to the preachers, the council, and the congregation at Eisleben. However, the new and enlarged edition (1541) of the catechism which Agricola had published in 1527 revealed the fact that also this last recantation was insincere; for in it he repeated his antinomistic teaching, though not in the original defiant manner. Little wonder, then, that, despite the formal settlement, cordial relations were not restored between Luther and Agricola. When the latter visited Wittenberg in 1545, Luther refused to see the man whom he regarded incurably dishonest. "Grickel," said he, "will remain Grickel to all eternity, *Grickel wird in alle Ewigkeit Grickel bleiben.*"

And "Grickel" he did remain; for in 1565 he published a sermon in which he said: "Every one who is to be appointed as teacher and preacher shall be asked: What do you intend to teach in the church? He shall answer: The Gospel of Jesus Christ. But when further asked: What does the Gospel preach? he shall answer: The Gospel preaches repentance and forgiveness of sins." Considering this a further evidence that Agricola still adhered to, and was now ready once more to champion, his old errors, the preachers of Mansfeld registered their protest in a publication of the same year. A controversy, however, did not materialize, for Agricola died the following year. (Planck 5, 1, 47; Frank 2, 267.)

### 193. False Propositions of Agricola.

Following are some of Agricola's radical statements concerning the Law and the Gospel. The first thesis of his *Positions* of 1537 reads: "Repentance is to be taught not from the Decalog or from any law of Moses, but from the violation of the Son through the Gospel. *Poenitentia docenda est non ex decalogo aut ulla lege Mosis, sed ex violatione Filii per evangelium.*" (E. 4. 420.) Thesis 13: "In order to keep the Christian doctrine pure, we must resist those [Luther and Melanchthon] who teach that the Gospel must be preached only to such whose hearts have previously been terrified and broken by the Law. *Quare pro conservanda puritate doctrinae resistendum est iis, qui docent, evangelium non praedicandum nisi animis prius quassatis et contritis per legem.*" (421.) Thesis 16: "The Law merely rebukes sin, and that, too, without the Holy Spirit; hence it rebukes to damnation." Thesis 17: "But there is need of a doctrine which does not only condemn with great efficacy, but which saves at the same time; this, however, is the Gospel, a doctrine which teaches conjointly repentance and remission of sins." (421.) In his *Brief Summary of the Gospel*, Agricola says: "In the New Testament and among Christians or in the Gospel we must not preach the violation of the Law when a man breaks or transgresses the Law, but the violation of the Son, to wit, that he who does not for the sake of the kingdom of heaven willingly omit what he should omit, and does not do what he should do, crucifies Christ anew." (St. L. 20, 1622 ff.; Frank

2, 313; Gieseler 3, 2, 137; Pieper, *Dogm.* 3, 265 ff.)

A commingling of the Law and Gospel always results in a corruption of the doctrines of conversion, faith, and justification. Such was the case also with respect to Agricola, who taught that justification follows a contrition which flows from, and hence is preceded by, love toward God. Turning matters topsy-turvy, he taught: Repentance consists in this, that the heart of man, experiencing the kindness of God which calls us to Christ and presents us with His grace, turns about, apprehends God's grace, thanks Him heartily for having spared it so graciously, begins to repent, and to grieve heartily and sorrowfully on account of its sins, wishes to abstain from them, and renounces its former sinful life. "This," says Agricola, "is repentance (*poenitentia, Buessen*) and the first stage of the new birth, the true breathing and afflation of the Holy Spirit. After this he acquires a hearty confidence in God, believing that He will condone his folly and not blame him for it, since he did not know any better, although he is much ashamed of it and wishes that it had never happened; he also resolves, since he has fared so well, never to sin any more or to do anything that might make him unworthy of the benefit received as if he were ungrateful and forgetful; he furthermore learns to work out, confirm, and preserve his salvation in fear and trembling . . . : this is forgiveness of sins." (Frank 2, 247.) These confused ideas plainly show that Agricola had a false conception, not only of the Law and Gospel, but also of original sin, repentance, faith, regeneration, and justification. Essentially, his was the Roman doctrine, which makes an antecedent of what in reality is an effect and a consequence of conversion and justification. Viewed from this angle, it occasions little surprise that Agricola consented to help formulate and introduce the Augsburg Interim, in which the essentials of Lutheranism were denied.

### 194. Poach, Otto, Musculus, Neander.

The antinomistic doctrines rejected, in particular, by Article VI of the *Formula of Concord*, were represented chiefly by Andrew Poach, Anton Otto, Andrew Musculus, and Michael Neander. Poach, born 1516, studied under Luther and was an opponent of the Philippists; he became pastor in Halle in 1541; in Nordhausen, 1547; in Erfurt, 1550; in Uttenbach, near Jena, 1572, where he died 1585. At Erfurt, Poach was deposed in 1572 on account of dissensions due to the antinomistic controversies. He signed the *Book of Concord.* — Otto [Otho; also called Herzberger, because he was born in Herzberg, 1505] studied under Luther; served as pastor in Graefenthal, and from 1543 in Nordhausen, where he was deposed in 1568 for adherence to Flacius. However, when Otto, while antagonizing Majorism and synergism, in sermons on the Letter to the Galatians of 1565, rejected the Third Use of the Law, he was opposed also by Flacius, who reminded him of the fact that here on earth the new man resembles a child, aye, an embryo, rather than a full-fledged man.

In his zealous opposition to the Majorists, Andrew Musculus (Meusel, born 1514; studied at Leipzig 1532—1538, then at Wittenberg; became a zealous and passionate adherent of Luther, whom he considered the greatest man since the days of the apostles; from 1540 till his death, September 29, 1581, professor and pastor, later on, General Superintendent, in Frankfurt-on-the-Oder) also made some extreme statements. Later on, however, he cooperated in preparing and revising the *Formula of Concord*. Musculus wrote of Luther: "There is as great a difference between the dear old teachers and Luther as there is between the light of the sun and that of the moon; and beyond all doubt, the ancient fathers, even the best and foremost among them, as Hilary and Augustine, had they lived contemporaneously with him, would not have hesitated to deliver the lamp to him, as the saying is." (Meusel, *Handl.* 4, 709; Richard, 450.)

The most prominent opponents of these Antinomians were the well-known theologians Moerlin, Flacius, Wigand, and Westphal (chiefly in letters to Poach). The controversy was carried on with moderation, and without any special efforts to cause trouble among the people. The main issue was not — as in the conflict with Agricola — whether the Law is necessary in order to effect contrition and prepare men for the Gospel, but the so-called Third Use of the Law (*tertius usus legis*), i. e., whether the Law is, and is intended to be, of service to Christians after their regeneration; in particular, whether the regenerate still need the Law with respect to their new obedience.

The conflict with Poach arose from the Majoristic controversy. Dealing in particular with the aberrations of Menius, the Synod at Eisenach, 1556, adopted seven theses which Menius was required to subscribe. The first declared: "Although the proposition, Good works are necessary to salvation, may be tolerated hypothetically and in an abstract way in the doctrine of the Law (*in doctrina legis abstractive et de idea tolerari potest*), nevertheless there are many weighty reasons why it ought and should be avoided no less than this one: Christ is a creature." (Preger 1, 383.) While Flacius, Wigand, and Moerlin defended the thesis, Amsdorf (who first, too, adopted it, but later on withdrew his assent; Seeberg 4, 488), Aurifaber, and especially Poach rejected it. This marked the beginning of the so-called Second Antinomistic Controversy. Poach denied that the Law has any promise of salvation. Even the most perfect fulfilment of the Law, said he, is but the fulfilment of a duty which merits no reward. The only thing one may acquire by a perfect fulfilment is freedom from guilt and punishment. Fulfilment of our duty (*solutio debiti*) does not warrant any claim on salvation. Yet Poach was careful to declare that this did not apply to the fulfilment of the Law which Christ

rendered for us. Why? Poach answered: Because Christ, being the Son of God, was not obliged to fulfil the Law. When, therefore, He did fulfil it in our stead, He rendered satisfaction to divine justice, so that righteousness can now be imputed to us and we become partakers of eternal life.

Poach wrote: "It would not be correct to say: In the doctrine of the Law all the works commanded in the Law are necessary to salvation. *In doctrina legis omnia opera mandata in lege sunt necessaria ad salutem.*" (Schluesselburg 4, 343.) Again: "The works of Christ, which are the fulfilment of the Law, are the merit of our salvation. Our works, which ought to have been the fulfilment of the Law, do not merit salvation, even though they were most perfect, as the Law requires, — which, however, is impossible. The reason is that we are debtors to the Law. Christ, however, is not a debtor to the Law. Even if we most perfectly fulfilled all the commandments of God and completely satisfied the righteousness of God, we would not be worthy of grace and salvation on that account, nor would God be obliged to give us grace and salvation as a debt. He justly demands the fulfilment of His Law from us as obedience due Him from His creature, which is bound to obey its Creator. *Etiamsi nos omnia mandata Dei perfectissime impleremus et iustitiae Dei penitus satisfaceremus, tamen non ideo digni essemus gratia et salute, nec Deus obligatus esset, ut nobis gratiam et salutem daret ex debito. Sed iure requirit impletionem legis suae a nobis, ut debitam obedientiam a sua creatura, quae conditori suo obedire tenetur.*" (274.) Again: "The Law has not the necessity of salvation, but the necessity of obligation (*non habet lex necessitatem salutis, sed necessitatem debiti*). For, as said, even though a man would most perfectly do the works of the Law, he would not obtain salvation on account of these works. Nor is God under obligation to man, but man is under obligation to God. And in the Law God requires of man the obedience he owes; He does not require an obedience with the promise of salvation." (276.)

As to Otto, he distinguished, in a series of Latin theses, a double office of the Law, the ecclesiastical and political — *officium ecclesiasticum* and *officium politicum*. The former is to give knowledge of sin; the latter, to coerce the old man and maintain order among the obstinate. He denied that the Law in any way serves Christians with respect to good works. Otto declared: "The Law is useful and necessary neither for justification nor for any good works. But faith in Christ the Mediator alone is useful and necessary both for justification and the good works themselves. *Lex enim non modo ad iustificationem sed neque ad ulla bona opera utilis et necessaria est. Sed sola fides in Christum mediatorem utilis et necessaria est tam ad iustificationem quam ad ipsa bona opera.*" Quoting Luther, he said: "The highest art of Christians is to know nothing of the Law, to ignore works. *Summa ars Christianorum est nescire legem, ignorare opera,*" i. e., in the article of

Justification, as Otto did not fail to add by way of explanation. (Luther, Weimar 40, 1, 43; Tschackert, 485.) Seeberg remarks that, in reality, Poach and Otto were merely opposed to such an interpretation of the Third Use of the Law as made the Law a motive of good works, and hence could not be charged with antinomianism proper. (4, 488 f.)

Planck, Frank, and other historians have fathered upon Otto also a series of radical German theses, which, however, were composed, not by Otto, but probably by some of his adherents. These theses, in which all of the errors of Agricola are revamped, were discussed at the Altenburg colloquy, 1568 to 1569; their author, however, was not mentioned. We submit the following: "1. The Law does not teach good works, nor should it be preached in order that we may do good works. 3. Moses knew nothing of our faith and religion. 5. Evangelical preachers are to preach the Gospel only, and no Law. 7. A Christian who believes should do absolutely nothing, neither what is good nor what is evil. 10. We should pray God that we may remain steadfast in faith till our end, without all works. 14. The Holy Spirit does not work according to the norm or rule of the Law, but by Himself, without the assistance of the Law. 16. A believing Christian is *supra omnem obedientiam*, above all Law and all obedience. 17. The rebuking sermons of the prophets do not at all pertain to Christians. 21. The Law, good works, and new obedience have no place in the kingdom of Christ, but in the world, just as Moses and the government of the Pope. 25. The Law has no place in the Church or in the pulpit, but in the court-house (*Rathaus*). 28. The Third Use of the Law is a blasphemy in theology and a monstrosity in the realm of nature (*portentum in rerum natura*). 29. No man can be saved if the Third Use of the Law is true and is to be taught in the Church. The Holy Spirit in man knows nothing of the Law; the flesh, however, is betimes in need of the Law." (Tschackert, 485; Planck 5, 1, 62.) Frank also quotes: "The Christians or the regenerate are deified (*vergoettert*); yea, they are themselves God and cannot sin. God has not given you His Word that you should be saved thereby (*dass du dadurch sollst selig werden*); and whoever seeks no more from God than salvation (*Seligkeit*) seeks just as much as a louse in a scab. Such Christians are the devil's own, together with all their good works." (2, 326. 275.)

Also Musculus is numbered among the theologians who were not always sufficiently discreet and guarded in their statements concerning the necessity of good works and the use of the Law. All expressions of the Apostle Paul regarding the spiritual use of the Law, said Musculus, must be understood as referring to such only as are to be justified, not to those who are justified (*de iustificandis, non de iustificatis*). But he added: "For these, in as far as they remain in Christ, are far outside of and above every law. *Hi enim, quatenus in Christo manent, longe extra et supra omnem legem sunt.*" (Tschackert, 486.)

Michael Neander of Ilfeld, a friend of Otto, was also suspected of antinomianism. He denied that there is any relation whatever between the Law and a regenerate Christian. But he, too, was careful enough to add: "in as far as he is just or lives by the spirit, *quatenus est iustus seu spiritu vivit.*" In a letter, Neander said: "I adhere to the opinion that the Law is not given to the just in any use or office whatsoever, in so far as he is just or lives by the spirit. . . . 'For the Law,' as Luther says in his marginal note to Jeremiah, chap. 31, 'is no longer over us, but under us, and does not surround us any more.' Love rules and governs all laws, and frequently something is true according to the Law, but false according to love (*saepeque aliquid lege verum, dilectione tamen falsum est*). For love is the statute, measure, norm, and rule of all things on earth. . . . The Law only accuses and damns, and apart from this it has no other use or office, *i. e.*, the Law remains the norm of good works to all eternity, also in hell after the Last Day, but for the unjust and reprobate, and for the flesh in every man. To the just, regenerated, and new man, however, it is not the norm of good works; *i. e.*, the Law does not govern, regulate, and teach the just man; *i. e.*, it is not active with respect to him as it is with respect to an unjust man; but is rather regulated and governed and taught by the just man. It no longer drives the just (as it did before conversion and as it still drives the flesh), but is now driven and suffers, since as just men we are no longer under the Law, but above the Law and lords of the Law. How, therefore, can the Law be a norm to the just man when he is the lord of the Law, commands the Law, and frequently does what is contrary to the Law (*cum iustus legis sit dominus, legi imperet et saepe legi contraria faciat*)? . . . When the just man meditates in the Law of the Lord day and night, when he establishes the Law by faith, when he loves the Law and admires the inexhaustible wisdom of the divine Law, when he does good works written and prescribed in the Law (as indeed he alone can), when he uses the Law aright, — all these are neither the third, nor the fourth, nor the twelfth, nor the fiftieth use or office of the Law, . . . but fruits of faith, of the Spirit, or regeneration. . . . But the Old Man, who is not yet new, or a part of him which is not as yet regenerated, has need of this Law, and he is to be commanded: 'Put on the new man; put off the old.' " (Schluesselburg 4, 61; Tschackert, 484.)

## 195. Melanchthon and the Philippists.

A further controversy concerning the proper distinction between the Law and the Gospel was caused by the Philippists in Wittenberg, whose teaching was somewhat akin to that of Agricola. They held that the Gospel, in the narrow sense of the term, and as distinguished from the Law, is "the most powerful preaching of repentance." (Frank 2, 327.) Taking his cue from Luther, Melanchthon, in his *Loci* of 1521 as well as in later writings, clearly distinguished between Law and Gospel. (*C. R.* 21, 139; 23, 49; 12, 576.) True, he had taught, also in the *Apology*, that, in the wider sense, the Gospel is both a preaching of repentance and forgiveness of sin. But this, as the *Formula of Concord* explains, was perfectly correct and in keeping with the Scriptures. However, in repeating the statement that the Gospel embraces both the preaching of repentance and forgiveness of sins, Melanchthon was not always sufficiently careful to preclude misapprehension and misunderstanding. Indeed, some of the statements he made after Luther's death are misleading, and did not escape the challenge of loyal Lutherans.

During a disputation in 1548, at which Melanchthon presided, Flacius criticized the unqualified assertion that the Gospel was a preaching of repentance, but was satisfied when Melanchthon explained that the term Gospel was here used in the wider sense, as comprising the entire doctrine of Christ. However, when Melanchthon, during another disputation, 1556, declared: The ministry of the Gospel "rebukes the other sins which the Law shows, as well as the saddest of sins which is revealed by the Gospel (*hoc tristissimum peccatum, quod in Evangelio ostenditur*), viz., that the world ignores and despises the Son of God," Flacius considered it his plain duty to register a public protest. It was a teaching which was, at least in part, the same error that Luther, and formerly also Melanchthon himself, had denounced when espoused by Agricola, viz., that genuine contrition is wrought, not by the Law, but by the Gospel; by the preaching, not of the violation of the Law, but of the violation of the Son. (*C. R.* 12, 634. 640.)

These misleading statements of Melanchthon were religiously cultivated and zealously defended by the Wittenberg Philippists. With a good deal of animosity they emphasized that the Gospel in its most proper sense is also a preaching of repentance (*praedicatio poenitentiae, Busspredigt*), inasmuch as it revealed the baseness of sin and the greatness of its offense against God, and, in particular, inasmuch as the Gospel alone uncovered, rebuked, and condemned the hidden sin (*arcanum peccatum*) and the chief sin of all, the sin of unbelief (*incredulitas et neglectio*

*Filii*), which alone condemns a man. These views, which evidently involved a commingling of the Law and the Gospel, were set forth by Paul Crell in his Disputation against John Wigand, 1571, and were defended in the *Propositions Concerning the Chief Controversies of These Times* (also of 1571), by Pezel and other Wittenberg theologians. (Frank 2, 277. 323.)

As a consequence, the Philippists, too, were charged with antinomianism, and were strenuously opposed by such theologians as Flacius, Amsdorf, and Wigand. Wigand attacked the Wittenberg *Propositions* in his book of 1571, *Concerning Antinomianism, Old and New.* Pezel answered in his *Apology of the True Doctrine on the Definition of the Gospel,* 1571; and Paul Crell, in *Spongia, or 150 Propositions Concerning the Definition of the Gospel, Opposed to the Stupid Accusation of John Wigand,* 1571. The teaching of the Philippists was formulated by Paul Crell as follows: "Since this greatest and chief sin [unbelief] is revealed, rebuked, and condemned by the Gospel alone, therefore also the Gospel alone is expressly and particularly, truly and properly, a preaching and a voice of repentance or conversion in its true and proper sense. *A solo evangelio, cum peccatum hoc summum et praecipuum monstretur, arguatur et damnetur, expresse ac nominatim solum etiam evangelium vere ac proprie praedicatio ac vox est poenitentiae sive conversionis vere et proprie ita dictae.*" (277. 327.)

This doctrine of the Philippists, according to which the Gospel in the narrow and proper sense, and as distinguished from the Law, is a preaching of repentance, was rejected by Article V of the *Formula of Concord* as follows: "But if the Law and the Gospel, likewise also Moses himself as a teacher of Law and Christ as a preacher of the Gospel, are contrasted with one another, we believe, teach, and confess that the Gospel is not a preaching of repentance or reproof, but properly nothing else than a preaching of consolation, and a joyful message which does not reprove or terrify, but comforts consciences against the terrors of the Law, points alone to the merit of Christ, and raises them up again by the lovely preaching of the grace and favor of God, obtained through Christ's merit." (803, 7.)

# XVIII. The Crypto-Calvinistic Controversy.

## 196. Contents and Purpose of Articles VII and VIII.

In all of its articles the *Formula of Concord* is but a reaffirmation of the doctrines taught and defended by Luther. The fire of prolonged and hot controversies through which these doctrines passed after his death had but strengthened the Lutherans in their conviction that in every point Luther's teaching was indeed nothing but the pure Word of God itself. It had increased the consciousness that, in believing and teaching as they did, they were not following mere human

authorities, such as Luther and the Lutheran Confessions, but the Holy Scriptures, by which alone their consciences were bound. Articles VII and VIII of the *Formula of Concord,* too, reassert Luther's doctrines on the Lord's Supper and the person of Christ as being in every particular the clear and unmistakable teaching of the divine Word, — two doctrines, by the way, which perhaps more than any other serve as the acid test whether the fundamental attitude of a church or a theologian is truly Scriptural and fully free from every rationalistic and enthusiastic infection.

The Seventh Article teaches the real and substantial presence of the true body and blood of Christ; their sacramental union in, with, and under the elements of bread and wine; the oral manducation, or eating and drinking of both substances by unbelieving as well as believing communicants. It maintains that this presence of the body and blood of Christ, though real, is neither an impanation nor a companation, neither a local inclusion nor a mixture of the two substances, but illocal and transcendent. It holds that the eating of the body and the drinking of the blood of Christ, though truly done with the mouth of the body, is not Capernaitic, or natural, but supernatural. It affirms that this real presence is effected, not by any human power, but by the omnipotent power of Christ in accordance with the words of the institution of the Sacrament.

The Eighth Article treats of the person of Christ, of the personal union of His two natures, of the communication of these natures as well as of their attributes, and, in particular, of the impartation of the truly divine majesty to His human nature and the terminology resulting therefrom. One particular object of Article VIII is also to show that the doctrine of the real presence of the body and blood of Christ in the Holy Supper, as taught by the Lutheran Church, does not, as was contended by her Zwinglian and Calvinistic adversaries, conflict in any way with what the Scriptures teach concerning the person of Christ, His human nature, His ascension, and His sitting at the right hand of God the Father Almighty. The so-called Appendix, or Catalogus, a collection of passages from the Bible and from the fathers of the ancient Church, prepared by Andreae and Chemnitz, was added to the Formula of Concord (though not as an authoritative part of it) in further support of the Lutheran doctrine particularly concerning the divine majesty of the human nature of Christ.

Both articles, the seventh as well as the eighth, were incorporated in the Formula of Concord in order thoroughly to purify the Lutheran Church from Reformed errors concerning the Lord's Supper and the person of Christ, which after Luther's death had wormed their way into some of her schools and churches, especially those of Electoral Saxony, and to make her forever immune against the infection of Calvinism (Crypto-Calvinism) — a term which, during the controversies preceding the Formula of Concord, did not, as is generally the case to-day, refer to Calvin's absolute decree of election and reprobation, but to his doctrine concerning the Lord's Supper, as formulated by himself in the Consensus Tigurinus (Zurich Consensus), issued 1549. The subtitle of this confession reads: "Consensio Mutua in Re Sacramentaria Ministrorum Tigurinae Ecclesiae, et D. Iohannis Calvini Ministri Genevensis Ecclesiae, iam nunc ab ipsis autoribus edita." In this confession, therefore, Calvin declares his agreement with the teaching of Zwingli as represented by his followers in Zurich,

notably Bullinger. Strenuous efforts were made by the Calvinists and Reformed everywhere to make the Consensus Tigurinus the basis of a pan-Protestant union, and at the same time the banner under which to conquer all Protestant countries, Lutheran Germany included, for what must be regarded as being essentially Zwinglianism. The Consensus was adopted in Switzerland, England, France, and Holland. In Lutheran territories, too, its teaching was rapidly gaining friends, notably in Southern Germany, where Bucer had prepared the way for it, and in Electoral Saxony, where the Philippists offered no resistance. Garnished as it was with glittering and seemingly orthodox phrases, the Consensus Tigurinus lent itself admirably for such Reformed propaganda. "The consequence was," says the Formula of Concord, "that many great men were deceived by these fine, plausible words — splendidis et magnificis verbis." (973, 6.) To counteract this deception, to establish Luther's doctrine of the real presence of the body and blood of Christ, and to defend it against the sophistries of the Sacramentarians: Zwinglians, Calvinists, and Crypto-Calvinists — such was the object of Articles VII and VIII of the Formula of Concord.

### 197. John Calvin.

Calvin was born July 10, 1509, in Noyon, France. He began his studies in Paris, 1523, preparing for theology. In 1529 his father induced him to take up law in Orleans and Bourges. In 1531 he returned to his theological studies in Paris. Here he experienced what he himself describes as a "sudden conversion." He joined the Reformed congregation, and before long was its acknowledged leader. In 1533 he was compelled to leave France because of his anti-Roman testimony. In Basel, 1535, he wrote the first draft of his Institutio Religionis Christianae. In Geneva, where he was constrained to remain by William Farel [born 1489; active as a fiery Protestant preacher in Meaux, Strassburg, Zurich, Bern, Basel, Moempelgard, Geneva, Metz, etc.; died 1565], Calvin developed and endeavored to put into practise his legalistic ideal of a theocratic and rigorous puritanical government. As a result he was banished, 1538. He removed to Strassburg, where he was held and engaged by Bucer. He attended the conventions in Frankfort, 1539; Hagenau, 1540; Worms, 1540; and Regensburg, 1541. Here he got acquainted with the Lutherans, notably Melanchthon. September 13, 1541, he returned to Geneva, where, woefully mixing State and Church, he continued his reformatory and puritanical efforts. One of the victims of his theocratic government was the anti-Trinitarian Michael Servetus, who, at the instance of Calvin, was burned at the stake, October 27, 1553. In 1559 Calvin established the Geneva School, which exercised a far-reaching theological influence. He died May 27, 1564.

Calvin repeatedly expressed his unbounded admiration for Luther as a "preeminent servant of Christ — praeclarus Christi servus."

(*C. R.* 37, 54.) In his *Answer* of 1543 against the Romanist Pighius he said: "Concerning Luther we testify without dissimulation now as heretofore that we esteem him as a distinguished apostle of Christ, by whose labor and service, above all, the purity of the Gospel has been restored at this time. *De Luthero nunc quoque sicut hactenus non dissimulanter testamur, eum nos habere pro insigni Christi apostolo, cuius maxime opera et ministerio restituta hoc tempore fuerit Evangelii puritas.*" (Gieseler 3, 2, 169.) Even after Luther had published his *Brief Confession*, in which he unsparingly denounces the Sacramentarians (deniers of the real presence of Christ's body and blood in the Lord's Supper), and severs all connection with them, Calvin admonished Bullinger in a letter dated November 25, 1544, to bear in mind what a great and wonderfully gifted man Luther was, and with what fortitude, ability, and powerful teaching he had shattered the kingdom of Antichrist and propagated the salutary doctrine. "I am frequently accustomed to say," he declared, "that, even if he should call me a devil, I would accord him the honor of acknowledging him to be an eminent servant of God." In the original the remarkable words of Calvin read as follows: "*Sed haec cupio vobis in mentem venire, primum quantus sit vir Lutherus, et quantis dotibus excellat, quanta animi fortitudine et constantia, quanta dexteritate, quanta doctrinae efficacia hactenus ad profligandum Antichristi regnum et simul propagandam salutis doctrinam incubuerit. Saepe dicere solitus sum, etiamsi me diabolum vocaret, me tamen hoc illi honoris habiturum, ut insignem Dei servum agnoscam, qui tamen, ut pollet eximiis virtutibus, ita magnis vitiis laboret.*" (Gieseler 3, 2, 169; *C. R.* 39 [*Calvini Opp.* 11], 774.)

However, though he admired the personality of Luther, Calvin, like Zwingli and Oecolampadius at Marburg 1529, revealed a theological spirit which was altogether different from Luther's. In particular, he was violently opposed to Luther's doctrines of the real presence in the Lord's Supper and of the majesty of the human nature of Christ. Revealing his animus, Calvin branded the staunch and earnest defenders of these doctrines as the "apes" of Luther. In his *Second Defense* against Westphal, 1556, he exclaimed: "O Luther, how few imitators of your excellences, but how many apes of your pious ostentation have you left behind! *O Luthere, quam paucos tuae praestantiae imitatores, quam multas vero sanctae tuae iactantiae simias reliquisti!*" (Gieseler 3, 2, 209.)

True, when in Strassburg, Calvin signed the *Augsburg Confession* (1539 or 1540), and was generally considered a Lutheran. However, in his *Last Admonition* to Westphal, of 1557, and in a letter of the same year to Martin Schalling, Calvin wrote: "Nor do I repudiate the *Augsburg Confession*, to which I have previously subscribed, *in the sense in which the author himself* [Melanchthon in the *Variata* of 1540] *has interpreted it. Nec vero Augustanam Confessionem repudio, cui pridem*

*volens ac libens subscripsi, sicut eam auctor ipse interpretatus est.*" (*C. R.* 37, 148.) According to his own confession, therefore, Calvin's subscription to the *Augustana*, at least as far as the article of the Lord's Supper is concerned, was insincere and nugatory. In fact, Calvin must be regarded as the real originator of the second controversy on the Lord's Supper between the Lutherans and the Reformed, even as the first conflict on this question was begun, not by Luther, but by his opponents, Carlstadt, Zwingli, and Oecolampadius. For the adoption of the *Consensus Tigurinus* in 1549, referred to above, cannot but be viewed as an overt act by which the Wittenberg Concord, signed 1536 by representative Lutheran and Reformed theologians, was publicly repudiated and abandoned by Calvin and his adherents, and whereby an anti-Lutheran propaganda on an essentially Zwinglian basis was inaugurated. Calvin confirmed the schism between the Lutherans and the Reformed which Carlstadt, Zwingli, and Oecolampadius had originated.

### 198. Calvin's Zwinglianism.

The doctrine of Calvin and his adherents concerning the Lord's Supper is frequently characterized as a materially modified Zwinglianism. Schaff maintains that "Calvin's theory took a middle course, retaining, on the basis of Zwingli's exegesis, the religious substance of Luther's faith, and giving it a more intellectual and spiritual form, triumphed in Switzerland, gained much favor in Germany, and opened a fair prospect for union." (*Creeds* 1, 280.) As a matter of fact, however, a fact admitted also by such Calvinists as Hodge and Shedd, Calvin's doctrine was a denial *in toto* of the real presence as taught by Luther. (Pieper, *Dogm.* 3, 354.) Calvin held that after His ascension Christ, according to His human nature, was locally enclosed in heaven, far away from the earth. Hence he denied also the real presence of Christ's body and blood in the Holy Supper. In fact, Calvin's doctrine was nothing but a polished form of Zwingli's crude teaching, couched in phrases approaching the Lutheran terminology as closely as possible. Even where he paraded as Luther, Calvin was but Zwingli disguised (and poorly at that) in a seemingly orthodox garb and promenading with several imitation Lutheran feathers in his hat.

In the *Formula of Concord* we read: "Although some Sacramentarians strive to employ words that come as close as possible to the *Augsburg Confession* and the form and mode of speech in its churches, and confess that in the Holy Supper the body of Christ is truly received by believers, still, when we insist that they state their meaning properly, sincerely, and clearly, they all declare themselves unanimously thus: that the true essential body and blood of Christ is absent from the consecrated bread and wine in the Holy Supper as far as the highest heaven is from the earth. . . . Therefore they understand this presence of the body of Christ not as a presence here upon earth, but only *respectu fidei* (with respect to faith), that is, that our faith, reminded and excited by the visible signs, just as by the Word preached, elevates itself and ascends above all heavens, and receives and enjoys the body of Christ, which is there in heaven present, yea, Christ Himself, together with all His benefits, in a manner true and essential, but nevertheless *spiritual only;* . . ., consequently nothing else is received by the mouth in the Holy Supper than bread and wine." (971, 2 f.) This is, and was intended to be, a presentation of Calvinism as being nothing but Zwinglianism clothed in seemingly orthodox phrases.

That this picture drawn by the *Formula of Concord* is not a caricature or in any point a misrepresentation of Calvinism appears from the *Consensus Tigurinus* itself, where we read: "In as far as Christ is a man, He is to be sought nowhere else than in heaven and in no other manner than with the mind and the understanding of faith. Therefore it is a perverse and impious superstition to include Him under elements of this world. *Christus, quatenus homo est, non alibi quam in coelo nec aliter quam mente et fidei intelligentia quaerendus est. Quare perversa et impia superstitio est, ipsum sub elementis huius mundi includere.*" Again: "We repudiate those [who urge the literal interpretation of the words of institution] as preposterous interpreters." "For beyond controversy, they are to be taken figuratively, . . . as when by metonymy the name of the symbolized thing is transferred to the sign — *ut per metonymiam ad signum transferatur rei figuratae nomen.*" Again: "Nor do we regard it as less absurd to place Christ under, and to unite Him with, the bread than to change the bread into His body. *Neque enim minus absurdum iudicamus, Christum sub pane locare vel cum pane copulare, quam panem transsubstantiare in corpus eius.*" Again: "When we say that Christ is to be sought in heaven, this mode of speech expresses a distance of place, . . . because the body of Christ, . . . being finite and contained in heaven, as in a place, must of necessity be removed from us by as great a distance as the heaven is removed from the earth — *necesse est, a nobis tanto locorum intervallo distare, quanto caelum abest a terra.*" (Niemeyer, *Collectio Confessionum*, 196.) Such was the teaching cunningly advocated by Calvin and his adherents, the Crypto-Calvinists in Germany included, but boldly and firmly opposed by the loyal Lutherans, and finally disposed of by Articles VII and VIII of the *Formula of Concord.*

### 199. Melanchthon's Public Attitude.

As stated, Calvin's doctrine of the Lord's Supper was received with increasing favor also in Lutheran territories, notably in Southern Germany and Electoral Saxony, where the number of theologians and laymen who secretly adopted and began to spread it was rapidly increasing. They were called Crypto-Calvinists (secret or masked Calvinists) because, while they subscribed to the *Augsburg Confession,* claimed to be loyal Lutherans, and occupied most important positions in the Lutheran Church, they in reality were propagandists of Calvinism, zealously endeavoring to suppress Luther's books and doctrines, and to substitute for them the views of Calvin. Indeed, Calvin claimed both privately and publicly that Melanchthon himself was his ally. And, entirely apart from what the latter may privately have confided to him, there can be little doubt that Calvin's assertions were not altogether without foundation. In fact, theologically as well as ethically, Melanchthon must be regarded as the spiritual father also of the Crypto-Calvinists.

True, originally Melanchthon fully shared Luther's views on the Lord's Supper. At Marburg, 1529, he was still violently opposed to the Zwinglians and their "profane" teaching. In an *Opinion* on Carlstadt's doctrine, of October 9, 1525, he affirms that Christ, both as God and man, *i. e.*, with His body and blood, is present in the Supper. (*C. R.* 1, 760.) In September of the following year he wrote to Philip Eberbach: "Know that Luther's teaching [concerning the Lord's Supper] is very old in the Church. *Hoc scito, Lutheri sententiam perveterem in ecclesia esse.*" (823.) This he repeats in a letter of November 11, also to Eberbach. In an *Opinion* of May 15, 1529: "I am satisfied that I shall not agree with the Strassburgers all my life, and I know that Zwingli and his compeers write falsely concerning the Sacrament." (1067.) June 20, 1529, to Jerome Baumgaertner: "I would rather die than see our people become contaminated by the society of the Zwinglian cause. *Nam mori malim, quam societate Cinglianae causae nostros contaminari.* My dear Jerome, it is a great cause, but few consider it. I shall be lashed to death on account of this matter." (*C. R.* 1, 1077; 2, 18.) November 2, 1529, to John Fesel: "I admonish you most earnestly to avoid the Zwinglian dogmas. Your Judimagister [Eberbach], I fear, loves these profane disputations too much. I know that the teaching of Zwingli can be upheld neither with the Scriptures nor with the authority of the ancients. Concerning the Lord's Supper, therefore, teach as Luther does." (1, 1109.) In February, 1530, he wrote: "The testimonies of ancient writers concerning the Lord's Supper which I have compiled are now being printed." (2, 18.) In this publication Melanchthon endeavored to show by quotations from Cyril, Chrysostom, Vulgarius, Hilary, Cyprian, Irenaeus, and Augustine that Zwingli's interpretation of the words of institution does not agree with that of the ancient Church. (23, 732.) According to his own statement, Melanchthon embodied Luther's doctrine in the *Augsburg Confession* and rejected that of the Zwinglians. (2, 142. 212.)

At Augsburg, Melanchthon was much provoked also when he heard that Bucer claimed to be in doctrinal agreement with the Lutherans. In his *Opinion Concerning the Doctrine of the Sacramentarians,* written in August, 1530, we read: "1. The Zwinglians believe that the body of the Lord can be present in but one place. 2. Likewise that the body of Christ cannot be anywhere except locally only. They vehemently contend that it is contrary to the nature of a body to be anywhere in a manner not local; also, that it is inconsistent with the nature of a body to be in different places at the same time. 3. For this reason they conclude that the body of Christ is circumscribed in heaven in a certain place, so that it can in no way be elsewhere at the same time, and that in truth and reality it is far away from the bread, and not in the bread and with the bread. 4. Bucer is therefore manifestly wrong in contending that they [the Zwinglians] are in agreement with us. For we say that it is not necessary for the body of Christ to be in but one place. We say that it can be in different places, whether this occurs locally or in some other secret way by which different places are as one point present at the same time to the person of Christ. We, therefore, affirm a true and real presence of the body of Christ with the bread. 5. If Bucer wishes to accept the opinion of Zwingli and Oecolampadius, he will never dare to say that the body of Christ is really with the bread without geometric distance. 9. Here they [the Zwinglians] wish the word 'presence' to be understood only concerning efficacy and the Holy Spirit. 10. We, however, require not only the presence of power, but of the body. This Bucer purposely disguises. 11. They simply hold that the body of Christ is in heaven, and that in reality it is neither with the bread nor in the bread. 12. Nevertheless they say that the body of Christ is truly present, but by contemplation of faith, i. e., by imagination. 13. Such is simply their opinion. They deceive men by saying that the body is truly present, yet adding afterwards, 'by contemplation of faith,' i. e., by imagination. 14. We teach that Christ's body is truly and really present with the bread or in the bread. 15. . . . Although we say that the body of Christ is really present, Luther does not say that it is present locally, namely, in some mass, by circumscription; but in the manner by which Christ's person or the entire Christ is present to all creatures. . . . We deny transubstantiation, and that the body is locally in the bread," etc. (2, 222. 311. 315.)

Such were the views of Melanchthon in and before 1530. And publicly and formally he continued to adhere to Luther's teaching. In an *Opinion* written 1534, prior to his convention with Bucer at Cassel, he said: "If Christ were a mere creature and not God, He would not be with us essentially, even if He had the government; but since He is God, He gives His body as a testimony that He is essentially with us always. This sense of the Sacrament is both simple and comforting. . . . Therefore I conclude that Christ's body and blood are truly with the bread and wine, that is to say, Christ essentially, not figuratively. But here we must cast aside the thoughts proffered by reason, *viz.*, how Christ ascends and descends, hides Himself in the bread, and is nowhere else." (2, 801.) In 1536 Melanchthon

signed the Wittenberg Concord, which plainly taught that the body and blood of Christ are received also by unworthy guests. (CONC. TRIGL. 977, 12 ff.) In 1537 he subscribed to the *Smalcald Articles*, in which Luther brought out his doctrine of the real presence in most unequivocal terms, declaring that "bread and wine in the Supper *are* the true body and blood of Christ, and are given and received not only by the godly, but also by wicked Christians." (CONC. TRIGL, 493, 1.) In his letter to Flacius of September 5, 1556, Melanchthon solemnly declared: "I have never changed the doctrine of the Confession." (*C. R.* 8, 841.) September 6, 1557, he wrote: "We all embrace and retain the Confession together with the *Apology* and the confession of Luther written previous to the Synod at Mantua." (9, 260.) Again, in November of the same year: "Regarding the Lord's Supper, we retain the *Augsburg Confession* and *Apology*." (9, 371.) In an *Opinion* of March 4, 1558, Melanchthon declared that in the Holy Supper the Son of God is truly and substantially present in such a manner that when we use it, He gives us with the bread and wine His body," etc., and that Zwingli was wrong when he declared "that it is a mere outward sign, and that Christ is not essentially present in it, and that it is a mere sign by which Christians know each other." (9, 472 f.) Several months before his death, in his preface to the *Corpus Philippicum*, Melanchthon declared that in the Holy Supper "Christ is truly and substantially present and truly administered to those who take the body and blood of Christ," and that in it "He gives His body and blood to him who eats and drinks." (Richard, 389.)

## 200. Melanchthon's Private Views.

While Melanchthon, in a public and formal way, continued, in the manner indicated, to maintain orthodox appearances till his death, he had inwardly and in reality since 1530 come to be more and more of a stranger to Luther's firmness of conviction, also with respect to the doctrine of the Lord's Supper. Influenced by an undue respect for the authority of the ancient fathers and misled by his reason or, as Luther put it, by his philosophy, he gradually lost his firm hold on the clear words of the institution of the Holy Supper. As a result he became a wavering reed, driven to and fro with the wind, now verging toward Luther, now toward Calvin. Always oscillating between truth and error, he was unable to rise to the certainty of firm doctrinal conviction, and the immovable stand which characterized Luther. In a letter dated May 24, 1538, in which he revealed the torments of his distracted and doubting soul, he wrote to Veit Dietrich: "Know that for ten years neither a night nor a day has passed in which I did not reflect on this matter," the Lord's Supper. (*C. R.* 3, 537.) And his doubts led to a departure from his own former position, — a fact for which also sufficient evidences are not wholly lacking. "Already in 1531," says Seeberg, "Melanchthon secretly expressed his opinion plainly enough to the effect that it was sufficient to acknowledge a presence of the divinity of Christ in the Lord's Supper, but not a union of the body and the bread. *Ep.*, p. 85." (*Dogg.* 4, 2, 447.)

That Melanchthon's, later public statements and protestations concerning his faithful adherence to the doctrine of the *Augsburg Confession* must be more or less discounted, appears, apart from other considerations, from his own admission that he was wont to dissimulate in these and other matters; from his private letters, in which he favorably refers to the symbolical interpretation of the words of institution; from his communication to Philip of Hesse with regard to Luther's article on the Lord's Supper at Smalcald, referred to in a previous chapter; from the changes which he made 1540 in Article X of the *Augsburg Confession;* from his later indefinite statements concerning the real presence in the Holy Supper; from his intimate relations and his cordial correspondence with Calvin; from his public indifference and neutrality during the eucharistic controversy with the Calvinists; and from his unfriendly attitude toward the champions of Luther in this conflict.

### 201. Misled by Oecolampadius and Bucer.

That Melanchthon permitted himself to be guided by human authorities rather than by the clear Word of God alone, appears from the fact that Oecolampadius's *Dialogus* of 1530 — which endeavored to show that the symbolical interpretation of the words of institution is found also in the writings of the Church Fathers, notably in those of St. Augustine, and which Melanchthon, in a letter to Luther (*C. R.* 2, 217), says, was written "with greater exactness (*accuratius*) than he is otherwise wont to write" — made such a profound impression on him that ever since, as is shown by some of his private letters, to which we shall presently refer, he looked with increasing favor on the figurative interpretation.

As a result, Melanchthon's attitude toward the Southern Germans and the Zwinglians also underwent a marked change. When he left to attend the conference with Bucer at Cassel, in December, 1534, Luther in strong terms enjoined him to defend the sacramental union and the oral eating and drinking; namely, that in and with the bread the body of Christ is truly present, distributed, and eaten. Luther's *Opinion* in this matter, dated December 17, 1534, concludes as follows: "Und ist Summa das unsere Meinung, dass wahrhaftig in und mit dem Brot der Leib Christi gegessen wird, also dass alles, was das Brot wirkt und leidet, der Leib Christi wirke und leide, dass er ausgeteilt [ge]gessen und mit den Zaehnen zerbissen werde." (St. L. 17, 2052.) Self-evidently, when writing thus, Luther had no Capernaitic eating and drinking in mind, his object merely being, as stated, to emphasize the reality of the sacramental union. January 10, 1535, however, the day

after his return from Cassel, Melanchthon wrote to his intimate friend Camerarius that at Cassel he had been the messenger, not of his own, but of a foreign opinion. (*C. R.* 2, 822.)

As a matter of fact, Melanchthon returned to Wittenberg a convert to the compromise formula of Bucer, according to which Christ's body and blood are truly and substantially received in the Sacrament, but are not really connected with the bread and wine, the signs or *signa exhibitiva*, as Bucer called them. Stating the difference between Luther and Bucer, as he now saw it, Melanchthon said: The only remaining question therefore is the one concerning the physical union of the bread and body, — and of what need is this question? *Tantum igitur reliqua est quaestio de physica coniunctione panis et corporis, qua quaestione quid opus est?"* (*C. R.* 2, 827. 842; St. L. 17, 2057.) To Erhard Schnepf he had written: "He [Bucer] confesses that, when these things, bread and wine, are given, Christ is truly and substantially present. As for me, I would not demand anything further." (*C. R.* 2, 787.) In February he wrote to Brenz: "I plainly judge that they [Bucer, etc.] are not far from the view of our men; indeed, in the matter itself they agree with us (*reipsa convenire*); nor do I condemn them." (2, 843; St. L. 17, 2065.) This, however, was not Luther's view. In a following letter Melanchthon said: "Although Luther does not openly condemn it [the formula of Bucer], yet he did not wish to give his opinion upon it as yet. *Lutherus, etsi non plane damnat, tamen nondum voluit pronuntiare."* (*C. R.* 2, 843; St. L. 17, 2062.) A letter of February 1, 1535, to Philip of Hesse and another of February 3, to Bucer, also both reveal, on the one hand, Melanchthon's desire for a union on Bucer's platform and, on the other, Luther's attitude of aloofness and distrust. (*C. R.* 2, 836. 841.)

### 202. Secret Letters and the Variata of 1540.

In the letter to Camerarius of January 10, 1535, referred to in the preceding paragraph, Melanchthon plainly indicates that his views of the Holy Supper no longer agreed with Luther's. "Do not ask for my opinion now," says he, "for I was the messenger of an opinion foreign to me, although, forsooth, I will not hide what I think when I shall have heard what our men answer. But concerning this entire matter either personally, or when I shall have more reliable messengers. *Meam sententiam noli nunc requirere; fui enim nuntius alienae, etsi profecto non dissimulabo, quid sentiam, ubi audiero, quid respondeant nostri. Ac de hac re tota aut coram, aut cum habebo certiores tabellarios."* (2, 822.) Two days later, January 12, 1535, Melanchthon wrote a letter to Brenz (partly in Greek, which language he employed when he imparted thoughts which he regarded as dangerous, as, *e. g.*, in his defamatory letter to Camerarius, July 24, 1525, on Luther's marriage; *C. R.* 1, 754), in which he lifted the veil still more and gave a clear glimpse of his own true inwardness. From this letter it plainly appears that Melanchthon was no longer sure of the correctness of the literal interpretation of the words of institution, the very foundation of Luther's entire doctrine concerning the Holy Supper.

The letter reads, in part, as follows: "You have written several times concerning the Sacramentarians, and you disadvise the Concord, even though they should incline towards Luther's opinion. My dear Brenz, if there are any who differ from us regarding the Trinity or other articles, I will have no alliance with them, but regard them as such who are to be execrated. . . . Concerning the Concord, however, no action whatever has as yet been taken. I have only brought Bucer's opinions here [to Wittenberg]. But I wish that I could talk to you personally concerning the contro-versy. I do not constitute myself a judge, and readily yield to you, who govern the Church, and I affirm the real presence of Christ in the Supper. I do not desire to be the author or defender of a new dogma in the Church, but I see that there are many testimonies of the ancient writers who without any ambiguity explain the mystery typically and tropically [περὶ τύπου καὶ τροπικῶς], while the opposing testimonies are either more modern or spurious. You, too, will have to investigate whether you defend the ancient opinion. But I do wish earnestly that the pious Church would decide this case without sophistry and tyranny. In France and at other places many are killed on account of this opinion. And many applaud such judgments without any good reason, and strengthen the fury of the tyrants. To tell the truth, this matter pains me not a little. Therefore my only request is that you do not pass on this matter rashly, but consult also the ancient Church. I most fervently desire that a concord be effected without any sophistry. But I desire also that good men may be able to confer on this great matter in a friendly manner. Thus a concord might be established without sophistry. For I do not doubt that the adversaries would gladly abandon the entire dogma if they believed that it was new. You know that among them are many very good men. Now they incline toward Luther, being moved by a few testimonies of ecclesiastical writers. What, then, do you think, ought to be done? Will you forbid also that we confer together? As for me, I desire that we may be able frequently to confer together on this matter as well as on many others. You see that in other articles they as well as we now explain many things more skilfully (dexterius) since they have begun to be agitated among us more diligently. However, I conclude and ask you to put the best construction on this letter, and, after reading it, to tear it up immediately, and to show it to nobody." (C. R. 2, 823 f.; Luther, St. L. 17, 2060.)

In a letter to Veit Dietrich, dated April 23, 1538, Melanchthon declares: "In order not to deviate too far from the ancients, I have maintained a sacramental presence in the use, and said that, when these things are given, Christ is truly present and efficacious. That is certainly enough. I have not added an inclusion or a connection by which the body is affixed to, concatenated or mixed with, the bread. Sacraments are covenants [assuring us] that something else is present when the things are received. Nec addidi inclusionem aut coniunctionem talem, qua affigeretur τῷ ἄρτῳ.τὸ σῶμα, aut ferruminaretur, aut misceretur. Sacramenta pacta sunt, ut rebus sumptis adsit aliud. . . . What more do you desire? And this will have to be resorted to lest you defend what some even now are saying, viz., that the body and blood are tendered separately — separatim tradi corpus et sanguinem. This, too, is new and will not even please the Papists. Error is fruitful, as the saying goes. That physical connection (illa physica coniunctio) breeds many questions: Whether the parts are separate; whether included; when [in what moment] they are present; whether [they are present] apart from the use. Of this nothing is read among the ancients. Nor do I, my dear Veit, carry these disputations into the Church; and in the Loci I have spoken so sparingly on this matter in order to lead the youth away from these questions. Such is in brief and categorically what I think. But I wish that the two most cruel tyrants, animosity and sophistry, would be removed for a while, and a just deliberation held concerning the entire matter. If I have not satisfied you by this simple answer, I shall expect of you a longer discussion. I judge that in this manner I am speaking piously, carefully, and modestly concerning the symbols, and approach as closely as possible to the opinion of the ancients." (C. R. 3, 514 f.) A month later, May 24, Melanchthon again added: "I have simply written you what I think, nor do I detract anything from the words. For I know that Christ is truly and substantially present and efficacious when we use the symbols. You also admit a synecdoche. But to add a division and separation of the body and blood, that is something altogether new and unheard of in the universal ancient Church." (3, 536; 7, 882.)

Evidently, then, Melanchthon's attitude toward the Reformed and his views concerning the Lord's Supper had undergone remarkable changes since 1530. And in order to clear the track for his own changed sentiments and to enable the Reformed, in the interest of an ultimate union, to subscribe the Augsburg Confession, Melanchthon, in 1540, altered its Tenth Article in the manner set forth in a previous chapter. Schaff remarks: Calvin's view of the Lord's Supper "was in various ways officially recognized in the Augsburg Confession of 1540." (1, 280.) Such at any rate was the construction the Reformed everywhere put on the alteration. It was generally regarded by them to be an essential concession to Calvinism. Melanchthon, too, was well aware of this; but he did absolutely nothing to obviate this interpretation — no doubt, because it certainly was not very far from the truth.

## 203. Not in Sympathy with Lutheran Champions.

When Westphal, in 1552, pointed out the Calvinistic menace and sounded the tocsin, loyal Lutherans everywhere enlisted in the controversy to defend Luther's doctrine concerning the real presence and the divine majesty of Christ's human nature. But Melanchthon again utterly failed the Lutheran Church both as a leader and a private. For although Lutheranism in this controversy was fighting for its very existence, Master Philip remained silent, non-committal, neutral. Viewed in the light of the conditions then prevailing, it was impossible to construe this attitude as pro-Lutheran. Moreover, whenever and wherever Melanchthon, in his letters and opinions written during this controversy, did show his colors to some extent, it was but too apparent that his mind and heart was with the enemies rather than with the champions of Lutheranism. For while his letters abound with flings and thrusts against the men who defended the doctrines of the sacramental union and the omnipresence of the human nature of Christ, he led Calvin and his adherents to believe that he was in sympathy with them and their cause.

Melanchthon's animosity ran high not only against such extremists as Saliger (Beatus) and Fredeland (both were deposed in Luebeck 1568, and Saliger again in Rostock 1569), who taught that in virtue of the consecration before the use (*ante usum*) bread and wine are the body and blood of Christ, denouncing all who denied this as Sacramentarians (Gieseler 3, 2, 257), but also against all those who faithfully adhered to, and defended, Luther's phraseology concerning the Lord's Supper. He rejected the teaching of Westphal and the Hamburg ministers, according to which, in the Lord's Supper, the bread is properly called the body of Christ and the wine the blood of Christ, and stigmatized their doctrine as "bread-worship, ἀρτολατρεία." (*C. R.* 8, 362. 660. 791; 9, 470. 962.)

In a similar manner Melanchthon ridiculed the old Lutheran teaching of the omnipresence of Christ according to His human nature as a new and foolish doctrine. Concerning the *Confession and Report of the Wuerttemberg Theologians*, framed by Brenz and adopted 1559, which emphatically asserted the real presence, as well as the omnipresence of Christ also according to His human nature, Melanchthon remarked contemptuously in a letter to Jacob Runge, dated February 1, 1560, and in a letter to G. Cracow, dated February 3, 1560, that he could not characterize "the decree of the Wuerttemberg Fathers (*Abbates Wirtebergenses*) more aptly than as Hechinger Latin (*Hechingense Latinum, Hechinger Latein*)," *i. e.*, as absurd and insipid teaching. (9, 1035 f.; 7, 780. 884.)

## 204. Melanchthon Claimed by Calvin.

In 1554 Nicholas Gallus of Regensburg republished, with a preface of his own, *Philip Melanchthon's Opinions of Some Ancient Writers Concerning the Lord's Supper.* The timely reappearance of this book, which Melanchthon, in 1530, had directed against the Zwinglians, was most embarrassing to him as well as to his friend Calvin. The latter, therefore, now urged him to break his silence and come out openly against his public assailants. But Melanchthon did not consider it expedient to comply with this request. Privately, however, he answered, October 14, 1554: "As regards your admonition in your last letter that I repress the ignorant clamors of those who renew the strife concerning the bread-worship, know that some of them carry on this disputation out of hatred toward me in order to have a plausible reason for oppressing me. *Quod me hortaris, ut reprimam incruditos clamores illorum, qui renovant certamen περὶ ἀρτολατρείας, scito, quosdam praecipue odio mei eam disputationem movere, ut habeant plausibilem causam ad me opprimendum.*" (8, 362.)

Fully persuaded that he was in complete doctrinal agreement with his Wittenberg friend on the controverted questions, Calvin finally, in his *Last Admonition (Ultima Admonitio) to Westphal,* 1557, publicly claimed Melanchthon as his ally, and implored him to give public testimony "that they [the Calvinists and Zwinglians] teach nothing foreign to the *Augsburg Confession, nihil alienum nos tradere a Confessione Augustana.*" "I confirm," Calvin here declared, "that in this cause [concerning the Lord's Supper] Philip can no more be torn from me than from his own bowels. *Confirmo, non magis a me Philippum quam a propriis visceribus in hac causa posse divelli.*" (*C. R.* 37 [*Calvini Opp.* 9], 148. 149. 193. 466; Gieseler 3, 2, 219; Tschackert, 536.) Melanchthon, however, continued to preserve his sphinxlike silence, which indeed declared as loud as words could have done that he favored the Calvinists, and was opposed to those who defended Luther's doctrine. To Mordeisen he wrote, November 15, 1557: "If you will permit me to live at a different place, I shall reply, both truthfully and earnestly, to these unlearned sycophants, and say things that are useful to the Church," (*C. R.* 9, 374.)

After the death of Melanchthon, Calvin wrote in his *Dilucida Explicatio* against Hesshusius, 1561: "O Philip Melanchthon! For it is to you that I appeal, who art living with Christ in the presence of God and there waiting for us until we shall be assembled with you into blessed rest. A hundred times you have said, when, fatigued with labor and overwhelmed with cares, you, as an intimate friend, familiarly laid your head upon my breast: Would to God I might die on this bosom! But afterwards I have wished a thousand times that we might be granted to be together. You would certainly have been more courageous to engage in battle and stronger to despise envy, and disregard false accusations. In this way, too, the wickedness of many would have been restrained whose audacity to revile grew from your pliability, as they called it. *O Philippe Melanchthon! Te enim appello, qui apud Deum cum Christo vivis, nosque illic exspectas, donec tecum in beatam quietem colligamur. Dixisti centies, quum fessus laboribus et molestiis oppressus caput familiariter in sinum meum deponeres: Utinam, utinam moriar in hoc sinu! Ego vero millies postea optavi nobis contingere, ut simul essemus. Certe animosior fuisses ad obeunda certamina et ad spernendam invidiam falsasque criminationes pro nihilo ducendas fortior. Hoc quoque modo cohibita fuisset multorum improbitas, quibus ex tua mollitie, quam vocabant, crevit insultandi audacia."* (*C. R.* 37 [*Calvini Opp.* 9], 461 f.) It was not Melanchthon, but Westphal, who disputed Calvin's claim by publishing (1557) extracts from Melanchthon's former writings under the title: *Clarissimi Viri Ph. Melanchthonis Sententia de Coena Domini, ex scriptis eius collecta.* But, alas, the voice of the later Melanchthon was not that of the former!

### 205. Advising the Crypto-Calvinists.

In various other ways Melanchthon showed his impatience with the defenders of Luther's doctrine and his sympathy with their Calvinistic opponents. When Timann of Bremen, who sided with Westphal, opposed Hardenberg, a secret, but decided Calvinist, Melanchthon admonished the latter not to rush into a conflict with his colleagues, but to dissimulate. He says in a letter of April 23, 1556: *"Te autem oro, ne properes ad certamen cum collegis. Oro etiam, ut multa dissimules."* (*C. R.* 8, 736.) Another letter (May 9, 1557), in which he advises Hardenberg how to proceed against his opponents, begins as follows: "Reverend Sir and Dear Brother. As you see, not only the controversy, but also the madness (*rabies*) of the writers who establish the bread-worship is growing." (9, 154.) He meant theologians who, like Timann and Westphal, defended Luther's doctrine that in the Lord's Supper the bread is truly the body of Christ and the wine truly the blood of Christ, and that Christ is truly present also according to His human nature. Again, when at Heidelberg, in 1559, Hesshusius refused to acknowledge the Calvinist Klebitz (who had publicly defended the Reformed doctrine) as his assistant in the distribution of the Lord's Supper, and Elector Frederick III, the patron of the Crypto-Calvinists, who soon after joined the Reformed Church, demanded that Hesshusius come to an agreement with Klebitz, and finally deposed the former and dismissed the latter, Melanchthon approved of the unionistic methods of the Elector, and prepared ambiguous formulas to satisfy both parties.

In the *Opinion* requested by the Elector, dated November 1, 1559, Melanchthon said: "To answer is not difficult, but dangerous. . . . Therefore I approve of the measure of the illustrious Elector, commanding silence to the disputants on both sides [Hesshusius and the Calvinist Klebitz], lest dissension occur in the weak church. . . . The contentious men having been removed, it will be profitable that the rest agree on one form of words. It would be best in this controversy to retain the words

of Paul: 'The bread which we break is the communion (*κοινωνία*) of Christ.' Much ought to be said concerning the fruit of the Supper to invite men to love this pledge and to use it frequently. And the word 'communion' must be explained: Paul does not say that the nature of the bread is changed, as the Papists say; He does not say, as those of Bremen do, that the bread is the substantial body of Christ; he does not say that the bread is the true body of Christ, as Hesshusius does; but that it is the communion, *i. e.,* that by which the union occurs (*consociatio fit*) with the body of Christ, which occurs in the use, and certainly not without thinking, as when mice gnaw the bread. . . . The Son of God is present in the ministry of the Gospel, and there He is certainly efficacious in the believers, and He is present not on account of the bread, but on account of man, as He says, 'Abide in Me and I in you.' Again: 'I am in My Father, and you in Me, and I in you.' And in these true consolations He makes us members of His, and testifies that He will raise our bodies. Thus the ancients explain the Lord's Supper." (*C. R.* 9, 961.) No doubt, Calvin, too, would readily have subscribed to these ambiguous and indefinite statements. C. P. Krauth pertinently remarks: "Whatever may be the meaning of Melanchthon's words in the disputed cases, this much is certain, that they practically operated as if the worse sense were the real one, and their mischievousness was not diminished, but aggravated, by their obscurity and double meaning. They did the work of avowed error, and yet could not be reached as candid error might." (*Cons. Ref.,* 291.)

### 206. Historians on Melanchthon's Doctrinal Departures.

Modern historians are generally agreed that also with respect to the Lord's Supper the later Melanchthon was not identical with the earlier. Tschackert: "Melanchthon had long ago [before the outbreak of the second controversy on the Lord's Supper] receded from the peculiarities of the Lutheran doctrine of the Lord's Supper; he was satisfied with maintaining the personal presence of Christ during the Supper, leaving the mode of His presence and efficacy in doubt." (532.) Seeberg, who maintains that Melanchthon as early as 1531 departed from Luther's teaching concerning the Lord's Supper, declares: "Melanchthon merely does not want to admit that the body of Christ is really eaten in the Supper, and that it is omnipresent as such." (4, 2, 449.) Theo. Kolde: "It should never have been denied that these alterations in Article X of the *Augustana* involved real changes. . . . In view of his gradually changed conception of the Lord's Supper, there can be no doubt that he sought to leave open for himself and others the possibility of associating also with the Swiss." (25.) Schaff: "Melanchthon's later view of the Lord's Supper agreed essentially with that of Calvin." (1, 280.)

Such, then, being the attitude of Melanchthon as to the doctrine of the Lord's Supper, it was but natural and consistent that his pupils, who looked up to Master Philip with unbounded admiration, should become decided Calvinists. Melanchthon, chiefly, must be held responsible for the Calvinistic menace which threatened the Lutheran Church after the death of Luther. In the interest of fraternal relations with the Swiss, he was ready to compromise and modify the Lutheran truth. Had he had his way, and had not the tendency which he inaugurated been checked, the Lutheran Church would have lost its character and been transformed into a Reformed or, at least, a unionistic body. In a degree, this guilt was shared also by his older Wittenberg colleagues: Caspar Cruciger, Sr., Paul Eber, John Foerster, and others, who evidently inclined toward Melanchthon's view and attitude also in the matter concerning the Lord's Supper. Caspar Cruciger, for example, as appears from his letter to Veit Dietrich, dated April 18, 1538, taught the bodily presence of Christ in the use of the Lord's Supper, but not "the division or separation of the body and blood." (*C. R.* 3, 510.) Shortly before his death, as related in a previous chapter, Luther had charged these men with culpable silence with regard to the truth, declaring: "If you believe as you speak in my presence, then speak the same way in church, in public lectures, in sermons, and in private discussions, and strengthen your brethren, and lead the erring back to the right way, and contradict the wilful spirits; otherwise your confession is a mere sham and will be of no value whatever." (Walther, 40.) Refusal to confess the truth will ultimately always result in rejection of the truth. Silence here is the first step to open denial.

### 207. Westphal First to Sound Tocsin.

Foremost among the men who saw through Calvin's plan of propagating the Reformed doctrine of the Lord's Supper under phrases coming as close as possible to the Lutheran terminology, and who boldly, determinedly, and ably opposed the Calvinistic propaganda, was Joachim Westphal of Hamburg [born 1510; 1527 in Wittenberg; since 1541 pastor in Hamburg; died January 16, 1574]. Fully realizing the danger which threatened the entire Lutheran Church, he regarded it as his sacred duty to raise his voice and warn the Lutherans against the Calvinistic menace. He did so in a publication entitled: "*Farrago Confusanearum et inter se Dissidentium Opinionum de Coena Domini* — Medley of Confused and Mutually Dissenting Opinions on the Lord's Supper, compiled from the books of the Sacramentarians," 1552. In it he proved that in reality Calvin and his adherents, despite their seemingly orthodox phrases, denied the real presence of the body and blood of Christ in the Lord's Supper just as emphatically and decidedly as Zwingli had done. At the same time he refuted in strong terms the Reformed doctrine in the manner indicated by the title, and maintained the Lutheran doctrine of the real presence, the oral eating and drinking (*manducatio oralis*),

also of unbelievers. Finally he appealed to the Lutheran theologians and magistrates everywhere to guard their churches against the Calvinistic peril. "The *Farrago*," says Kruske, "signified the beginning of the end of Calvin's domination in Germany." Schaff: "The controversy of Westphal against Calvin and the subsequent overthrow of Melanchthonianism completed and consolidated separation of the two Confessions," Lutheran and Reformed. (*Creeds* 1, 280.) Thus Westphal stands preeminent among the men who saved the Lutheran Church from the Calvinistic peril. To add fuel to the anti-Calvinistic movement, Westphal, in the year following, published a second book: "*Correct Faith (Recta Fides) Concerning the Lord's Supper,* demonstrated and confirmed from the words of the Apostle Paul and the Evangelists," 1553. Here he again called upon all true disciples of Luther to save his doctrine from the onslaughts of the Calvinists, who, he declared, stooped to every method in order to conquer Germany for Zwinglianism.

Westphal's fiery appeals for Lutheran loyalty received a special emphasis and wide publicity when the Pole, John of Lasco (Laski), who in 1553, together with 175 members of his London congregation, had been driven from England by Bloody Mary, reached the Continent. The liberty which Lasco, who in 1552 had publicly adopted the *Consensus Tigurinus*, requested in Lutheran territories for himself and his Reformed congregation, was refused in Denmark, Wismar, Luebeck, and Hamburg, but finally granted in Frankfort-on-the-Main. Soon after, in 1554, the Calvinistic preacher Micronius, who also sought refuge in Hamburg, was forbidden to make that city the seat of Reformed activity and propaganda. As a result, Calvin decided to enter the arena against Westphal. In 1555 he published his *Defensio Sanae et Orthodoxae Doctrinae de Sacramentis,* "Defense of the Sound and Orthodox Doctrine Concerning the Sacraments and Their Nature, Power, Purpose, Use, and Fruit, which the pastors and ministers of the churches in Zurich and Geneva before this have comprised into a brief formula of the mutual Agreement" (*Consensus Tigurinus*). In it he attacked Westphal in such an insulting and overbearing manner (comparing him, *e. g.*, with "a mad dog") that from the very beginning the controversy was bound to assume a personal and acrimonious character.

### 208. Controversial Publications.

After Calvin had entered the controversy, Westphal was joined by such Lutherans as John Timann, Paul v. Eitzen, Erhard Schnepf, Alber, Gallus, Flacius, Judex, Brenz, Andreae, and others. Calvin, on the other hand, was supported by Lasco, Bullinger, Ochino, Valerandus Polanus, Beza (the most scurrillous of all the opponents of Lutheranism), and Biblicander. In 1555 Westphal published three additional books: *Collection (Collectanea) of Opinions of Aurelius Augustine Concerning the Lord's Supper,* and *Faith (Fides) of Cyril,*

*Bishop of Alexandria, Concerning the Presence of the Body and Blood of Christ,* and *Adversus cuiusdam Sacramentarii Falsam Criminationem Iusta Defensio,* "Just Defense against the False Accusation of a Certain Sacramentarian." The last publication was a personal defense against the insults and invectives of Calvin and a further proof of the claim that the Calvinists were united only in their denial of the real presence of Christ in the Lord's Supper. Coming to the support of Westphal, John Timann, Pastor in Bremen, published in 1555: "*Medley (Farrago) of Opinions Agreeing in the True and Catholic Doctrine Concerning the Lord's Supper,* which the churches of the Augsburg Confession have embraced with firm assent and in one spirit according to the divine Word."

In the following year Calvin wrote his *Secunda Defensio . . . contra J. Westphali Calumnias,* "Second Defense of the Pious and Orthodox Faith, against the Calumnies of J. Westphal," a vitriolic book, dedicated to the Crypto-Calvinists, *viz.,* "to all ministers of Christ who cultivate and follow the pure doctrine of the Gospel in the churches of Saxony and Lower Germany." In it Calvin declared: "I teach that Christ, though absent according to His body, is nevertheless not only present with us according to His divine power, but also makes His flesh vivifying for us." (*C. R.* 37 [*Calvini Opp.* 9], 79.) Lasco also wrote two books against Westphal and Timann, defending his congregation at Frankfort, and endeavoring to show the agreement between the Calvinian doctrine of the Lord's Supper and the *Augsburg Confession.* In 1556 Henry Bullinger appeared on the battlefield with his *Apologetical Exposition, Apologetica Expositio,* in which he endeavored to show that the ministers of the churches in Zurich do not follow any heretical dogma in the doctrine concerning the Lord's Supper.

In the same year, 1556, Westphal published *Epistola, qua Breviter Respondet ad Convicia I. Calvini —* "Letter in which He [Westphal] Answers Briefly to the Invectives of J. Calvin," and "*Answer (Responsum) to the Writing of John of Lasco,* in which he transforms the *Augsburg Confession* into Zwinglianism." In the same year Westphal published "*Confession of Faith (Confessio Fidei) Concerning the Sacrament of the Eucharist,* in which the ministers of the churches of Saxony maintain the presence of the body and blood of our Lord Jesus Christ in the Holy Supper, and answer regarding the book of Calvin dedicated to them." This publication contained opinions which Westphal had secured from the ministeriums of Magdeburg (including Wigand and Flacius), of Mansfeld, Bremen, Hildesheim, Hamburg, Luebeck, Lueneburg, Brunswick (Moerlin and Chemnitz), Hannover, Wismar, Schwerin, etc. All of these ministeriums declared themselves unanimously and definitely in favor of Luther's doctrine, appealing to the words of institution as they read. In 1557 Erhard Schnepf [born 1595; active in Nassau, Marburg, Speier, Augsburg; attended convents in Smalcald 1537; in Regensburg

1546; in Worms 1557; died 1558], then in Jena, published his *Confession Concerning the Supper.* In the same year Paul von Eitzen [born 1522; died 1598; refused to sign *Formula of Concord*] published his *Defense of the True Doctrine Concerning the Supper of Our Lord Jesus Christ.* Westphal also made a second attack on Lasco in his "*Just Defense against the Manifest Falsehoods of J. A. Lasco* which he spread in his letter to the King of Poland against the Saxon Churches," 1557. In it he denounces Lasco and his congregation of foreigners, and calls upon the magistrates to institute proceedings against them.

Calvin now published his *Ultima Admonitio,* "Last Admonition of John Calvin to J. Westphal, who, if he does not obey (*obtemperet*), must thenceforth be held in the manner as Paul commands us to hold obstinate heretics; in this writing the vain censures of the Magdeburgians and others, by which they endeavored to wreck heaven and earth, are also refuted," 1557. Here Calvin plainly reveals his Zwinglianism and says: "This is the summary of our doctrine, that the flesh of Christ is a vivifying bread because it truly nourishes and feeds our souls when by faith we coalesce with it. This, we teach, occurs spiritually only, because the bond of this sacred unity is the secret and incomprehensible power of the Holy Spirit." (*C. R.* 37 [*Calvini Opp.* 9], 162.) In this book Calvin also, as stated above, appeals to Melanchthon to add his testimony that "we [the Calvinists] teach nothing that conflicts with the *Augsburg Confession.*"

Though Calvin had withdrawn from the arena, Westphal continued to give public testimony to the truth. In 1558 he wrote several books against the Calvinists. One of them bears the title: "*Apologetical Writings (Apologetica Scripta) of J. W.,* in which he both defends the sound doctrine concerning the Eucharist and refutes the vile slanders of the Sacramentarians," etc. Another is entitled: *Apology of the Confession Concerning the Lord's Supper against the Corruptions and Calumnies of John Calvin.* In 1559 Theodore Beza donned the armor of Calvin and entered the controversy with his "*Treatise (Tractatio) Concerning the Lord's Supper,* in which the calumnies of J. Westphal are refuted." Lasco's *Reply to the Virulent Letter of That Furious Man J. Westphal,* of 1560, appeared posthumously, he having died shortly before in Poland.

## 209. Brenz and Chemnitz.

Foremost among the influential theologians who, besides Westphal, took a decided stand against the Calvinists and their secret abettors in Lutheran territories were John Brenz in Wuerttemberg and Martin Chemnitz in Brunswick. John Brenz [born 1499, persecuted during the Interim, since 1553 Provost at Stuttgart, died 1570], the most influential theologian in Wuerttemberg, was unanimously supported in his anti-Calvinistic attitude by the whole ministerium of the Duchy. He is the author of the *Confession and Report (Bekenntnis und Bericht) of the Theologians in*

*Wuerttemberg Concerning the True Presence of the Body and Blood of Christ in the Holy Supper,* adopted at the behest of Duke Christopher by the synod assembled in Stuttgart, 1559. The occasion for drafting and adopting this *Confessión* had been furnished by Bartholomew Hagen, a Calvinist. At the synod in Stuttgart he was required to dispute on the doctrine of the Lord's Supper with Jacob Andreae, with the result that Hagen admitted that he was now convinced of his error, and promised to return to the Lutheran teaching.

The *Confession* thereupon adopted teaches in plain and unmistakable terms that the body and blood of Christ are orally received by all who partake of the Sacrament, and that Christ, by reason of the personal union, is omnipresent also according to His human nature, and hence well able to fulfil the promise He gave at the institution of the Holy Supper. It teaches the real presence (*praesentia realis*), the sacramental union (*unio sacramentalis*), the oral eating and drinking (*manducatio oralis*), also of the wicked (*manducatio impiorum*). It holds "that in the Lord's Supper the true body and the true blood of our Lord Jesus Christ are, through the power of the word [of institution], truly and essentially tendered and given with the bread and wine to all men who partake of the Supper of Christ; and that, even as they are tendered by the hand of the minister, they are at the same time also received with the mouth of him who eats and drinks it." Furthermore, "that even as the substance and the essence of the bread and wine are present in the Lord's Supper, so also the substance and the essence of the body and blood of Christ are present and truly tendered and received with the signs of bread and wine." (Tschackert, 541.) It protests: "We do not assert any mixture of His body and blood with the bread and wine, nor any local inclusion in the bread." Again: "We do not imagine any diffusion of the human nature or expansion of the members of Christ (*ullam humanae naturae diffusionem aut membrorum Christi distractionem*), but we explain the majesty of the man Christ by which He, being placed at the right hand of God, fills all things not only by His divinity, but also as the man Christ, in a celestial manner and in a way that to human reason is past finding out, by virtue of which majesty His presence in the Supper is not abolished, but confirmed." (Gieseler 3, 2, 239 f.) Thus, without employing the term "ubiquity," this *Confession* prepared by Brenz restored, in substance, the doctrine concerning the Lord's Supper and the person of Christ which Luther had maintained over against Zwingli, Carlstadt, and the Sacramentarians generally.

As stated above, Melanchthon ridiculed this *Confession* as "Hechinger Latin." In 1561 Brenz was attacked by Bullinger in his *Treatise (Tractatio) on the Words of St. John 14.* In the same year Brenz replied to this attack in two writings: *Opinion (Sententia) on the Book of Bullinger* and *On the Personal Union (De Personali Unione) of the Two Natures in*

Christ and on the Ascension of Christ into Heaven and His Sitting at the Right Hand of the Father, etc. This called forth renewed assaults by Bullinger, Peter Martyr, and Beza. Bullinger wrote: "*Answer (Responsio)*, by which is shown that the meaning concerning 'heaven' and the 'right hand of God' still stands firm," 1562. Peter Martyr: *Dialogs (Dialogi) Concerning the Humanity of Christ, the Property of the Natures, and Ubiquity,* 1562. Beza: *Answers (Responsiones) to the Arguments of Brenz,* 1564. Brenz answered in two of his greatest writings, *Concerning the Divine Majesty of Christ (De Divina Maiestate Christi),* 1562, and *Recognition (Recognitio) of the Doctrine Concerning the True Majesty of Christ,* 1564. In the *Dresden Consensus (Consensus Dresdensis)* of 1571 the Philippists of Electoral Saxony also rejected the omnipresence (which they termed ubiquity) of the human nature of Christ.

In order to reclaim the Palatinate (which, as will be explained later, had turned Reformed) for Lutheranism, the Duke of Wuerttemberg, in April, 1564, arranged for the Religious Discussion at Maulbronn between the theologians of Wuerttemberg and the Palatinate. But the only result was a further exchange of polemical publications. In 1564 Brenz published *Epitome of the Maulbronn Colloquium . . . Concerning the Lord's Supper and the Majesty of Christ.* And in the following year the Wuerttemberg theologians published *Declaration and Confession (Declaratio et Confessio) of the Tuebingen Theologians Concerning the Majesty of the Man Christ.* Both of these writings were answered by the theologians of the Palatinate. After the death of Brenz, Jacob Andreae was the chief champion in Wuerttemberg of the doctrines set forth by Brenz.

In his various publications against the Calvinists, Brenz, appealing to Luther, taught concerning the majesty of Christ that by reason of the personal union the humanity of Christ is not only omnipotent and omniscient, but also omnipresent, and that the human nature of Christ received these as well as other divine attributes from the first moment of the incarnation of the Logos. Following are some of his statements: "Although the divine substance [in Christ] is not changed into the human, and each has its own properties, nevertheless these two substances are united in one person in Christ in such a manner that the one is never in reality separated from the other." "Wherever the deity is, there is also the humanity of Christ." "We do not ascribe to Christ many and various bodies, nor do we ascribe to His body local extension or diffusion; but we exalt Him beyond this corporeal world, outside of every creature and place, and place Him in accordance with the condition of the hypostatic union in celestial majesty, which He never lacked, though at the time of His flesh in this world He hid it or, as Paul says, He humbled Himself (*quam etsi tempore carnis suae in hoc saeculo dissimulavit, seu ea sese, ut Paulus loquitur, exinanivit, tamen numquam ea caruit*)." According to Brenz the man Christ was omnipotent, almighty, omniscient while He lay in the manger. In His majesty He darkened the sun, and kept alive all the living while in His humiliation He was dying on the cross. When dead in the grave, He at the same time was filling and ruling heaven and earth with His power. (Gieseler 3, 2, 240 f.)

In Brunswick, Martin Chemnitz (born 1522; died 1586), the Second Martin (*alter Martinus*) of the Lutheran Church, entered the controversy against the Calvinists in 1560 with his *Repetition (Repetitio) of the Sound Doctrine Concerning the True Presence of the Body and Blood of Christ in the Supper,* in which he based his arguments for the real presence on the words of institution. Ten years later he published his famous book, *Concerning the Two Natures in Christ (De Duabus Naturis in Christo,* etc., — preeminently the Lutheran classic on the subject it treats. Appealing also to Luther, he teaches that Christ, according to His human nature, was anointed with all divine gifts; that, in consequence of the personal union, the human nature of Christ can be and is present where, when, and in whatever way Christ will; that therefore, in accordance with His promise, He is in reality present in His Church and in His Supper. Chemnitz says: "This presence of the assumed nature in Christ of which we now treat is not natural or essential [flowing from the nature and essence of Christ's humanity], but voluntary and most free, depending on the will and power of the Son of God (*non est vel naturalis vel essentialis, sed voluntaria et liberrima, dependens a voluntate et potentia Filii Dei*); that is to say, when by a definite word He has told, promised, and asseverated that He would be present with His human nature, . . . let us retain this, which is most certainly true, that Christ can be with His body wherever, whenever, and in whatever manner He wills (*Christum suo corpore esse posse, ubicunque, quandocunque et quomodocunque vult*). But we must judge of His will from a definite, revealed word." (Tschackert, 544; Gieseler 3, 2, 259.)

The *Formula of Concord* plainly teaches, both that, in virtue of the personal union by His incarnation, Christ according to His human nature possesses also the divine attribute of omnipresence, and that He can be and is present wherever He will. In the Epitome we read: This majesty Christ always had according to the personal union, and yet He abstained from it in the state of His humiliation until His resurrection, "so that now not only as God, but also as man He knows all things, can do all things, *is present with all creatures,* and has under His feet and in His hand everything that is in heaven and on earth and under the earth. . . . And this His power He, *being present,* can exercise everywhere, and to Him everything is possible and everything is known." (821, 16. 27. 30.) The Thorough Declaration declares that Christ "truly fills all things, and, being present everywhere, not only as God, but also as man, rules from sea to sea and to the ends of the

earth." (1025, 27 ff.) Again: "We hold . . . that also according to His assumed human nature and with the same He [Christ] *can be, and also is,* present where He will, and especially that in His Church and congregation on earth He is present as Mediator, Head, King, and High Priest, not in part, or onehalf of Him only, but the entire person of Christ, to which both natures, the divine and the human, belong, is present not only according to His divinity, but also according to, and with, His assumed human nature, according to which He is our Brother, and we are flesh of His flesh and bone of His bone." (1043, 78 f.) In virtue of the personal union Christ is present everywhere also according to His human nature; while the peculiarly gracious manner of His presence in the Gospel, in the Church, and in the Lord's Supper depends upon His will and is based upon His definite promises.

### 210. Bremen and the Palatinate Lost for Lutheranism.

The indignation of the Lutherans against the Calvinistic propaganda, roused by Westphal and his comrades in their conflict with Calvin and his followers, was materially increased by the success of the crafty Calvinists in Bremen and in the Palatinate. In 1547 Hardenberg [Albert Rizaeus from Hardenberg, Holland, born 1510] was appointed Domepreacher in Bremen. He was a former priest whom Lasco had won for the Reformation. Regarding the doctrine of the Lord's Supper he inclined towards Zwingli. Self-evidently, when his views became known, the situation in Bremen became intolerable for his Lutheran colleagues. How could they associate with, and fellowship, a Calvinist! To acknowledge him would have been nothing short of surrendering their own views and the character of the Lutheran Church. The result was that John Timann [pastor in Bremen; wrote a tract against the Interim; died February 17, 1557], in order to compel Hardenberg to unmask and reveal his true inwardness, demanded that all the ministers of Bremen subscribe to the *Farrago Sententiarum Consentientium in Vera Doctrina et Coena Domini,* which he had published in 1555 against the Calvinists. Hardenberg and two other ministers refused to comply with the demand. In particular, Hardenberg objected to the omnipresence of the human nature of Christ taught in Timann's *Farrago.* In his *Doctrinal Summary (Summaria Doctrina)* Hardenberg taught: "St. Augustine and many other fathers write that the body of Christ is circumscribed by a certain space in heaven, and I regard this as the true doctrine of the Church." (Tschackert, 191.) Hardenberg also published the fable hatched at Heidelberg (*Heidelberger Landluege,* indirectly referred to also in the *Formula of Concord,* 981, 28), but immediately refuted by Joachim Moerlin, according to which Luther is said, toward the end of his life, to have confessed to Melanchthon that he had gone too far and overdone the matter in his controversy against the

Sacramentarians; that he, however, did not want to retract his doctrine concerning the Lord's Supper himself, because that would cast suspicion on his whole teaching; that therefore after his death the younger theologians might make amends for it and settle this matter. . . . In 1556 Timann began to preach against Hardenberg, but died the following year. The Lower Saxon Diet, however, decided February 8, 1561, that Hardenberg be dismissed within fourteen days, yet "without infamy or condemnation, *citra infamiam et condemnationem.*" Hardenberg submitted under protest and left Bremen February 18, 1561 (he died as a Reformed preacher at Emden, 1574). Simon Musaeus, who had just been expelled from Jena, was called as Superintendent to purge Bremen of Calvinism. Before long, however, the burgomaster of the city, Daniel von Bueren, whom Hardenberg had secretly won for the Reformed doctrine, succeeded in expelling the Lutheran ministers from the city and in filling their places with Philippists, who before long joined the Reformed Church. Thus ever since 1562 Bremen has been a Reformed city.

A much severer blow was dealt Lutheranism when the Palatinate, the home of Melanchthon, where the Philippists were largely represented, was Calvinized by Elector Frederick III. Tileman Hesshusius [Hesshusen, born 1527; 1553 superintendent at Goslar; 1556 professor and pastor at Rostock; 1557 at Heidelberg; 1560 pastor at Magdeburg; 1562 court-preacher at Neuburg; 1569 professor at Jena; 1573 bishop of Samland, at Koenigsberg; 1577 professor at Helmstedt, where he died 1588] was called in 1557 by Elector Otto Henry to Heidelberg both as professor and pastor and as superintendent of the Palatinate. Here the Calvinists and Crypto-Calvinists had already done much to undermine Lutheranism; and after the death of Otto Henry, February 12, 1559, Hesshusius, who endeavored to stem the Crypto-Calvinistic tide, was no longer able to hold his own. Under Elector Frederick III, who succeeded Otto Henry, the Calvinists came out into the open. This led to scandalous clashes, of which the Klebitz affair was a typical and consequential instance. In order to obtain the degree of Bachelor of Divinity, William Klebitz, the deacon of Hesshusius, published, in 1560, a number of Calvinistic theses. As a result, Hesshusius most emphatically forbade him henceforth to assist at the distribution of the Holy Supper. When Klebitz nevertheless appeared at the altar, Hesshusius endeavored to wrest the cup from his hands. Elector Frederick ordered both Hesshusius and Klebitz to settle their trouble in accordance with the *Augustana* (Variata). Failing to comply with this unionistic demand, Hesshusius was deposed, September 16, 1559, and Klebitz, too, was dismissed. In a theological opinion, referred to above, Melanchthon approved of the action. Hereupon Hesshusius entered the public controversy against Calvinism. In 1560 he published *Concerning the Presence (De Praesentia) of the Body of Christ in the Lord's* *Supper* and his *Answer (Responsio) to the Prejudicial Judgment (Praeiudicium) of Philip Melanchthon on the Controversy Concerning the Lord's Supper* [with Klebitz].

After the dismissal of Hesshusius, Elector Frederick III, who had shortly before played a conspicuous rôle in endeavoring to win the day for Melanchthonianism at the Lutheran Assembly of Naumburg, immediately began to Calvinize his territory. In reading the controversial books published on the Lord's Supper, he suffered himself to be guided by the renowned physician Thomas Erastus [died 1583], who was a Calvinist and had himself published Calvinistic books concerning the Lord's Supper and the person and natures of Christ. As a result the Elector, having become a decided Reformedist, determined to de-Lutheranize the Palatinate in every particular, regarding practise and divine service as well as with respect to confessional books, doctrines, and teachers. The large number of Philippists, who had been secret Calvinists before, was increased by such Reformed theologians as Caspar Olevianus (1560), Zacharias Ursinus (1561), and Tremellius (1561). Images, baptismal fonts, and altars were removed from the churches; wafers were replaced by bread, which was broken; the organs were closed; the festivals of Mary, the apostles, and saints were abolished. Ministers refusing to submit to the new order of things were deposed and their charges filled with Reformed men from the Netherlands. The Calvinistic *Heidelberg Catechism*, composed by Olevianus and Ursinus and published 1563 in German and Latin, took the place of Luther's Catechism. This process of Calvinization was completed by the introduction of the new Church Order of November 15, 1563. At the behest of Frederick III the *Swiss Confession (Confessio Helvetica)* was published in 1566, in order to prove by this out-and-out Zwinglian document, framed by Bullinger, "that he [the Elector of the Palatinate] entertained no separate doctrine, but the very same that was preached also in many other and populous churches, and that the charge was untrue that the Reformed disagreed among themselves and were divided into sects." Thus the Palatinate was lost to the Lutheran Confession, for though Ludwig VI (1576—1583), the successor of Frederick III, temporarily restored Lutheranism, Frederick IV (1583 to 1610) returned to Calvinism.

## 211. Saxony in the Grip of Crypto-Calvinists.

It was a severe blow to the Lutheran Church when Bremen and the Palatinate fell a prey to Calvinism. And the fears were not unfounded that before long the Electorate of Saxony would follow in their wake, and Wittenberg, the citadel of the Lutheran Reformation, be captured by Calvin. That this misfortune, which, no doubt, would have dealt a final and fatal blow to Lutheranism, was warded off, must be regarded as a special providence of God. For the men (Melanchthon, Major, etc.) whom Luther had accused of culpable silence regarding the true doctrine of the Lord's Supper, were, naturally enough, succeeded by theologians who, while claiming to be true Lutherans adhering to the *Augsburg Confession* and, in a shameful manner, deceiving and misleading Elector August, zealously championed and developed the Melanchthonian aberrations, in particular with respect to the doctrines concerning the Lord's Supper and the person of Christ, and sedulously propagated the views of Calvin, at first secretly and guardedly, but finally with boldness and *abandon*. Gieseler says of these Philippists in Wittenberg: "Inwardly they were out-and-out Calvinists, although they endeavored to appear as genuine Lutherans before their master," Elector August. (3, 2, 250.)

The most prominent and influential of these so-called Philippists or Crypto-Calvinists were Dr. Caspar Cruciger, Jr., Dr. Christopher Pezel, Dr. Frederick Widebram, and Dr. Henry Moeller. The schemes of these men were aided and abetted by a number of non-theological professors: Wolfgang Crell, professor of ethics; Esrom Ruedinger, professor of philosophy; George Cracow, professor of jurisprudence and, later, privy councilor of Elector August; Melanchthon's son-in-law, Caspar Peucer, professor of medicine and physician in ordinary of the Elector, who naturally had a great influence on August and the ecclesiastical affairs of the Electorate. He held that Luther's doctrine of the real presence had no more foundation in the Bible than did the Roman transubstantiation. To these must be added John Stoessel, confessor to the Elector and superintendent at Pirna; Christian Schuetze, court-preacher at Dresden; Andrew Freyhub and Wolfgang Harder, professors in Leipzig; and others. The real leaders of these Philippists were Peucer and Cracow. Their scheme was to prepossess the Elector against the loyal adherents of Luther, especially Flacius, gradually to win him over to their liberal views, and, at the proper moment, to surrender and deliver Electoral Saxony to the Calvinists. In prosecuting this sinister plan, they were unscrupulous also in the choice of their means. Thus Wittenberg, during Luther's days the fountainhead of the pure Gospel and the stronghold of uncompromising fidelity to the truth, had become a veritable nest of fanatical Crypto-Calvinistic schemers and dishonest anti-Lutheran plotters, who also controlled the situation in the entire Electorate.

The first public step to accomplish their purpose was the publication of the *Corpus Doctrinae Christianae*, or *Corpus Doctrinae Misnicum*, or *Philippicum*, as it was also called. This collection of symbolical books was published 1560 at Leipzig by Caspar Peucer, Melanchthon's son-in-law, with a preface to both the German and Latin editions written by Melanchthon and dated September 29, 1559, and February 16, 1560, respectively, — an act by which, perhaps without sufficiently realizing it, Melanchthon immodestly assumed for himself and his views the place within the Lutheran Church which belonged not to him, but to Luther. The title, which reveals the insincerity and the purpose of this publication, runs as follows: "*Corpus Doctrinae, i. e.*, the entire sum of the true and Christian doctrine . . . as a testimony of the steadfast and unanimous confession of the pure and true religion in which the schools and churches of these Electoral Saxon and Meissen territories have remained and persevered in all points according to the *Augsburg Confession* for now almost thirty years against the unfounded false charges and accusations of all lying spirits, 1560." As a matter of fact, however, this *Corpus* contained, besides the Ecumenical Symbols, only writings of Melanchthon, notably the altered *Augsburg Confession* and the altered *Apology* of 1542, the Saxon Confession of 1551, the changed *Loci*, the *Examen Ordinandorum* of 1554, and the *Responsiones ad Impios Articulos Inquisitionis Bavaricae*.

Evidently this *Corpus Philippicum*, which was introduced also in churches outside of Electoral Saxony, particularly where the princes or leading theologians were Melanchthonians, was intended to alienate the Electorate from the old teaching of Luther, to sanction and further the Melanchthonian tendency, and thus to pave the way for Calvinism. It was foisted upon, and rigorously enforced in, all the churches of Electoral Saxony. All professors, ministers, and teachers were pledged by an oath to teach according to it. Such as refused to subscribe were deposed, imprisoned, or banished. Among the persecuted pastors we find the following names: Tettelbach, superintendent in Chemnitz; George Herbst, deacon in Chemnitz and later superintendent in Eisleben; Graf, superintendent in Sangerhausen; Schade, Heine, and Schuetz, pastors in Freiberg. When ministers who refused their signatures appealed to Luther's writings, they were told that Luther's books must be understood and explained according to Melanchthon's *Corpus*. At Wittenberg the opposition to Luther and his teaching bordered on fanaticism. When, for example, in 1568 Conrad Schluesselburg and Albert Schirmer, two Wittenberg students, entered a complaint against Professors Pezel and Peucer because of their deviations from Luther in the doctrine of the Lord's Supper, and refused to admit that Peucer and his colleagues represented the pure doctrine in this matter, they were expelled from the university, anathematized, and driven from the city. (Schluesselburg 13, 609. 730; Gieseler 3, 2, 250.)

Immediately after its appearance, the *Corpus Philippicum* was denounced by loyal Lutherans, notably those of Reuss, Schoenfeld, and Jena. When the charges of false teaching against the Wittenberg theologians increased in number and force, Elector August arranged a colloquy between the theologians of Jena and Wittenberg. It was held at Altenburg and lasted from October, 1568, to March, 1569, because the Wittenbergers, evidently afraid of compromising themselves, insisted on its being conducted in writing only. The result of this colloquy was a public declaration on the part of Wigand, Coelestinus, Kirchner, Rosinus, and others to the effect that the Wittenberg and Leipzig theologians had unmistakably revealed themselves as false teachers. At the colloquy the Jena theologians objected in particular also to the *Corpus Misnicum* because it contained the altered *Augustana*, concerning which they declared: Melanchthon "has changed the said *Augsburg Confession* so often -that finally he has opened a window through which the Sacramentarians and Calvinists can sneak into it. One must watch carefully, lest in course of time the Papists also find such a loophole to twist themselves into it." (Gieseler 3, 2, 252.)

The Philippists of Leipzig and Wittenberg, in turn, denounced the Jena theologians as Flacian fighting cocks (*Flacianische Haderkatzen*). They also succeeded in persuading Elector August to adopt more rigorous measures against the malcontents in his territories. For in addition to the adoption of the *Corpus Philippicum* the ministers were now required to subscribe to a declaration which was tantamount to an endorsement of all of the false doctrines entertained by the Wittenbergers. The declaration read: "I do not adhere to the dangerous Flacian Illyrian errors, contentions, poisonous backbitings, and fanaticism (*zaenkischem Geschmeiss, giftigem Gebeiss und Schwaermerei*) with which the schools and churches of this country are burdened [by Flacius] concerning the imagined adiaphorism, synergism, and Majorism and other false accusations, nor have I any pleasure in it [the quarreling], and in the future I intend, by the help of God, to abstain from it altogether, to damn, flee, and avoid it, and, as much as I am able, to prevent it." (Gieseler 3, 2, 253; Walther, 49.)

### 212. Bold Strides Forward.

Feeling themselves firm and safe in the saddle, the Wittenberg Philippists now decided on further public steps in the direction of Calvinism. In 1570 they published *Propositions (Propositiones) Concerning the Chief Controversies of This Time*, in which the Lutheran doctrine regarding the majesty of the human nature of Christ was repudiated. In the following year they added a new Catechism, entitled: "*Catechesis continens explicationem simplicem et brevem decalogi, Symboli Apostolici, orationis dominicae, doctrinae Christianae, quod amplectuntur ac tuentur Ecclesiae regionum Saxonicarum et Misnicarum, quae sunt subiectae ditioni Ducis Electoris Saxoniae, edita in Academia Witebergensi et accommodata ad usum scholarum puerilium. 1571.*"

This Catechism, written, according to Wigand, by Pezel, appeared anonymously. Its preface, signed by the Wittenberg theological faculty, explains that the new Catechism was an epitome of the *Corpus Doctrinae Misnicum* and merely intended as a supplement of Luther's Catechism for progressed scholars who were in need of additional instruction. As a

matter of fact, however, its doctrine concerning the person of Christ and the Lord's Supper was in substantial agreement with the teaching of Calvin. Under the odious name of "ubiquity" it rejected the omnipresence of Christ according to His human nature, and sanctioned Calvin's teaching concerning the local inclusion of Christ in heaven. Acts 3, 21 was rendered in Beza's translation: "*Quem oportet coelo capi.* Who must be received by the heaven."

The Catechism declares: "The ascension was visible and corporeal; the entire Antiquity has always written that Christ's body is restricted to a certain place, wherever He wishes it to be; and a bodily ascension was made upwards. *Ascensio fuit visibilis et corporalis, et semper ita scripsit tota antiquitas, Christum corporali locatione in aliquo loco esse, ubicumque vult, et ascensio corporalis facta est sursum.*" Concerning the real presence, the Catechism merely states: "The Lord's Supper is the communication of the body and blood of our Lord Jesus Christ as it is instituted in the words of the Gospel; in which eating (*sumptione*) the Son of God is truly and substantially present, and testifies that He applies His benefits to the believers. He also testifies that He has assumed the human nature for the purpose of making us, who are ingrafted into Him by faith, His members. He finally testifies that He wishes to be in the believers, to teach, quicken and govern them." (Gieseler 3, 2, 263.) The sacramental union, oral eating and drinking, and the eating and drinking of the wicked are not mentioned. Tschackert remarks that every Calvinist would readily have subscribed to the teaching of this Catechism. (545.)

When the Wittenberg Catechism was warned against and designated as Calvinistic by Chemnitz, Moerlin, and other theologians of Brunswick, Lueneburg, Mansfeld, Jena, and Halle, the Wittenbergers answered and endeavored to defend their position in the so-called *Grundfeste*, Firm Foundation, of 1571. It was a coarse and slanderous publication, as even the title indicates, which reads: "Firm Foundation of the True Christian Church Concerning the Person and Incarnation of Our Lord Jesus Christ against the Modern Marcionites, Samosatenes, Sabellians, Arians, Nestorians, Eutychians, and Monothelites among the Flacian Rabble Published by the Theologians in Wittenberg." In this *Grundfeste* the Wittenbergers present the matter as though the real issue were not the Lord's Supper, but Christology. They enumerate as heretics also the "Ubiquitists," including Brenz, Andreae, and Chemnitz. With respect to their own agreement with Calvin, they remark that their teaching is the doctrine of the early Church, in which point, they said, also Calvin agreed. (Tschackert, 546.)

This daring Calvinistic publication again resulted in numerous protests against the Wittenbergers on the part of alarmed Lutherans everywhere outside of Electoral Saxony, which induced Elector August to require his theologians to deliver at Dresden, October 10, 1571, a definite statement of their faith. The confession which they presented was entitled: *Brief Christian and Simple Repetition of the Confession of the Churches of God in the Territories of the Elector of Saxony Concerning the Holy Supper,*" etc. The *Consensus Dresdensis,* as the document was called, satisfied the Elector at least temporarily, and was published also in Latin and Low German. Essentially, however, the indefinite and dubious language of the Catechism was here but repeated. Concerning the majesty of Christ the *Dresden Consensus* declares that after the resurrection and ascension the human nature of Christ "was adorned with higher gifts than all angels and men." In His ascension, the *Consensus* continues, Christ "passed through the visible heavens and occupied the heavenly dwelling, where He in glory and splendor retains the essence, property, form, and shape of His true body, and from there He, at the last day, will come again unto Judgment in great splendor, visibly."

In a similar vague, ambiguous, and misleading manner Christ's sitting at the right hand of God is spoken of. Omitting the oral eating and drinking and the eating and drinking of the wicked, the *Consensus* states concerning the Lord's Supper that "in this Sacrament Christ gives us with the bread and wine His true body sacrificed for us on the cross, and His true blood shed for us, and thereby testifies that He receives us, makes us members of His body, washes us with His blood, presents forgiveness of sins, and wishes truly to dwell and to be efficacious in us." (Tschackert, 546.) The opponents of the Wittenbergers are branded as unruly men, who, seeking neither truth nor peace, excite offensive disputations concerning the real presence in the Lord's Supper as well as with regard to other articles. Their doctrine of the real communication ("*realis seu physica communicatio*") is characterized as a corruption of the article of the two natures in Christ and as a revamping of the heresies of the Marcionites, Valentinians, Manicheans, Samosatenes, Sabellians, Arians, Nestorians, Eutychians, and Monothelites. (Gieseler 3, 2, 264 f.)

### 213. Apparently Victorious.

All the Crypto-Calvinistic publications of the Wittenberg and Leipzig Philippists were duly unmasked by the Lutherans outside of Electoral Saxony, especially in Northern Germany. Their various opinions were published at Jena, 1572, under the title: "*Unanimous Confession (Einhelliges Bekenntnis) of Many Highly Learned Theologians and Prominent Churches* 1. concerning the New Catechism of the New Wittenbergers, and 2. concerning their *New Foundation (Grundfeste),* also 3. concerning their *New Confession (Consensus Dresdensis),* thereupon adopted." However, all this and the repeated warnings that came from every quarter outside of his own territories, from Lutheran princes as well as theologians, do not seem to have made the least impression on Elector August. Yet he

evidently was, and always intended to be, a sincere, devoted, true-hearted, and single-minded Lutheran. When, for example, in 1572 Beza, at the instance of the Wittenberg Philippists, dedicated his book against Selneccer to Elector August, the latter advised him not to trouble him any further with such writings, as he would never allow any other doctrine in his territory than that of the *Augsburg Confession.*

However, blind and credulous as he was, and filled with prejudice and suspicion against Flacius and the Jena theologians generally, whom he, being the brother of the usurper Maurice, instinctively feared as possibly also political enemies, Elector August was easily duped and completely hypnotized, as it were, by the men surrounding him, who led him to believe that they, too, were in entire agreement with Luther and merely opposed the trouble-breeding Flacians, whom they never tired of denouncing as zealots, fanatics, bigots, wranglers, barkers, alarmists, etc. While in reality they rejected the doctrine that the true body and blood of Christ is truly and essentially present in the Holy Supper, these Crypto-Calvinists pretended (and Elector August believed them) that they merely objected to a *local* presence and to a Capernaitic eating and drinking of the body and blood of Christ in the Holy Supper. And while in reality they clearly repudiated Luther's teaching, according to which the divine attributes (omnipotence, omnipresence, etc.) are communicated to the human nature of Christ, they caused the Elector to believe that they merely opposed a delusion of the "Ubiquitists," who, they said, taught that the body of Christ was *locally extended* over the entire universe. This cross localism, they maintained, was the teaching of their opponents, while they themselves faithfully adhered to the teachings of Luther and Philip, and, in general, were opposed only to the exaggerations and excrescences advocated by the bigoted Flacians. (Walther, 43.)

Such was the manner in which the Elector allowed himself to be duped by the Philippists who surrounded him, — men who gradually developed the art of dissimulation to premeditated deceit, falsehood, and perjury. Even the Reformed theologian Simon Stenius, a student at Wittenberg during the Crypto-Calvinistic period, charges the Wittenbergers with dishonesty and systematic dissimulation. The same accusation was raised 1561 by the jurist Justus Jonas in his letters to Duke Albrecht of Prussia. (Gieseler 3, 2, 249.) And evidently believing that Elector August could be fooled all the time, they became increasingly bold in their theological publications, and in their intrigues as well.

To all practical purposes the University of Wittenberg was already Calvinized. Calvinistic books appeared and were popular. Even the work of a Jesuit against the book of Jacob Andreae on the Majesty of the Person of Christ was published at Wittenberg. The same was done with a treatise of Beza, although, in order to deceive the public, the title-page gave Geneva as the place of publication. Hans Lufft, the Wittenberg printer, later declared that during this time he did not know how to dispose of the books of Luther which he still had in stock, but that, if he had printed twenty or thirty times as many Calvinistic books, he would have sold all of them very rapidly.

Even Providence seemed to bless and favor the plans of the plotters. For when on March 3, 1573, Duke John William, the patron and protector of the faithful Lutherans, died, Elector August became the guardian of his two sons. And fanaticized by his advisers, the Elector, immediately upon taking hold of the government in Ducal Saxony, banished Wigand, Hesshusius, Caspar Melissander [born 1540; 1571 professor of theology in Jena; 1578 superintendent in Altenburg; died 1591], Rosinus [born 1520; 1559 superintendent in Weimar; 1574 superintendent in Regensburg; died 1586], Gernhard, court-preacher in Weimar, and more than 100 preachers and teachers of Ducal Saxony. The reason for this cruel procedure was their refusal to adopt the *Corpus Philippicum*, and because they declined to promise silence with respect to the Philippists.

### 214. "Exegesis Perspicua."

In 1573, the Calvinization of Electoral and Ducal Saxony was, apparently, an accomplished fact. But the very next year marked the ignominious downfall and the unmasking of the dishonest Philippists. For in this year appeared the infamous *Exegesis*, which finally opened the eyes of Elector August. Its complete title ran: "*Exegesis Perspicua et ferme Integra Controversiae de Sacra Coena* — Perspicuous and Almost Complete Explanation of the Controversy Concerning the Holy Supper." The contents and make-up of the book as well as the secret methods adopted for its circulation clearly revealed that its purpose was to deal a final blow to Lutheranism in order to banish it forever from Saxony. Neither the author, nor the publisher, nor the place and date of publication were anywhere indicated in the book. The paper bore Geneva mark and the lettering was French. The *prima facie* impression was that it came from abroad.

Before long, however, it was established that the *Exegesis* had been published in Leipzig by the printer Voegelin, who at first also claimed its authorship. But when the impossibility of this was shown, Voegelin, in a public hearing, stated that Joachim Curaeus of Silesia, a physician who had left Saxony and died 1573, was the author of the book. Valentin Loescher, however, relates (*Historia Motuum* 3, 195) that probably Pezel and the son-in-law of Melanchthon, Peucer, had a hand in it; that the Crypto-Calvinist Esram Ruedinger [born 1523, son-in-law of Camerarius, professor of physics in Wittenberg, died 1591] was its real author; that it was printed at Leipzig in order to keep the real originators of it hidden; and that, for the same purpose, the Silesian Candidate of Medicine Curaeus

had taken the responsibility of its authorship upon himself. (Tschackert, 547.)

Self-evidently, the Wittenberg theologians disclaimed any knowledge of, or any connection with, the origin of the *Exegesis*. However, they were everywhere believed to share its radical teachings, and known to have spread it among the students of the university, and suspected also of having before this resorted to tactics similar to those employed in the *Exegesis*. As early as 1561, for example, rhymes had secretly been circulated in Wittenberg, the burden of which was that faith alone effects the presence of Christ in the Lord's Supper, and that the mouth receives nothing but natural bread. One of these ran as follows: "Allein der Glaub' an Jesum Christ Schafft, dass er gegenwaertig ist, Und speist uns mit sei'm Fleisch und Blut Und sich mit uns einigen tut. Der Mund empfaeht natuerlich Brot, Die Seel' aber speist selber Gott." (Walther, 46.) Of course, the purpose of such dodgers was to prepare the way for Calvinism. And on the very face of it, the *Exegesis Perspicua* was intended to serve similar secret propaganda.

The chief difference between the preceding publications of the Philippists and the *Exegesis* was that here they came out in clear and unmistakable language. The sacramental union, the oral eating and drinking (*manducatio oralis*), and the eating and drinking of the wicked, which before were passed by in silence, are dealt with extensively and repudiated. The *Exegesis* teaches: The body of Christ is inclosed in heaven; in the Holy Supper it is present only according to its efficacy; there is no union of the body of Christ with the bread and wine; hence, there neither is nor can be such a thing as oral eating and drinking or eating and drinking of unbelievers. The "ubiquity," as the *Exegesis* terms the omnipresence of Christ's human nature, is condemned as Eutychian heresy. The *Exegesis* declared: "In the use of the bread and wine the believers by faith become true and living members of the body of Christ, who is present and efficacious through these symbols, as through a ministry inflaming and renewing our hearts by His Holy Spirit. The unbelieving, however, do not become partakers, or *xοινωνοί*, but because of their contempt are guilty of the body of Christ." (Seeberg, *Grundriss* 146.)

After fulsome praise of the Reformed, whose doctrine, the *Exegesis* says, is in agreement with the symbols of the ancient Church, and who as to martyrdom surpass the Lutherans, and after a corresponding depreciation of Luther, who in the heat of the controversy was said frequently to have gone too far, the *Exegesis* recommends that the wisest thing would be to follow the men whom God had placed at the side of Luther, and who had spoken more correctly than Luther. Following Melanchthon, all might unite in the neutral formula, "The bread is the communion of the body of Christ," avoiding all further definition regarding the ubiquity [the omnipresence of Christ's human nature] and the eating of the true body of Christ, until a synod had definitely decided these matters. (Tschackert, 547.)

All purified churches (all churches in Germany, Switzerland, etc., purified from Roman errors), the *Exegesis* urges, "ought to be in accord with one another; and this pious concord should not be disturbed on account of this difference [regarding the Holy Supper]. Let us be united in Christ and discontinue those dangerous teachings concerning the ubiquity, the eating of the true body on the part of the wicked, and similar things. The teachers should agree on a formula which could not create offense. They should employ the modes of speech found in the writings of Melanchthon. It is best to suppress public disputations, and when contentious men create strife and disquiet among the people, the proper thing to do, as Philip advised [in his opinion to the Elector of the Palatinate], is to depose such persons of either party, and to fill their places with more modest men. The teachers must promote unity, and recommend the churches and teachers of the opposite party." (Walther, 51.) Such was the teaching and the theological attitude of the *Exegesis*. It advocated a union of the Lutherans and the Reformed based on indifferentism, and a surrender in all important doctrinal points to Calvinism, the Lutherans merely retaining their name. This unionistic attitude of the *Exegesis* has been generally, also in America, termed Melanchthonianism.

### 215. Plotters Unmasked.

The plain and unmistakable language of the *Exegesis* cleared the atmosphere, and everywhere dispelled all doubts as to the real nature of the theological trend at Wittenberg and Leipzig. Now it was plain to everybody beyond the shadow of a doubt that Electoral Saxony was indeed infested with decided Calvinists. And before long also the web of deceit and falsehood which they had spun around the Elector was torn into shreds. The appearance of the *Exegesis* resulted in a cry of indignation throughout Lutheran Germany against the Wittenberg and Leipzig Philippists. Yet, in 1574, only few books appeared against the document, which, indeed, was not in need of a special refutation. Wigand published *Analysis of the New Exegesis*, and Hesshusius: *Assertion (Assertio) of the True Doctrine Concerning the Supper, against the Calvinian Exegesis*. At the same time Elector August was again urged by Lutheran princes, notably the King of Denmark and Duke Ludwig of Wuerttemberg, also by private persons, to proceed against the Calvinists in his country and not to spare them any longer. (Gieseler 3, 2, 267.) The aged Count of Henneberg made it a point to see the Elector personally in this matter. But there was little need for further admonitions, for the *Exegesis* had opened the Elector's eyes. And soon after its publication discoveries were made which filled August with deep humiliation and burning indignation at the base deception practised on him by the very men whom he had trusted implicitly and placed in most im-

portant positions. By lying and deceit the Philippists had for a long period succeeded in holding the confidence of Elector August; but now the time for their complete and inglorious unmasking had arrived.

Shortly after the *Exegesis* had appeared, Peucer wrote a letter to the Crypto-Calvinist Christian Schuetze, then court-preacher in Dresden [who studied at Leipzig; became superintendent at Chemnitz in 1550; court-preacher of Elector August in 1554; when he was buried, boys threw a black hen over his coffin, crying, 'Here flies the Calvinistic devil'; Joecher, *Lexicon* 4, 372], which he had addressed to the wife of the court-preacher in order to avoid suspicion. By mistake the letter was delivered to the wife of the court-preacher Lysthenius [born 1532; studied in Wittenberg; became court-preacher of Elector August in 1572 and later on his confessor; opposed Crypto-Calvinism; was dismissed 1590 by Chancellor Crell; 1591 restored to his position in Dresden; died 1596]. After opening the letter and finding it to be written in Latin, she gave it to her husband, who, in turn, delivered it to the Elector. In it Peucer requested Schuetze dexterously to slip into the hands of Anna, the wife of the Elector, a Calvinistic prayer-book which he had sent with the letter. Peucer added: "If first we have Mother Anna on our side, there will be no difficulty in winning His Lordship [her husband] too."

Additional implicating material was discovered when Augustus now confiscated the correspondence of Peucer, Schuetze, Stoessel, and Cracow. The letters found revealed the consummate perfidy, dishonesty, cunning, and treachery of the men who had been the trusted advisers of the Elector, who had enjoyed his implicit confidence, and who by their falsehoods had caused him to persecute hundreds of innocent and faithful Lutheran ministers. The fact was clearly established that these Philippists had been systematically plotting to Calvinize Saxony. The very arguments with which Luther's doctrine of the Lord's Supper and the Person of Christ might best be refuted were enumerated in these letters. However, when asked by the Elector whether they were Calvinists, these self-convicted deceivers are said to have answered that "they would not see the face of God in eternity if in any point they were addicted to the doctrines of the Sacramentarians or deviated in the least from Dr. Luther's teaching." (Walther, 56.) The leaders of the conspiracy were incarcerated. Cracow died in prison, 1575; Stoessel, 1576. It was as late as 1586 that Peucer regained his liberty, Schuetze in 1589.

### 216. Lutheranism Restored.

In all the churches of Saxony thanksgiving services were held to praise God for the final triumph of genuine Lutheranism. A memorial coin celebrating the victory over the Crypto-Calvinists, bearing the date 1574, was struck at Torgau. The obverse exhibits Elector August handing a book to Elector John George of Brandenburg. The inscription above reads:

"*Conserva Apud Nos Verbum Tuum, Domine.*
Preserve Thy Word among Us, O Lord." Below, the inscription runs: "*Augustus, Dei Gratia Dux Saxoniae et Elector.* Augustus, by the Grace of God Duke of Saxony and Elector." The reverse represents Torgau and its surroundings, with Wittenberg in the distance. The Elector, clad in his armor, is standing on a rock bearing the inscription: "*Schloss Hartenfels*" (castle at Torgau). In his right hand he is holding a sword, in his left a balance, whose falling scale, in which the Child Jesus is sitting, bears the inscription: "*Die Allmacht,* Omnipotence." The lighter and rising pan, in which four Wittenberg Crypto-Calvinists are vainly exerting themselves to the utmost in pulling on the chains of their pan in order to increase its weight, and on the beam of which also the devil is sitting, is inscribed: "*Die Vernunft,* Reason." Above, God appears, saying to the Elector, "Joshua 1, 5. 6: *Confide, Non Derelinquam Te.* Trust, I will not forsake thee." Below we read: "*Apud Deum Non Est Impossibile Verbum Ullum,* Lucae 1. *Conserva Apud Nos Verbum Tuum, Domine.* 1574. Nothing is impossible with God, Luke 1. Preserve Thy Word among us, Lord 1574."

The obverse of a smaller medal, also of 1574, shows the bust of Elector August with the inscription: "*Augustus, Dei Gratia Dux Saxoniae Et Elector.*" The reverse exhibits a ship in troubled waters with the crucified Christ in her expanded sails, and the Elector, in his armor and with the sword on his shoulder, standing at the foot of the mast. In the roaring ocean are enemies, shooting with arrows and striking with swords, making an assault upon the ship. The fearlessness of the Elector is expressed in the inscription: "*Te Gubernatore,* Thou [Christ] being the pilot." Among the jubilee medals of 1617 there is one which evidently, too, celebrates the victory over Zwinglianism and Calvinism. Its obverse exhibits Frederick in his electoral garb pointing with two fingers of his right hand to the name Jehovah at the head of the medal. At his left Luther is standing with a burning light in his right hand and pointing with the forefinger of his left hand to a book lying on a table and bearing the title: "*Biblia Sacra: V[erbum] D[ei] M[anet] I[n] Ae[ternum].*" The reverse represents the Elector standing on a rock inscribed: "*Schloss Hartenfels,* Castle Hartenfels." In his right hand he is holding the sword and in his left a balance. Under the falling scale, containing the Child Jesus, we read: "*Die Allmacht,* Omnipotence," and under the rising pan, in which the serpent is lying: "*Die Vernunft,* Reason." The marginal inscription runs: "*Iosua 1: Confide. Non Derelinquam Te.* Joshua 1: Trust. I will not forsake thee." (Ch. Junker, *Ehrengedaechtnis Dr. M. Luthers,* 353. 383.)

Self-evidently, Elector August immediately took measures also to reestablish in his territories Luther's doctrine of the Lord's Supper. The beginning was made by introducing a confession prepared by reliable superintendents, and discussed, adopted, and subscribed at the Diet of Torgau, September, 1574, and published simultaneously in German and Latin. Its German title ran: "*Brief Confession (Kurz Bekenntnis) and Articles Concerning the Holy Supper of the Body and Blood of Christ,* from which may clearly be seen what heretofore has been publicly taught, believed, and confessed concerning it in both universities of Leipzig and Wittenberg, and elsewhere in all churches and schools of the Elector of Saxony; also what has been rebuked and is still rebuked as Sacramentarian error and enthusiasm." The Torgau Confession, therefore, does not reject the *Corpus Doctrinae Misnicum* of 1560 nor even the *Consensus Dresdensis* of 1571, and pretends that Melanchthon was in doctrinal agreement with Luther, and that only a few Crypto-Calvinists had of late been discovered in the Electorate. This pretense was the chief reason why the Confession did not escape criticism. In 1575 Wigand published: "Whether the New Wittenbergers had hitherto always taught harmoniously and agreeably with the Old, and whether Luther's and Philip's writings were throughout in entire harmony and agreement."

As for its doctrine, however, the Torgau Confession plainly upholds the Lutheran teaching. Article VII contends that in the distribution of the Lord's Supper the body and blood of Christ "are truly received also by the unworthy." Article VIII maintains the "oral eating and drinking, *oris manducatio.*" Calvin, Beza, Bullinger, Peter Martyr, and the Heidelberg theologians are rejected, and their names expressly mentioned. On the other hand, the "ubiquity [local extension] of the flesh of Christ" is disavowed and a discussion of the mode and possibility of the presence of the body and blood of Christ is declined as something inscrutable. The Latin passage reads: "*Ac ne carnis quidem ubiquitatem, aut quidquam, quod vel veritatem corporis Christi tollat, vel ulli fidei articulo repugnet, propter praesentiam in Coena fingimus aut probamus. Denique de modo et possibilitate praesentiae corporis et sanguinis Domini plane nihil disputamus. Nam omnia haec imperscrutabilia statuimus.*" (Gieseler 3, 2, 268.)

Caspar Cruciger, Jr., Henry Moeller, Christopher Pezel, and Frederick Widebram, who refused to subscribe the *Brief Confession,* were first arrested, then, after subscribing with a qualification, released, but finally (1574) banished. Widebram and Pezel removed to Nassau, Moeller to Hamburg, and Cruciger to Hesse. At Leipzig, Andrew Freyhub, who, appealing to the *Consensus Dresdensis,* taught that Christ was exalted according to both natures, that divine properties were not communicated to His humanity, and that His body was inclosed in a certain place in heaven, was deposed in 1576.

Thus ended the Crypto-Calvinistic drama in Electoral Saxony. Henceforth such men as Andreae, Chemnitz, and Selnecker were the trusted advisers of August, who now became the enthusiastic, devoted, and self-sacrificing leader of the larger movement for settling all of the controversies distracting the Lutheran Church, which finally resulted in the adoption of the *Formula of Concord*.

### 217. Visitation Articles.

Elector August, the stanch defender of genuine Lutheranism, died 1586. Under his successor, Christian I, and Chancellor Nicholas Crell, Crypto-Calvinism once more raised its head in Electoral Saxony. But it was for a short period only, for Christian I died September 25, 1591, and during the regency of Duke Frederick William, who acted as guardian of Christian II, Lutheranism was reestablished. In order effectually and permanently to suppress the Crypto-Calvinistic intrigues, the Duke, in February of 1592, ordered a general visitation of all the churches in the entire Electorate. For this purpose Aegidius Hunnius [born 1550; 1576 professor in Marburg and later superintendent and professor in Wittenberg; attended colloquy at Regensburg 1601; wrote numerous books, particularly against Papists and Calvinists; died 1603], Martin Mirus [born 1532, died 1593], George Mylius [born 1544; 1584 expelled from Augsburg because he was opposed to the Gregorian almanac; since 1585 professor in Wittenberg and Jena; died 1607], Wolfgang Mamphrasius [born 1557; superintendent in

Wurtzen; died 1616], and others, who were to conduct the visitation, composed the so-called *Visitation Articles*, which were printed in 1593. The complete title of these articles runs: "*Visitation Articles in the Entire Electorate of Saxony*, together with the Negative and Contrary Doctrines of the Calvinists, and the Form of Subscription, as Presented to be Signed by Both Parties."

As a result of the visitation, the Crypto-Calvinistic professors in Wittenberg and Leipzig were exiled. John Salmuth [born 1575; court-preacher in Dresden since 1584; died 1592] and Prierius, also a minister in Dresden were imprisoned. As a bloody *finale* of the Crypto-Calvinistic drama enacted in Electoral Saxony, Chancellor Crell was beheaded, October 9, 1601, after an imprisonment of ten years. Crell was punished, according to his epitaph, as "an enemy of peace and a disturber of the public quiet — *hostis pacis et quietis publicae turbator*," or, as Hutter remarks in his *Concordia Concors*, "not on account of his religion, but on account of his manifold perfidy — *non ob religionem, sed ob perfidiam multiplicem*." (448. 1258.) For a long period (till 1836) all teachers and ministers in Electoral Saxony were required to subscribe also to the Visitation Articles as a doctrinal norm. Self-evidently they are not an integral part of the *Book of Concord*.

# XIX. Controversy on Christ's Descent into Hell.

### 218. Luther's Doctrine.

While according to medieval theologians the descent into hell was regarded as an act by which Christ, with His soul only, entered the abode of the dead; and while according to Calvin and the Reformed generally the descent into hell is but a figurative expression for the sufferings of Christ, particularly of His soul, on the cross, Luther, especially in a sermon delivered 1533 at Torgau, taught in accordance with the Scriptures that Christ, the God-man, body and soul, descended into hell as Victor over Satan and his host. With special reference to Ps. 16, 10 and Acts 2, 24. 27, Luther explained: After His burial the whole person of Christ, the God-man, descended into hell, conquered the devil, and destroyed the power of hell and Satan. The mode and manner, however, in which this was done can no more be comprehended by human reason than His sitting at the right hand of the Father, and must therefore not be investigated, but believed and accepted in simple faith. It is sufficient if we retain the consolation that neither hell nor devil are any longer able to harm us. Accordingly, Luther did not regard the descent into hell as an act belonging to the state of humiliation, by which He paid the penalty for our sins, but as an act of exaltation, in which Christ, as it were, plucked for us the fruits of His sufferings which were finished when He died upon the cross.

Luther's sermon at Torgau graphically describes the descent as a triumphant march of

our victorious Savior into the stronghold of the dismayed infernal hosts. From it we quote the following: "Before Christ arose and ascended into heaven, and while yet lying in the grave, He also descended into hell in order to deliver also us from it, who were to be held in it as prisoners. . . . However, I shall not discuss this article in a profound and subtle manner, as to how it was done or what it means to 'descend into hell,' but adhere to the simplest meaning conveyed by these words, as we must represent it to children and uneducated people." "Therefore, whoever would not go wrong or stumble had best adhere to the words and understand them in a simple way as well as he can. Accordingly, it is customary to represent Christ in paintings on walls, as He descends, appears before hell, clad in a priestly robe and with a banner in His hand, with which He beats the devil and puts him to flight, takes hell by storm, and rescues those that are His. Thus it was also acted the night before Easter as a play for children. And I am well pleased with the fact that it is painted, played, sung, and said in this manner for the benefit of simple people. We, too, should let it go at that, and not trouble ourselves with profound and subtle thoughts as to how it may have happened, since it surely did not occur bodily, inasmuch as He remained in the grave three days."

Luther continues: "However, since we cannot but conceive thoughts and images of what is presented to us in words, and are unable to think of or understand anything without such images, it is appropriate and right that we view it literally, just as it is painted, that He descends with the banner, shattering and destroying the gates of hell; and we should put aside thoughts that are too deep and incomprehensible for us." "But we ought . . . simply to fix and fasten our hearts and thoughts on the words of the Creed, which says: 'I believe in the Lord Jesus Christ, the Son of God, dead, buried, and descended into hell,' that is, in the entire person, God and man, with body and soul, undivided, 'born of the Virgin, suffered, died, and buried'; *in like manner I must not divide it here either, but believe and say that the same Christ, God and man in one person, descended into hell,* but did not remain in it; as Ps. 16, 10 says of Him: 'Thou wilt not leave My soul in hell, nor suffer Thine Holy One to see corruption.' By the word 'soul,' He, in accordance with the language of the Scripture, does not mean, as we do, a being separated from the body, but the entire man, the Holy One of God, as He here calls Himself. But how it may have occurred that the man lies there in the grave, and yet descends into hell — that, indeed, we shall and must leave unexplained and uncomprehended; for it certainly did not take place in a bodily and tangible manner, although we can only paint and conceive it in a coarse and bodily way and speak of it in pictures." "Such, therefore is the plainest manner to speak of this article, that we may adhere to the words and cling to this main point, that for us, through Christ, hell has been torn to pieces and the devil's kingdom and power utterly destroyed, for which purpose He died, was buried, and descended, — so that it should no longer harm or overwhelm us, as He Himself says, Matt. 16, 18. . . ." (CONC. TRIGL., 1050.)

## 219. Aepinus in Hamburg.

The two outstanding features of Luther's sermon are that Christ descended into hell, body and soul, and that He descended as a triumphant Victor, and not in order to complete His suffering and the work of atonement. The denial of these two points, in particular, caused a new controversy, which, however, was of brief duration only, and practically confined to the city of Hamburg, hence also called the Hamburg Church Controversy, *der Hamburger Kirchenstreit.* Its author was John Aepinus [Huck or Hoeck; born 1499; studied under Luther; persecuted in Brandenburg and banished; rector in Stralsund; 1532 pastor and later superintendent in Hamburg; wrote 1547 against the Interim; sided with Flacius against the Philippists; published books in Latin and Low German; dealt with Christ's descent to hell especially in his *Commentary on Psalm 16,* of 1544, and in his *Explanation of Psalm 68,* of 1553; died May 13, 1553].

Aepinus taught that Christ's descent is a part of His suffering and atonement. While the body was lying in the grave, His soul descended into hell in order to suffer the qualms and pangs required to satisfy the wrath of God, complete the work of redemption, and render a plenary satisfaction, *satisfactio plenaria.* The descent is the last stage of Christ's humiliation and suffering, His triumph first beginning with the resurrection. Though we know His sufferings in hell to have been most sad and bitter, yet we are unable to say and define what they were in particular, or to describe them concretely, because Scripture is silent on this question.

But while Aepinus originally held that the soul of Christ suffered in hell the punishment of *eternal* death, he later on distinguished between the first and the second death (eternal damnation), asserting the suffering Christ endured in hell to have been a part of the punishment of the first death, and that He did not suffer the *cruciatus* AETERNI *tartarei ignis.* — Such were the views advocated, developed, and variously modified by Aepinus in his theological lectures and publications. From the Latin *"Consummatum est,* It is finished," the teaching that Christ finished His suffering and the work of atonement by His death on the cross was stigmatized by Aepinus as *"error consummaticus,"* and its advocates as "Consummatists," while these, in turn, dubbed Aepinus and his adherents "Infernalists." (Frank 3, 440.)

Among the statements of Aepinus are the following: "I believe that hell is a place prepared by divine justice to punish the devils and wicked men according to the quality of their sins." (437.) "On account of our redemption Christ descended to hell, just as He suffered and died for us." (437.) "Theologians who either deny that the soul of Christ descended into hell, or say that Christ was present in hell only in effect and power, and not by His presence, deprive the Church of faith in the sufficient, complete, and perfect satisfaction and redemption of Christ, and leave to Satan the right over pious souls after their separation from the body. For by denying that Christ sustained and bore those punishments of death and hell which the souls were obliged to bear after their separation from the body, they assert that complete satisfaction has not been made for them." (439.) "I believe that the descent of the soul of Christ to hell is a part of the Passion of Christ, *i. e.,* of the struggles, dangers, anguish, pains, and punishments which He took upon Himself and bore in our behalf; for, in the Scriptures, to descend to hell signifies to be involved in the highest struggles, pain, and distress. I believe that the descent of Christ to hell is a part of His obedience foretold by the prophets and imposed on Him because of our sins." (440.) "I believe that the descent of Christ pertains to His humiliation, not to His glorification and triumph." (441.) "The descent to hell was by God's judgment laid upon Christ as the last degree of His humiliation and exinanition and as the extreme part of His obedience and satisfaction." (441.) "Peter clearly teaches, Acts 2, that the soul of

Christ felt the pangs of hell and death while His body was resting in the sepulcher." (441.) "What Christ experienced when He descended into hell is known to Himself, not to us; may we acknowledge and accept with grateful minds that He descended into hell for us. But let us not inquire what it was that He experienced for us in His descent, for we may piously remain ignorant of matters which God did not reveal to His Church, and which He does not demand that she know." (444.)

### 220. Opposed by His Colleagues.

The views of Aepinus, first presented in lectures delivered 1544 before the ministers of Hamburg, called forth dissent and opposition on the part of his colleagues. Before long, however (1549), the controversy began to assume a virulent character. While the conduct of Aepinus was always marked by dignity, moderation, and mildness, his opponents, Tileman Epping, John Gartz, and Caspar Hackrott, ventilated and assailed his teaching in their pulpits.

The chief argument against Aepinus was that his doctrine conflicted with, and invalidated, the words of Christ, "It is finished," "To-day shalt thou be with Me in Paradise." Aepinus rejoined that the word "to-day" is an ambiguous term, denoting both the immediate presence and the indefinite near future (*pro praesenti et imminente tempore indefinito*). (414.) However, it was not in every respect Luther's position which was occupied by some of the opponents of Aepinus. Gratz is reported to have taught that the article concerning the descent of Christ was not necessary to salvation; that *descendere* (descend) was identical with *sepeliri* (to be buried); that the descent to hell referred to the anguish and temptation of Christ during His life; that Christ immediately after His death entered paradise together with the malefactor; that the work of atonement and satisfaction was completed with His death. (446.)

In 1550 the city council of Hamburg asked Melanchthon for his opinion. But Melanchthon's answer of September, 1550, signed also by Bugenhagen, was rather indefinite, vague, and evasive. He said, in substance: Although we have frequently heard the Reverend Doctor Luther speak on this matter and read his writings, yet, since a controversy has now been raised, we have written also to others for their views, in order to present a unanimous opinion, and thus avoid dissensions later on. In his *Commentary on Genesis* and in his Torgau sermon, Luther referred Descent only to the victory of the Son of God, indicating that the rest must not be searched out. The Son of God did indeed overcome the torments of hell; but the Psalms show that the pains of hell are not to be restricted only to the time after the separation of the soul (*dolores inferorum non restringendos esse tantum ad tempus post animae separationem*): Luther, said Melanchthon, expressed it as his opinion "that this article concerning the Descent must be retained even when referred

only to the victory of Christ, confessing that the tyranny of the devil and hell is destroyed, *i. e.*, that all who believe in Christ are liberated from the power of the devil and hell, according to the word: 'No one shall pluck My sheep out of My hands.' And in a certain way the Son of God manifested this victory to the devils, and, no doubt, the devils felt that their power was broken by this Victor, and that the head of the serpent was truly bruised by the Seed of the Woman, by Christ, God and man. And among the signs of His victory was the resurrection of many dead." With respect to the controverted point, concerning the sufferings of the soul of Christ after its separation from the body, Melanchthon advised that the council of Hamburg "enjoin both parties to await the opinions of others also, and in the mean time to avoid mentioning this question in sermons, schools, or other public meetings." Not the article concerning the Descent itself, but "only the investigation of this particular point, concerning the suffering of His departed soul in hell, is to be omitted, an inquiry which also Dr. Luther did not consider necessary." (*C. R.* 7, 667.)

Before this Melanchthon had written in a similar vein of compromise to Aepinus and his colleague, John Gartz. "I wish," said he in a letter of April 4, 1550, "that there would be an amnesty between you in this entire strife" about the descent of Christ. "Let us cultivate peace with one another, and cover up certain wounds of ours, lest sadder disputations originate." (7, 569; compare 6, 116.) In the following year the Hamburg Council, acting on the advice of Melanchthon, deposed and expelled the leaders of the opposition to Aepinus, which, however, was not intended as a decision in favor of the doctrine of Aepinus, but merely as a measure to restore peace and silence in the city.

### 221. Other Participants in This Controversy.

Though the controversy was suppressed in Hamburg, and Aepinus died May 13, 1553, the theological questions involved were not settled, nor had all of the advocates of the views set forth by Aepinus disappeared from the scene. Even such theologians as Westphal, Flacius, Gallus, and Osiander were partly agreed with him. Osiander says in an opinion: "I am asked whether the descent of Christ pertains to the satisfaction made for us or only to His triumph over the enemies. I answer briefly that the descent of Christ into hell pertained to the satisfaction He merited for us as well as to the triumph over the enemies, just as His death on the cross does not belong to the one only, but to both. . . . Thus by descending into hell He rendered satisfaction for us who merited hell, according to Ps. 16." On the other hand, a synod held July 11, 1554, at Greifswald made it a point expressly to deny that the descent of Christ involved any suffering of His soul, or that it was of an expiatory nature, or that this article referred to the anguish of His soul before His death, or that it was identical with His burial. They affirmed the teaching of Luther, *viz.*, that the entire Christ, God and man, body and soul, descended into hell after His burial and before His resurrection, etc. (Frank, 446 f.; 416.)

Furthermore, in a letter to John Parsimonius, court-preacher in Stuttgart, dated February 1, 1565, John Matsperger of Augsburg taught that, in the article of the descent of Christ, the word "hell" must not be taken figuratively for torments, death, burial, etc., but literally, as the kingdom of Satan and the place of the damned spirits and souls, wherever that might be; that the entire Christ descended into this place according to both divinity and humanity, with His body and soul, and not only with the latter, while the former remained in the grave; that this occurred immediately after His vivification or the reunion of body and soul in the grave and before His resurrection; that the Descent was accomplished in an instant, *viz.*, in the moment after His vivification and before His resurrection; and that Christ descended, not to suffer, but, as a triumphant Victor, to destroy the portals of hell for all believers. Parsimonius, too, maintained that Christ did not in any way suffer after His death, but denied emphatically that "hell" was a definite physical locality or place in space, and that the descent involved a local motion of the body. Brenz assented to the views of Parsimonius, and the preachers of Augsburg also assented to them. In order to check his zeal against his opponents, Matsperger was deposed and imprisoned. (Frank, 450 f.)

Such being the situation within the Lutheran Church concerning the questions involved in the Hamburg Controversy, which, by the way, had been mentioned also in the Imperial Instruction for the Diet at Augsburg, 1555, the *Formula of Concord* considered it advisable to pass also on this matter. It did so, in Article IX, by simply reproducing what Luther had taught in the sermon referred to above. Here we read: "We simply believe that the entire person, God and man, after the burial, descended into hell, conquered the devil, destroyed the power of hell, and took from the devil all his might." (1051, 3.) "But how this occurred we should [not curiously investigate, but] reserve until the other world, where not only this point [this mystery], but also still others will be revealed, which we here simply believe, and cannot comprehend with our blind reason." (827, 4.) Tschackert remarks: "Ever since [the adoption of the Ninth Article of the *Formula of Concord*] Lutheran theology has regarded the Descent of Christ as the beginning of the state of exaltation of the human nature of the God-man." (559.)

# XX. The Eleventh Article of the Formula of Concord: On Predestination.

## 222. Why Article XI was Embodied in the Formula.

The reason why Article XI was embodied in the *Formula of Concord* is stated in the opening paragraph of this article: "Although among the theologians of the *Augsburg Confession* there has not occurred as yet any public dissension whatever concerning the eternal election of the children of God that has caused offense; and has become wide-spread, yet since this article has been brought into very painful controversy in other places, and even among our theologians there has been some agitation concerning it; moreover, since the same expressions were not always employed concerning it by the theologians: therefore, in order, by the aid of divine grace, to prevent disagreement and separation on its account in the future among our successors, we, as much as in us lies, have desired also to present an explanation of the same here, so that every one may know what is our unanimous doctrine, faith, and confession also concerning this article." (1063, 1.)

The statements contained in these introductory remarks are in agreement with the historical facts. For, while serious dissensions pertaining to election did occur in Reformed countries, the Lutheran Church, ever since the great conflict with Erasmus on free will, in 1525, had not been disturbed by any general, public, and offensive controversy on this question, neither *ad intra* among themselves, nor *ad extra* with the Calvinists. Hence the chief purpose for embodying Article XI in the *Formula* was not to settle past or present disputes, but rather, as stated in the paragraph quoted, to be of service in avoiding future differences and conflicts.

This earnest concern for the future peace of our Church, as well as for the maintenance of its doctrinal purity, was partly due to apprehensions, which, indeed, were not without foundation. As a matter of fact, long before the *Formula* was drafted, the theological atmosphere was surcharged with polemical possibilities and probabilities regarding predestination, — a doctrine which is simple enough as long as faith adheres to the plain Word of God, without making rationalistic and sophistical inferences, but which in public controversies has always proved to be a most intricate, crucial, and dangerous question.

Calvin and his adherents boldly rejected the universality of God's grace, of Christ's redemption, and of the Spirit's efficacious operation through the means of grace, and taught that, in the last analysis, also the eternal doom of the damned was solely due to an absolute decree of divine reprobation (in their estimation the logical complement of election), and this at the very time when they pretended adherence to the *Augsburg Confession* and were making heavy inroads into Lutheran territory with their doctrine concerning the Lord's Supper and the person of Christ, — which in itself was sufficient reason for a public discussion and determined resentment of their absolute predestinarianism. The Synergists, on the other hand, had long ago been busy explaining that the only way to escape the Stoic dogma of Calvinism, and to account for the difference why some are accepted and elected, while the rest are rejected, was to assume a different conduct in man — *aliqua actio dissimilis in homine.* And as for their Lutheran opponents, it cannot be denied that some of their statements were not always sufficiently guarded to preclude all misapprehensions and false inferences.

Thus controversial material had been everywhere heaped up in considerable quantities. Considering these factors, which for decades had been making for a theological storm, one may feel rather surprised that a controversy on predestination had not arisen long ago. Tschackert says: "They [the Lutheran theologians] evidently feared an endless debate if the intricate question concerning predestination were made a subject of discussion." (559.) Sooner or later, however, the conflict was bound to come with dire results for the Church, unless provisions were made to escape it, or to meet it in the proper way. Well aware of this entire critical situation and the imminent dangers lurking therein, the framers of the *Formula of Concord* wisely resolved to embody in it also an article on election in order to clear the theological atmosphere, maintain the divine truth, ward off a future controversy, and insure the peace of our Church.

### 223. Unguarded Statements of Anti-Synergists.

That the occasional dissimilar and inadequate references to eternal election and related subjects made by some opponents of the Synergists were a matter of grave concern to the authors of the *Formula of Concord* appears from the passage quoted from Article XI, enumerating, among the reasons why the article on predestination was embodied in the *Formula*, also the fact that "the same expressions were not always employed concerning it [eternal election] by the theologians." These theologians had stanchly defended the *sola gratia* doctrine, but not always without some stumbling in their language. In their expositions they had occasionally employed phrases which, especially when torn from their context, admitted a synergistic or Calvinistic interpretation. The framers of the *Formula* probably had in mind such inadequate and unguarded statements of Bucer, Amsdorf, and others as the following.

Bucer had written: "The Scriptures do not hesitate to say that God delivers some men into a reprobate mind and drives them to perdition. Why, then, is it improper to say that God has afore-determined to deliver these into a reprobate mind and to drive them to perdition? *Scriptura non veretur dicere, Deum tradere quosdam homines in sensum reprobum*

*et agere in perniciem. Quid igitur indignum Deo, dicere, etiam statuisse antea, ut illos in sensum reprobum traderet et ageret in perniciem?"* (Frank 4, 264.) The *Formula of Concord,* however, is careful to explain: "Moreover, it is to be diligently considered that when God punishes sin with sins, that is, when He afterwards punishes with obduracy and blindness those who had been converted, because of their subsequent security, impenitence, and wilful sins, this should not be interpreted to mean *that it never had been God's good pleasure* that such persons should come to the knowledge of the truth and be saved." (1001, 83.)

Brenz had said: 'To the one of the entire mass of the human race God gives faith in Christ, whereby he is justified and saved, while He leaves the other in his incredulity that he may perish. *Deus ex universa generis humani massa alteri quidem donat fidem in Christum, qua iustificetur et salvetur, alterum autem relinquit in sua incredulitate, ut pereat."* (Frank 4, 256.) Again: It was God's will to elect Jacob and to leave Esau in his sin. What is said of these two must be understood of the election and rejection of all men in general. *"Potuisset Deus optimo iure ambos abiicere; . . . sed sic proposuerat Deus, sic visum est Deo, sic erat voluntas Dei, sic erat bene placitum Dei, ut Iacobum eligeret, Esau autem in peccato suo relinqueret; quod de his duobus dictum est, hoc intelligendum erit generaliter de omnium hominum electione et abiectione."* (256.) Hesshusius: "In this respect God does not will that all be saved, for He has not elected all. *Hoc respectu Deus non vult, ut omnes salventur; non enim omnes elegit."* (Schluesselburg 5, 320. 548.) Such statements, when torn from their context, gave color to the inference that God's grace was not universal. The *Formula of Concord,* therefore, carefully urges that God earnestly endeavors to save all men, also those who are finally lost, and that man alone is the cause of his damnation.

In his *Sententia de Declaratione Victorini* 'of 1562 Nicholas Amsdorf said: "God has but one mode of working in all creatures. . . . Therefore God works in the same way in man who has a will and intellect as in all other creatures, rocks and blocks included, *viz.,* through His willing and saying alone. . . . As rocks and blocks are in the power of God, so and in the same manner man's will and intellect are in the will of God, so that man can will and choose absolutely nothing else than what God wills and says, be it from grace or from wrath. *Non est nisi unus modus agendi Dei cum omnibus creaturis. . . . Quare eodem modo cum homine volente et intelligente agit Deus, quemadmodum cum omnibus creaturis reliquis, lapide et trunco, per solum suum velle et dicere. . . . Sicut lapides et trunci sunt in potestate Dei, ita et eodem modo voluntas et intellectus hominis sunt in voluntate Dei, ut homo nihil prorsus velle et eligere possit nisi id, quod vult et dicit Deus, sive ex gratia, sive ex ira, derelinquens eum in manu consilii eius."* (Schlb. 5, 547; Gieseler 3, 2, 230; Frank

4, 259.) This, too, was not embodied in the *Formula of Concord*, which teaches that, although man before his conversion has no mode of working anything good in spiritual things, God nevertheless has a different way of working in rational creatures than in irrational, and that man is not coerced, neither in his sinning nor in his conversion. (905, 60 ff.)

## 224. Synergistic Predestination.

The connection between the doctrines of conversion and election is most intimate. A correct presentation of the former naturally leads to a correct presentation of the latter, and *vice versa*. Hence Melanchthon, the father of synergism in conversion, was also the author of a synergistic predestination. In his first period he speaks of predestination as Luther did, but, as Frank puts it, "with less of mysticism, conformably to reason, following the same line of thought as Zwingli (*mit weniger Mystik, auf verstandesmaessige, Zwinglis Ausfuehrungen aehnliche Weise.*" (1, 125; *C. R.* 21, 88. 93.) In reality he probably had never fully grasped the truly religious and evangelical view of Luther, which, indeed, would account for his later synergistic deviations as well as for the charges of Stoicism he preferred against Luther. After abandoning his former doctrine, he, as a rule, was noncommittal as to his exact views on election. But whenever he ventured an opinion, it savored of synergism. September 30, 1531, he wrote to Brenz: "But in the entire *Apology* I have avoided that long and inexplicable disputation concerning predestination. Everywhere I speak as though predestination follows our faith and works. And this I do intentionally; for I do not wish to perturb consciences with these inexplicable labyrinths. *Sed ego in tota Apologia fugi illam longam et inexplicabilem disputationem de praedestinatione. Ubique sic loquor, quasi praedestinatio sequatur nostram fidem et opera. Ac facio hoc certo consilio; non enim volo conscientias perturbare illis inexplicabilibus labyrinthis.* (*C. R.* 2, 547.)

In the third, revised edition of his *Explanation of the Epistle to the Romans*, 1532, he suggests "that divine compassion is truly the cause of election, but that there is some cause also in him who accepts, namely, in as far as he does not repudiate the grace offered. *Verecundius est, quod aliquamdiu placuit Augustino, misericordiam Dei vere causam electionis esse, sed tamen eatenus aliquam causam in accipiente esse, quatenus promissionem oblatam non repudiat, quia malum ex nobis est.*" (Gieseler 3, 2, 192; Seeberg 4, 2, 442.) In an addition to his *Loci* in 1533, Melanchthon again speaks of a cause of justification and election residing in man, in order to harmonize the statements that the promise of the Gospel is both gratis and universal. (*C. R.* 21, 332.) In the *Loci* edition of 1543 we read: "God elected because He had decreed to call us to the knowledge of His Son, and desires His will and benefits to be known to the human race. He therefore approves and

elected those who obey the call. *Elegit Deus, quia vocare nos ad Filii agnitionem decrevit et vult generi humano suam voluntatem et sua beneficia innotescere. Approbat igitur ac elegit obtemperantes vocationi.*" (21, 917.)

The bold synergistic views concerning conversion later on developed by Melanchthon plainly involve the doctrine that there must be in man a cause of discrimination why some are elected while others are rejected. In his *Loci* of 1548 he had written: "Since the promise is universal, and since there are no contradictory wills in God, some cause of discrimination must be in us why Saul is rejected and David accepted (*cur Saul abiiciatur, David recipiatur*), that is, there must be some dissimilar action in these two." (21, 659.) Self-evidently Melanchthon would not have hesitated to replace the phrase, "why Saul was rejected and David accepted," with, "why Saul was rejected and David elected."

Melanchthon held that the sole alternative of, and hence the only escape from, the doctrine of absolute necessity (*Stoica ἀνάγκη*) and from the absolute decree, which makes God responsible also for sin and eternal damnation, was the synergistic assumption of man's "ability to apply himself to grace — *facultas applicandi se ad gratiam.*" Accordingly, as he dubbed those who opposed his Calvinizing views on the Lord's Supper as "bread-worshipers," so he stigmatized as Stoics all Lutherans who opposed his synergistic tendencies. (*C. R.* 8, 782. 783. 916; 9, 100. 565. 733; 23, 392.) Seeberg summarizes Melanchthon's doctrine as follows: "Grace alone saves, but it saves by imparting to man the freedom to decide for himself. This synergistic element reappears in his doctrine of election." (4, 2, 446.) "God elects all men who desire to believe." (*Grundriss*, 144.)

Naturally the Synergists of Wittenberg and other places followed Master Philip also in the doctrine of election. In 1555, John Pfeffinger declared in his *Quaestiones Quinque* (extensively quoted from in the chapter on the Synergistic Controversy), thesis 17: "If the will were idle or purely passive [in conversion], there would be no distinction between the pious and the impious, or the elect and the damned, as between Saul and David, between Judas and Peter. God would become a respecter of persons and the author of contumacy in the wicked and damned. Moreover, contradictory wills would be ascribed to God, which conflicts with the entire Scripture. Hence it follows that there is in us some cause why some assent while others do not assent." Thesis 23: "For we are elected and received *because* we believe in the Son. (*Ideo enim electi sumus et recepti, quia credimus in Filium.*) But our apprehension must concur. For since the promise of grace is universal, and we must obey the promise, it follows that between the elect and the rejected some difference must be inferred from our will, *viz.*, that those are rejected who resist the promise, while contrariwise those are accepted who embrace the promise."

The Synergists argued: If in every respect

*See Rom 8:28-30 Eph 1:4-5*

grace alone is the cause of our salvation, conversion, and election, grace cannot be universal. Or, since man's contempt of God's Word is the cause of his reprobation, man's acceptance of God's grace must be regarded as a cause of his election. Joachim Ernest of Anhalt, for instance, in a letter to Landgrave William of Hesse, dated April 20, 1577, criticized the *Formula of Concord* for not allowing and admitting this argument. (Frank 4, 135. 267.)

## 225. Calvinistic Predestination.

While the Synergists, in answering the question why only some are saved, denied the *sola gratia* and taught a conversion and predestination conditioned by the conduct of man, John Calvin and his adherents, on the other hand, made rapid progress in the opposite direction, developing with increasing clearness and boldness an absolute, bifurcated predestination, *i. e.,* a capricious election to eternal damnation as well as to salvation, and in accordance therewith denied the universality of God's grace, of Christ's redemption, and of the efficacious operation of the Holy Spirit through the means of grace. In his "*Institutio Religionis Christianae,* Instruction in the Christian Religion," of which the first edition appeared 1535, the second in 1539, and the third in 1559, Calvin taught that God created and foreordained some to eternal life, others to eternal damnation. Man's election means that he has been created for eternal life; man's reprobation, that he has been created for eternal damnation. We read (*Lib.* 3, cap. 21, 5): "*Praedestinationem vocamus aeternum Dei decretum, quo apud se constitutum habuit, quid de unoquoque homine fieri vellet. Non enim pari conditione creantur omnes; sed aliis vita aeterna, aliis damnatio aeterna praeordinatur. Itaque prout in alterutrum finem quisque conditus est, ita vel ad vitam, vel ad mortem praedestinatum dicimus.*" (Tholuck, *Calvini Institutio* 2, 133.) In the edition of 1559 Calvin says that eternal election illustrates the grace of God by showing "that He does not adopt all promiscuously unto the hope of salvation, but bestows on some what He denies to others — *quod non omnes promiscue adoptat in spem salutis, sed dat aliis, quod aliis negat.*" (Gieseler 3, 2, 172.) Again: "I certainly admit that all the sons of Adam have fallen by the will of God into the miserable condition of bondage, in which they are now fettered; for, as I said in the beginning, one must always finally go back to the decision of the divine will alone, whose cause is hidden in itself. *Fateor sane, in hanc qua nunc illigati sunt conditionis miseriam Dei voluntate cecidisse universos filios Adam; atque id est, quod principio dicebam, redeundum tandem semper esse ad solum divinae voluntatis arbitrium, cuius causa sit in ipso abscondita.*" (173.) Calvin's successor in Geneva, Theodore Beza, was also a strict supralapsarian. At the colloquy of Moempelgard (Montbeliard), 1586, in disputing with Andreae, he defended the proposition "that Adam had indeed of his own

accord fallen into these calamities, yet, nevertheless, not only according to the prescience, but also according to the ordination and decree of God — *sponte quidem, sed tamen non modo praesciente, sed etiam iuste ordinante et decernente Deo.*" (186.) "There never has been, nor is, nor will be a time," said he, "when God has wished, wishes, or will wish to have compassion on every individual person. *Nullum tempus fuit vel est vel erit, quo voluerit, velit aut voliturus sit Deus singulorum misereri.*" (Pieper, *Dogm.* 2, 25. 50.)

In foisting his doctrine of election on the Reformed churches, Calvin met with at least some opposition. The words in the paragraph of the *Formula of Concord* quoted above: "Yet, since this article [of predestination] has been brought into very painful controversy in other places," probably refer to the conflicts in Geneva and Switzerland. October 16, 1551, Jerome Bolsec [a Carmelite in Paris; secretly spread Pelagianism in Geneva; sided with the Protestants in Paris and Orleans after his banishment from Geneva; reembraced Romanism when persecution set in; wrote against Calvin and Beza; died 1584] was imprisoned in Geneva because of his opposition to Calvin's doctrine of predestination. Melanchthon remarks in a letter of February 1, 1552: "Laelius [Socinus] wrote me that in Geneva the struggle concerning the Stoic necessity is so great that a certain one who dissented from Zeno [Calvin] was incarcerated. What a miserable affair! The doctrine of salvation is obscured by disputations foreign to it." (*C. R.* 7, 932.) Although the German cantons (Zurich, Bern, Basel) advised moderation, Bolsec was banished from Geneva, with the result, however, that he continued his agitation against Calvin in other parts of Switzerland. In Bern all discussions on predestination were prohibited by the city council. Calvin complained in a letter of September 18, 1554: "The preachers of Bern publicly declare that I am a heretic worse than all the Papists." (Gieseler 3, 2, 178.) January 26, 1555, the council of Bern renewed its decree against public doctrinal discussions, notably those on predestination — "*principalement touchant la matière de la divine prédestination, qui nous semble non être nécessaire,*" etc. (179.) Later on the doctrine of Calvin was opposed by the Arminians from Semi-Pelagian principles.

## 226. Calvinistic Confessions.

The essential features of Calvin's doctrine of predestination were embodied in most of the Reformed confessions. The *Consensus Genevensis* of January 1, 1552, written by Calvin against Albert Pighius [a fanatical defender of Popery against Luther, Bucer, Calvin; died December 26, 1542] and adopted by the pastors of Geneva, is entitled: "*Concerning God's Eternal Predestination,* by which He has elected some to salvation and left the others to their perdition — *qua in salutem alios ex hominibus elegit, alios suo exitio reliquit.*" (Niemeyer, *Collectio Confessionum,* 218. 221.) The *Confessio Belgica,* of 1559, and the *Confessio Gallicana,* of 1561, teach the same absolute predestinarianism. In Article XVI of the Belgic Confession we read: In predestination God proved Himself to be what He is in reality, *viz.,* merciful and just. "Merciful by liberating and saving from damnation and perdition those whom . . . He elected; just, by leaving the others in their fall and in the perdition into which they precipitated themselves. *Iustum vero, alios in illo suo lapsu et perditione relinquendo, in quam sese ipsi praecipites dederunt.*" (Niemeyer, 370.) The *Gallic Confession* [prepared by Calvin and his pupil, De Chandieu; approved by a synod at Paris 1559; delivered by Beza to Charles IX, 1561; translated into German, 1562, and into Latin, 1566; adopted 1571 by the Synod of La Rochelle] maintains that God elected some, but left the others in their corruption and damnation. In Article XII we read: "We believe that from this corruption and general damnation in which all men are plunged, God, according to His eternal and immutable counsel, calls those whom He has chosen by His goodness and mercy alone in our Lord Jesus Christ, without consideration of their works, to display in them the riches of His mercy, leaving the rest in this same corruption and condemnation to show in them His justice. *Credimus ex hac corruptione et damnatione universali, in qua omnes homines natura sunt submersi, Deum alios quidem eripere, quos videlicet aeterno et immutabili suo consilio sola sua bonitate et misericordia, nulloque operum ipsorum respectu in Iesu Christo elegit; alios vero in ea corruptione et damnatione relinquere, in quibus nimirum iuste suo tempore damnandis iustitiam suam demonstret, sicut in aliis divitias misericordiae suae declarat.*" (Niemeyer, 332; Schaff 3, 366.) The *Formula Consensus Helveticae* of 1675 says, canon 13: "As from eternity Christ was elected Head, Leader, and Heir of all those who in time are saved by His grace, thus also in the time of the New Covenant He has been the Bondsman *for those only* who by eternal election were given to Him to be His peculiar people, seed, and heredity. *Sicut Christus ab aeterno electus est ut Caput, Princeps et Haeres omnium eorum, qui in tempore per gratiam eius salvantur, ita etiam in tempore Novi Foederis Sponsor factus est pro iis solis, qui per aeternam electionem dati ipsi sunt ut populus peculii, semen et haereditas eius,*" etc. (Niemeyer, 733.) The same Calvinistic doctrines were subsequently embodied in the *Canons of the Synod of Dort,* promulgated May 6, 1619, and in the *Westminster Confession of Faith,* published 1647. In the former we read: "That some receive the gift of faith from God, and others do not receive it, proceeds from God's eternal election. . . . According to this just judgment He leaves the non-elect to their own wickedness and obduracy." (Schaff 3, 582.) "The elect, in due time, though in various degrees and in different measures, attain the assurance of this eternal and unchangeable election, not by inquisitively prying into the secret and deep things of God, but by observ-

ing in themselves, with a spiritual joy and holy pleasure, the infallible fruits of election pointed out in the Word of God, such as a true faith in Christ, filial fear, a godly sorrow for sin, a hungering and thirsting after righteousness, etc." (583.) "Not all, but some only, are elected, while others are passed by in the eternal decree; whom God, out of His sovereign, most just, irreprehensible, and unchangeable good pleasure, hath decreed to leave in the common misery into which they have wilfully plunged themselves, and not to bestow upon them saving faith and the grace of conversion." . . . (584.) "For this was the sovereign counsel and most gracious will and purpose of God the Father, that the quickening and saving efficacy of the most precious death of His Son should extend to all the elect, for bestowing *upon them alone* the gift of justifying faith, thereby to bring them infallibly to salvation; that is, it was the will of God that Christ by the blood of the cross, whereby He confirmed the New Covenant, should effectually redeem out of every people, tribe, nation, and language all those, *and those only,* who were from eternity chosen to salvation, and given to Him by the Father." (587.) "But God, who is rich in mercy, according to His unchangeable purpose of election, does not *wholly* withdraw the Holy Spirit from His own people, even in their melancholy falls, nor suffer them to proceed so far as to lose the grace of adoption and forfeit the state of justification," etc. (Schaff 3, 593; Niemeyer, 716.)

The *Westminster Confession* declares: "By the decree of God, for the manifestation of His glory, some men and angels are predestinated unto everlasting life, and others foreordained to everlasting death." (Schaff 3, 608.) "As God hath appointed the elect unto glory, so hath He, by the eternal and most free purpose of His will, foreordained all the means thereunto. Wherefore they who are elected, being fallen in Adam, are redeemed by Christ, are effectually called unto faith in Christ by His Spirit working in due season; are justified, adopted, sanctified, and kept by His power through faith unto salvation. Neither are any other redeemed by Christ, effectually called, justified, adopted, sanctified, and saved but the elect only." (609.) "The rest of mankind God was pleased, according to the unsearchable counsel of His own will, whereby He extends or withholds mercy as He pleases, for the glory of His sovereign power over His creatures, *to pass by,* and to ordain them to dishonor and wrath for their sin, to the praise of His glorious justice." (610; Niemeyer, *Appendix* 6. 7.)

## 227. Marbach and Zanchi in Strassburg.

In view of the situation portrayed in the preceding paragraphs, it is certainly remarkable that a general public controversy, particularly with the Calvinists and Synergists, had not been inaugurated long before the *Formula of Concord* was able to write that such a conflict had not yet occurred. Surely the

powder required for a predestinarian conflagration was everywhere stored up in considerable quantities, within as well as without the
Lutheran Church. Nor was a local skirmish
lacking which might have served as the spark
and been welcomed as a signal for a general
attack. It was the conflict between Marbach
and Zanchi, probably referred to by the words
quoted above from Article XI: "Something of
it [of a discussion concerning eternal election]
has been mooted also among our theologians."
This controversy took place from 1561 to 1563,
at Strassburg, where Lutheranism and Calvinism came into immediate contact. In 1536
Strassburg had adopted the *Wittenberg Concord* and with it the *Augsburg Confession*,
which since took the place of the *Tetrapolitana* delivered to Emperor Charles at the Diet
of Augsburg, 1530. The efficient and zealous
leader in Lutheranizing the city was John
Marbach, a graduate of Wittenberg and, together with Mathesius, a former guest at Luther's table. He was born in 1521 and labored
in Strassburg from 1545 to 1581, the year of
his death. He had Bucer's Catechism replaced
by Luther's, and entered the public controversy against the Calvinists with a publication entitled, *Concerning the Lord's Supper,
against the Sacramentarians*, which defends
the omnipresence of Christ also according to
His human nature.

In his efforts to Lutheranize the city, Marbach was opposed by the Crypto-Calvinist
Jerome Zanchi (born 1516, died 1590), a converted Italian and a pupil of Peter Martyr
[born September 8, 1500; won for Protestantism by reading books of Bucer, Zwingli,
and others; professor, first in Strassburg,
1547 in Oxford; compelled to return to the
Continent (Strassburg and Zurich) by Bloody
Mary; died November 12, 1562, when just
about to write a book against Brenz]. From
1553 to 1563 Zanchi was professor of Old
Testament exegesis in Strassburg. Though he
had signed the *Augsburg Confession*, he was
and remained a rigid Calvinist, both with respect to the doctrine of predestination and
that of the Lord's Supper, but withheld his
public dissent until about 1561. It was the
Calvinistic doctrine of the perseverance of the
saints, according to which grace once received
cannot be lost, upon which Zanchi now laid
especial emphasis. According to Loescher
(*Historia Motuum* 3, 30) he taught: "1. To
the elect in this world faith is given by God
only once. 2. The elect who have once been
endowed with true faith . . . can never again
lose faith altogether. 3. The elect never sin
with their whole mind or their entire will.
4. When Peter denied Christ, he, indeed, lacked
the *confession* of the mouth, but not the faith
of the heart. 1. *Electis in hoc saeculo semel
tantum vera fides a Deo datur.* 2. *Electi
semel vera fide donati Christoque per Spiritum Sanctum insiti fidem prorsus amittere . . .
non possunt.* 3. *In electis regeneratis duo
sunt homines, interior et exterior. Ii, quum
peccant, secundum tantum hominem exterio-
rem, i. e., ea tantum parte, qua non sunt re-
geniti, peccant; secundum vero interiorem*

*hominem nolunt peccatum et condelectantur
legi Dei; quare non toto animo aut plena
voluntate peccant.* 4. *Petrum, quum negavit
Christum, defecit quidem fidei confessio in
ore, sed non defecit fides in corde.*" (Tschackert, 560; Frank 4, 261.)

This tenet, that believers can neither lose
their faith nor be eternally lost, had been
plainly rejected by Luther. In the *Smalcald
Articles* we read: "On the other hand, if certain sectarists would arise, some of whom are
perhaps already extant, and in the time of the
insurrection [of the peasants, 1525] came to
my own view, holding that all those who had
once received the Spirit or the forgiveness of
sins, or had become believers, even though
they should afterwards sin, would still remain
in the faith, and such sin would not harm
them, and hence crying thus: 'Do whatever
you please; if you believe, it all amounts to
nothing: faith blots out all sins,' etc. — they
say, besides, that if any one sins after he has
received faith and the Spirit, he never truly
had the Spirit and faith: I have had before
me many such insane men, and I fear that in
some such a devil is still remaining [hiding
and dwelling]. It is, accordingly, necessary
to know and to teach that when holy men,
still having and feeling original sin, also daily
repenting of and striving with it, happen to
fall into manifest sins, as David into adultery,
murder, and blasphemy, that then faith and
the Holy Ghost has departed from them. For
the Holy Ghost does not permit sin to have
dominion, to gain the upper hand, so as to be
accomplished, but represses and restrains it,
so that it must not do what it wishes. But
if it does what it wishes, the Holy Ghost and
faith are not present. For St. John says,
1 Ep. 3, 9: 'Whosoever is born of God doth
not commit sin, . . . and he cannot sin.' And
yet it is also the truth when the same St. John
says, 1 Ep. 1, 8: 'If we say that we have no
sin, we deceive ourselves and the truth is not
in us.'" (491, 42 f.)

In an opinion of March 9, 1559, Melanchthon remarks that about 1529 some Antinomians maintained and argued "that, since
in this life sin remains in saints, they remain
holy and retain the Holy Spirit and salvation
even when they commit adultery and other
sins against their conscience. . . . There are
many at many places who are imbued with
this error [that righteousness, Holy Spirit,
and sins against the conscience can remain in
a man at the same time], regard themselves
holy although they live and persevere in sins
against their consciences." (*C. R.* 9, 764. 405.
473; 8, 411.)

The perseverance of saints as taught by
Zanchi was the point to which Marbach immediately took exception. A long discussion
followed, which was finally settled by the
*Strassburg Formula of Concord* of 1563, outside theologians participating and acting as
arbiters. This *Formula*, which was probably
prepared by Jacob Andreae, treated in its first
article the Lord's Supper; in its second, predestination. It rejected the doctrine that,
once received, faith cannot be lost, and pre-

scribed the *Wittenberg Concord* of 1536 as the doctrinal rule regarding the Holy Supper. The document was signed by both parties, Zanchi stating over his signature: *"Hanc doctrinae formam ut piam agnosco, ita eam recipio."* Evidently his mental reservation was that he be permitted to withdraw from it in as far as he did not regard it as pious. Later Zanchi declared openly that he had subscribed the *Formula* only conditionally. Soon after his subscription he left Strassburg, serving till 1568 as preacher of a Reformed Italian congregation in Chiavenna, till 1576 as professor in the Reformed University of Heidelberg, and till 1582 as professor in Neustadt. He died at Heidelberg as professor emeritus, November 19, 1590. Marbach continued his work at Strassburg, and was active also in promoting the cause of the *Formula of Concord.* His controversy with Zanchi, though of a local character, may be regarded as the immediate cause for adding Article XI. The thorough Lutheranizing of the city was completed by Pappus, a pupil of Marbach. In 1597 Strassburg adopted the *Formula of Concord.*

### 228. The Strassburg Formula.

The *Strassburg Formula of Concord* sets forth the Scriptural and peculiarly Lutheran point of view in the doctrine of election, according to which a Christian, in order to attain to a truly divine assurance of his election and final salvation, is to consider predestination not *a priori*, but *a posteriori.* That is to say, he is not to speculate on the act of eternal election as such, but to consider it as manifested to him in Christ and the Gospel of Christ. Judging from his own false conception of predestination, Calvin remarked that the *Strassburg Formula* did not deny, but rather veiled, the doctrine of election,— a stricture frequently made also on Article XI of the *Formula of Concord,* whose truly Scriptural and evangelical view of election the Reformed have never fully grasped and realized.

The *Strassburg Formula* taught that, in accordance with Rom. 15, 4, the doctrine of predestination must be presented so as not to bring it into conflict with the doctrines of repentance and justification nor to deprive alarmed consciences of the consolation of the Gospel, nor in any way to violate the truth that the only cause of our salvation is the grace of God alone; that the consolation afforded by election, especially in tribulations (that no one shall pluck us out of the hands of Christ), remains firm and solid only as long as the universality of God's promises is kept inviolate; that Christ died and earned salvation for all, and earnestly invites all to partake of it by faith, which is the gift of grace, and which alone receives the salvation proffered to all; that the reason why the gift of faith is not bestowed upon all men, though Christ seriously invites all to come to Him, is a mystery known to God alone, which human reason cannot fathom; that the will of God proposed in Christ and revealed in the Bible, to which all men are directed, and

in which it is most safe to acquiesce, is not contradictory of the hidden will of God. (Loescher, *Hist Mot.* 2, 229; Frank 4, 126. 262; Tschackert, 560.)

Particularly with respect to the "mystery," the *Strassburg Formula* says: "The fact that this grace or this gift of faith is not given by God to all when He calls all to Himself, and, according to His infinite goodness, certainly calls earnestly: 'Come unto the marriage, for all things are now ready,' is a sealed mystery, known to God alone, past finding out for human reason; a secret that must be contemplated with fear and be adored, as it is written: 'O the depth of the riches both of the wisdom and knowledge of God! How unsearchable are His judgments, and His ways past finding out!' Rom. 11, 33. And Christ gives thanks to the Father because He has hid these things from the wise and prudent, and revealed them unto babes. Matt. 11, 25. Troubled consciences, however, must not take offense at this hidden way of the divine will, but look upon the will of God revealed in Christ, who calls all sinners to Himself." This was also the teaching of the contemporary theologians. Moerlin wrote: "God has revealed to us that He will save only those who believe in Christ, and that unbelief is chargeable to us. Hidden, however, are God's judgments — why He converts Paul, but does not convert Caiaphas; why He receives fallen Peter again and abandons Judas to despair." Chemnitz: "Why, then, is it that God does not put such faith into the heart of Judas, so that he, too, might have believed and been saved through Christ? Here we must leave off questioning and say, Rom. 11: 'O the depth!' . . . We cannot and must not search this nor meditate too deeply upon such questions." Kirchner: "Since, therefore, faith in Christ is a special gift of God, why does He not bestow it upon all? Answer: We must defer the discussion of this question unto eternal life, and in the mean time be content to know that God does not want us to search His secret judgments, Rom. 11: 'O the depth,' etc." In a similar way Chemnitz, Selneccer, and Kirchner expressed themselves in their *Apology of the Book of Concord,* of 1582, declaring that, when asked why God does not convert all men, we must answer with the apostle: 'How unsearchable are His judgments and His ways past finding out!' but not ascribe to God the Lord the willing and real cause of the reprobation or damnation of the impenitent." (Pieper, *Dogm.* 2, 585 f.)

### 229. Predestination according to Article XI of Formula of Concord.

In keeping with her fundamental teaching of *sola gratia* and *gratia universalis,* according to which God's grace is the only cause of man's salvation, and man's evil will the sole cause of his damnation, the Lutheran Church holds that eternal election is an election of grace, *i. e.,* a predestination to salvation only. God's eternal election, says the *Formula of Concord,* "does not extend at once over the godly and the wicked, but only over the children of God, who were elected and ordained to eternal life before the foundation of the world was laid, as Paul says, Eph. 1, 4. 5: 'He hath chosen us in Him, having predestinated us unto the adoption of children by Jesus Christ.'" (1065, 5.) This election, the *Formula* continues, "not only foresees and foreknows the salvation of the elect, but is also, from the gracious will and pleasure of God in Christ Jesus, a cause which procures, works, helps, and promotes our salvation, and what pertains thereto; and upon this [divine predestination] our salvation is so founded that the gates of hell cannot prevail against it, Matt. 16, 18, as is written John 10, 28: 'Neither shall any man pluck My sheep out of My hand.' And again, Acts 13, 48: 'And as many as were ordained to eternal life believed.'" (1065, 8; 1833, 5.) While thus election is a cause of faith and salvation, there is no cause of election in man. The teaching "that not only the mercy of God and the most holy merit of Christ, but also in us there is a cause of God's election on account of which God has elected us to everlasting life," is rejected by the *Formula of Concord* as one of the "blasphemous and dreadful erroneous doctrines whereby all the comfort which they have in the holy Gospel and the use of the holy Sacraments is taken from Christians." (837, 20 f.)

Concerning the way of considering eternal election, the *Formula* writes: "If we wish to think or speak correctly and profitably concerning eternal election, or the predestination and ordination of the children of God to eternal life, we should accustom ourselves not to speculate concerning the bare, secret, concealed, inscrutable foreknowledge of God, but how the counsel, purpose, and ordination of God in Christ Jesus, who is the true Book of Life, is revealed to us through the Word, namely, that the entire doctrine concerning the purpose, counsel, will, and ordination of God pertaining to our redemption, call, justification, and salvation should be taken together; as Paul treats and has explained this article Rom. 8, 29 f.; Eph. 1, 4 f., as also Christ in the parable, Matt. 22, 1 ff." (1067, 13.)

While according to the Lutheran Church election is the cause of faith and salvation, there is no such a thing as an election of wrath or a predestination to sin and damnation, of both of which God is not the cause and author. According to the *Formula* the vessels of mercy are prepared by God alone, but the vessels of dishonor are prepared for damnation, not by God, but by themselves. Moreover, God earnestly desires that all men turn from their wicked ways and live. We read: "For all preparation for condemnation is by the devil and man, through sin, and in no respect by God, who does not wish that any man be damned; how, then, should He Himself prepare any man for condemnation? For as God is not a cause of sins, so, too, He is no cause of punishment, of damnation; but the only cause of damnation is sin; for the wages of sin is death, Rom. 6, 23. And as God does

not will sin, and has no pleasure in sin, so He does not wish the death of the sinner either, Ezek. 33, 11, nor has He pleasure in his condemnation. For He is not willing that any one should perish, but that all should come to repentance, 2 Pet. 3, 9. So, too, it is written in Ezek. 18, 23; 33, 11: 'As I live, saith the Lord God, I have no pleasure in the death of the wicked, but that the wicked turn from his way and live.' And St. Paul testifies in clear words that from vessels of dishonor vessels of honor may be made by God's power and working, when he writes 2 Tim. 2, 21: 'If a man, therefore, purge himself from these, he shall be a vessel unto honor, sanctified and meet for the Master's use, and prepared unto every good work.' For he who is to purge himself must first have been unclean, and hence a vessel of dishonor. But concerning the vessels of mercy he says clearly that the Lord Himself has prepared them for glory, which he does not say concerning the damned, who themselves, and not God, have prepared themselves as vessels of damnation." (1089, 81 f.) "Hence the apostle distinguishes with especial care the work of God, who alone makes vessels of honor, and the work of the devil and of man, who by the instigation of the devil, and not of God, has made himself a vessel of dishonor. For thus it is written, Rom. 9, 22 f.: 'God endured with much long-suffering the vessels of wrath fitted to destruction, that He might make known the riches of His glory on the vessels of mercy, which He had afore prepared unto glory.' Here, then, the apostle clearly says that God endured with much long-suffering the vessels of wrath, but does not say that He made them vessels of wrath; for if this had been His will, He would not have required any great long-suffering for it. The fault, however, that they are fitted for destruction belongs to the devil and to men themselves, and not to God." (1089, 79 f.)

It is man's own fault when he is not converted by the Word or afterwards falls away again. We read: "But the reason why not all who hear it [the Word of God] believe and are therefore condemned the more deeply, is not because God had begrudged them their salvation; but it is their own fault, as they have heard the Word in such a manner as not to learn, but only to despise, blaspheme, and disgrace it, and have resisted the Holy Ghost, who through the Word wished to work in them, as was the case at the time of Christ with the Pharisees and their adherents." (1089, 78.) "For few receive the Word and follow it; the greatest number despise the Word, and will not come to the wedding, Matt. 22, 3 ff. The cause of this contempt for the Word is not God's foreknowledge [or predestination], but the perverse will of man, which rejects or perverts the means and instrument of the Holy Ghost, which God offers him through the call, and resists the Holy Ghost, who wishes to be efficacious, and works through the Word, as Christ says: 'How often would I have gathered you together, and ye would not!' Matt. 23, 37. Thus many receive the Word with joy, but afterwards fall away again, Luke 8, 13. But the cause is not as though God were unwilling to grant grace for perseverance to those in whom He has begun the good work, for that is contrary to St. Paul, Phil. 1, 6; but the cause is that they wilfully turn away again from the holy commandment, grieve and embitter the Holy Ghost, implicate themselves again in the filth of the world, and garnish again the habitation of the heart for the devil. With them the last state is worse than the first." (1077, 41 f.; 835, 12.)

It is not because of any deficiency in God that men are lost; for His grace is universal as well as serious and efficacious. The *Formula of Concord* declares: "However, that many are called and few chosen is not owing to the fact that the call of God, which is made through the Word, had the meaning as though God said: Outwardly, through the Word, I indeed call to My kingdom all of you to whom I give My Word; however, in My heart I do not mean this with respect to all, but only with respect to a few; for it is My will that the greatest part of those whom I call through the Word shall not be enlightened nor converted, but be and remain damned, although through the Word, in the call, I declare Myself to them otherwise. *Hoc enim esset Deo contradictorias voluntates affingere.* For this would be to assign contradictory wills to God. That is, in this way it would be taught that God, who surely is Eternal Truth, would be contrary to Himself [or say one thing, but revolve another in His heart], while, on the contrary, God [rebukes and] punishes also in men this wickedness, when a person declares himself to one purpose, and thinks and means another in the heart, Ps. 5, 9; 12, 2 f." (1075, 34.)

It is a punishment of their previous sins and not a result of God's predestination when sinners are hardened; nor does such hardening signify that it never was God's good pleasure to save them. "Moreover," says the *Formula*, "it is to be diligently considered that when God punishes sin with sins, that is, when He afterwards punishes with obduracy and blindness those who had been converted, because of their subsequent security, impenitence, and wilful sins, this should not be interpreted to mean that it never had been God's good pleasure that such persons should come to the knowledge of the truth and be saved. For both these facts are God's revealed will: first, that God will receive into grace all who repent and believe in Christ; secondly, that He also will punish those who wilfully turn away from the holy commandment, and again entangle themselves in the filth of the world, 2 Pet. 2, 20, and garnish their hearts for Satan, Luke 11, 25 f., and do despite unto the Spirit of God, Heb. 10, 29, and that they shall be hardened, blinded, and eternally condemned if they persist therein." (1091, 83.)

"But that God . . . hardened Pharaoh's heart, namely, that Pharaoh always sinned again and again, and became the more obdurate, the more he was admonished, that was a punishment of his antecedent sin and horrible tyranny, which in many and manifold ways he practised inhumanly and against the accusations of his heart towards the children of Israel. And since God caused His Word to be preached and His will to be proclaimed to him, and Pharaoh nevertheless wilfully reared up straightway against all admonitions and warnings, God withdrew His hand from him, and thus his heart became hardened and obdurate, and God executed His judgment upon him; for he was guilty of nothing else than hell-fire. Accordingly, the holy apostle also introduces the example of Pharaoh for no other reason than to prove by it the justice of God which He exercises towards the impenitent and despisers of His Word; by no means, however, has he intended or understood it to mean that God begrudged salvation to him or any person, but had so ordained him to eternal damnation in His secret counsel that he should not be able, or that it should not be possible for him, to be saved." (1091, 85 f.)

## 230. Agreement of Articles XI and II.

In the *Formula of Concord*, Article XI is closely related to most of the other articles, particularly to Article I, Of Original Sin, and Article II, Of Free Will and Conversion. Election is to conversion what the concave side of a lens is to the convex. Both correspond to each other in every particular. What God does for and in man when He converts, justifies, sanctifies, preserves, and finally glorifies him, He has in eternity resolved to do, — that is one way in which eternal election may be defined. Synergists and Calvinists, however, have always maintained that the Second Article is in a hopeless conflict with the Eleventh. But the truth is, the Second fully confirms and corroborates the Eleventh, and *vice versa;* for both maintain the *sola gratia* as well as the *universalis gratia.*

Both articles teach that in every respect grace alone is the cause of our conversion and salvation, and that this grace is not confined to some men only, but is a grace for all. Both teach that man, though contributing absolutely nothing to his conversion and salvation, is nevertheless the sole cause of his own damnation. Both disavow Calvinism, which denies the universality of grace. Both reject synergism, which corrupts grace by teaching a cooperation of man towards his own conversion and salvation. Teaching, therefore, as they do, the same truths, both articles will and must ever stand and fall together. It was, no doubt, chiefly due to this complete harmony between the Second and the Eleventh Article that, after the former (which received its present shape only after repeated changes and additions) had been decided upon, the revision of the latter (the Eleventh) caused but little delay. (Frank 4, V. 133.)

Concerning the alleged conflict between Articles II and XI, we read in Schaff's *Creeds of Christendom:* "There is an obvious and irreconcilable antagonism between Article II and Article XI. They contain not simply opposite truths to be reconciled by theological science, but contradictory assertions, which ought never to be put into a creed. The *Formula* adopts one part of Luther's book *De Servo Arbitrio*, 1525, and rejects the other, which follows with logical necessity. It is Augustinian, yea, hyper-Augustinian and hyper-Calvinistic in the doctrine of human depravity, and anti-Augustinian in the doctrine of divine predestination. It endorses the anthropological premise, and denies the theological conclusion. If man is by nature like a stone and block, and unable even to accept the grace of God, as Article II teaches, he can only be converted by an act of almighty power and *irresistible* grace, which Article XI denies. If some men are saved without any cooperation on their part, while others, with the same inability and the same opportunities, are lost, the difference points to a particular predestination and the inscrutable decree of God. On the other hand, if God sincerely wills the salvation of all men, as Article XI teaches, and yet only a part are actually saved, there must be some difference in the attitude of the saved and the lost towards converting grace, which is denied in Article II. The Lutheran system, then, to be consistent, must rectify itself, and develop either from Article II in the direction of Augustinianism and Calvinism, or from Article XI in the direction of synergism and Arminianism. The former would be simply returning to Luther's original doctrine [?], which he never recalled, though he may have modified it a little; the latter is the path pointed out by Melanchthon, and adopted more or less by some of the ablest modern Lutherans." (1, 314. 330.) Prior to Schaff, similar charges had been raised by Planck, Schweizer, Heppe, and others, who maintained that Article XI suffers from a "theological confusion otherwise not found in the *Formula*."

Apart from other unwarranted assertions in the passage quoted from Schaff, the chief charges there raised against the *Formula of Concord* are: 1. that Articles XI and II are contradictory to each other; 2. that the Lutheran Church has failed to harmonize the doctrines of *sola gratia* and *gratia universalis*. However, the first of these strictures is based on gross ignorance of the facts, resulting from a superficial investigation of the articles involved; for the alleged disagreement is purely imaginary. As a matter of fact, no one can read the two articles attentively without being everywhere impressed with their complete harmony. In every possible way Article XI excludes synergism, and corroborates the *sola gratia* doctrine of Article II. And Article II, in turn, nowhere denies, rather everywhere, directly or indirectly, confirms, the universal grace particularly emphasized in Article XI.

The framers of the *Formula* were well aware of the fact that the least error in the doctrine of free will and conversion was bound to manifest itself also in the doctrine of election, and that perhaps in a form much more

difficult to detect. Hence Article XI was not only intended to be a bulwark against the assaults on the doctrine of grace coming from Calvinistic quarters, but also an additional reenforcement of the article of Free Will against the Synergists, in order to prevent a future recrudescence of their errors in the sphere of predestination. Its object is clearly to maintain the doctrine of the Bible, according to which it is grace alone that saves, a grace which, at the same time, is a grace for all, and thus to stear clear of synergism as well as of Calvinism, and forever to close the doors of the Lutheran Church to every form of these two errors.

According to the Second Article, Christians cannot be assured of their election if the doctrine of conversion [by grace alone] is not properly presented. (900, 47. 57.) And Article XI most emphatically supports Article II in its efforts to weed out every kind of synergistic or Romanistic corruption. For here we read: "Thus far the mystery of predestination is revealed to us in God's Word; and if we abide thereby and cleave thereto, it is a very useful, salutary, consolatory doctrine; for it establishes very effectually the article that we are justified and saved without all works and merits of ours, purely out of grace alone, for Christ's sake. For before the time of the world, before we existed, yea, before the foundation of the world was laid, when, of course, we could do nothing good, we were according to God's purpose chosen by grace in Christ to salvation, Rom. 9, 11; 2 Tim. 1, 9. Moreover, all opinions and erroneous doctrines concerning the powers of our natural will are thereby overthrown, because God in His counsel, before the time of the world, decided and ordained that He Himself, by the power of His Holy Ghost, would produce and work in us, through the Word, everything that pertains to our conversion." (1077, 43 f.; 837, 20.)

Again: "By this doctrine and explanation of the eternal and saving choice of the elect children of God, His own glory is entirely and fully given to God, that in Christ He saves us out of pure [and free] mercy, without any merits or good works of ours, according to the purpose of His will, as it is written Eph. 1, 5 f.: 'Having predestinated us.' . . . Therefore it is false and wrong when it is taught that not alone the mercy of God and the most holy merit of Christ, but that also in us there is a cause of God's predestination on account of which God has chosen us to eternal life." Indeed, one of the most exclusive formulations against every possible kind of subtile synergism is found in Article XI when it teaches that the reason why some are converted and saved while others are lost, must not be sought in man, *i. e.*, in any minor guilt or less faulty conduct toward grace shown by those who are saved, as compared with the guilt and conduct of those who are lost. (1081, 57 f.) If, therefore, the argument of the Calvinists and Synergists that the *sola gratia* doctrine involves a denial of universal grace were correct, the charge of Calvinism would have to be raised against Article XI as well as against Article II.

In a similar manner the Second Article confirms the Eleventh by corroborating its anti-Calvinistic teaching of universal grace and redemption; of man's responsibility for his own damnation; of man's conversion, not by compulsion or coercion, etc. The Second Article most emphatically teaches the *sola gratia*, but without in any way limiting, violating, or encroaching upon, universal grace. It is not merely opposed to Pelagian, Semi-Pelagian, and synergistic errors, but to Stoic and Calvinistic aberrations as well. While it is not the special object of the Second Article to set forth the universality of God's grace, its anti-Calvinistic attitude is nevertheless everywhere apparent.

Article II plainly teaches that "it is not God's will that any one should be damned, but that all men should be converted to Him and be saved eternally. Ezek. 33, 11: 'As I live.'" (901, 49.) It teaches that "Christ, in whom we are chosen, offers to all men His grace in the Word and holy Sacraments, and wishes earnestly that it be heard, and has promised that where two or three are gathered together in His name and are occupied with His holy Word, He will be in their midst." (903, 57.) It maintains that through the Gospel the Holy Ghost offers man grace and salvation, effects conversion through the preaching and hearing of God's Word, and is present with this Word in order to convert men. (787, 4 ff.; 889, 18.) It holds that "all who wish to be saved ought to hear this preaching, because the preaching and hearing of God's Word are the instruments of the Holy Ghost, by, with, and through which He desires to work efficaciously, and to convert men to God, and to work in them both to will and to do." (901, 52 ff.) It admonishes that no one should doubt that the power and efficacy of the Holy Ghost is present with, and efficacious in, the Word when it is preached purely and listened to attentively, and that we should base our certainty concerning the presence, operation, and gifts of the Holy Ghost not on our feeling, but on the promise that the Word of God preached and heard is truly an office and work of the Holy Ghost, by which He is certainly efficacious and works in our hearts, 2 Cor. 2, 14 ff.; 3, 5 ff." (903, 56.) It asserts that men who refuse to hear the Word of God are not converted because they despised the instrument of the Holy Spirit and would not hear (903, 58); that God does not force men to become godly; that those who always resist the Holy Ghost and persistently oppose the known truth are not converted (905, 60). If, therefore, the inference were correct that the doctrine of universal grace involved a denial of the *sola gratia*, then the charge of synergism would have to be raised against Article II as well as against Article XI. Both articles will always stand and fall together; for both teach that the grace of God is the only cause of our conversion and salvation, and that this grace is truly universal.

## 231. Mystery in Doctrine of Grace.

The second charge raised by Calvinists and Synergists against the *Formula of Concord* is its failure to harmonize "logically" what they term "contradictory doctrines": *sola gratia* and *universalis gratia*, — a stricture which must be characterized as flowing from rationalistic premises, mistaking a divine mystery for a real contradiction, and in reality directed against the clear Word of God itself. Says Schaff, who also in this point voices the views of Calvinists as well as Synergists: "The *Formula of Concord* sanctioned a compromise between Augustinianism and universalism, or between the original Luther and the later Melanchthon, by teaching both the absolute inability of man and the universality of divine grace, without an attempt to solve these contradictory positions." (304.) "Thus the particularism of election and the universalism of vocation, the absolute inability of fallen man, and the guilt of the unbeliever for rejecting what he cannot accept, are illogically combined." (1, 330.) The real charge here raised against the *Formula of Concord* is, that it fails to modify the doctrines of *sola gratia* or *universalis gratia* in a manner satisfactory to the demands of human reason; for Synergists and Calvinists are agreed that, in the interest of rational harmony, one or the other must be abandoned, either *universalis gratia seria et efficax*, or *sola gratia*.

In judging of the charge in question, it should not be overlooked that, according to the *Formula of Concord*, all Christians, theologians included, are bound to derive their entire doctrine from the Bible alone; that matters of faith must be decided exclusively by clear passages of Holy Scripture; that human reason ought not in any point to criticize and lord it over the infallible Word of God; that reason must be subjected to the obedience of Christ, and dare not hinder faith in believing the divine testimonies even when they seemingly contradict each other. We are not commanded to harmonize, says the *Formula*, but to believe, confess, defend, and faithfully to adhere to the teachings of the Bible. (1078, 52 ff.) In the doctrine of conversion and salvation, therefore, Lutherans confess both the *sola gratia* and the *universalis gratia*, because they are convinced that both are clearly taught in the Bible, and that to reject or modify either of them would amount to a criticism of the Word of God, and hence of God Himself. Synergists differ from Lutherans, not in maintaining universal grace (which in reality they deny as to intention as well as extension, for they corrupt the Scriptural content of grace by making it dependent on man's conduct, and thereby limit its extension to such only as comply with its conditions), but in denying the *sola gratia*, and teaching that the will of man enters conversion as a factor alongside of grace. And Calvinists differ from Lutherans not in maintaining the *sola gratia*, but in denying universal grace.

But while, in accordance with the clear

Word of God, faithfully adhering to both the *sola gratia* and *universalis gratia,* and firmly maintaining that whoever is saved is saved by grace alone, and whoever is lost is lost through his own fault alone, the *Formula of Concord* at the same time fully acknowledges the difficulty presenting itself to human reason when we hold fast to this teaching. In particular, it admits that the question, not answered in the Bible, *viz.,* why some are saved while others are lost, embraces a mystery which we lack the means and ability of solving, as well as the data. Accordingly, the *Formula* also makes no efforts whatever to harmonize them, but rather discountenances and warns against all attempts to cater to human reason in this respect, and insists that both doctrines be maintained intact and taught conjointly. Lutherans are fully satisfied that here every effort at rational harmonization cannot but lead either to Calvinistic corruption of universal grace or to synergistic modification of *sola gratia.*

Thus the Lutheran Church not only admits, but zealously guards, the mystery contained in the doctrine of grace and election. It distinguishes between God in as far as He is known and not known; in as far as He has revealed Himself, and in as far as He is still hidden to us, but as we shall learn to know Him hereafter. The truths which may be known concerning God are contained in the Gospel, revealed in the Bible. The things still hidden from us include the unsearchable judgments of God, His wonderful ways with men, and, in particular, the question why some are saved while others are lost. God has not seen fit to reveal these mysteries. And since reason cannot search or fathom God, man's quest for an answer is both presumptuous and vain. That is to say, we are utterly unable to uncover the divine counsels, which would show that the mysterious judgments and ways proceeding from them are in complete harmony with the universal grace proclaimed by the Gospel.

Yet Lutherans believe that the hidden God is not in real conflict with God as revealed in the Bible, and that the secret will of God does not in the least invalidate the gracious will of the Gospel. According to the *Formula of Concord* there are no real contradictions in God; in Him everything is yea and amen; His very being is pure reality and truth. Hence, when relying on God as revealed in Christ, that is to say, relying on grace which is pure grace only and at the same time grace for all, Christians may be assured that there is absolutely nothing in the unknown God, *i. e.,* in as far as He has not revealed Himself to them, which might subvert their simple faith in His gracious promises. The face of God depicted in the Gospel is the true face of God. Whoever has seen Christ has seen the Father as He is in reality.

Indeed, also the hidden God, together with His secret counsels, unsearchable judgments, and ways past finding out, even the majestic God, in whom we live and move and have our

being, the God who has all things well in hand, and without whom nothing can be or occur, must, in the light of the Scriptures, be viewed as an additional guarantee that, in spite of all contingencies, the merciful divine promises of the Gospel shall stand firm and immovable. Upon eternal election, says the *Formula of Concord,* "our salvation is so [firmly] founded 'that the gates of hell cannot prevail against it.'" (1065, 8.) As for us, therefore, it remains our joyous privilege not to investigate what God has withheld from us, or to climb into the adyton of God's transcendent majesty, but merely to rely on, and securely trust in, the blessed Gospel, which proclaims grace for all and salvation by grace alone, and teaches that whoever is saved must praise God alone for it, while whoever is damned must blame only himself.

Regarding the mystery involved in predestination, the *Formula of Concord* explains: "A distinction must be observed with especial care between that which is expressly revealed concerning it [predestination] in God's Word and what is not revealed. For in addition to what has been revealed in Christ concerning this, of which we have hitherto spoken, God has still kept secret and concealed much concerning this mystery, and reserved it for His wisdom and knowledge alone, which we should not investigate, nor should we indulge our thoughts in this matter, nor draw conclusions, nor inquire curiously, but should adhere to the revealed Word. This admonition is most urgently needed. For our curiosity has always much more pleasure in concerning itself with these matters [investigating things abstruse and hidden] than with what God has revealed to us concerning this in His Word, because we cannot harmonize it [cannot by the acumen of our natural ability harmonize the intricate and involved things occurring in this mystery], which, moreover, we have not been commanded to do."

The *Formula* enumerates as such inscrutable mysteries: Why God gives His Word at one place, but not at another; why He removes it from one place, and allows it to remain at another; why one is hardened, while another, who is in the same guilt, is converted again. Such and similar questions, says the *Formula,* we cannot answer and must not endeavor to solve. On the contrary, we are to adhere unflinchingly to both truths, *viz.,* that those who are converted are saved, not because they are better than others, but by pure grace alone; and that those who are not converted and not saved cannot accuse God of any neglect or injustice, but are lost by their own fault. The *Formula* concludes its paragraphs on the mysteries in predestination by saying: "When we proceed thus far in this article [maintaining that God alone is the cause of man's salvation and man alone is the cause of his damnation, and refusing to solve the problems involved], we remain on the right [safe and royal] way, as it is written Hos. 13, 9: 'O Israel, thou hast destroyed thyself; but in Me is thy help.' However, as regards these things in this disputation which would soar too high and beyond these limits, we should, with Paul, place the finger upon our lips, remember and say, Rom. 9, 20: 'O man, who art thou that repliest against God?' " (1078, 52 ff.)

### 232. Predestination a Comforting Article.

Christian doctrines, or doctrines of the Church, are such only as are in exact harmony with the Scriptures. They alone, too, are able to serve the purpose for which the Scriptures are given, viz., to convert and save sinners, and to comfort troubled Christians. Scriptural doctrines are always profitable, and detrimental doctrines are never Scriptural. This is true also of the article of eternal election. It is a truly edifying doctrine as also the *Formula of Concord* is solicitous to explain. (1092, 89 ff.) However, it is comforting only when taught in its purity, *i. e.*, when presented and preserved in strict adherence to the Bible; that is to say, when both the *sola gratia* and *gratia universalis* are kept inviolate. Whenever the doctrine of predestination causes despair or carnal security, it has been either misrepresented or misunderstood.

In the introductory paragraphs of Article XI we read: "For the doctrine concerning this article, if taught from, and according to, the pattern of the divine Word, neither can nor should be regarded as useless or unnecessary, much less as offensive or injurious, because the Holy Scriptures not only in but one place and incidentally, but in many places, thoroughly treat and urge the same. Moreover, we should not neglect or reject the doctrine of the divine Word on account of abuse or misunderstanding, but precisely on that account, in order to avert all abuse and misunderstanding, the true meaning should and must be explained from the foundation of the Scriptures." (1063, 2; 1067, 13.)

"If it is treated properly," says also the Epitome, the doctrine of predestination "is a consolatory article" (830, 1); that is to say, if predestination is viewed in the light of the Gospel, and particularly, if *sola gratia* as well as *gratia universalis* are kept inviolate. Outside of God's revelation in the Gospel there is no true and wholesome knowledge whatever concerning election, but mere noxious human dreams. And when the universality of grace is denied, it is impossible for any one to know whether he is elected, and whether the grace spoken of in the Gospel is intended for or belongs to him. "Therefore," says the *Formula of Concord*, "if we wish to consider our eternal election to salvation with profit, we must in every way hold sturdily and firmly to this, that, as the preaching of repentance, so also the promise of the Gospel is *universalis* (universal), that is, it pertains to all men, Luke 24, 47," etc. (1071, 28.) By denying that universal grace is meant seriously and discounting the universal promises of the Gospel, "the necessary consolatory foundation is rendered altogether uncertain and void, as we are daily reminded and admonished that only from God's Word, through which He treats with us and calls us, we are to learn and conclude what His will toward us is, and that we should believe and not doubt what it affirms to us and promises." (1075, 36.) If God cannot be trusted in His universal promises, absolutely nothing in the Bible can be relied upon. A doctrine of election from which universal grace is eliminated, necessarily leads to despair or to contumaciousness and carnal security. Calvin was right when he designated his predestination theory, which denies universal grace, a "horrible decree." It left him without any objective foundation whatever upon which to rest his faith and hope.

In like manner, when the doctrine of election and grace is modified synergistically, no one can know for certain whether he has really been pardoned and will be saved finally, because salvation is not exclusively based on the sure and immovable grace and promises of God, but, at least in part, on man's own doubtful conduct — a rotten plank which can serve neither foot for safely crossing the great abyss of sin and death. Only when presented and taught in strict adherence to the Bible is the doctrine of election and grace fully qualified to engender divine certainty of our present adoption and final salvation as well, since it assures us that God sincerely desires to save all men (us included), that He alone does, and has promised to do, everything pertaining thereto, and that nothing is able to thwart His promises, since He who made them and confirmed them with an oath is none other than the majestic God Himself.

Accordingly, when Calvinists and Synergists criticize the *Formula of Concord* for not harmonizing (modifying in the interest of rational harmony) the clear doctrines of the Bible, which they brand as contradictions, they merely display their own conflicting, untenable position. For while professing to follow the Scriptures, they at the same time demand that its doctrines be corrected according to the dictate of reason, thus plainly revealing that their theology is not founded on the Bible, but orientated in rationalism, the true ultimate principle of Calvinism as well as synergism.

In the last analysis, therefore, the charge of inconsistency against the *Formula of Concord* is tantamount to an indirect admission that the Lutheran Church is both a consistently Scriptural and a truly evangelical Church. Consistently Scriptural, because it receives in simple faith and with implicit obedience every clear Word of God, all counter-arguments to the contrary notwithstanding. Truly evangelical, because in adhering with unswerving loyalty to the seemingly contradictory, but truly Scriptural doctrine of grace, it serves the purpose of the Scriptures, which — praise the Lord — is none other than to save, edify, and comfort poor disconsolate sinners.

### 233. Statements of Article XI on Consolation Offered by Predestination.

The purpose of the entire Scripture, says the *Formula of Concord*, is to comfort penitent sinners. If we therefore abide by, and cleave to, predestination as it is revealed to us in God's Word, "it is a very useful, salutary, consolatory doctrine." Every presentation of eternal election, however, which produces carnal security or despair, is false. We read: "If any one presents the doctrine concerning the gracious election of God in such a manner that troubled Christians cannot derive comfort from it, but are thereby incited to despair, or that the impenitent are confirmed in their wantonness, it is undoubtedly sure and true that such a doctrine is taught, not according to the Word and will of God, but according to [the blind judgment of human] reason and the instigation of the devil. For, as the apostle testifies, Rom. 15, 4: 'Whatsoever things were written aforetime were written for our learning, that we through patience and comfort of the Scriptures might have hope.' But when this consolation and hope are weakened or entirely removed by Scripture, it is certain that it is understood and explained contrary to the will and meaning of the Holy Ghost." (1093, 91 f.; 837, 16; 1077, 43.)

Predestination is comforting when Christians are taught to seek their election in Christ. We read: "Moreover, this doctrine gives no one a cause either for despondency or for a shameless, dissolute life, namely, when men are taught that they must seek eternal election in Christ and His holy Gospel, as in the Book of Life, which excludes no penitent sinner, but beckons and calls all the poor, heavy-laden, and troubled sinners who are disturbed by the sense of God's wrath, to repentance and the knowledge of their sins and to faith in Christ, and promises the Holy Ghost for purification and renewal, and thus gives the most enduring consolation to all troubled, afflicted men, that they know that their salvation is not placed in their own hands (for otherwise they would lose it much more easily than was the case with Adam and Eve in Paradise, yea, every hour and moment), but in the gracious election of God, which He has revealed to us in Christ, out of whose hand no man shall pluck us, John 10, 28; 2 Tim. 2, 19." (1093, 89.)

In order to manifest its consolatory power, predestination must be presented in proper relation to the revealed order of salvation. We read: "With this revealed will of God [His universal gracious promises in the Gospel] we should concern ourselves, follow and be diligently engaged upon it, because through the Word, whereby He calls us, the Holy Ghost bestows grace, power, and ability to this end [to begin and complete our salvation], and should not [attempt to] sound the abyss of God's hidden predestination, as it is written in Luke 13, 24, where one asks: Lord, are there few that be saved?' and Christ answers: 'Strive to enter in at the strait gate.' Accordingly, Luther says [in his Preface to the Epistle to the Romans]: 'Follow the Epistle to the Romans in its order, concern yourself first with Christ and His Gospel, that you may recognize your sins and His grace; next, that you contend with sin, as Paul teaches

from the first to the eighth chapter; then, when in the eighth chapter you will come into [will have been exercised by] temptation under the cross and afflictions, — this will teach you in the ninth, tenth, and eleventh chapters how consolatory predestination is,' etc." (1073, 33.)

Predestination, properly taught, affords the glorious comfort that no one shall pluck us out of the almighty hands of Christ. The *Formula* says: "Thus this doctrine affords also the excellent, glorious consolation that God was so greatly concerned about the conversion, righteousness, and salvation of every Christian, and so faithfully purposed it [provided therefor] that before the foundation of the world was laid, He deliberated concerning it, and in His [secret] purpose ordained how He would bring me thereto [call and lead me to salvation], and preserve me therein. Also, that He wished to secure my salvation so well and certainly that, since through the weakness and wickedness of our flesh it could easily be lost from our hands, or through craft and might of the devil and the world be snatched and taken from us, He ordained it in His eternal purpose, which cannot fail or be overthrown, and placed it for preservation in the almighty hand of our Savior Jesus Christ, from which no one can pluck us, John 10, 28. Hence Paul also says, Rom. 8, 28. 39: 'Because we have been called according to the purpose of God, who will separate us from the love of God in Christ?' [Paul builds the certainty of our blessedness upon the foundation of the divine purpose, when, from our being called according to the purpose of God, he infers that no one can separate us, etc.] (1079, 45.) "This article also affords a glorious testimony that the Church of God will exist and abide in opposition to all the gates of hell, and likewise teaches which is the true Church of God, lest we be offended by the great authority [and majestic appearance] of the false Church, Rom. 9, 24. 25." (1079, 50.)

Especially in temptations and tribulations the doctrine of eternal election reveals its comforting power. We read: "Moreover, this doctrine affords glorious consolation under the cross and amid temptations, namely, that God in His counsel, before the time of the world, determined and decreed that He would assist us in all distresses [anxieties and perplexities], grant patience, give consolation, excite [nourish and encourage] hope, and produce such an outcome as would contribute to our salvation. Also, as Paul in a very consolatory way treats this, Rom. 8, 28. 29. 35. 38. 39, that God in His purpose has ordained before the time of the world by what crosses and sufferings He would conform every one of His elect to the image of His Son, and that to every one his cross shall and must work together for good, because they are called according to the purpose, whence Paul has concluded that it is certain and indubitable that neither tribulation nor distress, nor death, nor life, etc., shall be able to separate us from the love of God which is in Christ Jesus, our Lord." (1079, 48.)

# XXI. Luther and Article XI of the Formula of Concord.

## 234. Luther Falsely Charged with Calvinism.

Calvinists and Synergists have always contended that Luther's original doctrine of predestination was essentially identical with that of John Calvin. Melanchthon was among the first who raised a charge to this effect. In his *Opinion* to Elector August, dated March 9, 1559, we read: "During Luther's life and afterwards I rejected these Stoic and Manichean deliria, when Luther and others wrote: All works, good and bad, in all men, good and bad, must occur as they do. Now it is apparent that such speech contradicts the Word of God, is detrimental to all discipline, and blasphemes God. Therefore I have sedulously made a distinction, showing to what extent man has a free will to observe outward discipline, also before regeneration," etc. (*C. R.* 9, 766.) Instead of referring to his own early statements, which were liable to misinterpretation more than anything that Luther had written, Melanchthon disingenuously mentions Luther, whose real meaning he misrepresents and probably had never fully grasped. The true reason why Melanchthon charged Luther and his loyal adherents with Stoicism was his own synergistic departure from the Lutheran doctrine of original sin and of salvation by grace alone. Following Melanchthon, rationalizing Synergists everywhere have always held that without abandoning Luther's doctrine of original sin and of the *gratia sola* there is no escape from Calvinism.

In this point Reformed theologians agree with the Synergists, and have therefore always claimed Luther as their ally. I. Mueller declared in *Lutheri de Praedestinatione et Libero Arbitrio Doctrina* of 1832: "As to the chief point (*quod ad caput rei attinet*), Zwingli's view of predestination is in harmony with Luther's *De Servo Arbitrio.*" In his *Zentraldogmen* of 1854 Alexander Schweizer endeavored to prove that the identical doctrine of predestination was originally the central dogma of the Lutheran as well as of the Zwinglian reformation. "It is not so much the dogma [of predestination] itself," said he (1, 445), "as its position which is in dispute" among Lutherans and Calvinists. Schweizer (1, 483) based his assertion on the false assumption "that the doctrines of the captive will and of absolute predestination [denial of universal grace] are two halves of the same ring." (Frank 1, 12. 118. 128; 4, 262.) Similar contentions were made in America by Schaff, Hodge, Shedd, and other Reformed theologians.

As a matter of fact, however, also in the doctrine of predestination Zwingli and Calvin were just as far and as fundamentally apart from Luther as their entire rationalistic theology differed from the simple and implicit Scripturalism of Luther. Frank truly says that the agreement between Luther's doctrine and that of Zwingli and Calvin is "only specious, *nur scheinbar.*" (1, 118.) Tschackert remarks: "Whoever [among the theologians before the *Formula of Concord*] was acquainted with the facts could not but see that in this doctrine [of predestination] there was a far-reaching difference between the Lutheran and the Calvinistic theology." (559.) F. Pieper declares that Luther and Calvin agree only in certain expressions, but differ entirely as to substance. (*Dogm.* 3, 554.)

The *Visitation Articles*, adopted 1592 as a norm of doctrine for Electoral Saxony, enumerate the following propositions on "Predestination and the Eternal Providence of God" which must be upheld over against the Calvinists as "the pure and true doctrine of our [Lutheran] churches": "1. That Christ has died for all men, and as the Lamb of God has borne the sins of the whole world. 2. That God created no one for condemnation, but will have all men to be saved, and to come to the knowledge of the truth. He commands all to hear His Son Christ in the Gospel, and promises by it the power and working of the Holy Ghost for conversion and salvation. 3. That many men are condemned by their own guilt, who are either unwilling to hear the Gospel of Christ, or again fall from grace, by error against the foundation or by sins against conscience. 4. That all sinners who repent are received into grace, and no one is excluded, even though his sins were as scarlet, since God's mercy is much greater than the sins of all the world, and God has compassion on all His works." (Conc. Trigl., 1153.) Not one of these propositions, which have always been regarded as a summary of the Lutheran teaching in contradistinction from Calvinism, was ever denied by Luther.

## 235. Summary of Luther's Views.

Luther distinguished between the hidden and the revealed or "proclaimed" God; the secret and revealed will of God; the majestic God in whom we live and move and have our being, and God manifest in Christ; God's unsearchable judgments and ways past finding out, and His merciful promises in the Gospel. Being truly God and not an idol, God, according to Luther, is both actually omnipotent and omniscient. Nothing can exist or occur without His power, and everything surely will occur as He has foreseen it. This is true of the thoughts, volitions, and acts of all His creatures. He would not be God if there were any power not derived from, or supplied by Him, or if the actual course of events could annul His decrees and stultify His knowledge. Also the devils and the wicked are not beyond His control.

As for evil, though God does not will or cause it, — for, on the contrary, He prohibits sin and truly deplores the death of a sinner, — yet sin and death could never have entered the world without His permission. Also the will of fallen man receives its power to will from God, and its every resolve and consequent act proceeds just as God has foreseen, ordained, or permitted it. The evil quality of all such acts, however, does not emanate from God, but from the corrupt will of man. Hence free will, when defined as the power of man to nullify and subvert what God's majesty has foreseen and decreed, is a nonent, a mere empty title. This, however, does not involve that the human will is coerced or compelled to do evil, nor does it exclude in fallen man the ability to choose in matters temporal and subject to reason.

But while holding that we must not deny the majesty and the mysteries of God, Luther did not regard these, but Christ crucified and justification by faith in the promises of the Gospel, as the true objects of our concern. Nor does he, as did Calvin, employ predestination as a corrective and regulative norm for interpreting, limiting, invalidating, annulling, or casting doubt upon, any of the blessed truths of the Gospel. Luther does not modify the revealed will of God in order to harmonize it with God's sovereignty. He does not place the hidden God in opposition to the revealed God, nor does he reject the one in order to maintain the other. He denies neither the revealed universality of God's grace, of Christ's redemption, and of the efficaciousness of the Holy Spirit in the means of grace, nor the unsearchable judgments and ways of God's majesty. Even the Reformed theologian A. Schweizer admits as much when he says in his *Zentraldogmen* (1, 445): "In the Zwinglio-Calvinian type of doctrine, predestination is a dogma important as such and *regulating* the other doctrines, yea, as Martyr, Beza, and others say, the chief part of Christian doctrine; while in the Lutheran type of doctrine it is merely a dogma supporting other, more important central doctrines." (Frank 4, 264.)

Moreover, Luther most earnestly warns against all speculations concerning the hidden God as futile, foolish, presumptuous, and wicked. The secret counsels, judgments, and ways of God cannot and must not be investigated. God's majesty is unfathomable, His judgments are unsearchable, His ways past finding out. Hence, there is not, and there cannot be, any human knowledge, understanding, or faith whatever concerning God in so far as He has not revealed Himself. For while the fact that there are indeed such things as mysteries, unsearchable judgments, and incomprehensible ways in God is plainly taught in the Bible, their nature, their how, why, and wherefore, has not been revealed to us, and no amount of human ingenuity is able to supply the deficiency. Hence, in as far as God is still hidden and veiled, He cannot serve as a norm by which we are able to regulate our faith and life. Particularly when considering the question how God is disposed toward us individually, we must not take refuge in the secret counsels of God, which reason cannot spy and pry into. According to Luther, all human speculations concerning the hidden God are mere diabolical inspirations, bound to lead away from the

saving truth of the Gospel into despair and destruction.

What God, therefore, would have men believe about His attitude toward them, must, according to Luther, be learned from the Gospel alone. The Bible tells us how God is disposed toward poor sinners, and how He wants to deal with them. Not His hidden majesty, but His only-begotten Son, born in Bethlehem, is the divinely appointed object of human investigation. Christ crucified is God manifest and visible to men. Whoever has seen Christ has seen God. The Gospel is God's only revelation to sinful human beings. The Bible, the ministry of the Word, Baptism, the Lord's Supper, and absolution are the only means of knowing how God is disposed toward us. To these alone God has directed us. With these alone men should occupy and concern themselves.

And the Gospel being the Word of God, the knowledge furnished therein is most reliable. Alarmed sinners may trust in its comforting promises with firm assurance and unwavering confidence. In *De Servo Arbitrio* Luther earnestly warns men not to investigate the hidden God, but to look to revelation for an answer to the question how God is minded toward them, and how He intends to deal with them. In his *Commentary on Genesis* he refers to this admonition and repeats it, protesting that he is innocent if any one is misled to take a different course. "I have added" [to the statements in *De Servo Arbitrio* concerning necessity and the hidden God], Luther here declares, "that we must look upon the revealed God. *Addidi, quod aspiciendus sit Deus revelatus.*" (CONC. TRIGL. 898.)

This Bible-revelation, however, by which alone Luther would have men guided in judging God, plainly teaches both, that grace is universal, and that salvation is by grace alone. Luther always taught the universality of God's love and mercy, as well as of Christ's redemption, and the operation of the Holy Spirit in the means of grace. Also according to *De Servo Arbitrio*, God wants all men to be saved, and does not wish the death of sinners, but deplores and endeavors to remove it. Luther fairly revels in such texts as Ezek. 18, 23 and 31, 11: "As I live, saith the Lord God, I have no pleasure in the death of the wicked, but that the wicked turn from his way and live. Turn ye from your evil ways; for why will ye die, O house of Israel?" He calls the above a "glorious passage" and "that sweetest Gospel voice — *illam vocem dulcissimi Evangelii.*" (E. v. a. 7, 218.)

Thus Luther rejoiced in universal grace, because it alone was able to convince him that the Gospel promises embraced and included also him. In like manner he considered the doctrine that salvation is by grace *alone* to be most necessary and most comforting. Without this truth divine assurance of salvation is impossible; with it, all doubts about the final victory of faith are removed. Luther was convinced that, if he were required to contribute anything to his own conversion, preservation, and salvation, he could never attain these blessings. Nothing can save but the grace which is grace alone. In *De Servo Arbitrio* everything is pressed into service to disprove and explode the assertion of Erasmus that the human will is able to and does "work something in matters pertaining to salvation," and to establish the monergism or sole activity of grace in man's conversion. (St. L. 18, 1686, 1688.)

At the same time Luther maintained that man alone is at fault when he is lost. In *De Servo Arbitrio* he argues: Since it is God's will that all men should be saved, it must be attributed to man's will if any one perishes. The cause of damnation is unbelief, which thwarts the gracious will of God so clearly revealed in the Gospel. The question, however, why some are lost while others are saved, though their guilt is equal, or why God does not save all men, since it is grace alone that saves, and since grace is universal, Luther declines to answer. Moreover, he demands that we both acknowledge and adore the unsearchable judgments of God, and at the same time firmly adhere to the Gospel as revealed in the Bible. All efforts to solve this mystery or to harmonize the hidden and the revealed God, Luther denounces as folly and presumption.

Yet Luther maintains that the conflict is seeming rather than real. Whatever may be true of the majestic God, it certainly cannot annul or invalidate what He has made known of Himself in the Gospel. There are and can be no contradictory wills in God. Despite appearances to the contrary, therefore Christians are firmly to believe that, in His dealings with men, God, who saves so few and damns so many, is nevertheless both truly merciful and just. And what we now believe we shall see hereafter. When the veil will have been lifted and we shall know God even as we are known by Him, then we shall see with our eyes no other face of God than the most lovable one which our faith beheld in Jesus. The light of glory will not correct, but confirm, the truths of the Bible, and reveal the fact that in all His ways God was always in perfect harmony with Himself.

Indeed, according to Luther, the truth concerning the majestic God in whom we live and move and have our being, and without whom nothing can be or occur, in a way serves both repentance and faith. It serves repentance and the Law inasmuch as it humbles man, causing him to despair of himself and of the powers of his own unregenerate will. It serves faith inasmuch as it guarantees God's merciful promises in the Gospel. For if God is supreme, as He truly is, then there can be nothing more reliable than the covenant of grace to which He has pledged Himself by an oath. And if God, as He truly does, controls all contingencies, then there remains no room for any fear whether He will be able to fulfil His glorious promises, also the promise that nothing shall pluck us out of the hands of Christ. — Such, essentially, was the teaching set forth by Luther in *De Servo Arbitrio* and in his other publications.

### 236. Object of Luther's "De Servo Arbitrio."

The true scope of *De Servo Arbitrio* is to prove that man is saved, not by any ability or efforts of his own, but solely by grace. Luther says: "We are not arguing the question what we can do when God works [moves us], but what *we* can do *ourselves*, *viz.*, whether, after being created out of nothing, we can do or endeavor [to do] anything through that general movement of omnipotence toward preparing ourselves for being a new creation of His Spirit. This question should have been answered, instead of turning aside to another." Luther continues: "We go on to say: Man, before he is renewed to become a new creature of the kingdom of the Spirit, does nothing, endeavors nothing, toward preparing himself for renewal and the kingdom; and afterwards, when he has been created anew, he does nothing, endeavors nothing, toward preserving himself in that kingdom; but the Spirit alone does each of these things in us, both creating us anew without our cooperation and preserving us when recreated, — even as Jas. 1, 18 says: 'Of His own will begat He us by the Word of Truth that we should be a kind of firstfruits of His creatures.' He is speaking here of the renewed creature." (E. v. a. 7, 317; St. L. 18, 1909; compare here and in the following quotations Vaughan's *Martin Luther on the Bondage of the Will*, London, 1823.)

Man lacks also the ability to do what is good before God. Luther: "I reply: The words of the Prophet [Ps. 14, 2: "The Lord looketh down from heaven upon the children of men to see if there were any that did understand and seek God. They are all gone aside," etc.] include both act and power; and it is the same thing to say, 'Man does not seek after God,' as it would be to say, 'Man cannot seek after God.'" (E. 330; St. L. 1923.) Again: "Since, therefore, men are flesh, as God Himself testifies, they cannot but be carnally minded (*nihil sapere possunt nisi carnem*); hence free will has power only to sin. And since they grow worse even when the Spirit of God calls and teaches them, what would they do if left to themselves, without the Spirit of God?" (E. 290; St. L. 1876.) "In brief, you will observe in Scripture that, wherever flesh is treated in opposition to the Spirit, you may understand by flesh about everything that is contrary to the Spirit, as in the passage [John 6, 63]: 'The flesh profiteth nothing.'" (E. 291; St. L. 1877.) "Thus also Holy Scripture, by way of emphasis (*per epitasin*), calls man 'flesh,' as though he were carnality itself, because his mind is occupied with nothing but carnal things. *Quod nimio ac nihil aliud sapit quam ea, quae carnis sunt.*" (E. 302; St. L. 1890.)

According to Luther there is no such thing as a neutral willing in man. He says: "It is a mere logical fiction to say that there is in man a neutral and pure volition (*medium et purum velle*); nor can those prove it who assert it. It was born of ignorance of things and servile regard to words, as if something must straightway be such in substance as we state it to be in words, which sort of figments are numberless among the Sophists [Scholastic theologians]. The truth of the matter is stated by Christ when He says [Luke 11, 23]: 'He that is not with Me is against Me.' He does not say, 'He that is neither with Me nor against Me, but in the middle.' For if God be in us, Satan is absent, and only the will for good is present with us. If God be absent, Satan is present, and there is no will in us but towards evil. Neither God nor Satan allows a mere and pure volition in us; but, as you have rightly said, having lost our liberty, we are compelled to serve sin; that is, sin and wickedness we will, sin and wickedness we speak, sin and wickedness we act." (E. 199; St. L. 1768.)

In support of his denial of man's ability in spiritual matters Luther quotes numerous Bible-passages, and thoroughly refutes as fallacies *a debito ad posse*, etc., the arguments drawn by Erasmus from mandatory and conditional passages of Scripture. His own arguments he summarizes as follows: "For if we believe it to be true that God foreknows and preordains everything, also, that He can neither be deceived nor hindered in His foreknowledge and predestination; furthermore, that nothing occurs without His will (a truth which reason itself is compelled to concede), then, according to the testimony of the selfsame reason, there can be no free will in man or angel or any creature. Likewise, if we believe Satan to be the prince of the world, who is perpetually plotting and fighting against the kingdom of Christ with all his might, so that he does not release captive men unless he be driven out by the divine power of the Spirit, it is again manifest that there can be no such thing as free will. Again, if we believe original sin to have so ruined us that, by striving against what is good, it makes most troublesome work even for those who are led by the Spirit, then it is clear that in man devoid of the Spirit nothing is left which can turn itself to good, but only [what turns itself] to evil. Again, if the Jews, following after righteousness with all their might, rushed forth into unrighteousness, and the Gentiles, who were following after unrighteousness, have freely and unexpectedly attained to righteousness, it is likewise manifest, even by very deed and experience, that man without grace can will nothing but evil. In brief, if we believe Christ to have redeemed man by His blood, then we are compelled to confess that the whole man was lost; else we shall make Christ either superfluous, or the Redeemer only of the vilest part [of man], which is blasphemous and sacrilegious." (E. 366; St. L. 1969.)

### 237. Relation of Man's Will toward God's Majesty.

According to Luther man has power over things beneath himself, but not over God in His majesty. We read: "We know that man is constituted lord of the things beneath him,

over which he has power and free will, that they may obey him and do what he wills and thinks. But the point of our inquiry is whether he has a free will toward God, so that God obeys and does what man wills; or, whether it is not rather God who has a free will over man, so that the latter wills and does what God wills, and can do nothing but what God has willed and does. Here the Baptist says that man can receive nothing except it be given him from heaven: wherefore free will is nothing." (E. 359; St. L. 1957.)

God as revealed in the Word may, according to Luther, be opposed and resisted by man, but not God in His majesty. We read: "Lest any one should suppose this to be *my* own distinction, [let him know that] I follow Paul, who writes to the Thessalonians concerning Antichrist (2 Thess. 2, 4) that he will exalt himself above every God that is proclaimed and worshiped, plainly indicating that one may be exalted above God, so far as He is proclaimed and worshiped, that is, above the Word and worship by which God is known to us, and maintains intercourse with us. Nothing, however, can be exalted above God as He is in His nature and majesty (as not worshiped and proclaimed); rather, everything is under His powerful hand." (E. 221; St. L. 1794.)

God in His majesty is supreme and man cannot resist His omnipotence, nor thwart His decrees, nor foil His plans, nor render His omniscience fallible. Luther: "For all men find this opinion written in their hearts, and, when hearing this matter discussed, they, though against their will, acknowledge and assent to it, first, that God is omnipotent, not only as regards His power, but also, as stated, His action; else He would be a ridiculous God; secondly, that He knows and foreknows all things, and can neither err nor be deceived. These two things, however, being conceded by the hearts and senses of all men, they are presently, by an inevitable consequence, compelled to admit that, even as we are not made by our own will, but by necessity, so likewise we do nothing according to the right of free will, but just as God has foreknown and acts by a counsel and an energy which is infallible and immutable. So, then, we find it written in all hearts alike that free will [defined as a power independent of God's power] is nothing, although this writing [in the hearts of men] be obscured through so many contrary disputations and the great authority of so many persons who during so many ages have been teaching differently." (E. 268; St. L. 1851.)

The very idea of God and omnipotence involves that free will is not, and cannot be, a power independent of God. Luther: "However, even natural reason is obliged to confess that the living and true God must be such a one who by His freedom imposes necessity upon us; for, evidently, He would be a ridiculous God or, more properly, an idol, who would either foresee future events in an uncertain way, or be deceived by the events, as the Gentiles have asserted an inescapable fate also for their gods. God would be equally ridiculous if He could not do or did not do all things, or if anything occurred without Him. Now, if foreknowledge and omnipotence are conceded, it naturally follows as an irrefutable consequence that we have not been made by ourselves, nor that we live or do anything by ourselves, but through His omnipotence. Since, therefore, He foreknew that we should be such [as we actually are], and even now makes, moves, and governs us as such, pray, what can be imagined that is free in us so as to occur differently than He has foreknown or now works? God's foreknowledge and omnipotence, therefore, conflict directly with our free will [when defined as a power independent of God]. For either God will be mistaken in foreknowing, err also in acting (which is impossible), or we shall act, and be acted upon, according to His foreknowledge and action. By the omnipotence of God, however, I do not mean that power by which He can do many things which He does not do, but that active omnipotence by means of which He powerfully works all things in all, in which manner Scripture calls Him omnipotent. This omnipotence and prescience of God, I say, entirely abolish the dogma of free will. Nor can the obscurity of Scripture or the difficulty of the matter be made a pretext here. The *words* are most clear, known even to children; the *subject-matter* is plain and easy, judged to be so even by the natural reason common to all, so that ever so long a series of ages, times, and persons writing and teaching otherwise will avail nothing." (E. 267; St. L. 1849.)

According to Luther, therefore, nothing can or does occur independently of God, or differently from what His omniscience has foreseen. Luther: "Hence it follows irrefutably that all things which we do, and all things which happen, although to us they seem to happen changeably and contingently, do in reality happen necessarily and immutably, *if one views the will of God*. For the will of God is efficacious and cannot be thwarted, since it is God's natural power itself. It is also wise, so that it cannot be deceived. And since His will is not thwarted, the work itself cannot be prevented, but must occur in the very place, time, manner, and degree which He Himself both foresees and wills." (E. 134; St. L. 1692.)

### 238. God Not the Cause of Sin.

Regarding God's relation to the sinful actions of men, Luther held that God is not the cause of sin. True, His omnipotence impels also the ungodly; but the resulting acts are evil because of man's evil nature. He writes: "Since, therefore, God moves and works all in all, He necessarily moves and acts also in Satan and in the wicked. But He acts in them precisely according to what they are, and what He finds them to be (*agit in illis taliter, quales illi sunt, et quales invenit*). That is to say, since they are turned away [from Him] and wicked, and [as such] are

impelled to action by divine omnipotence, they do only such things as are averse [to God] and wicked, just as a horseman driving a horse which has only three or two [sound] feet (*equum tripedem vel bipedem*) will drive him in a manner corresponding to the condition of the horse (*agit quidem taliter, qualis equus est*), *i. e.*, the horse goes at a sorry gait. But what can the horseman do? He drives such a horse together with sound horses, so that it sadly limps along, while the others take a good gait. He cannot do otherwise, unless the horse is cured. Here you see that, when God works in the wicked and through the wicked, the result indeed is evil (*mala quidem fieri*), but that nevertheless God cannot act wickedly, although He works that which is evil through the wicked; for He, being good, cannot Himself act wickedly, although He uses evil instruments, which cannot escape the impulse and motion of His power. The fault, therefore, is in the instruments, which God does not suffer to remain idle, so that evil occurs, God Himself impelling them, but in no other manner than a carpenter who, using an ax that is notched and toothed, would do poor work with it. Hence it is that a wicked man cannot but err and sin continually, because, being impelled by divine power, he is not allowed to remain idle, but wills, desires, and acts, according to what he is (*velit, cupiat, faciat taliter, qualis ipse est*)." (E. 255; St. L. 1834.) "For although God does not make sin, still He ceases not to form and to multiply a nature which, the Spirit having been withdrawn, is corrupted by sin, just as when a carpenter makes statues of rotten wood. Thus men become what their nature is, God creating and forming them of such nature." (E. 254; St. L. 1833.)

Though God works all things in all things, the wickedness of an action flows from the sinful nature of the creature. Luther: "Whoever would have any understanding of such matters, let him consider that God works evil in us, *i. e.*, through us, not by any fault of His, but through our own fault. For since we are by nature evil, while God is good, and since He impels us to action according to the nature of His omnipotence, He, who Himself is good, cannot do otherwise than do evil with an evil instrument, although, according to His wisdom, He causes this evil to turn out unto His own glory and to our salvation." (E. 257; St. L. 1837.) "For this is what we assert and contend, that, when God works without the grace of His Spirit [in His majesty, outside of Word and Sacrament], He works all in all, even in the wicked; for He alone moves all things, which He alone has created, and drives and impels all things by virtue of His omnipotence, which they [the created things] cannot escape or change, but necessarily follow and obey, according to the power which God has given to each of them, — such is the manner in which all, even wicked, things cooperate with Him. Furthermore, when He acts by the Spirit of Grace in those whom He has made righteous, *i. e.*, in

His own kingdom, He in like manner impels and moves them; and, being new creatures, they follow and cooperate with Him; or rather, ås Paul says, they are led by Him." (E. 317; St. L. 1908.) "For we say that, without the grace of God, man still remains under the general omnipotence of God, who does, moves, impels all things, so that they take their course necessarily and without fail, but that what man, so impelled, does, is nothing, *i. e.*, avails nothing before God, and is accounted nothing but sin." (E. 315; St. L. 1906.)

Though everything occurs as God has foreseen, this, according to Luther, does not at all involve that man is coerced in his actions. Luther: "But pray, are we disputing now concerning coercion and force? Have we not in so many books testified that we speak of the necessity of immutability? We know . . . that Judas of his own volition betrayed Christ. But we affirm that, if God foreknew it, this volition would certainly and without fail occur in this very Judas. . . . We are not discussing the point whether Judas became a traitor unwillingly or willingly, but whether at the time foreappointed by God it infallibly had to happen that Judas of his own volition betrayed Christ." (E. 270; St. L. 1853.) Again: "What is it to me that free will is not coerced, but does what it does willingly? It is enough for me to have you concede that it must necessarily happen, that he [Judas] does what he does of his own volition, and that he cannot conduct himself otherwise if God has so foreknown it. If God foreknows that Judas will betray, or that he will change his mind about it, — whichever of the two He shall have foreknown will necessarily come to pass; else God would be mistaken in foreknowing and foretelling, — which is impossible. Necessity of consequence effects this: if God foreknows an event, it necessarily happens. In other words, free will is nothing" [it is not a power independent of God or able to nullify God's prescience]. (E. 272; St. L. 1855.)

To wish that God would abstain from impelling the wicked is, according to Luther, tantamount to wishing that He cease to be God. Luther: "There is still this question which some one may ask, 'Why does God not cease to impel by His omnipotence, in consequence of which the will of the wicked is moved to continue being wicked and even growing worse?' The answer is: This is equivalent to desiring that God cease to be God for the sake of the wicked, since one wishes His power and action to cease, *i. e.*, that He cease to be good, lest they become worse!" (E. 259; St. L. 1839.)

### 239. Free Will a Mere Empty Title.

Luther considers free will (when defined as an ability in spiritual matters or as a power independent of God) a mere word without anything corresponding to it in reality (*figmentum in rebus seu titulus sine re*, E. v. a. 5, 230), because natural will has powers only

in matters temporal and subject to reason, but none in spiritual things, and because of itself and independently of God's omnipotence it has no power whatever. We read: "Now it follows that free will is a title altogether divine and cannot belong to any other being, save only divine majesty, for He, as the Psalmist sings [Ps. 115, 3], can do and does all that He wills in heaven and in earth. Now, when this title is ascribed to men, it is so ascribed with no more right than if also divinity itself were ascribed to them, — a sacrilege than which there is none greater. Accordingly it was the duty of theologians to abstain from this word when they intended to speak of human power, and to reserve it exclusively for God, thereupon also to remove it from the mouth and discourse of men, claiming it as a sacred and venerable title for their God. And if they would at all ascribe some power to man, they should have taught that it be called by some other name than 'free will,' especially since we all know and see that the common people are miserably deceived and led astray by this term; for by it they hear and conceive something very far different from what theologians mean and discuss. 'Free will' is too magnificent, extensive, and comprehensive a term; by it common people understand (as also the import and nature of the word require) a power which can freely turn to either side, and neither yields nor is subject to any one." (E. 158; St. L. 1720.)

If the term "free will" be retained, it should, according to Luther, be conceived of as a power, not in divine things, but only in matters subject to human reason. We read: "So, then, according to Erasmus, free will is the power of the will which is able of itself to will and not to will the Word and work of God, whereby it is led to things which exceed both its comprehension and perception. For if it is able to will and not to will, it is able also to love and to hate. If it is able to love and to hate, it is able also, in some small degree, to keep the Law and to believe the Gospel. For if you will, or do not will, a certain thing, it is impossible that by that will you should not be able to do something of the work, even though, when hindered by another, you cannot complete it." (E. 191; St. L. 1759.) "If, then, we are not willing to abandon this term altogether, which would be the safest and most pious course to follow, let us at least teach men to use it in good faith (*bona fide*) only in the sense that free will be conceded to man, with respect to such matters only as are not superior, but inferior to himself; *i. e.*, man is to know that, with regard to his means and possessions, he has the right of using, of doing, and of forbearing to do according to his free will; although also this is directed by the free will of God alone whithersoever it pleases Him. But with respect to God, or in things pertaining to salvation or damnation, he has no free will, but is the captive, subject, and servant, either of the will of God or of the will of Satan." (E. 160; St. L. 1722.) "Perhaps you might properly attribute some will (*aliquod arbitrium*) to man; but to attribute free will to him in divine things is too much, since in the judgment of all who hear it the term 'free will' is properly applied to that which can do and does with respect to God whatsoever it pleases, without being hindered by any law or authority. You would not call a slave free who acts under the authority of his master. With how much less propriety do we call men or angels truly free, who, to say nothing of sin and death, live under the most complete authority of God, unable to subsist for a moment by their own power." (E. 189; St. L. 1756.)

Lost liberty, says Luther, is no liberty, just as lost health is no health. We read: "When it has been conceded and settled that free will, having lost its freedom, is compelled to serve sin, and has no power to will anything good, I can conceive nothing else from these expressions than that free will is an empty word, with the substance lost. My grammar calls a lost liberty no liberty. But to attribute the title of liberty to that which has no liberty is to attribute an empty name. If here I go astray, let who can correct me; if my words are obscure and ambiguous, let who can make them plain and definite. I cannot call health that is lost health. If I should ascribe it to a sick man, I believe to have ascribed to him nothing but an empty name. But away with monstrous words! For who can tolerate that abuse of speech by which we affirm that man has free will, and in the same breath assert that he, having lost his liberty, is compelled to serve sin, and can will nothing good? It conflicts with common sense, and utterly destroys the use of speech. The *Diatribe* is rather to be accused of blurting out its words as if it were asleep, and giving no heed to those of others. It does not consider, I say, what it means, and what it all includes, if I declare: Man has lost his liberty, is compelled to serve sin, and has no power to will anything good." (E. 200; St. L. 1769.)

Satan causes his captives to believe themselves free and happy. Luther: "The Scriptures set before us a man who is not only bound, wretched, captive, sick, dead, but who (through the operation of Satan, his prince) adds this plague of blindness to his other plagues, that he believes himself to be free, happy, unfettered, strong, healthy, alive. For Satan knows that, if man were to realize his own misery, he would not be able to retain any one in his kingdom, because God could not but at once pity and help him who recognizes his misery and cries for relief. For throughout all Scripture He is extolled and greatly praised for being nigh unto the contrite in heart, as also Christ testifies, Isaiah 61, 1. 2, that He has been sent to preach the Gospel to the poor and to heal the broken-hearted. Accordingly, it is Satan's business to keep his grip on men, lest they recognize their misery, but rather take it for granted that they are able to do everything that is said." (E. 213; St. L. 1785.)

## 240. The Gospel to be Our Only Guide.

According to *De Servo Arbitrio* God's majesty and His mysterious judgments and ways must not be searched, nor should speculations concerning them be made the guide of our faith and life. Luther says: "Of God or of the will of God proclaimed and revealed, and offered to us, and which we meditate upon, we must treat in a different way than of God in so far as He is not proclaimed, not revealed, and not offered to us, and is not the object of our meditations. For in so far as God hides Himself, and desires not to be known of us, we have nothing to do with Him. Here the saying truly applies, 'What is above us does not concern us.'" (E. 221; St. L. 1794.) "We say, as we have done before, that one must not discuss the secret will of [divine] majesty, and that man's temerity, which, due to continual perverseness, disregards necessary matters and always attacks and encounters this [secret will], should be called away and withdrawn from occupying itself with scrutinizing those secrets of divine majesty which it is impossible to approach; for it dwells 'in the light which no man can approach unto,' as Paul testifies, 1 Tim. 6, 16." (E. 227; St. L. 1801.) This statement, that God's majesty must not be investigated, says Luther, "is not our invention, but an injunction confirmed by Holy Scripture. For Paul says Rom. 9, 19—21: 'Why doth God yet find fault? For who hath resisted His will? Nay but, O man, who art thou that repliest against God? . . . Hath not the potter power,' etc.? And before him Isaiah, chapter 58, 2: 'Yet they seek Me daily, and delight to know My ways, as a nation that did righteousness, and forsook not the ordinance of their God. They ask of Me the ordinances of justice; they take delight in approaching to God.' These words, I take it, show abundantly that it is unlawful for men to scrutinize the will of majesty." (E. 228; St. L. 1803.)

Instead of searching the Scriptures, as they are commanded to do, men unlawfully crave to investigate the hidden judgments of God. We read: "But we are nowhere more irreverent and rash than when we invade and argue these very mysteries and judgments which are unsearchable. Meanwhile we imagine that we are exercising incredible reverence in searching the Holy Scriptures, which God has commanded us to search. Here we do not search, but where He has forbidden us to search, there we do nothing but search with perpetual temerity, not to say blasphemy. Or is it not such a search when we rashly endeavor to make that wholly free foreknowledge of God accord with our liberty, and are ready to detract from the prescience of God, if it does not allow us liberty, or if it induces necessity, to say with the murmurers and blasphemers, 'Why doth He find fault? Who shall resist His will? What is become of the most merciful God? What of Him who wills not the death of the sinner? Has He made men that He might delight Himself with their torments?' and the like, which will be howled out

forever among the devils and the damned."
(E. 266; St. L. 1848.)

God's unknowable will is not and cannot be
our guide. Luther: "The *Diatribe* beguiles
herself through her ignorance, making no distinction between the proclaimed and the hidden God, that is, between the Word of God
and God Himself. God does many things
which He has not shown us in His Word. He
also wills many things concerning which He
has not shown us in His Word that He wills
them. For instance, He does not will the
death of a sinner, namely, according to His
Word, but He wills it according to His inscrutable will. Now, our business is to look
at His Word, disregarding the inscrutable
will; for we must be directed by the Word,
not by that inscrutable will (*nobis spectan-
dum est Verbum relinquendaque illa voluntas
imperscrutabilis; Verbo enim nos dirigi, non
voluntate illa inscrutabili oportet*). Indeed,
who could direct himself by that inscrutable
and unknowable will? It is enough merely to
know that there is such an inscrutable will
in God; but what, why, and how far it wills,
that is altogether unlawful for us to inquire
into, to wish [to know], and to trouble or occupy ourselves with; on the contrary, we
should fear and adore it." (E. 222; St. L.
1795.)

Instead of investigating the mysteries of
divine majesty, men ought to concern themselves with God's revelation in the Gospel.
Luther: "But let her [human temerity] occupy herself with the incarnate God or, as
Paul says, with Jesus Crucified, in whom are
hidden all the treasures of wisdom and knowledge. For through Him she has abundantly
what she ought to know and not to know. It
is the incarnate God, then, who speaks here
[Matt. 23]: 'I would, and thou wouldest not.'
The incarnate God, I say, was sent for this
purpose, that He might will, speak, do, suffer,
and offer to all men all things which are
necessary to salvation, although He offends
very many who, being either abandoned or
hardened by that secret will of His majesty,
do not receive Him who wills, speaks, works,
offers, even as John says: 'The light shineth
in darkness, and the darkness comprehendeth
it not'; and again: 'He came unto His own,
and His own received Him not.'" (E. 227 f.;
St. L. 1802.)

### 241. God's Grace Is Universal and Serious.

All men are in need of the saving Gospel,
and it should be preached to all. We read in
*De Servo Arbitrio:* "Paul had said just before: 'The Gospel is the power of God unto
salvation to every one that believeth; to the
Jew first and also to the Greek.' These words
are not obscure or ambiguous: 'To the Jews
and to the Greeks,' that is, to all men, the
Gospel of the power of God is necessary, in
order that, believing, they may be saved from
the revealed wrath." (E. 322; St. L. 1915.)
"He [God] knows what, when, how, and to
whom we ought to speak. Now, His injunction is that His Gospel, which is necessary
for all, should be limited by neither place nor

time, but be preached to all, at all times, and
in all places." (E. 149; St. L. 1709.)

The universal promises of the Gospel offer
firm and sweet consolation to poor sinners.
Luther: "It is the voice of the Gospel and the
sweetest consolation to poor miserable sinners
when Ezekiel says [18, 23. 32]: 'I have no
pleasure in the death of a sinner, but rather
that he be converted and live.' Just so also
the thirtieth Psalm [v. 5]: 'For His anger en-
dureth but a moment; in His favor is life
[His will rather is life].' And the sixty-
ninth [v. 16]: 'For Thy loving-kindness is
good [How sweet is Thy mercy, Lord!]' Also:
'Because I am merciful.' And that saying of
Christ, Matt. 11, 28: 'Come unto Me, all ye
that labor and are heavy laden, and I will refresh you.' Also that of Exodus [20, 6],
'I show mercy unto thousands of them that
love Me.' Indeed, almost more than half of
Holy Scripture, — what is it but genuine
promises of grace, by which mercy, life, peace,
and salvation are offered by God to men?
And what else do the words of promise sound
forth than this: 'I have no pleasure in the
death of a sinner'? Is it not the same thing
to say, 'I am merciful,' as to say, 'I am not
angry,' 'I do not wish to punish,' 'I do not
wish you to die,' 'I desire to pardon,' 'I desire to spare'? Now, if these divine promises
did not stand [firm], so as to raise up afflicted
consciences terrified by the sense of sin and
the fear of death and judgment, what place
would there be for pardon or for hope? What
sinner would not despair?" (E. 218; St. L.
1791.)

God, who would have all men to be saved,
deplores and endeavors to remove death, so
that man must blame himself if he is lost.
Luther: "God in His majesty and nature
therefore must be left untouched [unsearched],
for in this respect we have nothing to do with
Him; nor did He want us to deal with Him
in this respect; but we deal with Him in so
far as He has clothed Himself and come forth
in His Word, by which He has offered Himself to us. This [Word] is His glory and
beauty with which the Psalmist, 21, 6, celebrates Him as being clothed." Emphasizing
the seriousness of universal grace, Luther continues: "Therefore we affirm that the holy
God does not deplore the death of the people
which He works in them, but deplores the
death which He finds in the people, and endeavors to remove (*sed deplorat mortem, quam
invenit in populo, et amovere studet*). For
this is the work of the proclaimed God to take
away sin and death, that we may be saved.
For He has sent His Word and healed them."
(E. 222; St. L. 1795.) "Hence it is rightly
said, If God wills not death, it must be
charged to our own will that we perish.
'Rightly,' I say, if you speak of the proclaimed
God. For He would have all men to be saved,
coming, as He does, with His Word of salvation to all men; and the fault is in the will,
which does not admit Him; as He says, Matt.
23, 37: 'How often would I have gathered
thy children together, and ye would not!'"
(E. 222; St. L. 1795.)

## 242. Sola Gratia Doctrine Engenders Assurance.

Luther rejoices in the doctrine of *sola gratia* because it alone is able to engender assurance of salvation. He writes: "As for myself, I certainly confess that, if such a thing could somehow be, I should be unwilling to have free will given me, or anything left in my own hand, which might enable me to make an effort at salvation; not only because in the midst of so many dangers and adversities and also of so many assaulting devils I should not be strong enough to remain standing and keep my hold of it (for one devil is mightier than all men put together, and not a single man would be saved), but because, even if there were no dangers and no adversities and no devils, I should still be compelled to toil forever uncertainly, and to beat the air in my struggle. For though I should live and work to eternity, my own conscience would never be sure and at ease as to how much it ought to do in order to satisfy God. No matter how perfect a work might be, there would be left a doubt whether it pleased God, or whether He required anything more; as is proved by the experience of all who endeavor to be saved by the Law (*iustitiariorum*), and as I, to my own great misery, have learned abundantly during so many years. But now, since God has taken my salvation out of the hands of my will, and placed it into those of His own and has promised to save me, not by my own work or running, but by His grace and mercy, I feel perfectly secure, because He is faithful and will not lie to me; moreover, He is powerful and great, so that neither devils nor adversities can crush Him, or pluck me out of His hand. No one, says He, shall pluck them out of My hand; for My Father, who gave them unto Me, is greater than all. Thus it comes to pass that, though not all are saved, at least some, nay, many are, whereas by the power of free will absolutely none would be saved, but every one of us would be lost. We are also certain and sure that we please God, not by the merit of our own work, but by the favor of His mercy which He has promised us; and that, if we have done less than we ought, or have done anything amiss, He does not impute it to us, but, as a father, forgives and amends it. Such is the boast of every saint in his God." (E. 362; St. L. 1961 f.)

In the *Apology of the Augsburg Confession* this thought of Luther's is repeated as follows: "If the matter [our salvation] were to depend upon our merits, the promise would be uncertain and useless, because we never could determine when we would have sufficient merit. And this experienced consciences can easily understand [and would not, for a thousand worlds, have our salvation depend upon ourselves]." (CONC. TRIGL. 145, 84; compare 1079, 45 f.)

## 243. Truth of God's Majesty Serves God's Gracious Will.

Luther regarded the teaching that everything is subject to God's majesty as being of service to His gracious will. We read: "Two

things require the preaching of these truths [concerning the infallibility of God's foreknowledge, etc.]; the first is, the humbling of our pride and the knowledge of the grace of God; the second, Christian faith itself. First, God has certainly promised His grace to the humbled, *i. e.*, to those who deplore their sins and despair [of themselves]. But man cannot be thoroughly humbled until he knows that his salvation is altogether beyond his own powers, counsels, efforts, will, and works, and depends altogether upon the decision, counsel, will, and work of another, *i. e.*, of God only. For as long as he is persuaded that he can do anything toward gaining salvation, though it be ever so little, he continues in self-confidence, and does not wholly despair of himself; accordingly he is not humbled before God, but anticipates, or hopes for, or at least wishes for, a place, a time, and some work by which he may finally obtain salvation." (E. 153. 133; St. L. 1715. 1691.) "More than once," says Luther, "I myself have been offended at it [the teaching concerning God's majesty] to such an extent that I was at the brink of despair, so that I even wished I had never been created a man, — until I learned how salutary that despair was and how close to grace." (E. 268; St. L. 1850.)

Of the manner in which, according to Luther, the truth concerning God's majesty serves the Gospel, we read: "Moreover, I do not only wish to speak of how true these things are, . . . but also how becoming to a Christian, how pious, and how necessary it is to know them. For if these things are not known, it is impossible for either faith or any worship of God to be maintained. That would be ignorance of God indeed; and if we do not know Him, we cannot obtain salvation, as is well known. For if you doubt that God foreknows and wills all things, not contingently, but necessarily and immutably, or if you scorn such knowledge, how will you be able to believe His promises, and with full assurance trust and rely upon them? When He promises, you ought to be sure that He knows what He is promising, and is able and willing to accomplish it, else you will account Him neither true nor faithful. That, however, is unbelief, extreme impiety, and a denial of the most high God. But how will you be confident and sure if you do not know that He certainly, infallibly, unchangeably, and necessarily knows, and wills, and will perform what He promises? Nor should we merely be certain that God necessarily and immutably wills and will perform [what He has promised], but we should even glory in this very thing, as Paul does, Rom. 3, 4: 'Let God be true, but every man a liar.' And again, Rom. 9, 6; 4, 21; 1 Sam. 3, 19: 'Not that the Word of God hath taken none effect.' And in another place, 2 Tim. 2, 19: 'The foundation of God standeth sure, having this seal, The Lord knoweth them that are His.' And in Titus 1, 2: 'Which God, that cannot lie, hath promised before the world began.' And in Heb. 11, 6: 'He that cometh to God must believe that God is, and that He is a rewarder of them that hope in Him.' So, then, Christian faith is altogether extinguished, the promises of God and the entire Gospel fall absolutely to the ground, if we are taught and believe that we have no need of knowing the fore-knowledge of God to be necessary and the necessity of all things that must be done. For this is the only and highest possible conso-lation of Christians in all adversities to know that God does not lie, but does all things im-mutably, and that His will can neither be re-sisted, nor altered, nor hindered." (E. 137. 264; St. L. 1695. 1845.)

## 244. There Are No Real Contradictions in God.

Among the mysteries which we are unable to solve Luther enumerates the questions: Why did God permit the fall of Adam? Why did He suffer us to be infected with original sin? Why does God not change the evil will? Why is it that some are converted while others are lost? We read: "But why does He not at the same time change the evil will which He moves? This pertains to the secrets of His majesty, where His judgments are in-comprehensible. Nor is it our business to in-vestigate, but to adore these mysteries. If, therefore, flesh and blood here take offense and murmur, let them murmur; but they will effect nothing, God will not be changed on that account. And if the ungodly are scandalized and leave in ever so great numbers, the elect will nevertheless remain. The same answer should be given to those who ask, 'Why did He allow Adam to fall, and why does He create all of us infected with the same sin when He could have preserved him [Adam], and created us from something else, or after first having purged the seed?' He is God, for whose will there is no cause or reason which might be prescribed for it as a standard and rule of action; for it has no equal or superior, but is itself the rule for everything. If it had any rule or standard, cause or reason, it could no longer be the will of God. For what He wills is right, not because He is or was in duty bound so to will, but, on the contrary, because He wills so, therefore what occurs must be right. Cause and reason are pre-scribed to a creature's will, but not to the will of the Creator, unless you would set an-other Creator over Him." (E. 259; St. L. 1840.)

Regarding the question why some are con-verted while others are not, we read: "But why this majesty does not remove this fault of our will, or change it in all men (seeing that it is not in the power of man to do so), or why He imputes this [fault of the will] to man when he cannot be without it, it is not lawful to search, and although you search much, you will never discover it, as Paul says, Rom. 9, 20: 'O man, who art thou that re-pliest against God?'" (E. 223; St. L. 1796.) "But as to why some are touched by the Law and others are not, so that the former receive, and the latter despise, the grace offered, this is another question, and one not treated by Ezekiel in this place, who speaks, not of the preached and offered mercy of God, not of the

secret and to-be-feared will of God, who by His counsel ordains what and what kind of persons He wills to be capable and partakers of His preached and offered mercy. This will of God must not be searched, but reverently adored, as being by far the most profound and sacred secret of divine majesty, reserved for Himself alone, and prohibited to us much more religiously than countless multitudes of Corycian Caves." (E. 221; St. L. 1794.)

Christians firmly believe that in His deal-ings with men God is always wise and just and good. Luther: "According to the judg-ment of reason it remains absurd that this just and good God should demand things that are impossible of fulfilment by free will, and, although it cannot will that which is good, but necessarily serves sin, should nevertheless charge this to free will; and that, when He does not confer the Spirit, He should not act a whit more kindly or more mercifully than when He hardens or permits men to harden themselves. Reason will declare that these are not the acts of a kind and merciful God. These things exceed her understanding too far, nor can she take herself into captivity to believe God to be good, who acts and judges thus; but setting faith aside, she wants to feel and see and comprehend how He is just and not cruel. She would indeed comprehend if it were said of God: 'He hardens nobody, He damns nobody, rather pities everybody, saves everybody,' so that, hell being destroyed and the fear of death removed, no future pun-ishment need be dreaded. This is the reason why she is so hot in striving to excuse and defend God as just and good. *But faith and the spirit judge differently, believing God to be good though He were to destroy all men.*" (E. 252; St. L. 1832.) "The reason why of the divine will must not be investigated, but simply adored, and we must give the glory to God that, being alone just and wise, *He does wrong to none, nor can He do anything fool-ish or rash, though it may appear far other-wise to us. Godly men are content with this answer.*" (E. 153; St. L. 1714.)

According to Luther, divine justice must be just as incomprehensible to human reason as God's entire essence. We read: "But when we feel ill at ease for the reason that it is difficult to vindicate the mercy and equity of God because He damns the undeserving, *i. e.*, such ungodly men as are born in ungodliness, and hence cannot in any way prevent being and remaining ungodly and damned, and are compelled by their nature to sin and perish, as Paul says [Eph. 2, 3]: 'We were all the sons of wrath even as others,' they being cre-ated such by God Himself out of the seed which was corrupted through the sin of the one Adam, — then the most merciful God is to be honored and revered in [His dealings with] those whom He justifies and saves, although they are most unworthy, and at least a little something ought to be credited to His divine wisdom by believing Him to be just where to us He seems unjust. For if His justice were such as could be declared just by human understanding, it would clearly not be divine, differing nothing from human justice. But since He is the one true God, and entirely incomprehensible and inaccessible to human reason, it is proper, nay, necessary, *that His justice also be incomprehensible,* even as Paul also exclaims, Rom. 11, 33, saying: 'O the depth of the riches both of the wisdom and knowledge of God! How unsearchable are His judgments, and His ways past finding out!' Now, they would not be incomprehensible if we were able, in everything He does, to comprehend why they are just. What is man compared with God? How much is our power capable of as compared with His? What is our strength compared with His powers? What is our knowledge compared with His wisdom? What is our substance compared with His substance? In short, what is everything that is ours as compared with everything that is His?" (E. 363; St. L. 1962.)

Christians embrace the opportunity offered by the mysterious ways of God to exercise their faith. Luther: "This is the highest degree of faith, to believe that He is merciful, who saves so few and condemns so many; to believe Him just, who by His will [creating us out of sinful seed] necessarily makes us damnable, thus, according to Erasmus, seeming to be delighted with the torments of the wretched, and worthy of hatred rather than of love. If, then, I could in any way comprehend how this God is merciful and just who shows such great wrath and [seeming] injustice, there would be no need of faith. But now, since this cannot be comprehended there is to be an opportunity for the exercise of faith when these things are preached and published, even as when God kills, our faith in life is exercised in death." (E. 154; St. L. 1716.)

### 245. Seeming Contradictions Solved in Light of Glory.

Christians are fully satisfied that hereafter they will see and understand what they here believed, viz., that in His dealings with men God truly is and always was absolutely just. Luther: "If you are pleased with God for crowning the unworthy, you ought not to be displeased with Him for condemning the undeserving [who were not worse or more guilty than those who are crowned]. If He is just in the former case, why not in the latter? In the former case He scatters favor and mercy upon the unworthy; in the latter He scatters wrath and severity upon the undeserving [who are guilty in no higher degree than those who are saved]. In both cases He is excessive and unrighteous before [in the judgment of] men, but just and true in His own mind. For how it is just that He crowns the unworthy is incomprehensible to us now; *but we shall understand it when we have come to that place where we shall no longer believe, but behold with our face unveiled.* So, too, how it is just that He condemns the undeserving we cannot comprehend now; yet we believe it until the Son of Man shall be revealed." (E. 284; St. L. 1870.) "Of course, in all other things we concede divine majesty to God;

only in His judgment we are ready to deny it, and cannot even for a little while believe that He is just, since He has promised us that, *when He will reveal His glory, we all shall then both see and feel that He has been, and is, just.*" (E. 364; St. L. 1964.)

Again: "Do you not think that since the light of grace has so readily solved a question which could not be solved by the light of nature, the light of glory will be able to solve with the greatest ease the question which in the light of the Word or of grace is unsolvable? In accordance with the common and good distinction let it be conceded that there are three lights — the light of nature, the light of grace, and the light of glory. In the light of nature it is unsolvable that it should be just that the good are afflicted while the wicked prosper. The light of grace, however, solves this [mystery]. In the light of grace it is unsolvable how God may condemn him who cannot by any power of his own do otherwise than sin and be guilty. There the light of nature as well as the light of grace declares that the fault is not in wretched man, but in the unjust God. For they cannot judge otherwise of God, who crowns a wicked man gratuitously without any merits, and does not crown another, but condemns him, who perhaps is less, or at least not more wicked [than the one who is crowned]. *But the light of glory pronounces a different verdict,* and when it arrives, it will show God, whose judgment is now that of incomprehensible justice, to be a Being of most just and manifest justice, which meanwhile we are to believe, admonished and confirmed by the example of the light of grace, which accomplishes a like miracle with respect to the light of nature." (E. 365; St. L. 1965.)

### 246. Statements Made by Luther before Publication of "De Servo Arbitrio."

Wherever Luther touches on predestination, both before and after 1525, essentially the same thoughts are found, though not developed as extensively as in *De Servo Arbitrio.* He consistently maintains that God's majesty must be neither denied nor searched, and that Christians should be admonished to look and rely solely upon the revealed universal promises of the Gospel. In his *Church Postil* of 1521 we read: "The third class of men who also approve this [the words of Paul, Rom. 11, 34. 35: 'For who hath known the mind of the Lord? Or who hath been His counselor? Or who hath first given to Him, and it shall be recompensed unto Him again?'] are those who indeed hear the Word of Revelation. For I am not now speaking of such as deliberately persecute the Word (they belong to the first class, who do not at all inquire about God), but of those who disregard the revelation and, led by the devil, go beyond and beside it, seeking to grasp the ways and judgments of God which He has not revealed. Now, if they were Christians, they would be satisfied and thank God for giving His Word, in which He shows what is pleasing to Him, and how we are to be saved. But they suffer the devil to lead them, insist on seeking other revelations, ponder what God may be in His invisible majesty, how He secretly governs the world, and what He has in particular decreed for each one in the future. For nature and human reason cannot desist; they *will* meddle in His judgment with their wisdom, sit in His most secret council, instruct Him and master Him. This is the pride of the foul fiend, who was cast into the abyss of hell for trying to meddle in [matters of] divine majesty, and who in the same way eagerly seeks to bring man to fall, and to cast him down with himself, as he did in Paradise in the beginning, tempting also the saints and even Christ with the same thing, when he set Him on the pinnacle of the Temple, etc. Against such in particular St. Paul here introduces these words [Rom. 11, 34. 35] to the inquisitive questions of wise reason: Why did God thus punish and reject the Jews while He permitted the condemned heathen to come to the Gospel? Again, Why does He govern on this wise, that wicked and evil men are exalted while the pious are allowed to undergo misfortune and be suppressed? Why does He call Judas to be an apostle and later on reject him while He accepts the murderer and malefactor? By them [his words, Rom. 11] Paul would order such to cease climbing up to the secret Majesty, and to adhere to the revelation which God has given us. For such searching and climbing is not only in vain, but also harmful. Though you search in all eternity, you will never attain anything, but only break your neck."

"But if you desire to proceed in the right way, you can do no better than busying yourself with His Word and works, in which He has revealed Himself and permits Himself to be heard and apprehended, to wit, how He sets before you His Son Christ upon the cross. That is the work of your redemption. There you can certainly apprehend God, and see that He does not wish to condemn you on account of your sins if you believe, but to give you eternal life, as Christ says: 'God so loved the world that He gave His only-begotten Son, that whosoever believeth in Him should not perish, but have everlasting life.' (John 3, 16.) In this Christ, says Paul, are hid all the treasures of wisdom and knowledge. (Col. 2, 3.) And that will be more than enough for you to learn, study, and consider. This lofty revelation of God will also make you marvel and will engender a desire and love for God. It is a work which in this life you will never finish studying; a work of which, as Peter says, even the angels cannot see enough, but which they contemplate unceasingly with joy and delight. (1 Pet. 1, 12.)"

"This I say that we may know how to instruct and direct those (if such we should meet with) who are being afflicted and tormented by such thoughts of the devil to tempt God, when he entices them to search the devious ways of God outside of revelation, and to grope about trying to fathom what God plans for them — whereby they are led into such doubt and despair that they know not

how they will survive. Such people must be reminded of these words [Rom. 11], and be rebuked with them (as St. Paul rebukes his Jews and wiseacres) for seeking to apprehend God with their wisdom and to school Him, as His advisers and masters, and for dealing with Him by themselves without means, and for giving Him so much that He must requite them again. For nothing will come of it; He has carefully built so high that you will not thus scale Him by your climbing. His wisdom, counsel, and riches are so great that you will never be able to fathom or to exhaust them. Therefore be glad that He permits you to know and receive these things somewhat by revelation." (E. 9, 15 sqq.; St. L. 12, 641 sqq.)

In a sermon on 2 Pet. 1, 10, delivered in 1523 and published in 1524, Luther said: "Here a limit [beyond which we may not go] has been set for us how to treat of predestination. Many frivolous spirits, who have not felt much of faith, tumble in, strike at the top, concerning themselves first of all with this matter, and seek to determine by means of their reason whether they are elected in order to be certain of their standing. From this you must desist; it is not the hilt of the matter. If you would be certain, you must attain to this goal by taking the way which Peter here proposes. Take another, and you have already gone astray; your own experience must teach you. If faith is well exercised and stressed, you will finally become sure of the matter, so that you will not fail." (E. 52, 224; St. L. 9, 1353.)

After a discussion at Wittenberg with a fanatic from Antwerp, in 1525, Luther wrote a letter of warning to the Christians of Antwerp, in which he speaks of God's will with respect to sin in an illuminating manner as follows: "Most of all he [the fanatic] fiercely contended that God's command was good, and that God did not desire sin, which is true without a doubt; and the fact that we also confessed this did not do us any good. But he would not admit that, although God does not desire sin, He nevertheless permits (*verhaengt*) it to happen, and such permission certainly does not come to pass without His will. For who compels Him to permit it? Aye, how could He permit it if it was not His will to permit it? Here he exalted his reason, and sought to comprehend how God could not desire sin, and still, by permitting sin, will it, imagining that he could exhaust the abyss of divine majesty: how these two wills may exist side by side. . . . Nor do I doubt that he will quote me to you as saying that God desires sin. To this I would herewith reply that he wrongs me, and as he is otherwise full of lies, so also he does not speak the truth in this matter. I say that God has forbidden sin, and does not desire it. This will has been revealed to us, and it is necessary for us to know it. But in what manner God permits or wills sin, this we are not to know; for He has not revealed it. St. Paul himself would not and could not know it, saying, Rom. 9, 20: 'O man, who art thou that repliest against God?' Therefore I beseech you, in case this spirit should trouble you much with the lofty question regarding the secret will of God, to depart from him and to speak thus: 'Is it too little that God instructs us in His public [proclaimed] will, which He has revealed to us? Why, then, do you gull us, seeking to lead us into that which we are forbidden to know, are unable to know, and which you do not know yourself? Let the manner in which that comes to pass be commended to God; it suffices us to know that He desires no sin. In what way, however, He permits or wills sin, this we shall leave unanswered (*sollen wir gehen lassen*). The servant is not to know his master's secrets, but what his master enjoins upon him; much less is a poor creature to explore and desire to know the secrets of the majesty of its God.' — Behold, my dear friends, here you may perceive that the devil always makes a practise of presenting unnecessary, vain, and impossible things in order thereby to tempt the frivolous to forsake the right path. Therefore take heed that you abide by that which is needful, and which God has commanded us to know, as the wise man says: 'Do not inquire for that which is too high for you, but always remain with that which God has commanded you.' We all have work enough to learn all our lifetime God's command and His Son Christ." (E. 53, 345; St. L. 10, 1531; Weimar 18, 549 f.)

## 247. Statements Made by Luther in 1528.

In a letter of comfort written July 20, 1528, Luther says: "A few days ago my dear brother Caspar Cruciger, Doctor of Divinity, informed me with grief that on his various visitations he learned from your friends that you are afflicted with abnormal and strange thoughts pertaining to God's predestination, and are completely confused by them; also, that you grow dull and distracted on account of them; and that finally it must be feared that you might commit suicide, — from which Almighty God may preserve you! . . . Your proposition and complaints are: God Almighty knows from eternity who are to be and who will be saved, be they dead, living, or still to live in days to come, — which is true, and shall and must be conceded; for He knows all things, and there is nothing hidden from Him, since He has counted and knows exactly the drops in the sea, the stars in the heavens, the roots, branches, twigs, leaves of all trees, also all the hair of men. From this you finally conclude that, do what you will, good or evil, God still knows whether you shall be saved or not (which is indeed true); yet, at the same time, you think more of damnation than of salvation and on that account you are faint-hearted, nor do you know how God is minded toward you; hence you grow dispirited and altogether doubtful."

"Against this I, as a servant of my dear Lord Jesus Christ, give you this advice and comfort, that you may know how God Almighty is disposed toward you, whether you are elected unto salvation or damnation. Although God Almighty knows all things, and all works and thoughts in all creatures must come to pass according to His will (*iuxta decretum voluntatis suae*), it is nevertheless His earnest will and purpose, aye, His command, decreed from eternity, to save all men and make them partakers of eternal joy, as is clearly stated Ezek. 18, 23, where He says: God does not desire the death of the wicked, but that the wicked turn and live. Now, if He desires to save and to have saved the sinners who live and move under the wide and high heaven, then you must not separate yourself from the grace of God by your foolish thoughts, inspired by the devil. For God's grace extends and stretches from east to west, from south to north, overshadowing all who turn, truly repent, and make themselves partakers of His mercy and desire help. For He is 'rich unto all that call upon Him', Rom. 10, 12. This, however, requires true and genuine faith, which expels such faint-heartedness and despair and is our righteousness, as it is written Rom. 3, 22: 'the righteousness of God through faith in Jesus Christ unto all and upon all.' Mark these words, *in omnes, super omnes* (unto all, upon all), whether you also belong to them, and are one of those who lie and grovel under the banner of the sinners." "Think also as constantly and earnestly of salvation as you [now] do of damnation, and comfort yourself with God's Word, which is true and everlasting, then such ill winds will cease and pass entirely."

"Thus we are to comfort our hearts and consciences, silence and resist the evil thoughts by and with the divine Scriptures. For one must not speculate about God's Word, but be still, drop reason and, holding the Word to be true, believe it, and not cast it to the winds, nor give the Evil Spirit so much power as to suffer ourselves to be overcome, and thus to sink and perish. For the Word, by which all things and creatures in all the wide world, no matter what they are called, have been created and made, and by which all that lives and moves is still richly preserved, is true and eternal; and it must be accounted and held to be greater and more important, mightier and more powerful than the fluttering, empty, and vain thoughts which the devil inspires in men. For the Word is true, but the thoughts of men are useless and vain. One must also think thus: God Almighty has not created, predestinated, and elected us to perdition, but to salvation, as Paul asserts, Eph. 1, 4; nor should we begin to dispute about God's predestination from the Law or reason, but from the grace of God and the Gospel, which is proclaimed to all men." "Hence these and similar thoughts about God's predestination must be judged and decided from the Word of God's grace and mercy. When this is done, there remains no room or occasion for a man thus to pester and torment himself, — which neither avails anything, even if he should draw the marrow out of his bones, leaving only skin and hair." (E. 54, 21 ff.)

## 248. Statements Made by Luther in 1531 and 1533.

In a letter of comfort, dated April 30, 1531, Luther refers to the fact that he, too, had passed through temptation concerning predestination. "For," says he, "I am well acquainted with this malady, having lain in this hospital sick unto eternal death. Now, in addition to my prayer I would gladly advise and comfort you, though writing is weak in such an affair. However, I shall not omit what I am able to do (perhaps God will bless it), and show you how God helped me out of this affliction, and by what art I still daily maintain myself against it. In the first place, you must be firmly assured in your heart that such thoughts are without doubt the inspiration and the fiery darts of the foul fiend. . . . Hence it is certain that they do not proceed from God, but from the devil, who therewith plagues a heart that man may become an enemy of God and despair,—all of which God has strictly forbidden in the First Commandment, bidding men to trust, love, and praise Him—whereby we live. Secondly: When such thoughts come to you, you must learn to ask yourself, 'Friend, in what commandment is it written that I must think or treat of this?' . . . Fourthly: The chief of all the commandments of God is that we picture before our eyes His dear Son, our Lord Jesus Christ. He is to be the daily and the chief mirror of our heart, in which we see how dear we are to God, and how much He has cared for us as a good God, so that He even gave His dear Son for us."

"Here, here, I say, and nowhere else, a man can learn the true art of predestination. Then it will come to pass that you believe on Christ. And if you believe, then you are called; if you are called, then you are also surely predestinated. Do not suffer this mirror and throne of grace to be plucked from the eyes of your heart. On the contrary, when such thoughts come and bite like fiery serpents, then under no circumstances look at the thoughts or the fiery serpents, but turn your eyes away from them and look upon the brazen serpent, i. e., Christ delivered for us. Then, by the grace of God, matters will mend." (St. L. 10, 1744 sq.; E. 54, 228.)

In Luther's *House Postil* of 1533 we read: "From the last passage: 'Many are called, but few are chosen,' wiseacres draw various false and ungodly conclusions. They argue: He whom God has elected is saved without means; but as for him who is not elected, may he do what he will, be as pious and believing as he will, it is nevertheless ordained that he must fall and cannot be saved; hence I will let matters take what course they will. If I am to be saved, it is accomplished without my assistance; if not, all I may do and undertake is nevertheless in vain. Now every one may readily see for himself what sort of wicked, secure people develop from such thoughts. However, in treating of the passage from the Prophet Micah on the day of Epiphany, we have sufficiently shown that one must guard against such thoughts as against

the devil, undertake another manner of studying and thinking of God's will, and let God in His majesty and with respect to election untouched [unsearched]; for there He is incomprehensible. Nor is it possible that a man should not be offended by such thoughts, and either fall into despair or become altogether wicked and reckless."

"But whoever would know God and His will aright must walk the right way. Then he will not be offended, but be made better. The right way, however, is the Lord Jesus Christ, as He says: 'No one cometh unto the Father but by Me.' Whoever knows the Father aright and would come unto Him must first come to Christ and learn to know Him, viz., as follows: Christ is God's Son, and is almighty, eternal God. What does the Son of God now do? He becomes man for our sakes, is made under the Law to redeem us from the Law, and was Himself crucified in order to pay for our sins. He rises again from the dead, in order by His resurrection to pave the way to eternal life for us, and to aid us against eternal death. He sits at the right hand of God in order to represent us, to give us the Holy Spirit, to govern and lead us by Him, and to protect His believers against all tribulations and insinuations of Satan. That means knowing Christ rightly."

"Now when this knowledge has been clearly and firmly established in your heart, then begin to ascend into heaven and make this conclusion: Since the Son of God has done this for the sake of men, how, then, must God's heart be disposed to us, seeing that His Son did it by the Father's will and command? Is it not true that your own reason will compel you to say: Since God has thus delivered His only-begotten Son for us, and has not spared Him for our sakes, He surely cannot harbor evil intentions against us? Evidently He does not desire our death, for He seeks and employs the very best means toward assisting us to obtain eternal life. In this manner one comes to God in the right way, as Christ Himself declares, John 3, 16: 'God so loved the world that He gave His only-begotten Son, that whosoever believeth in Him should not perish, but have everlasting life.' Now contrast these thoughts with those that grow out of the former opinion, and they will be found to be the thoughts of the foul fiend, which must offend a man, causing him either to despair, or to become reckless and ungodly, since he can expect nothing good from God."

"Some conceive other thoughts, explaining the words thus: 'Many are called,' i. e., God offers His grace to many, 'but few are chosen,' i. e., He imparts such grace to only a few; for only a few are saved. This is an altogether wicked explanation. For how is it possible for one who holds and believes nothing else of God not to be an enemy of God, whose will alone must be blamed for the fact that not all of us are saved? Contrast this opinion with the one that is formed when a man first learns to know the Lord Christ, and it will be found to be nothing but devilish blasphemy. Hence the sense of this passage, 'Many are called,' etc., is far different. For the preaching of the Gospel is general and public, so that whoever will may hear and accept it. Furthermore, God has it preached so generally and publicly that every one should hear, believe, and accept it, and be saved. But what happens? As the Gospel states: 'Few are chosen,' i. e., few conduct themselves toward the Gospel in such a manner that God has pleasure in them. For some do not hear and heed it; others hear it, but do not cling to it, being loath either to risk or suffer anything for it; still others hear it, but are more concerned about money and goods, or the pleasures of the world. This, however, is displeasing to God, who has no pleasure in such people. This Christ calls 'not to be chosen,' i. e., conducting oneself so that God has no pleasure in one. Those men are chosen of God and well-pleasing to Him who diligently hear the Gospel, believe in Christ, prove their faith by good fruits, and suffer on that account what they are called to suffer."

"This is the true sense, which can offend no one, but makes men better, so that they think: Very well, if I am to please God and be elected, I cannot afford to live so as to have an evil conscience, sin against God's commandments, and be unwilling to resist sin; but I must go to church, and pray God for His Holy Spirit; nor must I permit the Word to be taken out of my heart, but resist the devil and his suggestions, and pray for protection, patience, and help. This makes good Christians, whereas those who think that God begrudges salvation to any one either become reckless or secure, wicked people, who live like brutes, thinking: It has already been ordained whether I am to be saved or not; why, then, should I stint myself anything? To think thus is wrong; for you are commanded to hear God's Word and to believe Christ to be your Savior, who has paid for your sin. Remember this command and obey it. If you notice that you are lacking faith, or that your faith is weak, pray God to grant you His Holy Ghost, and do not doubt that Christ is your Savior, and that if you believe in Him, i. e., if you take comfort in Him, you shall by Him be saved. Dear Lord Jesus Christ, grant this unto us all! Amen." (E. 1, 204; St. L. 13, 199.)

## 249. Statements Made by Luther in 1538 and 1545.

In his remarks of 1538 on Matt. 11, 25. 26, Luther says: "Christ speaks especially against those who would be wise and judge in religious matters, because they have on their side the Law and human reason, which is overwise, exalting itself against the true religion both by teaching and by judging. Hence Christ here praises God as doing right when He conceals His secrets from the wise and prudent, because they want to be over and not under God. Not as though He hid it in fact or desired to hide it (for He commands it to be preached publicly under the entire heaven and in all lands), but that He has chosen that kind of preaching which the wise and prudent abhor by nature, and which is hidden from them through their own fault, since they do not want to have it — as is written Is. 6, 9: 'See ye indeed, but perceive not.' Lo, they see, i. e., they have the doctrine which is preached both plainly and publicly. Still they do not perceive, for they turn away from it and refuse to have it. Thus they hide the truth from themselves by their own blindness. And so, on the other hand, He reveals it to the babes; for the babes receive it when it is revealed to them. To them the truth is revealed since they wish and desire it." (W. 7, 133.)

In a letter giving comfort concerning predestination, dated August 8, 1545, Luther wrote: "My dear master and friend N. has informed me that you are at times in tribulation about God's eternal predestination, and requested me to write you this short letter on that matter. Now to be sure, this is a sore tribulation. But to overcome it one must know that we are forbidden to understand this or to speculate about it. For what God wants to conceal we should be glad not to know. This is the apple the eating of which brought death upon Adam and Eve and upon all their children, when they wanted to know what they were not to know. For as it is sin to commit murder, to steal, or to curse, so it is also sin to busy oneself searching such things. As an antidote to this God has given us His Son, Jesus Christ. Of Him we must daily think; in Him we must consider ourselves (uns in ihm spiegeln). Then predestination will appear lovely. For outside of Christ everything is only danger, death, and the devil; in Him, however, there is nothing but peace and joy. For if one forever torments himself with predestination, all one gains is anguish of soul. Hence flee and avoid such thoughts as the affliction of the serpent of Paradise, and, instead, look upon Christ. God preserve you!" (E. 56, 140; St. L. 10, 1748.)

## 250. Statements Made by Luther in His Commentary on Genesis.

Luther's caeterum censeo, that we are neither to deny nor to search the hidden God (who cannot be apprehended in His bare majesty — qui in nuda sua maiestate non potest apprehendi, E., Op. Lat. 2, 171), but to adhere to the revelation He has given us in the Gospel, is repeated again and again also in his Commentary on Genesis, which was begun in 1536 and completed in 1545. In the explanation of chap. 26, 9 we read, in part: "I gladly take occasion from this passage to discuss the question concerning doubt, concerning God and God's will. For I hear that everywhere among the nobles and magnates profane sayings are spread concerning predestination or divine prescience. For they say: 'If I am predestinated, I shall be saved, whether I have done good or evil. If I am not predestinated, I shall be damned, without any regard whatever to my works.' Against these ungodly sayings I would gladly argue at length if my ill health would permit. For if these sayings are true, as they believe them to be, then the incarnation of the Son of God, His suffering and resurrection, and whatever He did for the salvation of the world, is entirely abolished. What would the prophets and the entire Holy Scriptures profit us? what the Sacraments? Let us therefore abandon and crush all this," all these ungodly sayings.

Luther proceeds: "These thoughts must be opposed by the true and firm knowledge of Christ, even as I frequently admonish that above all it is useful and necessary that our knowledge of God be absolutely certain, and, being apprehended by firm assent of the mind, cleave in us, as otherwise our faith will be in vain. For if God does not stand by His promises, then our salvation is done for, while on the contrary this is to be our consolation, that, although we change, we may nevertheless flee to Him who is unchangeable. For this is what He affirms of Himself, Mal. 3, 6: 'I am the Lord, I change not,' and Rom. 11, 29: 'For the gifts and calling of God are without repentance.' Accordingly, in the book De Servo Arbitrio and elsewhere I have taught that we must distinguish when we treat of the knowledge of God or, rather, of His essence. For one must argue either concerning the hidden or the revealed God. Concerning God, in so far as He has not been revealed to us, there is no faith, no knowledge, no cognition whatever. Here one must apply the saying: What is above us does not concern us (Quae supra nos, nihil ad nos). For such thoughts as search for something higher, beyond or without the revelation of God, are altogether diabolical; and by them nothing else is achieved than that we plunge ourselves into perdition, because they are occupied with an unsearchable object, i. e., the unrevealed God. Indeed, rather let God keep His decrees and mysteries concealed from us; for there is no reason why we should labor so much that they be disclosed to us. Moses, too, asked God to show His face, or glory, to him. But the Lord answered, Ex. 33, 23: 'Thou shalt see My back parts; but My face shall not be seen. Posteriora mea tibi ostendam, faciem autem meam videre non poteris.' For this curiosity is original sin itself, by which we are impelled to seek for a way to God by natural speculation. But it is an enormous sin and a useless and vain endeavor. For Christ says, John 6, 65; 14, 6: 'No man cometh unto the Father but by Me.' Hence, when we approach the non-revealed God, there is no faith, no word, nor any knowledge, because He is an invisible God whom you will not make visible."

With special reference to his book De Servo Arbitrio Luther continues: "It was my desire to urge and set forth these things, because after my death many will quote my books and by them try to prove and confirm all manner of errors and follies of their own. Now, among others I have written that all things are absolute and necessary; but at the same time (and very often at other times) I added that we must look upon the revealed God, as we sing in the Psalm: 'Er heisst Jesus Christ, der Herr Zebaoth, und ist kein andrer Gott,' 'Jesus Christ it is, of Sabaoth Lord, and there's none other God.' But they will pass by all these passages, and pick out those only concerning the hidden God. You, therefore, who are now hearing me, remember that I have taught that we must not inquire concerning the predestination of the hidden God, but acquiesce in that which is revealed by the call and the ministry of the Word. For there you can be certain regarding your faith and salvation and say: I believe in the Son of God who said: 'He that believeth on the Son hath everlasting life,' John 3, 36. In Him therefore is no damnation or wrath, but the good will of God the Father. But these very things I have set forth also elsewhere in my books, and now I transmit them orally, too, viva voce; hence I am excused — ideo sum excusatus." (E., Op. Exeg. 6, 200. 292. 300; Conc. Trigl., 897 f.)

### 251. Luther Never Retracted His Doctrine of Grace.

It has frequently been asserted that Luther in his later years recalled his book De Servo Arbitrio, and retracted, changed, and essentially modified his original doctrine of grace, or, at least silently, abandoned it and relegated it to oblivion. Philippi says in his Glaubenslehre (4, 1, 37): "In the beginning of the Reformation [before 1525] the doctrine of predestination fell completely into the background. But when Erasmus, in his endeavors to restore Semi-Pelagianism, injected into the issue also the question of predestination, Luther, in his De Servo Arbitrio, with an overbold defiance, did not shrink from drawing also the inferences from his position. He, however, not only never afterwards repeated this doctrine, but in reality taught the very opposite in his unequivocal proclamation of the universality of divine grace, of the all-sufficiency of the merits of Christ, and of the universal operation of the means of grace; and he even opposed that doctrine [of De Servo Arbitrio] expressly as erroneous, and by his corrections took back his earlier utterances on that subject." Endorsing Philippi's view as "according well with the facts in the case," J. W. Richard, who, too, charges the early Luther with "absolute predestinarianism," remarks: "But this is certain: the older Luther became, the more did he drop his earlier predestinarianism into the background, and the more did he lay stress on the grace of God and on the means of grace, which offer salvation to all men (in omnes, super omnes) without partiality, and convey salvation to all who believe." (Conf. Hist., 336.)

Time and again similar assertions have been repeated, particularly by synergistic theologians. But they are not supported by the facts. Luther, as his books abundantly show, was never a preacher of predestinarianism (limited grace, limited redemption, etc.), but always a messenger of God's universal grace in Christ, offered in the means of grace to all poor and penitent sinners. In his public preaching and teaching predestination never predominated. Christ Crucified and His merits offered in the Gospel always stood in the foreground. In *De Servo Arbitrio* Luther truly says: "We, too, teach nothing else than Christ Crucified." (St. L. 18, 1723; E. v. a. 7, 160.) Luther's sermons and books preached and published before as well as after 1525 refute the idea that he ever made predestination, let alone predestinarianism, the center of his teaching and preaching. It is a fiction that only very gradually Luther became a preacher of universal grace and of the means of grace. In fact, he himself as well as his entire reformation were products of the preaching, not of predestinarianism, but of God's grace and pardon offered to all in absolution and in the means of grace. The bent of Luther's mind was not speculative, but truly evangelical and Scriptural. Nor is it probable that he would ever have entered upon the question of predestination to such an extent as he did in *De Servo Arbitrio*, if the provocation had not come from without. It was the rationalistic, Semi-Pelagian attack of Erasmus on the fundamental Christian truths concerning man's inability in spiritual matters and his salvation by grace alone, which, in Luther's opinion, called for just such an answer as he gave in *De Servo Arbitrio*. Wherever the occasion demanded it, Luther was ready to defend also the truth concerning God's majesty and supremacy, but he always was and remained a preacher of the universal mercy of God as revealed in Christ Crucified.

Nor is there any solid foundation whatever for the assertion that Luther later on retracted his book against Erasmus or abandoned its doctrine, — a fact at present generally admitted also by disinterested historians. (Frank 1, 129. 135. 125.) In his criticism of the *Book of Confutation*, dated March 7, 1559, Landgrave Philip of Hesse declared: "As to free will, we a long time ago have read the writings of Luther and Erasmus of Rotterdam as well as their respective replies; and, although in the beginning they were far apart, Luther some years later saw the disposition of the common people and gave a better explanation (*und sich besser erklaeret*); and we believe, if a synod were held and one would hear the other, they would come to a brotherly agreement in this article." (*C. R.* 9, 760.) But Flacius immediately declared that this assertion was false, as appeared from Luther's *Commentary on Genesis* and his letter to the Elector concerning the Regensburg Interim. (Preger 2, 82.) Schaff writes: "The Philippist [Christopher] Lasius first asserted, 1568, that Luther had recalled his book *De Servo Arbitrio;* but this was indignantly characterized by Flacius and Westphal as a wretched lie and an insult to the evangelical church. The fact is that Luther emphatically reaffirmed this book, in a letter to Capito [July 9], 1537, as one of his very best." (*Creeds* 1, 303.) In his letter to Capito, Luther says: "*Nullum enim agnosco meum iustum librum nisi forte 'De Servo Arbitrio' et 'Catechismum,'*" thus endorsing *De Servo*

*Arbitrio* in the same manner as his Catechism. (Enders 11, 247.) Before this Luther had said at his table: "Erasmus has written against me in his booklet *Hyperaspistes*, in which he endeavors to defend his book *On Free Will*, against which I wrote my book *On the Enslaved Will*, which as yet he has not refuted, and will never in eternity be able to refute. This I know for certain, and I defy and challenge the devil together with all his minions to refute it. For I am certain that it is the immutable truth of God." (St. L. 20, 1081.) Despite numerous endeavors, down to the present day, not a shred of convincing evidence has been produced showing that Luther ever wavered in this position, or changed his doctrine of grace.

Luther's extensive reference to *De Servo Arbitrio* in his *Commentary on Genesis*, from which we freely quoted above, has frequently been interpreted as a quasi-retraction. But according to the *Formula of Concord* these expositions of Luther's merely "repeat and explain" his former position. They certainly do not offer any corrections of his former fundamental views. Luther does not speak of any errors of his own, but of errors of others which they would endeavor to corroborate by quoting from his books — "*post meam mortem multi meos libros proferrent in medium et inde omnis generis errores et deliria sua confirmabunt.*" Moreover, he declares that he is innocent if some should misuse his statements concerning necessity and the hidden God, because he had expressly added that we must not search the hidden majesty of God, but look upon the revealed God to judge of His disposition toward us — "*addidi, quod aspiciendus sit Deus revelatus. . . . Ideo sum excusatus.*" (CONC. TRIGL., 898.) Luther's entire theological activity, before as well as after 1525, was an application of the principle stressed also in *De Servo Arbitrio*, viz., that we must neither deny nor investigate or be concerned about the hidden God, but study God as He has revealed Himself in the Gospel and firmly rely on His gracious promises in the means of grace.

### 252. Luther's Doctrine Approved by Formula of Concord.

Flacius, who himself did not deny the universality of grace, declared at the colloquy in Weimar, 1560, that, when taken in their context, Luther's statements in *De Servo Arbitrio* contained no inapt expressions (*nihil incommodi*). He added: "I do not want to be the reformer of Luther, but let us leave the judgment and discussion concerning this book to the Church of sound doctrine. *Nolo reformator esse Lutheri, sed iudicium et discussionem istius libri permittamus sanae ecclesiae.*" (Planck 4, 704; Frank 4, 255.) In Article II of the *Formula of Concord* the Church passed on Luther's book on the bondage of the will together with his declarations in his *Commentary on Genesis*. In referring to this matter, the *Formula* gives utterance to the following thoughts: 1. that in *De Servo Arbitrio* Luther "elucidated and supported this position [on free will, occupied also by the *Formula of Concord*] well and thoroughly, *egregie et solide"*; 2. that "afterwards he repeated and explained it in his glorious exposition of the Book of Genesis, especially of chapter 26"; 3. that in this exposition also "his meaning and understanding of some other peculiar disputations, introduced incidentally by Erasmus, as of absolute necessity, etc., have been secured by him in the best and most careful way against all misunderstanding and perversion"; 4. that the *Formula of Concord* "appeals and refers others" to these deliverances of Luther. (CONC. TRIGL. 896, 44.)

The *Formula of Concord*, therefore, endorsed Luther's *De Servo Arbitrio* without expressing any strictures or reservations whatever, and, particularly in Articles I, II, and XI, also embodied its essential thoughts, though not all of its phrases, statements, and arguments. The said articles contain a guarded reproduction and affirmation of Luther's doctrine of grace, according to which God alone is the cause of man's salvation, while man alone is the cause of his damnation. In particular they reaffirm Luther's teaching concerning man's depravity and the inability of his will to cooperate in conversion; the divine monergism in man's salvation; the universality of grace and of the efficaciousness of the means of grace; man's responsibility for the rejection of grace and for his damnation; God's unsearchable judgments and mysterious ways; the mystery why some are lost while others are saved, though all are equally guilty and equally loved by God; the solution of this problem in the light of glory, where it will be made apparent that there never were contradictory wills in God. In its doctrine of predestination as well as of free will, therefore, the *Formula of Concord* is not a compromise between synergism and monergism, but signifies a victory of Luther over the later Melanchthon.

### 253. Attitude of Apology of the Book of Concord.

The attitude of the *Formula of Concord* with respect to Luther's *De Servo Arbitrio* was shared by contemporary Lutheran theologians. They expressed objections neither to the book itself nor to its public endorsement by the *Formula of Concord*. In 1569 the theologians of Ducal Saxony publicly declared their adherence to the doctrine "set forth most luminously and skilfully (*summa luce et dexteritate traditum*)" in *De Servo Arbitrio*, the *Commentary on Genesis*, and other books of Luther. (Schluesselburg 5, 133.) That the authors of the *Formula of Concord* were fully conscious of their agreement with Luther's *De Servo Arbitrio* and his *Commentary on Genesis* appears also from the *Apology of the Book of Concord*, composed 1582 by Kirchner, Selneccer, and Chemnitz. Instead of charging Luther with errors, these theologians, who were prominent in the drafting of the *Formula of Concord*, endorse and defend his position, *viz.*, that we must neither deny nor investigate the hidden God, but search the

Gospel for an answer to the question how God is disposed toward us.

In this *Apology* the opening paragraph of the section defending Article XI of the *Formula of Concord* against the Neustadt theologians reads as follows: "In their antilog [antilogia-attack on Article XI of the *Formula of Concord*] regarding God's eternal election and predestination they merely endeavor to persuade the people that in this article the doctrine of the *Christian Book of Concord* [*Formula of Concord*] conflicts with the teaching of Doctor Luther and his book *De Servo Arbitrio*, while otherwise we ourselves are accustomed to appeal to Luther's writings. They accordingly charge the *Book of Concord* with condemning Luther, who in the book called *Servum Arbitrium* maintained the proposition that it was not superfluous, but highly necessary and useful for a Christian to know whether God's foreknowledge (*Versehung*) is certain or uncertain, changeable, etc. Now, praise the Lord, these words of Dr. Luther are not unknown to us, but, besides, we also well know how Dr. Luther in his last explanation of the 26th chapter of the First Book of Moses explains and guards these words of his." (Fol. 204 a.) After quoting the passages from Luther's Genesis, which we cited above (p. 223 f.), the *Apology* continues: "With this explanation of Luther we let the matter rest. If our opponents [the Neustadt theologians] wish to brood over it any further and in their investigating and disputing dive into the abyss or unfathomable depth of this mystery, they may do so for themselves [at their own risk] and suffer the consequences of such an attempt. As for us, we are content to adhere to God in so far as He has revealed Himself in His Word, and lead and direct Christianity thereto, reserving the rest for the life to come." (405 a.)

### 254. Agreement of Apology with Formula of Concord and Luther.

Doctrinally also, the *Apology of the Book of Concord* is in agreement with both Luther and the *Formula of Concord*. This appears from the following excerpts: "Nor does the *Christian Book of Concord* [*Formula of Concord*] deny that there is a reprobation in God, or that God rejects some; hence also it does not oppose Luther's statement when he writes in *De Servo Arbitrio* against Erasmus that it is the highest degree of faith to believe that God, who saves so few, is nevertheless most merciful; but it does not intend to ascribe to God the efficient cause of such reprobation or damnation as the doctrine of our opponents teaches; it rather holds that, when this question is discussed, all men should put their finger on their lips and first say with the Apostle Paul, Rom. 11, 20: '*Propter incredulitatem defracti sunt* — Because of unbelief they were broken off,' and Rom. 6, 23: 'For the wages of sin is death.' In the second place: When the question is asked why God the Lord does not through His Holy Spirit convert, and bestow faith upon, all men, etc. (which He is certainly able to do — *das er* doch wohl koennte), that we furthermore say with the Apostle [Rom. 11, 33]: *'Quam incomprehensibilia sunt iudicia eius et imper-vestigabiles viae eius* — How unsearchable are His judgments and His ways past finding out,' but not in any way ascribe to the Lord God Himself the willing and efficient cause of the reprobation and damnation of the impenitent."

"But when they, pressing us, declare, 'Since you admit the election of the elect, you must also admit the other thing, *viz.*, that in God Himself there is from eternity a cause of reprobation, also apart from sin,' etc., then we declare that we are not at all minded to make God the author [*Ursacher*] of reprobation (the cause of which properly lies not in God, but in sin), nor to ascribe to Him the efficient cause of the damnation of the ungodly, but intend to adhere to the word of the Prophet Hosea, chapter 13, where God Himself says: 'O Israel, thou hast destroyed thyself; but in Me is thy help.' Nor do we intend to search our dear God in so far as He is hidden and has not revealed Himself. For it is too high for us anyway, and we cannot comprehend it. And the more we occupy ourselves with this matter, the farther we depart from our dear God, and the more we doubt His gracious will toward us." (206.)

The *Apology* continues: "Likewise the *Book of Concord* [*Formula of Concord*] does not deny that God does not work in all men in the same manner. For at all times there are many whom He has not called through the public ministry. However, our opponents shall nevermore persuade us to infer with them that God is an efficient [*wirkliche*] *cause* of the reprobation of such people, and that He decreed absolutely from His mere counsel [*fuer sich aus blossem Rat*] to reject and cast them away eternally, even irrespective of their sin [*auch ausserhalb der Suende*]. For when we arrive at this abyss of the mysteries of God, it is sufficient to say with the Apostle, Rom. 11: 'His judgments are unsearchable'; and 1 Cor. 15, 57: 'But thanks be to God, which giveth us the victory through our Lord Jesus Christ.' Whatever goes beyond this our Savior Christ Himself will reveal to us in eternal life."

"Nor is there any cause for the cry that the *Book of Concord* did not distinguish between *malum culpae, i. e.*, sin which God neither wills, nor approves, nor works, and *malum poenae*, or the punishments which He wills and works. For there [in Article XI] the purpose was not to discuss all questions which occur and might be treated in this matter concerning God's eternal election, but merely to give a summary statement of the chief points of this article; and elsewhere this distinction is clearly explained by our theologians. Nor is there any one among us who approves of this blasphemy, that God wills sin, is pleased with it, and works it; moreover, we reject such speech as a blasphemy against God Himself. Besides, it is plainly stated, p. 318 [edition of 1580; CONC. TRIGL. 1065, 6], that God does not will evil acts and works, from which it is apparent

that the *Book* [*Formula*] *of Concord* does not at all teach that God is the author of *malum culpae* or of sins in the same manner as He executes and works the punishments of sins." (206 b.)

### 255. Apology on Universalis Gratia Seria et Efficax.

Emphasizing the universality and seriousness of God's grace and the possibility of conversion and salvation even for those who are finally damned, the *Apology* proceeds: "And why should we not also reject [the proposition]: 'The reprobate cannot be converted and saved,' since it is undoubtedly true that, with respect to those who are finally rejected and damned, we are unable to judge with certainty who they are, and there is hope for the conversion of all men as long as they are still alive? For the malefactor, Luke 23, was converted to God at his last end; concerning whom, according to the judgment of reason, everybody might have said that he was one of the reprobates. The passage John 12, 39: 'Therefore they could not believe,' etc., does not properly treat of eternal reprobation, nor does it say with so many words that no reprobate can be converted and saved. . . . It is therefore the meaning neither of the prophet [Is. 6, 9. 10] nor of the evangelist [John 12, 39] that God, irrespective of the sins and wickedness of such people, solely from His mere counsel, purpose, and will, ordains them to damnation so that they cannot be saved. Moreover, the meaning and correct understanding of this passage is, that in the obstinate and impenitent God punishes sin with sins, and day by day permits them to become more blind, but not that He has pleasure in their sin and wickedness, effectually works in them blindness and obstinacy, or that He, solely from His purpose and mere counsel, irrespective also of sins, has foreordained them to damnation so that they cannot convert themselves and be saved. In all such and similar passages, therefore, we shall and must be sedulously on our guard, lest we spin therefrom this blasphemy, that out of His free purpose and counsel, irrespective also of sin, God has decreed to reject eternally these or others. . . ." (207.)

With respect to the seriousness of universal grace we furthermore read: "They [the Neustadt theologians] say that in His Word God declares what He approves in, and earnestly demands of, all men, but not what He wishes to work and effect in all of them. For, they say, He reveals His secret counsel in no other way than by working in man, *viz.*, through conversion or final hardening of those who are either converted or hardened and damned. . . . With regard to this we give the following correct answer, *viz.*: that we are not minded in the least to carry on a dispute or discussion with our opponents concerning God and His secret counsel, purpose, or will in so far as He has not in His Word revealed Himself and His counsel. The reason is the one quoted above from the words of Luther himself, *viz.*, that concerning God, so far as He has not been revealed [to us], or has not made Himself known in His Word, there is neither faith nor knowledge, and one cannot know anything of Him, etc., which also in itself is true. Why, then, should we, together with our opponents, dive into the abyss of the incomprehensible judgments of God and presumptuously assert with them that from His mere counsel, purpose, and will, irrespective also of sin, God has ordained some to damnation who cannot be converted, moreover, whom He, according to His secret purpose, does not want to be converted, despite the fact that through the office of the ministry He declares Himself friendly towards them and offers them His grace and mercy? My dear friend, where is it written in the Word of God that it is not the will of God that all should be saved, but that, irrespective of their sin, He has ordained some to damnation only from His mere counsel, purpose, and will, so that they cannot be saved? Never in all eternity, try as they may, will they prove this proposition from God's revealed Word. For nowhere do the Holy Scriptures speak thus. Yet from sheer fool-hardiness they dare employ, contrary to Scripture, such blasphemous doctrine and speech, and spread it in all Christendom." (108 b.)

### 256. Apology on God's Mysterious Judgments and Ways.

Concerning the mysterious judgments and ways of God the *Apology* says: "At the same time we do not deny that God does not work alike in all men, enlightening all, — for neither does He give His Word to all, — and that nevertheless He is and remains both just and merciful, and that nobody can justly accuse Him of any unfaithfulness, envy, or tyranny, although He does not, as said, give His Word to all and enlighten them. But we add that, when arriving at this mystery, one should put his finger on his lips and not dispute or brood over it [*gruebeln* — from the facts conceded infer doctrines subversive of God's universal serious grace], but say with the apostle: 'How unsearchable are His judgments, and His ways past finding out!' Much less should one rashly say, as our opponents do, that of His free will, and irrespective of sin, God has ordained that some should be damned. For as to what God holds and has decreed in His secret, hidden counsel, nothing certain can be said. Nor should one discuss this deeply hidden mystery, but reserve it for yonder life, and meanwhile adhere to the revealed Word of God by which we are called to repentance, and by which salvation is faithfully offered us. And this Word, or revealed will, of God concerning the giving rest to all those that labor and are heavy laden, is certain, infallible, unwavering, and not at all opposed to the secret counsel of God, with which alone our opponents are occupied. Accordingly, nothing that conflicts with the will revealed in the Word of God should be inferred from it, even as God Himself in His Word has not directed us to it. Because of the fact, therefore, that not all accept this call, we must not declare that from His free purpose and will, without regard to sin, God, in His secret counsel, has ordained those who do not repent to damnation, so that they cannot be converted and saved (for this has not been revealed to us in the Word), but adhere to this, that God's judgments in these cases are unsearchable and incomprehensible."

"It is impossible that the doctrine of the opponents concerning this article should not produce in the hearers either despair or Epicurean security, when in this doctrine it is taught that God, from His mere counsel and purpose and irrespective of sin, has ordained some to damnation so that they cannot be converted. For as soon as a heart hears this, it cannot but despair of its salvation, or fall into these Epicurean thoughts: If you are among the reprobate whom, from His free purpose and without regard to sin, God has ordained to damnation, then you cannot be saved, do what you will. But if you are among those who shall be saved, then you cannot fail; do what you will, you must nevertheless be saved, etc. We do not in the least intend to join our opponents in giving occasion for such things. God also shall protect us from it." (209.)

Again: "They [the opponents] also say that we stress the universal promises of grace, but fail to add that these belong and pertain to believers. But herein they wrong us. For we urge both, *viz.*, that the promises of grace are universal, and that, nevertheless, only believers, who labor and are heavy laden, Matt. 11, become partakers of them. But their [our opponents'] object is to have us join them in saying that some are ordained to damnation from the free purpose of God, also without regard to sin, whom He does not want to be saved, even though He calls them through the Word and offers His grace and salvation to them, — which, however, we shall never do. For our heart is filled with horror against such a Stoic and Manichean doctrine." (209 b.)

# XXII. Article XII of the Formula of Concord: Of Other Heretics and Sects.

### 257. Purpose of Article XII.

The purpose of the first eleven articles of the *Formula of Concord* was not only to establish peace within the Lutheran Church and to ward off future controversies, but also to meet the ridicule and obloquy of the Papists, and to brand before the whole world as slander, pure and simple, their assertions that the Lutherans were hopelessly disagreed and had abandoned the *Augsburg Confession*, and that the Reformation was bound to end in utter confusion and dissolution. The *Formula of Concord* was to leave no doubt regarding the fact that the Lutheran Church offers a united front in every direction: against the

Romanists, the Calvinists, the errorists that had arisen in their own midst, and self-evidently also against the sects and fanatics, old and modern, with whom the Romanists slanderously identified them.

Summarizing the errors which Lutherans repudiate, the *Formula of Concord* declares: "First, we reject and condemn all heresies and errors which were rejected and condemned in the primitive, ancient, orthodox Church, upon the true, firm ground of the holy divine Scriptures. Secondly, we reject and condemn all sects and heresies which are rejected in the writings, just mentioned, of the comprehensive summary of the confession of our churches [the Lutheran symbols, preceding the *Formula of Concord*]. Thirdly, we reject also all those errors which caused dissension within the Lutheran Church, and which are dealt with and refuted in the first eleven articles of the *Formula of Concord*." (857, 17 ff.) Among the errors rejected in the *Augsburg Confession* and the subsequent Lutheran symbols were those also of the Anabaptists, Antitrinitarians, and others. (CONC. TRIGL. 42, 6; 44, 4; 46, 3; 48, 7; 50, 3. 4; 138, 66; 244, 52; 310, 13; 356, 43; 436, 49; 744, 55; 746, 58.) And this is the class of errorists which Article XII of the *Formula of Concord* makes it a special point to characterize summarily and reject by name. Before this the *Book of Confutation*, composed 1559 by the theologians of Duke John Frederick, had enumerated and rejected the doctrines of such errorists as Servetus, Schwenckfeld, and the Anabaptists.

From the very beginning of the Reformation, and especially at Augsburg, 1530, Eck and other Romanists had either identified the Lutherans with the Anabaptists and other sects, or had, at least, held them responsible for their origin and growth. Both charges are denied by the *Formula of Concord*. For here we read: "However, lest there be silently ascribed to us the condemned errors of the above enumerated factions and sects (which, as is the nature of such spirits, for the most part, secretly stole in at localities, and especially at a time when no place or room was given to the pure word of the holy Gospel, but all its sincere teachers and confessors were persecuted, and the deep darkness of the Papacy still prevailed and poor simple men who could not help but feel the manifest idolatry and false faith of the Papacy, in their simplicity, alas! embraced whatever was called Gospel, and was not papistic), we could not forbear testifying also against them publicly, before all Christendom, that we have neither part nor fellowship with their errors, be they many or few, but reject and condemn them, one and all, as wrong and heretical, and contrary to the Scriptures of the prophets and apostles, and to our Christian *Augsburg Confession*, well grounded in God's Word." (1097, 7 f.)

## 258. The Anabaptists.

The Anabaptistic movement originated in Zurich. Their leaders were Conrad Grebel, Felix Manz, and the monk George of Chur

(also called *Blaurock*, Bluecoat), who was the first to introduce anabaptism. In rapid succession Anabaptistic congregations sprang up in Swabia, Tyrol, Austria, Moravia, etc. Because of their attitude toward the civil government the Anabaptists were regarded as rebels and treated accordingly. As early as January, 1527, some of them were executed in Zurich. Persecution increased after the council held by Anabaptists in the autumn of 1527 at Augsburg, which then harbored a congregation of more than 1,100 "Apostolic Brethren," as the Anabaptists there called themselves. In Germany the imperial mandate of September 23, 1529, authorized the governments to punish Anabaptists, men and women of every age, by fire or sword "without previous inquisition by spiritual judges." They suffered most in Catholic territories. By 1531 about 1,000 (according to Sebastian Franck 2,000) had been executed in Tyrol and Goerz.

The most prominent of the early Anabaptistic leaders and protagonists were Hubmaier, Denk, Dachser, and Hans Hutt. Besides these we mention: Ludwig Haetzer, published a translation of the prophets from the Hebrew, 1527, for which he was praised by Luther, was executed as adulterer February 4, 1529, at Constance; Eitelhans Langenmantel, a former soldier and son of the Augsburg burgomaster, expelled from the city October 14, 1527, impassionate in his writings against the "old and new Papists," *i. e.*, Luther and others who adhered to the real presence of Christ in the Lord's Supper, decapitated May 12, 1528, at Weissenburg; Christian Entfelder, 1527 leader of the Brethren at Eisenschuetz, Moravia, and later on counselor of Duke Albrecht of Prussia; Hans Schlaffer, a former priest, active as Anabaptistic preacher and author, executed 1528; Joerg Haug, pastor in Bibra; Wolfgang Vogel, pastor near Nuernberg, executed 1527; Siegmund Salminger, imprisoned 1527 in Augsburg; Leonard Schiemer, former Franciscan, bishop of the Brethren in Austria, an Antitrinitarian, executed 1528; Ulrich Hugwald, professor in Basel; Melchior Rinck, pastor in Hesse; Pilgram Marbeck; Jacob Buenderlin; Jacob Kautz, preacher and author in Worms; Clemens Ziegler; Peter Riedemann, an Anabaptistic author and preacher, who was frequently imprisoned and died 1556; Melchior Hofmann, an Anabaptistic lay-preacher and prolific author, who died in prison at Strassburg, 1543. (Tschackert, 148 ff.; Schlottenloher, *Philipp Ulhart, ein Augsburger Winkeldrucker und Helfershelfer der "Schwaermer" und "Wiedertaeufer,"* 1523—1529, p. 59 ff.)

The various errors of the Anabaptists are enumerated in the Twelfth Article of the *Formula of Concord.* The Epitome remarks: "The Anabaptists are divided among themselves into many factions, as one contends for more, another for less errors; however, they all in common propound such doctrine as is to be tolerated or allowed neither in the church, nor in the commonwealth and secular government, nor in domestic life." (839, 2.)

Urbanus Regius said in his book *Against the New Baptistic Order:* "Not all [of the Anabaptists] know of all of these errors [enumerated in his book]; it is therefore not our intention to do an injustice to any one; we mean such public deceivers in the Baptistic Order as John Denk and Balthasar Friedberger," Hubmaier. (Schlottenloher, 80.)

While some of the Anabaptists, as Hubmaier, were more conservative, others (Denk, Schiemer) went so far as to deny even the doctrine of the Trinity. They all were agreed, however, in their opposition to infant baptism, and to the Lutheran doctrines of justification, of the means of grace, of the Sacraments, etc. What their preachers stressed was not faith in the atonement made by Christ, but medieval mysticism, sensation-faith (*Gefuehlsglaube*), and the law of love as exemplified by Christ. Tschackert quotes from one of their sermons: "Whoever follows the voice which constantly speaks in his heart always finds in himself the true testimony to sin no more, and an admonition to resist the evil." (153.) In his introduction to a publication of hymns of Breuning, Salminger said: "Whoever speaks in truth to what his own heart testifies will be received by God." Schlottenloher remarks: "It was medieval mysticism from which they [the Anabaptists] derived their consuming desire for the complete union of the soul with God and the Spirit." (83.)

### 259. Balthasar Hubmaier.

Hubmaier (Hubmoer, Friedberger, Pacimontanus) was born at Friedberg, near Augsburg, and studied under Eck. In 1512 he became Doctor and professor of theology at Ingolstadt; 1516 preacher in Regensburg; 1522 pastor in Waldshut on the Rhine. Before he came to Waldshut, he had read the books of Luther. He joined Zwingli in his opposition to Romanism. In January, 1525, however, he wrote to Oecolampadius that now "he proclaimed publicly what before he had kept to himself," referring in particular to his views on infant baptism. On Easter Day of the same year he was rebaptized together with 60 other persons, after which he continued to baptize more than 300. In July of 1525 he published his book *Concerning Christian Baptism of Believers*, which was directed against Zwingli, whose name, however, was not mentioned. At Zurich, whither he had fled from Waldshut after the defeat of the peasants in their rebellion of 1525, he was compelled to hold a public disputation with Zwingli on infant baptism. This led to his imprisonment, from which he was released only after a public recantation, 1526. He escaped to Nicolsburg, Moravia, where, under the protection of a powerful nobleman, he developed a feverish activity and rebaptized about 12,000 persons. When the persecutions of the Anabaptists began, Hubmaier was arrested, and after sulphur and powder had been well rubbed into his long beard, he was burned at the stake, in Vienna, March 10, 1528. Three days after,

his wife, with a stone about her neck, was thrust from the bridge into the Danube.

Hubmaier denounced infant baptism as "an abominable idolatry." He taught: Children are incapable of making the public confession required by Baptism; there is no Scriptural reason for infant baptism; it robs us of the true baptism, since people believe that children are baptized while in reality they are nothing less than baptized. He says: "Since the alleged infant baptism is no baptism, those who now receive water-baptism according to the institution of Christ cannot be charged with anabaptism."

Concerning the Lord's Supper, Hubmaier taught: "Here it is apparent that the bread is not the body of Christ, but only a reminder of it. Likewise the wine is not the blood of Christ, but also a mere memorial that He has shed and given His blood to wash all believers from their sins." "In the Lord's Supper the body and blood of Christ are received spiritually and by faith only." In the Supper of Christ "bread is bread and wine is wine, and not Christ. For He has ascended to heaven and sits at the right hand of God, His Father."

Hubmaier did not regard the Word as a means of grace nor Baptism and the Lord's Supper as gracious acts of God, but as mere works of man. "In believers," he says, "God works both to will and to do, by the inward anointing of His Holy Spirit." Concerning church discipline he taught: Where the Christian ban is not established and used according to the command of Christ, there sin, shame, and vice control everything. A person who is expelled must be denied all communion until he repents. In connection with his deliverances on the ban, Hubmaier, after the fashion of the Papists, made the Gospel of Christian liberty as preached by Luther responsible for the carnal way in which many abused it. The socialistic trend of Anabaptism, however, was not developed by Hubmaier. (Tschackert 132. 179. 234.)

### 260. Dachser and Hutt.

Jacob Dachser was one of the most zealous members and leaders of the large Anabaptistic congregation in Augsburg, where he was also imprisoned, 1527. He, not Langenmantel, is the author of the "*Offenbarung von den wahrhaftigen Wiedertaeufern. Revelation of the True Anabaptists*," secretly published by the Anabaptistic printer Philip Ulhart in Augsburg and accepted as a sort of confession by the council held by the Anabaptists in the fall of 1527 at Augsburg. The book of Urban Regius: "*Wider den neuen Tauforden notwendige Warnung an alle Christenglaeubigen* — Against the new Baptistic Order, a Necessary Warning to All Christians," was directed against Dachser's *Revelation*. In 1529 Dachser published his *Form and Order of Spiritual Songs*, the first hymn-book of the Anabaptists, containing hymns of Luther, Speratus, Muenzer, Hutt, Pollio, and Dachser.

In his *Revelation* Dachser said: "The entire world is against each other; we don't know any more where the truth is. While all are convinced that the Pope has erred and deceived us, the new preachers, by reviling and maligning each other, betray that they, too, are not sent by God." "In their pulpits the false teachers [Lutherans, etc.] themselves confess that the longer they preach, the less good is done. But since they do not forsake a place where they see no fruits of their doctrine, they thereby reveal that they are not sent by God." "God draws us to Himself through the power which is in us, and warns us against wickedness and through the Teacher Christ, who in His Word has taught us the will of God." "Christ sent His disciples to preach the Gospel to all creatures and to baptize such as believe. And such as obey this command are called 'Anabaptists'!" "By our evil will original purity has been defiled; from this uncleanness we must purge our heart. Who does not find this uncleanness in himself, neither without nor within, is a true child of God, obedient to the Word of God. Who, in accordance with the command of Christ, preaches and baptizes such as believe, is not an Anabaptist, but a co-baptist [*Mittaeufer*] of Christ and the Apostles." "All such as preach, teach, and baptize otherwise than Christ commanded, are the real Anabaptists [opponents of Baptism], acting contrary to the Son of God, by first baptizing, instead of first teaching and awaiting faith, as Christ commanded." "We need but strive with Christ to do the will of the Father, then we receive from God through the Holy Ghost the power to fulfil the divine command." (Schlottenloher, 72 ff.)

Hans Hutt (Hut), a restless bookbinder in Franconia, attended the Anabaptistic council in Augsburg, where he was opposed by Regius and incarcerated. He died 1527 in an attempt to escape from prison. As a punishment his body was burned. Hutt must not be confounded with Jacob Huter or Hueter, an Anabaptist in Tyrol. The followers of Hans Hutt in the city of Steyr developed the socialistic tendencies of Anabaptism. They taught: Private ownership is sinful; all things are to be held in common; Judgment Day is imminent; then the Anabaptists will reign with Christ on earth. Some also taught that finally the devil and all the damned would be saved; others held that there is neither a devil nor a hell, because Christ had destroyed them. (Tschackert 134 ff. 141. 153.) Article XVII of the *Augsburg Confession* condemns "the Anabaptists, who think that there will be an end to the punishments of condemned men and devils . . .; also others, who are now spreading certain Jewish opinions, that before the resurrection of the dead the godly shall take possession of the kingdom of the world, the ungodly being everywhere suppressed." (CONC. TRIGL., 51.)

### 261. John Denk.

Denk, who was called the "Archbaptist," the "Bishop," "Pope," and "Apollo" of the Anabaptists, was born in Bavaria and trained

in Basel. In 1523 he became Rector of St. Sebald in Nuernberg, where he was opposed by Osiander. Banished in the following year, he escaped to St. Gallen. Expelled again, he fled to Augsburg. Here he was rebaptized by immersion and became an active member of the Anabaptistic "Apostolic Brethren," who at that time numbered about 1,100 persons. Denk was the leader of the council held by the Anabaptists in 1527 in Augsburg. Expelled from the city, Denk died during his flight, 1527, at Basel. His "Retraction, *Widerruf*" (a title probably chosen by the printer), published 1527 after his death, does not contain a retraction, but a summary of his teaching. (Schlottenloher, 84.) The mystic mind of Denk runs a good deal in the channels of the author of the "German Theology, *Deutsche Theologie*," and of his pantheistic contemporary, Sebastian Franck.

Denk taught: God is one, and the source of unity. To return from all divisions to this unity must be our constant aim. The only way is entire surrender to God and submission in tranquillity. He says: "Nothing is necessary for this salvation [reunion with God] but to obey Him who is in us, and to be tranquil and wait for Him in the true real Sabbath and tranquillity, losing ourselves and all that is ours, so that God may both work and suffer in us. He who is in us is ready every hour and moment to follow, if we are but willing. His hour is always, but ours is not. He calls and stretches forth His arms the entire day, always ready; nobody answers Him, nobody admits Him or suffers Him to enter. Do but seek the Lord, then you will find Him; yea, He is already seeking you; only suffer yourselves to be found. Indeed, He has already found you, and even now is knocking. Do but open unto Him and let Him in. Apprehend and know the Lord, even as you are apprehended and known of Him."

Denk held that the source of religious and moral knowledge is not the Scriptures, but the voice of God in the heart of man, or Christ Himself, who speaks and writes the divine Law into the hearts of those who are His. [Before Denk, Thomas Muenzer had said: "Was Bibel! Bibel, Bubel, Babel!"] Whoever has this divine Law in his heart lacks nothing that is needed to fulfil the will of God. According to Denk a man may be saved without the preaching of the Word, without the Scriptures, and without any knowledge of the historical Christ and His work. Nor can the Scriptures be understood without heeding the revelation of God in our own bosom. The Scriptures must indeed be regarded as higher than "all human treasures, but not as high as God's Word" [in our own bosom]. Baptism is a mere outward sign that one has joined the number of believers; hence it can be administered to such only as are conscious of their faith. Ceremonies in themselves are not sin, says Denk; "but whoever imagines to obtain grace through them, either by Baptism or by the Breaking of Bread, is given to superstition." (Tschackert, 143; Meusel, *Handl.* 2, 142.)

## 262. The Schwenckfeldians.

Caspar Schwenckfeldt, of Ossig in Liegnitz, a descendent of a noble family in Silesia, was born 1490 and studied in Cologne. In 1524 he helped to introduce the Reformation in Liegnitz. He was twice in Wittenberg; 1522, when he met Carlstadt and Thomas Muenzer, and 1525, when he visited Luther. He endeavored to interest Luther in the formation of conventicles, and particularly in his mystical theory concerning the Lord's Supper, which he considered the correct middle ground on which Lutherans and Zwinglians might compromise. But Luther had no confidence in the enthusiast, whom he characterized as a "mad fool," "possessed by the devil." He said: "In Silesia Schwenckfeldt has kindled a fire which as yet has not been quenched and will burn on him eternally."

Because of the troubles and dissensions created in Liegnitz, Schwenckfeldt, in 1529, was compelled to leave. Having removed to Strassburg, he was zealous in propagating his enthusiasm in Southern Germany by establishing conventicles of "Lovers of the Glory of Christ," as the adherents of Schwenckfeldt called themselves. At a colloquy in Tuebingen, 1535, he promised not to disquiet the Church. In 1539 he published his *Summary of Several Arguments that Christ according to His Humanity Is To-day No Creature, but Entirely Our God and Lord.* He called it the doctrine of the "Deification of the Flesh of Christ." When this teaching was rejected as Eutychianism, Schwenckfeldt published his *Large Confession,* 1540. At the convention of Smalcald, also 1540, his views were condemned, and his books prohibited and burned. Compelled to leave Strassburg, he spent the remainder of his life in Augsburg, in Speier, and in Ulm (where he died, December 10, 1561). Schwenckfeldt exchanged controversial writings with many contemporary theologians, whom he kept in constant excitement. In Liegnitz he was supported by the ministers Valentin Krautwald, Fabian Eckel, Sigismund Werner, and Valerius Rosenheyn. His adherents were called "Neutrals," because they declined to affiliate with any of the existing churches.

## 263. Schwenckfeldt's Doctrine.

In 1526 Schwenckfeldt wrote to Paul Speratus: Since by the preaching of the Gospel as set forth by Luther so few people amended their lives, the thought had occurred to him that "something must still be lacking, whatever that may be." Endeavoring to supply this defect, Schwenckfeldt taught: Grace cannot be imparted by any creature, bodily word, writing, or sacrament, but only by the omnipotent, eternal Word proceeding from the mouth of God. Whatever is external is a mere symbol and image of God, able neither to bring God into the soul nor to produce faith or an inward experience of divine life. "Mark well," says he, "God is not in need of external things and means for His internal grace and spiritual action. For even Christ, according to the flesh, was a hindrance to

grace and [the Spirit] of God, and had to be translated into the heavenly mode of being that the grace of the Holy Spirit might come to us. . . . Whoever endeavors to come from without and through external means into the inner [the heart] does not understand the course of grace. God works without all means and pictures. . . . Man must forget and drop everything, and be free and tranquil for the inbreathing [*Einsprechen*, inspiration], and be drawn away from all creatures, giving himself up to God altogether."

Schwenckfeldt continues: The Holy Spirit enters the quiet soul only through the eternal Word, which "proceeds from the mouth of God without means and not at all through Scripture, external Word, Sacrament, or any creature in heaven or on earth. God wants to have this honor reserved solely to Himself; through Himself [without any means] He wants to pardon man, teach him, impart the Holy Spirit to him, and save him. He does not want to grant His grace, and effect illumination and salvation through any creature; for even the flesh of Christ was not a sufficient instrument for this purpose before He was glorified, translated into the heavenly places, and removed from our eyes." "Scripture is for the external man; the Holy Spirit teaches everything to the elect inwardly and is not in need of Scripture to give faith to them and to save them." Schwenckfeldt, who employed the term "revelation" for this immediate operation of God, was inconsistent in not rejecting Scripture, preaching, etc., altogether. But when admitting these, he adds that he distinguishes "God's own inner work from the external service."

Self-evidently, these views concerning the means of grace had a corrupting influence also on other doctrines. Saving faith, according to Schwenckfeldt, is not trust in God's promise of pardon for Christ's sake, but an immediate mystical relation of the soul to God. Justification, says he, "is not only forgiveness and non-imputation of sin, but also renewal of the heart." "We must seek our justification and righteousness not in Christ according to His first state [of humiliation], in a manner historical," but according to His state of glorification, in which He governs the Church. In order to enhance the "glory of Christ" and have it shine and radiate in a new light, Schwenckfeldt taught the "deification of the flesh of Christ," thus corrupting the doctrine of the exaltation and of the person of Christ in the direction of Monophysitism. And the more his views were opposed, the more he was enamored of, and engrossed by, them, calling himself the "confessor and lover of the glory of Christ."

Concerning the Lord's Supper, Schwenckfeldt taught that the deified humanity of Christ is really imparted and appropriated, not indeed through bread and wine, but immediately (without the intervention of any medium), internally, spiritually. The words of institution mean: My body, which is given for you, is what bread is, a food, *i. e.*, a food for souls; and the new testament in My blood is a chalice, *i. e.*, a drink for the elect to drink in the kingdom of God. Baptism, says Schwenckfeldt, is the "baptizing of the heavenly High Priest Jesus Christ, which occurs in the believing soul by the Holy Ghost and by fire. Infant baptism is a human ordinance, not merely useless, but detrimental to the baptism of Christ." (Tschackert, 159 ff.)

### 264. The Antitrinitarians.

The first article of the *Augsburg Confession* makes a special point of rejecting not only the ancient, but also the "modern Samosatenes," *i. e.*, the Antitrinitarians, who in the beginning of the Reformation began their activity in Italy, Spain, Switzerland, and Germany. Most of these "modern Arians and Antitrinitarians," as they are called in the Twelfth Article of the *Formula of Concord*, came from the skeptical circles of Humanists in Italy. Concerning these rationalists and Epicureans the *Apology* remarks: "Many [in Italy and elsewhere] even publicly ridicule all religions, or, if they approve anything, they approve such things only as are in harmony with human reason, and regard the rest as fabulous and like the tragedies of the poets." (CONC. TRIGL. 235, 28; *C. R.* 9, 763.) Pope Leo X was generally regarded as being one of those who spoke of the profitable "fables concerning Christ."

According to a letter of warning to the Christians in Antwerp, 1525, a fanatic (*Rumpelgeist*) there taught: "Every man has the Holy Spirit. The Holy Spirit is our reason and understanding (*ingenium et ratio naturalis*). Every man believes. There is neither hell nor damnation. Every one will obtain eternal life. Nature teaches that I should do unto my neighbor as I would have him do unto me — to desire which is faith. The Law is not violated by evil lust as long as I do not consent to lust. Who has not the Holy Ghost has no sin, for he has no reason." (E. 53, 344; St. L. 21 a, 730; Enders 5, 147.)

In his report on the Marburg Colloquy, October 5, 1529, Melanchthon remarks: "We have heard that some of them [the Strassburgers] speak of the Deity as the Jews do, as though Christ were not God by nature. (*C. R.* 1, 1099. At Marburg, Zwingli remarked that some had spoken incorrectly concerning the Trinity, and that Haetzer had written a book against the divinity of Christ, which he, Zwingli, had not permitted to be published. (1103.)

In a letter of Luther to Bugenhagen, 1532, we read: "Your undertaking [of publishing a writing of Athanasius concerning the Trinity] is Christian and wholesome in this our most corrupt time, in which all articles of faith in general are attacked by the servants of Satan, and the one concerning the Trinity is in particular beginning to be derided confidently by some skeptics and Epicureans. These are ably assisted not only by those Italian grammarians [Humanists] and orators, which they flatter themselves to be, but also by some Italico-German vipers and others, or, as you are accustomed to call them, viper-

aspides, who sow their seed here and there in their discourses and writings, and, as Paul says [2 Tim. 2, 17], eat as doth a canker (*gar sehr um sich fressen*) and promote godlessness, about which they, when among themselves, laugh so complacently and are so happy that one can hardly believe it." (St. L. 14, 326; Enders 9, 252.)

Some Antitrinitarians who affiliated with the Anabaptists have already been referred to. Denk, Haetzer, and others rejected the Apostles' Creed because of their opposition to the doctrine of the Trinity. Haetzer, as stated, wrote a book against the deity of Christ in which he denied the tripersonality of God and the preexistence of the Logos, and blasphemously designated the belief in the deity of Christ as "superstition" and the trust in His satisfaction as "drinking on the score of Christ (*ein Zechen auf die Kreide Christi*)." According to Denk, Christ is merely an example showing us how to redeem ourselves, which we are all able to do because there is still within us a seed of the divine Word and light. (Tschackert, 143, 461.) It was of Denk that Capito wrote, 1526: "At Nuernberg the schoolteacher at St. Sebald denied that the Holy Ghost and the Son are equal to the Father, and for this reason he was expelled." (Plitt, *Augustana* 1, 153.)

At Strassburg the Anabaptists were publicly charged, in 1526, with denying the Trinity; in 1529, with denying the deity of Christ. In 1527 Urban Regius spoke of the Anabaptists in Augsburg as maintaining that Christ was merely a teacher of a Christian life. In the same year Althamer of Nuernberg published his book *Against the New Jews and Arians under the Christian Name Who Deny the Deity of Christ*. In 1529 Osiander wrote concerning Anabaptists in Nuernberg: "It is well known, and may be proved by their own writings, that they deny and contradict the sublime article of our faith concerning the Holy Trinity, from which it follows immediately that they also deny the deity of Christ." "Christ is not the natural, true Son of God," such was also the accusation made by Justus Menius in his book concerning the *Doctrines and Secrets of the Anabaptists*. In his *Sermons on the Life of Luther*, Mathesius said: "Now the Anabaptists speak most contemptuously of the deity of Jesus Christ. . . . This was their chief article that they despised the written Word, the Holy Bible, and believed nothing or very little of Jesus Christ, the eternal Son of God."

### 265. Franck, Campanus, Ochino, Servetus, Blandrata, etc.

Sebastian Franck and John Campanus must also be numbered among the Antitrinitarians. Franck was a pantheist, who had been pastor in the vicinity of Nuernberg till 1528, when he resigned and engaged in soap manufacturing, writing, and printing. Campanus appeared in Wittenberg, 1527. At the Colloquy of Marburg he endeavored to unite Luther and Zwingli by explaining the words: "This is My body" to mean: This is a body created by Me. In 1530 he published a book:

"Against the Entire World after the Apostles — *Contra Totum post Apostolos Mundum*," in which he taught that the Son is inferior to the Father, and denied the personality of the Holy Spirit. "He argues," says Melanchthon, who in his letters frequently refers to the "blasphemies of Campanus," "that Christ is not God; that the Holy Spirit is not God; that original sin is an empty word. Finally there is nothing which he does not transform into philosophy," (*C. R.* 2, 33. 34. 93. 29. 513; 9, 763; 10, 132.) When Campanus endeavored to spread his doctrines, he was banished from Saxony, 1531. He returned to Juelich, where he preached on the imminence of Judgment Day, with the result that the peasants sold their property and declined to work any longer. Campanus was imprisoned for twenty years and died 1575.

Prominent among the numerous Antitrinitarians who came from Italy were Ochino, Servetus, Gribaldo, Gentile, Blandrata, and Alciati. Bernardino Ochino, born 1487, was Vicar-General of the Capuchins and a renowned pulpit orator in Siena. In 1542 he was compelled to leave Italy in order to escape the Inquisition. He served the Italian congregation in Zurich from 1555 to 1564, when he was banished because he had defended polygamy. He died in Austerlitz, 1565. In his *Thirty Dialogs*, published 1563, he rejects the doctrines of the Trinity, of the deity of Christ, and of the atonement. (*Herzog R.* 14, 256.) — Michael Servetus was born in 1511 and educated at Saragossa and Toulouse. In 1531, at Hagenau, Alsace, he published *De Trinitatis Erroribus Libri VII.* He was opposed by Zwingli and Oecolampadius. In 1540 he wrote his *Christianismi Restitutio*, a voluminous book, which he published in 1553. In it he opposes the Trinity as an unbiblical and satanic doctrine, and at the same time rejects original sin and infant baptism. The result was that, while passing through Geneva, on his way to Italy, he was arrested at the instance of Calvin, tried, condemned, and burned at the stake, October 27, 1553 — an act which was approved also by Melanchthon. (*C. R.* 8, 362; 9, 763.) — Matteo Gribaldo, in 1554, uttered tritheistic views concerning the Trinity in the Italian congregation at Geneva. Arrested in Bern, he retracted his doctrine. He died 1564. — John Valentine Gentile also belonged to the Italian fugitives in Geneva. In 1558 he signed an orthodox confession concerning the Trinity. Before long, however, he relapsed into his Antitrinitarian errors. He was finally beheaded at Bern. (*Herzog R.* 6, 518.)

George Blandrata, born 1515, was influenced by Gribaldo. Fearing for his liberty, he left Geneva and went to Poland and thence to Transylvania. Here he published his *Confessio Antitrinitaria*, and was instrumental in introducing Unitarianism into Transylvania. He died after 1585. In 1558 Gianpaolo Alciati of Piedmont accompanied Blandrata to Poland. He taught that Christ was inferior to the Father, and denied that there were two natures in Christ.

**266. Davidis and Socinus.**

Francis Davidis in Transylvania was an Antitrinitarian of the most radical stripe. He had studied in Wittenberg 1545 and 1548. In 1552 he joined the Lutherans, in 1559 the Calvinists. Secretly after 1560 and publicly since 1566 he cooperated with Blandrata to introduce Unitarianism in Transylvania. In numerous disputations he attacked the doctrine of the Trinity as unscriptural and contradictory. In 1567 he published his views in *De Falso et Vera Unius Dei Patris, Filii et Spiritus Sancti Cognitione Libri Duo.* He contended that the doctrine of the Trinity was the source of all idolatry in the Church; that Christ, though born of Mary in a supernatural way, was preexistent only in the decree of God, and that the Holy Spirit was merely a power emanating from God for our sanctification. He also rejected infant baptism and the Lord's Supper. After the prince and the greater part of the nobility had been won for Unitarianism, Davidis, in 1568, was made Superintendent of the Unitarian Church in Transylvania. In 1571 religious liberty was proclaimed, and Unitarians, Catholics, Lutherans, and Calvinists were tolerated equally. Before long, however, a reaction set in. The Catholic Stephan Bathory, who succeeded to the throne, removed the Unitarians from his court and surrounded himself with Jesuits. On March 29, 1579, Davidis delivered a sermon against the adoration of Christ, declaring it to be the same idolatry as the invocation of Mary and the saints. Three days after he was deposed and imprisoned. In the proceedings instituted against him he was convicted as a blasphemer and sentenced to imprisonment for life. He died in prison, November 15, 1579, prophesying the final downfall of all "false dogmas," meaning, of course, the doctrines which he had combated.

In Poland, especially since 1548, the humanistic and liberal-minded nobility opposed the Catholic clergy and protected Protestants and later on also fugitive Antitrinitarians. Among these were the Italians Francis Lismanio, Gregory Pauli, and Peter Statorius. These Unitarians, however, lacked unity and harmony. They disagreed on infant baptism, the preexistence and adoration of Christ, etc. These dissensions continued until Faustus Socinus (born at Siena 1539, died 1604 in Poland) arrived. He was the nephew of the skeptical and liberal-minded Laelius Socinus (Lelio Sozzini) who left Italy in 1542, when the Inquisition was established there, and died in Zurich, 1562.

Faustus Socinus claimed that he had received his ideas from his uncle Laelius. In 1562 he published anonymously an explanation of the first chapter of the Gospel of St. John, which contained the entire program of Unitarianism. In 1578 he followed an invitation of Blandrata to oppose non-adorantism (the doctrine that Christ must not be adored) as taught by Davidis. In the following year Faustus removed to Poland, where he endeavored to unite the various Unitarian parties: the Anabaptists, Non-adorantes, the believers in the

*Learn this name* (margin annotation)

*Learn this name*
*Big name in Unitarianism* (bottom annotation)

preexistence of Christ, etc., and their opponents. The growth of Unitarianism in Poland was rapid. A school flourished in Rakow, numbering in its palmy days about 1,000 scholars. However, here, too, a Jesuitic reaction set in. In 1638 the school at Rakow was destroyed, the printery closed, and the teachers and ministers expelled. In 1658 the Unitarians generally were banished as traitors, and in 1661 the rigorous laws against Unitarianism were confirmed.

The chief source of the Antitrinitarian and Socinian doctrine is the Racovian Catechism, published 1605 in the Polish and 1609 in the Latin language under the title: "*Catechism of the Churches in the Kingdom of Poland* which affirm that no one besides the Father of our Lord Jesus Christ is that One God of Israel." It teaches: There is but one divine person; Christ is a mere man; the doctrine concerning the deity of Christ is false; as a reward for His sinless life, God has given Christ all power in heaven and on earth; as such, as God's representative (*homo Deus factus*, the man made God), He may be adored; there is no original sin; with the help of God, that is to say, with the commandments and promises of God revealed by Christ, man may acquire salvation; he is able to keep these commandments, though not perfectly; man's shortcomings are pardoned by God on account of his good intention; an atonement by Christ is not required for this purpose; moreover, the doctrine of atonement must be opposed as false and pernicious; by His death Christ merely sealed His doctrine; all who obey His commandments are adherents of Christ; these will participate in His dominion; the wicked and the devils will be annihilated; there is no such thing as eternal punishment; whatever in the Bible comports with human reason and serves moral ends is inspired; the Old Testament is superfluous for Christians, because all matters pertaining to religion are contained better and clearer in the New Testament. (Tschackert, 473.)

Evidently, in every detail, Antitrinitarianism and Socinianism are absolutely incompatible with, and destructive of, the very essence of Christianity. The *Apology* declares that the deniers of the doctrine of the Holy Trinity "are outside of the Church of Christ, and are idolaters, and insult God." (103, 1.) This verdict is confirmed by Article XII of the *Formula of Concord*. (843, 30; 1103, 39.)

# XXIII. Origin, Subscription, Character, etc., of Formula of Concord.

### 267. Lutherans Yearning for a Godly Peace.

A holy zeal for the purity and unity of doctrine is not at all incompatible, rather always and of necessity connected with an earnest desire for peace; not, indeed, a peace at any price, but a truly Christian and godly peace, a peace consistent with the divine truth. Also in the loyal Lutherans, who during the controversies after Luther's death faithfully adhered to their Confessions, the fervent desire for such a godly peace grew in proportion as the dissensions increased. While Calvinists and Crypto-Calvinists were the advocates of a unionistic compromise, true Lutherans everywhere stood for a union based on the truth as taught by Luther and contained in the Lutheran Confessions. Though yearning for peace and praying that the controversies might cease, they were determined that the Lutheran Church should never be contaminated with indifferentism or unionism, nor with any teaching deviating in the least from the divine truth.

As a result, earnest and repeated efforts to restore unity and peace were made everywhere by Lutheran princes as well as by theologians, especially the theologians who had not participated in the controversies, but for all that were no less concerned about the maintenance of pure Lutheranism and no less opposed to a peace at the expense of the divine truth than the others. As early as 1553 Flacius and Gallus published their *Provokation oder Erbieten der adiaphorischen Sachen halben, auf Erkenntnis und Urteil der Kirchen*. In this Appeal they urged that ten or twenty competent men who hitherto had not participated in the public controversy be appointed to decide the chief differences between themselves and the Interimists. In the two following years Flacius and Gallus continued their endeavors to interest influential men in Saxony and other places for their plan. Melanchthon and his Wittenberg colleagues, however, maintained silence in the matter.

At the behest of the dukes of Thuringia, Amsdorf, Stolz, Aurifaber, Schnepf, and Strigel met at Weimar in the early part of 1556 to discuss the conditions of peace. Opposed as they were to a peace by agreeing to disagree or by ignoring the differences and past contentions, they demanded that synergism, Majorism, adiaphorism, as also the doctrines of Zwingli, Osiander, and Schwenckfeldt, be publicly rejected by the Wittenbergers. (Preger 2, 4. 7.)

### 268. Pacific Overtures of Flacius.

Soon after the convention in Weimar, Gottschalk Praetorius, rector of the school in Magdeburg, and Hubertus Languet from Burgundy (an intimate friend of Melanchthon and a guest at his table, who later on maliciously slandered Flacius) had an interview with Flacius, in which the latter submitted the conditions on which peace might be established. However, a letter written in this matter by Praetorius, in April, 1556, was not answered by Melanchthon, who, moreover, insinuated that Flacius's object merely was to kindle hatred. (*C. R.* 8, 794.)

In May, 1556, Flacius, continuing his peace efforts, forwarded to Paul Eber his "Mild Pro-

posals, *Linde Vorschlaege,* dadurch man gott-
selige und notwendige friedliche Vergleichung
machen koennte zwischen den Wittenbergi-
schen und Leipzigischen Theologen in causa
Adiaphoristica und den andern, so wider sie
geschrieben haben." According to these *Proposals,* Flacius demanded that, in a publication signed by the theologians of both parties,
the Pope be denounced as the true Antichrist,
the Augsburg Interim be rejected, the proposition: "Good works are necessary to salvation," be condemned, also the errors of Zwingli
and Osiander. "The good Lord knows," said
Flacius, "that every day and hour I consider
and plan earnestly how the affair of the Adiaphorists might be settled in a Christian manner." But he added that he could not be satisfied until, by repentance, they wipe out their
sin, denial, apostasy, and persecution, instead
of increasing them by their excuses." But
Flacius received an answer neither from Eber
nor from Melanchthon. Instead, the Wittenbergers, with the silent consent of Melanchthon, circulated a caricature in which Flacius
was accorded the rôle of a braying ass being
crowned by other asses with a soiled crown.
(Preger 2, 11. 13.)

Another offer of Flacius to meet Melanchthon in Wittenberg and discuss the matter
personally was also declined. July 15, 1556,
Melanchthon wrote: "I enjoyed a sweet
friendship and familiarity with Illyricus, and
I would gladly confer with him on the entire
doctrine. But before this he has spread
things which I had neither said nor thought,
wherefore now, too, I fear treachery (*insidias
metuo*)." Timid as he was, Melanchthon
really feared for his life at the contemplated
colloquy, because the statement of Chytraeus:
"As long as Flacius and Melanchthon are
alive, unity will not be restored," had been reported to him in the form: unless Philip
were put out of the way, unity would not be
possible. "None of my friends," he wrote,
is willing to attend the colloquy, and they believe that it is not safe for me to confer with
him [Flacius] alone." (*C. R.* 8, 798.) Considering Melanchthon's answer as insincere
and sophistical, Flacius declared that, after
having earnestly sought peace in a private
way, he would now appeal to the Church.
He did so by publishing "*Von der Einigkeit,*
Concerning Unity," a book which he had written before he made his pacific overtures to
Melanchthon. (Preger 2, 17. 22.)

However, induced by a letter of Fabricius
of Meissen (August 24, 1556), Flacius made
a further effort, addressing Melanchthon in a
letter of September 1, 1556, in which he implored him to make his peace with God and
the Church by an unequivocal disavowal of
Adiaphorism. As a result, Melanchthon wrote
his famous letter of September 5, 1556, referred to in our chapter on the Adiaphoristic
Controversy, in which he admitted in a qualified way that he had sinned in the matter.
In his reply of September 16, 1556, Flacius
again declared that his object was not any
triumph or glory for himself, but "only the
maintenance of truth and the rooting out of

error," and that nothing was able to remove
the offense given by Melanchthon and the
Adiaphorists but a clear confession of the
truth and an unequivocal rejection of error.
Melanchthon, however, broke off the correspondence and continued to nurse his animosity against Flacius. (Preger 2, 29 f.)

**269. Lower Saxons Endeavoring to Me-
diate between Melanchthon and Flacius.**

Despite his experiences with Melanchthon,
Flacius did not allow himself to be discouraged in his efforts to bring about unity
and peace. Embracing an opportunity which
a correspondence with the clergy of Lower
Saxony concerning Schwenckfeldt offered him,
he requested the Lower Saxons to mediate
between himself and Melanchthon, submitting
for this purpose articles, differing from the
*Mild Proposals* only in expressly mentioning
also the Leipzig Interim. The request was
granted, and four superintendents, accompanied by four ministers, were delegated for the
purpose to Wittenberg. The delegates were:
from Luebeck: Valentin Curtius and Dionysius Schunemann; from Hamburg: Paul von
Eitzen and Westphal; from Lueneburg: F.
Henning and Antonius Wippermann; from
Brunswick: Moerlin and Chemnitz. After
agreeing, at Brunswick, January 14, 1557, on
theses based on those of Flacius, and after
conferring with Flacius in Magdeburg, January 17, 1557, they unexpectedly, January 19,
arrived in Wittenberg, offering their services
as mediators.

Melanchthon received them in a friendly
manner; but when, on the following day,
Moerlin read the articles of agreement, he
denounced Flacius and Gallus as having slandered him, and declined to treat with the
Lower Saxons on the basis of the "Flacian
theses." On January 21 the delegation submitted eight new articles. Of these the third
read: "All corruptions which militate against
the pure apostolic doctrine and that of the
*Augsburg Confession* shall be eliminated from
the article of justification, in particular the
corruption concerning the necessity of good
works to salvation." Article VII requested
Melanchthon to make a public statement concerning the adiaphora and the necessity of
good works, declaring his agreement with the
confession of our Church. (Preger 2, 37.)

The presentation of these articles had a
most unfavorable effect on Melanchthon. The
Saxon mediators report that he was excited
to such an extent that they feared he would
be taken seriously ill. In a most violent manner Melanchthon charged the delegation with
treacherously conspiring with Flacius to ensnare him. However, appeased by Paul Eber,
he finally consented to reply in writing on the
morrow, January 22. In his answer Melanchthon declared: For thirty years he had borne
the heavy burdens of the Church and encoun-
tered most insidious conflicts; they therefore
ought now to have had compassion with him
instead of assaulting him alone; it was being
fulfilled what Sturm had once told him on
leaving: We shall meet again to crucify you.

Sparing Flacius, they had presented articles with the sole purpose of forcing him and others to cut their own throats. As to the articles themselves, Melanchthon objected to the third, because, he said, it falsely charged him and others with having taught and defended errors regarding justification. He declined Article VII because the publication there required was unnecessary, since it might easily be learned from his many writings what he had taught in the matter there referred to. (Preger 2, 38. 40.)

Fearing that the Lower Saxon mediators might yield and make concessions detrimental to the truth, Flacius and his adherents (Wigand, Baumgartner, Judex, Albert Christiani, P. Arbiter, H. Brenz, Antonius Otto) assembled in Coswig, a place not very far from Wittenberg. In a letter, dated January 21, 1557, they admonished the Saxon mediators not to yield anything contrary to the divine truth, but firmly to insist on the elimination of the errors connected with the Interim (*ut id iugulum recte iuguletis*). Flacius also requested Count of Ungnad first to meet them in Coswig, and then go to Wittenberg in order to assist in winning Melanchthon for his peace proposals. In the letter to the Count, Flacius remarked: he feared that the mediators were administering to Melanchthon "sweet rather than wholesome and strong medicine." (Preger 2, 42.) In a similar manner Pastor Michael Stiefel was urged to go to Wittenberg to influence Melanchthon. At the same time Judex was sent to implore the Saxon delegates not to discontinue their efforts, and adopt no resolution before submitting it also to them [the Magdeburgers] for consideration. No news having arrived by Saturday, January 23, an additional letter was dispatched to Wittenberg, written in the same spirit· of anxiety, and urging the mediators to stand firm, not to yield, and to continue their efforts until successful, since failure, they said, would not only expose them to ridicule, but greatly damage the Church. (2, 42 f.)

On the evening of the same day Moerlin, Hennig, and Westphal arrived in Coswig. Moerlin reported on their discussions, and submitted the articles presented to Melanchthon together with the latter's answer. At the same time he requested the Flacians to overlook the harsh language of Philip, telling also of the animosity and general opposition they had met with in Wittenberg, where the students, he said, had even threatened to stone them. Having heard the report, the Flacians withdrew for a brief consultation. Their impression was (which they neither made any efforts to hide) that in deference to Melanchthon the Saxons had not been sufficiently careful in seeking only the honor of God, the welfare of the Church, and the true conversion of sinners. In a meeting held on Sunday, January 24, Wigand and Flacius declared their dissatisfaction with the proceedings in Wittenberg. Referring particularly to the shocking stubbornness of Melanchthon, the former urged the Saxon delegates to regard God higher than men, and earnestly

and openly to call the Wittenbergers to repentance. He thereupon handed the delegates, besides a list of Adiaphoristic errors and of offensive statements culled from Major's homilies, two sealed letters, which contained their strictures on the eight articles presented to Melanchthon, their answer to Melanchthon's charges, etc. Flacius said in the meeting: This matter troubled him day and night; hope for the conversion of the Adiaphorists, who had despised the admonition, not of men, but of the Holy Spirit, was constantly decreasing; having already yielded more than he should have done, he now must insist that, in a publication signed by both parties, the Leipzig Interim be condemned by name, and ·that also in the future the people be warned against such sins and be called to repentance. Flacius furthermore declared that his theses should have been either retained or refuted. In this he was supported by Otto of Nordhausen. Moerlin answered, irritated:· They had presented other articles because Melanchthon had declined the first; if any one was able to frame better theses, he was at liberty to do so. Discouraged and ill-humored, the delegation returned to Wittenberg, where, too, animosity had reached its climax. For in his sermon, delivered Sunday in Bugenhagen's pulpit, and in the presence of Melanchthon and the other professors, John Curio had spoken of Flacius as "the rascal and knave (*Schalk und Bube*)," and even referred to the Lower Saxon delegates in unfriendly terms. Also a filthy and insulting pasquil, perhaps composed by Paul Crell, in which Flacius and the Saxon delegates were reviled, was circulated in Wittenberg and even sent to Coswig. (Preger 2, 49.) The first lines of the pasquil ran thus: "*Qui huc venistis legati Illyrici permerdati, Ab illo concacati, Polypragmones inflati, Illius natibus nati, Quae communio veritati, Mendacio et vanitati?*" (*C. R.* 9, 50. 235.)

Having read the sealed letters and convinced themselves that Melanchthon could never be induced to accede to the demands of the Magdeburgers, the delegation (with the exception of Chemnitz) immediately returned to Coswig, January 25. Here they declared: They had not delivered the list of errors to Melanchthon; if they had done so, deliberations would have been broken off immediately; only the charges with respect to justification had been transmitted; they therefore requested the Magdeburgers to declare their agreement with the articles already submitted to Melanchthon. Seeing no other course, the Magdeburgers finally yielded, though reluctantly, and not without protests and some changes in the articles. Flacius, too, consented, but "only with a wounded conscience," as he declared. Having returned to Wittenberg, the delegates transmitted the modified articles together with the additions of the Magdeburgers to Melanchthon.

In his answer of January 27 to the Lower Saxon pastors, Melanchthon said in part: "You know that in the last thirty years a great confusion of opinions obtained in which it was difficult not to stumble somewhere. And many hypocrites have been, and still are, hostile in particular to me. I was also drawn into the insidious deliberations of the princes. If, therefore, I have either stumbled anywhere or been too lukewarm in any matter, I ask God and the churches to forgive me and shall submit to the verdict of the Church. . . . As to the Flacian quarrels, however, concerning which you are now treating with me so eagerly, and into which Flacius has injected many foreign matters, you yourselves know that this affair pertains also to many others, and that, without offending them, I cannot decide and settle anything (*me aliquid statuere posse*). . . . This now I desire to be my last answer (*hanc volo nunc meam postremam responsionem esse*); if it does not satisfy you, I appeal to the verdict of the Church, in which you, too, will be judges. May the Son of God govern all of us, and grant that we be one in Him!" As to the articles submitted by the delegates, Melanchthon rejected all the changes and additions suggested by the Magdeburgers. He declared that he was not willing to enter into a discussion of the adiaphora, nor in any way to censure the honorable men who had participated in the deliberations concerning the Leipzig Interim. (*C. R.* 9, 62.)

Toward evening Flacius received Melanchthon's answer, together with the information that the Saxon delegates would depart on the morrow, and that now the Magdeburgers might do what seemed best to them. Early next morning they dispatched another letter written by Flacius, in which they modified their demands, and urged the Saxon delegates to continue their efforts to induce the Wittenbergers to reject the Adiaphoristic errors. "We call upon God as our witness," they said, "that we most earnestly desire a godly peace, and that, if it is not brought about, the fault lies not with us, but with them, who expressly say and confess concerning themselves that they absolutely refuse to condemn the Adiaphoristic errors — the real issue of the entire controversy." (*C. R.* 9, 67.) But the messenger arrived too late; he met the delegation when they were about to leave the gates of Wittenberg. Increased animosity on both sides was the only result of the mediation-efforts of the Lower Saxon theologians.

### 270. Futile Efforts of Duke John Albrecht.

Four weeks later Duke John Albrecht of Mecklenburg sent messengers to Wittenberg for the same purpose, *viz.,* of mediating between Melanchthon and Flacius, Melanchthon in particular having previously requested him to frame articles which might serve as a basis of peace. The articles, composed by the theologians and counselors of the Duke, were more severe than those of the Lower Saxons. George Venetus, professor at Rostock, and Counselor Andrew Mylius were commissioned to present them, first at Wittenberg, then at Magdeburg. When the articles were submitted to Melanchthon, he again fell into a state

of violent agitation. The report says: "As soon as he noticed that Adiaphorism was criticized, and that he was requested to reject it, even if only in a mild form, he instantly sprang up with great impatience and would not permit them [the delegates] to finish their speech (although they most earnestly, in the name of their prince, requested to be heard), but burst forth into invectives and denunciations of Illyricus and others, and finally also declaimed against the prince himself and his delegates, vociferating that Illyricus secretly entertained many repulsive errors, etc." On February 27, Melanchthon delivered his answer to the delegates. When these urged him to give a more favorable reply, he again interrupted them, exclaiming: "Oppress me, if you so desire; such is the lot of the peaceful. . . . I commend myself to God." After Melanchthon had left, Peucer, who had accompanied him, harshly told the delegates: "Don't trouble my father-in-law any more with such matters. *Ihr sollt forthin meinen Schwaeher zufrieden lassen mit solchen Haendeln.*" (9, 106 f.)

Regarding the last (8) of the articles submitted by the delegates of Duke Albrecht which dealt with the Adiaphora, Melanchthon declared in his answer of February 27: "I should not be astonished to have these two conditions [to confess the Adiaphoristic errors, etc.] imposed on me if I had been an enemy. The action of the Saxon pastors was milder. I may have been lukewarm in some transactions, but I certainly have never been an enemy. . . . Therefore I clearly state that I do not assent to these presentations [of Duke Albrecht], which are cunningly framed, so that, if I accept them, I myself may cut my throat (*ut me, si eas recepero, ipse iugulem*)." (*C. R.* 9, 104.)

The Magdeburgers refused to participate in these efforts of Count Albrecht, chiefly because, as they said, there was no hope for peace as long as Melanchthon remained under the influence of his Wittenberg friends. But even now Flacius did not entirely abandon his attempts to bring about a godly peace. In 1557 he asked Paul Vergerius, who passed Jena on his way to Wittenberg, to treat with Melanchthon on the Adiaphoristic question. Melanchthon, however, is reported to have said: "Omit that; let us treat of other things." Flacius also wrote to King Christian III of Denmark to influence Elector August to abolish the Adiaphoristic errors, but apparently without any result.

### 271. Clash at Colloquy in Worms, 1557.

The Diet at Regensburg, which adjourned in March of 1557, resolved that a colloquy be held at Worms to bring about an agreement between the Lutheran and Roman parties of the Empire. In order to prepare for the colloquy, a convention was held by the Lutherans in June, 1557, at Frankfort-on-the-Main. June 30 a resolution was adopted to the effect that all controversies among the Lutherans be suspended, and the Romanists be told at the prospective colloquy that the Lutherans were all agreed in the chief points of doctrine. Against this resolution Nicholas Gallus and several others entered their protest. Self-evidently, also Flacius and his adherents, who had always held that the controverted issues involved essential points of doctrine, could not assent to the resolution without violating their conscience, and denying their convictions and the truth as they saw it. Such being the situation, the wise thing for the Lutherans to do would have been to decline the colloquy. For, since also Ducal Saxony with its stanch Lutherans was held to attend it, a public humiliating clash of the Lutherans was unavoidable.

Before the formal opening of the colloquy, the Thuringian delegates at Worms received a letter from Flacius, dated August 9, 1557, in which he admonished them to make a determined confession, and to induce the other Lutheran theologians to reject the Interim, Adiaphorism, Majorism, Osiandrism, and Zwinglianism. This was necessary, said Flacius, because the Romanists would, no doubt, exploit the concessions made in the Leipzig Interim and the dissensions existing among the Lutherans. (*C. R.* 9, 199 ff.) Flacius expressed the same views in an opinion to the dukes of Saxony, who, in turn, gave corresponding instructions to their delegates in Worms. In a letter dated August 20, 1557, Duke John Frederick said it was impossible that, in defending the *Augsburg Confession* against the Romanists, the Lutherans could stand as one man and speak as with one mouth (*fuer einen Mann und also ex uno ore*), if they had not previously come to an agreement among themselves and condemned the errors. For otherwise the Papists would be able to defeat the Lutherans with their own sword, *i. e.*, their own polemical publications. (231.) On the same day, August 20, 1557, Flacius repeated his sentiments and admonitions in letters to Schnepf, Moerlin, and Sarcerius. (232 ff.)

In a meeting of the Lutheran theologians at Worms, held September 5, Dr. Basilius Monner, professor of jurisprudence at Jena, made a motion in keeping with his instructions and the admonitions of Flacius, whereupon Erhard Schnepf, professor in Jena, read a list of the errors that ought to be rejected. But the majority, led by Melanchthon, opposed the motion. A breach seemed unavoidable. For Duke John Frederick had decided that his theologians could not participate in the colloquy with Lutherans who refused to reject errors conflicting with the *Augsburg Confession*, nor recognize them as pure, faithful, loyal, and true members and adherents of the *Augsburg Confession*, the *Apology*, and the *Smalcald Articles*. (Preger 2, 67.) The imminent clash was temporarily warded off by the concession on the part of the Melanchthonians that the Thuringian theologians should be allowed freely to express their opinion on any article discussed at the colloquy. At the session held September 11, 1557, however, Bishop Michael Helding demanded to know whether the Lutherans ex-

cluded the Zwinglians, Calvinists, Osiandrists, and Flacians (in the doctrine *de servo arbitrio*) from the *Augsburg Confession*. The Jesuit Canisius plied the Lutherans with similar questions: Whether they considered Osiander, Major, and others adherents of the *Augustana*. Melanchthon declared evasively that all evangelical delegates and pastors present were agreed in the *Augsburg Confession*. As a result the Thuringians decided to enter their protest. In a special meeting of the Lutherans the majority threatened to exclude the Thuringians from all following sessions if they dared to express their protest [containing the list of errors which they rejected] before the Papists. The consequence was that the Thuringians presented their protest in writing to the President, Julius Pflug, and departed from Worms. The Romanists, who from the beginning had been opposed to the colloquy, refused to treat with the remaining Lutheran theologians, because, they said, it was impossible to know who the true adherents of the *Augsburg Confession* were with whom, according to the Regensburg Resolution, they were to deal.

## 272. Efforts of Princes to Restore Unity: Frankfort Recess.

The Colloquy of Worms had increased the enmity and animosity among the Lutherans. It had brought their quarrels to a climax, and given official publicity to the dissensions existing among them, — a situation which was unscrupulously exploited by the Romanists, also politically, their sinister object being to rob the Lutherans of the privileges guaranteed by the Augsburg Peace, and to compel them to return to the Roman fold. In particular the Jesuits stressed the point that the dissensions among the Lutherans proved conclusively that they had abandoned the *Augsburg Confession*, to the adherents of which alone the provisions of the Augsburg Peace of 1555 applied. At the same time they embraced the opportunity to spread false reports concerning all manner of heresies that were tolerated in the Lutheran churches. This roused the Lutheran princes, who according to the Augsburg Peace Treaty were responsible to the Empire for the religious conditions within their territories, to bend all their energies toward healing the breach and restoring religious unity within their churches. Efforts to this effect were made especially at Frankfort-on-the-Main, 1558, and at Naumburg, 1561. But instead of promoting peace among the Lutherans also these conventions of the princes merely poured oil into the flames by adding new subjects of dissension, increasing the general distrust, and confirming the conviction that Luther's doctrine of the Lord's Supper was in danger indeed. For, instead of insisting on a clear confession of the truth and an unequivocal rejection of error, the princes endeavored to establish peace by ignoring, veiling, and compromising the differences.

At Frankfort, Otto Henry of the Palatinate, Augustus of Saxony, Joachim of Brandenburg,

Wolfgang of Zweibruecken, Christopher of Wuerttemberg, and Philip of Hesse discussed the religious situation and, on March 18, 1558, signed the so-called *Frankfort Recess* (Agreement), in which they again solemnly pledged their adherence to the Holy Scriptures, the Ecumenical Symbols, the *Augsburg Confession* of 1530, and its *Apology*. (*C. R.* 9, 494.) In the *Recess* the princes stated that the existing dissensions encouraged the Romanists to proceed against the Lutherans, who, the princes declared, were not disagreed in their confession. In four articles the controverted questions concerning justification, good works, the Lord's Supper, and the adiaphora were dealt with, but in vague and ambiguous terms, the articles being based on Melanchthon's anti-Flacian opinion of March 4, 1558. (499 ff.; 462 ff.)

When the *Frankfort Recess* was submitted for subscription) to the estates who had not been present at Frankfort, it failed to receive the expected approval. It was criticized by the theologians of Anhalt, Henneberg, Mecklenburg, Pomerania, the Lower Saxon cities, and Regensburg. The strongest opposition, however, came from Ducal Saxony, where Flacius attacked the *Recess* in two books. The first was entitled: "*Refutatio Samaritani Interim,* in quo vera religio cum sectis et corruptelis scelerate et perniciose confunditur — Refutation of the Samaritan Interim, in which the true religion is criminally and perniciously confounded with the sects." The other: "*Grund und Ursach', warum das Frankfurtisch Interim in keinem Wege anzunehmen sei* — Reason and Cause why the Frankfort Interim must Not be Adopted." The chief objections of Flacius were: 1. The *Smalcald Articles* should have been included in the confessions subscribed to. 2. The differences within the Lutheran Church should not have been treated as questions of minor import. 3. Major's statement should have been rejected as simply false, and not merely when falsely interpreted. 4. The statements concerning the Lord's Supper are "dark, general, and ambiguous," hence Crypto-Calvinistic. 5. The article on the adiaphora is ambiguous and altogether unsatisfactory. 6. The measures adopted to suppress theological discussions and controversies would lead to suppression of the truth ("binding the mouth of the Holy Ghost") and tyrannizing of the churches by the princes. (Preger 2, 74.)

In his attitude Flacius was supported by his colleagues in Jena and by Duke John Frederick. When a delegation appeared requesting him to sign the *Recess,* he declined and ordered his theologians to set forth his objection in a special book. Elector August, in turn, charged Melanchthon to write an apology of the *Recess* against the ducal theologians; which, again, was answered by Flacius. In order to unite the opponents of the *Recess,* John Frederick invited the Lower Saxons to attend a convention in Magdeburg. When this failed, Flacius induced the Duke to publish a book treating particularly the doctrinal differences within the Lutheran

Church. In the drafting and revision of this *Book of Confutation,* as it was called, the following theologians participated: Strigel, Schnepf, Andrew Huegel, John Stoessel, Simon Musaeus, Joachim Moerlin, Sarcerius, Aurifaber, and Flacius. November 28, 1558, it received the sanction of the dukes. Among the Melanchthonians the *Book of Confutation,* which had made it a special point to refute and reject the errors of the Wittenberg Philippists, caused consternation and bitter resentment. For evidently its theological attitude was incompatible with the *Recess,* and hence the breach now seemed incurable and permanent. By order of Elector August, Melanchthon, in the name of the Wittenberg faculty, wrote an opinion of the *Book of Confutation.* (*C. R.* 9, 763.) But contents as well as form of this opinion merely served to confirm the ducal theologians in their position. The Philippists also fortified themselves by publishing the *Corpus Doctrinae* (*Corpus Philippicum* or *Misnicum*), which contained writings only of Melanchthon. The *Frankfort Recess,* therefore, instead of bringing relief to the Lutherans, only increased their mutual enmity and distrust. In order to reconcile John Frederick, the Duke of Wuerttemberg suggested a convention of princes at Fulda, on January 20, 1559. But when Elector August heard that besides the Duke of Saxony also other opponents of the *Frankfort Recess* were invited, he foiled the plan by declining to attend.

### 273. General Lutheran Council Advocated by Flacianists.

To heal the breach and end the public scandal, Flacius and his adherents fervently advocated the convocation of a General Lutheran Synod. In 1559 they published "*Supplicatio Quorundam Theologorum . . . pro Libera Christiana et Legitima Synodo,* Supplication of Some Theologians . . . for a Free, Christian, and Lawful Synod." The document was signed by 51 superintendents, professors, and pastors, "who after Luther's death," as they emphasized, "had contended orally and in writing against the corruptions and sects." The signatures represented theologians from Ducal Saxony, Hamburg, Bremen, Luebeck, Rostock, Wismar, Brunswick, Magdeburg, Halberstadt, Koethen, Nordhausen, Schweinfurt, Regensburg, Lindau, Upper Palatinate, Hesse, Brandenburg, Electoral Saxony, Nuernberg, Augsburg, Baden, etc. Some of the first were: Amsdorf, Musaeus, Joachim Moerlin, Hesshusius, Max Moerlin, Gallus, Wigand, Judex, Westphal, John Freder of Wismar, Anton Otto of Nordhausen, Flacius. The *Supplication* showed why a General Synod was necessary and how it was to be conducted. Its chief object, the *Supplication* said, would be to pass on adiaphorism, Majorism, and synergism, all participants in the Synod having previously been pledged on the *Augsburg Confession,* the *Apology,* and the *Smalcald Articles,* according to which all questions were to be decided. (Preger 2, 86 f.)

The most violent opponent of this plan was

Melanchthon. Fearing that the Flacianists might get control of the prospective general council, he, in advance, denounced and branded it as a "Robber Synod (*Raeubersynode*), advocated by the ignorant Flacian rabble." Three weeks before his death, March 28, 1560, he wrote: "Since they [the Flacians] cannot kill me, the object of these hypocrites is to expel me. For long ago they have said that they would not leave a foot of ground for me in Germany. *Hoc agunt isti hypocritae, ut me pellant, cum sanguinem meum haurire non possint; et quidem oratio istorum vetus est, qua dixerunt, se mihi non relicturos esse in Germania vestigium pedis.*" (*C. R.* 9, 1079.) Philip of Hesse consented to attend the general synod with the proviso that the power of the Jena theologians be curbed and also the Swiss be admitted. (Preger 2, 93.) That the plan of the Flacianists failed was chiefly due to Elector August, who declined to attend the synod.

### 274. Futile Efforts of Princes at Naumburg.

In lieu of the General Lutheran Council advocated by the Flacians, Christopher of Wuerttemberg, in March, 1559, recommended as the best means to heal the breach a convention of all the Lutheran princes and estates to be held at Naumburg, deliberations to begin January 20, 1561. The object of this assembly, he said, was neither to discuss the differences among the Lutherans, nor to formulate any condemnations, but only to renew the subscription to the *Augsburg Confession*, and to consider how the Lutherans might present a united front and a unanimous confession at the next diet and at the prospective papal council. All finally consented to attend, including Duke John Frederick, Elector August (who, instigated by Melanchthon, first had declined participation), and the Crypto-Calvinist, Elector Frederick of the Palatinate. Expecting no results favorable to genuine Lutheranism from this assembly, the Jena theologians renewed their request for a general synod and sent their *Supplication* to Naumburg with an additional writing, dated January 23, 1561, in which they admonished the princes not to enter into an ungodly and unionistic agreement, rather to eliminate the errors of Major, Osiander, etc. But the princes, whose object was to settle matters without the theologians, declined to consider their petition, and, on February 8, the last day of the convention, returned the documents to their authors in Jena.

After comparing the various editions of the *Augsburg Confession*, the Naumburg Assembly decided to subscribe to the *Confession* as delivered 1530 in Augsburg and published 1531 in German and Latin at Wittenberg. But when, in the interest of Calvinism, whither he at that time already was openly tending, Elector Frederick, supported by Elector August, demanded that the edition of 1540 be recognized as the correct explanation of the original *Augustana*, the majority of the princes yielded, and, as a result, the Variata

of 1540 alone was mentioned in the Preface (*Praefatio*), in which the princes stated the reasons for renewing their subscription to the *Augsburg Confession* at Naumburg. This Preface, prepared by Elector Frederick and the Wittenberg Crypto-Calvinist Cracow, also asserted that hitherto no doctrinal corruptions or deviations from the *Augsburg Confession* had been tolerated among the Lutherans. It mentioned neither the controversies within the Lutheran Church nor the *Smalcald Articles*.

Evidently, to subscribe to this Preface was impossible for genuine Lutherans. Duke John Frederick was told by his theologians Moerlin and Stoessel that, if he signed it, they would resign and leave. The duke replied that he, too, would mount his horse and depart rather than put his signature to a document in which the errors introduced by the Philippists, etc., were not rejected. Ulrich of Mecklenburg took the same stand. And failing in his efforts to have the Preface changed in accordance with his convictions, the Duke entered his protest and left Naumburg without any further conference with the princes. When hereupon the latter sent messengers to Weimar, John Frederick remained firm. As conditions of his subscription the Duke demanded that in the Preface the apostasy during the Interim be confessed, the distinctive features of the Lutheran doctrine concerning the Lord's Supper be brought out clearly, the recognition of the Variata of 1540 as a doctrinal norm be eliminated, and the *Smalcald Articles* be recognized with the rest of the Lutheran symbols. Unwilling to accede to these demands, the princes closed the discussions at Naumburg without the Duke, — hence also without having attained their goal: peace among the Lutherans.

The Preface containing the objectionable features was signed by the Electors of the Palatinate, Saxony, and Brandenburg, by Christopher of Wuerttemberg, Philip of Hesse, Carl of Baden, and quite a number of other princes and cities. However, Duke John Frederick did not by any means stand alone in his opposition to the ambiguous, unionistic Naumburg document. He was supported by Ulrich of Mecklenburg (who also left Naumburg before the close of the convention), Ernest and Philip of Brunswick, Albrecht of Mecklenburg, Adolf of Holstein, Francis of Saxon-Lauenburg, the counts of Schwartzburg, Mansfeld, Stolberg, Barby, and a number of other princes and cities, among the latter Regensburg, Augsburg, Strassburg, Nuernberg, and Windsheim. Besides, the loyal Lutherans were represented also in the territories of almost all the princes who had signed the Preface. Margrave John of Brandenburg emphatically declared his dissatisfaction with the subscription of his delegate at Naumburg. Before long also August of Saxony, Wolfgang of the Palatinate, Christopher of Wuerttemberg, and Joachim of Brandenburg signified their willingness to alter the Preface in accordance with the views and wishes of John Frederick, especially regarding the doctrine of the Lord's Supper. Indeed, the princes declared that from the beginning they had understood the Preface in the strict Lutheran sense. In the Preface of the *Book of Concord* signed by the Lutheran princes, we read: "Now, our conferences and those of our illustrious predecessors, which were undertaken with a godly and sincere intention, first at Frankfort-on-the-Main and afterwards at Naumburg, and were recorded in writing, not only did not accomplish that end and peaceful settlement which was desired, but from them even a defense for errors and false doctrines was sought by some, while it had never entered our mind, by this writing of ours, either to introduce, furnish a cover for, and establish any false doctrine, or in the least even to recede from the Confession presented in the year 1530 at Augsburg, but rather, as many of us as participated in the transactions at Naumburg, wholly reserved it to ourselves, and promised besides that if, in the course of time, anything would be desired with respect to the *Augsburg Confession*, or as often as necessity would seem to demand it, we would further declare all things thoroughly and at length." (CONC. TRIGL. 15.) Even Philip of Hesse finally consented to the changes demanded by Duke John Frederick. Elector Frederick of the Palatinate, however, who had misled and, as it were, hypnotized the Lutheran princes at Naumburg, openly embraced the Reformed confession and expelled all consistent Lutherans. For the cause of Lutheranism the loss of the Palatinate proved a great gain internally, and helped to pave the way for true unity and the formulation and adoption of the *Formula of Concord*. And more than any other individual it was Flacius who had helped to bring about this result. (Preger 2, 102.)

### 275. Andreae and Chemnitz.

The theologians who were first in adopting effective methods and measures to satisfy the general yearning for a real peace in the divine truth were Jacob Andreae and Martin Chemnitz. Andreae was born 1528 in Weiblingen, Wuerttemberg. He studied at Stuttgart and Tuebingen. In 1546 he became pastor in Stuttgart, where, two years later, he was deposed because of his refusal to consent to the Interim. In 1549 he became pastor and later on superintendent in Tuebingen. Since 1562 he was also professor and chancellor of the university. He died 1590. Andreae has been called "the spiritual heir of John Brenz." Hoping against hope, he incessantly labored for the unity and peace of the Lutheran Church. Being a man of great energy and diplomatic skill, he served her at numerous occasions and in various capacities. In his pacification efforts he made more than 120 journeys, visiting nearly all evangelical courts, cities, and universities in Northern and Southern Germany. With the consent of the Duke of Wuerttemberg, Andreae entered the service of Elector August, April 9, 1567, and lived with his family in Saxony till his dismissal in December, 1580. Here he was engaged in directing the affairs of the churches and universities, and in promoting the work of Lutheran pacification and concord at large. During his efforts to unite the Lutherans he was maligned by the Philippists, and severely criticized also by the strict Lutherans. The latter was largely due to the fact that in his first attempts at pacification he allowed himself to be duped by the Wittenberg Philippists, being even blind enough to defend them against the charges of Calvinism in the doctrine of the Lord's Supper made by their opponents in Jena and in Lower Saxony. While thus Andreae was the able and enthusiastic promoter of the pacification which culminated in the adoption of the *Formula of Concord*, he lacked the theological insight, acumen, and consistency which characterized Martin Chemnitz.

Martin Chemnitz was born November 9, 1522, at Treuenbritzen in Brandenburg. As a boy he attended, for a brief period, the school in Wittenberg, where he "rejoiced to see the renowned men of whom he had heard so much at home, and to hear Luther preach." From 1539 to 1542 he attended the *Gymnasium* at Magdeburg; from 1543 to 1545 he studied in Frankfort-on-the-Oder; in 1545 he went to Wittenberg, where Melanchthon directed his studies. In 1548 he became rector of the school in Koenigsberg, and 1550 librarian of Duke Albrecht, with a good salary. Owing to his participation in the Osiandrian controversy, Chemnitz lost the favor of Albrecht, and in 1553 he removed to Wittenberg. On June 9, 1554, he began his lectures on Melanchthon's *Loci Communes* before a large and enthusiastic audience, Melanchthon himself being one of his hearers. In November, 1554, he accepted a position as pastor, and in 1567 as superintendent, in the city of Brunswick. He died April 8, 1586. Chemnitz was the prince of the Lutheran divines of his age and, next to Luther, the greatest theologian of our Church. Referring to Luther and Chemnitz, the Romanists said: "You Lutherans have two Martins; if the second had not appeared, the first would have disappeared (*si posterior non fuisset, prior non stetisset*)." Besides the two Lutheran classics: *Examen Concilii Tridentini*, published 1565—1573, and *De Duabus Naturis in Christo*, 1570, Chemnitz wrote, among other books: *Harmonia Evangelica*, continued and published 1593 by Leyser and completed by John Gerhard, and Foundations (*Die Fundamente*) of the Sound Doctrine concerning the Substantial Presence, Tendering, and Eating and Drinking of the Body and Blood of the Lord in the Supper, 1569.

Andreae and Chemnitz became acquainted with each other in 1568, when Duke Julius invited the former to conduct the visitation in Brunswick together with Chemnitz. They jointly also composed the Brunswick Church Order of 1569, which was preceded by the *Corpus Doctrinae Iulium*, compiled by Chemnitz and containing the *Augsburg Confession*, the *Apology*, the *Smalcald Articles*, the Catechisms of Luther, and a "short [rather long], simple, and necessary treatise on the prevalent corruptions." Andreae and Chemnitz are the theologians to whom more than any other two men our Church owes the *Formula of Concord* and the unification of our Church in the one true Christian faith as taught by Luther. However, it is Chemnitz who, more than Andreae or any other theologian, must be credited with the theological clarity and correctness which characterizes the *Formula.*

### 276. First Peace Efforts of Andreae Fail.

In his first attempts to unify the Lutheran Church, Andreae endeavored to reconcile all parties, including the Wittenberg Philippists, who then were contemplating an agreement with the Calvinists. In 1567, at the instance of Landgrave William of Hesse-Cassel and Duke Christopher of Wuerttemberg, Andreae composed his "*Confession and Brief Explanation of Several Controverted Articles,* according to which a Christian unity might be effected in the churches adhering to the *Augsburg Confession,* and the offensive and wearisome dissension might be settled." In five articles he treated: 1. Justification, 2. Good Works, 3. Free Will, 4. The Adiaphora, 5. The Lord's Supper. The second article maintains that we are neither justified nor saved by good works, since Christ has earned for us both salvation and righteousness by His innocent obedience, suffering, and death alone, which is imputed as righteousness to all believers solely by faith. It rejects all those who teach otherwise, but not directly and expressly the statement: Good works are necessary to salvation. The third article maintains that, also after the Fall, man is not a block, but a rational creature having a free, though weak, will in external things; but that in divine and spiritual matters his intellect is utterly blind and his will is dead; and that hence, unless God creates a new volition in him, man is unable of himself, of his own powers, to accept the grace of God offered in Christ. It rejects all who teach otherwise. The fourth article states that ceremonies are no longer free, but must be abandoned, when their adoption is connected with a denial of the Christian religion, doctrine, and confession. It rejects all those who teach otherwise. The fifth article emphasizes that also the wicked, when they partake of the Lord's Supper, receive the body of Christ, but to their damnation. It furthermore declares: Since it is objected that the body and blood cannot be present in the Holy Supper because Christ ascended to heaven with His body, it is necessary "to explain the article of the incarnation of the Son of God, and to indicate, in as simple a way as possible, the manner in which both natures, divine and human, are united in Christ, wherefrom it appears to what height the human nature in Christ has been exalted by the personal union." (Hutter, *Concordia Concors,* 110 ff.)

In 1568, at the Brunswick Visitation, referred to above, Andreae submitted his five articles to Duke Julius, and succeeded in winning him for his plan. In the same interest he came to Wittenberg, January 9, 1569. Furnished with letters of commendation from Duke Julius and Landgrave William of Hesse, he obtained an interview also with Elector August, who referred him to his theologians. On August 18, 1569, Andreae held a conference with the Wittenbergers. They insisted that the basis of the contemplated agreement must be the *Corpus Misnicum (Philippicum).* When Andreae, unsophisticated as he still was with respect to the real character of Philippism, publicly declared that the Wittenbergers were orthodox teachers, and that the *Corpus Misnicum* contained no false doctrine, he was supplied with a testimonial in which the Wittenbergers refer to their *Corpus,* but not to Andreae's articles, to which also they had not fully consented. The result was that the Jena theologians, in particular Tilemann Hesshusius, denounced Andreae's efforts as a unionistic scheme and a betrayal of true Lutheranism in the interest of Crypto-Calvinism. They rejected Andreae's articles because they were incomplete, and contained no specific rejection of the errors of the Philippists.

At the instance of Andreae, May 7, 1570, a conference met at Zerbst in Anhalt, at which twenty theologians represented Electoral Saxony, Brunswick, Hesse, Brandenburg, Anhalt, and Lower Saxony (the Ducal Saxon theologians declining to participate). The conference decided that a new confession was not needed, and unanimously recognized the *Augsburg Confession,* its *Apology,* the *Smalcald Articles,* and the Catechisms of Luther. Andreae was elated. In his "Report" to the Emperor and the princes he gloried in "the Christian unity" attained at Zerbst. But also this apparent victory for peace and true Lutheranism was illusory rather than real, for the Wittenberg theologians qualified their subscription by formally declaring that they interpreted and received the confessions enumerated only in as far as they agreed with the *Corpus Philippicum.* And before long the Crypto-Calvinistic publications, referred to in the chapter on the Crypto-Calvinistic Controversy, began to make their appearance. The only result of these first peace efforts of Andreae, which lacked in single-minded devotion to the truth, and did not sufficiently exclude every form of indifferentism and unionism, was that he himself was regarded with increasing suspicion by the opponents of the Philippists. As for Andreae, however, the dealings which he had with the dishonest Wittenbergers opened his eyes and convinced him that it was impossible to win Electoral Saxony for a truly Lutheran union as long as the Crypto-Calvinists were firmly seated in the saddle.

### 277. Andreae's Sermons and the Swabian Concordia.

Abandoning his original scheme, which had merely served to increase the animosity among the Lutherans and to discredit himself, Andreae resolved henceforth to confine his peace efforts to true Lutherans, especially those of Swabia and Lower Saxony, and to unite them in opposition to the Zwinglians, Calvinists, and Philippists, who, outside of Electoral Saxony, were by this time generally regarded as traitors to the cause of Lutheranism. In 1573 he made his first move to carry out this new plan of his by publishing sermons which he had delivered 1572 on the doctrines controverted within the Lutheran Church. The title ran: "*Six Christian Sermons* concerning the dissensions which from the year 1548 to this 1573d year have gradually arisen among the theologians of the Augsburg Confession, as to what attitude a plain pastor and a common Christian layman who may have been offended thereby should assume toward them according to his Catechism." These sermons treat of justification, good works, original sin, free will, the adiaphora, Law and Gospel, and the person of Christ. As the title indicates, Andreae appealed not so much to the theologians as to the pastors and the people of the Lutheran Church, concerning whom he was convinced that, adhering as they did, to Luther's Catechism, they in reality, at least in their hearts, were even then, and always had been, agreed. Andreae sent these sermons to Chemnitz, Chytraeus, Hesshusius, Wigand, and other theologians with the request that they be accepted as a basis of agreement. In the preface, dated February 17, 1573, he dedicated them to Duke Julius of Brunswick, whose good will and consent in the matter he had won in 1568, when he assisted in introducing the Reformation in his territories. Before this Nicholas Selneccer, then superintendent of Wolfenbuettel, in order to cultivate the friendly relations between Swabia and Lower Saxony, had dedicated his *Instruction in the Christian Religion (Institutio Religionis Christianae)* to the Duke of Wuerttemberg, praising the writings of Brenz, and lauding the services rendered by Andreae to the duchy of Brunswick.

The sermons of Andreae were welcomed by Chemnitz, Westphal in Hamburg, David Chytraeus in Rostock, and others. They also endeavored to obtain recognition for them from various ecclesiastical ministries of Lower Saxony. But having convinced themselves that the sermonic form was not adapted for a confession, they, led by Chemnitz, advised that their contents be reduced to articles in "thesis and antithesis," and that this be done "with the assistance of other theologians." Andreae immediately acted on this suggestion, and the result was what is known as the *Swabian Concordia (Schwaebische Konkordie)*, — the first draft of the *Formula of Concord.* This document, also called the Tuebingen Book, was submitted to, and approved by, the theologians of Tuebingen and by the Stuttgart Consistory. In substance it was an elaboration of the *Six Sermons* with the addition of the last two articles. It contains eleven articles, treating 1. Original Sin; 2. Free Will; 3. The Righteousness of Faith before God; 4. Good Works; 5. Law and Gospel; 6. The Third Use of the Law; 7. The Church Usages Called Adiaphora; 8. The Lord's Supper; 9. The Person of Christ; 10. Eternal

Election; 11. Other Factions and Sects. In the introduction Andreae also emphasizes the necessity of adopting those symbols which were afterwards received into the *Book of Concord.*

### 278. The Swabian-Saxon Concordia.

On March 22, 1574, Andreae sent the *Swabian Concordia* to Duke Julius and Chemnitz with the request to examine it and to have it discussed in the churches of Lower Saxony. On the twelfth of May the Duke ordered Chemnitz to prepare an opinion on the book and to present it to the clergy for their examination and approval. Under the leadership of Chemnitz numerous conferences were held, and the various criticisms offered led to a revision of the document. This work was begun in April, 1575, by the theological faculty of Rostock. Apart from numerous changes and additions everywhere, the articles on Free Will and on the Lord's Supper were completely remodeled by Chytraeus and Chemnitz.

The new confession, known as the *Swabian-[Lower] Saxon Concordia*, was subscribed by the theologians and pastors of the duchies of Brunswick, Mecklenburg, Mansfeld, Hoya, and Oldenburg. It acknowledges as its doctrinal basis the Holy Scriptures, the three Ecumenical Creeds, the *Augsburg Confession*, its *Apology*, the *Smalcald Articles*, and Luther's two Catechisms. It discusses the following articles in the following order: 1. Of Original Sin; 2. Of the Person of Christ; 3. Of the Righteousness of Faith before God; 4. Of Good Works; 5. Of the Law and the Gospel; 6. Of the Third Use of the Law of God; 7. Of the Holy Supper; 8. Of God's Eternal Providence and Election; 9. Of Church Usages which are Called Adiaphora or Things Indifferent; 10. Of Free Will or Human Powers; 11. Of Other Factions and Sects which have Never Acknowledged the *Augsburg Confession.*

While this new *Concordia* was adopted in Lower Saxony, the Swabians, to whom it was forwarded, September 5, 1575, were not quite satisfied with its form, but did not object to its doctrinal contents. They criticized the unevenness of its style, its frequent use of Latin technical terms, its quotations (now approved, now rejected) from Melanchthon, etc. Particularly regarding the last mentioned point, they feared that the references to Melanchthon might lead to new dissensions; hence they preferred that citations be taken from Luther's writings only, which was done in the *Formula of Concord* as finally adopted.

### 279. The Maulbronn Formula.

The movement for a general unity within the Lutheran Church received a powerful impetus by the sudden and ignominious collapse of Crypto-Calvinism in Electoral Saxony, 1574. By unmasking the Philippists, God had removed the chief obstacle of a godly and general peace among the Lutherans. Now the clouds of dissension began to disappear rapidly. As long as the eyes of Elector August were closed to the dishonesty of his theologians, there was no hope for a peace embracing the entire Lutheran Church in Germany. Even before the public exposure of the Philippists, August had been told as much by Count Henneberg and other princes, viz., that the Wittenberg theologians were universally suspected, and that peace could not be established until their Calvinistic errors had been condemned. For in the doctrines of the Lord's Supper and of the person of Christ, as has been shown in the chapter on the Crypto-Calvinistic Controversy, the Philippists of Electoral Saxony and of other sections of Germany were Calvinists rather than Lutherans. It was the appearance of the Calvinistic *Exegesis Perspicua* of 1574 which left no doubt in the mind of the Elector that for years he had been surrounded by a clique of dishonest theologians and unscrupulous schemers, who, though claiming to be Lutherans, were secret adherents of Calvinism. And after the Elector, as Chemnitz remarks, had discovered the deception of his theologians in the article on the Lord's Supper, he began to doubt their entire contention. (Richard, 426.)

Among Lutherans generally the humiliating events in Saxony increased the feeling of shame at the conditions prevailing within their Church as well as the earnest desire for a genuine and lasting peace in the old Lutheran truths. And now Elector August, who, despite his continued animosity against Flacius, always wished to be a true Lutheran, but up to 1574 had not realized that the Philippistic type of doctrine dominant in his country departed from Luther's teaching, was determined to satisfy this universal longing for unity and peace. Immediately after the unmasking of the Philippists he took measures to secure the restoration of orthodox Lutheranism in his own lands. At the same time he placed himself at the head of the larger movement for the establishment of religious peace among the Lutherans generally by the elaboration and adoption of a doctrinal formula settling the pending controversies. To restore unity and peace to the Lutheran Church, which his own theologians had done so much to disturb, was now his uppermost desire. He prosecuted the plan of pacification with great zeal and perseverance. He also paid the heavy expenses (80,000 gulden), incurred by the numerous conventions, etc. And when, in the interest of such peace and unity, the theologians were engaged in conferences, the pious Elector and his wife were on their knees, asking God that He would crown their labor with success.

The specific plan of the Elector was, as appears from his rescript of November 21, 1575, to his counselors, that pacific theologians, appointed by the various Lutheran princes, "meet in order to deliberate how, by the grace of God, all [the existing various *corpora doctrinae*] might be reduced to one *corpus*, which we all could adopt, and that this book or *corpus doctrinae* be printed anew and the ministers in the lands of each ruler be required to be guided thereby." Before this

Elector August had requested Count George Ernest of Henneberg to take the initiative in the matter. Accordingly, in November, 1575, Henneberg, Duke Ludwig of Wuerttemberg, and Margrave Carl of Baden agreed to ask a number of theologians to give their opinion concerning the question as to how a document might be prepared which would serve as a beginning to bring about true Christian concord among the churches of the *Augsburg Confession*. The theologians appointed were the Wuerttemberg court-preacher Lucas Osiander (born 1534; died 1604), the Stuttgart provost Balthasar Bidembach (born 1533; died 1578), and several theologians of Henneberg and Baden. Their opinion, delivered November 14, 1575, was approved by the princes, and Osiander and Bidembach were ordered to prepare a formula of agreement in accordance with it. The document which they submitted was discussed with theologians from Henneberg and Baden at Cloister Maulbronn, Wuerttemberg, and subscribed January 19, 1576.

The *Maulbronn Formula*, as the document was called, differs from the *Swabian-Saxon Concordia* in being much briefer (about half as voluminous), in avoiding technical Latin terms, in making no reference whatever to Melanchthon, in quoting from Luther's works only, and in omitting such doctrinal points (Anabaptism, Schwenckfeldianism, Antitrinitarianism, etc.) as had not been controverted among the Lutherans. Following the order of the *Augustana*, this *Formula* treats the following articles: 1. Of Original Sin; 2. Of the Person of Christ; 3. Of Justification of Faith; 4. Of the Law and Gospel; 5. Of Good Works; 6. Of the Holy Supper of Our Lord Christ; 7. Of Church Usages, Called Adiaphora or Things Indifferent; 8. Of Free Will; 9. Of the Third Use of God's Law.

### 280. The Torgau Book.

On February 9, 1576, the *Maulbronn Formula*, approved by Count Ludwig of Wuerttemberg, Margrave Carl of Baden, and Count George Ernest of Henneberg, was transmitted to Elector August, who had already received a copy of the Swabian-Saxon Concordia from Duke Julius of Brunswick. The Elector submitted both to Andreae for an opinion, whom formal reasons induced to decide in favor of the *Maulbronn Formula*. At the same time Andreae advised the Elector to arrange a general conference of prominent theologians to act and decide in this matter, suggesting as two of its members Chemnitz and Chytraeus of Rostock. This being in agreement with his own plans, the Elector, at the convention at Lichtenberg, February 15, 1576, submitted the suggestions of Andreae to twelve of his own theologians, headed by Nicholas Selnecker, then professor in Leipzig. [Selnecker was born December 6, 1530. In 1550 he took up his studies in Wittenberg, where he was much impressed and influenced by Melanchthon. In 1557 he was appointed court-preacher in Dresden. Beginning with 1565, after the banishment of Flacius and his colleagues, he was professor in Jena. He returned to Leipzig in

1568. In 1570 he accepted a call from Duke Julius as court-preacher and superintendent in Brunswick, but returned to Leipzig in 1574. Before the unmasking of the Crypto-Calvinists his theological attitude lacked clearness and determination. Ever after, however, he was the leader of the Lutheran forces in Electoral Saxony. At the Lichtenberg Convention, convoked February 16, 1576, by Elector August, Selneccer successfully advocated the removal of the Wittenberg Catechism, the *Consensus Dresdensis*, and the *Corpus Philippicum*. In their place he recommended the adoption of a new *corpus doctrinae* containing the three Ecumenical Creeds, the *Unaltered Augsburg Confession*, the *Apology*, the *Smalcald Articles*, the Catechisms of Luther, and, if desired, Luther's *Commentary on Galatians*. Finally he advised that the electors and princes arrange a convention of such representative theologians as, *e. g.*, Chytraeus, Chemnitz, Andreae, and Marbach, to discuss the doctrinal differences. Selneccer's recommendations were adopted by the convention and transmitted to Elector August. Though contributing little to the contents of the *Formula of Concord*, Selneccer heartily cooperated in its preparation, revision, and adoption. In 1580, of his own accord, he published the Latin *Book of Concord*, which was followed in 1584 by an edition authorized by the princes. Selneccer also participated in preparing the *Apology of the Book of Concord*, first published 1582 in Magdeburg. In May, 1589, after the Crypto-Calvinistic reaction under Christian I, Selneccer, whom the Calvinists hated more than others of the theologians who had participated in the promulgation of the *Formula of Concord*, was deposed, harassed, and reduced to poverty because of his testimony against Chancellor Crell and his earnest and continued warnings against the Calvinists. After the death of Christian I, Selneccer was recalled to Leipzig, where he arrived May 19, 1592, five days before his death, May 24, 1592.]

Having through the influence of Selneccer, at Lichtenberg, obtained the consent of his clergy to his plans of unification, and, also in accordance with their desire, called Andreae to Saxony, Elector August immediately made arrangements for the contemplated general convention of theologians. It was held at Torgau, from May 28 to June 7, 1576, and attended by Selneccer, the Saxon ministers who had participated in the Lichtenberg convention, Andreae, Chemnitz, Andrew Musculus [General Superintendent of Brandenburg], Christopher Cornerus [professor in Frankfurt-on-the-Oder; born 1518; died 1549], and David Chytraeus [born February 26, 1530, in Wuerttemberg; awarded degree of magister in Tuebingen when only fourteen years old; began his studies 1544 in Wittenberg, where he also heard Luther; was professor in Rostock from 1551 till his death, June 25, 1600]. The result of the Torgau deliberations, in which much time was spent on the articles of Original Sin and Free Will, was the so-called *Torgau Book*. On the seventh of June the theologians informed the Elector that, on the basis of the Swabian-Saxon and the Maulbronn documents, they, as desired by him, had agreed on a *corpus doctrinae*.

The *Torgau Book* was essentially the *Swabian-Saxon Concordia*, recast and revised, as urged by Andreae, with special reference to the desirable features (enumerated above) of the *Maulbronn Formula*. The majority decided, says Chemnitz, that the Saxon Concordia should be retained, but in such a manner as to incorporate also the quotations from Luther, and whatever else might be regarded as useful in the *Maulbronn Formula*. The *Torgau Book* contained the twelve articles of the later *Formula of Concord* and in the same sequence; Article IX, "Of the Descent of Christ into Hell," had been added at Torgau. The Book was entitled: *"Opinion* as to how the dissensions prevailing among the theologians of the *Augsburg Confession* may, according to the Word of God, be agreed upon and settled in a Christian manner." It was signed as "their faith, doctrine, and confession" by the six men who were chiefly responsible for its form and contents: Jacob Andreae, Martin Chemnitz, Nicholas Selneccer, David Chytraeus, Andrew Musculus, and Christopher Cornerus. The convention was closed with a service of thanksgiving to Almighty God for the blessed results of their labors and the happy termination and favorable issue of their discussions, Selneccer delivering the sermon. Similar services were held at other places, notably in Mecklenburg and Lower Saxony.

In a letter to Hesshusius, Chemnitz says concerning the Torgau Convention: "Everything in this entire transaction occurred aside from, beyond, above, and contrary to the hope, expectation, and thought of all. I was utterly astounded, and could scarcely believe that these things were done when they were done. It seemed like a dream to me. Certainly a good happy and desired beginning has been made toward the restoration of purity of doctrine, toward the elimination of corruptions, toward the establishment of a godly confession." In a letter of July 24, 1576, to Hesshusius and Wigand, Andreae wrote in a similar vein, saying: "Often were they [Chemnitz and Chytraeus] almost overwhelmed with rejoicing and wonder that we were there [at Torgau] brought to such deliberation. Truly, this is the change of the right hand of the Most High, which ought also to remind us that since the truth no longer suffers, we should do everything that may contribute to the restoration of good feeling." (Richard, 428. 430.)

## 281. The Bergic Book or the Formula of Concord.

In accordance with the recommendation of the Torgau convention the Elector of Saxony examined the *Torgau Book* himself and had copies of it sent to the various Lutheran princes and estates in Germany with the request to have it tested by their theologians, and to return their opinions and censures to

Dresden. Of these (about 25) the majority were favorable. The churches in Pomerania and Holstein desired that Melanchthon's authority be recognized alongside of Luther's. On the other hand, Hesshusius and Wigand demanded that Flacius, Osiander, Major, Melanchthon, and other "originators and patrons of corruptions" be referred to by name and condemned as errorists. Quite a number of theologians objected to the *Torgau Book* because it was too bulky. To meet this objection the *Epitome*, a summary of the contents of the *Torgau Book*, was prepared by Andreae, with the consent of the Elector. Originally its title read: *"Brief Summary* of the articles which, controverted among the theologians of the *Augsburg Confession* for many years, were settled in a Christian manner at Torgau in the month of June, 1576, by the theologians which there met and subscribed."

After most of the censures had arrived, the "triumvirate" of the *Formula of Concord* (as Chytraeus called them 1581), Andreae, Selneccer, and Chemnitz, by order of the Elector, met on March 1, 1577, at Cloister Bergen, near Magdeburg, for the consideration of the criticisms and final editing of the new confession. They finished their work on March 14. Later, when other criticisms arrived and a further revision took place (also at Bergen, in May, 1577), Musculus, Cornerus, and Chytraeus were added to their number. Though numerous changes, additions, and omissions were made at Bergen, and in Article IX the present form was substituted for the sermon of Luther, the doctrinal substance of the *Torgau Book* remained unchanged. The chief object of the revisers was to eliminate misunderstandings and to replace ambiguous and dark terms with clear ones. At the last meeting of the six revisers (at Bergen, in May) the *Solid Declaration* was quickly and finally agreed upon, only a few changes of a purely verbal and formal nature being made. On May 28, 1577, the revised form of the *Torgau Book* was submitted to Elector August. It is known as the *Bergic Book*, or the *Solid Declaration*, or the *Formula of Concord*, also as the *Book of Concord* (a title which was afterwards reserved for the collection of all the Lutheran symbols). Of course, the *Epitome*, prepared by Andreae, was also examined and approved by the revisers at Cloister Bergen.

In order to remove a number of misunderstandings appearing after the completion of the *Bergic Book*, a "Preface" (Introduction to the *Book of Concord*) was prepared by the theologians and signed by the princes. The *Catalog of Testimonies*, added first with the caption "Appendix" and later without the same, or omitted entirely, is a private work of Andreae and Chemnitz, and not a part of the confession. Its special purpose is to prove that the Lutheran doctrine concerning the person of Christ and the majesty of His human nature as set forth in Article VII of the *Formula of Concord*, is clearly taught by the Scriptures as well as by the Fathers of the ancient Church. The *Formula of Concord* (German) was first published at Dresden,

1580, as a part of the *Book of Concord*. The first authentic Latin edition appeared in Leipzig, 1584. (Compare chapter on "The Book of Concord.")

## 282. Subscription to the Formula of Concord.

Originally Elector August planned to submit the *Bergic Book* to a general convention of the evangelical estates for approval. But, fearing that this might lead to new discussions and dissensions, the six theologians, in their report (May 28, 1577) on the final revision of the *Bergic Book*, submitted and recommended a plan of immediate subscription instead of an adoption at a general convention. Consenting to their views, the Electors of Saxony and Brandenburg forthwith sent copies of the *Bergic Book* to such princes and estates as were expected to consent. These were requested to multiply the copies, and everywhere to circulate and submit them for discussion and subscription. As a result the *Formula of Concord* was signed by the electors of Saxony, of Brandenburg, and of the Palatinate; furthermore by 20 dukes and princes, 24 counts, 4 barons, 35 imperial cities, and about 8,000 pastors and teachers, embracing about two-thirds of the Lutheran territories of Germany.

The first signatures were those of Andreae, Selneccer, Musculus, Cornerus, Chytraeus, and Chemnitz, who on May 29, 1577, signed both the *Epitome* and the *Thorough Declaration*, the latter with the following solemn protestation: "Since now, in the sight of God and of all Christendom, we wish to testify to those now living and those who shall come after us that this declaration herewith presented concerning all the controverted articles aforementioned and explained, and no other, is our faith, doctrine, and confession, in which we are also willing, by God's grace, to appear with intrepid hearts before the judgment-seat of Jesus Christ, and give an account of it; and that we will neither privately nor publicly speak or write anything contrary to it, but, by the help of God's grace, intend to abide thereby: therefore, after mature deliberation, we have, in God's fear and with the invocation of His name, attached our signatures with our own hands." (CONC. TRIGL. 1103, 40; 842, 31.)

Kolde remarks: "Wherever the civil authorities were in favor of the *Bergic Book*, the pastors and teachers also were won for its subscription. That the wish of the ruler contributed to this result cannot be denied and is confirmed by the Crypto-Calvinistic troubles reappearing later on in Saxony. But that the influence of the rulers must not be overestimated, appears, apart from other things, from the frequent additions to the signatures: 'With mouth and heart (*cum ore et corde*).'"

Self-evidently the Crypto-Calvinists as well as other errorists had to face the alternative of either subscribing or being suspended from the ministry. The very object of the *Formula of Concord* was to purge the Lutheran Church from Calvinists and others who were not in sympathy and agreement with the Lutheran

Confessions and constituted a foreign and disturbing element in the Lutheran Church.

As to the manner in which the *Formula* was submitted for subscription, it was certainly not indifferentistic, but most solemn and serious, and perhaps, in some instances, even severe. Coercion, however, was nowhere employed for obtaining the signatures. At any rate, no instance is recorded in which compulsion was used to secure its adoption. Moreover, the campaign of public subscription, for which about two years were allowed, was everywhere conducted on the principle that such only were to be admitted to subscription as had read the *Formula* and were in complete agreement with its doctrinal contents. Yet it was probably true that some, as Hutter assumes, signed with a bad conscience [Hutter: *"Deinde esto: subscripserunt aliqui mala conscientia Formulae Concordiae"*; Mueller, *Einleitung*, 115]; for among those who affixed their names are quite a few of former Crypto-Calvinists — men who had always found a way of escaping martyrdom, and, also in this instance, may have preferred the retaining of their livings to following their conviction. The fact is that no other confession can be mentioned in the elaboration of which so much time, labor, and care was expended to bring out clearly the divine truth, to convince every one of its complete harmony with the Bible and the Lutheran symbols, and to hear and meet all objections, as was the case with respect to the *Formula of Concord*.

"In reply to the criticism [of the Calvinists in the *Neustadt Admonition*, etc.] that it was unjust for only six theologians to write a Confession for the whole Church, and that a General Synod should have been held before the signing of the Confession, the Convention of Quedlinburg, in 1583, declared it untrue that the *Formula of Concord* had been composed by only six theologians, and reminded the critics how, on the contrary, the articles had first been sent, a number of times, to all the Lutheran churches in Germany; how, in order to consider them, synods and conferences had been held on every side, and the articles had been thoroughly tested; how criticisms had been made upon them; and how the criticisms had been conscientiously taken in hand by a special commission. The Quedlinburg Convention therefore declared in its minutes that, indeed, 'such a frequent revision and testing of the *Christian Book of Concord*, many times repeated, is a much greater work than if a General Synod had been assembled respecting it, to which every province would have commissioned two or three theologians, who in the name of all the rest would have helped to test and approve the book. For in that way only one synod would have been held for the comparing and testing of this work, but, as it was, many synods were held; and it was sent to many provinces, which had it tested by the weighty and mature judgment of their theologians, in such manner as has never occurred in the case of any book or any matter of religion since the beginning of Christianity, as is evident from the history of the Church.' . . . We are solemnly told [by Andreae, Selneccer, etc.] that no one was forced by threats to sign the *Formula of Concord*, and that no one was tempted to do so by promises. We know that no one was taken suddenly by surprise. Every one was given time to think. As the work of composition extended through years, so several years were given for the work of signing. We very much doubt whether the Lutheran Church to-day could secure any democratic subscription so clean, so conscientious, so united, or so large as that which was given to the *Book of Concord*." (Schmauk, 663 f.)

## 283. Subscription in Electoral Saxony, Brandenburg, etc.

In Electoral Saxony, where Crypto-Calvinism had reigned supreme for many years, prevailing conditions naturally called for a strict procedure. For Calvinists could certainly not be tolerated as preachers in Lutheran churches or as teachers in Lutheran schools. Such was also the settled conviction and determination of Elector August. When he learned that the Wittenberg professors were trying to evade an unqualified subscription, he declared: By the help of God I am determined, as long as I live, to keep my churches and schools pure and in agreement with the *Formula of Concord*. Whoever does not want to cooperate with me may go; I have no desire for him. God protect me, and those belonging to me, from Papists and Calvinists — I have experienced it. (Richard, 529.)

The Elector demanded that every pastor affix his own signature to the *Formula*. Accordingly, in every place, beginning with Wittenberg, the commissioners addressed the ministers and schoolteachers, who had been summoned from the smaller towns and villages, read the *Formula* to them, exhorted them to examine it and to express their doubts or scruples, if they had any, and finally demanded subscription of all those who could not bring any charge of false doctrine against it. According to Planck only one pastor, one superintendent (Kolditz, who later on subscribed), and one schoolteacher refused to subscribe. (6, 560.) Several professors in Leipzig and Wittenberg who declined to acknowledge the *Formula* were disturbed.

However, as stated, also in Electoral Saxony coercion was not employed. Moreover, objections were listened to with patience, and time was allowed for consideration. Indeed, in the name of the Elector every one was admonished not to subscribe against his conscience. I. F. Mueller says in his *Historico-Theological Introduction to the Lutheran Symbols:* "At the Herzberg Convention, 1578, Andreae felt justified in stating: 'I can truthfully say that no one was coerced to subscribe or banished on that account. If this is not true, the Son of God has not redeemed me with His blood; for otherwise I do not want to become a partaker of the blood of Christ.' Pursuant to this declaration the opponents were publicly challenged to mention a single person who had subscribed by compulsion, but they were unable to do so. Moreover, even the Nuernbergers, who did not adopt the *Formula of Concord,* acknowledged that the signatures had been affixed without employment of force." (115.) True, October 8, 1578, Andreae wrote to Chemnitz: "We treated the pastors with such severity that a certain truly good man and sincere minister of the church afterwards said to us in the lodging that, when the matter was proposed so severely, his mind was seized with a great consternation, which caused him to think that he, being near Mount Sinai, was hearing the promulgation of the Mosaic Law (*se animo adeo consternato fuisse, cum negotium tam severiter proponeretur, ut existimaret, se monti Sinai proximum legis Mosaicae promulgationem audire*). . . . I do not believe that anywhere a similar severity has been employed." (116.) But the term "severity" here employed does not mean force or compulsion, but merely signifies religious seriousness and moral determination to eliminate Crypto-Calvinism from the Lutheran Church in Electoral Saxony. The spirit in which also Andreae desired this matter to be conducted appears from his letter of November 20, 1579, to Count Wolfgang, in which he says: Although as yet some ministers in his country had not subscribed to the *Formula,* he should not make too much of that, much less press or persuade them; for whoever did not subscribe spontaneously and with a good conscience should abstain from subscribing altogether much rather than pledge himself with word and hand when his heart did not concur — *denn wer es nicht mit seinem Geist und gutem Gewissen tue, bleibe viel besser davon, als dass er sich mit Worten und mit der Hand dazu bekenne und das Herz nicht daran waere.* (115.)

Also Selneccer testifies to the general willingness with which the ministers in Saxony affixed their signatures. With respect to the universities of Wittenberg and Leipzig, however, he remarks that there some were found who, while willing to acknowledge the first part of the *Book of Concord,* begged to be excused from signing the *Formula,* but that they had been told by the Elector: If they agreed with the first part, there was no reason why they should refuse to sign the second, since it was based on the first. (Carpzov, *Isagoge* 20.) While thus in Electoral Saxony subscription to the *Formula* was indeed demanded of all professors and ministers, there is not a single case on record in which compulsion was employed to obtain it.

In Brandenburg the clergy subscribed unconditionally, spontaneously, and with thankfulness toward God and to their "faithful, pious ruler for his fatherly care of the Church." Nor was any opposition met with in Wuerttemberg, where the subscription was completed in October, 1577. In Mecklenburg the ministers were kindly invited to subscribe. Such as refused were suspended and given time for deliberation, with the proviso that they abstain from criticizing the *Formula* be-

fore the people. When the superintendent of Wismar and several pastors declined finally to adopt the *Formula,* they were deposed.

Accordingly, it was in keeping with the facts when the Lutheran electors and princes declared in the Preface to the *Formula of Concord* "that their theologians, ministers, and schoolteachers" "did with glad heart and heartfelt thanks to God the Almighty voluntarily and with well-considered courage adopt, approve, and subscribe this *Book of Concord* [*Formula of Concord*] as the true and Christian sense of the *Augsburg Confession,* and did publicly testify thereto with heart, mouth, and hand. Wherefore also this Christian Agreement is not the confession of some few of our theologians only, but is called, and is, in general, the unanimous confession of each and every one of the ministers and schoolteachers of our lands and provinces." (CONC. TRIGL., 12 f.)

## 284. Where and Why Formula of Concord was Rejected.

Apart from the territories which were really Calvinistic (Anhalt, Lower Hesse, the Palatinate, etc.), comparatively few of the German princes and estates considered adherents of the *Augsburg Confession* declined to accept the *Formula of Concord* because of any doctrinal disagreement. Some refused to append their names for political reasons; others, because they were opposed on principle to a new symbol. With still others, notably some of the imperial cities, it was a case of religious particularism, which would not brook any disturbance of its own mode of church-life. Also injured pride, for not having been consulted in the matter, nor called upon to participate in the preparation and revision of the *Formula,* was not altogether lacking as a motive for withholding one's signature. In some instances personal spite figured as a reason. Because Andreae had given offense to Paul von Eitzen, Holstein rejected the *Formula,* stating that all the articles it treated were clearly set forth in the existing symbols. Duke Julius of Brunswick, though at first most zealous in promoting the work of pacification and the adoption of the *Book of Concord,* withdrew in 1583, because Chemnitz had rebuked him for allowing his son to be consecrated Bishop of Halberstadt. (Kolde, 73 f.) However, despite the unfriendly attitude of Duke Julius, some of the Brunswick theologians openly declared their agreement with the *Formula* as well as their determination, by the help of God, to adhere to its doctrine. No doubt but that much more pressure was exercised in hindering than in urging Lutherans to subscribe to the *Formula.*

For the reasons enumerated the *Formula of Concord* was not adopted in Brunswick, Wolfenbuettel, Holstein, Hesse, Pomerania (where, however, the *Formula* was received later), Anhalt, the Palatinate (which, after a short Lutheran interregnum, readopted the Heidelberg Catechism under John Casimir, 1583), Zweibruecken, Nassau, Bentheim, Tecklenburg, Solms, Ortenburg, Liegnitz, Brieg, Wohlau,

Bremen, Danzig, Magdeburg, Nuernberg, Weissenburg, Windsheim, Frankfort-on-the-Main, Worms, Speyer, Strassburg.

In Sweden and Denmark, Frederick II issued an edict, July 24, 1580, forbidding (for political reasons) the importation and publication of the *Formula of Concord* on penalty of execution and confiscation of property. He is said to have cast the two elegantly bound copies of the *Formula* sent him by his sister, the wife of Elector August of Saxony, into the fireplace. Later on, however, the *Formula* came to be esteemed also in the Danish Church and to be regarded as a symbol, at least in fact, if not in form.

While some of the original signatories subsequently withdrew from the *Formula of Concord*, a larger number acceded to it. Among the latter were Holstein, Pomerania, Krain, Kaernthen, Steiermark, etc. In Sweden the *Formula* was adopted 1593 by the Council of Upsala; in Hungary, in 1597. With few exceptions the Lutheran synods in America and Australia all subscribed also to the *Formula of Concord*.

### 285. Formula Not a New Confession Doctrinally.

The *Formula of Concord* purified the Lutheran Church from Romanism, Calvinism, indifferentism, unionism, synergism, and other errors and unsound tendencies. It did so, not by proclaiming new exclusive laws and doctrines, but by showing that these corruptions were already excluded by the spirit and letter of the existing Lutheran symbols. Doctrinally the *Formula of Concord* is not a new confession, but merely a repetition and explanation of the old Lutheran confessions. It does not set forth or formulate a new faith or tenets hitherto unknown to the Lutheran Church. Nor does it correct, change, or in any way modify any of her doctrines. On the contrary, its very object was to defend and maintain the teaching of her old symbols against all manner of attacks coming from without as well as from within the Lutheran Church. The *Formula* merely presents, repeats, reaffirms, explains, defends, clearly defines, and consistently applies the truths directly or indirectly, explicitly or implicitly confessed and taught in the antecedent Lutheran confessions. The *Augsburg Confession* concludes its last paragraph: "If there is anything that any one might desire in this Confession, we are ready, God willing, to present ampler information (*latiorem informationem*) according to the Scriptures." (94, 7.) Close scrutiny will reveal the fact that in every detail the *Formula* must be regarded as just such an "*ampler information*, according to the Scriptures." The Lutheran Church, therefore, has always held that whoever candidly adopts the *Augsburg Confession* cannot and will not reject the *Formula of Concord* either.

As for the *Formula* itself, it most emphatically disclaims to be anything really new. In their Preface to the *Book of Concord* the Lutheran princes declared: "We indeed (to repeat in conclusion what we have mentioned several times above) have wished, in this work of concord, *in no way to devise anything new*, or to depart from the truth of the heavenly doctrine, which our ancestors (renowned for their piety) as well as we ourselves have acknowledged and professed. We mean that doctrine, which, having been derived from the prophetic and apostolic Scriptures, is contained in the three ancient Creeds, in the *Augsburg Confession*, presented in the year 1530 to Emperor Charles V, of excellent memory, then in the *Apology*, which was added to this, in the *Smalcald Articles*, and lastly in both the Catechisms of that excellent man, Dr. Luther. *Therefore we also have determined not to depart even a finger's breadth either from the subjects themselves, or from the phrases which are found in them*, but, the Spirit of the Lord aiding us, to persevere constantly, with the greatest harmony, in this godly agreement, and we intend to examine all controversies according to this true norm and declaration of the pure doctrine." (Conc. Trigl., 23.) In the Comprehensive Summary we read: "We [the framers and signers of the *Formula of Concord*] have declared to one another with heart and mouth that we will not make or receive a *separate or new confession* of our faith, but confess the public common writings which always and everywhere were held and used as such symbols or common confessions in all the churches of the *Augsburg Confession* before the dissensions arose among those who accept the *Augsburg Confession*, and as long as in all articles there was on all sides a unanimous adherence to the pure doctrine of the divine Word, as the sainted Dr. Luther explained it." (851, 2. 9.) The *Formula of Concord* therefore did not wish to offer anything that was new doctrinally. It merely expressed the consensus of all loyal Lutherans, and applied the truths contained in the existing symbols to the questions raised in the various controversies.

### 286. Formula a Reaffirmation of Genuine Lutheranism.

To restore Luther's doctrine, such was the declared purpose of the promoters and authors of the *Formula of Concord*. And in deciding the controverted questions, they certainly did most faithfully adhere to Luther's teaching. The *Formula* is an exact, clear, consistent, and guarded statement of original Lutheranism, purified of all foreign elements later on injected into it by the Philippists and other errorists. It embodies the old Lutheran doctrine, as distinguished not merely from Romanism and Calvinism, but also from Melanchthonianism and other innovations after the death of Luther. Surely Luther would not have hesitated to endorse each and all of its articles or doctrinal statements. Even Planck, who poured contempt and sarcasm on the loyal Lutherans, admits: "It was almost beyond controversy that the *Formula*, in every controverted article, established and authorized precisely the view which was most clearly sanctioned by the *Unaltered Augsburg Confession*, by its *Apology* according to the edition of the year 1531, by the *Smalcald Articles*, and by the Catechisms of Luther." (6, 697.) This complete agreement with Luther also accounts for the fact that the *Formula* was immediately acknowledged by two-thirds of the Protestants in Germany.

As for Luther, the *Formula of Concord* regards him as the God-given Reformer and teacher of the Church. We read: "By the special grace and mercy of the Almighty the doctrine concerning the chief articles of our Christian religion (which under the Papacy had been horribly obscured by human teachings and ordinances) *were explained and purified again from God's Word by Dr. Luther, of blessed and holy memory.*" (847, 1.) Again: "In these last times God, out of special grace, has brought the truth of His Word to light again from the darkness of the Papacy *through the faithful service of the precious man of God, Dr. Luther.*" (851, 5.) Luther is spoken of as "this highly illumined man," "the hero illumined with unparalleled and most excellent gifts of the Holy Ghost," "the leading teacher of the *Augsburg Confession*." (980, 28; 983, 34.) "Dr. Luther," says the *Formula*, "is to be regarded as the most distinguished (*vornehmste, praecipuus*) teacher of the Churches which confess the *Augsburg Confession*, whose entire doctrine as to sum and substance is comprised in the articles of the *Augsburg Confession*." (985, 41.) Again: "Dr. Luther, who, above others, certainly understood the true and proper meaning of the *Augsburg Confession*, and who constantly remained steadfast thereto till his end, and defended it, shortly before his death repeated his faith concerning this article [of the Lord's Supper] with great zeal in his last Confession." (983, 33.) Accordingly, only from Luther's writings quotations are introduced by the *Formula* to prove the truly Lutheran character of a doctrine. In this respect Luther was considered the highest authority, outweighing by far that of Melanchthon or any other Lutheran divine. Everywhere Luther's books are referred and appealed to, *e. g.*, his "beautiful and glorious exposition of the Epistle of St. Paul to the Galatians," his book concerning Councils, his *Large Confession*, his *De Servo Arbitrio*, his *Commentary on Genesis*, his sermon of 1533 at Torgau, etc. (925, 28; 937, 67; 823, 21; 897, 43; 827, 2; 1051, 1; cf. 1213 ff.)

Luther's doctrine, according to the *Formula of Concord*, is embodied in the old Lutheran symbols, and was "collected into the articles and chapters of the *Augsburg Confession*." (851, 5.) The *Augsburg Confession*, the *Apology*, the *Smalcald Articles*, and the *Small* and the *Large Catechism*, says the *Formula*, "have always been regarded as the norm and model of the doctrine which Dr. Luther, of blessed memory, has admirably deduced from God's Word, and firmly established against the Papacy and other sects; and to his full explanations in his doctrinal and polemical writings we wish to appeal, in the manner

and as far as Dr. Luther himself in the Latin preface to his published works has given necessary and Christian admonition concerning his writings." (853, 9.) According to the *Formula* there were no dissensions among the Lutherans "as long as in all articles there was on all sides a unanimous adherence to the pure doctrine of the divine Word *as the sainted Dr. Luther explained it.*" (851, 2.) Melanchthon, Agricola, Osiander, Major, and the Philippists, departing from Luther, struck out on paths of their own, and thus gave rise to the controversies finally settled by the *Formula of Concord*.

As for the *Formula of Concord* itself, the distinct object also of its promoters and authors was to restore, reaffirm, and vindicate the doctrine of Luther. In a letter of July 24, 1576, to Hesshusius and Wigand, Andreae, giving an account of the results of the Torgau Convention, remarks: "For this I dare affirm and promise sacredly that the illustrious Elector of Saxony is bent on this alone, that the doctrine of Luther, which has been partly obscured, partly corrupted, partly condemned openly or secretly, shall again be restored pure and unadulterated in the schools and churches, and accordingly shall Luther live, *i. e.*, Christ, whose faithful servant Luther was — *adeoque Lutherus, hoc est, Christus, cuius fidelis minister Lutherus fuit, vivat.* What more do you desire? Here [in the *Torgau Book*] nothing is colored, nothing is dressed up, nothing is concealed, but everything is in keeping with the spirit of Luther, which is Christ's. *Nihil hic fucatum, nihil palliatum, nihil tectum est, sed iuxta spiritum Lutheri, qui Christi est.*" (Schaff 1, 339.) Also the *Formula of Concord*, therefore, contains Luther's theology.

It has been asserted that the *Formula of Concord* is a compromise between Luther and Melanchthon, a "synthesis or combination of the two antagonistic forces of the Reformation, a balance of mutually destructive principles," etc. The *Formula*, says also Seeberg, represents a "Melanchthonian Lutheranism." But the plain truth is that the *Formula* is a complete victory of Luther over the later Melanchthon as well as the other errorists who had raised their heads, within the Lutheran Church. It gave the floor, not to Philip, but to Martin. True, it was the avowed object of the *Formula* to restore peace to the Lutheran Church, but not by compromising in any shape or form the doctrine of Luther, which, its authors were convinced, is nothing but divine truth itself. In thesis and antithesis, moreover, the *Formula* takes a clearly defined stand against all the errorists of those days: Anabaptists, Schwenckfeldians, Antitrinitarians, Romanists, Zwinglians, Calvinists, Crypto-Calvinists, Adiaphorists, Antinomians, Synergists, Majorists, the later Flacianists, etc. It did not acknowledge, or leave room for, any doctrines or doctrinal tendencies deviating in the least from original genuine Scriptural Lutheranism. At every point it occupied the old Lutheran ground. Everywhere it observed a correct balance between two errors (*e. g.*, Romanism and Zwinglianism, Calvinism and synergism, Majorism and antinomianism); it steered clear of Scylla as well as Charybdis, avoiding errors to the right as well as pitfalls to the left. The golden highway of truth on which it travels was not Melanchthon nor a middle ground between Luther and Melanchthon, but simply Luther and the truths which he had brought to light again.

Melanchthonianism may be defined as an effort to inoculate Lutheranism with a unionistic and Calvinistic virus. The distinct object of the *Formula*, however, was not merely to reduce, but to purge the Lutheran Church entirely from, this as well as other leaven. The *Formula's* theology is not Lutheranism modified by, but thoroughly cleansed from, antinomianism, Osiandrianism, and particularly from Philippism. Accordingly, while in the *Formula* Luther is celebrated and quoted as the true and reliable exponent of Lutheranism, Melanchthon is nowhere appealed to as an authority in this respect. It is only in the Preface of the *Book of Concord* that his writings are referred to as not to be "rejected and condemned"; but the proviso is added, "in as far as (*quatenus*) they agree throughout with the norm laid down in the *Book of Concord*." (16.)

### 287. Scripture Sole Standard and Rule.

From the high estimation in which Luther was held by the *Formula of Concord* it has falsely been inferred that this Confession accords Luther the "highest authority," as Hase says, or considers him "the regulative and almost infallible expounder" of the Bible, as Schaff asserts. (*Creeds* 1, 313.) But according to the *Formula* the supreme arbiter and only final rule in all matters of religion is the inspired Word of God; and absolutely all human teachers and books, including Luther and the Lutheran symbols, are subject to its verdict. When, after Luther's death, God permitted doctrinal controversies to distract the Church, His purpose, no doubt, being also to have her fully realize not only that Luther's doctrine is in complete harmony with Scripture, but, in addition, that in matters of faith and doctrine not Luther, not the Church, not the symbols, nor any other human authority, but His Word alone is the sole rule and norm. The *Formula* certainly learned this lesson well. In its opening paragraph we read: "We believe, teach, and confess that the sole rule and standard according to which both all doctrines and all teachers should be estimated and judged are the prophetic and apostolic Scriptures of the Old and the New Testament alone. . . . Other writings, however, of ancient or modern teachers, whatever name they bear, must not be regarded as equal to the Holy Scriptures, but all of them together be subjected to them." (777, 1.) And in this, too, the *Formula* was conscious of being in agreement with Luther. Luther himself, it declares, "has expressly drawn this distinction, namely, that the Word of God alone should

be and remain the only standard and rule of doctrine, to which the writings of no man should be regarded as equal, but to which everything should be subjected." (853, 9.) Scripture is, and always must remain, the only *norma normans*, the standard that rules everything, — such was the attitude of the *Formula of Concord*.

Accordingly, the proof proper for the truth of any doctrinal statement is taken by the *Formula* neither from the Lutheran symbols nor the writings of Luther, but from the Word of God. And the only reason why the promoters and framers of the *Formula* were determined to restore the unadulterated teaching of Luther was because, in the controversies following his death, they had thoroughly convinced themselves that, on the one hand, the doctrines proclaimed by Luther were nothing but the purest gold mined from the shafts of God's Word, and that, on the other hand, the various deviations from Luther's teaching, which had caused the dissensions, were aberrations not only from the original Lutheran Confessions, but also from Holy Scripture. The thirty years of theological discussion had satisfied the Lutherans that to adhere to the Bible was tantamount to adhering to the teaching of Luther, and *vice versa*. Accordingly, the *Formula* also declared it as its object to prove that the doctrines it presented were in harmony with the Bible, as well as with the teaching of Luther and the *Augsburg Confession*. (856, 19.) This agreement with the Word of God and the preceding Lutheran symbols constitutes the *Formula* a Lutheran confession, which no one who is a true Lutheran can reject or, for doctrinal reasons, refuse to accept.

### 288. Formula Benefited Lutheran Church.

It has frequently been asserted that the *Formula of Concord* greatly damaged Lutheranism, causing bitter controversies, and driving many Lutherans into the fold of Calvinism, *e. g.*, in the Palatinate (1583), in Anhalt, in Hesse, and in Brandenburg (1613). Richard says: "The *Formula of Concord* was the cause of the most bitter controversies, dissensions, and alienations. The position taken by the adherents of the *Formula of Concord* that this document is the true historical and logical explanation of the older confessions, and is therefore the test and touchstone of Lutheranism, had the effect, as one extreme generates a counter-extreme, of driving many individual Lutherans and many Lutheran churches into the Calvinistic fold, as that fold was represented in Germany by the Heidelberg Catechism as the chief confession of faith." (516.)

But this entire view is founded on indifferentism and unionism flowing from the false principle that quality must be sacrificed to quantity, eternal truth to temporal peace, and unity to external progress and temporary success. Viewed in the light of God's Word, error is the centrifugal force and the real cause of dissension and separations among

Christians, while divine truth always acts as a centripetal or a truly unifying power. The *Formula* therefore, standing clearly as it does for divine truth only, cannot be charged with causing dissension and breeding trouble among Christians. It settled many controversies and healed dissensions, but produced none. True, the *Formula* was condemned by many, but with no greater justice and for no other reasons than those for which the truths of God's Word have always been assailed by their enemies.

Nor is the statement correct that the *Formula of Concord* drove loyal Lutherans out of their own churches into Calvinistic folds. It clearly stated what, according to God's Word and their old confessions, Lutherans always will believe, teach, and confess, as also what they always must reject as false and detrimental to the cause of the Church of Christ; however, in so doing, it did not drive Lutherans into the ranks of the Calvinists, but drove masked Calvinists out of the ranks of loyal Lutherans into those folds to which they really belonged. Indeed, the *Formula* failed to make true Lutherans of all the errorists; but neither did the *Augsburg Confession* succeed in making friends and Lutherans of all Papists, nor the Bible, in making Christians of all unbelievers. However, by clearly stating its position in thesis and antithesis, the *Formula* did succeed in bringing about a wholesome separation, ridding the Lutheran Church of antagonistic spirits, unsound tendencies, and false doctrines. In fact, it saved the Church from slow, but sure poisoning at the hands of the Crypto-Calvinists; it restored purity, unity, *morale*, courage, and hope when she was demoralized, distracted, and disfigured by many dissensions and corruptions. Whatever, by adopting the *Formula of Concord*, the Lutheran Church therefore may have lost in extension, it won in intention; what it lost in numbers, it won in unity, solidity, and firmness in the truth.

True, the *Formula of Concord* completely foiled Melanchthon's plan of a union between the Lutheran and Reformed churches on the basis of the Variata of 1540, — a fact which more than anything else roused the ire of Philippists and Calvinists. But that was an ungodly union, contrary to the Word of God; a union involving a denial of essential Christian truths; a union incompatible with the spirit of Lutheranism, which cannot survive where faith is gagged and open confession of the truth is smothered; a union in which Calvinism, engrafted on Lutheranism, would have reduced the latter to a mere feeder of a foreign life. However, though it shattered the ungodly plans of the Philippists and Calvinists, the *Formula* did not in the least destroy the hope of, or block the way for, a truly Christian agreement. On the contrary, it formulated the only true basis for such a union, which it also realized among the Lutherans. And if the Lutheran and Reformed churches will ever unite in a true and godly manner, it must be done on the basis of the truths set forth by the *Formula*.

## 289. Necessity of Formula of Concord.

Several Lutheran states, as related above, declined to accept the *Formula of Concord*, giving as their reason for such action that there was no need of a new confession. The fact, however, that the *Formula* was adopted by the great majority of Lutheran princes, professors, preachers, and congregations proves conclusively that they were of a different opinion. A new confession was necessary, not indeed because new truths had been discovered which called for confessional coining or formulation, but because the old doctrines, assailed by errorists, were in need of vindication, and the Lutheran Church, distracted by prolonged theological warfare, was sorely in need of being restored to unity, peace, and stability. The question-marks suspended everywhere in Germany after Luther's death were: Is Lutheranism to die or live? Are its old standards and doctrines to be scrapped or vindicated? Is the Church of Luther to remain, or to be transformed into a unionistic or Reformed body? Is it to retain its unity, or will it become a house divided against itself and infested with all manner of sects?

Evidently, then, if the Lutheran Church was not to go down ingloriously, a new confession was needed which would not only clear the religious and theological atmosphere, but restore confidence, hope, and normalcy. A confession was needed which would bring out clearly the truths for which Lutherans must firmly stand if they would be true to God, true to His Word, true to their Church, true to themselves, and true to their traditions. A confession was needed which would draw exactly, clearly, and unmistakably the lines which separate Lutherans, not only from Romanists, but also from Zwinglians, Calvinists, Crypto-Calvinists, unionists, and the advocates of other errors and unsound tendencies. Being essentially the Church of the pure Word and Sacrament, the only way for the Lutheran Church to maintain her identity and independence was to settle her controversies, not by evading or compromising the doctrinal issues involved, but by honestly facing and definitely deciding them in accordance with her principles: the Word of God and the old confessions. Particularly with respect to the doctrine of the Lord's Supper, Melanchthon, by constantly altering the *Augsburg Confession*, had muddied the water to such an extent that the adoption of the *Augustana* was no longer a clear test of Lutheran orthodoxy and loyalty. Even Calvin, and the German Reformed generally, subscribed to it; "in the sense," they said, "in which Melanchthon has explained it." The result was a corruption of Lutheranism and a pernicious Calvinistic propaganda in Lutheran territories. A new confession was the only means of ending the confusion and checking the invasion.

## 290. Formula Fully Met Requirements.

The *Formula of Concord* was just such a confession as the situation called for. The Preface to the *Apology of the Book of Con-*

cord, signed by Kirchner, Selneccer, and Chemnitz, remarks that the purpose of the *Formula* was "to establish and propagate unity in the Lutheran churches and schools, and to check the Sacramentarian leaven and other corruptions and sects." This purpose was fully attained by the *Formula*. It maintained and vindicated the old Lutheran symbols. It cleared our Church from all manner of foreign spirits which threatened to transform its very character. It settled the controversies by rendering a clear and correct decision on all doctrinal questions involved. It unified our Church when she was threatened with hopeless division, anarchy, and utter ruin. It surrounded her with a wall of fire against all her enemies. It made her a most uncomfortable place for such opponents of Lutheranism as Crypto-Calvinists, unionists, etc. It infused her with confidence, self-consciousness, conviction, a clear knowledge of her own position over against the errors of other churches and sects, and last, but not least, with a most remarkable vitality.

Wherever and whenever, in the course of time, the *Formula of Concord* was ignored, despised, or rejected, the Lutheran Church fell an easy prey to unionism and sectarianism; but wherever and whenever the *Formula* was held in high esteem, Lutheranism flourished, and its enemies were confounded. Says Schaff: "Outside of Germany the Lutheran Church is stunted in its normal growth, or undergoes, with the change of language and nationality, an ecclesiastical transformation. This is the case with the great majority of Anglicized and Americanized Lutherans, who adopt Reformed views on the Sacraments, the observance of Sunday, church discipline, and other points." But the fact is that, since Schaff wrote the above, the Lutheran Church developed and flourished nowhere as in America, owing chiefly to the return of American Lutherans to their confessions, including the *Formula of Concord*. The *Formula of Concord* fully supplied the dire need created by the controversies after Luther's death; and, despite many subsequent controversies, also in America, down to the present day, no further confessional deliverances have been necessary, and most likely such will not be needed in the future either.

The *Formula of Concord*, therefore, must ever be regarded as a great blessing of God. "But for the *Formula of Concord*," says Krauth, "it may be questioned whether Protestantism could have been saved to the world. It staunched the wounds at which Lutheranism was bleeding to death; and crises were at hand in history in which Lutheranism was essential to the salvation of the Reformatory interest in Europe. The Thirty Years' War, the war of martyrs, which saved our modern world, lay indeed in the future of another century, yet it was fought and settled in the Cloister of Bergen. But for the pen of the peaceful triumvirate, the sword of Gustavus had not been drawn. Intestine treachery and division in the Church of the Reformation would have done what the arts and arms of

Rome failed to do. But the miracle of restoration was wrought. From being the most distracted Church on earth, the Lutheran Church had become the most stable. The blossom put forth at Augsburg, despite the storm, the mildew, and the worm, had ripened into the full round fruit of the amplest and clearest Confession in which the Christian Church has ever embodied her faith." (Schmauk, 830.)

### 291. Formula Attacked and Defended.

Drawing accurately and deeply, as it did, the lines of demarcation between Lutheranism, on the one hand, and Calvinism, Philippism, etc., on the other, and thus also putting an end to the Calvinistic propaganda successfully carried on for decades within the Lutheran Church, the *Formula of Concord* was bound to become a rock of offense and to meet with opposition on the part of all enemies of genuine Lutheranism within as well as without the Lutheran Church. Both Romanists and Calvinists had long ago accustomed themselves to viewing the Lutheran Church as moribund and merely to be preyed upon by others. Accordingly, when, contrary to all expectations, our Church, united by the *Formula*, rose once more to her pristine power and glory, it roused the envy and inflamed the ire and rage of her enemies. Numerous protests against the *Formula*, emanating chiefly from Reformed and Crypto-Calvinistic sources, were lodged with Elector August and other Lutheran princes. Even Queen Elizabeth of England sent a deputation urging the Elector not to allow the promulgation of the new confession. John Casimir of the Palatinate, also at the instigation of the English queen, endeavored to organize the Reformed in order to prevent its adoption. Also later on the Calvinists insisted that a general council (of course, participated in by Calvinists and Crypto-Calvinists) should have been held to decide on its formal and final adoption!

Numerous attacks on the *Formula of Concord* were published 1578, 1579, 1581, and later, some of them anonymously. They were directed chiefly against its doctrine of the real presence in the Lord's Supper, the majesty of the human nature of Christ, and eternal election, particularly its refusal to solve, either in a synergistic or in a Calvinistic manner, the mystery presented to human reason in the teaching of the Bible that God alone is the cause of man's salvation, while man alone is the cause of his damnation. In a letter to Beza, Ursinus, the chief author of the Heidelberg Catechism, shrewdly advised the Reformed to continue accepting the *Augsburg Confession*, but to agitate against the *Formula*. He himself led the Reformed attacks by publishing, 1581, "*Admonitio Christiana de Libro Concordiae*, Christian Admonition Concerning the Book of Concord," also called "*Admonitio Neostadiensis*, Neustadt Admonition." Its charges were refuted in the "Apology or Defense of the Christian Book of Concord — *Apologia oder Verantwortung des christlichen Konkordienbuchs*, in welcher die wahre christliche Lehre, so im Konkordien-buch verfasst, mit gutem Grunde heiliger, goettlicher Schrift verteidiget, die Verkehrung aber und Kalumnien, so von unruhigen Leuten wider gedachtes christliche Buch ausgespren-get, widerlegt worden," 1583 (1582). Having been prepared by command of the Lutheran electors, and composed by Kirchner, Selneccer, and Chemnitz, and before its publication also submitted to other theologians for their ap-proval, this guardedly written *Apology*, also called the Erfurt Book, gained considerable authority and influence.

The Preface of this Erfurt Book enumerates, besides the Christian Admonition of Ursinus and the Neustadt theologians, the following writings published against the *Formula of Concord:* 1. *Opinion and Apology (Bedencken und Apologie)* of Some Anhalt Theologians; 2. *Defense (Verantwortung)* of the Bremen Preachers; Christian Irenaeus on Original Sin; *Nova Novorum* ("ein famos Libell"); other libelli, satyrae et pasquilli; *Calumniae et Scurrilia Convitia of Brother Nass (Bruder Nass)*; and the history of the *Augsburg Con-fession* by Ambrosius Wolf, in which the author asserts that from the beginning the doctrine of Zwingli and Calvin predominated in all Protestant churches. The theologians of Neustadt, Bremen, and Anhalt replied to the Erfurt Apology; which, in turn, called forth counter-replies from the Lutherans. Beza wrote: *Refutation of the Dogma Con-cerning the Fictitious Omnipresence of the Flesh of Christ.* In 1607 Hospinian published his *Concordia Discors*," to which Hutter re-plied in his *Concordia Concors.* The papal detractors of the *Formula* were led by the Jesuit Cardinal Bellarmin, who in 1589 pub-lished his *Judgment of the Book of Concord.*

### 292. Modern Strictures on Formula of Concord.

Down to the present day the *Formula of Concord* has been assailed particularly by unionistic and Reformed opponents of true Lutheranism. Schaff criticizes: "Religion was confounded with theology, piety with orthodoxy, and orthodoxy with an exclusive confessionalism." (1, 259.) However, the sub-jects treated in the *Formula* are the most vital doctrines of the Christian religion: con-cerning sin and grace, the person and work of Christ, justification and faith, the means of grace, — truths without which neither Chris-tian theology nor Christian religion can re-main. "Here, then," says Schmauk, "is the one symbol of the ages which treats almost exclusively of Christ — of His work, His pres-ence, His person. Here is the Christ-symbol of the Lutheran Church. One might almost say that the *Formula of Concord* is a devel-oped witness of Luther's explanation of the Second and Third Articles of the Apostles' Creed, meeting the modern errors of Protes-tantism, those cropping up from the sixteenth to the twentieth century, in a really modern way." (751.) Tschackert also designates the assertion that the authors of the *Formula of* Concord "abandoned Luther's idea of faith and established a dead scholasticism" as an unjust charge. (478.) Indeed, it may be ques-tioned whether the doctrine of grace, the real heart of Christianity, would have been saved to the Church without the *Formula*.

R. Seeberg speaks of the "ossification of Lutheran theology" caused by the *Formula of Concord*, and Tschackert charges it with transforming the Gospel into a "doctrine." (571.) But what else is the Gospel of Christ than the divine doctrine or statement and proclamation of the truth that we are saved, not by our own works, but by grace and faith alone, for the sake of Christ and His merits? The *Formula of Concord* truly says: *"The Gospel is properly a doctrine which teaches what man should believe*, that he may obtain forgiveness of sins with God, namely, that the Son of God, our Lord Christ, has taken upon Himself and borne the curse of the Law, has expiated and paid for all our sins, through whom alone we again enter into favor with God, obtain forgiveness of sins by faith, are delivered from death and all the punishments of sins, and eternally saved." (959, 20.) Says Schmauk: "The *Formula of Concord* was . . . the very substance of the Gospel and of the *Augsburg Confession*, kneaded through the ex-perience of the first generation of Protes-tantism, by incessant and agonizing conflict, and coming forth from that experience as a true and tried teaching, a standard recognized by many." (821.) The *Formula of Concord* is truly Scriptural, not only because all its doctrines are derived from the Bible, but also because the burden of the Scriptures, the doc-trine of justification, is the burden also of all its expositions, the living breath, as it were, pervading all its articles.

Another modern objection to the *Formula* is that it binds the future generations to the *Book of Concord.* This charge is correct, for the *Formula* expressly states that its decisions are to be "a public, definite testimony, not only for those now living, but also for our posterity, what is and should remain (*sei und bleiben solle — esseque perpetuo debeat*) the unanimous understanding and judgment of our churches in reference to the articles in controversy." (857, 16.) However, the criti-cism implied in the charge is unwarranted. For the Lutheran Confessions, as promoters, authors, and signers of the *Formula* were fully persuaded, are in perfect agreement with the eternal and unchangeable Word of God. As to their contents, therefore, they must always remain the confession of every Church which really is and would remain loyal to the Word of God.

### 293. Formula Unrefuted.

From the day of its birth down to the present time the *Formula of Concord* has always been in the limelight of theological discussion. But what its framers said in praise of the *Augsburg Confession*, viz., that, in spite of numerous enemies, it had remained unrefuted, may be applied also to the *For-*

*mula:* it stood the test of centuries and emerged unscathed from the fire of every controversy. It is true to-day what Thomasius wrote 1848 with special reference to the *Formula:* "Numerous as they may be who at present revile our Confession, not one has ever appeared who has refuted its chief propositions from the Bible." (*Bekenntnis der ev.- luth. Kirche,* 227.)

Nor *can* the *Formula* ever be refuted, for its doctrinal contents are unadulterated truths of the infallible Word of God. It confesses the doctrine which Christians everywhere will finally admit as true and divine, indeed, which they all in their hearts believe even now, if not explicitly and consciously, at least implicitly and in principle. The doctrines of the *Formula* are the ecumenical truths of Christendom; for true Lutheranism is nothing but consistent Christianity. The *Formula,* says Krauth, is "the completest and clearest confession in which the Christian Church has ever embodied her faith." Such being the case, the *Formula of Concord* must be regarded also as the key to a godly peace and true unity of entire Christendom.

The authors of the *Formula* solemnly declare: "We entertain heartfelt pleasure and love for, and are on our part sincerely inclined and anxious to advance with our utmost power that unity [and peace] by which His glory remains to God uninjured, nothing of the divine truth of the Holy Gospel is surrendered, no room is given to the least error, poor sinners are brought to true, genuine repentance, raised up by faith, confirmed in new obedience, and thus justified and eternally saved alone through the sole merit of Christ." (1095, 96.) Such was the godly peace and true Christian unity restored by the *Formula of Concord* to the Lutheran Church. And what it did for *her* it is able also to do for the Church at large. Being in complete agreement with Scripture, it is well qualified to become the regeneration center of the entire present-day corrupted, disrupted, and demoralized Christendom.

Accordingly Lutherans, the natural advocates of a truly wholesome and God-pleasing union based on unity in divine truth, will not only themselves hold fast what they possess in their glorious Confession, but strive to impart its blessings also to others, all the while praying incessantly, fervently, and trustingly with the pious framers of the *Formula:* "May Almighty God and the Father of our Lord Jesus grant the grace of His Holy Ghost that *we all* may be one in Him, and constantly abide in this Christian unity, which is well pleasing to Him! Amen." (837, 23.)

**SOLI DEO GLORIA!**

# INDEX TO HISTORICAL INTRODUCTIONS.